Teaching Students to Write

SECOND EDITION

BETH S. NEMAN

New York   Oxford
OXFORD UNIVERSITY PRESS
1995

Oxford University Press

Oxford   New York
Athens   Auckland   Bangkok   Bombay
Calcutta   Cape Town   Dar es Salaam   Delhi
Florence   Hong Kong   Istanbul   Karachi
Kuala Lumpur   Madras   Madrid   Melbourne
Mexico City   Nairobi   Paris   Singapore
Taipei   Tokyo   Toronto

and associated companies in
Berlin   Ibadan

Copyright © 1980 by Bell & Howell Company
Copyright © 1995 by Beth Neman

Pages iii–iv constitute an extension of this copyright page.

Published by Oxford University Press, Inc.,
198 Madison Avenue, New York, New York 10016

Oxford is a registered trademark of Oxford University Press

Library of Congress Cataloging-in-Publication Data
Neman, Beth.
Teaching students to write / Beth S. Neman. — 2nd ed.
p.   cm.   ISBN 0-19-506428-3
1. English language — Rhetoric.
I. Title.
PE1408.N417   1995   808'.042 — dc20   94-13018

9 8 7 6 5 4 3 2 1

Printed in the United States of America
on acid-free paper

Preface

When the first edition of *Teaching Students to Write* was published in 1980, it was a pioneer text. Though composition pedagogy was at last beginning to be accepted as a serious discipline, there were almost no textbooks on this subject. In the decade and a half since, there has been a surge of scholarly inquiry and research and a proliferation of books and articles in this field.

Then why should there be another book on composition pedagogy?

- Because we still need a research-based text that is student centered.
- Because we need a text that combines scholarly theory with practical pedagogy.
- And because we need a text that offers a wide variety of strategies to meet the diverse needs of our students.

While scholars have given us carefully structured research on almost every aspect of composition pedagogy, we still need a text whose first consideration is reaching and teaching students, a well researched book focused on the basic substance of pedagogy—the nurturing of the student mind.

Although the new scholarship has also provided us with serious, well-reasoned publications relating postmodern philosophical, political, social, or psychological theory to composition pedagogy, we still need a text that approaches theory and research with a nonpolemic eye, gleans the scholars' wisdom, and turns it into counsel useful in the classroom.

And though we now have an abundance of books setting forth the individual teaching techniques of gifted teachers—books such as those by Nancie Atwell, Peter Elbow, and the Tchudis, we still have need for a text that offers a wide range of differing strategies. For no technique, however sound, will work for every teacher or reach every student.

Teaching Students to Write, Second Edition, I believe, is such a book. In writing it, I have read just about everything skillful teachers and researchers have produced since the first edition; I have also interviewed many master teachers and scholars. With their input I have selected a variety of strategies that have proven effective. Readers can build a wide-ranging repertoire of techniques from these ideas to reach the "mute inglorious Miltons" in our classrooms.

HOW DOES THE NEW EDITION DIFFER FROM THE FIRST?

The first edition of *Teaching Students to Write* was conceived as a balanced approach in the midst of the extreme counterswings of the day. It attempted to achieve an equilibrium between competing points of view by championing the idea that in our classrooms we "can teach both students and subject matter," can have "both fun and laughter and the hard, sometimes even painful, reality of learning," and that "we can simultaneously go both back to the basics and to a real concern for the intellectual and emotional well-being of every individual soul in our charge."

These goals still seem to me well worth pursuing and are reflected throughout the second edition. I have revised the book, however, not only to take advantage of the findings of current research and thus bring it up to date, but also to suggest, in addition to the balances of the first edition, the following new equilibriums:

- A balance between self expression and communication
- A balance between one's "own language" and academic discourse
- A balance between theoretical idealism and practical pedagogy.

Teaching Students to Write, Second Edition, has been extensively rewritten to reflect the abundance of scholarship published over the last fifteen years. I have revised the entire book in light of the new knowledge and nomenclature. For example, the Second Edition puts a new emphasis on strategies connected to collaborative learning, experiential (sometimes called "discovery") learning, learning by writing, Hillocks' "Environmental Mode" learning, and Perry's very useful scale.

Drawing further on this contemporary emphasis, the Second Edition devotes full chapters to teaching invention and prewriting heuristics (Chapter 3), composing effective assignments (Chapter 14), and teaching the rhetorical analysis, including practical suggestions for making use of contemporary critical theory (Chapter 10).

Wilmington, Ohio   B. S. N.
October 1994

Preface to the First Edition

Teaching Students to Write provides the theoretical background and the practical techniques needed to teach composition. It is intended primarily for college courses in Advanced Composition for Teachers, English Teaching Methods, and seminars for instructors of Freshman Composition, but should also be a useful text for in-service courses and seminars. Firmly rooted in the research and personal experience of master teachers who have succeeded in reaching the "mute inglorious Miltons" in their classrooms, this text shares their advice and reproduces their strategies. It suggests explicit procedures and proposes alternative methods for every step in the writing process. . . .

Addressing the needs of the students who will use this book, the text discusses the writing process throughout with enough specificity to enable future teachers who may themselves be inexperienced writers to master the craft. The "Ideas for Essay or Discussion" at the end of each chapter encourage further writing practice; and the very specific "Guidelines" and "Strategies" sections throughout the text provide new teachers with explicit directions for solving such perplexing writing problems as inventing generative ideas, planning the structure of support about a thesis, and writing with an effective voice. These sections also offer aid in grappling with such thorny teaching situations as conducting student conferences, interesting a class in syntactical intricacies, and responding to student papers. Though the book's approach is thus experiential and pragmatic, its focus is our composition students and their needs.

For many years pedagogy based on the principle that "life is real and life is earnest" was pursued so relentlessly in the classroom that most students sat through the droning lectures with clenched teeth and closed minds. Then came the revolutionary pendulum-swing of the sixties. Every effort was made to eliminate anything associated with the old joyless education. Anything that was considered dull or hard or tedious or irrelevant was eliminated; only the joy of learning was to remain. But when the Palace of Learning became a Pleasure Dome, the Sacred River of knowledge ran down to an extraordinarily Sunless Sea; and educators discovered to their horror that the joy of learning cannot exist where learning itself does not exist. Now with College Board scores plummeting and some college texts being rewritten to the sixth-grade level, the outcry presaging another great swing of the pendulum begins again; and the whole dreadful cycle may be upon us once more.

This book is written in the belief that some sort of equilibrium in teaching can be achieved; that we can teach both students AND subject matter; that our classrooms can accommodate both fun and laughter AND the hard, sometimes even painful, reality of learning; that we can simultaneously go both back to the basics AND back to a real concern for the intellectual and emotional well-being of every individual soul in our charge.

This dual concern for both the personal and the academic suffuses *Teaching Students to Write*. The book begins with a close look at the Student, discussing special difficulties in learning to write, the painful ego-involvement of the writer with his or her work in a learning environment where growth is impossible without correction. Having examined what is known of relevant learning theory, it then suggests an approach which in itself epitomizes these ideas: the teacher should be at once personally supportive and academically demanding; for, perhaps paradoxically, only this combination can give the learner the self-confidence needed to write well. The book concludes with a similar look at the Teacher and offers guidance for establishing the sort of atmosphere in the classroom and the sort of relationship with students which would best promote the development of writing skills. The heart of the book, however, consists of concrete, practical advice on how to write and how to teach writing. The presentation of this practical advice is in itself consistent with our dual concern. The teaching of expository writing is emphasized, but the teaching of creative writing is not overlooked. Throughout, the book emphasizes both self-expression and form.

Underlying the practical guidance offered to help teach students to write are a number of assumptions and biases:

Basic Assumption

- Writing can be taught. It is a skill that can be developed and a craft that can be learned. To a large extent, writing handicaps can be overcome and native talent can be enhanced, by thoughtful and skilled instruction.

Rhetorical Biases

- Good writing is purposive. All expository prose has an essentially persuasive element.
- Writing style can be influenced—if not created—by a writer's decisions about the voice to employ and the audience to be reached and by specific

choices of the syntax and diction in which to phrase the ideas. Style, therefore, can be improved by a writer's learning to make these decisions and choices more consciously and with greater understanding.

Pedagogical Biases

- The most effective teaching comes through intellectual tussle, through argument and counterargument. Students learn best when they have a chance to develop an understanding for themselves through free debate. Therefore, for the most part, eliciting is a wiser technique than lecturing; induction a more useful method than declamation.
- The greatest growth in writing takes place when students, under supervision, revise and rewrite their work.

Teaching Students to Write did not spring full-grown, like Athena, from its author's head. It is rather a product of the advice and experience of many people—not only the authors of books and articles I have read, but also, as the dedication suggests, my own teachers, my colleagues, and my students, to all of whom I am most grateful. Some people have been particularly helpful, and I would like to thank them individually. They include Mary Sohngen from Miami University, Susan Glick from Charles Merrill, who copy-edited the entire manuscript and Cindy Peck, the production editor; Judith Frankel and Floyd Ogburn from the University of Cincinnati and Andrew Kerek from Miami, who gave expert advice on portions of the manuscript; and Gerald Sullivan from California State University at Long Beach, Margaret Fleming from the University of Arizona, and Ron Fortune from Ohio State University, whose readings offered much helpful guidance. I would also like to express my appreciation to the following master teachers whose students participated in portions of the book: Ellen Layne (William Howard Taft High School), Diane Menendez (University of Cincinnati), Max Morenberg (Miami), Pauline Smolin (University College, University of Cincinnati), Catherine Tuck (Madeira High School), Linda White (University College), and Sandra Wittstein (Hughes High School), and to Stephen Carroll, Lois Frankel, Deborah Levinrad, and Daniel Neman, students who participated individually. I would also like to thank Elayne Bleill for her first-rate typing, Gil Imholz and Tom Hutchinson from Merrill for their faith in the project, and my other colleagues in the English department at Miami, especially Paul Anderson, Donald Daiker, Rebecca Lukens, our chairman Robert Johnson, and director of freshman English, William Gracie, for their helpful discussions and continuing support.

Oxford, Ohio   B. S. N.
May 1979

Acknowledgments

I continue to be grateful to all those who helped create the first edition and to all the students and colleagues from whose experience and advice this edition was derived. In addition I wish to thank particularly Carolyn Boiarsky of Illinois Community College in Peoria, Gloria Flaherty of Wilmington College, and Barbara Wenner of the University of Cincinnati, who read the entire manuscript and whose comments and suggestions proved invaluable. And special thanks to Judith Frankel of University of Cincinnati, Max Morenberg of Miami University, Stephen Spencer of Wilmington College and Nancy Kline of the Melton School of Adult Education, who were very helpful with individual parts of the book.

Thanks also to the high school English teachers who participated with me in writing workshops during the gestation of this book and whose classroom experiences helped shape it; they include: Gloria Appleby, Mark Baughman, Lyn Brendel, Jane Brewer, Angel Gerard, Susan Herman, Jennifer Hostetler, Jeffrey Karnofel, Dan Pearce, Bonnie Pritchard, George Shoemaker, Melissa Snyder, Marion West, and Joan Winner. I also very much appreciate the exceedingly useful from-the-horse's-mouth counsel of my Wilmington College methods students, who studied from the manuscript: Anna Adams, Cynthia Asmus, Thomas Burriss, Michael Daugherty, Dawn Davis, Nicole Driver, Mary Hartz, Lisa McConnaughy, Kassie Penn, Kim Robbins, Andrea Stevens, Patti Wallingford, Amy Walters, Shari West, Christopher Westbay, Marcia Williams, and Tammy Wrightsel.

I am grateful to Mary Rose Zink and her students in the Wilmington College inmate education programs and to Donna McClughen for helping me prepare the manuscript. And finally, I would like to thank the people at Oxford University Press for all they have done; among them, Elda Rotor, for her helpful efficiency, and especially Colby Stong, for his discerning mind and his sympathetic ear.

Contents

PART III   TEACHING CREATIVE WRITING

PART IV   THE TEACHER

Abbreviations to Notes and Works Cited

CCC	*College Composition and Communication*
CCCC	College Composition and Communication Conference
CE	*College English*
DAI	*Dissertation Abstracts International*
EJ	*English Journal*
HER	*Harvard Education REview*
JEP	*Journal of Educational Psychology*
JER	*Journal of Educational Research*
NCTE	National Council of Teachers of English
RER	*Review of Educational Research*
RTE	*Research in the Teaching of English*

□ □ □ **Part I**

THE STUDENT

A good teacher begins with belief—belief that writing can be taught and that it is worth teaching. . . . A good teacher is one who cares and one for whom students care. . . . A good teacher recognizes diversity in students and works with the grain that they show, not against it, to turn their natural tendencies to advantage.

—William Irmscher

□ □ □

□ □ □   **1**

Teaching the Student

A Writer is a person with his skin off.
—Donald Graves

□ □ □

PROBLEMS IN LEARNING TO WRITE

Since many of our students seriously believe—and some are eager to proclaim—that they "hate to write," "don't want to write," and "can't write anyhow," it would seem that we who set out to teach them to write face a formidable task. And although we know that we can win over students and change their attitudes by establishing an atmosphere of warmth and a relationship of mutual trust, there are contradictions inherent in the very nature of the teaching/writing situation that work to exacerbate the problem of students' attitudes.

The Skinless Student

The primary difficulty stems from the intense ego involvement of writers with their work. For most people, writing seems almost an extension of their person. Criticize it and you criticize them; insult it and they suffer hurt; dismiss it and they are devastated. Writing is a material manifestation of the very processes of thought; and in our essential selves, we are what we think.

Extreme sensitivity about one's writing is almost universal. Surely, we teachers have felt it ourselves. Even those who have reason to think especially highly of themselves and of their writing suffer from such sensitivity. A lawyer of my acquaintance, for example, a man of acknowledged intellect who writes well and is aware of his ability, recently had a rather distressing experience in this regard while collaborating on a case with another lawyer. He had prepared the first draft of a brief for the case and then turned it over to his partner, commenting, "Revise it all you want; I have no pride of authorship." His partner took him at his word and made extensive revisions in the brief.

The intensity of my friend's feelings upon seeing the finished product took him by surprise.

Such a response can offer us insight into how our students, lacking the confidence of achievement and already battered by adolescent self-doubt, must feel when their compositions and — by subconscious extension — they themselves are shown to be worthless. Thus, when they cry, "I can't write; I don't want to write," they are actually erecting a defense to protect a profoundly personal part of themselves from public discovery of what they assume are hidden and ignominious flaws.

Writing: Both Personal Expression and Craft

Unfortunately, perhaps, writing is not only a personal embodiment of its author's thoughts and voice. It is also a craft, an artistic process with techniques and conventions that can be learned, employing skills that can be improved. As with other crafts, improvement of writing skills comes about through trial and error. But most apprentice writers — unlike apprentice potters, for instance — are not immediately aware of their specific problems nor do they know ways to remedy them. Until they develop this knowledge internally, they will need an outsider to intervene and point to the source of the difficulty. For growth to take place, students must recognize their writing problems, at least enough to rewrite the current paper and to avoid similar difficulties in future work. But almost inevitably this necessary recognition entails a blow to self-confidence.

THE IMPORTANCE OF SELF-CONFIDENCE. If that blow to a student's self-confidence is strong enough — because of the severity of the criticism, the circumstances of its delivery, or the emotional state of the student at the time — it can be incapacitating. Thus, the criticism that is necessary for growth in writing skill can actually be self-defeating, for it can destroy self-confidence, the very element that empowers the skill. T. S. Eliot's J. Alfred Prufrock vividly characterizes the internal situation that can thus be created:

> And I have know the eyes already, known them all —
> The eyes that fix you in a formulated phase,
> And when I am formulated, sprawling on a pin,
> When I am pinned and wriggling on the wall,
> Then how should I begin
> To spit out all the butt-ends of my days and ways?
> And how should I presume?

Students who are convinced that they write badly will write badly; students who are convinced that they have nothing worthwhile to offer will probably not offer anything worthwhile. Robert Rosenthal and Leonore Jacobson, in their classic text *Pygmalion in the Classroom*, cite study after careful study to prove that a student's "self concept, his expectations of his own behavior, has everything to do with how well he actually performs." Researchers Thomas L. Good and Jere E. Brophy confirm that "[s]tudents with poor self-concepts may give up hope and expect mediocrity or worse as inevitable."[1]

THE DILEMMA.   Attempting to teach students to write therefore puts instructors on the horns of a seemingly insoluble dilemma. Because writing has two dimensions—craft and expression of self—writing well requires both knowledge of the craft and the self-confidence to exercise this knowledge. On the one hand, remedying writing problems is a necessary component of learning the writing craft. On the other hand, because writing is so intimately bound up with self-image, criticism of a person's writing—however well intentioned—reflects immediately upon the ego of the writer, and to that extent corrodes self-confidence and retards writing performance. Furthermore, because of the nature of the teacher–student relationship, vigorous teacher intervention—again, however well intentioned—can undermine the self-expressive dimension of a student's writing and turn it instead into a mere teacher-pleasing exercise.

We want to assist our students in both dimensions of their writing. We want to help them to learn strategies effective in the writing situations they face and will face, and to learn the conventions appropriate to the linguistic communities they address and will address. And we want to help them to develop their own written thoughts in their own voices. But given the dilemma, how can we go about doing it?

Let's look at what other teachers do.

THE CRAFT-CENTERED SOLUTION

Teachers who follow the methods of what is sometimes called—rather erroneously—the "traditional" approach and whose primary concern is the finished product solve the dilemma by, in effect, ignoring its psychological implications and making correction and criticism the heart of their program. They mark students' papers liberally with red pencil and make caustic comments in the margins. During class discussion some even try to encourage correct reasoning through the use of sarcasm and ridicule. They invoke the rationale that they are upholding high standards and pursuing excellence, and they argue that "those who can't stand the heat should get out of the kitchen."

Teaching through correction and negative criticism was the dominant approach for centuries. " 'Riting," we must remember, as well as "reading and 'rithmetic," were customarily "taught to the tune of the hickory stick." It continued to be so taught until relatively recently, in practice if not in theory. A. Confrey's classic study, "Comments Made by Instructors on Student Themes," indicates that 36 percent of teacher comments are "not encouraging."[2]

Although this approach is no longer dominant, it continues to be commonplace in our day. Robert J. Connors and Andrea A. Lunsford surveyed three thousand graded student papers and found that the majority had errors that went unidentified—either through teacher compassion or inadvertence. But they also found a good number of papers "annotated marginally until they looked like the Book of Kells."[3] And only a week before this chapter was written, for instance, at one of the finest midwestern state universities, the chair of the English Department had a pertinent conversation with a colleague. The chair asked why nine students had withdrawn from the professor's advanced composition course in the six weeks since the beginning of the semester. The professor replied with a shrug and a chuckle, "It's simple—I give them F's and I tell them why."

Evaluation of the Craft-Centered Solution

The pursuit of excellence and the maintenance of standards are wholly admirable goals. Nevertheless, teaching through shame and ridicule can in no way be condoned. Educational psychologists, such as Kelvin L. Seifert and Thomas L. Good and Jere E. Brophy, condemn this method out of hand. And research scholars such as S. Tobias and J. P. Wine have conducted studies of the effect upon students of anxiety-producing classroom situations. Without exception, these situations, exacerbated by the special anxieties inherent in the writing context, were found to be detrimental to learning and to achievement.[4]

INEFFECTIVE.   Even if we ignore the psychological damage that abuses of the totally craft-centered method almost inevitably inflict upon at least some of our students, we must still condemn the correctionist approach because it does not adequately meet the goals toward which it is directed. Study after study has shown that the correctionist approach is counterproductive.[5] And little wonder. For when a student is "pinned and wriggling on the wall," "how should [she] begin" to write her theme? and "how should [she] presume" to strive for excellence in thought and expression? The point is that such a student cannot and does not.

THE AFFECT-CENTERED SOLUTION

If the correctionists have been able to avoid the criticism/self-actualization dilemma inherent in the teaching of composition by ignoring the psychological implications of their practices, other teachers avoid it by discounting the necessity for correction and criticism altogether. They solve the problem by defining the purpose of the composition class solely in terms of the personal development of the learner. Timothy McCracken and Allen Ashby, for example, suggest that its purpose is "to help create vital human beings . . . [and] to encourage creative responses to a complex world." Gregory Jay defines the writing teacher's primary task almost psychiatrically as "bringing to discourse unconscious thoughts (or resistances to thought)." And Joy Ritchie describes "the emerging, often powerful, sense of self which develop[s] in such classes."[6] With the affect-centered approach, the primary goal is no longer that of helping students to acquire the skills necessary for good writing, but of letting them use the opportunity writing offers to achieve a better understanding of themselves and their world.

The instructor's role in this self-actualizing approach is what researcher George Hillocks calls "nondirectional." He notes that teachers "consider themselves 'facilitator[s]' whose role is to free the student's imagination and promote growth by sustaining a positive classroom atmosphere." Lou Kelly, herself a master teacher, argues that no explicit instruction is necessary:

> If everybody becomes involved in finding the answers to the questions raised about the experiences shared, we do not have to "teach" [students] how to organize and support their ideas. They will learn to—experientially—in their dialogues with teacher and with each other.[7]

With this approach, the problems caused by negative criticism are eliminated. When self-actualization is the goal, encouragement is all that is required. Criticism and correction may be dispensed with completely.

Evaluation of the Affect-Centered Solution

Unlike totally craft-centered teaching, much can be said in favor of this student-centered approach. Taken on its own terms and skillfully taught, it has fostered results that are altogether praiseworthy. The method aims at establishing trust; when students find their class truly nonthreatening, this approach helps them to acquire some important writing skills. It can, for example, help them to find their voices and the courage to use them. It can give students the confidence to experiment with ideas and form. When creatively employed, it can foster metacognition, and help students become more conscious in their use of writing strategies.

CREATIVE OPPORTUNITIES.   Students in such classes, exhilarated by the unaccustomed freedom and motivated by the energy and excitement generated by an enthusiastic teacher and the experimental situation, have reacted creatively and have produced genuinely fine work—particularly in the personal narrative genre. Numerous articles in the professional journals bear witness to the success of such experiments.[8]

But despite some truly successful prototypes, many of us retain reservations about this approach. And though we would recommend adoption of many of its features, we would not suggest that teachers embrace it as the heart of their entire writing program.

POSSIBILITIES FOR ABUSE.   Our first reservation concerning the affect-centered approach lies in the possibilities for abuse. This policy can lend itself to excesses that may be just as destructive to the student as those of the correctional method. When self-actualization is the goal, and freedom and intimacy the classroom atmosphere, inexperienced teachers may run into structural and/or psychological difficulties using this approach. The unstructured format this approach fosters has been known to degenerate into anarchy.

A greater threat is that the student–teacher closeness engendered by this method may draw untrained instructors into possibly damaging attempts at amateur psychiatry. Some influential theoreticians' recent coupling of composition pedagogy with Freud's or Lacan's psychoanalytic strategies may have increased the threat.[9] Ann Murphy addresses the problem candidly:

> When we . . . assign [students] tasks which push them inward to explore their own lives and selves, we may very well elicit material we are utterly unqualified to handle. . . . We must acknowledge the potentially ungovernable forces which can be unleashed by ill-trained pseudo-analysts.[10]

The affect-centered mode of instruction can also allow a disturbed teacher to exercise unwholesome influence. Long ago Louise Rosenblatt warned against these transference/countertransference dangers:

> Given the right to meddle in this way, . . . teachers [who] are themselves laboring under emotional tensions and frustrations . . . might be tempted to find solutions for their own problems by vicariously sharing the student's life.[11]

Rosenblatt concluded that "even worse than the old indifference to what is happening psychologically to the student is the tampering with personality carried on by well-intentioned but ill-informed adults" (207).

Excesses, of course, must be considered aberrations; but they are not as rare as one would like to think and thus should not be altogether discounted.

INSUFFICIENT GOAL.   Positing self-actualization as the major purpose of the composition program may in itself be problematic. Without question, we all hope that a certain maturation in self-understanding will come out of our students' writing experiences, yet should this not be an important possible by-product of learning the craft of writing rather than the chief aim of that experience? Should the program be so defined that instruction in the craft itself is all but eliminated?

Absence of Nonnarrative Writing.   Almost all the writing in self-actualizing classrooms is personal narrative. Students have few opportunities to learn expository writing and the analytical thinking concomitant with it. Certainly, personal narrative is an important genre, but many thoughtful teachers question whether it should be taught exclusively. Even Peter Elbow, a strong defender of personal narrative, expresses concern about not teaching academic writing:

> Many or even most of [our students' other] teachers will expect them to write in the language of the academy. If we don't prepare them for these tasks, we'll be shortchanging them.

But giving our students experience with expository or analytic writing in addition to personal or narrative writing can be defended on grounds far broader than the strictly academic. As Mike Rose argues,

> Students must, early on, begin wrestling with academically oriented topics that . . . [not only] will assist them in the courses they take . . . [but also] help them develop into more critical thinkers, [and] provide them with some of the tools of the examined life.[12]

To deny our students help in learning to write the clear, expository prose they need to communicate their meaning in writing is to keep from them one of the essential tools for living a productive, communicative life. As Susan Belasco Smith observes,

> While it is important for students to write about what they know, [this sort of] pedagogy gives far too little attention to how students come to terms with what they don't know. . . . Students need more than instruction in airing their feelings and expressing their own experiences. [They] need to learn that real power in writing occurs when one overcomes the self, reaches beyond personal experience, and moves into the wider realm of social and political reality.[13]

For our students to become truly self-actualized, they need not only confidence and self-knowledge, but skills as well.

Authenticity as a Criterion. Self-actualization as the objective of a composition course also presents a problem in assessment. Those who accept this goal equate good student writing with "honest" or "authentic" or "sincere" writing. Ericka Lindemann, for example, writes, "Good writing is most effective when we tell the truth about who we are and what we think." In Joseph Harris's words, "Either your guts are out there on the page or they're not." But as Lester Faigley quite reasonably asks, "Why is writing about potentially embarrassing aspects of one's life more honest than, say, the efforts of [a] student who tries to figure out what Thucydides was up to in writing about the Peloponnesian War?"[14]

Unhappily, when we evaluate writing in terms of its honesty or authenticity, we may not be judging the skill of our students but instead attempting to assess their very souls.

QUESTIONS OF EFFECTIVENESS. Despite the current respect for student self-actualizing, nondirective teaching, and the really remarkable success it sometimes enjoys, this pedagogy is not always effective. It works very well for charismatic teachers such as Don Murray, Peter Elbow, and Ken Macrorie, but it is far from uniformly successful. Not all students are comfortable with this kind of teaching. And the outcome of comparative research has often been disappointing.

Student Reactions.   Affect-centered teaching is not for everybody. Even charismatic teachers cannot reach *all* of their students with this technique. Robert Brooke notes that both Peter Elbow and Don Murray urge students who do not find the work congenial or who cannot commit to regular free-writing to drop their classes.[15] And some of Lou Kelly's students also express discomfort. Take these journal entries, for example:

- I am really bothered about having to write things down and letting some one else read them or show them to the class.
- How can I write honestly about myself when I don't know who I am? (649)

Why do some students experience difficulty with an affect-centered composition classroom? A teaching-methods student's thoughtful journal response to some readings on the subject may offer insight. She writes:

Seems more like a psychological free-writing therapy session than an English class. I know from personal experience that it may lead to uncomfortable — unwanted — dangerous — psychological and emotional unburdening.[16]

These examples are admittedly anecdotal, but research shows that this sort of troubled student feeling is widespread. Hillocks, in a massive survey, compared the attitudes of students taught in nondirective (mainly affect-centered), presentational (lecture — mainly craft-centered), and "environmental" (balanced) composition courses and discovered the least positive student attitude in the nondirectional classes. By a "highly significant margin," these students even viewed the straight lecture courses more favorably.[17]

FINAL CONSIDERATION.   These results do not point to the wisdom of a thoroughgoing endorsement of the self-actualizing approach. A totally affect-centered solution to the craft–criticism dilemma therefore must, to a degree, remain suspect. Surely, we must entertain strong doubts about an approach to teaching a craft that, in order to eliminate the sometimes damaging tool of correction, would eliminate teaching the craft itself.

A PROPOSED SOLUTION:
PERSONAL SUPPORT AND ACADEMIC DEMAND

Students, then, cannot effectively learn to write when teachers emphasize the craft of writing at the expense of their psyches nor when teachers emphasize psychological development and disregard the craft. Most assuredly, however, students can learn to write. There have always been teachers whose students year after year confide to their friends, "You know, I really learned something about writing this year" or "Be sure to sign up for Mrs. Brown [Dr. Jones, Mr. Cohen] — she [he] really teaches you to write." Many of the Mrs. Browns, Dr. Joneses, and Mr. Cohens share markedly similar approaches to the teaching of writing. Almost without exception they are aware of the difficulties of the dilemma discussed here, and again almost without exception—though, of course, each with his or her own style and in his or her own manner—they attack the problem by adopting an approach that is at once personally supportive and academically demanding.

Research Confirmation of the Balanced Approach

Though most of those teachers arrived at their methods instinctively or through experience, endorsement of this dual approach is grounded in a wide base of research.

INTERVENTIONAL BALANCE.   George Hillocks, Jr., in particular, did a careful meta-analysis of a large body of studies on the various approaches and found a balanced approach overwhelmingly the most effective. He compared studies on "the presentational [craft-centered] mode [which] emphasizes the teacher as presenter of knowledge about writing" and the "natural process [affect-centered] mode [which] emphasizes the student as generator of ideas, criteria, and forms" with studies on the "environmental [balanced] mode [which] appears to place teacher and student more nearly in balance, with the teacher planning activities and selecting materials through which students interact with each other to generate ideas and learn identifiable writing skills." He found that research results using the balanced approach were four times more effective than those using a craft-centered approach and three times more effective than those using an affect-centered approach (*Research on Written Composition* 123, 247).

AFFECTIVE BALANCE.   Research demonstrates the importance of balance on the affective level too. On the one hand, the fact that a teacher's personal support and warmth favorably influence student learning is well documented experimentally. Alberta D. J. Goodman's research, for example, found it of particular importance for writing students:

> Within an environment of acceptance and positive feedback, learners . . . gain both in their self-concept of their ability to communicate and in their actual ability.[18]

But on the other hand, there is a sizable body of research that suggests that warmth and acceptance alone do not ensure achievement. Neither Jere E. Brophy's functional analysis nor B. Ware's study, for example, found teacher praise to have a completely reinforcing effect.[19] Students tend to be skeptical when praise seems indiscriminate and rarely respond unless they perceive it to be warranted. The same principle is at work when students perceive an assignment to be too easy. Certainly, it is important to let our students experience success, but we must understand that they experience a sense of success more readily when they feel they have met a challenge. As Mike Rose points out:

> We should not assume that the successful completion of an assignment the
> student might well perceive as being simple, even juvenile, is going to make
> him feel better about himself or his writing. (113)

Praise for such work, like praise based only on simple kindness, does not
elevate students' levels of self-esteem. Thus, though unfairly placed or excessive criticism is harmful, warmth and praise are also ineffectual where quality
is not insisted upon and standards do not exist.

Teacher Expectation of Student Success

Teaching practices that combine both personal support and academic demand may seem at first glance to be paradoxical. On further consideration,
however, we can see that they are not really antagonistic attitudes at all, but
rather symbiotic ones. Both practices demonstrate the teacher's abiding sense
of the student's worth. Simple kindness coupled with no particular demands
may cause a student to think "Mr. Jones is awfully nice, but he doesn't think
too highly of my writing ability; he doesn't expect very much of me. And he
is probably right." After a conference with an equally kind, but more demanding, teacher, a student is more likely to think: "Ms. Wilson is really
hard! There is so much still to do. But she's fair, and she thinks I can do it.
Guess I better get to work."

Expectation makes a difference. The influence of teacher expectation on
student work can be amazing, as Rosenthal and Jacobson have verified experimentally. In their study, a group of children, distinguished from their classmates only by their teacher's (researcher-planted) expectations of achievement, did in fact achieve eleven IQ points more than the control students.[20]
Teacher expectation must work similarly in the teaching of writing. Thus,
for our students to learn the writing craft, we must approach them in a way
that is at the same time both personally supportive and academically demanding, a way that conveys to each student both that we expect him to
produce work that is clear, cogent, and good, and that we know with a certainty that he has what it takes to do so.[21]

INSISTING ON QUALITY. How, specifically, can teachers of writing
make manifest in the classroom their dual concern for student and craft?
First, for every assignment we must set up goals consistent with the particular
intellectual capacity and stage of development of our students. Although
there is little point in striving for writing of a professional caliber, we must
take care not to underestimate our students. For example, in teaching expository writing, it is not too much to expect all students to learn to write to a
point—that is, to be able to create a valid controlling idea and to support it
with logically ordered arguments or examples, even if the work produced is
only a paragraph in length or is confined to a very simple line of thought.
Once we are certain that our aims are realistic in terms of the particular
student, we must insist that these aims be achieved. Doing so, especially in
the beginning, will probably require our students to do a good bit of revision

and rewriting. And we must encourage that revision and rewriting so that they can succeed.

GIVING PERSONAL SUPPORT. Insistence upon such goals is the "demanding" aspect of the dual approach. Even though modification for individual differences should not be discounted, we should not waver from these demands. However, at the same time, everything should be done to make our demands as acceptable and as little threatening as possible. There are at least three basic ways to make learning to write more agreeable and more effective:

1. By establishing an accepting classroom atmosphere and building warm, supportive teacher–student and student–student relationships
2. By using teaching strategies aimed at reaching our students in all their individual diversity
3. By helping each of our students to the autonomy needed to develop his or her own thoughts in his or her own individual composing and writing style

In the remainder of this chapter, let's examine these general techniques in specific, practical terms.

ESTABLISHING AN ACCEPTING ATMOSPHERE

The ways in which we establish our relationship with our students and the atmosphere in our classrooms are as diverse as those of us who teach and as numerous as the classes we each meet, for the relationship between a teacher and her or his class is a very personal thing indeed. Whether it will be formal or informal, quiet or boisterous, "modern" or "old-fashioned" will reflect our individual personalities. The suggestions in the following Teaching Strategies are ideas that have fitted well into the styles of a number of successful teachers and have served them effectively.

TEACHING STRATEGIES

Establishing Relationships with Students

1. Establish a warm and personal atmosphere from the first day.
   a. For example, introduce yourself with a few words about your own background (where you received your education, whether you have a dog, whether you enjoy concerts or tennis, and so on), and then as you call the roll, ask each student to do the same. Comment or respond in some friendly way to what each has to say.
   b. Or have each student chat for a moment with his or her neighbor and then introduce each other to the class.
2. Observe the students closely and get to know and care about them as individuals.

continued

continued

    a. Learn your student's names as soon as possible. (Sometimes associating the student's names in your memory with some idiosyncracy of appearance or personality helps.)

    b. Mark the roll list with diacritical marks the first time you call the roll in order to prevent mispronouncing anyone's name twice. The correct pronunciation of one's name is disproportionately important to many people. By saying his name right, you just could make Joe Pieczonka a friend for life. At this time, it is also a good idea to write in nicknames and preferred names. Is Elizabeth Ann called "Liz"? "Bessie"? "Beth Ann"? "Annie"? "Betty"? Or maybe even "Elizabeth Ann"?

    c. Always avoid ridicule and sarcasm. Even a very witty retort can wound or embarrass.

    d. If you notice something pleasant about a student—something you would comment on in an acquaintance—go ahead and mention it. But think carefully first because such comments can sometimes become too personal and cause discomfort. Nevertheless, most people, students included, are flattered to be noticed and respond with pleasure to an honest compliment such as "What a handsome new coat."

3. Encourage interaction among the students.

    a. Have small groups work together to do or correct exercises, to explore ideas before sharing them with the class as a whole, and with even smaller groups (of two or three) to respond to one another's papers and help each other revise. (For strategies for small-group work, see Chapter 5.)

    b. In whole-class sessions, prompt real exchange rather than a simple teacher questions/student answers format. Placing the chairs in a circle so the students can see one another and respond to each other is the first step toward genuine discussion.

4. Never close the door on writing improvement.

    a. Encourage students to rewrite their papers by grading the revised work at its full value. After all, there's no point in penalizing students for something they hadn't learned yet.

    b. Rather than confronting a student with a discouraging grade, try withholding the mark, as many successful teachers do, until after revision. (Always give the student the option, however, of asking about and accepting the grade instead of rewriting—though very few will take this option.)

    c. Nevertheless, don't expect most papers to improve by simply asking a student to rewrite. Most students do as well as they can the first time and need help in re-visioning before they revise.

    d. It would be foolish to pretend that for many students rewriting is anything but onerous and difficult work. Nevertheless, it is in rethinking their ideas and organization that students come to see how confusion can be made to give way to clarity. It is in struggling with the complexities of one's own thoughts and sentences that a person really learns to write.

INDIVIDUALIZING OUR TEACHING

Because we face our students in great numbers—as many as twenty-five or thirty at a time—it is easy to forget that each one is an individual, totally different from all the others. Our students differ in size and shape and color. They differ in socioeconomic, religious, philosophical, and national background. They differ in degree of shyness or bravado—in how well they hide their sensitivity—but all are sensitive. They differ in knowledge, skills, and capability. They differ in physical, emotional, and cognitive development. And they differ profoundly in their learning styles. They differ from each other and they differ from us as well.

Responding to Difference

How can our teaching handle all these differences? We need to understand and appreciate the difference in each student and still identify with the fellow-suffering human being at the core.

TEACHING STRATEGIES

Basic Principles

1. Try to *reach the students where they are* and take them further.
2. Look for strategies that will *engage* their minds and use these strategies. And because our students differ so markedly, we need to *use a whole variety of strategies.*

RESPONDING TO DIFFERENCES IN CAPABILITY. Since our classes have students with a whole range of ability levels, we tend to aim our teaching at the middle of the range. And so we should. Our general lessons should engage as many minds as possible. But we also need to reach the students at the ends of the range.

For the Student Who Has a Hard Time Catching On. This is the student most of us have the greatest trouble identifying with, since most of us who choose to teach English are pretty fair scholars ourselves. Sometimes we think: "If this kid weren't so lazy—if she *really* tried, she'd be doing a whole lot better." And we find ourselves secretly growing annoyed with her.

My own solution to this problem is to remember how I felt when I, with only the most desultory preparation, was placed in a Latin class where the teacher and most of the students had been studying that language together for three years. I remained completely muddled no matter how hard I tried to figure out what Caesar was doing in the Gallic Wars—and I tried very hard indeed. The experience was traumatic, but looking back I think that, when it comes to my own teaching, that Latin class may have been the most valuable course I ever took. Perhaps you have had a similar experience. If so, you too can empathize with your student when you remember what it felt like *not* to be able to catch on—no matter what.

Beyond being empathic, we can take some practical steps to reach our less able or less prepared students. Ordinarily, they respond best to a highly structured approach. Provide them with a design and let them work within it—to fill in the blanks, so to speak—with their own ideas. For example, once they catch on to the rhythm (the dum-de-dums) of the ballad form and fill it with the story they want to tell, they will be writing iambic tetrameter-trimeter quatrains that sound surprisingly good and give them—and us—much pleasure. Even the (deservedly) despised five-paragraph-essay exercise has its use with these students. It gives them a place to hang their ideas. With a number of well-scaffolded assignments and plenty of personal help—peer tutoring, for example, and teacher conferencing—many of these students can experience an especially rewarding success.

For the Student Who Is Way Ahead.   Because we don't have to worry about especially able students, we may give them less attention than they deserve. Fairness alone suggests that they not be neglected. And with a little nourishing, they grow and blossom remarkably before our very eyes.

Some of these students delight in helping other students—and helping us. It is a good idea to put *these* students to work, for, as we well know, we learn best when we teach. They make wonderful peer-group leaders and effective tutors. But some gifted students don't enjoy this sort of thing, and they need stimulation too.

The poet Robert Browning hit the mark when he wrote, "A man's reach should exceed his grasp." We need to find projects for all our students—especially the particularly able—that will challenge them and engage them fully. When the class studies invention, for example, try assigning the advanced students an Aristotelian *topoi* heuristic while their classmates are practicing the five W's. On language days, let them learn, for instance, the basics of transformational-generative grammar while the others are struggling with the usual usage and syntax problems. Some gifted students need more time with their papers. They become really absorbed in the ideas they encounter and need time to follow through. By all means, give them that time. No reason a student can't skip an occasional assignment to let one longer, or more intensely worked, paper count for two. The trick is to enrich their assignments, rather than simply to require them to do more work. And we mustn't stint on conferencing for these students; nor should we forget that able and self-sufficient students need warmth and attention too.

RESPONDING TO DIFFERENCES IN COMPOSING STYLES. We are doomed to see only through our own eyes. And thus we may not be aware of multiplicity in composing styles. In fact, not until a chat a few years ago with a well-respected colleague did I (or he) ever have any idea that all competent writers did not set out to compose exactly as we did. But when we compared notes, we found that he habitually began by freewriting and I by listing. And, naturally, we had both been teaching invention in just the way we personally found effective. Since that day we have done some research on the invention question and have discovered an almost even split: half our students are planners, half are freewriters.[22]

The same diversity also occurs in other aspects of the composing process. Some writers, for instance, work better with collaborative assistance; others are more comfortable working alone. Some writers almost always do some sort of global revision; others prefer simply to edit a single draft. Furthermore, whatever one's individual composing preferences, they also vary with the purpose of the writing task and the kind of writing appropriate to it. How should we as teachers handle this diversity?

Teaching a Variety of Composing Styles. We need to help each student to find his or her own most comfortable writing style and to learn strategies to use it effectively.[23] And since most beginning writers are unaware of either their style or these strategies, we must give them the widest possible exposure to different styles and lots of opportunities to try out and practice various strategies. Once they have mastered a variety of techniques, we should give them the freedom to use the ones they prefer.

In approaching the diversity of invention practices I mentioned above, for example, we need to teach both the ins and the outs of the freewriting strategy and a variety of planning techniques — for instance, listing, clustering, and outlining — and to provide writing assignments requiring all the students to use these techniques (see Chapter 2). But when all our students have experienced a variety of inventing procedures, they should be free to use whatever they find most comfortable and effective for them individually.

We even need to provide students with an eventual choice for procedures as vital as global rewriting. Inexperienced writers need the opportunity to rewrite in order to develop a basic sense of structure, and it is essential that we encourage them to do so (see Chapter 5). Experienced writers, however, differ in their revising practices, as research has shown.[24] And thus we ought ultimately to permit our students this choice too.

Providing a Variety of Composing Opportunities. We also need to vary our own teaching approaches to accommodate our students varying learning proclivities. To learn, all students must be engaged. But they engage in varying ways. For instance, some learn best aurally and some visually. We thus must make information available to them through both speaking and reading. We should also enrich our oral presentation with appropriate visual support. To take another example, some students sometimes engage best through class discussion; others when involved in small groups; still others during individual conferences. We must be sure to provide an abundance of all these learning environments.

To accommodate differences, we must use a variety of approaches and teach a variety of methods, genres, and strategies. And we must be particularly sensitive to the needs of those whose styles of learning differ from our own.

RESPONDING TO DIFFERENCES IN COGNITIVE LEVEL The fact that our students can react to our teaching in totally contradictory ways may be the most disconcerting indication of student differences. Here is an all-too-familiar example. You're preparing your class for a *Beowulf* paper. You've asked your students to mark all the Christian and all the pagan references they can find. They come in prepared and have a rousing discussion. But as the students leave, you get the following contradictory reactions:

- Enthusiasm: "It was a great class! One of the best we've ever had. Allota evidence came out on both sides. I've got to decide which is the strongest. Maybe I'll find my way to compromise it for my paper."
- Determination: "If we just hang around acting interested long enough, she'll tell us 'The Answer,' and then we can write our papers."
- Indignation: "Why does she impose her views on us? She obviously favored the pagan interpretation. But my opinion is as good as hers."
- Anger: "If she is unable or unwilling to tell us 'The Facts,' she is just wasting our time."
- Shrewdness: "Clearly, she's biased for the Christian side. All I have to do is write a Christian-influence thesis and find some support for it in the text."
- Thoughtfulness: "I haven't quite made up my mind yet; I'll need to think the question through again. Maybe I'll read some critics. Then I'll be ready to write."

On days like that we can be grateful to William G. Perry, who—having probably been inspired by days like that himself—researched the mind-sets of his Harvard students and found that such conflicting reactions are natural to various stages of cognitive development. From his research, Perry developed a scheme upon which we can map the stages of our students' intellectual development.

Perry's Scales. Modeled in general on Piaget's developmental scales,[25] Perry sets up a four-part scheme charting the growing mind's progress upward through

- Duality: right and wrong securely distinguishable
- Multiplicity: there are many right answers, equally true
- Relativity: some partial truths are more valid than others
- Commitment: a selection of the ideas whose validity one will stand by.

Perry divides these parts into nine stages separated by transitional periods of self-questioning. He suggests that the stages are intellectual plateaus where growth is consolidated and characterizes the transitional periods as times of disequilibrium preceding growth.[26]

The following Teaching Strategies, offers an abbreviated adaptation of Perry's model.[27]

TEACHING STRATEGIES

Perry's Scheme

DUALITY

1. Authorities know.
   [Transition: But authorities disagree.]
2. *True* authorities know. (The others are frauds.)
   [Transition: But even good authorities admit they don't know all the answers.]
3. True authorities *will* know, once they complete their research.
   [Transition: But there are so *many* things they need to research, and they won't know for a very long *time*.]

MULTIPLICITY

4a. If even authorities don't know, then everyone's opinion is as good as anyone else's.
[or]
4b. It doesn't matter to Them what I say; They just want me to support it with data.
   [Transition: Supporting opinion with data seems to work, in school and out.]

RELATIVITY

5. Everything is relative but *not* equally valid.
   [Transition: Then how can I know I'm making the Right Choice?]
6. I'm going to have to make my own decisions in an uncertain world—not by relying on any authority, but by weighing varying authoritative data as best I can.

Using the Perry Scheme. Perry's work is not only interesting theoretically, but can be genuinely useful in the classroom.[28] It can help us to understand our students' reactions. With it we can identify the particular cognitive set motivating a student's thinking and thus figure out how to respond to it appropriately. Knowledge of Perry's scheme also helps us to empathize with our students, especially when they are experiencing the often painful transitional periods between one stage of intellectual growth and another. We need to make allowances for strong student reactions during these periods of disequilibrium, for as Perry (and Piaget) contends, cognitive growth is necessarily accompanied by psychic pain.

Perry's scheme will also help us to develop individual goals for our students. They come to us at various stages of intellectual growth. Thinking in terms of the Perry's scale, we can understand "where they are" and try to take them a little farther. In teaching our students to write, we can gently urge them to independent thinking and help them toward the goal of intellectual autonomy.

HELPING OUR STUDENTS TOWARD AUTONOMY

The third approach to a simultaneous accepting and demanding teacher–student relationship involves another paradox, the paradox of dependence and independence. The ultimate aim of teaching, like that of parenting, is to put ourselves out of business. Like good parents, we teachers aim to help our students gain the strength and skill that will continue to serve them when we are no longer by their sides. But exercising power to empower may be for many of us the most difficult part of our teaching responsibilities. Successful teachers, however, do achieve this balance.

Teaching Counts

Part of the difficulty stems from our own diffidence, our reluctance to assume an authoritative role. We're worried about being perceived in terms of the old-fashioned, discredited theory of the teacher-pitcher pouring knowledge into student-receptacles (a theory, by the way, to which most effective teachers never did subscribe). We know very well that teaching and learning is an interactive process. At present, however, the teaching component of the process may be underrated. Nevertheless, teaching does count. And that fact has been well substantiated by research. In a recent study, for instance, David L. Wallace and John R. Hayes were "able to produce a significant increase in global revision and improvement in revision quality . . . in a substantial proportion of treatment group members . . . with just eight minutes of instruction."[29] Good teaching is still one of the most valuable skills in the world, and we should not be timid about using it.

Students Count Too

On the other hand, we must take care not to dominate the learning process. To become better writers, better scholars, and better citizens, students need to develop confidence and a sense of themselves as individuals. There is much we can do in the writing classroom to further this end:

- We can recognize each student's individuality—and give him or her recognition for that individuality.
- We can give students plenty of opportunity to express themselves in writing—without teacher intervention.
- And when we intervene, we can do so as a coach—or as an editor in the Maxwell Perkins' sense—not as an adversary.
- We can encourage student participation and make sure that such participation is meaningful.
- And we can help our students acquire the communicating skills with which they can become truly autonomous.

Each of these ideas is also rich in pedagogical possibilities. Let's examine them in more detail.

RECOGNIZE INDIVIDUALITY. By following strategies for responding to individual differences, such as those suggested above (pages 15–20), we acknowledge students as individuals and help them to establish a sense of personal identity. One way to promote a positive self-image is to encourage students to write about the ideas that make them themselves, their values, their religion, their background. We can then engender a favorable response from their classmates by responding positively to these ideas ourselves.

Whenever we can, we should help them rejoice in their own particular identities. Such recognition, though, must be tactfully handled. For example, in teaching poetic meter, we might ask a student of Greek descent to count in Greek for the class. Pronouncing the Greek numbers would not only clarify the *dimeter*, *trimeter*, *tetrameter*, *pentameter*, and so on, for the class, but would also give recognition to the student in terms of his or her family heritage. Favorable recognition is especially important for students whose backgrounds are sometimes targeted for bigotry. We can, for instance, bring out some of the more interesting facts about the family languages and dialects of our students in linguistic discussions (see Chapter 7 for suggestions).

OFFER OPPORTUNITIES FOR SELF-EXPRESSION. Students need to learn how to use writing to explore their thinking. And they need some writing opportunities to get a sense of their own thought processes. Assigned journal responses are useful for both purposes and also serve as a reservoir of composition ideas. But whether the responses are kept in a notebook meant to be turned in on a regular basis or are written in class for immediate sharing, they belong to their student authors in a way distinctive from other academic writing. And we need to respect that ownership. Whether to read an entry aloud or not should be the student's decision. When we collect and read student journals, we should respond to the content, and comment as we would in correspondence or in written conversation. We should show our interest, perhaps model a better choice, but not correct the form. Students need some private ground in their writing, territory where teachers do not intervene.

BE A TEACHER–COACH.   In the less private writing, where we do intervene, our comments and advice should not convey the impression of a teacher-adversary. We are, after all, on the same side; we have the same goal: that the students succeed. Many effective writing teachers say they take the athletic coach as their model, working with their students to improve their writing skills.

MAKE STUDENT PARTICIPATION MEANINGFUL.   When students participate, they are open to learning. They also gain a sense of autonomy. How can we encourage participation? First, by establishing an atmosphere of trust, where all students know that they will not be mocked, that their thoughts will not be put down. Students must feel free to speak or write whatever they wish within the bounds of civility. And they must be able to count on teacher-backed civility to preserve that freedom.

The second way to encourage student participation is to make participation significant. Students who think that what they say or write makes little difference will not want to participate. If we give them the feeling that all decisions have been made and all the answers are known, they will not want to make suggestions or to answer questions. We must make them feel that what they say and do in our classes has consequence.

Effective teachers promote this assurance throughout the full variety of pedagogical situations.

In Class Discussion.   Our most successful writing teachers rarely lecture, but rather present instruction through class discussion and by eliciting responses. Most of the questions they ask when they lead these discussions are open-ended, inviting unrestricted responses. And even when they have a good idea of what sort of answer they hope to elicit, they do not reject the unexpected out of hand, but instead hear the student out and genuinely consider what he has to say.

A student responding in such class discussions feels listened to. Her classmates feel comfortable questioning her, arguing with her, or augmenting or clarifying what she has to say. And so does the teacher as he picks up the thread and leads the discussion further.

In Student Groups.   Small groups offer students a chance for even greater involvement. The shy student usually feels less intimidated in a small group, and since there are fewer people to share the talking time, more students are able to participate. When small-group teaching works, students believe that the task they are assigned is worth doing and that their participation is consequential. Such positive student belief directly reflects the teacher's attitude and behavior.

In successful peer groups, students *know* that what they say actually counts. When they help one another revise, reviewers take their reviewing seriously because they know that the writer will either follow their suggestions or at least weigh and consider them. When students are asked to come to a decision, they know that their decision will be implemented, as far as possible.

In Conferences. The key to a successful student–teacher conference is a teacher who really listens. Our aim is to discover what the student truly wants to say and to help her discover the best way to say it. We are free to make—even obliged to make—suggestions to help the student achieve his writing goal. But the goal remains the student's, and we must be quick to back off if we have misconceived it. And even when our advice is valid, the paper remains the student's and the final decision must always be hers.

MAKE SURE STUDENTS HAVE SKILLS. Gaining confidence and a sense of autonomy is an important goal which we as writing teachers can help our students to achieve. But confidence is empty if it is not grounded in genuine skill, and a sense of autonomy remains useless without the skills to exercise it. So the most important help we can give our students in this regard is to make sure they can communicate their ideas effectively in writing.

In Summary

For good work to be produced despite the problems of the intense ego involvement of the writer with his work, we teachers of writing must, in the particular style of our own personalities, lavish upon our students enough warmth and good humor to let them know we care about them as individuals and permit them to glimpse enough strength in our own characters to make them secure in the knowledge that we can—and, when necessary, will—help them to achieve in their writing.

And whatever style we choose to adopt in our classrooms, I hope all of us will include lots of good talk and some laughter to make the learning sweet.

IDEAS FOR DISCUSSION OR ESSAY

1. Can the "traditional" approach be employed without resorting to any sort of psychological "hickory stick"?
2. Is there anything in your personal experience that would confirm or refute Rosenthal and Jacobson's findings on the importance of teacher expectations to what a student learns?

3. At which stage on the Perry Scheme would you place each of the Beowulf class students quoted on page 18?

4. The accompanying article was written in frustration by a disillusioned young idealist who pinned his hopes on a nondirective, affect-centered approach to the teaching of college freshman composition. How would you respond to him?

IN SHORT, WHY DID THE CLASS FAIL?*

By Henry F. Ottinger

And now, like it or not, I'd like to say a few parting words. As you know, I began the semester in a way that departed from the manner in which I had taught composition classes in the past. Much of my attitude at that time was influenced by Jerry Farber's book, *The Student as Nigger*. On the first day of class, I read to you the following:

> School is where you let the dying society put its trip on you. Our schools may seem useful: to make children into doctors, sociologists, engineers — to discover things. But they're poisonous as well. They exploit and enslave students; they petrify society; they make democracy unlikely. And it's not what you're taught that does the harm, but how you're taught. Our schools teach you by pushing you around, by stealing your will and your sense of power, by making timid, apathetic slaves of you — authority addicts.

That sounded like a breath of fresh air back in February — and I suggested that we try to break the mold, that we could write papers on any subject we wanted, that we could spend class time discussing things — either "the burning issues of the day," or otherwise. You seemed to agree, and we spent a lot of time agreeing together that indeed Farber had the word and we would do what we could to break out of the mold.

As you know, things went from initial ecstasy to final catastrophe. And recently, I fell back — no, you forced me back — into assigning general topics. As a result of that action, and several other factors, this semester has been the worst I've ever taught. In fact, I even debated with myself whether or not to go on teaching next year. But in some ways the semester was valuable because I learned something, if you didn't.

*This article was derived from a final lecture delivered in 1972 by Henry F. Ottinger, an instructor of English and a doctoral candidate at the University of Missouri. The text has been revised slightly by the author. Copyright 1971 by the New York Times Company. Reprinted by permission.

continued

Let me share with you some of the things I learned: and keep in mind that this does not apply to all of you, but it does to the majority.

I learned that all this bull about "getting it together" or "working to-gether" (be it for peace or a grade) is just that—bull. The 1950's [students] were labeled by pop sociologists the "silent generation." I assure you they have nothing on you. Ten years ago, the people around the fountains wore saddle shoes and chinos, and had crewcuts. Now they're barefoot, wear Army fatigues, and have long hair. Big revelation: it's the same bunch of people.

Generally, this class has been the most silent, reticent, paranoid bunch of people in a group I have ever experienced. If you are indicative of the generation that's supposed to change things, good luck. Change is predicated on, among other things, communication between people, "which in your case," as the poem "Naming of Parts" goes, "you have not got."

You had an opportunity to exchange ideas (which it often turned out "you have not got,") and you were too embarrassed to do so.

You had an opportunity to find out about each other—you didn't. (Or perhaps you found out some of the same things I did: if so, congratulations: the semester has not been a waste for you.)

You had an opportunity to find out something about yourselves. This, by the way, is the crux of education. And, as far as I can see, you found out very little.

You had an opportunity to exchange ideas—on your own—and didn't. Most of the papers hashed over the usual cliche-ridden topics: abortion, the SST, the population explosion. One person went so far as to churn out a masterpiece on the pros and cons of fraternities, a topic that was really hot back around 1956.

Most of all, you had the opportunity to be free—free from the usual absurdities of a composition class where topics are assigned, thesis state-ments are submitted, and so on. You also had freedom of thought, as long as it was confined to the standards of formal English. You had the opportunity to be free—to be responsible to yourselves—and you succeeded in proving to me and to yourselves that "Freedom is Slav-ery," a line from *1984* which I hope, for the sake of all of us, isn't pro-phetic.

continued

continued

But you protest! (Oh, how I wished you would): "We're incapable of handling all this freedom at once. You see, Mr. Ottinger, we've been conditioned; we're not used to all this!"

Well, I read that in Farber, too, and it's bull. Rats and dogs are conditioned, and are usually incapable of breaking that conditioning. Human beings can break conditioning, if it's to their advantage. But here, it's too good an excuse to say "I'm conditioned." Obviously, then, it's to your advantage not to break out of the mold.

Why is it to your advantage not to break the mold? In short, why did the class fail?

It failed because, as Dostoevski's "Underground Man" pointed out, thinking causes pain. And, like good little utilitarians, you want to avoid pain. No, it's much easier to come up with instant aesthetics, instant solutions, instant salvation, instant thoughts. After all, instant things, like breakfasts and TV dinners, are easily digestible—and easily regurgitated—and not terribly nourishing.

One of the more atrocious remarks I've heard this semester is, "Gosh, college is no fun," or, when an idea is presented, "It doesn't turn me on."

If you don't believe that knowledge for its own sake is a valid and valuable goal, then you are in the wrong place, and you'd do much better in a vocational school, studying how to be a plumber or a beautician. And if you don't believe, along with Ezra Pound, that "real education must ultimately be limited to men who INSIST on knowing," you are definitely in the wrong place. You are merely clutter.

Granted, there are problems within the University itself—serious problems—that, despite what you may think, show some sign of possible solution. One step they could take (but probably won't) is to limit enrollment, and keep the forty-five percent of you out who don't belong here, because it's no fun.

Well, it's time, I suppose, to bring this to halt, and let you go over to the Union, or wherever. Until then, I invite you to listen to the lyrics of the Beatles' "Nowhere Man," and if it fits, take it to heart.

Last, I will bid good-bye (until the final) and say that if at any time some sly hint, or cluc, or (God forbid) a half-truth slipped out of my unconscious and slid out the corner of my mouth and, pardon

continued

the expression, "turned one of you on," then we have not failed, you and I.

And, to paraphrase Theodore Roethke: I love you for what you might be; I'm deeply disturbed by what you are.

NOTES

The part-opening epigraph is from William Irmsher's *Teaching Expository Writing* (New York: Holt, 1979), 50–51.

The chapter-opening epigraph is from Donald Graves, quoted in Charles W. Bridges, Toni A. Lopez, Ronald F. Lunsford, eds. *Training the New Teacher of College Composition*, (Urbana: NCTE, 1985), 7.

1. Robert Rosenthal and Leonore Jacobson, *Pygmalion in the Classroom* (New York: Holt, 1968; Thomas L. Good and Jere E. Brophy, *Educational Psychology: A Realistic Approach*, (New York: Longman, 1990), 456.

2. A. Confrey, "Comments Made by Instructors on Student Themes," *Catholic Educational Digest* 24 (1927): 335–40.

3. Robert J. Connors and Andrea A. Lumsford, "Frequency of Formal Errors in Current College Writing, or Ma and Pa Kettle Do Research," *CCC* 39 (1988): 398.

4. Kelvin L. Seifert, *Educational Psychology*, 2nd ed. (Boston: Houghton, 1991) writes about the "negative effects of sarcasm [and] criticism" (285); Thomas L. Good and Jere Brophy, *Looking in Classrooms*, 4th ed. (New York: Harper, 1987) say that "severe personal criticism cannot be justified. . . It has no corrective function" (269). See also S. Tobias, "Test Anxiety: Interference, Defective Skills, and Cognitive Capacity," *Educational Psychologist* 20 (1985): 135–42; and J. P. Wine, "Theory of Test Anxiety," in *Test Anxiety; Theory, Research, and Applications to Reduce the Negative Implications*, ed. I. Sarason, (Hillsdale, N.J.: Erlbaum, 1980).

In addition, Lee Odell documents examples of anxiety-produced agitated—even irrational—student behavior: "Whenever I see a mark on my paper, I panic," one student explained; see "Responding to Responses: Good News, Bad News, and Unanswered Questions," in *Encountering Student Texts: Interpretive Issues in Reading Student Writing*, eds. Bruce Lawson, Susan Sterr Ryan, and W. Ross Winterowd, (Urbana: NCTE, 1989) 221. And Ericka Lindemann, like many experienced teachers, attributes the familiar student–writer's block to "past teachers' finding fault with every paper." See *A Rhetoric for Teachers* (New York: Oxford UP, 1987), 14. Psychologists John A. Daly and Michael Miller discovered that writing apprehension correlates not only with remembered anxiety-ridden learning situations but also with a number of undesirable later results, including, for example, a tendency to avoid occupations perceived to involve writing; see "The Empirical Development of an Instrument to Measure Writing Apprehension" and "Further Studies in Writing Apprehension: SAT Scores, Success Expectations, Willingness to Take Advance Courses and Sex Differences," *RTE* 9 (1975): 242–49, 250–56.

See also Ned Flanders, "Personal-Social Anxiety as a Factor in Experimental Learning Situations," *JER*, 55 (1951): 100–10; R. Spalding, *Achievement, Creativity, and Self-Concept Correlates of Teacher-Pupil Transactions in Elementary Schools* (Champaign: U of Illinois P, 1962); and Seymour B. Sarason et al., *Anxiety in Elementary School Children* (New York: Wiley, 1960).

5. Thomas C. Gee, "Students' Responses to Teacher Comments," *RTE* 6 (1972): 216; Dwight L. Burton and Lois V. Arnold, *Effects of Frequency of Writing and Intensity of Teacher Evaluation upon High School Students' Performance in Written Composition* (Tallahassee: Florida State UP, 1963); and Sayra B. Nikoloff, *The Relationship of Teacher Standards to the Written Expression of Fifth and Sixth Grade Children* (Urbana: NCTE, 1967).

6. See Timothy McCracken and Allen Ashby, "The Widow's Walk: An Alternative for English 101 — Creative Communications," *CE* 36 (1975): 555–78; Gregory Jay, "The Subject of Pedagogy: Lessons in Psychoanalysis and Politics," *CE* 49 (1987): 789; Joy Ritchie, "Beginning Writers: Diverse Voices and Individual Identity," *CCC* 40 (1989): 156.

7. George Hillocks, Jr., *Research on Written Composition: New Directions for Teaching* (Urbana: NCRE and ERIC, 1987): 119; Lou Kelly, "Toward Competence and Creativity in an Open Class," *CE* 34 (1973): 644–660.

8. For just a few outstanding examples, see the articles by McCracken, Ashby, and Ritchie cited in note 5 and the article by Kelly cited in note 6; see also Jean Pumphrey, "Teaching English Composition as a Creative Art," *CE* 34 (1973): 666–673; Ken Macrorie, "To Be Read," *EJ* (1968): 686–692; and Donald M. Murray, "Teach Writing as a Process not Product," in the New England Association of Teachers of English *Leaflet* (November 1972), 11–14.

9. *EJ*, for instance, devoted its October and November 1987 issues to "Psychoanalysis and Pedagogy."

10. Ann Murphy, "Transference and Resistance in the Basic Writing Classroom: Problematics and Praxis," *CCC* 40 (1989): 178, 181.

11. Louise Rosenblatt, *Literature as Exploration* (New York: Appleton, 1938) 207. In this connection, consider this ardent young teacher's words: "In my writing courses, I *want* to meddle with my students' emotional lives, and I *want* their writing to meddle with mine"; see Lad Tobin, "Reading Students, Reading Ourselves: Revising the Teacher's Role in the Writing Class," *CE* 53 (1991): 342.

12. Peter Elbow, "Reflections on Academic Discourse: How It Relates to Freshmen and Colleagues," *CE* 53 (1991): 135. Other experts agree. Mike Rose reviewed over 500 across-the-curriculum writing assignments and discovered that personal narrative is not the academic genre:

> There were simply no assignments calling for the student to narrate or describe personal experiences, to observe relatively immediate objects or events . . . , to express a general opinion on something not studied closely, to reflect on self. ("Remedial Writing Courses: A Critique and a Proposal, *CE* 45 [February 1983]: 110.)

13. Susan Belasco Smith's review of Ken Macrorie's *The I-Search Paper*, *CCC* 40 (1989): 360–61. And other experts agree. Ann Murphy writes: "Our explicit focus (or governmental mandate) concerns not the exploration of student psyches, but the enhancement of their skills in wielding . . . written discourse" (178).

14. See *What Makes Writing Good*, eds. William Coles and James Vopat (Lexington, Mass.: Heath, 1985), 161 for Lindemann and Harris's comment. See also Lester Faigley, "Judging Writing, Judging Selves," *CCC* 40 (1989): 404–05 and his response

to Bruce Holland *CCC* (1991) 89–90. The Coles and Vopat book is an anthology of student papers selected for their excellence by a number of well known writing instructors, who also included explanations for their choices. In analyzing the anthology, Faigley discovered that at least 30 of the 48 selections were "personal experience essays."

15. Robert Brooke, "Lacan, Transference, and Writing Instruction," *CE* 49 (1987): 683; Peter Elbow, *Writing Without Teachers*, 78; Don Murray: *A Writer Teaches Writing*, 203.

Brooke offers an interesting, though perhaps somewhat disturbing, analysis of the achievement of charismatic teachers. He explains the success of "response" teaching like Murray's and Elbow's in terms of Lacan's willing psychiatric transference to the teacher, "who is supposed to know." The idea is that since truth can't be taught (Plato) and each individual must find his/her own way, students find their way by projecting their ideas on to the nonresponding teacher and behaving (that is, writing) as they believe Teacher would approve. As Brooke puts it, "The real dialogue is within the patient [student] and the voice he puts into your mouth" (686).

16. Student, Wilmington College, 1991.

17. George Hillocks, Jr. "The Responses of College Freshmen to Three Modes of Instruction," *American Journal of Education*, 89 (1981): 373–95.

18. Alberta D. J. Goodman, "Utilization of Positive Feedback in a Classroom Environment of Acceptance to Promote Enhanced Learner Self-Concept and Improved Writer Performance," *DAI* 36 (1975), 6550A, U of Michigan. For the effect of teacher acceptance in other disciplines see: Howard A. Maynard, Jr., "Student Perceived Teacher Effectiveness in Business Communications," *DAI* 35 (1974) 4867A (Georgia State U); and Horace B. Reed, "Implications for Science Education of a Teacher Competence Research," *Science Education* 46 (1962): 473–86.

19. Jere E. Brophy, "Teacher Praise: A Functional Analysis," *RER* 5 (1981): 5–32; B. Ware, "What Rewards Do Students Want?" *Phi Delta Kappan* 59 (1978): 355–56.

20. Though no other experimenters have been able to duplicate the positive results of the Rosenthal and Jacobson experiment (see Note 1) quite as spectacularly, other researchers have documented similar sized negative results, where a teacher's low expectations has lead to lower achievement. Studies reporting statistically significant positive or negative effect on students include C. Cornbleth, O. Davis, and C. Button, "Teacher-Pupil Interaction and Teacher Expectations for Pupil Achievement in Secondary Social Studies Classes" (paper presented at the annual meeting of the American Educational Research Association [AERA], 1972); J. Jeter and O. Davis, "Elementary School Teachers' Differential Classroom Interaction with Children as a Function of Differential Expectations of Pupil Achievements, AERA annual meeting, 1973; Jere Brophy and Thomas Good, *Teacher-Student Relationships: Causes and Consequences*, (New York: Holt, 1974); H. Cooper, *"Intervening and Expectation Communication: A Follow-Up Study to the "Personal Control" Study* (Hamilton, New York: Colgate UP, 1976); and Thomas Good, H. Cooper, and S. Blakey, "Classroom Interaction as a Function of Teacher Expectations, Student Sex, and Time of Year," *JEP* 72 (1980): 378–385.

21. This combination, which B. McCandless and E. Evans call "noncontingent acceptance and provision of sensitive but realistic and honest feedback" (*Children and Youth: Psychosocial Development* [Hinsdale, Ill: Dryden, 1973]), has been found to be successful almost universally. For example, when J. Kleinfeld studied "Effective teachers of Indian and Eskimo Students," she discovered that the most effective teachers

elicited high intellectual performance from the village Indian and Eskimo students by creating warm personal relationships and demanding a level of academic work 'that the student does not suspect he can attain.' Village students interpreted the teachers demandingness not as bossiness or hostility but rather as another expression of personal concern. (As quoted in Good and Brophy [1990] 458.)

22. Professor William Guthrie, Wilmington College. Our last survey of 88 freshman composition students, for example, came out precisely 44 free-writers and 44 planners. See also Joy Reid, "The Radical Outliner and the Radical Brainstormer: A Perspective on Composing Processes," *TESOL Quarterly* 18 (1985): 529–34.

23. George H. Jensen and John K. DiTiberio in "Personality and Individual Writing Processes," (*CCC* 35 [1984]) point out that

> If teachers deliver the same advice to all students, they may, despite good intentions, render more harm than good. Then students will begin to write as the teachers wish, not necessarily as they write best. (287)

And Jack Selzer in "Exploring Options in Composing," (*CCC* 35 [Oct 1984]) writes:

> Teachers need to concentrate on expanding and directing students' composing repertoires, in much the same way they expand and direct students' stylistic repertoires. (281)

24. In studying the practices of expert writers, Lester Faigley and Stephen Witte found "extreme diversity." In "Analyzing Revision," (*CCC* 32 [1981]) they write:

> One expert in the present study made almost no revisions; another started with an almost stream-of-consciousness text that she then converted to an organized essay in the second draft; another limited his major revisions to a single long insert; and another revised mostly by pruning. (410)

Other studies have had similar results. See Lillian S. Bridwell, "Revising Strategies in Twelfth Grade Students' Transactional Writing," *RTE* 14 (1980): 197–222; Linda Flower, John R. Hayes et al, "Detection, Diagnosis, and the Strategies of Revision," *CCC* 36 (1986): 16–55; Joan Henley, "A Revisionist View of Revision," *Washington English Journal* 8 (1986): 5–7; and Stephen P. Witte, "Pre-text and Composing," *CCC* 38 (1987): 397–425. For a comprehensive discussion, see Muriel Harris, "Composing Behaviors of One- and Multi-Draft Writers," *CE* 51 (1989): 174–191.

25. Walter L. Bateman suggests that Perry's scheme "could be considered as . . . a nine-rung ladder on which the student climbs from [Piaget's] stage three to stage four." See *Open to Question: The Art of Teaching and Learning by Inquiry* (San Francisco: Jossey-Bass, 1990), 37.

26. Joseph Williams has pointed out that one can respond to different situations at different cognitive stages. Facing an unfamiliar intellectual demand or entering a new cognitive community (the doctor's office, for instance) often sends us back a stage or two.

27. William G. Perry, *Forms of Intellectual and Ethical Development in the College Years: A Scheme*, (New York: Holt, 1970). My version is derived from the scheme appearing in "Cognitive and Ethical Growth: The Making of Meaning" in *The Modern American College*, ed. Arthur W. Chickering, (San Francisco: Jossey, 1981). I have omitted the Commitment stages as beyond our focus.

28. It would be unwise, however, to teach directly to the Scheme as a few Perry enthusiasts suggest. Perry's purpose is descriptive, not prescriptive. Besides, such a plan is illogical on its face: If confronted by a series of assignments cued to rungs on Perry's ladder, students would react at their current stage of development—just as they do to any assignment.

29. David L. Wallace and John R. Hayes, "Redefining Revision for Freshmen," *RTE* 25 (1991): 63. Such conclusions may appear self-evident. But recent challenges to the usefulness of teaching—such as that implied by the title of Peter Elbow's popular text, *Writing without Teachers*, for instance, have called all into question. See also Hillocks's *Research* where, in discussing L. M. Calkins's "Case Study of a Nine Year Old Writer," he speculates that "more direct teaching would have helped Andrea develop more quickly. If the instructor knows the rules, or some rules, for generating a stronger lead, . . . why not help the child become privy to them?" (18).

□ □ □   Part II

THE WRITING PROCESS

TEACHING THE WRITING PROCESS

What Should We Teach?

Despite the fact that the traditional modes of discourse have been largely discredited (and quite properly so),[1] we teachers of writing need to find some comprehensive way to approach our discipline. The following scheme, based on categories devised by Toby Fulwiler,[2] may be useful to us for that purpose:

AUDIENCE-FOCUSED WRITING

- *Writing to communicate:* to convey an idea clearly and logically. [usually called expository writing.]
- *Writing to imagine:* to create art—poetry, fiction, drama, and song—something to do with beauty, play, emotion, and personal expression. [usually called creative writing.]

NON-AUDIENCE-FOCUSED WRITING

- *Writing to think:* writing to yourself—concentrat[ing] on thoughts, feelings, problems, whatever—not on audience; personal, expressive, exploratory, or merely informal writing; honest writing—there's no point in pretending; diaries, journals, jotted notes, free-writing, personal letters.

READER-BASED AND WRITER-BASED PROSE. Linda Flower, a highly respected researcher-teacher, suggests an approach to teaching writing based roughly on categories such as Fulwiler's.[3] The point of this approach—and it's a good one—is to help students use their non-audience-focused "writing to think" work toward creating audience-focused "writing to communicate" and "writing to imagine." Flower calls non-audience-focused writing *writer-based prose* and audience-focused writing *reader-based prose*. She defines reader-based prose in this way:

> Reader-Based prose is a deliberate attempt to communicate something to a reader. (77)

By contrast,

> Writer-Based prose is a verbal expression written by a writer to himself and for himself. It is the record and the working of his own verbal thought. (77)

Writer-based prose, the language of journals, diaries, and freewriting, is often deeply satisfying to its writer. And, as Flower points out, it can be exceedingly useful as a "medium for thinking"; it also helps the writer to "solve problems" (86). And, for some, it "appears to be a tapline to the rich sources of episodic memory" (97). On the other hand, Flower notes, that although writer-based prose can be "a masterful method for searching memory, [it also can be] a dud for communicating that information to anyone else" (89).

Writer-based prose often communicates poorly because it is so personal that readers do not understand it. Like the "egocentric talk" that Piaget noticed in children and the "inner speech" Lev Vygotsky describes, writer-based prose is elliptical: subjects and other referents needed by the reader are so well known to the writer that he or she often omits them. Its words, though frequently rich in private associations and personal connotations, do not communicate their meaning to the reader who is unaware of these associations and experiences. The sentences tend to lack logical or causal relationships (78–79). In fact, as Flower appraises it, though writer-based prose "is natural and adequate for a writer writing to himself or herself . . . , it is the source of some of the most common and pervasive problems in academic and professional writing" (76).

Flower writes that

> ineffective writers . . . merely "express" themselves by offering up an unretouched and underprocessed version of their own thought, [while] . . . effective writers do not simply *express* thought, [they] *transform* it . . . for the needs of a reader. (76)

Flower's analysis—backed by solid research—suggests an approach to teaching writing: we should help our students make that transformation. Our aim should be to help them turn their natural writer-based prose to reader-based prose when they need to communicate through their writing.

Throughout the discussion of "writing to communicate" (expository writing) and "writing to imagine" (creative writing) in the rest of this book, we will seek ways to help students use their "inner voice" to achieve writing that communicates effectively and persuasively to their readers.

EXPOSITORY AND CREATIVE WRITING.   The basic subject matter of a composition program are expository writing (Fulwiler's "writing to communicate") and creative writing (Fulwiler's "writing to imagine"). These two distinctive genres are distinguished from one another by their structure.

They cannot be differentiated by subject matter. All subjects are appropriate for both. Many authors (Ellen Goodman and E. B. White, for instance), write expository essays about personal topics; and many poets, novelists, and playwrights (Ibsen with his *Enemy of the People*, for example, or Dickens with *Hard Times*) write technical or didactic creative works. Nor can expository and creative writing really be distinguished by purpose since all audience-focused work shares an essentially persuasive purpose: the authors of both kinds of writing aim to persuade the reader to accept what they are saying as worthy of consideration.

Structure Alone Accounts for the Difference.   Poetry and drama differ structurally from prose, of course. But structural differences also distinguish expository writing from fictional or personal narratives. Fiction and personal narratives relate a story. Their narrative structure is based on chronology; that is, they are organized according to a time scheme and follow a pattern of "and then, and then, and then." Expository prose, on the other hand, is structured around a controlling idea; it is organized so as best to persuade its readers to accept the point of view expressed. And most of the teachable conventions of these genres are structurally related.

WHERE TO BEGIN TEACHING.   Storytelling and poetry is indigenous to the human family. Every culture the world has ever known has its songs and stories. And these arts even seem to come naturally to children. But exposition, the workaday writing of the adult world, involves learned logical structures. And students often find learning these structures difficult.[4]

Expository structure, then, is both difficult and important for our students to learn. It looks as if our work is cut out for us. Let's start here.

NOTES

1. For a historical analysis see Robert J. Connors, "The Rise and Fall of the Modes of Discourse," *CCC* 32 (1981): 444–55, in which he concludes that "the only teachers still making real classroom use of the modes are those out of touch with current theory" (453). See also Albert Kitzhaber, "Rhetoric in American Colleges, 1850–1900," Diss. U of Washington, 1953, 221; James Kinneavy, *A Theory of Discourse* (Englewood Cliffs, NJ: Prentice, 1971), 28, who writes: "[the modes] represent an unrealistic view of the writing process, a view that assumes writing is done by formula and in a social vacuum," and argues against "a stress on modes of discourse rather than aims of discourse" (28).

The four traditional modes, narration, description, exposition, and argument or, more likely, an expanded list of some eight to ten are still used to organize a good number of syllabi and textbooks. But though they provide a handy structural scheme, most of what are called "modes" are not generic at all. Some, such as exposition and argument, are not really distinguishable from each other. Others, such as description and definition, are actually ways of supporting or expanding ideas. And still others, such as comparison and contrast, classification, and cause and effect, are ways of organizing ideas.

2. Toby Fulwiler, *College Writing* (Glenview, Ill.: Scott, 1988), adapted from pages 13–18 by means of direct quotation. Fulwiler and I do not fully agree, however, on the best pedagogical use for these categories. He places "writing to think" at the center of his composition program; but in the academic setting I see writing to think mainly as subservient to writing meant for an audience.

3. Linda Flower, "Writer-Based Prose: A Cognitive Basis for Problems in Writing," in *To Compose: Teaching Writing in the High School*, ed. Thomas Newkirk (Portsmouth: Heinemann, 1986), 76–93.

4. See Beverly E. Cox, Timothy Shanahan, and Margaret B. Tinzmann, "Children's Knowledge of Organization, Cohesion, and Voice in Written Exposition," *RTE* 25 (1991): 179–212, who argue that expository writing is more difficult for children than it should be because they "have [such] severely limited experiences with it" (180). Their research demonstrates that "children, even at an early age, [can] learn important information about expository text" (206).

Section A

Teaching Expository Structure

Form . . . is an arousing and fulfillment of desire. A work has form in so far as one part of it leads a reader to anticipate another part, to be gratified by the sequence.

— Kenneth Burke

The writer understands that people have a hunger for form, and he feels this need of structure very strongly himself. He wants to discover patterns — meanings, reasons, explanations — in his world.

— Donald M. Murray

□ □ □ 2

Understanding Expository Structure

The convention of explicitness and straightforward organization in [expository writing] teaches that we can figure out what we really mean and get enough control over language to actually say it—directly and clearly.

—Peter Elbow

□ □ □

WHAT IS EXPOSITORY WRITING?

Expository writing is the sort of writing found in nonfiction books, in magazines, and in many newspaper articles; the sort of writing required for college exams and business reports; the workaday, useful writing that makes the world's intellectual wheels go round. Expository writing expounds, explains, and sets forth information and ideas. Its function is not that of poetry—to sing a lyric or a ballad—nor that of fiction—to tell a tale; it is, rather, to make a statement. Its purpose, however, like that of all writing, is essentially persuasive.

All writing is an expression of an author's ideas, feelings, or view of the facts of the world. Whether consciously or unconsciously, authors write to persuade their readers of the truth of these ideas, feelings, or facts. Lyric poets charm us with rhythm, alliteration, and metaphor to convince us of the power of their love or the beauty of their lovers; humorists employ the comic tools of incongruity, wit, or farce to point out the funny disparity between what *is* and what *should be* in this world. And fiction writers present their view of life by narrating the actions and describing the thoughts of their characters.

The purpose of expository writers is to persuade their readers to understand and, as far as possible, to accept the truth of what they are setting forth, of the statement they are making. To do so,

- They gather as much persuasive supporting material as they can find
and
- They arrange and order it so as to bring out their point most convincingly.

TEACHING THE ORGANIZING IDEA

That point expository writers set forth, the essence of a piece of expository writing, is its organizing idea. For a given work, the organizing idea is what the author seeks to persuade the reader to accept as true. Some call the organizing idea the *thesis*—a useful term, for both in its Greek derivation and in its nontechnical definition *thesis* means "a proposition . . . that is maintained by argument" *(American Heritage Dictionary)*. This definition exactly captures the rhetorical function of the organizing idea.

You can usually find at least a hint of the organizing idea toward the end of the introductory portion of a piece of expository prose; and it almost always appears somewhere in the concluding segment. Sometimes the organizing idea is not stated in so many words, and occasionally it is only implied; but there can be no good expository writing without it. Without an organizing idea, or thesis, expository writing appears literally pointless to the reader.[1]

The Point in Having a Point

It is no exaggeration to say that the most important skills we can teach our students are how to come to grips with an effective organizing idea and how to support it effectively. (Teaching support skills is discussed in Chapter 4.) When students complain that they "can't write," almost inevitably what they actually mean is that they lack these skills. And if, in later years, they announce triumphantly, "Old Jenkins really taught me to write," it is to the acquisition of these skills that they refer. Structuring support around a sound organizing idea is fundamental to the solution of the problems associated with the traditional composition-class triumvirate: unity, coherence, and emphasis. Such structure is also the direct answer to papers that are pointless and lack focus.[2]

Knowing how to express and support an organizing idea is the heart of reader-based expository prose and thus the key to communication. With this knowledge, our students will be able to make themselves understood in writing—even if they are never able to express themselves in an elegant style or even in a completely standard dialect. In a purely practical sense, this knowledge will permit them to be evaluated throughout their educational and professional careers in terms of what they really know and understand. As Toby Fulwiler wisely notes,

If there is one general "set" guideline to follow in academic writing, one you would do well to internalize, it's to write your papers with clear thesis statements—a guideline that presumes, of course, that you have information and ideas about which to have theses.[3]

We cannot endow all our students with brilliant minds, nor can we make sure they always have command of the facts of their history lessons or of what went on in the industrial study or how to use the latest software, but we can make sure that they can be credited for whatever intelligence and knowledge they actually possess by giving them, as an intellectual tool, a method of expressing their ideas coherently and intelligibly.

THE TEACHING PROBLEM. Understanding the concept of the organizing idea is the key to good expository writing. But like other truths that we hold to be self-evident, this idea seems to be honored more in the breach than in the observance.

When students untrained in structural skills are given an assignment to write a paper on "The Things I Did Last Summer," "My Dog Spot," or "Important Issues on the Peloponnesian War," their typical behavior is to begin writing down whatever they can think of that may relate to the subject—and more often than not—in whatever order it occurs to them. Lacking purpose or any notion of audience, the essay they write is usually one of the two kinds of writer-based prose Linda Flower describes. It is either "a narrative of their own discovery process . . . , a home movie of the writer's mind at work" or "a survey of the data before them."[4] Even when there is a research base to the assignment, students commonly employ the same chain-of-consciousness organization.

EXPLANATION. Before we can take steps to conquer this problem, we must understand its causes. Why do students seem to have such a difficult time shaping their essays to a central purpose? Surely, the explanation lies in the nature of student motivation for writing. The perceptive teacher who is privileged to hear students' candid discussion of the subject soon discovers that students' motives range from getting a grade, to pleasing the teacher, to fulfilling the assignment. Only under extraordinary circumstances (or with extraordinary students) do they see themselves as writing to communicate—or even to express—an opinion or a thought to a reader.

Students simply do not identify the point of their composition with their purposes in writing. It is not that they are particularly adverse to such an idea; rather, the notion seems simply not to occur to them.

Clearly, then, our first step is to persuade our students to make this identification between purpose and point, to adopt the rhetorical point of view. To do this, we need to convince them of the importance of working from an organizing idea.

REMINISCENCES OF AN ENGLISH TEACHING-METHODS STUDENT

by Patti Wallingford

Late August. Junior Year. Eastern High School. English Comp. Miss Reinsmith. A blank sheet of paper. "Thesis," she says. "Our papers NEED a thesis."

Not many of us knew exactly what she meant by "thesis" at the beginning of the hour-long period (I question now whether any of us did). But, by golly, walking down the narrow, dimly lit hallways after class I was certain I had the whole thing under my belt. Five minutes later I found myself sitting behind one of the familiar white tables that adorned the study hall. In front of me lay a piece of notebook paper. Its blank face stared up at mine—which must have been equally bare and just as white.

I remembered the thesis that we had developed as a class and Miss Reinsmith had jotted on the new green chalkboard in our room. Yet sitting there in the study hall things were very much different. The flow of ideas was gone. The open discussion had vanished and now the occasional, sharp "Shh" of the study-hall monitor followed by a glare of apparent annoyance were all that filled the air—and my thoughts. Things were definitely different from the encouraging classroom atmosphere I had left behind, and it occurred to me that I had been left to conquer a new concept single-handed.

BACK TO THE PRESENT
Developing a thesis wasn't as traumatic as it seemed at the time. I did learn to do it. But what I find myself trying to say is merely this: waging war on any new concept can be frightening. Therefore, it is important for us (as future teachers) to remember that though we have already waged such wars ourselves in past years, we may now be exposing our students to what they deem frightening, unfamiliar opponents at best. Remembering this, perhaps we will have a better understanding of our students' apprehension and will not cry out in frustration, "WHY AREN'T YOU GETTING THIS?" but will work with patience toward the goal of helping students make a life-long friend of an apparent enemy.

TEACHING THE RHETORICAL POINT OF VIEW

As "Reminiscences of an English Teaching-Methods Student" demonstrates, the rhetorical point of view is not easy to grasp. To teach it requires persistence, empathy, humor, and—yes—some rhetorical skill of our own.

Why Do We Write?

We might begin by getting our class to think about their purpose in writing. We might ask: "Why do you write?" We would probably be able to write on the board such answers as these:

- To find a job
- To thank grandmother
- Because teacher says to.

We can then go over their answers orally and elicit the idea that in every case they are writing to communicate *something* to *someone*. When we get to asking the "what?" and the "why?" of each communication, we can get them to see that in every case we write to persuade a reader. In the examples, for instance, the writer means, in general, to persuade the reader:

- To offer an interview—maybe even a job
- That I care about grandma and like the present she sent
- That I understand the subject and should get a good grade.

Our students should catch on to the communicating and persuasive pattern rather quickly. When they do, we can move them on to the next step.

Why Do Expository Writers Write?

What will you want to communicate in the expository essays you've just been assigned? What do professional expository writers want to persuade their readers of? The best way for our students to answer these questions is to go to the source, to experience some expository writing and to find out for themselves.[5] Whatever we have at hand will do. We can photocopy and bring in—or have our students bring in—newspaper or magazine clippings of brief articles by such first-rate syndicated writers as Ellen Goodman, William Raspberry, George Will, or Jeff Greenfield. If such material is not convenient, history and social studies classrooms often have supplementary reading texts, and essay anthologies are available to many English classes.[6]

Working in groups (or individually—if that's their preference), students can decide why Goodman wrote that article; what Raspberry wanted to get across; what Greenfield's purpose was. They should be able to see for themselves that each of the authors has an idea to communicate to his or her readers, and they should enjoy reaching a consensus about what that idea is. When they have decided, we might ask them to

- Write down the central, controlling idea of the professionally written essay
- Then go back over the article and mark the place or places where the author comes closest to stating this central point.

In this way our students can figure out for themselves what an organizing idea is. And when they return to a general class discussion, they can share their discoveries with one another. Enough articles should be explored to convince our students of the universality of the principle.

IMPORTANCE. Once students understand the general notion of an organizing idea, we can anticipate less difficulty in gaining their assent to its importance in their own writing. Because of the inherent logic of the thing, they can fairly easily be brought to realize, at least in a superficial way, that there is not much point in writing except to get across something they want to say.

The Dual Function of the Organizing Idea

The next step is for our students to see how the central point functions in someone else's expository work and then to see how it might function in their own. Just what does it do? Here we might supplement our students' thinking with some definitions of the organizational idea borrowed from expert rhetoricians:

- The main point of the essay, the one main idea to which all others should be subordinate (Frederick Crews)
- Pure extract of essay, the one major point you want to make with everything else stripped away. (Lucille Vaughn Payne)[7]

These definitions explain the central point in terms of its double function: persuasive and structural. It is, of course, *both* the rhetorical focus and the organizing idea of a work.

THE RHETORICAL FUNCTION. Despite our students glib, and sometimes even enthusiastic, acceptance of the concept of the organizing idea, we must not be too surprised to discover, upon our asking them to supply their own examples, that many have not fully grasped its real meaning. In all likelihood, when asked to think of an organizing idea they might use and told to boil it down to a concise statement, they tend to produce topics or subjects instead of real organizing ideas. Some of these pseudo–organizing ideas will be phrased as titles, such as "How I Learned My Lessons" or "My Most Interesting Experience"; some as questions, such as "Do cats make better pets than dogs?" or "Is athletics overemphasized?" and yet others as simple topics: "the water buffalo," "vacation days," or "the Peloponnesian wars."

If we get examples of this sort, we can be sure our students still do not realize that the notion of organizing idea, of thesis, infers argument, and thus that they have yet to understand the persuasiveness inherent in the concept. We must somehow bring them to know that when they write their papers, they will not be simply talking *around* a subject but that they will be saying something *about* it, answering the reader's question, "So what?" They will be making some point about their subject. In a manner of speaking, they will be asserting or arguing this statement or point. Their papers will, in Crews's words, "contain a thread of argument — that is, they [will] defend one position against possible alternatives to it." The organizing idea, then, still as Crews phrases it, "represent[s] a commitment of some sort, a stand that requires support in the body of [the] essay" (23).

"But Why Must the Organizing Idea Be Arguable?"   Our students may be reluctant to accept the rhetorical — persuasive — function of an organizing idea. When we encourage them to express themselves candidly, we may well find them troubled. They will let us know that they have "caught on" and can phrase their central point as a statement if we "want," but that they still do not really see the relevance of what we are asking them to do. They may say, "I don't want to argue anything; I just want to tell about the Peloponnesian Wars" or "I don't see how I can argue anything about what happened on my vacation." And there will be a general murmur of assent if some courageous lad or lass politely challenges: "I don't mean to be disrespectful, Mrs. Jones, but what you are saying just won't work for this assignment. It would make sense if we were assigned to defend or oppose Senator Smith's election, or the women's movement, or something like that, but not for this."

In voicing this concern, the student would be touching upon the crux of the whole matter. For as odd as it may seem to our students, what we really are asking them to do is to regard all expository writing as if it were a defense/opposition assignment. In other words, we are asking them to view all expository writing as if it were, in a manner of speaking, persuasive writing and to understand that the obviously persuasive paper is just a more blatant example of what *all* good expository writing actually is.

A Lyrical Example.   Perhaps the most emphatic way of conveying the universality of the persuasive nature of written expression is to carry the point to its extreme and show that it is valid even there. We might, for instance, recite the opening octave of Wordsworth's sonnet "On the Beach at Calais," and — after assuring the students that an organizing idea is not obligatory in lyric poetry — then show them that even lines as apparently nonpersuasive as these may be viewed as arguing a point. Wordsworth states his "thesis" in the first line: "It is a beauteous evening." This being a poem, he "argues" his "thesis" not only with factual statements, but also with the devices of poetry. In the next lines he persuades with simile and connotative language:

> It is a beauteous evening, calm and free.
> The holy time is quiet as a Nun
> Breathless with adoration;

Then he entices with rhyme, alliteration, and personification:

> . . . The broad sun
> Is sinking down in its tranquility;
> The gentleness of Heaven broods o'er the Sea.

And he convinces with onomatopoeia:

> Listen! the mighty Being is awake
> And doth with His eternal motion make
> A sound like thunder — everlastingly.

Wordsworth thus has not simply described an evening: he has offered powerful emotional arguments to support his convictions about its beauty and its holiness. In doing so, he has effectively set up the philosophical conclusions expressed in the final sestet of his sonnet.

Once our students can concede that there is something very like a controlling idea at work even here in a romantic sonnet, they should be able to understand that what is going on even in the least controversial of expository compositions is the demonstrating or supporting of the author's point.

THE STRUCTURAL FUNCTION.   Returning to the sample essays as a class should give our students a firmer grasp of the rhetorical function of the organizing idea. Such study should also help them understand the structural function because it should demonstrate that all good expository writing is structured so as to best support the organizing idea. We might lead them in close reading, insisting that the students keep asking themselves one focusing question: "What is the author trying to say?" Once the students have determined the organizing idea (and have found the places in the text where it is most clearly stated or suggested), we can help them point out the way in which every portion of the article is geared to its demonstration. If the essay's point is implicit, a reader has all the more reason to identify it. We need to show our students that all the author's ideas and techniques combine to point it up, imply it, or support it — no less than in the case of works with an explicitly stated organizational idea.

Omnipresent.   It is also useful to show our students that inclusion of an organizing idea is not a factor of length. We can demonstrate that essays as brief as one paragraph have them — though in this case they are usually called topic sentences — and that even works as long as Gibbon's multivolumed *Decline and Fall of the Roman Empire* are organized around a single central point. We may then face a challenge: "Oh, that can't be so. A work that long must have lots and lots of points!" Such an observation gives us a chance to bring out in a natural way the notion of subtheses. Taking *Decline and Fall* as our example, we can tell our students that Gibbon's basic thesis is that Rome fell because of its moral decadence and that every word in all his volumes helps to illustrate this idea. Since the work covers most of the major events of Western civilization for some thirteen centuries, however, it supports a number of related points as well. An example is the famous subordinate thesis for which Gibbon was so severely criticized: that the rise of Christianity had a negative rather than a positive moral effect on the Roman Empire.

In working with professional essays, we can help our students discover how the author structures a specific essay to communicate the organizational idea to the reader and help them visualize the strategy by making an outline or a tree on the board. After students have worked through such structural analysis as a class, they may wish to return to their groups to try another essay on their own.

APPLYING THE ORGANIZATIONAL IDEA CONCEPT

Once students have reached this understanding of how the organizational idea functions, they are ready to apply it to their own work and use it to structure their own papers.

The Working Thesis

It is then time to introduce the concept of the working thesis:

- The working thesis (according to Payne) is what the writer wants to say—the writer's "opinion—boiled down into a single *arguable statement*." (And it must be a statement because a question or phrase is not arguable, not supportable.)
- This statement condenses an organizational idea into a single sentence to help writers structure their expository writing.

If a working thesis is well thought out and carefully phrased (see the examples in the Strategies Student Guidelines), a writer can base an effective expository structure upon it. And though our students must understand that they will very seldom use their working thesis in just those words in the finished work, it is still an especially valuable composing tool. For writers can actually develop a structural plan (even an outline) from its wording. A working thesis is the pragmatic essence of the organizational idea.

Formulating a Working Thesis Statement

Once the students have come to accept the practicality of a working thesis, they will be impatient to formulate their own and will want to learn exactly how to do so. In satisfying students' desire for specific techniques, we face the danger of providing a learning exercise that can harden into formulaic restrictions unless properly qualified and understood. But even at the risk of offering simplistic solutions to complex problems, I think it is appropriate at this point to satisfy our students' perceived need for a step-by-step method. And so with a cautionary word or two about the number of ways of skinning cats, we might provide them with illustrative strategies like those in the Student Guidelines.

STUDENT GUIDELINES

Strategies for Formulating the Arguable Statement That Is the Working Thesis

1. Think of a subject. Examples:
   - Water buffalo
   - The Peloponnesian Wars
2. Narrow your chosen subject to a workable size by asking yourself "What about it interests me most?" or "What is most likely to interest others?" Answers:
   - The usefulness of the water buffalo
   - Why the Athenians lost the Peloponnesian Wars
3. Put what Sheridan Baker calls "an argumentive edge." (19) on the narrowed subject, either by
   a. syntactically turning the topic into a statement or by
   b. finding the answer to the title question.
   Examples:
   - The water buffalo is useful. (a)
   - The Athenians lost the Peloponnesian Wars because they had a foolish foreign policy. (b)

[Continuation for students who have mastered 1 through 3]:
4. Sharpen the "argumentative edge" still further by asking yourself "What am I arguing against? What is the position of the 'other side'?" Answers:
   - A person wouldn't think water buffalo could be useful, since they are so awkward and ungainly.
   - The Athenians were so much more highly civilized and intelligent than their opponents, it hardly seems possible that they could have lost.
5. Add this dimension to the working thesis in the form of an "Although clause." Examples:
   - Although the water buffalo is an ungainly beast, it is remarkably useful to the lives of many peoples of Asia.
   - Despite the undeniable superiority of the Athenian civilization, the Athenians were foolhardy in their foreign policy and thus lost the Peloponnesian Wars.

The most effective way to convey this material is to elicit it in as open discussion as possible. Those who participate will be touched more directly. The following section suggests patterns for how this discussion might work out in the classroom.

Finding a Working Thesis: The Preliminary Steps

STEP 1. THE SUBJECT.   We might ask the students to propose a likely subject, or if no ideas are forthcoming, we could make suggestions ourselves. In a similar exercise Robert P. Saalbach works with the topic "My Brother."[8] Since the idea of a semireal/semi-imaginary sibling is almost universally appealing, the notion works out well in practice. College freshmen respond with enthusiasm to the topic "My Roommate," probably for the same reason. "Our Lunchroom" will arouse peals of mischievous laughter from junior high school students and probably prompt them on to heights of satiric creativity. A social studies teacher might try "Capital Punishment" or "The Women's Movement." Just about any area about which the class has knowledge, however, will do — even the proverbial "The Things I Did Last Summer" or "My Dog Spot."

STEP 2. THE NARROWING DOWN.   After such a subject is agreed upon, we might point out that unless the paper about it is to be a very long one indeed, "My Brother," or "My Roommate," or even "My Dog Spot" is far too broad a topic to begin to be comprehended within it. Whatever its length, a paper written with no more focus than being "about" such a subject would be hopelessly diffuse. It might also be wise to mention to our students that topics assigned for papers are very often of this degree of generality, and that therefore assigned topics, like the one here agreed upon, must be narrowed into a workable compass or scope.

How does a writer go about narrowing? One way is to answer the question "What about it?" We can demonstrate this technique by asking our students "what about" their topic and recording their answers on the chalkboard. What about my brother? What about my roommate? What is he like? What first comes to mind about her? How would you describe him? Friendly. Lazy. Sloppy. Studious. What is the most interesting, most important thing about the lunchroom? Funny smell. Inedible food. About last summer? Busy. Lazy. Satisfying. Dreary. Student responses often come in the form of modifying words or phrases such as these. Sometimes, though, the answers come as questions themselves: What about capital punishment? Does it deter crime? Should it be abolished?

STEP 3. THE "ARGUMENTATIVE EDGE."   When we ask whether our narrowed topics — "My studious brother," "My sloppy roommate," "My busy summer," "Should capital punishment be abolished?" — are now working theses, most of our students should call out their "No's" with a fair amount of confidence. They understand that they need to put their idea into the form of a statement that can serve as an arguable proposition. But they will want to know how to go about doing it.

Finding the Deep Structure.   They might try putting Sheridan Baker's "argumentative edge" on their subject by taking their topics and finding the deep structure beneath the surface syntax. For example, "my studious brother" becomes "my brother is studious," a statement around which the writer can order support. "My sloppy roommate" turns into "My roommate is sloppy," and "my busy summer" becomes "My summer was busy," each now an arguable proposition.

Answering the Question.   Topics phrased as questions—such as "Should capital punishment be abolished?"—must be handled a little differently. The working theses formed when such topics receive their argumentative edge are the answers to the indicated questions: Capital punishment should be abolished, Capital punishment should not be abolished, Capital punishment is a deterrent to crime, or Capital punishment is not an effective deterrent. The students can turn all their ideas into potential theses by using these two approaches.

Once students have developed the ability to put an argumentative edge on their chosen topic and have acquired an understanding of the function and importance of the working thesis, they should be skilled enough to begin writing expository prose, at least in a preliminary, unsophisticated way. Late high school and college classes—especially those composed of particularly able students—ordinarily profit from an introductory exposure to the full range of working-thesis strategies. For many classes of younger, less linguistically experienced or less able students, however, the material already covered is sufficient introduction and the culminating strategies are better reserved for later in the term or for future years. Postponing for now discussion of the final strategies, let us go on to the evaluation of working-thesis statements. Evaluation is a good next step for those classes that will have completed their thesis-formulating exercises and an excellent way into the final thesis-formulating strategies for those who will be continuing with them.

Evaluating Statements for Working-Thesis Potential

If all has gone well, every one of the suggested ideas has been narrowed to a feasible topic and phrased as an arguable statement. The chalkboard is now filled with potential working theses. How does one go about discriminating among them? How do we choose the one (or ones) that would serve us best? We might suggest that there are two major considerations that can serve as touchstones in the evaluating process:

1. How much evidence can I bring to bear to support this thesis?
2. Is it a proposition worth supporting?

Using these as criteria, our students can determine the relative quality of the suggested statements on the board.

SUFFICIENT EVIDENCE?   One by one, each of the potential working-thesis statements can be examined in terms of whether we have enough material to support it properly. There are many well-worded theses that would not make good compositions because they make an assertion about which little can be said. For example,

- "My roommate tosses our books on the floor" or "George Washington wore false teeth" are arguable statements, but probably too specific to provide much more than a paragraph.
- Some statements—such as "The ptitze mold is a little known organism"— are self-limiting on their face. Although they might serve well as an introductory remark or as a way of arousing interest, the impossibility of their exemplification deprives them of value as theses.
- Again, if a student knows nothing about ptitze mold and there are no books about it at an accessible library, the working thesis "Ptitze mold is an interesting species" can yield no adequate composition.
- By the same token, a writer will not be able to find sufficient evidence to demonstrate a thesis that, upon investigation or reflection, turns out to be patently false.

WORTH SUPPORTING?   The second way to evaluate statements for their potential is to consider whether the proposition expressed is worth supporting at all. Students sometimes have a tendency to propose self-evident or platitudinous theses. Chances are that some of those statements under consideration will be of this sort. We will need to point out that although an organizing idea certainly need not be blatantly controversial, a less-than-exciting composition will result from an attempt to argue such an idea as "grass is green" when no one has ever proposed otherwise. *Implicit in all effective working theses is the notion that something or someone argues against it.* Since one cannot truthfully claim concerning the greenness of grass that "Despite its appearance to the contrary . . ." or that "Although noted authorities suggest differently . . ." or even that "There is substantial reason for believing otherwise . . . ," the value of "Grass is green" as an organizing idea is, to say the least, questionable. "Grass is not green" would make a far better thesis, if it could escape elimination by the first criterion and could be demonstrated, perhaps in terms of some little-known scientific explanation.

On the other hand, we must guard against inflexibility in the use of this criterion. For the most exciting implicit opposition argument of all is "No one has ever pointed it out before, but. . . ." Even though we cannot, of course, *expect* truly original thinking from our students, happily it does occasionally occur.

Exercising these criteria should result in the class's selection of a particular working thesis with which to continue. Some of our classes will then be ready to begin their prewriting (see Chapter 3), while others will want to continue sharpening the argumentative edge of their chosen working-thesis statement.

Finding a Working Thesis: The "Although Clause"

STEP 4. FURTHER SHARPENING.   Work with the second evaluative criterion should have convinced our students that all working theses have within them, either implicitly or explicitly, a sense of what is being argued against. They are, after all, by definition arguable propositions. The discussion may also have given the students the hint that a more interesting paper can be developed when its working thesis is formulated with the opposition argument in mind. What we yet need to do, then, is to encourage our students to think through their working theses from this point of view and to give them some direction in how to do so.

STEP 5. THE "ALTHOUGH CLAUSE."   It is often helpful for this purpose to introduce the concept of the *although clause.* The "although clause" is a syntactic device that permits writers to get a handle on opposition arguments by phrasing them as a subordinate clause attached to the main statement—as, for example, in:

- "Although capital punishment has been proved to exert no deterrent effect upon crime, it should not be abolished because it serves some important psychological needs of society;" or
- "Despite capital punishment's overwhelming popularity in a country ideally run by the wishes of the majority, it should nevertheless be abolished because it serves no useful purpose and is inherently uncivilized."

"Although clauses" might be similarly phrased for our other sample topics:

- "Although my family might claim that I did nothing but sit in the sun all summer, it actually was a very productive vacation for me, because I took the time to do a lot of growing up," or
- "Even though my dog Spot is less than a foot high and has a yelping little bark, he is as courageous as a lion and has a very strong character."

In each of these cases, the addition of an "although clause" serves not only to sharpen the point of contention, but also to clarify the issues upon which the argument will depend.

EXPLAINING THE "ALTHOUGH CLAUSE."   How do we get this idea across to our students? Again, I would suggest working through classroom discussion. Let us suppose that the class has chosen "My brother is sloppy" as their working-thesis statement. We should help them to think through their ideas about what sort of a statement about Brother's sloppiness they want to make. Why is his sloppiness noteworthy? Is it because people (including the reader) are neat and he is messy? "Although most people are neat, . . ." is the implied clause in "My brother is sloppy" papers that relate anecdotes and list examples in an attempt to amuse or disgust the reader.

From another angle, is Brother's sloppiness worth writing about because *I* am neat and *he* is sloppy? ("Although I am neat, my brother is very sloppy.") Because he is neat about *some* things but incredibly sloppy about *others*? ("Although my brother is neat about some things . . ."). Or is his sloppiness all of a piece? Are we really interested in using Brother to make a generalization about human nature? Or do we want to talk about our relationship with Brother? Or would we rather write a character sketch of him or make him the subject of a psychological study? Depending upon what rationale the students decide upon, the working thesis could be anything from "Although my brother and I get along about as well as brothers can, his sloppiness is one fault that really bugs me" to "Although the human character appears to be all of a piece because of the dominance of one trait that impresses, actually each human being is an amalgam of traits — many of them contradictory — as the sloppy room of my otherwise meticulous brother attests."

Because of the extraordinary usefulness of the "although clause" as a tool, both for thinking and for composing, I recommend encouraging students to formulate their working theses in this way — and I do so with my own classes. But some students tend to mistake the scaffolding for the structure. And so if we want to avoid prototypical "although clauses" appearing in theme after theme, we must take care to emphasize the distinction between working thesis and thesis and insist that students not try to insert their working theses into the finished papers.

Our students should find the "Although Clause" Student Guidelines particularly helpful.

STUDENT GUIDELINES

What Every Student Should Know about the "Although Clause"

1. The clause need NOT begin with the word *although*.
   Examples: "*Despite* capital punishment's overwhelming popularity, . . ."
   "*Although* my family might claim that I did nothing but sit in the sun all summer, . . ."
   "*Even though* my dog Spot is less than a foot high and has a yelping little bark, . . ."
   'Spot is very small, *but* . . ."
                              yet . . ."
                              nevertheless . . ."
                              however, . . . "
                              on the other hand, . . ."

continued

2. There is NO single "correct" "although clause" for a given proposition. Usually a number of alternatives will do as well.

    Examples:

    > "Although most people are neat, . . ."
    > "Although I am neat, . . ."
    > "Although my brother is neat about some things, . . ."
    > "Although my brother and I get along about as well as brothers can, . . ."
    > "Although some think people are all alike, . . ."

3. The "although" material is subordinate to the central point and should thus be mentioned, or developed, BEFORE IT in the expository structure (see Chapter 3).

4. The more controversial the "although" material, the greater attention it needs in the expository structure (See Chapter 6).

5. Useful as the "although clause" part of the working thesis is in constructing an expository composition, it NEED NOT—and often SHOULD NOT—appear (especially in the same phrasing) in the finished composition.

A Word or Two about Assignments

Discussion of the organizing idea will fall upon much more receptive ears if it is occasioned by what the students perceive to be a real need. It is therefore a good idea to precede such discussion by assigning a paper, the first expository paper of the term, and to mention the assignment from time to time whenever relevant throughout the preparation period.

The assignment that best gets across the concepts we are aiming at is the personal assignment. "How It Feels to Be a Freshman," "How It Feels to Be a Senior," "Why This Fall Is Different for Me," "Life at Our House," "Life in the Dormitory"—all of these have served successfully as topics for the first expository theme. For courses in history, science, literature, and other disciplines that emphasize subject matter, the writing assignments are necessarily determined by the content, but teachers of classes devoted in whole or in part to the teaching of composition per se would do best assigning a more or less personal topic.

There are a number of advantages to this choice. On the practical level, there is so much to be learned with the first assignment that it would be a mistake to complicate the issue by calling for subject matter beyond that which is already present in the student's mind. More importantly, such a choice helps further the purposes of the lesson this assignment is designed to teach. Working on a personal topic should diffuse the tendency toward excessive confrontation that may be engendered by the argumentative emphasis. On the other hand, writing the first expository paper on a personal topic gives each student a chance to demonstrate to herself or himself that all subjects really can be treated persuasively.

IDEAS FOR DISCUSSION OR ESSAY

1. Complete the following exercises. Assess their learning potential. How would you teach them to get your point across?

    A. Study three expository essays in newspapers, magazines, journals, or in an essay anthology. Answer these questions for each essay:
    - What do you think is the author's organizing idea? Is it stated or simply implied?
    - Read through the introduction (remember it may well be several paragraphs) and record whatever hint or statement of the organizing idea you find toward its close (or topping the first paragraph of the next segment).
    - How well does the material in the central portion of the essay tend to explain or support that idea?
    - Review the concluding portion. Record the most persuasive phrasing of the organizing idea you find there.

    B. The following are topics that could be made into potential working theses. Select several and take them through the five steps of the thesis-formulating strategies:

Relations with South Africa	Fraternities and sororities
Elephants	Chinese food
ERA (Equal Rights Amendment)	Beethoven
Nuclear power plants	Crime in the streets
Conscientious objection	Vegetarianism
High school athletics	The Grand Canyon
MTV	Computer Banking

2. If your students came to you with the following theses for you to evaluate, which ones would you discourage them from using. Explain why. Discuss how you would help the student think through and rephrase each one.
    - Thomas Jefferson was the third president of the United States.
    - I plan to discuss the effect of the Federal Reserve Bank on the stock market.
    - Why John Donne wrote "A Hymn to God the Father."
    - The differences between the French and English political systems.
    - The sadness of Life.
    - Should inflation be defeated at the expense of full employment?
    - Ernest Hemingway influenced Shakespeare.

NOTES

The section opening epigraphs are from Kenneth Burke, *Counter-Statement*, 3rd Ed. (Berkeley and Los Angeles: U of California P), 124, and from Donald M. Murray, *A*

Writer Teaches Writing: A Practical Method of Teaching Composition (Boston: Houghton, 1968), 19.

The chapter-opening epigraph is from Peter Elbow's "Reflections on Academic Discourse: How It Relates to Freshmen and Colleagues," *CE* 53 (1991): 147.

1. Professor Sheridan Baker, dean of composition pedagogues, writes: "If your essay falls apart, it probably has no primary idea, no thesis to hold it together. . . . Your thesis is your essay's life and spirit. If it is sufficiently firm, it may tell you immediately how to organize your supporting material. But if you do not find a thesis, your essay will be a tour through the miscellaneous, replete with scaffolds and cat-walks—"We have just seen this; now let us turn to this"—an essay with no vital idea." See his *The Practical Stylist*, 7th ed. (New York: Harper, 1990), 18–19.

See also Rise B. Axelrod and Charles R. Cooper, *The St.. Martin's Guide to Writing*, 2nd ed.: "Readers by necessity look for something that will tell them the point of an essay, a focus for the many diverse details and ideas they encounter as they read. The lack of an explicit thesis statement can make this task more difficult." (402)

2. Although the pendulum swing against rigid composition instruction has in some quarters gone so far as to attempt to discredit even the central concept of thesis, more thoughtful reformers, such as Fulwiler, continue to recognize its importance. Erica Lindeman, to take another example, calling thesis statements "promise sentences," writes: "When we write, we initially make a promise to our readers which the rest of the piece should fulfill." *A Rhetoric for Writing Teachers*, 2nd ed (New York: Oxford UP, 161–162.

3. Toby Fulwiler, *College Writing* (Glenview, Ill.: Scott, 1988), 88.

4. Linda Flower, "Writer-Based Prose: A Cognitive Basis for Problems in Writing," in *To Compose: Teaching Writing in the High School*, ed. Thomas Newkirk (Portsmouth: Heinemann, 1986), 84, 87.

5. George Hillocks, Jr., in *Research on Written Composition: New Directions for Teaching* (Urbana: NCRE and ERIC, 1987) describes such experiential teaching:

> Principles . . . are approached through concrete materials and problems, the working through of which not only illustrates the principles but engages students in its use. (122)

For documentation supporting the effectiveness of experiential (or inquiry) teaching, see Hillocks, *Research*, 247–48, and tables 5, 7, and 6. For a discussion of this approach, see Hillocks, 122–26, 194, and 224–25 and Walter L. Batemen, *Open to Question: The Art of Teaching and Learning by Inquiry* (San Francisco: Jossey, 1990). Bateman's book also offers a wide variety of examples of such teaching.

6. One caution. Although most of the selections in such anthologies are expository essays—which will exemplify the conventions discussed here, some texts also include excerpts from longer works—with incomplete structural patterns—or short stories and autobiographical narratives—which follow other structural conventions.

7. Frederick Crews, *The Random House Handbook* (New York: Random House, 1974), 22; Lucille Vaughn Payne, *The Lively Art of Writing* (Chicago: Follett, 1965), 26.

8. Robert P. Saalbach, "Teaching Students to Organize," *EJ*, 48 (1958): 505–07.

□ □ □   **3**

Teaching Prewriting: Invention and Arrangement

A writer's difficulty getting started has to do with his difficulty knowing and understanding the structure of the utterance he is setting out to make — not what he wants to say (although naturally that may create some problems too), but how he wants to say it. Once we know, however vaguely, the order or form of our discourse, we can begin that discourse, but not before.

— Kenneth Bruffee

□ □ □

Writing is a single process. Nevertheless, it can be analyzed into three stages — prewriting, writing, and rewriting, or more explicitly, planning, composing, and revising. Experienced writers tend to combine these stages as they compose.[1] But since almost everyone who writes follows them in one way or another, we can, for teaching purposes, break down the process into these three stages so that our students can experience the process in learnable chunks. This is a workable approach to a difficult subject; but in adopting it, we must make sure our students understand that it is merely pedagogically useful, and not mandatory, for writing well.

INVENTION: PREWRITING, PART I

Good writing is produced when writers have something they truly want to express to their readers. Finding something significant to say is often the most difficult problem a writer faces. We have all seen it: a paper is assigned, and instantaneously all youthful animation fades and sparkling eyes go blank and fearful. A teacher needs a far stonier heart than mine not to feel a surge of sympathy toward those profoundly blank postassignment faces gazing raptly into space as they wait for inspiration to strike. But our sympathy alone is not likely to help them very much. Except for those miraculous moments when inspiration—or something akin to it—really does seem to strike, all prospective writers at this stage have to give some serious thought to the problems of invention.

Invention is the term that has been used since the days of Aristotle, but it does not accurately describe the process of finding ideas. Nobody really *invents* ideas: people discover them, they find them through research, or they bring ideas out of their subconscious into the light where their conscious minds can examine and work with them.

And what is it that expository writers need to invent? An organizing idea and support to make it convincing to readers. And thus for our students to try expository invention, they must first understand the concept of the organizing idea (which is why we discussed it early on, in Chapter 2).

Deductive and Inductive Invention

The organizing idea and its support are interdependent. When we invent ideas for compositions, sometimes one comes to mind first and sometimes the other. Thus there are two ways to approach the discovery process. A subject will either spontaneously suggest an organizing idea to the writer or it will not. If an organizing idea spontaneously comes to mind, the writer evaluates it and refines it by sorting out possible supporting ideas. During this process the writer employs *deductive reasoning:* working from the general to the specific, from the theoretical to the concrete.

If no organizing idea occurs, however, then the writer must find one by brainstorming—freewriting, or researching up a battery of information and ideas, and then by analyzing the collection into possible chains of support, and deriving an organizing idea to which they lead. This latter approach is based on *inductive reasoning*, the process in which the thinker reasons from the specific to the general. Our students need to learn how to work from both approaches.

THE DEDUCTIVE APPROACH. Explanation to a class is best begun with the deductive approach, since it is the one with which our students will already be familiar. Until recent years, deductive invention was often the only approach to expository writing taught. But the limitations this process places on creative or exploratory thought have now been recognized. Still, it is the best method for quickly structuring already known material—for instance, an essay exam answer. And although our students may not find it the most useful approach for their more mature composition needs, we can guess with fair certainty that it will have been the approach they had most frequently adopted in attempting composition assignments up to this point. What they require now, is only a brief lesson that will systematize an already familiar process and permit students to use deductive reasoning in a more self-conscious and deliberate way.

Sample Lesson.   How does the deductive approach work? Let us take an example from the last chapter's demonstrations, where the subject "My Brother" spontaneously suggested the putative working thesis "My brother is sloppy." To find out if such an organizing idea would be worth pursuing, the writer must discover and then evaluate the support through which it might be communicated persuasively to the reader. As the class invents "arguments" to test out and — if satisfactory — to demonstrate this organizing idea, they are reasoning deductively.

Ask the students for "proof" that Brother is sloppy, and they will gleefully provide it. They will, for example, suggest that Brother keeps a sloppy room or that Brother is very sloppy with his homework. Push them harder, and the students will provide the evidence to illustrate their arguments. They will describe the heap of dirty laundry on the floor of his room; or they will self-righteously reveal his never-made bed in all its wrinkled ignominy; or they may refer indelicately to the odor of his uncleaned gerbil cage. Someone is sure to relate an illustrative anecdote. One sister might tell of the day Brother turned in a paper so ink-blotched and scribbled over that his teacher insisted he stay after class to write "I will be neat" one hundred times on the chalk-board.

If we record this information in outline form on our own chalkboards, (see Table 3–1) we can then ask, "Will this working thesis do? Can you see the paper you might write from this?" With such an outline, most students would probably be able to envisage their way fairly clearly through the whole composition, and would be eager to say so. When the exercise is complete, we can trace back the processes of thought that went into it. We can lead the class to discover that they had begun with a generalization and were able to support it through the accumulation of relevant evidential details; and they can discover that, in so doing, they had validated their organizing idea and constructed about it a working structure for a paper.

Table 3–1 Structural Plan

Working Thesis: My brother is sloppy.
   1. Introduction
   2. Sloppy Room
         Dirty laundry
         Unmade bed
         Uncleaned gerbil cage
   3. Sloppy Homework
         "I will be neat" incident
   4. Conclusion (?)

THE INDUCTIVE APPROACH.   The inductive approach may be less familiar to our students; but as they mature, they will be increasingly confronted by subjects that do not immediately suggest their own organizing ideas, subjects about which they frequently will have little or no prior knowledge. In such cases, the students will have to gather their information, either by doing research of one kind or another (see Chapter 9) or by summoning it up from their memories.[2] A memory search can be made either freely or systematically. For a systematic search, students can use heuristics (see pages 70–76). A free search of the mind is usually called brainstorming. Writers brainstorm in two ways: by deliberately inventorying the mind and then listing what they find or by letting the subconscious take over through freewriting.

Listing and Freewriting.   Writers, as I noted in Chapter 1 (pages 17, 29, fn. 22) divide almost exactly in half in their preference for listing or freewriting composing styles. But most of our students are not aware of their own predilections. Because these techniques are fundamental to effective inventing, it is essential that we teach both styles and give our students ample opportunity to experience both techniques.

Listing or Inventorying Ideas.   We might first demonstrate brainstorming by means of an "inventory of ideas." That involves—we can explain to our students—placing before themselves, either mentally or in writing, a sort of inventory of information and ideas on the subject they want to write on, information they have gathered or ideas they have summoned up from their memories. Once they have made an inventory of their ideas, they should play with them, relating them to each other, paralleling them, subordinating one to another, and forming categories until a pattern begins to emerge. This pattern may suggest a structure of support, which will in turn suggest an organizing idea, or it may suggest an organizing idea from which they can derive a structure of support.

Despite the usefulness of this method, it is difficult to convey to students in a theoretical form. Students grasp the technique easily, however, when they can confront it experientially. For this reason, I enthusiastically recommend trying an inventory-of-ideas exercise. Here the class as a whole works together as a single entity to summon up an inventory of ideas from its collective memory. Because such an exercise tends to involve each student imaginatively in the essentials of prewriting thought, it proves to be especially effective. One successful version of this exercise is demonstrated in a videotape transcript called A Class in Action, Part 1, below.

PREWRITING EXERCISE: TAKING AN INVENTORY OF IDEAS.   As class begins, the teacher asks the students to select a topic about which everyone is knowledgeable—for example, "George Washington," "Abraham Lincoln," or "The Pilgrims."—even "Madonna" has made a successful session. The teacher then goes rapidly around the room, asking every student to suggest a fact about the subject. The teacher records the facts on the chalkboard as quickly as possible. When all the students have made their contribution, the teacher suggests that the chalkboard list represents an inventory of the group's ideas on the subject, much like the sort of inventory an individual can construct mentally before tackling a writing assignment.

At this point the teacher can assure the class that, although at present their ideas appear confused, disorderly, and too variegated ever to be the foundation of a paper, these confused ideas can and indeed soon will be fashioned into an organizing idea and a supporting structure from which a good paper could easily be written. The teacher assures them that all it will take is the relating of the ideas one to the other by a process of coordination and subordination.

The teacher then asks the students to connect the ideas, and draws lines between related items as the students do so. While this work is in progress, the teacher asks student contributors for their reasoning, using such questions as "Why did they make a particular link?" and "What is the coordinating principle?" These principles become the categories under which the items are subordinated. All should be indicated on the blackboard. By doing the whole process on the blackboard, the teacher makes the ideas visually as well as intellectually clear to the students.

A CLASS IN ACTION, PART 1

Quotation from a transcript of a class working through this exercise should demonstrate dramatically how it functions and give a clearer notion of its value. The videotape from which this excerpt is taken was made of a class of seventeen- and eighteen-year-old students.

The class met, the exercise was introduced, a topic was selected, and the lesson itself began in this way:

Teacher: . . . "George Washington." That's a good idea. Its a topic everybody knows something about, and what's more, he's a figure that the revisionist historians are beginning to rethink. We'll start with you, Curt. Tell me something about George Washington. Anything.

Curt: He had white hair.

Teacher: That wasn't hair.

Curt: A white wig.

Teacher: (Aside) I understand he had red hair underneath it. Missy?

Missy: He had wooden teeth.

Teacher: Jason?

Jason: He liked to throw dollars.

Teacher: (Laughing) Any particular place he liked to throw dollars?

Jason: In rivers. (General laughter)

Teacher: All right. Doug?

Doug: He was a surveyor.

Teacher: Renee?

Renee: He was a president?

Teacher: Any particular president?

Renee: The first.

Jason: He is literally the father of our country.

Heather: His wife's name was Martha.

Steve: Yes, his face is on a dollar bill.

Teacher: Jeff.

Jeff: A fine military leader.

Teacher: The other Jeff.

Jeff: He spent the winter at Valley Forge. . . . [After every student had an opportunity to contribute and the class was drained of further suggestions, all of which were duly recorded, the chalkboard looked like that shown in Chalkboard 1.]

Teacher: Anything else? Well, anyway, we have quite a lot of things here. And now we have to get all of this diverse stuff together — in order to write our paper on Washington. Catch that: "ON Washington." All we still really know is our general subject.

Doug: We have to put these items into an outline.

Teacher: Yes, but we can't do anything with all this various stuff. A paper that is made from an outline that has thirty different items is bound to come out "And then, and then, and then." We first have to get these topics to fit together. We have to get them under and over

CHALKBOARD 1.

White wig
Wooden teeth
$ in Potomac
Surveyor
1ST Pres.
Fath. of Country
Face on $
Military leader
Valley Forge
Chopped Cherry Tree
Crossed Delaware
Washington Monument

French & Indian War
Vice Pres. = Adams
Farewell Address:
    Strong Union
    Strong Central Gov.
Large Plantation
Slaves
Born Feb 22, 1732
Pres. Day = Holiday
Capital named Wash.
Mt. Rushmore
Death = being bled too often
Refused Crown

and together. And a good way to begin is just to attach them to each other. What things can we put with what things?

Heather: Oh. I'd say we can put stuff together like monuments. Like his monument; the capital is named after him; he's on Mt. Rushmore.

Teacher: Okay. Could you just tell me where to write? You probably could come up and do it better. Would you like to come up, Heather?

Heather: Yeah.

Teacher: Okay. Just attach the monuments together. I like the way you're doing it because you're thinking in terms of a category and these things go under it.

Heather: (Speaking aloud as she joins the items with colored chalk) The capital's named after him.

Steve: Over there.

Heather: "Mt. Vernon." That's it. (Murmured voices: "Mt. Rushmore") Yeah, where's "Mt. Rushmore?"

Tyrone: Bottom right.

Heather: Okay. What's that one? No, that's "military leader."

Jason: There's "Face on the $." We should add that . . . not "Mt. Vernon."

Curt: Yeah, why did you put "Mt. Vernon" on there?

Heather: Sure, "Mt. Vernon." You pay to get in there.

Doug: Mt. Vernon is where he lived. That wouldn't do at all.

Ginger: Sure it would.

Heather: But you pay to get in. (General laughter) Okay.

Tyrone: "President's Day?"

Heather: Oh, sure. (Many thinking aloud: Mmm, uhmm) Well, I guess that's it.

Teacher: Let me just collect them here. (At another board, the teacher lists the items marked under the category "Monuments")

Renee: Another category might be "Appearance." We have "White wig," "Wooden teeth," "White horse." . . .

Heather: Okay. I'll connect.

Teacher: Do you want the category "Appearance"? Or? Or . . .?

Jeff: "Image." (Others give assent)

Maria: But what do you mean by "Image?"

Renee: Oh, like when you think of Washington, you think of a white wig, on a big horse, standing with the flag waving behind him.

Teacher: But would the wooden teeth fit with that?

Heather: The wig, the wooden teeth. Homey details really. I don't know if the horse. . . .

Class: (Voices in assent) All right. "Homey details."

Ginger: How about "Father of his country," "First president." . . .

Maria: That's not right.

Ginger: That's what he's known for.

Heather: Oh, a different category. "Accomplishments" and that sort of thing.

Ginger: Okay.

Jason: How about "Washington as a leader?"

Teacher: Do you want to mark those, Heather, or are you marking "Homey details?" Why not get those Jason, while she is doing the others. And let me get caught up too. (At another board the teacher lists the items under the suggested categories) The first is "Monuments." And then you had "Homey details." And then "Heroic accomplishments."

Jason: No.

Teacher: What did you call it?

Jason: "Washington as a leader."

Teacher: "As leader." These things, by the way, are all different kinds of categories; and if we're going to use them eventually, its better to get them into the same kind of syntax.

Susan: Parallel.

Teacher: Yes, parallel syntax. If you get your structural plan that way, then the whole paper falls into shape. I'm not sure why it works, but it always does. After "as Leader?"

Heather: Do you think we should include "Turning down the crown" under "As leader?"

Jeff: That would be "As a leader."

Jason: Instead of "Homey details," would you put something like his "Private life?" . . . like "Mt. Vernon," his plantation, what he looked like . . . things like that.

Teacher: Why don't I put that here as an idea? Later we'll play with both of these terms. As we work it out, maybe one will turn out to be better than the other.

Heather: (Still at the board) Is that all for his accomplishments?

Steve: Well, "Valley Forge."

Steve: (Marking) "Valley Forge."

Renee: Then there's the "French and Indian War." Of course, that's early in his life.

Jason: That was also leadership.

Teacher: Yes, that was early leadership.

Heather: As a leader, he gave his "Farewell Address."

Teacher: Yes . . . I guess so.

Heather: It would be a good idea to do his "Farewell Address" and . . .

Jeff: His "Turning down the Crown" . . .

Heather: And his "Turning down the Crown" . . . something about his political career.

Teacher: Well, all right. Under "As a leader," do you want to put "Political" and "Military."

Class: (General assent) Yes . . . (Some say, "As subtopics")

Jason: How about "Legends?"

Teacher: All right. (Writing) "Legends."

Jason: "Chopping down the cherry tree" . . .

Renee: Being "Bled to death."

Curt: That's not a legend. That happened!

Jason: "Father of our country." Things like that.

Teacher: The "Father of our country" you had under "Monuments." So "Legends" and "Monuments" pretty well go together, don't they? That other legend—that dollar thing—didn't really happen, did it? . . .

Susan: I doubt it.

Curt: Even if it happened, it was a legend. (Laughter)

Heather: Is that all there is?

Teacher: Yes. I think . . . Yes. Now what don't we have? (Looking at first board) Let's see. What would you do with "Surveyor?" (No immediate response) You know, once you inventory your ideas, you can always drop things. We're trying to make our base as broad as we can, take in everybody's ideas; but we can always drop. You don't have to get everything into a paper—you can always save it for another essay.

Greg: "Surveyor." "Mt. Vernon." And "Slavery" and "Plantation." They would all go into "Private life."

Teacher: (Writing) Under "Private life."

Renee: "Martha" does too then. (General laughter)

Teacher: "Surveyor," "Mt. Vernon." Anything else? Oh, "Plantation." . . . That takes in everything then? We have got things related. (Laughter of relief)

Teacher: And having put all that material into some sort of categories, we have shaped it into a form which we can, at least, hold in our minds; and so now we are able to work with it.

At this point the category blackboard looked like that shown in Chalkboard 2.

Teacher: Now for the hard part—the organizing idea.

* * *

Finding the Organizing Idea and Structuring Around It. After this beginning, students are asked to suggest possible organizing ideas (or working theses) that would include as many of the categories as possible.

Ordinarily, the first suggestions are rather simple. Using the George Washington topic of the videotaped class, for instance, some typical responses might include: "George Washington was a great man" or "George Washington was the subject of many legends." Usually one student will argue that these grandiose topics do not include such pedestrian items as the wooden false teeth or George's problems with his stepson—facts which the protesting student, as least, is unwilling to relinquish. She might prefer a topic such as "George Washington was a human being, just like us." At this

CHALKBOARD 2.

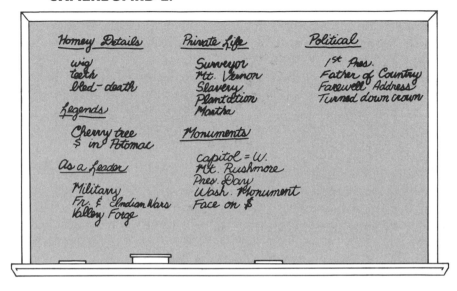

point, most students are convinced that these single-idea theses are the total yield of the inventory of ideas, and they are satisfied with having brought order out of chaos.

Usually, however, one bright pupil will observe—or can be prompted to observe—that all the ideas can be combined for a much more interesting organizing idea: for example, "George Washington was human, just like us, yet he was a great man who became the subject of much American folklore."

Advantages to the Inventory of Ideas Exercise.   There are a number of advantages to using this exercise as a preliminary to the first theme assignment.

- Total participation builds widespread interest and attention.
- The very diversity of the examples reflects the students' own jumbled thoughts when approaching a topic.
- The exercise presents an intriguing challenge to student ingenuity, especially when backed by the teacher's promise that an orderly solution will be found. (Thus the students experience a double satisfaction when the solution is indeed discovered.)
- Because the exercise also provides group practice before the students have to face writing their first theme all on their own, it lets them bring to it the confidence that comes from experience.

Furthermore, this exercise also leads quite naturally—perhaps at the next class meeting—into a more detailed analysis of the process of structural planning. That analysis accompanied by a practical discussion of how to write a theme from a structural plan—that is, how to approach the particular problems and conventions associated with the composition of the introduction, middle, and conclusion of the paper—should give the students the basic information to set off knowledgeably to do this work. Later in the chapter, we will discuss these subsequent steps in preparing our students for their first papers.

Freewriting

For about half of our students—if my research is correct—listing and structuring is *not* the most effective preliminary inventing technique. These students ask, in James McCrimmon's words, "How can I tell what I mean until I see what I've written?"[3] They think by writing. They brainstorm by writing. Their kind of brainstorming is called *freewriting*.

The point of freewriting is to get at ideas in the subconscious. It thus must be totally unrestricted, as its name implies. Only one thing is required of the freewriter: to keep writing until a set time is up. As Peter Elbow, perhaps the best known advocate of this method, describes it:

> The idea is simply to write for ten minutes. . . . Don't stop for anything. Go quickly without rushing. Never stop to look back, to cross something out, to wonder how to spell something, to wonder what word or thought to use, to think about what you are doing. If you can't think of a word or a spelling, just use a squiggle or else write, "I can't think of it." Just put down something. The easiest thing is just to put down whatever is in your mind. If you get stuck, it's fine to write, "I can't think what to say, I can't think what to say" as many times as you want; or repeat the last word you wrote over and over; or anything else. The only requirement is that you *never* stop.[4]

TEACHING FREEWRITING. Freewriting is writer-based prose in its purest form. Because of its personal nature, successful freewriting is grounded in trust. Students need to know that their thoughts are their own, that these writings are for their use only, and that they will never be *required* to share them. Needless to say, they must understand that we will never grade them. Once this trust is established, most students, most of the time—ironically enough—have no problem sharing their freewritings so that we or their collaborative partner or group can help them make use of them.

When introducing the activity, it is a good idea to participate in it ourselves. Then, if an atmosphere of trust has been established, if students are absolutely sure that "this won't count" and "errors really don't matter," a sufficient number of brave souls will come forward and read their writings when we call for volunteers.

Purpose. What should our students be looking for in their freewritings? It depends on why they write. When they freewrite to brainstorm for a paper, the preliminary freewriting is as general as the assignment. If the topic is the students' choice, then their purpose in freewriting is to find out what they want to write about. If the topic is more specific, they freewrite to discover their approach to that topic, even to discover an organizing idea for that topic. When the topic is specified, students often find it useful to write the topic at the top of the page. This procedure helps to focus their freewriting because they can let the wording of the topic suggest ideas that they can follow wherever they lead.[5]

Buried Treasure.   When students complete their preliminary freewriting (or when the time is up), they need to read over what they have written. They should, however, make no effort to correct it or to turn it into a finished composition. Instead, they should use it as a storage bank of ideas. We should encourage them to underline, circle, or highlight ideas they think worth pursuing. They can also look for and mark any graceful turns of phrase they may want to incorporate into the final essay. Once their freewriting is annotated, they can use it as an inventory of ideas; they can ask themselves:

- What is the most interesting idea here?
- Is there anything like a general principle here that ties most of the rest together?

Focused Freewriting.   Often students find it helpful to try another, more focused, freewriting session as a follow-up to the first. This time they can start with that most interesting thought or that general principle, write it at the top of a new page, and then let their minds wander from there. The second attempt will probably turn out to be more structured than the first. From it (or a third attempt, if need be) the student may be able to work out a plan that will lead directly to a first draft.

ILLUSTRATIVE MODEL

A Freewriting Invention Model

The following example is that of Melissa Snyder, a gifted eleventh-grade teacher taking part in a workshop on teaching writing.

   Prompt: What I thought, felt, did on first learning about the Challenger explosion.

STEP 1: FREEWRITING
She wrote:

> I remember some kids watching TV in the AV room. They usually watched old game tapes, but today they, along with every other student in America, wanted to see the first teacher go into space. I wonder how many of them wished I was on that thing being blasted off.

continued

continued

They came back to the lounge saying it had exploded. Of course we — I — figured they were kidding, but their tone told me otherwise; so then I thought, cynically, that they misunderstood. Finally, I viewed the ugly scene myself. I know I felt like crying — that rush of emotion that comes when you get death-news.

We watched the rerun all the rest of the day.

STEP 2: FIRST DRAFT
Using the most significant phrase in the freewriting as a prompt:

Prompt: "That rush of emotion that comes when you get death-news"

[Mrs. Snyder's first draft is similar in structure to the final draft — see below. The major differences are in the self-analytical passages.]

STEP 3: SCRATCH OUTLINE
Having studied her draft, she finally understood what she really wanted to say and wrote this outline:

Organizing idea: Humanizing education
Working thesis: It's important to see kids as humans

— Way in: the shuttle incident [intro]
— Problems in seeing kids as human [*although* material]
— Realizations
— Ramifications [concl]

STEP 4: SECOND DRAFT
[The second draft is a revised version of the first, emphasizing the points in the structural plan.]

STEP 5: REVISIONS AND FINAL DRAFT
[The final draft is a carefully edited and reformatted version of the second draft.] I quote it in full:

"Hey Mrs. Snyder — it's not too late. Maybe we could blast you off into space!"

Yeah, except we'd have you keep on going!"

I gritted my teeth in a "real-cute-guys" smile as I walked from the AV room. I was not in the mood for these goons right now.

Just as I settled in the lounge, though, Mike came back to me.

"It blew up — the shuttle — it blew up!"

Without looking up, I sarcastically said, "Too bad I wasn't on it, right?" Then I turned and saw this big jock — cool, tough, aloof — with tears in his eyes.

The death-news that shook us all. As we watched the scene over and over, I realized that we — these kids and I — were no different. We are all vulnerable, sensitive, insecure about our ability to deal with life.

continued

I forget this similarity occasionally. I become jaded and view their "teen-age angst" as insignificant, somehow less than real, unimportant. It's a shame that something like the shuttle has to happen to rein me in, pull me down off my pedestal, and make me treat these students "as if they really were fellow passengers to the grave and not another race of creatures bound on other journeys" (Dickens).

As I grieved with my students, I caught a glimpse of myself at fifteen. I realized that their worlds—with all of their "trivial" problems—are really just microcosms of my own. Each rejection, each failure is, to them, another explosion shaking their foundation, making them question their values, their station, their meaning. My students' behavior is merely a reflection of what they are dealing with, a sign of the struggle to validate themselves as members of the human race.

I have to remember this as a teacher. I have to lose this "they-are-manipulating-me" attitude.

I had that attitude in 1987 when Martie Baskins was in class. He was sneaky, underhanded. I always thought he was cheating. I never gave him full credit on papers, though he was a good writer. I hated to call on him in class because I didn't want him to get the best of me. He wasn't fooling me. About midyear, Martie put the end of a shotgun in his mouth and pulled the trigger with his toe.

When my patience is very short, when I hate dealing with "stupid kids," I close my eyes and see these two explosions simultaneously.

Then I stop and listen to what the arrogant jock and the class punk have to say.

USEFULNESS OF FREEWRITING. Some critics question the usefulness of teaching freewriting when, after it's all done, the writer still has to make a list. Why not start right out listing? they sometimes ask. There are sound reasons why not:

1. Some people, especially inexperienced writers, seem to need to begin in this way. If it takes an extra step or two—well, then it takes an extra step or two.
2. With its potential as "a mode of learning" (Emig) or "a way of knowing" (McCrimmon), surely freewriting is the most useful of all writer-centered writing.[6] Many writers discover their own thoughts this way. Note how Mrs. Snyder uses it in the model, for example.
3. Freewriting helps conquer writer's block. Many of our students are so fearful of "getting it wrong," of "not doing it right," that they become pen-tied and can scarcely write at all. Freewriting helps to loosen up the compulsive perfectionist. Because it forbids proofreading and insists on forging ahead at all costs, freewriting forces students who are hamstrung by the desire never to make a mistake at least to set down their ideas.

4. Freewriting can also aid in unblocking the mental channels of those who cannot write a word because they cannot settle down to thinking about a subject.

5. Students can use freewriting to harvest turns of phrase. Although the greater part of the writing so produced may be little more than babble or, at best, unrestrained and undigested thought, most writers from time to time produce some pure gems of expression, retrievable for future use.

6. Perhaps the best carryover from freewriting is the development of the student's own personal voice. The student's voice naturally cannot be denied in freewriting; and, after its habitual exercise here, it often manages to transfer to planned work as well.

A Caveat.   Freewriting thus can be a truly fruitful invention strategy, and one our students should learn. A word of caution though. Our students need to understand that a freewriting is ordinarily quite a different thing from a finished composition. As Erica Lindemann writes:

> A freewriting represents a writer talking out an idea; it is not a polished communication intended for an outside audience.[7]

Far from being a completed work, a freewriting is actually just the beginning of the writing process.

Heuristics

The temporarily uninspired have no alternative but to take some sort of inventory of their ideas. This inventory can be accomplished by a freely associating flow of thought—either by listing or freewriting. Indeed, this method is used by most writers most of the time. There are, however, a number of people who usually do better with a more systematic spur to creativity. And from time to time most people can benefit from employing such strategies, called heuristics. A *heuristic*, as defined by Linda Flower and John Hayes, is

> The codification of a useful technique of cognitive skill . . . as an alternative to trial and error [which] can operate as a discovery procedure.

It is, in Richard Young and Alton Becker's words,

> A method of solving problems, a series of steps or questions which are likely to lead an intelligent analyst to a reasonable solution of a problem.[8]

A wide variety of rhetorical heuristics has been developed. They range from the *topoi* of ancient rhetoricians to the cubing techniques of contemporary educators. They vary in complexity from the Five W's of journalism to the intricate slotted grids derived from tagmemic linguistics. But the purpose behind all of them is to help writers originate and clarify their ideas and to get a firmer grasp on their material. So although I would not recommend teaching heuristics for the first few compositions, our students might find it useful to learn some of them in later class sessions.

THE FIVE W'S OF JOURNALISM. Journalists learn early in their reporting days to ask the traditional journalistic questions:

- Who?
- What?
- Where?
- When?
- Why?
- [and How, if applicable]

This familiar trick of the newsman's trade is actually a translation of the *Quis? Quid? Quibus auxiliis? Ubi? Cur? Quomodo? Quando?* of the scholastic philosophers. Even today, every good newspaper story builds its "lead" around the answers to these questions. These same questions, when employed as a rhetorical heuristic, can be highly effective in summoning up all relevant information about the subject under consideration.

The "Five W's of Journalism," as they are called, have special value because they offer what W. Ross Winterowd calls "a finite set of topics," that is, one cannot ask questions "within the terms covered by the set . . . that cannot be classed under one of the items."[9] Using the Five W's therefore guarantees a fairly thorough survey of one's own information on a topic. If the class working with "George Washington," for instance, had used the Ws, their inventory of ideas may have been far more extensive. *Who?*, for example, should have generated not only "Martha" and "slaves," but also probably a number of other people important in Washington's life.

To Generate Support. The Five W's are useful not only in expanding one's inventory of ideas about a general topic but also in generating supporting details once the particular theme has been decided upon. A student can pose any one of the questions, answer it with whatever comes first to mind, and then ask the other questions in terms of that answer. Let's say, for example, that the assigned topic is "My Vacation." Our student starts with the question *When?* and answers it, "The day we went gathering shells." Thinking now in terms of the particular incident, she answers the question *Where?* "At the beach"; *Who?* brings "Bill and Lisa and I," and so on.

KENNETH BURKE'S PENTAD. The questions in Kenneth Burke's Pentad are almost identical to the Five W's. They include: What was done? (act), When or where was it done? (scene), How was it done? (agency), Who did it? (agent), and Why? (purpose). But, at least according to Richard Young, "Burke's procedure is capable of far more complex analysis than the journalistic questions." For, as Young points out, "the terms of the Pentad can be combined together for a more searching impact."[10] Significance can be attached to every item, for example, by including the question Why? as in the combinations Act/Purpose, Agent/Purpose, Scene/Purpose, and so on.

The Five W's have an instant appeal for the many students who have some interest in journalism. Burke's Pentad is especially useful for narrative writing. And both of these heuristics can be used to good effect by younger or less able groups.

ARISTOTLE'S TOPOI. Almost twenty-four centuries ago, Aristotle worked out a strategy for discovering and developing relationships among ideas.

Aristotle suggested that support for any point of view could be discovered by considering that subject in terms of modes of thought he called *topoi* (roughly, "topics"). The idea was for orators (now writers) to ask themselves questions about their subject that the "topics" suggested to them. Aristotle's method is aimed at the essential process of invention: the drawing of connections, the discovery of relationships between diverse facts until a unifying pattern emerges. His strategy was to consider the subject in relationship to its genre or class, its cause and its consequences, and its similarities to and differences from other comparable things.

The study of this grandsire of all our heuristics can provide an intriguing enrichment project for our gifted students.[11] And when we scale down his original five topics and seventeen subtopics to a workable few and teach students practical ways of implementing them, Aristotle's topoi can also make a useful alternative classroom heuristic. The Student Guidelines lists the most teachable topics and includes some thought-probing questions with each.

STUDENT GUIDELINES

Teachable Topoi

1. *Definition:* What kind of thing is my subject? To what grouping or category does it belong? How is it distinguished from other members of that group?
2. *Comparison:* How is this subject similar to others in its group? How does it differ from them?
3. *Causal Relationships:* What does the subject cause or bring about? What are the effects, the consequences of this subject?
4. *Authority:* What do the experts have to say about my subject?

Working from the Topoi. How can our students use this heuristic to invent? If the videotaped class, for example, had reasoned from Aristotle's "topics" with their same ideas about George Washington in mind, they would probably have arrived at an organizing idea rather similar to the one they found by freely associated thought. But the class might have created a more sophisticated and sensitive version of that organizing idea, one almost certainly backed by stronger and more convincing support. For instance, the class might have approached the topic first from Definition and reason: GW was a man, good—though flawed, great soldier, revolutionary hero, capable leader. Then they might have analyzed by using Comparison in this way:

> What other good, but flawed men were also great soldiers, revolutionary he-roes, capable leaders of men and became their countries' chief executive?
> Napoleon, Mao Tse-tung, Castro
> How does George Washington differ from these other leaders?
> G. W. turned down the crown.
> No other revolutionary leader ever voluntarily stepped down.
> All others attempted to perpetuate their power.

The usefulness of the technique, however, is not limited to factual material. It can work with equally creative generative power on more personal matters as well. Take, for example, the subject "My Vacation":

ILLUSTRATIVE MODEL

Using the Topoi on a Personal Topic

1. Definition [of my vacation]
   - Free time
   - Learning experience
2. Comparison (with other kinds of free time, other learning experiences)
   - More time
   - More solitude
   - Different way of being with friends, family
   - Sun and sand and sea
3. Consequences
   - Vacation threw new light on my relationship with others.
   - Vacation gave me more time alone to think about those things.
   - The background of the great eternals lent everything new perspective.
   - I learned some important things about myself.

Despite the triteness of the assignment, there is a thoughtful theme in the making here once each idea is supported by specific details.

As effective as the topoi are for generating and developing theses, they were designed originally to aid an orator (writer) searching for arguments to support controversial positions. And that purpose is still where they can achieve their greatest effectiveness. Let us look, for instance, at positions for and against legislation on equal rights for women and see how the topoi might help a partisan develop arguments.

ILLUSTRATIVE MODEL

Using the Topoi to Support a Controversial Position

The Question: Should equal rights for women be guaranteed by law?

The Answers: Yes   No

The Arguments:

From Definition:
Women, like men, are people, and therefore should be regarded so in the eyes of the law.

From Definition:
Men are men and women are women. Although neither should be favored, the difference should be legally recognized.

From Comparison (to the past)
1. Psychological difference: In the past, many women found their entire sense of identity and worth through the service they rendered to parents, husband, and children. Today more women recognize that they need something from life in their own right. The law must, therefore, grant women legal personhood and equality, so that they will have an equal chance with men to achieve their desires.

From Comparison
1. Psychological difference: In the past, women found fulfillment in their traditional role. Now women who choose to continue in that role suffer a sense of degradation and many women feel so degraded that they believe they must work out of the home, thus contributing to the downfall of the family and of the moral fabric of society itself.

2. Economic difference: In the past, most women had economic security: if they remained single they remained a part of a larger family circle which would provide for them. If they married, their husbands took care of them financially and they took care of their husbands in return. Now only the nuclear family remains, and it does not offer support to the unmarried relative. Married women now have to fear the possibility of divorce — a common occurrence — and even if they remain married, the rise in the cost of living often requires two breadwinners. Women, therefore, now need to be economically effective, just as men are.

2. Economic difference: In the past, when men were the major breadwinners with most women content to be helpmates at home, massive unemployment existed only during infrequent periods of economic depression. But now many women have been persuaded to seek "personal fulfillment" with a job outside the home. In neglecting their own families, these women are also displacing others, heads of families, from their work; and our society suffers the ills of continuous unemployment. The new legislation will further all these destructive trends.

continued

From Consequence:
If the legislation is passed, justice will be served and the promises of "freedom and justice for all" may then be fulfilled.

From Consequence:
If passed, all that is unnatural will triumph. Women will lose all their special privileges; they will be required to serve in combat; they will be forced to share lavatories with men; and they will lose all special financial protection in divorce and special physical protection in factories.

From Authority:
The Declaration of Independence.
The Constitution (especially the 14th Amendment)
Betty Friedan, Gloria Steinem.

From Authority:
The Bible

Phylis Schlafly, Mirabelle Morgan

FREEWRITING PLUS. This heuristic combines the probing apparatus of some of the other strategies with freewriting. Those students of ours who find freewriting helpful will find this technique especially useful. The idea is for the student to choose a heuristic—for instance, the Five W questions or each of Aristotle's "topics." Then, while considering each of the items (questions or topics) in turn, students freewrite the ideas that each item suggests. In this way, students who think through writing have the opportunity to explore their thoughts on a topic in some depth.

Cubing. An especially popular form of freewriting plus is a heuristic known as "cubing." When cubing, the writer considers a topic as if it were a cube—holding it up, so to speak, and examining each of its six sides. Elizabeth Cowan Neeld's version suggests the following six "sides":

- Describing it
- Comparing it
- Associating it (with other ideas)
- Analyzing it
- Applying it
- Arguing for and against it.[12]

Neeld explains that "cubing works well" when "writers can't get going on a subject because they are locked into a single way of looking at the topic." Her directions to the student include:

- Move fast.
- Don't allow yourself more than 3 to 5 minutes on each side of the cube.
- Use all six sides of the cube. (35)

OTHER HEURISTICS.   Other heuristics show promise of helping writers with the inventive process, but they have not yet been as solidly worked out. Interesting experimentation is in progress to convert portions of Kenneth Pike's tagmemic linguistic theory into a workable strategy for rhetorical invention. A good deal of work is also being done which attacks the problems of invention from the cognitive angle. See, for example, Linda Flower's *Problem-Solving Strategies for Writing.*[13]

TEACHING HEURISTIC STRATEGIES.   When the term is well underway, and students' initial enthusiasm has begun to flag, and even our most imaginative assignments no longer seem to inspire, the time is ripe for introducing one of the heuristics. The choice of method depends on the capability of the class, the teacher's personal predilection, or perhaps the recent subject of the class's studies. Completion of a unit on journalism, for example, would suggest the Five W's, while study of ancient Greece or Rome would naturally lead to the *topoi.* Whichever one we choose, we should offer the students a brief exposure to background theory and definition, followed by intensive practical experience using the strategy to "invent" a composition.

A Caveat.   A word of caution is in order here, however. Research has pointed to dangers associated with instructor insistence on student use of heuristics or, indeed, any prewriting strategy. Overconscientious students tend to confuse the complex heuristic means with the simple end of a well-written paper. Having conducted two studies of these problems, James D. Williams writes:

> It seems extremely easy for [prewriting activities] to become systematized to the point where they simply fail to help students plan, . . . [for] students come to believe that no writing can take place unless the designated prewriting activity is completed.[14]

With foreknowledge, however, we can make sure our students get their priorities straight. If a student doesn't find a strategy useful after a fair trial, then she should try generating her ideas in a different way. Students understand that their writing a paper just to demonstrate the workings of a heuristic strategy is as futile as a greyhound running a race just to give the mechanical rabbit a workout.

ARRANGEMENT: PREWRITING, PART II

To help our students learn to write, it is a good idea to single out for special study another component of the writing process, arrangement—Aristotle's term for organizing. In expository writing, arrangement means structuring the material so as best to support its central point.

The Pedagogical Problem

As teachers and writers, we know that the easiest and most effective way to figure out this structuring is to make a structural plan: a mental list, a balloon map, a jotted outline. Even those writers most oriented toward freewriting—writers such as Toby Fulwiler—make use of structural plans. As Fulwiler writes,

> Outlines are always generative. . . . I use them in the formative stages of determining what to write and where to direct my writing. . . . I think outlines are important in that they let you think through a project roughly before actually beginning it. . . . [They] prove especially useful in long projects.[15]

But too few students perceive a structural plan in this way. Ask them about outlines, and they will quickly agree to their importance. They will say: "Oh, yes. A plan is undoubtedly very important. Certainly. Of course. But I never use one myself. No. Never have. I'm one of those who can do just as well without one." If we dramatize just such a refrain to our students and then watch their faces, we will see embarrassed blushes and knowing twinkles as "the shoe" uncomfortably "fits." Make inclusion of an outline mandatory, and perhaps half the papers we receive will have outlines concocted after the paper was written. Most see the structural plan, I'm afraid, as Williams describes it, as "yet one more specified part of an assignment, . . . doing nothing but adding to the difficulty of the task" (41).

Faced with passive resistance of this sort, is there any way we can really convince our students of the value of a structural plan and so make this extraordinarily useful tool available to them? Probably the only way we might succeed is by somehow getting students to use one often enough to discover the truth for themselves.

The ABCD Experiment.   The best way I know to get students to try using plans was originated by Albert Joseph for the hardheaded businesspeople who are the clients of his Industrial Writing Institute in Cleveland, Ohio. He performs an experiment that proves to his sophisticated and skeptical clientele that a structural plan is necessary to their writing. Through it he clearly demonstrates the importance of establishing a logical pattern, and for more lengthy procedures, the importance of writing things down:

> The instructor begins by asking how many combinations can be made of the letters A and B. If the students are puzzled, they can be encouraged to envision the letters side by side as they would be typed. Once students understand, they should have no difficulty in arriving at the answer, "Two: AB and BA."
>
> The next question asks how many combinations can be made of A, B, C. In this case, there are six: ABC, ACB, BAC, BCA, CAB, and CBA. Most people cannot answer this correctly without resorting to pen and paper. There are too many items to hold easily in memory and oral trial and error does not work well. Those who arrive at the right answer will do so by following a

pattern, the sequence called "three factorial" by mathematicians $(3 \times 2 \times 1)$. They will note that there are three starting letters, and for each, two ways of arranging the remaining letters, ABC, ACB, and so on.

Once most students have caught on to the pattern, the teacher can surprise the group by asking them to recite all the possible combinations for A, B, C, and D. The odds are very much against anyone being able to apply the "four factorial" $(4 \times 3 \times 2 \times 1)$ and correctly name the 24 combinations without any kind of visual aid. (Experiments have shown that only one of 100 adults is able to manage the feat.) Very few will succeed even if the teacher coaches a little.[16]

Joseph's demonstration works equally well in the classroom. When our students begin reaching for their pencils and paper, our point has been made. For when the students can see the items as they try to arrange them, suddenly they are able to comprehend the pattern and reproduce it correctly. Before five minutes have elapsed, almost the entire class will have successfully completed the exercise. Nor will they have much difficulty afterward in understanding the importance of making a structural plan before writing a paper or report. As Joseph explains:

> If your report contains as many as three ideas, and if they are at least as complicated as A, B, and C, you cannot mentally examine all the possible combinations. [And when you're trying to start writing], that is exactly what you're trying to do. (169)

Overcoming Misconceptions

Even after our students are convinced that a structural plan is a necessity whenever they want to work with three ideas at least as complicated as the letters of the alphabet, the idea of "outline" may still bear a stigma for them. They will almost certainly harbor misconceptions about it. The words "make an outline" conjure up for most of our students a mental picture either of an interminable list of unrelated items numbered I to XXVI or of three painstakingly typed pages of topic sentences—and possibly both. Our first step in teaching the organizing process, therefore, must be to dispel these images.

WHAT AN EFFECTIVE STRUCTURAL PLAN ISN'T. We need to assure our students that the only kind of plans we care about must be useful to *them.*

Structural Plans Should NOT Be Teacher-Centered. Since working outlines are a writer's own personal tools, students should feel free to make their structural plans in whatever shape works best for them. We need to introduce them to possibilities of mapping with balloons or boxes as well as making linear lists and outlines. (See pages 91–93, for examples.)

They also should feel free to make their plans as neat or as mussed as their own work habits demand. They should be reconciled to the idea that there will be false starts, revisions, and scratch-outs.

If we ask students to share their plans with us in conference or when they hand in a paper—so we can offer some organizational help—we should request only the *working* outline, in whatever shape it might be in.

Structural Plans Should NOT Be Carved in Stone. If an outline isn't flexibly correctable, it isn't useful. The whole point of an outline is that it is a much *easier* way of trying out and adjusting structure than rewriting an entire paper would be.

Structural Plans Must NOT Be Long. Research shows that human minds can deal with a maximum of seven items—and most do much better with fewer. If the function of an outline is to set up the structure of the paper so that the writer can "see it steadily and see it whole" (to use Matthew Arnold's phrase), then a useful structural plan must be brief enough to hold complete in the memory. It is thus sensible for structural plans to contain no more than six or seven major points—including points for the introduction and the conclusion. Nor should any idea have more than a handful of subordinated points.

Structural Plans Should NOT Be "Sentence Outlines." Sentence outlines, where all items are recorded in sentence form, are cumbersome and tend to obscure the overall vision. Besides, the vested interest students have in sentences already composed inhibits the necessary flexibility of the outline, and student writers become locked in not only to the outlines but even to the phrasing of topic sentences.

WHAT AN EFFECTIVE STRUCTURAL PLAN IS. Once we reassure students that outlines need not—and indeed should not—be the busywork bores they're often thought to be, students will be more interested in what they actually are and how they can serve their needs. Metaphor is often useful for this purpose. Images that have proved especially helpful for teachers include the test model, the road map, the X-ray, the blueprint, and the pie.

Structural Plan as Test Model. Just as an automobile company first develops a test model to try out new automotive ideas on a small scale and to "iron out the bugs" before going into the expensive manufacturing process, a writer puts together a structural plan. Both offer a flexible model to test out structural patterns; both can be adjusted, readjusted, or even scrapped without too much expenditure.

Structural Plan as Road Map. A structural plan can serve as a spur to the memory to keep the writer on track. As Sheridan Baker describes this function:

> Once you get the logic down on paper and out of the way, you can let yourself go, writing from heading to heading, sure of your direction. . . . You can push aside without worry the good ideas constantly crowding in for your notice: your outline has already scheduled them up ahead, each in its most logical and effective place.[17]

Structural Plan as X-Ray. Like a skeletal X-ray, a structural plan conveys a sense of divided wholeness.

Structural Plan as Blueprint. Like a blueprint, it both compactly displays a basic design of a complicated structure and provides measurements and directions for developing the finished product. It also permits the project to be worked on as a whole or part by part.

Structural Plan as a Segmented Pie. The pie represents the organizational idea; the slices, the subordinated points; subslices, subpoints. Through this metaphor our students can grasp in a concrete way that an outline is a plan for dividing up a whole, that each segment is an integral part of one totality: the slices of an apple pie remain apple. Students can also see that slices can be of varying sizes, and that slices can be divided.

DEFINITION. What then is a structural plan?

> A structural plan — a working outline — consists of a few written points standing for the structural divisions of a complete composition, a plan that can be used as a guide on a trial basis to direct the construction of that composition.

Once students reach some such understanding, they are ready to make and use their own structural plans.

How Effective Structural Plans Can Be Constructed

The key to a genuinely useful structural plan is, quite naturally, a good organizational idea. As Ken Macrorie writes:

> Without a controlling idea, you have nothing around which to organize your points for a paper. Once you have the idea, you must make sure that it really controls your materials. . . . You must learn to discard even well phrased and interesting parts if they disturb the organization of the whole. To be a strong writer, you must be in love, not with yourself or your words, but with your controlling ideas.[18]

Start with a controlling or organizational idea and phrase it as a working thesis. If our students construct a working thesis that is well phrased — or if it at least conveys the intended meaning — its very language can provide the major clues to the structure of a composition based upon it. How? The writer should follow the steps in the following Student Guidelines.

STUDENT GUIDELINES

Making a Structural Plan

1. Examine the working thesis analytically.
2. Select the key words and phrases that point to ideas that must be supported or demonstrated.
3. Find the necessary support.
4. Subordinate the support under its appropriate idea or point.

AN INTRODUCTORY EXAMPLE.   In order to bring as little confusion as possible to what may at first appear a complex procedure, we should select for our demonstration the simplest possible example. If our students are truly inexperienced, we might suggest that they consider a working thesis as uncomplicated, for instance, as "Our zoo has interesting animals." Even the least able students will be able to point to "interesting" and "animals" as the key words, and they will have little difficulty in understanding that in order to support that thesis they will have to supply the names of some of the zoo's more interesting animals as evidence. A plan such as the following can then be easily developed.

Table 3–2.

Working Thesis [organizing idea]: Our zoo has interesting animals.

1. Introduction[19]
2. Giraffe
3. Elephant
4. Platypus
5. – – – [Have students supply]
6. Conclusion

Next we might argue that a list of animals alone is not sufficient evidence to support our organizing idea persuasively. If we ask what support is lacking, the students should be able to point out that we would also need support to show that each of the suggested animals is interesting. In other words, to write a paragraph or essay based on this idea, we would have to follow a plan something like that in the Student Exercise.

STUDENT EXERCISE

Supporting a Working Thesis

Working Thesis: Our zoo has interesting animals.
1. Introduction
2. — Giraffe
    — Interesting because has a long neck   .
    — Interesting because is awkward and graceful at once   .
    — Interesting because ?   .
3. Platypus
    — Interesting because has both fur and bill   .
    — Interesting because both lays eggs and nurses young   .
    — Interesting because ?   .
4. Elephant
    [Have students supply support]
5. Student choice
    — — —

    — — —
6. Conclusion

AN INTRODUCTORY CLASS EXERCISE.   An alternative or additional full-class structuring exercise that I can heartily recommend is a continuation of the George Washington class brainstorming I described earlier in this chapter. As in the preliminary portion, the class as a whole continues to imagine that they are a single mass brain assigned a paper on George Washington (or a similar agreed-upon topic).

A Class in Action, Part 2, the videotaped continuation of the lesson already excerpted, offers an example of an actual class setting up its organizing idea, formulating a working thesis, and developing a structural plan to support it from their assembled inventory of ideas. When we interrupted the lesson (see page 64), the teacher had just said: "Now for the hard part. The organizing idea." After that, she continued.

A CLASS IN ACTION, PART 2

Teacher: Can you think of some theses? What do you want to say in your paper? (Pause) Remember your organizing idea doesn't have to take in everything. (Pause) What do you want to say? [But despite the fact that one girl remarked, "I'm sure there's more than one organizing idea here"—an observation to which the teacher gave hearty assent—in the end, this class actually only considered one. For in the next moment Jason ventured:

Jason: I can't phrase it in a sentence but I can give you some idea. Take into account, you know, that Washington was a very great leader but that he also had a private life. And since that he had a private life, was a very great leader and because of the combination of these two things, many monuments and legends . . . they made monuments and legends about him.

    [It is truly extraordinary when a complex, comprehensive organizing idea is proposed before discussion. I am not sure that I recall another instance. This class recognized the merit of Jason's suggestion and was reluctant to consider anything else. They were eager, however, to clarify the terminology. In doing so, they were struggling toward a working thesis.]

Teacher: What we're getting into here is something called the "although clause." Do you know about the "although clause"?

Susan: Sounds like a bad one.

Teacher: No, it's a good one. It's a very helpful thing to have. You've actually got two organizing ideas there, Jason. You say (1) "Washington is a great leader." And that could be an organizing idea. With it you would take all the items we've got down here under "Great Leader" and probably also take "Monuments and Legends" and show that Washington was really terrific, a really great leader. That would leave out half the other things. But, you're suggesting taking both halves in by saying, "Although Washington was a human being like the rest of us, he was a great leader." I'm not sure that's what you want to say. Maybe you want to say, "Although Washington was a great leader, he was a human being like the rest of us—had his faults and failures."

Jason: Which one?

Teacher: Either one is good. Which one do you want to say?

Jason: There's more up there about his leading than anything. Even his plantation, in a sense, is a leading because he built it up almost from nothing to something.

Teacher: So you think that with the facts, the data we have before us, making the leading the main part of the organizing idea would be best? Does anyone disagree? Do you like "Although he was a great leader, he was a human being" or "a fallible human being"?

Jason: That's fine.

Teacher: Do we have any other ideas? We came to this so quickly. Any more ideas?

Kim: Not other ideas, but I don't like the word "human being."

Teacher: All right. Let's think of a better term.

[And they were off. For the next ten or fifteen minutes, the class struggled to phrase their organizing idea in such a way that it would say exactly what they intended, and would make an effective working thesis. But they never really accomplished this task to their complete satisfaction. When it became clear that continued brainstorming would probably not be fruitful, the teacher interrupted the discussion.]

Teacher: How about agreeing that this is not exactly the way we want to phrase our organizing idea, and if, as we go along, someone thinks of a better way, we'll just cross this one out and substitute the better one. But we all know what we mean by it, and we can get a structural plan together, just knowing what we mean — and maybe thinking of better words as we go along. For you've got an organizing idea. It isn't phrased just the way you want it, but it is something we can work with. [Then she wrote down the tentative organizing idea. See Chalkboard 3.]

Teacher: So, let's begin the structural plan. There's a personal way that I begin a structural plan. Not everybody does it. But it gives me confidence and I'll share it with you. I like to start by putting down "I. Introduction." You have to start with an introduction, and when I get that on the page, the page isn't blank anymore. And it gives me courage to go on. You don't have to do that if you don't want, but I have always found it a great help. (Laughter)

Your organizing idea, when you get it phrased, will go into your introduction, and the rest of your paper — and for now your structural plan — will go to present it more fully.

Now for the rest of the structural plan. How do we divide it up?

Kim: (Pointing to the organizing idea) "Washington the Man" and "Washington the Leader."

Teacher: Good. Where do we begin?

Michael: You should show how his private life led to help him build upon his qualities as a leader. Like in this kind of structural plan: you start with his being born, and some of the things he did, like chopping down the cherry tree, being sure he didn't lie, becoming a

CHALKBOARD 3.

?? although W. is comparable to the rest of us, he is still one of the great leaders of all time surveyor, surveying property, not only for himself but for other people, becoming a good surveyor, and then owning Mt. Vernon, and then leading that into the French and Indian War.

Teacher: Well, it seems as if now you're just narrating the story of Washington's life. Rather than a narrative structural plan, which would lead to a biography or a fiction or a story, we're trying to make an structural plan for an expository essay where you will support your points. You *can* support your points through narration. But the way you're phrasing it now, it seems to be more like just narrating his life. Let's look more closely at the organizing idea and see if we can find clues to our structural plan there.

Missy: What about the "although clause?" Right here. (Pointing)

Teacher: Yes, it is often a good idea to do the "although clause" first. Start with the part that you're arguing against. Give their arguments, and then give your side last where the reader will remember it; and although we're arguing for both sides here, the same principle holds true. (Writing) So that is "Washington the Man" and then "Washington the Leader." [See Chalkboard 4.]

Michael: Yeah.

Teacher: And under there (Pointing to Point II), what would you put? Yes, Jeff?

Jeff: Well, the organizing idea states that he is comparable to the rest of us and he is a great leader, so in the paper wouldn't you have to show how he is comparable to the rest of us.

Teacher: Just so. That is the part we're doing now.

CHALKBOARD 4.

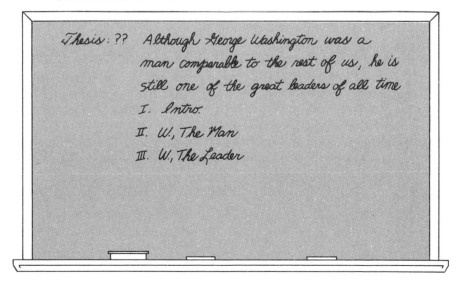

Thesis: ?? Although George Washington was a man comparable to the rest of us, he is still one of the great leaders of all time

I. Intro.

II. W, The Man

III. W, The Leader

Jeff: Okay. Good enough.

Teacher: We want to start with this. Even if the organizing idea is phrased in a way so that the main point came first, we would still start with whatever it is in the "although clause" part of it. And that would be so even if it were not phrased using the word "although." Does that make sense, Jeff?

Jeff: Yes.

Teacher: So that's what we're doing. "Washington, the Man" (Continuing). If we are going to support that Washington was a man . . .

Jeff: We have to take the facts we do know about him and use them.

Teacher: Right!

Jeff: Okay!

Teacher: And you support it. All the facts that will go in here will support that he is a "man," a human being. And then when we get to the next part, all those facts will support that he is a "great leader." Then you divide up the material. How would you divide it for Point II?

Heather: "Homey details," "Private life."

Steve: "The white wig," "The wooden teeth."

Teacher: That would be the "Homey details."

Michael: "Mt. Vernon," "Surveyor."

Teacher: That would be "Private life."

Jason: "Born February 22, 1732."

Teacher: Well, everybody's born. But I guess that makes him a man. Let me put these down. "Homey details," "Private life,": I don't know how parallel they are. But at least it gives you something to work with.

Missy: Put "Homey details" and "Details of private life."

Teacher: Okay, fine. All the "Homey details" will add up to Washington being a man, just like the rest of us and the "Details of private life" will add up the same way. Right?

Class: (Various sounds of assent.)

Teacher: And if you want to subdivide, each item in the subdivision, will add up to the category above. For instance, everything in the "Homey details" section (the false teeth, the wig, and so on) will serve to support that Washington had a lot of "homey details" about him. In other words (gesturing to the board), each step along the way will go to support the step above it, and the main steps will go to support the organizing idea. All along the line. Tight knit. Always supporting your point. [See Chalkboard 5.]

Teacher: Now we want to support Washington the "Great Leader." We had it divided into what?

Jason: "Military" and "Political."

Jeff: And "Monuments."

Class: (General assent)

Teacher: What would you do first?

Heather: Let's put it down, least to most important.

CHALKBOARD 5.

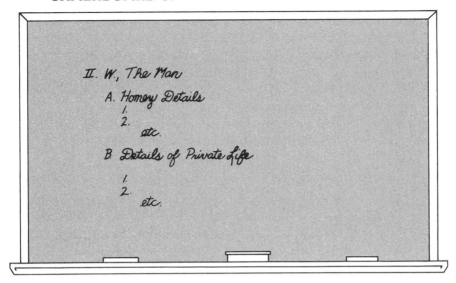

II. W., The Man
  A. Homey Details
    1.
    2.
        etc.
  B. Details of Private Life
    1.
    2.
      etc.

Teacher: Okay. What is the most important? What is the least important?
Michael: "Military" and then "Political."
Teacher: Would you all agree? (General assent) Instead of doing it this way, you might want to make it "Washington, the leader, Military," number III. And number IV: "Washington, the leader, Political." For V. "Washington, the Leader . . . what's the word? You want an adjective that means "after he was gone?" [See Chalkboard 6.]

CHALKBOARD 6.

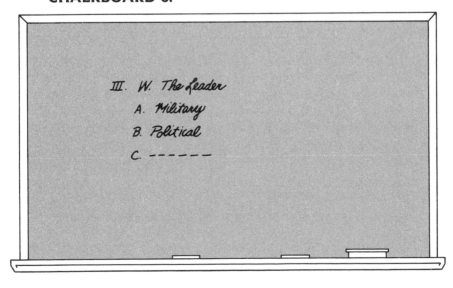

III. W. The Leader
  A. Military
  B. Political
  C. ------

Ginger: "Memorable?"
Susan: "Legendary?"
Several: Yes, "Legendary."
Teacher: "Legendary."
Steve: I don't think "legendary" goes with "Washington, the Leader" though.
Jason: But using "The Man" and then using "The Leader" — what became of that?
Heather: I think "Legendary" is . . .
Teacher: Would you rather have "Hero"? Washington, the Hero — Political, Military, and then Legendary?
H.,J.,S.: Yeah. (Then general assent)
Teacher: All right. That might be better. "Legendary" is a word that means more than just leadership. It puts Washington above; and that makes the idea more opposite to regular man. (Marking on board) Okay. Does that help? So, Washington, the Hero — Military; Washington the Hero — Political; and Washington, the Hero — Legendary. And then your conclusion, where you can really get into this thing you want to say. [See Chalkboard 7.]
Steve: Why not just put "Washington the Leader" and then put "Military"

CHALKBOARD 7.

II. W., The Man
   A. Homey Details
   B. Details of Private Life
III. W., The Hero — Military
IV. W., The Hero — Political
   W., The Hero — Legendary
VI. Conclusion

CHALKBOARD 8.

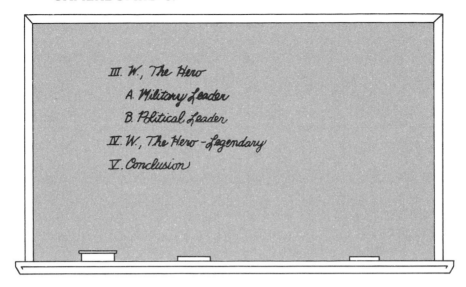

III. W., The Hero
   A. Military Leader
   B. Political Leader
IV. W., The Hero—Legendary
V. Conclusion

and "Political" under it there; and then just have "Legendary" as another number there.

Teacher: You'd rather put "Political" and "Military" together and keep the "Legendary" separate? All right. Do you all like that? These two really are different; the "Legendary" is . . .

Steve: Something else.

Jason: The "Legendary is a result of the leader . . .

Others: Yes . . .

Randy: Yes, and "Legendary" could be part of the "Conclusion."

Teacher: Yes. Okay, it can really be part of the "Conclusion." (Erases and writes) [See Chalkboard 8.]

Teacher: Are you all happy with this? (Assent and laughter) Still not, Heather?

Heather: You know, the legends, I think can be made enough of their own. And then, you can have a conclusion that draws from the private, the military, political, and legendary all in one.

Teacher: Okay. (Writing) "Conclusion—maybe." If you haven't said it already. If you've got some kind of whamo way to conclude. Otherwise, you could conclude with Number IV. (Dramatically) This man is not only a hero in his own time; but, legendary, he has become a hero . . .

CHALKBOARD 9.

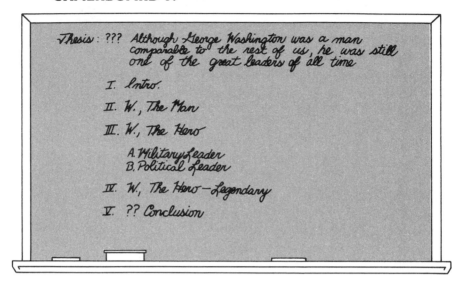

Thesis: ??? Although George Washington was a man comparable to the rest of us, he was still one of the great leaders of all time

I. Intro.

II. W., The Man

III. W., The Hero

    A. Military Leader
    B. Political Leader

IV. W., The Hero—Legendary

V. ?? Conclusion

Various Students: "Throughout the world," "Throughout American history" . . .

The general voice: "Throughout all time."

    Teacher: Yes, This'd be good. This would be very good. . . . But, of course, then you'd have to support it with big, strong evidence. [See Chalkboard 9.]

After such a workout, our abler or more mature students should grasp the concepts of structuring from an organizing idea and of subordinating the support in a logical way. On the other hand, we must not underestimate the difficulty of these ideas for many of our students. The concepts that seem to be the most troubling are the interactive, contrasting ideas of unity and subordination.

Teaching Unity and Subordination

The pie metaphor mentioned earlier can be particularly useful in helping our students understand these principles most essential to the organizing skills. The self-evident appleness of the entire pie demonstrates the fundamental unity of every composition. We can show our students that just as every piece of the pie is clearly apple, so every point in their structural plan (and every portion of the essay that results from it) must contribute to the whole (Figure 3–1). The pie metaphor helps students understand why we insist that they

Figure 3–1.

make sure that all subpoints support or develop their points and that all points support and develop the organizing idea.

BOARDWORK.   To get these ideas across experientially, we might send students to the chalkboard with the organizing ideas and support they had worked out in an earlier lesson (see pages 48–53). We could then ask them to make some sort of a diagram that would represent breaking their idea down into its component parts and still convey its essential unity. Some experienced students may choose to write a conventional linear outline, and we certainly should not discourage them. But to those who await our advice, we could suggest they base their diagrams on a literal rendition of the word *subordination*—that is, they should "order" their support "under" the appropriate points. Using whatever boxes or balloons that occur to them, they should produce graphic outlines such as the ones portrayed in Figures 3–2 and 3–3. (taken from examples in Chapter 2). Subordination, the heart of

Figure 3–2. Structural Plan Model A

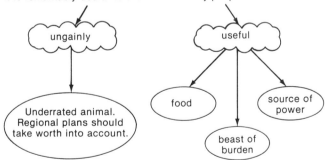

meaningful structure, seems to be a particularly difficult concept for some students. These students may need a good bit of practice at this stage: in class discussion, in an individual conference, or with exercises of progressive complexity such as those suggested at the end of this chapter or those included by Mina Shaughnessy in her most insightful book *Errors and Expectations: A Guide for the Teacher of Basic Writing.*[20]

Teaching the Ordering of Points and Subpoints

The second most problematic area in the structuring process is how to order the supporting evidence. The students in A Class in Action, for instance, having divided the "pie" of their organizing idea into appropriate supporting "slices," still spent a good portion of their organizing time deciding upon the order they felt would express their ideas most effectively. But how do individual writers decide how to order the points they want to make? Does the order matter very much anyway?

Figure 3–3. Structural Plan Model B

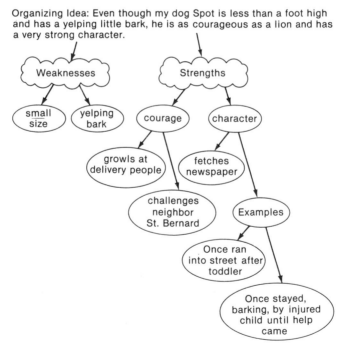

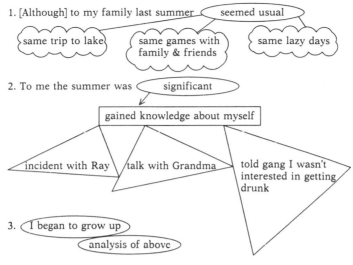

1. [Although] to my family last summer *seemed usual*
   - *same trip to lake*
   - *same games with family & friends*
   - *same lazy days*

2. To me the summer was *significant*

   gained knowledge about myself

   - incident with Ray
   - talk with Grandma
   - told gang I wasn't interested in getting drunk

3. *I began to grow up*
   analysis of above

Figure 3–4. Structural Plan Model C

Although we as teachers can admit frankly that rarely is the order of subpoints of crucial importance to the finished composition, we should maintain that the order of the main topics can often make a real difference. In any case, since all writing takes place in time, some order must necessarily be selected. What is important, then, is for the writer to make these decisions in a deliberate rather than a haphazard way. To this end, we teachers can make our students familiar with a number of principles upon which they may logically base their choices.

ORGANIZING FROM THE RHETORICAL PRINCIPLE. Perhaps the most important of these ordering principles is the rhetorical principle, the principle of persuasion. The sole criterion for arrangements based upon this principle is their degree of persuasiveness.

"Although Clause" Material First. An important axiom founded on this principle is to place the material in the subordinate clause of the organizing idea first. Whenever an organizing idea has anything approaching an overt "although clause" or other subordinate clause, the material it contains should be given less weight and should be dispatched as early in the paper as possible. As Sheridan Baker explains:

Table 3–3 Structural Plan Model D

Working Thesis: Although capital punishment has been proved to exert no deterrent effect upon crime, it should not be abolished because it serves some important economic and psychological needs of society.

I. Introduction (importance of issue . . . leading to preliminary statement of thesis)
II. Capital punishment does not deter
   A. Proof from study 1
   B. Proof from study 2
III. Should nevertheless be retained
   A. C.P. serves economic needs
      1. Example
      2. Example
   B. C.P. serves psychological needs.
      1. Example
      2. Example
IV. Conclusion (keep C.P.)

> The subordinate clause states the subordinate part of your argument, which is your concession to the con viewpoint; your main clause states your main argument. . . . You want, and your readers want, to get the opposition out of the way. And you want to end on your best foot. (32)

This precept holds true for most expository writing and is especially important when the subject is controversial. Often the "although" material makes an interesting introduction. See Figure 3–4. Even when no "although" is explicitly expressed, the latent negation inherent in all organizing ideas may be briefly explicated in the introduction. For instance, latent in the organizing idea "Spring is a beautiful season" is the subordinate clause, "Although other seasons have much to be said for them," a thought that can be developed into an introduction leading into a statement of the point that will be demonstrated in the body of the paper. Other examples of confining the "although clause" to the introduction may be found in Structural Plan Model A, illustrated in Figure 3–2, page 91 and also Chalkboard 9, page 90, where the Class in Action used this formulation.

Sometimes, however, the subordinate clause contains material that needs to be developed in some fullness in order to clarify the main point. And often the "although" material is controversial and needs to be treated more fully to concede what must be conceded to the other side. In these cases it is especially important to lead off with this material in order to de-emphasize it. See, for example, Structural Plan Models D and E, on the controversial capital punishment issue, illustrated in Table 3–3 and Table 3–4, respectively.

Though there are doubtless exceptional cases, the precept of using the "although clause" first is ignored at the writer's peril. How often have we

Table 3–4 Structural Plan Model E

Organizing Idea: Despite that fact that capital punishment is still overwhelmingly popular in a country ideally run by the wishes of the majority, it should nevertheless be abolished because it serves no useful purpose and is inherently uncivilized.

  I. Introduction (examples of the popularity of capital punishment . . . leading to an abbreviated statement of working thesis)
 II. C.P. purposeless
    A. Deterrence only conceivable useful purpose
    B. C.P. not a deterrent
      1. Proof
      2. Proof
      3. Proof
    C. C.P. therefore not useful
III. C.P. uncivilized
    A. Religious argument
    B. Humanistic argument
    C. Sociological argument
 IV. Conclusion (abolish C.P.)

been puzzled by student papers that begin with organizing ideas that strongly support one point of view but seem to come out at the end even more strongly on the other side? And such papers whose concluding paragraphs dutifully restate the original organizing ideas make the situation even more confusing. If there is any difficulty in convincing a skeptical student of the rightness of placing the subordinate material first, I recommend assigning the exercise Baker suggests for such cases:

> You might try putting the opposition last, just to see how peculiarly the last word insists on seeming best, and how, when stated last by you, the opposition's case seems to be your own. (32)

ORGANIZING THROUGH COMPARISON. If we have the opportunity to teach our students only one ordering formula, I recommend teaching the conventions governing the comparative presentation of material. These comparison-structuring techniques can prove useful in a large variety of contexts within students' ordinary work, in English class and across the curriculum. They are even helpful in working with "although clause" structuring, especially when a major portion of the paper will be taken up presenting and opposing the other or "although" point of view. Our time is well spent teaching these conventions because most students find them difficult to use successfully without some instruction.

Divided and Alternating Pattern. Students should come to understand how to use both the divided and the alternating patterns for comparison.

Once understood, the writer can choose between the patterns on the basis of the particular qualities of the material to be presented. The arrangements are:

Alternating Pattern   Divided Pattern

Alternating Pattern	Divided Pattern
I. Their side	I. Point 1
A. Point 1	A. Their side
B. Point 2	B. Our side
C. Point 3, etc.	II. Point 2
II. Our side	A. Their side
A. Point 1	B. Our side
B. Point 2	III. Point 3
C. Point 3, etc.	A. Their side
	B. Our side

If the student wants to make quite a number of points or if the points are not strongly distinguished from one another, the divided pattern can become repetitive, somewhat tedious, and sometimes even confusing. On the other hand, if there is a direct interplay between the arguments, the divided approach may be preferable. Note, however, that either way, the opposition idea is presented first and thus is refuted last.

We have been discussing the comparison arrangements as if they were necessarily linked with controversial material. In fact, quite the opposite is the case. They are used at least as often simply as a means of organizing contrastive material as, for example, in Structural Plan Model F, portrayed in Table 3–5.

ORGANIZING BY ORDER OF IMPORTANCE.   Arrangement according to order of importance is universally considered rhetorically effective. But there is little agreement among the experts as to which order of importance is best. Some, like Sheridan Baker, suggest organizing from least to most important:

> A reader's normal line of attention progressively declines, arching down like a wintry graph. Against this decline you must oppose your forces, making each successive point more interesting. And save the best till last. It is as simple as that. (30)

But journalists and business writing specialists argue that since many pieces of writing are skimmed by their readers, the most important ideas should be first. They point out that the inverted pyramid—most to least important—is the conventional organization for business communications, for example. The reason: business correspondents, constrained by time and profit considerations, frequently do not read through the whole.

There is yet a third point of view on arrangements by importance. Psychological surveys have shown that reader retention and reader interest is

Table 3–5 Structural Plan Model F

Working Thesis: Despite the undeniable superiority of the Athenian civilization, the Athenians were foolhardy in their foreign policy and thus lost the Peloponnesian Wars.

  I. Introduction (poses the paradox)

 II. Superiority of Athenian civilization

A. The arts		A. Sparta
1. Sparta		1. The arts
2. Athens		2. Philosophy
B. Philosophy		3. Government
1. Sparta	or	B. Athens
2. Athens		1. The arts
C. Government		2. Philosophy
1. Sparta		3. Government
2. Athens		

III. Foolishness of Athenian foreign policy

    A. Example ⎫

    B. Example ⎬ Chronologically arranged

    C. Example ⎭

    D. Example

IV. Loss of Peloponnesian Wars

    A. Chronological account

    B. Evaluation, emphasizing III as the cause

  V. Conclusion (generalization)

greatest for the material at the end of a work, then for that at the beginning, and least for that in the middle.[21] Guiding one's arrangement by these findings would suggest an ordering of points in this fashion: 2, 3, 4, 1 (the numbers indicating the degree of importance).

As teachers of writing, it is not really necessary for us to choose between these alternatives. Each has its appropriate validity. When we teach journalistic or business writing, we should recommend the inverted pyramid. But for writing that is intended to be read through and considered as a whole—in short, for almost all academic composition—we should, I think, teach our students to build toward their conclusions and to place the point with greatest rhetorical significance last.

ORGANIZING BY PROBLEM AND SOLUTION. When puzzled students approach us for help in structuring their ideas, surprisingly often they can find their way by looking at their topic in terms of a problem and its solution. This would seem an obvious approach to essay-test questions, but it also offers a useful structure for thinking out such diverse working theses as:

    • Lunchroom scheduling should be improved
     [Problems of current schedule; suggested solution]

- I was bored to death all last summer, but next year's vacation will be different
- Privately owned prison facilities can ameliorate dangerously overcrowded conditions.

Structural Plan Model G, illustrated in Table 3–6, is based on the problem-solution scheme.

ORGANIZING BY CHRONOLOGICAL ORDER. Chronological sequencing, the way narrative writing is structured, can also be useful for organizing ideas supporting an expository thesis. Students should certainly consider this organization when arranging the support for most theses with a historical dimension. See, for instance, Part III in Structural Plan Model F (see Table 3–5, page 97).

Beware the Narrative Urge. Nevertheless, we need to help our students be wary of a tendency toward overusing chronological structuring. Because people seem to have a natural affinity for the narrative form of exposition, chronological order exerts a powerful attraction, often with inappropriate— sometimes even ludicrous—results. Only too typical is the student who supported his organizing idea that *When Isaac Newton discovered the law of gravity, he revolutionized scientific thought* with (1) *Newton's childhood*, (2) *youth*, (3) *adulthood*, and (4) *old age*.

ORGANIZING FROM PRINCIPLES OF FORMAL LOGIC. There are a number of arrangements based upon principles originating with the study of logic which our students might well find useful. Among these, for instance, are arrangements based upon inductive or deductive reasoning. The deductive approach begins with a generalization and develops it through specific details. The inductive approach begins with the specifics and, as in a mystery story, builds into a generalization.

Academic writing is conventionally deductive. But the inductive approach holds a strong attraction for some students. With it they can go back and trace the thought processes that led them to the discovery of their organizing

Table 3–6 Structural Plan Model G

Problem: Prisons are overcrowded
  —danger
  —danger
  —danger
Solution: Privatization can help
  —Description of private sector prisons
  —Benefits
    1. How it will help eliminate dangers discussed above
    2. Other benefits
Conclusion:

idea. Journalists of the 1970s and 80s developed this format into a popular genre dubbed "the new journalism." In inexperienced hands, however, inductive structuring can make a composition inappropriately writer-focused. More importantly, student compositions of this sort tend to be unclear. The reader loses interest as well as the point while waiting to find out that "the butler done it." We should warn our students that except in rare cases, holding back on any hint of their organizing idea till the conclusion is likely to cause more confusion than suspense.

Cause and Effect.   Another useful logic-grounded structure is based upon cause and effect. A writer might start with an effect, such as World War II, and, one by one, trace the causes leading to it. Another student might start with a cause, such as World War II, and consider individually the effects that it produced. The writer might also choose to construct a chain of cause and effect: a cause leading to its effect which in turn itself becomes a cause leading to other effects.

Syllogistic Structuring.   Some of us offer a unit in formal logic. A number of useful organizational schemes might well come out of such study. The syllogism, for instance, can make a very effective base for the ordering of ideas in a tightly reasoned paper. See, for example, Structural Plan Model E (Table 3–4, page 95) where Point II is argued syllogistically:

> II. Capital punishment is purposeless
>   A. Deterrence is the only conceivable useful purpose
>   B. C.P. is not a deterrent
>   1. Proof
>   2. Proof
>   3. Proof
>   C. C.P. is therefore not useful

Dialectic Structuring.   The thesis-antithesis-synthesis format of the dialectic can also be a productive tool for our more intellectually sophisticated students. As a structural plan, it works in this way:

> I. Thesis [an accepted idea]: To be educated a student needs some acquaintance with "the best that has been thought and said in the world."
>   A. Support
>   B. Support, etc.
>
> II. Antithesis [valid objection to I]: But to be professionally qualified, a student must have a large quantity of specialized knowledge.
>   A. Support
>   B. Support, etc.
>
> III. Synthesis [a compromise]: Therefore, many colleges require for graduation a general liberal arts program as well as specialization in a major field.

Principle of Logical Progression.   The more general principle of logical progression can be especially useful to our students. It can be applied to any quantitative or qualitative relationship, any sort of least-to-most or best-to-worst order. Progression is the backbone of the degree-of-importance ordering already discussed.

Almost any topic has progressions natural to it, ones that students, once they understand the advantage of placing their items in some logical series, have little problem discovering. For example, a paper might describe a ranking of the most garish to the most subdued painting in the art gallery or a similar ranking of the kind of caribou most likely to hibernate to the kind least likely. The opposite order, of course, is usually another possible progression.

Spacial Sequence.   If we anticipate students having difficulty with the idea of progression, we might consider introducing them first to spacial sequencing, perhaps the most concrete application of the progression principle. We might get out a map or point to objects in the room to demonstrate spacial sequence.

If the items to be ordered in their composition are spatially related, students may organize them according to the degree or nature of their proximity to one another—for instance, from the closest to the farthest from a particular point, or as they occur going east, or by their position ascending a mountain or descending a river. Any sort of progression of sequential sites appropriate to the subject matter will serve to guide the reader's mind through the organization of the writer's ideas.

TEACHING THE PRINCIPLES OF ORDERING.   Although ordering ideas is a subject teachers might profitably study themselves in order to be ready to give knowledgeable assistance to individual students, it is not a topic on which to spend much class time. A plethora of information on this subject may actually result in student confusion. All that is really important for the students to understand about the ordering of the items in their structural plans are the following basic ideas:

- Items in a structural plan should be arranged in some logically defensible order.
- Many such arrangements are available.
- The arrangement selected should be followed consistently.

Providing Opportunities for Practice

Students can get a feeling for when a structural plan works and what makes it work only from personal experience. We should therefore try to provide them with a rich set of experiences that will engage them with the subject. The following paragraphs offer ideas for such experiential learning.

PRACTICE IN ANALYZING READINGS FOR STRUCTURE.   Since reading and writing are the obverse of one another, students can learn a good deal about writing by analyzing what they read. The structure of a well-written essay should be apparent to the sensitive reader. We might ask students to discover the structure of an assigned essay and write a structural plan for it. This exercise not only gives the student an understanding of how professional writers organize their work, but also provides valuable practice in reading comprehension. And reconstructing the underlying plan makes a good collaborative project.

Identifying Professional Structure. In a more elaborate exercise, the teacher can introduce the class to an essay she has already screened to make sure that the organizing idea is stated in a moderately complete form within the introductory paragraphs. The class goes over these paragraphs together and identifies the organizing-idea sentence. Then the teacher asks the class—either individually or in collaborative groups—to assume that they would be writing an essay based upon this organizing idea and to jot down a structural plan from it that would guide their own compositions.

After the students have completed their structural plans, they go on to read the rest of the article. When all are finished, the teacher can lead the class into abstracting the underlying organization from the article until they have put together something very close to what the author's structural plan must have been. A good discussion can develop from a comparison of the student structural plans with that of the author. Do they coincide? In what ways do they differ? On mature consideration, do the students have any organizational suggestions that would have improved the clarity or the effectiveness of the article? To everyone's delight, not infrequently they do.

PRACTICE PROBING THE ORGANIZING IDEA-STRUCTURAL PLAN RELATIONSHIP. Students can come to understand the derivative relationship of thesis and plan by studying examples of structural plans constructed from working theses:

- Teacher-made working theses
- Those of their own devising
- Those taken from essays and articles.

Providing our students with sample structural plans such as the models in this chapter should demonstrate the way a plan can be developed from a working-thesis statement. In a number of the models, I have omitted specific supporting examples in order to underscore the notion that the specific facts are not of central importance to the logic of a structural plan. (And, as a pedagogical corollary to this idea, it is comforting to note that a teacher need not be an expert on the students' subject matter to check out the logical validity of their structural plans.)

PRACTICE CONSTRUCTING PLANS FROM WORKING THESES. Students can practice making structural plans from working theses and evaluating and revising those already constructed. We should offer as many opportunities as possible

- For students to work privately, collaboratively, or with our guidance, on structural plans leading to their own papers
- To help classmates with their plans
- To become personally involved in constructing a class structural plan.

A CHECKLIST. Composing structural plans involves such complex skills that students are often grateful for a checklist so that they can try to keep in mind everything they need to remember. The Points to Remember . . . Student Guidelines offer just such a practical guide.

STUDENT GUIDELINES

Points to Remember in Making a Structural Plan

1. Keep the structural plan brief—from four to seven major headings (including introduction and conclusion).

   A major purpose of outlining is to break down information into related groups small enough for the mind to encompass easily, and with five or six items we are reaching the outer limits for easy comprehension and memory.
2. Restrict the subheadings as well: resubdivide if a sequence becomes longer than five or six.
3. Make sure that all subpoints go to support their points and that all major points go to support the organizing idea.
4. Try to keep the headings in each sequence grammatically parallel.

   Syntactic and semantic symmetry in the structural plan is ordinarily reflected in the logical tightness of the composition.
5. Evaluate the completed plan for rhetorical effectiveness and logical consistency:
   a. Rhetorical effectiveness. How effectively does the arrangement permit the points and ideas to support the organizing idea?
   b. Logical consistency. Are the points structured in a balanced and consistent manner? Is there a logical rationale, what Macrorie calls "a discernible order," in the arrangement?

   But do remember there is no single "right" way to organize.
6. Do not hesitate to revise.
   - Revising the plan before the first draft is ever written can eliminate from that draft the awkwardness and inconsistency apparent in the plan.
   - Revising the plan midroute when a particular portion of the paper is discovered unworkable permits scrapping the offending section, going back to the structural plan, and working out the problem on a piece-by-piece basis.

continued

- If dissatisfied with a first draft, search out the source of the difficulties and test new ideas through the structural plan rather than through laborious redrafts.
7. Remember, when a structural plan works, the organization of the paper will work as well.

Help for Individual Problems

Although envisioning or constructing structural plans is a skill most of our students should be able to acquire without too much difficulty, we will probably have some students who will not "catch on" at all, at least not at first. To help these students, we will have to break down these skills into their conceptual components, diagnose the individual difficulties, and assign exercises on a personal basis.

PROBLEMS OF SUBORDINATION. The hardest concept for most of these students to understand is the notion of levels of abstraction. We can reach them through a sequence of subordination exercises, starting from what they already know. The sequence in the Student Exercise is designed to start from what the students already know, where they can experience instant success, and build on that by gradually adding new concepts.

A WORD ABOUT EXERCISES. As teachers we think in terms of students' overall writing goals. Students usually think in terms of the current assignment. Exercises can be helpful for students who clearly understand the relationship between the particular exercise and the goals of the assignment. Without this understanding, even the best-conceived exercise becomes busy work. Since there is no time for busy work when we are teaching composition, we must make sure that the purpose behind each assigned exercise is completely understood.

STUDENT EXERCISE

Subordination

1. *Finding categories.* In what group does each of the individuals in this set belong? Trout, catfish, pike   (a) _____
   This set? Grasshopper, cricket, ant   (b) _____
   This set? Robin, sparrow, jay   (c) _____
   Considering the answers a, b, & c as a set, to what group would they all belong?   _____

continued

continued

This much should be familiar and easy and the students should be able to follow when the teacher arranges the answers in structural plan format:

I. Animals
   A. Fish
      1. Trout
      2. Catfish
      3. Pike
   B. Insects
      1. Grasshopper
      2. Cricket
      3. Ant
   C. Birds
      1. Robin
      2. Sparrow
      3. Jay

Students should experience little or no difficulty in filling in the next set of topics in the structural plan:

II. Plants
   A. Trees
      1.
      2.
      3.
   B. Flowers
      1.
      2.
      3.

2. *Follow-up.* Reinforce this knowledge with a game of Twenty Questions (Animal-Vegetable-Mineral), pointing out that category formation is the key to winning the game. This game can become a popular time-filler for odds and ends of periods, "a consummation devoutly to be wished," because it provides a first-rate mental workout for students suffering from this particular conceptual handicap.

For any students still having difficulty understanding the first exercise, we might offer a similar follow up, having students fill in the support:

I. Sports Figures   II. Entertainers
   A. Football   A. Musicians
   B. Baseball   B. Actors
   C. Basketball   C. Comedians

3. *Developing a structural plan deductively.* As soon as the basic subordination principle is understood, it is important to direct these students toward the organizing idea as the reason for and focus of their categories. At this point, exercises similar to the one on pages 81–82 would be in order. Another version of the basic working-thesis structural plan might be—

Organizing idea: Spring is a beautiful season.
   I. Introduction
   II. Spring weather is beautiful.

continued

      a. beautiful because of _____
      b. beautiful because of _____
  III. Spring flowers are beautiful.
      a. beautiful because of _____
      b. beautiful because of _____
  IV. Spring feelings are beautiful.
      a. beautiful because of _____
      b. beautiful because of _____
      c. beautiful because of _____
  V. Conclusion

4. *Developing an organizing idea and structural plan inductively.* Since students with this conceptual handicap are often intimidated by printed ideas, it is wisest, as Mina Shaughnessy suggests, for them to learn how to draw inferences and make generalizations at first from specific, though nonliterary, sources. (246–47) She recommends showing pictures or slides of groups of people for students to make inferences from. In her classes, for instance, she used slides of older married couples (often look like brother and sister), pregnant women (react differently to their pregnancy), and children at play (can become deeply involved).

5. *For the next level of difficulty,* Shaughnessy recommends having the students make generalizations from the sort of factual data found in almanacs, or I might add, from one of the *Book of Lists* by David Wallechinsky, Irving Wallace, and Amy Wallace.[22] For example, one of Shaughnessy's students developed an interesting organizing idea and accompanying arguments based upon a list of forty-six major kidnapping crimes in the last one hundred years (247–48).

Collaborative Prewriting

We don't often think of learning invention and arrangement in terms of peer groups. Activities associated with this learning are usually of the classroom or individual variety, such as those described in this chapter. But Lois Rosen and her colleagues at Penn State at New Kensington have experimented with preplanning in two-student peer groups and have found this strategy very effective indeed.[23]

PLANNING IN PAIRS. To use this strategy, students follow their individual natural proclivities for preplanning an expository essay assignment, doing some freewriting or scratching out a structural plan. They do *not* write a draft. With only their preliminaries in hand, they meet with a fellow student and engage in a colloquy based on a teacher-supplied question-and-answer sheet. The following Student Guidelines (which I adapted from models provided by Rosen) offers an example of this strategy.

STUDENT GUIDELINES

Collaborative Prewriting Queries

1. *Questioner:* What point do you want the reader to get from your paper?
   Writer: Response
   Questioner: Response to Writer's response.
   Writer: Response
   Questioner: What is the significance of this point? Where do you plan to explain the significance? How?
   Questioner: Response
   Writer: Response

2. *Questioner:* How do you plan to support your point?
   Writer: Response
   Questioner: How will you arrange this information when you write your paper?
   Writer: Response
   Questioner: What will go first?   *Writer:* Response
   Questioner: What will go next?   *Writer:* Response.
   Questioner: Next? . . . etc.   *Writer:* Responses . . .
   Questioner: What will go last?   *Writer:* Response

3. *Questioner:* Can you tell me more about this?
   Writer: Response
   Questioner: What other examples or details can you provide your readers so that they will have a better understanding of what you want to say?
   Writer: Response
   Questioner: Response to Writer's response
   Writer: Response
   Questioner: Why do you include this idea/detail? How will it help the reader understand or share your perspective?
   Writer: Response
   Questioner: Or this idea/detail? *Writer:* Response
   Questioner: Or this? . . . etc.   *Writer:* Responses . . .
   Questioner: Response to Writer.
   Writer: Response

HOW PEER PREPLANNING WORKS.   When the peer-pair have finished discussing the first writer's paper, they should reverse roles and discuss the partner's paper.

The only rule students need observe is to follow the script exactly. They may add as much private discussion to it as seems appropriate to them, but they are required to cover each component. In this way each writer is compelled to think through every significant element of the paper being planned, at least well enough to explain it to another person. When the discussion is over, both writers have a fairly good notion of what they want to say, why they want to say it, and how they can go about saying it to make it clear to their readers.

Strategy Evaluated.   Both students and teachers have been delighted with this method. Students in the Rosen study claim that this is the most helpful preplanning strategy they have ever tried. An especially capable partner, who can offer a writer a number of creative approaches, is, of course, especially welcome. But even gifted students paired with the less able voice their appreciation for this opportunity.

Teachers who have tried this prewriting peer strategy have found it capable of producing well-focused compositions even without extensive one-on-one conferencing and total revisions, an outcome many of them were not able to achieve through peer groups who reviewed the composition *after* it had been written. Because of the increasing heaviness of the English teacher's load, these instructors consider this result a particularly welcome breakthrough.

Some Final Thoughts on Invention

Since only half of our students are likely to be natural listers or outliners, you may be wondering if the time spent on familiarizing all students with the nitty-gritty of structural planning is worthwhile. I would argue strongly that it is, for these three reasons:

1. Even if—or perhaps, especially if—we personally tend toward freewriting, we need to take into consideration that half of our students who do not find that strategy productive.
2. Those who brainstorm by freewriting eventually come to a point where they need to derive some sort of structural plan from their writing to assure a well-focused, structurally effective final composition. (See example on pages 67–69).
3. And those who never (or hardly ever) actually write down a nonrequired plan have special need for this practice to train their mental-structuring faculties and to keep them alert.

Yes, I would contend that time spent on lessons in finding organizing ideas and creating structural plans is far from wasted—especially in the beginning of a term's expository writing activities. But our real goal is to develop within each student the habit of approaching all expository writing in these terms.

Probably the most effective way to achieve this goal is to make this approach part of our own habitual classroom behavior, for the teacher is a powerful role model. Whenever the subject of expository writing comes up, whether we are talking to the class or conferring with an individual student, if we ask, "What is the organizing idea?" or reach for a pencil or a piece of chalk to scribble out a structural plan, we will soon find our students following suit. And when our students adopt the notion of an organizing idea and its supporting structure into their habitual thought pattern, the dividends they will accrue in writing ease—and in reading comprehension as well—will be immense.

IDEAS FOR DISCUSSION OR ESSAY

1. Make a critique of the videotaped lesson A Class in Action. You might wish to consider the following questions:

    a. What is the relationship between the teacher and the class?
    b. Do you find the teacher's style of teaching more or less formal than your own? For example, do you find the initial calling on each student in turn too formal? Or, on the other hand, are you bothered by the frequent interruptions of the speaker by the students? (This quality is perhaps more apparent on the tape.)
    c. How would you describe the interaction in this classroom? How is this interaction achieved?
    d. How would you describe the teacher's questioning technique? How does she handle responses that are clearly not to the point? How would you?

2. Try out some of the exercises suggested in the chapter and comment upon their effectiveness in getting across the ideas and techniques they are meant to convey.

3. The following are organizing ideas for student papers. For each provide a sample structural plan you might help the student formulate. Where support is not provided, supply the ideas we will assume you have elicited from the student.

    a. Harper Lee embodies the theme of *To Kill a Mockingbird* in its title and works it out in the character and plot segments about the symbolic mockingbirds: Dill, Tom Robinson, and especially Boo Radley.
    b. College fraternities can offer a congenial social group for students—especially those who are a bit shy, and they do provide the sense of identity and belonging so many students seem to need at large universities. But the faulty values that often govern the selection process, the terrible pain that this process causes in those excluded, and the excesses a sense of exclusivity often generates in those selected—including hazing of pledges and harassment of women and other excluded groups—casts serious doubts upon the appropriateness of such systems to college life.

4. Ignoring the preliminary material and limiting yourself to the essay alone, reread Melissa Snyder's essay (pages 67–69).

- First, derive an organizing idea and a structural plan from the essay.
- Then compare your idea with Mrs. Snyder's. How close did you come to her preliminary work? Would your suggestions result in a better essay? How?
- How useful do you think such an exercise would be for students? Explain your evaluation.

NOTES

1. Nancy Sommers' conclusions expressed in her "Revision Strategies of Student Writers and Experienced Writers," *CCC* 31 (1980) have proved to be seminal and have been confirmed by other researchers.

2. Of course, these are also the techniques writers employ if they should run into problems with the deductive approach, but less intensive brainstorming is usually necessary with this approach.

3. James M. McCrimmon, "Writing as a Way of Knowing," *The Promise of English: NCTE 1970 Distinguished Lectures* (Urbana: NCTE, 1970), 115.

4. Peter Elbow, *Writing without Teachers* (New York: Oxford UP, 1973), 3.

5. As an invention strategy is only one of the useful ways the freewriting strategy can be employed. Others include: as a response to readings, lectures, or discussions; psychological analysis for creating personal narratives or poetry; plot or character development for writing fiction; and a way to conquer writer's block. See also Chapter 11, pages 405–6.

6. Note titles of Janet Emig's "Writing as a Mode of Learning," *CCC* 28 (1977): 122–28 and McCrimmon's "Writing as a Way of Knowing."

7. Erica Lindemann, *A Rhetoric for Writing Teachers* (New York: Oxford U, 1982), 78.

8. Linda Flower and John Hayes, "Problem-Solving Strategies and the Writing Process," *CE* 39 (1977): 450; Young and Becker, "Toward a Modern Theory of Rhetoric: A Tagmemic Contribution," *Harvard Education Review*, 35 (Fall 1965), 456.

9. W. Ross Winterowd, "Topics and Levels in the Composing Process," *CE* 34 (1973): 703.

10. For Kenneth Burke's Pentad, see especially *A Grammar of Motives* (Berkeley: U of California P), xv and throughout. Richard Young, "Invention, A Topographical Survey," in *Teaching Composition: 10 Bibliographical Essays*, ed. Gary Tate (Fort Worth: Texas Christian UP, 1976), 13.

11. A good background for such a unit or study project can be obtained from Edward P. J. Corbett's *Classical Rhetoric for the Modern Student*, 3rd ed. (New York: Oxford UP, 1990).

12. Elizabeth Cowan Neeld, *Writing*, 2nd ed., Scott, 1986, 34–39.

13. For adaptations of Kenneth Pike's theory, see especially Richard Young, Alton L. Becker, and Kenneth Pike, *Rhetoric: Discovery and Change* (New York: Harcourt, 1981).

14. James E. Williams, *Preparing to Teach Writing* (Belmont, Cal: Wadsworth, 1989), 41. Williams earlier studies were described in his "Covert Language Behaviour during Writing," *RTE* (1983) 17: 473–491 and "Covert Linguistic Behavior during

Writing Tasks: Psychophysicological Differences between Above-Average and Below-average writers," *Written Communications*, (1987) 4:310–328.

See also Hubert M. English, "Linguistic Theory as an Aid to Invention," *CCC*, 15 (1964): 136–40, who comes to the same conclusion, having participated in a freshman composition program at the University of Michigan using a Pike's tagmemics-based heuristic strategy. The program's evaluators made this criticism: "Instead of writing good essays [the students] wrote papers that exemplified the theory elegantly."

15. Toby Fulwiler, *College Writing* (Glenview, Ill.: Scott, 1988), 30. My own research gives rather startling confirmation. I hypothesized that the 50 percent of writers who preferred to compose by freewriting would be less likely to use outlines. But when I surveyed experienced, able writers, I discovered that all of my sample, without exception, relied on some sort of structural plan for expository writing. Reported in a presentation, "Responding to Cognitive Differences" at the 1991 CCCC in Boston.

16. Albert Joseph, *Put It in Writing* (Cleveland: Industrial Writing Institute, 1977), 169.

17. Sheridan Baker, *The Compleat Stylist* (New York: Crowell, 1966), 30.

18. Ken Macrorie, *The Perceptive Writer, Reader, and Speaker*, (New York: Harcourt, 1959) 108–9.

19. Authorities do not agree on whether a writer's structural plan should formally recognize beginning, middle, and end divisions. In my own classroom, however, I find students more comfortable including headings for introduction and conclusion when they will be separately existing entities in the final composition.

20. Mina Shaughnessy, *Errors and Expectations: A Guide for the Teacher of Basic Writing* (New York: Oxford UP, 1977), especially Chapter 9.

21. B. B. Murdock, Jr., "The Serial Position Effects of Free Recall," *JEP* 64 (1962): 482–88; J. Deese and R. A. Kaufman, "Serial Effects in recall of Unorganized and Sequentially Organized Verbal Material," *Journal of Experimental Psychology*, 54 (1957), 180–87; and W. A. Bousefield, B. H. Cohen, and J. G. Silva, "The Extension of Marbe's Law to the Recall of Stimulus Words," as discussed in James Deese and Steward H. Hulse, *The Psychology of Learning*, 3rd ed. (New York: McGraw, 1967), 266–67.

22. David Wallechinsky, Irving Wallace, and Amy Wallace, *Book of Lists* (New York: Morrow, 1977–1983).

23. These ideas were presented by Lois Rosen and her colleagues at the annual spring meeting of the NCTE in Richmond, Virginia, March 1993.

4

Teaching the Writing Process

BEGINNING

The assignment has been discussed and understood. The students have brainstormed or free written and have found their organizing ideas and support. They have thought out structural plans which organize their supporting ideas in a logical and cogent manner. We, their teachers, know that their most important deliberations have been accomplished; but we will never convince those of our students who have blank-page jitters that this assessment is true.

Handling the Blank-Page Jitters

A large percentage of those who put pen to paper—or fingers to word-processor, including many professional authors, suffer almost unendurable tension at every first face-to-face confrontation with the task of actually writing a composition. There is nothing rational about this all-but-universal fear. Indeed, it seems to be grounded in something deep and primeval in the human consciousness. Sir Phillip Sidney described it with painful accuracy 400 years ago in the Astrophel and Stella sonnet sequence (1591):

> But words came halting forth, wanting Invention's stay. . .
> Thus great with child to speak, and helpless in my throes,
> Biting my traunt pen, beating myself for spite. . . .

Donald Murray, himself a professional writer, speaks of the feeling from personal experience:

> I am afraid of heights. I do not like to stand near the edge of a cliff, climb a ladder, look down from a skyscraper, or drive across a high bridge, but I served in the paratroops during World War II. I was trained to overcome my

fear, to jump despite it. Yet, as much terror as I felt stepping out of an airplane, I feel more terror facing the empty page.[1]

Murray also offers a highly perceptive explanation for this phenomenon:

> The most elemental reason that writers do not write, that scholars perish rather than publish, is the fact that . . . the writer exposes what he is to the reader . . . The writer is a doer, a person who expresses himself to other people. Before we write, our knowledge is our own, after we write we have revealed ourselves to other people. (8, 70)

How do we teachers confront the blank-page jitters in our students? First, we must really understand how they feel and show that we do. And our students also must be sure that we will not betray their trust. In addition, they need to know that a first draft is just preliminary; it is not written in stone. We will not judge it, nor will we judge them for writing it.

Then we will need to urge our reluctant writers to begin, to just start writing. Those students who do preliminary free-writing have a head start in letting go. And those who can compose on a word processor have instant revision at their fingertips. But we need to convince all worried students that their words are not indelible, that their phrasing and organization is not necessarily permanent, and that there will always be chances for revision.

Commitment of the Writer

Even though it is, of course, true that any word or phrase is subject to being rubbed out, scribbled over, or erased, still there is a sense in which the students are quite right about the significance of what they put down upon the paper. With every word, the author does make a commitment to the reader about what is to come. Every sentence both restricts the writer's options for what follows and makes some specific promises about what is to come. The author's commitment to the reader holds true throughout the composition of the manuscript until the final sentence is written.

TEACHING INTRODUCTIONS

There is, in addition, a special commitment in the introduction; for in the introduction the writer's commitment is more fully conscious. A major purpose of an introduction is to set up just such a commitment. For this reason, I do not hold with the school of thought that suggests the writer should begin with the body of the paper, with a presentation of discussion, and only add on an introduction when all else is finished. No, in order to achieve a sense of initial thrust and continuity, we should not hesitate to advise our students: Begin at the beginning; start with the introduction. We can then reassure them that an introduction can be rewritten, just like any other portion.

A Survey

In order to teach students how to write an effective introduction one has to know exactly what a good introduction is supposed to do. What should it contain? How should it be arranged? Determined not to be bound by what traditional rhetorics expound and with a strong desire to avoid the substitution of my own intuitive fancies for those of the authors of those rhetorics, I decided to make a private study of how some of our most acclaimed essayists introduce their expository compositions.

I read essays of Shana Alexander, Joan Beck, William Buckley, Eleanor Clift, Ellen Goodman, Jeff Greenfield, Meg Greenfield, and James Kilpatrick. And also those of Jeanne Kirkpatrick, Charles Krauthammer, William Raspberry, Mike Royko, Carl Rowen, Robert J. Samuelson, Ben Wattenberg, George Will, and Walter Williams—representing a wide variance of opinion, but first-rate writers all. In addition, to give some formal parameters to my research I systematically analyzed all the expository essays in two typical composition course readers. For the first edition I studied the 38 expository essays included in *Strategies in Prose* (1973); and, for this edition, the 46 expository essays in *The Winston Reader* (1991).[2]

DEFINING THE INTRODUCTION.   Despite the diversity of the essays I surveyed, my research reveals enough unity to establish the existence of an expository introduction definable in purpose and structure.

Purpose: to Introduce an Essay's Central Point.   The introduction is still very much a path for leading the wandering reader to at least a preliminary statement of the organizing or controlling idea. The thesis, it would seem, is still alive and well. Those few introductions in the samplings which did not contain some explicit statement of their controlling ideas had it covertly suggested or broadly implied. (Only two of the 1991 essays saved a clear statement of the main point for the final paragraph, and in only one did it remain implicit throughout.)

Statements of Controlling Ideas *CONCLUDE* Introductions.   Controlling idea statements occur overwhelmingly toward the end of the introduction or, when paragraphed differently, begin the first paragraph of the body. Despite the common misconception that a composition should begin with a statement of its main point, only two essays in the first survey and one in the second begin with such a statement.

That professional writers eschew this sort of opening should not surprise us. Instead of a statement of point serving in its appropriate role as a type of topic sentence for the entire paper, such a statement—when placed first—becomes merely the topic sentence for the introductory paragraph; the composition is thus robbed of an introduction. When such a preliminary statement is supported in the introduction, the rest of the paper becomes repetitious or even redundant.

Introductions Do Not Contain Support for the Central Point. The surveyed introductions lead the reader toward the main point, explain it, or amplify it; but almost without exception, support for the main point is saved for the composition proper. Supporting material in almost all of the introductions is limited to support for the introductory concept.

Introductions Vary Markedly in Length. The one-paragraph introduction, standard advice in some student rhetorics, was a rarity in the several-page articles and even in the briefer syndicated columns.

Successful Introductions Orient Readers to Their Topic and Interest Them in It. Most of the samplings did so by using

1. a personal strategy. Suggesting what lead the author to the subject;
2. an "although" material strategy. Presenting an opposing point of view to refute; or
3. a specific instance strategy. Offering a specific instance leading to, commenting on, or explaining the topic—an anecdote, description, apt quotation or the like.

Teaching Students to Write Introductions

Information, such as that derived from my surveys and summarized here—or from a survey you might undertake yourself, can serve as a kind of guidelines for teaching expository introductions. Professional models are valid teaching tools because they embody the writing conventions of our time, conventions that inexperienced writers must come to understand if they are to communicate. As Phillip Arrington writes:

> Conventions exist, for better or worse, so that writers can address readers with some greater hope of being understood, if not believed or agreed with. . . . They have enormous impact because they're publicly accessible. Without them, our understanding, however imperfect, of what writers mean would be the poorer, if not impossible.[3]

INTRODUCING THE CENTRAL POINT. We can share with our students that the purpose of expository introductions (confirmed by any survey) is to lead into the author's subject, ordinarily concluding with a preliminary statement of the author's approach to that subject. An introduction bridges the gap between the unfocused speculation within the mind of the reader and a working understanding of the author's approach to a topic. Sheridan Baker's metaphor of expository introduction as a funnel narrowing the unfocused to a point, or Lucille Vaughn Payne's representation of it as an inverted triangle, provides a pictorial image of this central purpose that can clarify the concept for students.[4] This teachable strategy appeals to students' desire for orderliness and logic and seems to make good sense to them.

Problems with the Funnel Approach. Despite its usefulness, however, this strategy can be misleading if it is interpreted to mean that students should always begin their introductions with a generalization or with a generality or two. Inexperienced writers sometimes follow the funnel metaphor too literally and produce opening generalizations that are fatuous or even false. Openings like the fairly typical "Everyone is fascinated by sea shells," for example, are demonstrably untrue. And such opening sentences as "Swimming (collecting coins, skiing, riding the roller-coaster, reading, bowling, playing tiddly winks) is an exciting activity" or "Philosophy (entomology, philately, politics, religion, sex) is an interesting subject" offer little information to the reader and are not likely to inspire a very strong inclination to continue reading. We can forestall such inanities by suggesting that our students apply Ken Macrorie's evaluation to their work:

> A good test of the worth of a statement is to ask whether it can be made
> about any number of other subjects. If it can, it is often not worth making.[5]

Although funneling down ideas to clarify or express the writer's central point is certainly an introduction's main function, my surveys of professional essays reveal very few initial generalizations. Actually quite the contrary is true. Far more often professional writers orient their readers by beginning with a specific instance of their subject.

ORIENTING THE READER. Introductions need to furnish enough background information to orient the reader. Professional writers are careful to provide this information. Inexperienced writers, however—perhaps because their ideas are so familiar to themselves—frequently do not appreciate their reader's ignorance and the necessity of offering the essential information. We need to raise our students' consciousness of readers' potential problems in catching on. We can do so by asking questions about topics they are studying in one of their other classes—or in our own—and constructing a group-made introduction on the blackboard for a paper on that topic. Suppose, we might ask the class, you wanted to comment on—or dispute—what writer X has said? What would your readers need to know before you get to your point about X's ideas? What about X? What about the ideas?

What the Reader needs to Know. Or we could show how professionals have handled similar problems. We might ask, suppose you wanted to write about how much better life is for African Americans in the south since segregation was outlawed. What would your readers need to know before you could support your point? We could elicit what the class itself would need to know. They would probably indicate needing answers to such questions as:

What was segregation? When did it start? When did it stop? We might then share how a professional writer handles such an introduction to have the students discover if their questions are answered to their satisfaction. For instance, to continue the example, Mary Mebane begins "The System" in this way:

> Historically, my lifetime is important because I was part of the last generation born into a world of total legal segregation in the Southern United States. When the Supreme Court outlawed segregation in the public schools in 1954, I was twenty-one. When Congress passed the Civil Rights Act of 1964, permitting blacks free access to public places, I was thirty-one. The world I was born into had been segregated for a long time—so long, in fact, that I never met anyone who had lived during the time when restrictive laws were not in existence, although some people spoke of parents and others who had lived during the "free" time. As far as anyone knew, the laws as they then existed would stand forever. They were meant to—and did—create a world that fixed black people at the bottom of society in all aspects of human life. It was a world without options. (*Winston Reader*, 587)

Why the Topic Needs Considering.   Dava Sobel is faced with a similarly typical composing problem in "Acid Test," for instance, and solves it with somewhat different strategy. Sobel sides with the "many educators [who] complain that most current [standardized] tests give everybody a raw deal." But before she can make this point and go on to suggest alternatives, she needs to explain something about these tests and especially about their importance. She begins her introduction with an explanatory set of specific details:

> Several times a year, approximately 40 million youngsters around the country pile into classrooms where they hunch over their desks and spend hours blackening tiny bubbles on a piece of paper. They are taking standardized multiple-choice tests—tests scored by machines and used to decide matters of considerable consequence. "What is this boy's IQ? for example. Or, "Should this girl enter a program for gifted children?" "Is this student college material?" "How do the kids in that school district stack up against the rest of the nation?"
>
> Forget, for the moment, accusations that IQ tests reflect racial discrimination and . . . favor males. Many educators complain that most current tests give everybody a raw deal. (*Winston Reader*, 533)

In brief, our students need to understand that an expository introduction must get the reader from anywhere to the point. And in getting there, it must give the reader enough background to be able to grasp the preliminary approach to—or statement of—the controlling idea at the introduction's end.

Scaffolding.   In the interest of this kind of clarity, the question arises whether we should teach students to use such phrases as "The subject of my paper will be. . . ," "In my theme I will try to prove. . . ," "My composition will discuss. . ," or "This paper seeks to. . . ." Although such phrases are almost transparent in their clarity, I would suggest that we do not. Such phrases and the similarly worded "organizers"—"I will explain the five reasons for my opinion," "I propose to prove my organizing idea in the following three ways"—are the equivalent of the structural plan written as prose. Miami University's Spiro Peterson likens such material to the scaffolding sometimes carelessly left standing outside completed buildings. Once the underlying structure is firmly in place, such material, like scaffolding, becomes an awkward and unnecessary incumbrance upon the completed work. Since this form of expression is essentially graceless, we should not encourage its use.

On the other hand, we will probably encounter students who have already been taught to write in this manner and are either uncomfortable without the use of a phraseology that is familiar to them or inarticulate without the structure upon which they have learned to depend. We should not, I think, deprive these students of this means of expression. Though the former group could be encouraged to try some variety in their approach and the latter group might be gradually weaned to be less dependent upon it, the chances are that both groups have other, more basic, writing difficulties to which we could more profitably direct our attention.

GETTING THE READER INTERESTED. Besides achieving clarity, a good introduction should be interesting enough to keep the reader going until the author's direction becomes clear. But students will ask, "How are we supposed to do that?" In answer, we can teach them the strategies the survey suggests, the techniques professional writers employ. We might start with the personal strategy.

"Look in Thy Heart and Write." In reply to the plea, "How do we begin," we can answer just as Sir Philip Sidney did in the famous Astrophel and Stella poem quoted at the beginning of this chapter: "Look in thy heart and write." Sidney tried the same sort of expediencies that our students resort to—he studied models of other people's writing and looked into rhetorics for ideas—but he found the results as most of our students do, artificial and false and not suitable for his purpose:

> I sought fit words to paint the blackest face of woe;
> Studying inventions fine, her wits to entertain,
> Oft turning others' leaves to see if thence would flow
> Some fresh and fruitful showers upon my sun-burned brain.
> But words came halting forth, wanting Invention's stay;
> Invention, Nature's child, fled step-dame Study's blows,
> And others' feet still seemed but strangers in my way.
> Thus great with child to speak, and helpless in my throes,
> Biting my truant pen, beating myself for spite.

In this state, Sydney came upon the answer, as true today as it was then: "Fool," said my Muse to me, "look in thy heart and write."

Sidney's words still ring true because the key to successful introductions, as again confirmed by research, lies in a transference to the reader of a sense of the excitement that lead the author to the subject.

So when our students ask us how to begin, we might suggest that they think back to what it was which first interested them in the topic. Was there some personal connection? Something that happened to them? A book they read? A movie or play that they watched? Was there something in the topic that connects to something currently in the news? Is there a subject much talked about now that touches upon this topic? Is it an old subject which the student has just seen in a new light? Does the student disagree with the prevailing view on the subject or with an important dissenting view? Is there something about the topic that cries for present attention?

Ellen Goodman, for example, uses a personal approach to introduce her essay, "The Communication Gap":

> I went back to college this week or, to be more accurate, back to colleges. I had an extensive course on the generation born circa 1960. I gathered enough material for a thesis on The Communication Gap Between the Sexes, Phase II. . . . (*Boston Globe*, March 1981).

This sort of introduction, which recalls the connection between the subject and the writer's interest, invites the attention of any reader who has potential concern for the topic because it is based upon the inherent appeal of the topic itself.

Lead in with a Presentation of "Although" Material.   Sometimes when students "look into [their] heart[s]," they discover disagreement. In fact, this is one of the most important reasons writers choose to compose an expository work. More than 50% of the expository essays in the 1973 anthology and almost 30% of those in the 1991 volume introduce their topic with ideas opposing their own. For example, economist Robert J. Samuelson begins a *Newsweek* essay, "The Value of College" in this way:

> Few ideas are more entrenched in the American popular consciousness than the value of a college education. It's the key to success. By and large, economists agree: college graduates earn much more than high-school graduates, and the gap widened in the 1980s. The conclusions seem obvious. Stay in school. In a high-tech world — with specialized skills in acute shortage — we'd all be better off if more Americans went to college.
>
> Not necessarily.
>
> The truth is that more and more Americans have been going to college, and the expected (and advertised) benefits haven't fully materialized. . . . (Aug 31, 1992)

Having considered a few such examples, our students might well think the "although" material introduction an option for them too.

Not only is it natural for writers to want to begin where their minds first took hold, but this sort of introduction makes good rhetorical sense. If it is rhetorically unsound to permit the contrary view to dominate the conclusion of the composition, then might it not be a good idea to start right out with this material? With controversial topics, such a move has the further rhetorical advantage of giving an immediate appearance of fair-mindedness. William Raspberry, for instance, uses this strategy to good effect in "Children of Two-Career Families":

> Maybe you have to be crazy to argue with two Harvard psychiatrists — particularly two such insightful psychiatrists as Barrie Greiff and Preston Hunter. So before I register my small objection to their article in the May-June issue of Harvard Magazine, let me say that nearly everything these two doctors have to say about the strains and stresses of dual-career families makes sense to me. The only paragraph that arched my eyebrows included this sentence: . . . . . (*Washington Post*, May 19, 1980)

With noncontroversial topics, "Although" material introductions can provide a graceful way into the subject. Take, for instance, Shana Alexander's opening to "Getting Old in Kid's Country":

> Children are a relatively modern invention. Until a few hundred years ago, they did not exist. In medieval and Renaissance painting, you see pint-size men and women wearing grown-up clothes and grown-up expressions, performing grown-up tasks. . . . Children today not only exist; they have taken over. (*Newsweek*, Dec. 11, 1972)

Introduce the Topic with a Specific Instance or Incident. We might also point out to our students that professional writers often employ preliminarily a specific instance of their subject to make their topic clear and bring it home vividly to their readers. Examples, such as the opening lines of George F. Will's "The Cult of Ethnicity Distorts History," are easily found:

> Congress is about to rename Montana's Custer Battlefield as Little Bighorn Battlefield with appropriate acknowledgment of the Indians who fought there. This small, suitable act of moral reparation *is but one skirmish* in a multi-front battle about the presentation of America's past, and hence the shape of its future. [Emphasis mine.]

To make sure students are not misled by examples of this sort, we should supply the rest of the introduction and let them figure out how the author uses the specific instance to lead into the more general issue to be addressed and to set up his point of view. (In this case, Will reaches his controlling idea by first acknowledging the merits of some of the "although" arguments.)

> The battle rages around "multiculturalism." The issue is how to give various participants in America's drama their due without damaging the nation's animating premise.
>
> In New York and California, the two most ethnically complex states, and elsewhere, school curricula are being revised, and sometimes improved. A valid aim is to show that baking bread, not just making laws has mattered to the nation — that history should not neglect the anonymous. But the din now

drowning civil conversation and common sense is the whine of axes being ground by groups trying to turn the teaching of history into political preaching. (*Washington Post*, August 1, 1991)

Sometimes the instance authors use to point to their topic and/or to their controlling idea is an anecdote, often a brief, personal narrative. Such narrative introductions are currently in vogue. Joyce Carol Oates, for example, begins her essay "On Boxing and Pain" in this way:

> Years ago in the early 1950s when my father first took me to a Golden Gloves boxing tournament in Buffalo, New York, I asked him why the boys wanted to fight one another, why they were willing to get hurt. As if it were an explanation, my father said, "Boxers don't feel pain quite the way we do."
> Pain, in the proper context, is something other than pain. (*Winston Reader*, 283)

Hooks: Interest-Provoking Rhetorical Openings

Oates, like many essayists who use this strategy, employs a specific instance — in this case a personal anecdote — not only to shed introductory light on and explain her central point, but also to engage her reader with the material. Journalists call strategies designed to engage readers' interest "hooks."

Teaching "hooks" is not without problems — some of which are discussed below; nevertheless, I would recommend that we provide our students with some training in the standard techniques for rhetorically effective openings. After all, all else being equal, an exciting opening is better than a dull one. If exposure to the standard rhetorical opening gambits might help our students — even occasionally — to develop exciting introductions, we certainly should not deny them access to knowledge of these techniques.

The Student Guidelines contains samples of some traditional "hooks" effectively used in the essays I surveyed to lead into a preliminary statement of the author's point:

STUDENT GUIDELINES

Samples of Introductory "Hooks"
As They Set Up Their Central Points

INTRODUCTORY RHETORICAL QUESTION
Inherent in the question are two important rhetorical advantages: (1) Since by its very nature a question involves direct communication between author and reader, it has the ability to involve the reader personally in whatever the author has to say. (2) Since a question asks, it

continued

presupposes an answering which gives the author a quick means into the organizing idea by way of reply.

1. The commonest question asked of historians by laymen is whether history serves a purpose. Is it useful? Can we learn from the lessons of history?
   When people want history to be utilitarian and teach us lessons, that means they also want to be sure that it meets scientific standards. This, in my opinion, it cannot do. . . . (Barbara Tuchman, "Is History a Guide to the Future?" *Winston Reader*, 462–63)
2. Does black socioeconomic progress necessarily depend upon whether blacks are liked by whites? Does it depend on the continuance of massive federal expenditures?
   (Walter Williams, "U.S. Blacks and a Free Market," Heritage Features Syndicate, May 1980.)

THE POINTEDLY BRIEF STATEMENT

Because most mature writing is expressed in sentences developed by amplifying and qualifying phrases and clauses, a blunt, affirmative statement of only a few words arrests the eye and startles the mind into attention. These openings may be flat statements of fact, but the brevity and the simplicity of the phrasing gives them an aphoristic quality:

All radiation is dangerous.
(Helen Caldicott, "What You Must Know About Radiation," *Winston Reader*, 413)

We fear what we don't understand.
(John Wideman, "Fear in the Streets," *Strategies in Prose*, 146)

This device also lends itself well to the establishment of a tone of colloquial informality:

Well, the fraternity house still exists.
(Herbert Gold, "Letter from a Far Frat," *Strategies in Prose* 375)

INTRODUCTORY QUOTATION

Quotations can set up a topic to be expanded upon or taken issue with.

. . . . The only paragraph [from Barrie Greiff and Preston Hunter's article] that arched my eyebrows included this sentence: "Dual-career parents . . . shouldn't overburden their children with responsibility for themselves or their siblings, or for running the household; that only cheats them out of their childhood and confuses them about parental roles."
(William Raspberry, *Washington Post*, May 19, 1980.)

Quotations can also provide authority—or familiarity—for the reader.

"E pluribus unum," says the motto on this country's coins. And we mean it, most of us. Most of the time. For most folks, anyway. At least those who don't need our tax dollars.

continued

continued

> One of the saving strengths of this country has always been its ability to absorb immigrants—welcome or not—and turn them into Americans.
>
> The problem now isn't so much that the "pluribus" is growing so large and so incredibly divers. It's that there is no longer a consensus supporting the idea that Americans should be one people.
>
> (Joan Beck, "Losing the Sense of 'Oneness' " *Chicago Tribune*, July 1, 1992)

ANALOGY

In prose as well as in poetry, drawing an analogy to the concrete helps elucidate the abstract. Introductory analogies often have the further merit of being striking or witty enough to intrigue even the most jaded reader.

> Trying to get a handle on scholastic cheating is as frustrating as surveying American-eating patterns. Everyone says he is watching his weight—yet the streets are full of overweight folk, and the snack-food industry reports record sales.
>
> Talk to students, and you get the same kind of dichotomy. Most say that, yes, they cheated when they were younger, but no, they would not dream of cheating now, and no, cheating is not a big problem at their schools.
>
> But talk to their teachers, and a very different picture emerges, one that shatters many of the comfortable middle class myths about who cheats and why. . . . of a problem that is more likely to get worse than to get better.
>
> (Claudia H. Deutsch, "Cheating: Alive and Flourishing," *Winston Reader*, 502)

PARADOX

The paradox, that which is and at the same time is not, is an exciting notion for the educated mind. Many a paper has been written to resolve the seeming paradox between an organizing idea and its "although" clause. Because of this curious appeal, the paradoxical statement makes an especially effective opening.

- A strange place it was, that place where the world began. A place of incredible happenings, splendours and revelations, despairs like multitudinous pits of isolated hells. A place of shadow-spookiness, inhabited by the unknowable dead. A place of jubilation and of mourning, horrible and beautiful.

  It was, in fact, a small prairie town.
  (Margaret Laurence, "Where the World Began," *Winston Reader*)

- The twenty-first century promises to explain the unexplainable.
  (Holcomb B. Nobel, "Beyond the Knowable: The Ultimate Exploration," *Winston Reader*, 471)

Paradox combines well with other devices. See, for instance, Deutsch's analogy above.

TEACHING "HOOKS."   Devices like these and other witty openings do make an introduction more interest-provoking. But students should not feel such pizzazz is necessary.

There are, in fact, some risks involved in teaching "hooks." Some students are intimidated by exposure to professional models ("How could I ever come up with something that terrific?"). Writers' block can attack students who feel they must find a witty opening to get started. And sometimes even a student's success with a gambit can poison future work. I remember a student who was complimented on her use of a rhetorical question to open a paper about student zoo volunteers:

> What could possibly be the reason 41 high school students spend much of their free time watching a gorilla eat, sleep and climb her cage? They are participants in the current pregnant gorilla watch at the Metropolitan Zoo.

For the rest of the semester her themes began:

> What could possibly be the reason that paratroopers would spend much of their waking hours jumping out of the open doors of airplanes?
> What could possibly be the reason that some state legislatures take such an outmoded stand on capital punishment?

Preventing Excess.   Such problems can be avoided, however. To keep students from becoming too focussed on impressive introductions, we probably should not mention opening gambits at all for the first few themes. It is time enough to bring them up after most students have mastered the fundamentals and are ready to concentrate upon presentation.

Inappropriate flamboyance can be handled with humor. We might, for instance, tell our students the old chestnut about the writer determined to write the best introduction possible. He mentally checked off all the sure-fire attention-getters he could think of. What gets a reader interested? A narrative. A quotation. A brief and pithy statement. Profanity. Mention of celebrities, sex, violence. He decided to include them all. And so he wrote:

"Dammit, King Henry, take your hand off my knee!" she said.

With this sort of hyperbole, students should come to understand that getting attention is not an end in itself. What really works in an introduction is not just ingenuity, but a combination of wit and appropriateness.

Wittily appropriate introductions are unquestionably delightful. But if a student never achieves such an introduction, he or she needs to know that that's acceptable too. Quite frankly, dullness is not the greatest sin the novice writer can commit. All we need really expect of the introductions written by inexperienced and/or immature authors is a logical development of thought, leading to a clear, preliminary expression of their organizing idea.

The Title

In discussing the introduction, some students may bring up the subject of the title. There is a fairly widespread misconception that the title is an integral part of the introduction. It may therefore be necessary to remind our students that the title is quite separate from the rest of the paper.

Since the title may even appear on a different page, as it does in books, monographs, and most longer student essays, it is not a good idea to make the title an indefinite antecedent. A paper that begins, "This idea will lead to no good," for instance, arouses unnecessary curiosity while the reader fumbles for the title page to find out whether the writer is referring to capital punishment or to kissing on the first date.

We can help our students see the title as a nice completing touch. It is, in fact, very much like the frosting on a cake. It adds a gloss and a finish to the end product, but it does not really affect the texture of the work.

TEACHING SUPPORT—IN TERMS OF STRUCTURE

Once the students have completed the beginning of their papers, introducing their controlling idea, they will need to support it. Teaching the central supporting portion, sometimes called the "body" of expository compositions, raises two pedagogical issues, which we will consider separately in this chapter:

- How to help students structure their support effectively
- How to help students use the specific and vivid illustrations that will support their points persuasively

How well students structure support for their points determines the clarity and thus, to an important degree, the effectiveness of their composition. But teaching structural support—especially too early—can bring problems of writer self-consciousness, leading at its extreme to blocking. The difficulty lies in helping students make the best use of their structural plans and in helping them construct clear, focussed paragraphs without inhibiting their spontaneity.

Helping Students Make Their Structural Plans Work for Them

Students should write the body of their first drafts as freely as they can, using their structural plan as a general guide. The ideas jotted down in their organizational plans, along with the thoughts they call to mind, should suggest the means of support for the ideas they committed to in their introductions and should help them structure that support.

Such plans help writers explain, expand upon, and develop each of these ideas in order to present their points in the most convincing way. They can be exceedingly useful to our students. But we must take care that student writers are not shackled by them. What we really want for our composing students is to get their ideas flowing. They should not feel a need to stop and consider every word, every sentence. They should not be afraid occasionally to leave their plan behind and follow a thought wherever it takes them. They should be comfortable in the assurance that the plan, as well as the essay, is always subject to revision.

Teaching the Paragraph

When we speak of writing the body of a composition, we are talking essentially about composing paragraphs. But the paragraph, however important, is a surprisingly problematical concept. To promote writing comfort, it is probably wise to put off discussing paragraphing with our students until the question arises or until they have drafted a paper or two. From a pedagogical prospect, the more technical aspects of paragraphing probably fit more appropriately with teaching revision; they are thus considered in this text in Chapter 5. (See pages 150–54.) But if students are to make any effective use of this basic structural building block, they will have to have a working understanding of its characteristics.

THE CONCEPTUALLY PROBLEMATIC PARAGRAPH. Unlike the sentence, which is defined by the presence of subject and predicate, a paragraph has no content requirements. Though it is therefore defined totally in terms of form, its form is almost completely arbitrary. Paragraphs vary widely in length. They can be, for instance, as brief as a single word. One exuberant journalist habitually opens his theater reviews in a midwestern morning newspaper with such one-word paragraphs as "Wow!" or "Zowie!" They can also be lengthy enough to encompass a fair-sized book, a not unusual 18th-century practice. In fact, paragraphs of several pages were common into the second quarter of this century.

Idiosyncratic Variance. Different writers may paragraph the same passage differently. Often the decision is based on an author's—or an editor's—sense of readability. Since the space following each paragraph offers a rest for the reader's eye and mind, how many words to include before that rest is needed becomes a decision dependent upon such nonsubstantive conditions as the width of the column of print and the size of the lettering. For example, a good editor might decide to break up a passage of, say, 150 words on the popularity of soccer into three paragraphs if it were to be printed in a narrow newspaper column or into two paragraphs for printing on the pages of a small book with large print, while that same editor might leave it as a single paragraph if the material were to appear in a wide-column journal (See Figure 4–1).

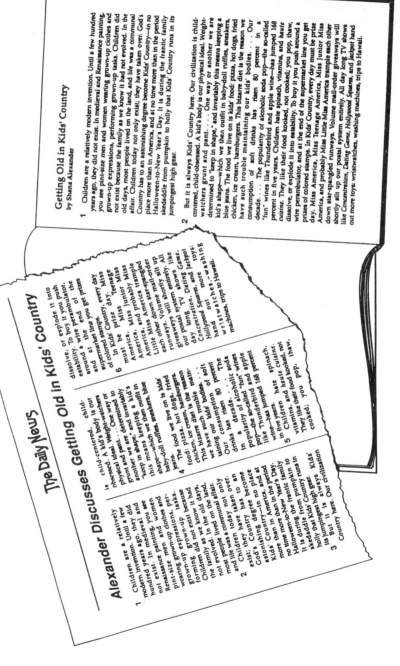

Figure 4–1. How Type Format Affects Paragraphing

The paragraph is thus a slippery concept to work with and an especially slippery one to teach, because, in its literal sense, we can make so few completely true statements about it. Actually, the only thing we can say about the concept which would encompass all of its representatives is that

> a paragraph consists of the material set off by conventional spacing and indentation on a page of print, type, or script.

"Paragraphs" and Topic Segments

Since paragraphs are such inconsistent things, our students may well wonder how any consistent advice can be given about them. The truth is that if we insist upon talking about the literal paragraph as it is variously printed on a page, no advice can be valid because no unvarying description can be made. The form of the middle paragraph in our example's newspaper column on soccer will probably have little in common with the form of the single 150-word soccer paragraph as it would appear in the wide-spaced journal. On the other hand, if we can look beyond the arbitrary mechanics of printing and concentrate on the 150-word passage as a whole—whether it appears on the page as a single paragraph or as a series of paragraphs—we can recognize characteristic features.

What we are really talking about here (and what is sometimes called "a paragraph" in rhetoric books) is a concept for which there is no universally recognized English term. We might call this concept a "topic segment" and define it as:

> A unit of prose in which a limited topic is stated and developed.

Whether this unit is spaced on the page as a single paragraph or as a cluster of paragraphs, it is the major building block of expository compositions.

USEFULNESS OF TOPIC SEGMENT CONCEPT. The problem with the current confusion of terminology is that it sets up a roadblock in effective student-teacher communication. When students hear us talk of "paragraphs," their minds comprehend the typographical paragraph, whose vagaries are outlined above. Misconceptions are thus inevitably created when, intending topic segments, teachers instruct their students that "Paragraphs must start with a topic sentence" or "The paragraph is a composition in miniature." Or when they say, "Every major point on your structural plan should be developed into a single paragraph."

Some students try to follow these admonitions rigidly in every one of their typographic paragraphs and in the process create ludicrously formulaic writing. More thoughtful students, realizing that in their own reading and writing experience they encounter many paragraphs to which these statements simply do not apply, become confused and distrustful. These apparent discrepancies engender Macrorie's Engfish writers on the one hand and credibility problems for us on the other.

More importantly, the notion of a topic segment or paragraph cluster can be useful for students because it gives them an understandable structure with which to structure their ideas.

PARAGRAPH CLUSTERS AND TOPIC SENTENCES. We know a good deal about the workings of these topic segments through the research of Francis Christensen and his followers.[6] Christensen's study of the paragraph clusters of professional writers has confirmed our intuitive knowledge of the primacy of the topic sentence to these "paragraphs" both in importance and in order. With the exception of those topic segments which open with transitional material harking back to the preceding segment, topic segments begin with their topic sentence. As Christensen defines it:

> The topic sentence is . . . the sentence on which the others depend. It is the sentence whose assertion is supported or whose meaning is explicated or whose parts are detailed by the sentences added to it. (79–80).

Topic sentences vary a great deal in nature, but as Christensen discovered through his research, their function remains uniform:

> In connected writing, the topic sentence varies greatly in how explicit it is in designating the organizing idea of the paragraph. Sometimes it is quite explicit; sometimes it is a mere sign pointing to the turn the new paragraph is going to take. Sometimes it is the shortest sentence of the paragraph; sometimes it is not even a grammatically complete sentence. Sometimes it is a question. It seems to me that these differences are irrelevant, provided only that the reader gets the signal and the writer remembers the signal he has called. (80)

What follows the topic sentence, then, either explains or restates it.

Researchers' analyses of topic segments in professional expository prose (research which our students can duplicate for themselves if they wish) show a number of shared characteristics, which I have listed in the Student Guidelines.

STUDENT GUIDELINES

**Characteristics of Well-Written
Expository Paragraphs
(Topic Segments or Paragraph Clusters)**

1. These units almost always contain a topic sentence that presents the subject of the paragraph (or cluster).
2. The rest of the sentences of the paragraph (or cluster) relate to the topic sentence in one of the following ways:

continued
     a. Lead into it
     b. Explain it, by expanding or restricting its meaning
     c. Support it
     d. Or support or explain a supporting sentence
3. The placement of the topic sentence can vary, but in paragraphs or clusters that are *not introductory*, the topic sentence ordinarily occurs at or near the beginning.
4. Introductory topic segments differ from other topic segments. They generally have the following characteristics:
     a. The topic sentence ordinarily occurs at or near the conclusion of an introductory paragraph or cluster.
     b. In "although clause" introductory paragraphs (or clusters), the topic sentence often occurs somewhere near the center, following the "although" material. There it often has the effect of altering, even reversing, the meaning of the paragraph to that point.
     c. These introductory patterns sometimes occur within the body of an essay as well. In particular, they provide the pattern for some transitional paragraphs that introduce new sets of ideas.

Topic Sentences

What can we help our students take from this knowledge of how good writers construct their paragraphs (or clusters), summarized in the Guidelines, that will be useful in constructing their own?

First, we can help them understand the importance of topic sentences for communicating their points to the reader. As Toby Fulwiler explains to his students:

> Topic Sentences . . . help you shape and control the direction of your thought; when you read them, they help you to follow where the author is going. If you want your readers to follow your writing with little chance of misinterpretation, uncertainty, or wandering, provide them with clear topic sentences. . . . What you lose in surprise you will gain in predictability. . . . [And] a reader who can predict where you are going next will understand you most clearly if you do, in fact, go there.[7]

Providing students with a page or two from a professional or even a student essay with the topic sentences whited out or otherwise omitted is a convincing way to demonstrate their importance for clarity of communication.

Second, we can suggest that our students help their readers by placing their topic sentences in a conventional position near the beginning of a paragraph. After conducting extensive research on reading, cognitive psychologist David Kieras determined that "The topic sentence of a passage really should be first, because that is where a reader expects to find the important information."[8] The other sentences in the paragraph unit can then perform their function of explaining or supporting their point.

Third, in revising, students will want to make sure that every sentence in the paragraph (or cluster)—except introductory transitional material—relates directly to their point and to eliminate any that do not.

To summarize, in teaching structural support it is a good idea to define paragraphs (or paragraph clusters) as the structural way a writer supports his organizing idea; and in terms of topic sentences, to explain paragraphs (or clusters) as a sort of contract a writer makes to her readers to satisfy their curiosity as to what their topic sentences mean or imply.[9]

TEACHING SUPPORT—IN TERMS OF CONTENT

To introduce contentual support, we might add that writers also tacitly commit to providing enough supporting data to permit readers to follow their point, their organizing idea, and, if not to accept it, at least to understand the writer's reasons for thinking it is so. The strength of an expository work lies in the strength of its supporting material. How well the point—and the supporting subpoints—are supported determines how persuasive readers will find it.

Teaching Specific Support

Unfortunately, it is with support that the novice writer is most likely to founder. Having made a point and rephrased it to his satisfaction, the student writer is often ready to get on to the next matter of business, not realizing that the reader may be left unconvinced and dissatisfied. Unrelieved generalization, in fact, may well be the chief hallmark of the inexperienced writer. We must help our students learn, in Donald Murray's phrase, "to show as well as tell."

Specifically detailed support is necessary whatever the subject. Most students have little difficulty acknowledging that the statement, "Capital punishment does not act as a deterrent," must be backed by the citing of statistical studies, court evidence, and/or criminal case histories. But we must make sure students also understand that it is no less urgent rhetorically to document the statement, "My brother keeps a messy room" with sense evidence and/or anecdotes and bits of conversation. Yes, Brother's room is messy, we might agree, but how exactly is it messy? What is messy about it? In what specific way is it untidy? The needed supporting evidence lies in the concrete answers to these questions.

Nor can unsupported simple adjectives and adverbs bear the brunt. Students need to understand that "The man was impatient" is far more effectively rendered "The man tapped nervously on the arm of his chair and every forty or fifty seconds glanced at his wristwatch."

EXERCISES IN SPECIFIC DETAIL. The concept of specificity is a difficult one for some students to master. Some are not even able to distinguish in their own work an adequately supported paragraph from one of simple assertions. With such students, "Be more specific" is fruitless advice. Fortunately, a number of first-rate exercises have been devised to help with these problems. James M. McCrimmon's apple-pie exercise is one of the best.[10]

Apple-Pie Exercise. McCrimmon presents his students with two identical, labeled pictures of a slice of apple pie. He first asks if the objects in the pictures are the same and inquires why, if they are different, are they both called apple pie? Having stimulated his students' curiosity, he describes in detail the "first quality" ingredients of the first pie and names the chef of the Waldorf Astoria as its baker. Then he turns the students' attention to the second pie and confides:

> I made the other pie. I got the apples off our driveway where they had fallen . . . I cut out all the worms and most of the bruised spots and I rejected any apples that had been run over by the car. I got the flour from an open package at the back of the kitchen cabinet. I don't know how long it had been there, but it had no weevils in it, at least none that I could see. . . . I was very careful preparing the crust, because I had never baked a pie before, but the recipe was so smudged that I had to guess at some of the measurements and ingredients. The crust got a little scorched [when] I baked it, . . . but except for that, it looked pretty good to me. (427)

After ascertaining which of the two pies his students would choose, McCrimmon leads them into some significant insights:

> What do we mean by the statement. "Apple pie1 is not Apple pie2"? So you think a similar distinction can be made between [student1] and [student2]? Between Democrat1 and Democrat2? Between X1 and X2 where X is any noun? (428)

A follow-up exercise lets the student put the apple-pie insights to practical writing use:

> Write a two-paragraph composition to illustrate one of the following statements: Woman driver1 is not a woman driver2; Redhead1 is not redhead2; X1 is not X2, where X can be any class name you choose. (428)

Evidential Use of Detail. Lynn Z. Bloom's suggestion in *Writing Exercises from "Exercise Exchange"*[11] is another one which might be particularly useful in teaching expository writing. She recommends that students compile lists of descriptive details of the external features and contents of their homes (or rooms) or those of others. Then, using the details as evidence, they are to draw conclusions from these lists about the nature of the people who live in these homes (or rooms). Finally, they write an exercise making a comparison of lives or characters of two of these people on the basis of this evidence.

NATURE OF SPECIFIC SUPPORT. Once students understand the necessity to support their assertions specifically, they are usually grateful to know that there is a wide variety of ways of doing so. Many of them may find a guide-list such as the following helpful:

1. Facts
2. Statistics
3. Quotations
4. Analogies and comparisons
5. Well-reasoned arguments
6. Anecdotes or other narratives
7. Evidence of the five senses (such as the details demonstrating the gentleman's impatience, above)

We might point out that all of these can be used as examples or illustrations either singly or appropriately combined to substantiate the given point.

HELPING STUDENTS FIND SPECIFIC SUPPORT. How can students find the detailed information they need? Sometimes when writers review their topic sentence or rethink the point they want to make in a particular topic segment, a series of pertinent examples, or perhaps a single extended example, come immediately to mind. Sometimes an illustrative anecdote occurs to them. Often a glance at their structural plans will remind them of an idea jotted down earlier.

But where can students find appropriate examples and illustrations when they do not come spontaneously? They can do research or they can search their memories.

Research. Detailed suggestions for helping students with research may be found in Chapter 9.

Heuristics. As for searching the memory, we might suggest that a blocked student turn again to one of the heuristics discussed earlier (pages 70–76) and continue the inventing process. In order to activate what Agatha Christie's detective, Hercule Poirot, calls "the little grey cells," such students might ask themselves, for example, the Aristotelian questions of definition, comparison, cause and effect, and authority, but ask them in terms of the point of their topic or subtopic sentences.

Writers should not limit themselves to any single line of reasoning, however. Instead, we should assure them that it is best to let their minds range freely among all the questions. Perhaps the shrewdest approach is to try to decide just what expectations their topic sentence would arouse in their readers, what questions it would create in their readers' minds. They might then plan their support to answer all of their readers' unasked questions.

Teaching Vivid Support

When we have convinced our students that specific support for all points and subpoints is essential in expository writing, our job is not finished. For, as we well know, in the most effective writing, the support is not only specific but vivid.

PROFESSIONAL PARAGRAPHS. Turn students lose with a batch of expository essays and they will discover the importance of vivid support soon enough for themselves. What do the appealing, convincing essays have in common? What distinguishes them from the duller or "just okay" ones? Not the source of the support—there they will find an overwhelming variety. In almost any collection they will find supporting material coming from literature (classical, popular, and historical); from statistical data and recorded facts; from memories or everyday knowledge; from personal observation or fantasy; from interviews and conversations; from television and movies; from knowledge derived from a whole alphabet of scholarly disciplines from archaeology, botany, chemistry all the way down the alphabet to zoology. Nevertheless, in the midst of all this diversity, supporting material in well-written paragraphs from whatever source is almost universally both specific and vivid.

NECESSARY SKILLS. What works for professional writers should also work for our students. The effectiveness of their expository paragraphs depends upon how well they can think up vivid, specific detail and how appropriately they can use it. Two skills are especially important in this effort:

- The ability to observe in the particular rather than just in the general
- The ability to find relationships, to uncover similarities within their diverse experiences and memories.

Both of these are the sort of skills that can be helped along by practice. And students seem to respond with real enthusiasm to exercises that give them this practice—exercises such as the following set, adapted from my *Writing Effectively* (HarperCollins, 1990).

EXERCISES IN OBSERVATION. First there must be a focus for observation. Students must choose a particular vista and an object (or person) within that vista. These exercises provide an excuse to break with the regular routine, and that is part of their appeal. So, if a field trip is at all feasible, it works well to take the class to an outdoor setting—or to the lunchroom, shop, library . . . to make their observations. If we assign the exercises as homework, students can, of course, have their choice of venues.

Gathering Sensual Information.   Visually, students can learn to observe an object, person, or portion of landscape (1) as a whole in relation to its surroundings and (2) as a sum of its parts. They should have the opportunity to view it from afar and then examine it at close range. We can ask them to record in their journals as many visual details as they can discover, with a minimum of ten. Then they can try to draw analogies from these observations to their own experience or memories and record these meditations in their journals as well.

Having made their visual observations, they should close their eyes and listen with concentration. They should then record in their journals every sound they hear and at least two details about it. If they have trouble describing a sound, we might encourage them to find a comparison or an analogy that will communicate what they have heard. In any case, they should also record the association[s] the sounds call up for them.

Finally, we can ask them to breathe deeply or sniff about and, concentrating on smell, record the predominant odor(s) and the association the odors bring to mind.

Selecting and Using Details.   A follow up exercise helps students learn to use their observed details discriminatingly. Inexperienced writers need to learn to narrow down the dozens of sense impressions that are part of every situation to those few telling details that convey the sense of what they want to say.

In this exercise, the students return to the original scene—if only in memory—and record the overall impression the place leaves in their minds. Perhaps it is a mood our students sense there. Perhaps it is a thought that the place suggests or a memory it calls up. Then we can ask them to:

1. Compose a sentence expressing this impression, mood, thought or memory.
2. Examine their list of specific details and associations, and check only those that have to do with the ideas expressed in their sentence.
3. Making this sentence their topic sentence, write a paragraph (or paragraph cluster) supporting the topic sentence with the details checked on their list.

This set of exercises offers the possibility for collaborative work. The gathering of impressions is best accomplished individually or in pairs, but many students enjoy working together in small groups to complete the assignment.

GROUP OBSERVATION.   Students, no less than the rest of us, can enjoy a good picture. If we show them a print or a slide of a richly evocative painting—such as Seurat's "Bathers," for instance, they can use it to hone their observation skills. Working with the class as a whole, we can ask first for our students' overall impression. They might then discuss briefly what they think the artist is trying to express through the painting.

We might then call on each student in turn and ask for one specific detail he or she notices in the picture. After the more obvious details have been mentioned, students begin to observe minutely and can come up with some surprisingly shrewd observations.

When the class's well of ideas has run dry, we can suggest they reexamine their interpretative theories. They may have to revise considerably in light of the details discovered.

The exercise can conclude with students writing paragraphs interpreting the picture. We can help them embody their interpretative theory in a topic sentence and support it with appropriate details.

Comparative Observation.   More experienced or older students also enjoy a more sophisticated version of the painting exercise. In this one the students have the opportunity to examine two paintings that are similar in subject matter, but vary widely in technique. They can compare, for example, rural landscapes from the early and the late 19th century, a Renaissance *memento mori* fruit and floral still-life with a similar painting by Cezanne. Comparison of portraits from different periods, such as Ingres' Madame Montessier and Matisse's Greta Moll, work especially well because students have a chance to observe details of both the model's pose and dress and the artist's technique.

Students might gather in groups to study and discuss the paintings. They should first look for a point[s] of similarity. For example, in the Ingres and Matisse portraits, careful scrutiny should reveal an underlying resemblance in the features of the women who sat as models for the portraits. What then explains the indisputable differences in the portraits? The groups list the specific details accounting for the differences and take the lists back to the class as a whole for general discussion.

To complete the exercise, students decide on the point of comparison they wish to discuss, phrase their view of it as a topic sentence, and then support it with comparative details from the pictures.

Practice such as these exercises afford can help reinforce students' sense of the form and content of a paragraph (cluster) or topic segment. The object is for them to develop this sense to a point of unselfconsciousness. That is, our students should be able to express and support their ideas without even having to think about paragraph structure—at least, until revision time.

TYING IT ALL TOGETHER: TEACHING THE EXPOSITORY CONCLUSION

The conclusion of a composition has but one purpose: to bring the work to a satisfying end. The reader should be brought to experience a feeling of finality, an understanding of the author's point, and a positive—or at least open-minded—attitude toward that point.

What kind of advice do we have to offer our students on achieving this purpose? We can serve them best by suggesting that they pause after they have completed the introduction and the body of their papers and read carefully through what they have written. Having reread and reconsidered, they can then let their ending flow out of what they have already written.

Stopping to Reread

Our students need to take the time to go back over their papers and reread them — preferably aloud so that they can get a feel for the rhythms and cadences — and then make the revisions that suggest themselves. Having worked diligently on their papers part by part, they need an opportunity to savor the work as a whole. After they have taken this pause and familiarized themselves with their work in its totality, it has been my experience that an appropriate way to end their essays will almost invariably suggest itself.

There are a number of reasons why this procedure is a good one. To begin with, it is possible that when the students have reread their composition, they may find that they have already said all they have to say, that anything else would just be filler. Especially in a very brief paper, a formal conclusion can be repetitive and unnecessary. It may be that instead of writing a concluding paragraph, all they will need to do is to be sure that the last paragraph of the body of their essay ends with a note of finality.

Then too, our students cannot know before they have written the essay just what its conclusion should say. Writing itself is part of the invention process. Unless they follow their original structural plan in a robot-like way, the chances are that they will be reshaping some of their ideas while they are writing them. Waiting to reread will leave our students free to find the most effective way of concluding the composition they have actually written.

Most important, drawing their conclusion from their rereading of the rest provides their essay with a sense of wholeness. When students write their closing after rereading, they will not be tempted to add on a pat ending. Instead, their conclusion will contain their final reflections upon their point and the ideas they have discussed in making it.

BEYOND REREADING.   When writers reread their essays, they sometimes discover that their work has already attained a sense of completeness. If this is the case, they should, of course, simply stop. More often they will discover a need to continue in order to achieve this sense of wholeness and completion.

To help them do so, we can introduce them to three basic concluding techniques:

1. restating their central point in terms of the ideas through which they have developed it;
2. providing echoes of these ideas and even of the language in which they have phrased them earlier; and

3. letting their natural enthusiasm for their topic gather force as they reach the end so that it heightens the emotional intensity of their language.

Let's look more closely at these techniques.

Definitive Stating of the Central Point

Besides the feeling of finality, the reader should experience from an expository conclusion an understanding of the author's point and a generally positive—or, at least, open-minded—feeling toward it. An eloquent statement of the controlling idea is thus the least dispensable component of a conclusion. It is a rare professionally written essay that does not include it, as the students can readily check out for themselves. Because last is the most influential position, the concluding section should contain the essay's strongest, most persuasive phrasing of the writer's point of view. It is the last thing the reader will read and will probably be that which is most readily remembered.

PLACEMENT OF CONTROLLING IDEA STATEMENT.   Where precisely in the conclusion should writers place their final statement of their central point? So as not to inhibit student spontaneity, we should, I think, postpone such technical discussion. But later in the term when the question comes up, we can send students back to professional essays to find out for themselves.

What they will discover is that although almost every professional expository essay makes its point fairly explicitly in its conclusion, there is no uniformity in where it occurs. It may simply conclude the essay, or it may draw the essay to a close and begin a paragraph [segment] that branches out from it.

Most of the essays I surveyed use the final paragraph[s] for a final expression, explanation, or amplification of their controlling idea. Others use what Sheridan Baker calls the "inverted funnel" format (50–54). This visual metaphor signifies a final statement of the controlling idea as a topic sentence upon which the author generalizes (according to Baker) or, more often, leads into a purposive conclusion that suggests a plan of action; for example, "Such and such being the case, we need to write our congresspeople or the school newspaper, and to be more understanding of others' needs ourselves." In scientific papers a purposive conclusion can lead into recommendations of paths for further research.

Summation by Echo

A summary statement of the central point brings an expository composition to closure, and that is sufficient. But if, in addition, the controlling idea can be stated in a way that echoes the ideas or phraseology of the points through which it was argued throughout the paper, or if the accompanying material in the rest of the conclusion can contain such echoes, the reader will not only

experience a more satisfying sense of wholeness and unity, but also a sublimi-
nal recapitulation of the most persuasive points and all they suggest. Although this recommendation may sound like a rephrasing of the last part of
the old saw which advises "Tell them what you're gonna say; say it; and tell
them you've said it," it is not so intended. Conclusions such as "I have argued
(1) . . . , (2) . . . , and (3) . . . ; and therefore, . . ." can be deathly, especially in a brief or nontechnical paper. It is quite another matter for these
points to suggest themselves to the reader through connecting links with the
rest of the paper.

FRAME CONCLUSION. It is difficult to exemplify the echo strategy without quoting an entire essay because its essence is that it reflects the whole.
Perhaps its effect may be suggested by an example of a related, but more
restricted, technique known as "framing." A frame conclusion picks up an
idea or an image suggested in the introduction so that, with the introduction,
it pulls the paper together within a sort of frame.

Shana Alexander, for instance, concludes her essay, "Getting Old in Kids
Country" by returning to the paradox of her introduction ("Until a few hundred years ago, [children] did not exist" and reversing it:

> If in the old days children did not exist, it seems equally true today that adults
> as a class have begun to disappear, condemning all of us to remain boys and
> girls forever, jogging and doing push-ups against all eternity. [See page 119
> for Alexander's introductory statement]

For another example, Samuelson, introduces "The Value of College," by first
negating and then expressing his controlling idea:

> The truth is that more and more Americans have been going to college, and
> the expected (and advertised) benefits haven't fully materialized. [*Newsweek*
> (August 31, 1992): 75]

Having supported this idea throughout his essay, he concludes by echoing
and this time definitively clarifying the meaning of that "although" introduction:

> The message here is emphatically *not* that college doesn't count—either for
> individuals or for society. It does. But what counts is not only how many
> students go to college but what they study, how hard they work and what
> they actually learn. The same is true of all our schools. What we need to
> improve most is quality, not the number of degrees we produce.

Echo Exercise. A good exercise to help students understand the use of
echoes is for them to work with colored pencils on duplicated copies of effective essays displaying this characteristic—essays by E. B. White, Ellen Goodman, or Lewis Thomas work especially well. We might ask our students to
underline in a separate color each pattern of recurring words and phrases and

in this way trace the development of ideas and images visually throughout the article and into the conclusion.

One of the most important advantages a writer gains by reading one's work through before completing it and by drawing a conclusion directly out of what has gone before is that often this process leads naturally to such rhetorically effective recapitulative borrowing.

Heightened Language

Because all writing is essentially persuasive, a good conclusion not only leaves the reader with something to remember or ponder, but also with a certain sense of conviction. To gain this sense of conviction, authors often close their essays with language that has more emotional intensity than the rest of the piece. They word their conclusions in a prose that is more rhythmical in its phrasing and more metaphorical in its content. Examples abound. There is scarcely an essay of quality in which the emotional impact of the writing does not intensify in the final sentences.

If we ask students to read essays with special concentration on the conclusion, they may become aware of the subtly heightened tone of the language in which the conclusions are written. Ask them to read the essays aloud, and they may find themselves using a different tone of voice for the conclusion than the rest of the article required. In trying together as a class to determine the reason why, students may point to the more emotionally charged connotative quality of the word choice, the heightened rhythmic quality of the syntax, and the use of imagery and repetition.

COLORFUL LANGUAGE; RHYTHMIC SYNTAX.   By studying how the effect is achieved professionally, our students can learn ways of adding such color to their own work. They may note the effect of the almost poetic rhythms created by parallel structure:

> • It is there we perceive Christmas — and the sheep quiet, and the world waiting (E. B. White, "The Distant Music of the Hounds," *Second House from the Corner*, New York: Harper & Row, 1949).

They may discover rousing exhortations:

> Black people need a fair chance to compete — nothing more and nothing less (Williams, "US Blacks and a Free Market," Heritage Features, [May 1980]).

Or they may find that sometimes the emotional charge comes in a final, very brief sentence — a sentence which often contrasts with the lengthy ones preceding it:

> • There is great joy in watching a tree grow (Carll Tucker, "On Splitting," *Saturday Review* [January 21, 1978]).

Sometimes students will discover the impact coming from a rhetorical question:

> Is this pain and disillusionment being nurtured now in the soil of our silence? (Ellen Goodman, "The Communication Gap," *Boston Globe* [March 1981]).

Sometimes they will note an effective use of metaphor, as in both the Tucker and Goodman concluding sentences.

CONCLUDING QUOTATIONS. Our students will almost certainly come across concluding quotations, a strategy expository writers frequently use to heighten the language and intensify the emotional quality of their conclusions. Authors who feel it would be inappropriate to employ ringing phrases themselves may choose another voice to speak for them. Sometimes the other voice selected is that of an authority. George Will, for example, uses a quotation of noted historian, Arthur Schlesinger, Jr. to conclude "The Cult of Ethnicity Distorts History":

> The cult of ethnicity produces what Schlesinger calls a culture of self-pity and victimization. There is a "contagion of inflammable sensitivities" which makes the bonds of national identity brittle. . . . The stakes are high because, as Schlesinger says, "history is to the nation as memory is to the individual." (See page 119–20 for Will's introductory material.)

An article based on interview research will often end with a quotation from one of the interviewees reinforcing the author's point. Claudia H. Deutsch uses this technique to conclude "Cheating: Alive and Flourishing":

> Said Beverly Betz, who teaches at New York City's High School for the Humanities, "Parents have got to make their kids feel that if they don't do well on a test it's not the end of the world, but just an indication that more work needs to be done." (See page 122 for Deutsch's introductory material.)

"CLINCHER" CLOSINGS. Our students may want to try to bring this sort of color to the endings of their own compositions. And we certainly don't want to discourage their experimenting. But, like the artifices sometimes used to achieve a striking introduction, these concluding devices can be pedagogically overemphasized. The same reasoning would seem to apply to both "hooks" and "clinchers": Though we should in no way pressure our students toward employing them, we should not deny them the opportunity of enhancing their papers in this way.

Concluding Hazards

Our advice to students might also include mentioning—without undue emphasis, of course, and not until after the first papers—the major hazards facing the novice conclusion-writer.

Writers should be careful not to distract their readers and disturb the unity of their essays by introducing new and extraneous material at the end. They should take special care not bring in "although" clause material at this time, which may confuse and even dissuade their readers.

Furthermore, a conclusion is rendered fatally ineffective by a final admission that "Of course the other side has much which can be said for it too" or by the inclusion of material which implies "Oh, by the way, I forgot to mention earlier that. . . ." We thus might warn our students that the conclusion is not the place for making either concessions or new points.

AVOIDING EXCESS. Our students should also be aware of the danger of overintensifying that exists whenever a writer is working in emotional linguistic patterns. The line between a ringing conclusion which captivates and enthralls the reader and a tear-jerking or bombastic finale which, in the common parlance, "turns the reader off," needs an experienced eye to determine. This matter of judgment presents a particular difficulty to our novice writers. The difficulty confronts us, their teachers, with a delicate problem as well: How do we encourage our students to be free to be creative and at the same discourage them from overuse of what one harassed junior-high instructor has termed "the flowery-bowery"? There is no good answer to this question. The young ego is so overwhelmingly bound up in personally written passages of this sort that I scarcely dare recommend even the mildest criticism of them. We have all probably encountered cases where a hasty word of reproof or, worse yet, a mocking remark concerning a passage that meant a great deal to the student personally has inhibited that student's writing for the rest of the semester, and often much longer. It seems to me that the solution— and it can be only a partial solution—lies in discouraging the writing of "flowery-bowery" conclusions before they are created:

- We can be careful not to praise unsuccessful attempts of this sort insincerely or to overpraise successful attempts.
- With more mature or more advanced students we can discuss the problem openly before it arises, perhaps bringing in some borderline or questionable sample conclusions and eliciting student reaction. A collection of mid-19th-century essays can be a fruitful source of such material.
- Most importantly, we can discourage that artificial striving for effect out of which arise most of the more blatantly flowery student conclusions.

FINAL HOPES. If our students will read their papers through and permit themselves to be—well, let's call it by name—inspired in a quite natural way by what they have written in the introduction and body, they may find that, without any artificial striving, they can achieve a genuinely effective conclusion. If not, they can at least produce a final restatement of their central point that has both solidity and clarity, in itself no small achievement.

IDEAS FOR DISCUSSION OR ESSAY

1. Conduct your own informal survey of the introductions and conclusions of contemporary expository essays and articles. Do your results conform fairly well to the results of the survey described in the Chapter? If there is a discrepancy, in what ways do they differ?

2. Mike Royko, a much beloved columnist for the *Chicago Tribune*, introduced a recent essay, "Israel Survives Amid Hostile Sea," in this way:

> When I look at a world map, I sometimes wonder what the insane fuss is all about. Sure, I listen to the experts, the pundits, and even Henry Kissinger. But then I look at the map and it still makes no sense. If I look closely and squint my eyes, I can find a country that has only about 8,000 square miles. That's Israel.

   What techniques does this passage exemplify that you could point out to your students? What controlling idea does it seem to be leading to?

3. Many teachers, especially beginning instructors, do not have the luxury of setting up their own curriculum; so, for many, teaching involves compromise and accommodation. Imagine yourself in the following situation and suggest practical ways of dealing with it. You are to teach a twelve week composition course using the following syllabus:

   Paper 1: Description

   Paper 2: Definition

   Paper 3: Comparison and contrast

   Paper 4: Classification

   Paper 5: Cause and effect argument

   Paper 6: Persuasion

   However, you have been convinced by the arguments cited here—as well as your own reasoning on the matter—that this sort of pattern is not the best way to structure student assignments. How would you handle the course in order to accommodate your teaching to the prescribed assignment schedule?

NOTES

1. Donald Murray, *A Writer Teaches Writing; A Practical Method of Teaching Composition* (Boston: Houghton, 1968), 8.

2. *Strategies in Prose*, eds. Wilfred A. Ferrell and Nicholas A. Salerno, 3rd ed. (New York: Holt, 1973) and *The Winston Reader*, eds. Bonnie Carter and Craig Skates (New York: Holt, 1991). Both anthologies are typical of popular composition-course readers in their selections. To make the studies comparable, both are published by Holt. Both accurately reflect the predilections of the composition-pedagogy scholarship of their times. For example, half the 1991 selections are personal narrative or short stories.

Comparative study reveals almost no change in the shape of the syndicated essays over the years and surprisingly little change in the anthologized expository essays. The only change I noted is that fewer of the 1991 anthologized introductions were controversial and more were anecdotal—in keeping with the current taste for narrative.

Perhaps because fewer of the 1991 anthologized essays were controversial, fewer of them opened with their "although" material: More than 50 percent of the 1973 reader; slightly under 30 percent of the 1991. But the fact that "although" introductions continue unabated in the syndicated essays makes me question whether the academics who selected the 1991 material reflect a general literary trend rather than simply the current academic climate.

3. Phillip Arrington, "Reflections on the Expository Principle," *CE* 54 (1992): 327, was once an outspoken critic of expository conventions.

4. Sheridan Baker, *The Practical Stylist*, 7th ed. (New York: Harper, 1990), 43–45; Lucille Vaughn Payne, *The Lively Art of Writing* (Chicago: Follett, 1965), 48–53.

5. Ken Macrorie, *The Perceptive Writer, Reader, and Speaker* (New York: Harcourt, 1959) 134.

6. Francis Christensen, *Notes toward a New Rhetoric: Nine Essays for Teachers*, 2nd ed. (New York: Harper, 1978). Christensen's findings have been confirmed by the research of others, most recently by R. I. Popkin in "A Study of Topic Sentence Use in Academic Writing," *Written Communication* 4 (1987): 57–66.

They are, nevertheless disputed by Richard Braddock in "The Frequency and Placement of Topic Sentences in Expository Prose," *RTE* 3 (1974): 287–302. Braddock, however, does not take into account the arbitrary division of topic segments and searches every typographical paragraph for its topic sentence. Christensen, on the other hand, gives consideration to sections which have been arbitrarily divided and creates a special category for paragraphs formed in this way. See "A Generative Rhetoric of the Paragraph" Sections 6 and 7 in *Notes*, 93–97.

7. Toby Fulwiler, *College Writing*, (Glenview, Ill.: Scott, 1982), 86. The few voices that have in recent years deprecated the importance of teaching the topic sentence are, I think, ill-advised. And some now feel they were in error. See, for example, Phillip Arrington, note 3 above.

8. David Kieras, "How Readers Abstract Main Ideas." a paper presented at the American Institute for Research, Washington D.C. November 17, 1980. 7. Compare with Arrington's remarks on page 114.

9. For a more detailed explication of this idea, see Patrick Hartwell, "Teaching Arrangement: A Pedagogy," *CE* 40 (1979): 548–54 and Robert M. Gorrell, "Not by Nature: Approaches to Rhetoric," *EJ* 55 (1966): 409–16.

10. James McCrimmon, "A Cumulative Sequence in Composition," *EJ* 55 (1966): 427–28.

11. Lynn Z. Bloom, "Be It Ever So Humble, They *Can* Go Home Again, Writing Exercises from *Exercise Exchange*, ed. Littleton Long (Urbana: NCTE, 1976), 89–92.

☐ ☐ ☐ **5**

Teaching the Rewriting Stage: Structural Revision

This chapter is devoted to issues related to teaching students how to approach major structural revision of their papers. Questions involved in teaching surface and stylistic revision as well as correction of errors will be discussed in Chapters 6, 7, and 8 of Section B.

TEACHING REVISING: THE PEDAGOGICAL ISSUES

Of all the composing stages—prewriting, writing, and rewriting—into which we divide the basically integral writing process for educational purposes, the final stage, rewriting, is arguably the most important pedagogically. And yet it also raises the most compelling questions. The wide variety of revising practices, and the varying effects of these practices, disclosed by recent research has caused thoughtful teachers to wonder: Should we require all our students to revise every paper? Should we teach all students to revise? Should we encourage all students to revise their work? The questions are valid. Let's examine each one in turn.

Should We Insist That All Students Revise Every Paper?

In light of current research, it is hard to justify doing so. Researchers looking to professional writers for a revision model for students find, in Lester Faigley and Stephen Witte's words, "extreme diversity in the ways expert writers revise"—and for some writers, this diversity includes no separate revision procedure at all. Nancy Sommers, among others, discovered that most experienced writers write recursively, revising as they go along, and that many have no need to do global revision at the end. Stephen Witte called our attention to some other writers, whose pre-text (the mental construction created before the act of transcription) is so complete that they manage to write a finished composition in one draft and need only cursory proofreading to bring their work to its best. As Muriel Harris writes:

> It is as hard for true one-drafters to suspend the need for closure as it is for multi-drafters to reach quick decisions and push themselves rapidly toward closure.[1]

NOT FOR EVERYONE.   Furthermore, some scholars who research revision pedagogy have found that compulsory revision (without intervention) does not always result in improved papers. (See, for example, the work of Barbara Hansen and R. J. Bracewell, et al.) A goodly number of researchers have found that the amount of change is not a key variable in revision and does not correlate with textual improvement. Among them, Linda Flower, John Hayes, and their colleagues, for instance, conclude that "revision as an obligatory stage required by teachers doesn't necessarily produce better writing."[2] How should we proceed in light of this research?

Provide Intervention.   First, we should not require revision without providing appropriate intervention. In researcher Barbara Hansen's words, "Rewriting, in and of itself, will not strengthen a student's composition skills. Revision needs to be taught, not assigned."[3]

Offer Freedom.   Second, we can give students the freedom to find and use their own natural composition strategies. As Muriel Harris writes, "[T]here is a very real danger in imposing a single, 'ideal' composing style on students" (190). We should, of course, provide instruction and help in revision for the large numbers of students who need this help. But the few who do all their revision recursively and the fewer who plan a polished text in their heads—revisions and all—should be encouraged to follow their own writing styles.

Be Flexible.   And third, we should be flexible in our revision requirements. Since the quantity of revision is not necessarily reflected in the quality of the writing, students should have the right to reject revision at any time in the history of a particular paper. If a student feels satisfied with a paper and, after considering suggestions, still decides "No, I'm finished" and asks for a grade, surely we should agree. It is, after all, her own creative work and we should take care to protect that ownership. Besides, she just may be right.

A student should also have the right to request a grade on a paper he is not yet completely satisfied with if he feels he has worked on it as much or as long as he can profitably work on it. It has been my experience that most student papers improve very little after one global revision and very few profit from more than two major rewriting efforts. There is only so much a student can learn from a particular essay, as the research confirms. After that point is reached, rewriting is a matter of diminishing returns. (See notes 1 and 2.) It is better to stop there and work on a new composition.

If revision is to entail the learning we hope it brings, we cannot make it compulsory.

Should We Teach Students to Revise?

I would most definitely recommend teaching revision skills. That most of us who are experienced writers revise recursively as we write cannot be denied. But, on the other hand, most experienced writers revise between drafts too; and, besides, most of our students are inexperienced writers. Revising includes a series of skills and perceptions that inexperienced writers need to learn—and *can* learn well from classroom instruction, as recent research attests.[4] And we cannot give such instruction recursively.

The best time to separate out revising skills from the writing process for teaching purposes is after the first draft.[5] It is at this point that student writers have done about all that they can do by themselves, and they will need some help if they are to improve their papers. And it is at this point, when student writers have used all the composing knowledge they currently possess, that real learning takes place.

Should We Encourage Revision?

Without question, in my judgment, we should encourage revision. Of course, not all papers need extensive revision, and all revision needs closure. Nevertheless, the single most important answer to: "How do students learn to write?" is "By rewriting."

This assumption, long held intuitively by successful teachers, has now been confirmed by research. Seventh and eighth grade students studied by George Hillocks, for example, who revised their papers according to brief, focused, teacher comments improved the quality of their future work twice as much as a group receiving similar comments who did not revise. The revised drafts of Louise Bridwell's high school seniors were significantly improved in both quality and mechanics over their first efforts. And the compositions of C. Effros's Yale freshman profitted measurably from guided revision and delayed grading.[6]

Beyond its role in improving the written product, rewriting promotes improvement in a student's command of the writing process—especially with expository writing. Expository structure, the key to this important genre, is not easily mastered through classroom presentations. Students can come to understand exposition through the sort of classroom work suggested in Chapters 2 through 4, but most cannot learn how to focus and support their ideas persuasively until they need to use these skills to structure an essay of their own. Typically, a student will discover this lack of knowledge when an outside reader responds to a first draft that lacks clear focus. And she will learn how to attain it when she rewrites. Students have described the moment when this knowledge is achieved as what we might call an epiphany:

> All of a sudden I figured it out. I know I'll still make lots of mistakes, but I think now I know how to write!

Because of the possibility of this "Aha" breakthrough, the importance of coaching students through this stage of the process can scarcely be overemphasized. As Matthew Doherty explains,

> Writing is basically a self-taught skill produced mainly by rewriting, and the teacher's primary role must be to guide the youngster through this difficult act of self-teaching. All good writing, as we know, is more perspiration than inspiration, and it is the culmination of rewriting, in the process of which the writer sweats, learns, and produces. . . . If students are not forced to involve themselves in actual, painful, total rewriting, then they are not writing; they may simply be playacting and conforming, and thus learning relatively little. In fact, they are learning the wrong lesson. . . . Writing *is* rewriting, and there exists no really valid shortcut or panacea.[7]

John J. Ruszkiewicz, in his advice to new teachers, does not, I think, put the case too strongly: "Perhaps the only stupid question an *experienced* teacher of writing can ask is 'Should I allow my students to revise?' You are not teaching writing if you are not allowing revision."[8]

HOW REVISION MAY BE ENCOURAGED. Allowing revision means encouraging students to revise by supplying motivation adequate to the task. Successful motivation rests on convincing students that their papers are an ongoing assignment. An assignment completed and graded is a project dead and gone; all students want to know then is "What's next?" How do we make an assignment an ongoing project? The best way I know is to delay grading until teacher and student agree that a paper has been satisfactorily completed. Teachers who are not comfortable in withholding a grade, or who are required to give one immediately, can encourage revision by permitting satisfactory major revision to raise the grade substantially or, better yet, by counting the revision as a new paper. (See Chapter 13 for discussion of these strategies.) Under these circumstances, students accept revision as a matter of course.

Teaching Revision

Teaching revision is probably the most important work writing teachers do. If there is any question of where our time is best spent, most successful teachers would argue for spending that time helping students revise their papers.

Our most important way to teach revision (and most of this chapter) involves strategies for working with a student and a particular paper, individually or in groups. But, there is a quantity of useful information that can help our students develop their own general revising strategies. Surely, part of our job in teaching revision is to help our students engage with that information. The following section is devoted to this material.

HELPING STUDENTS LEARN TO REWORK EXPOSITORY WRITING
Traditionally, when writers have worked on revising the structure of their compositions, they have analyzed them in terms of unity, coherence, and emphasis. These remain the most useful criteria. Donald Murray offers succinct definition of the three qualities:

> [Your essay] must have unity; it should all be about the same subject. It must have coherence; each point should lead to the next point. And it must have emphasis; the most important points should be in the most important places.[9]

We need to provide our students with techniques with which to review their own—or their partner's—draft to make sure that it has the appropriate unity, coherence, and emphasis, and we also need to teach them ways they can revise flawed text to correct whatever deficiencies they might discover.

Stylistic considerations are, of course, important for successful revision in these areas, especially for emphasis—and we will discuss these goals again when we take up style—but good structure alone can give a composition much of its needed unity and coherence, and a good part of its emphasis as well.

Diagnosing and Remedying Problems of Unity

A writer's organizing idea is the best tool for achieving unity in an expository composition. If students have focused their entire paper upon supporting their central point, their papers will automatically be unified. How can they tell? They can read over all the topic sentences of their—or their partner's—paragraph segments to make sure that each one somehow amplifies or supports their central point. If they do, then the paper has an overall focus.

So far so good. But an expository essay needs internal unity as well. To check for this, students will need to reread those topic sentences to be certain that each one also sets up the subject matter of its own particular paragraph segment. Then, within each paragraph unit, they can check to see if all the supporting material contributes to backing up the topic sentence.

We must urge our students to be brutal in eliminating any material they find not to the point. If they cannot bear to part with some of this material, they might seek a way of subordinating it under another topic or they might jot it down in a notebook or journal for development at another time. But whatever they do, they must not let a persistent but off-the-point idea wander in and disrupt. No matter how interesting this extra material might be, if it distracts from the line of thinking they are pursuing in this paper, it can only do harm.

FINDING THE IRRELEVANT. A few students may have trouble distinguishing the extraneous. They can be encouraged to remedy this problem by checking their work against a structural plan. If it corresponds, then they will want to check—or help their partner check—the plan itself for unity. They can go about this check in an almost algebraic way:

- Do points I + II + III + IV . . . = their organizing idea?
- Do subpoints IIA + IIB + IIC . . . = Point II?
- Do sub-subpoints IIA1 + IIA2 + IIA3 = Subpoint IIA? And so on?

Where they find a discrepancy, they should find it easier to rework their structural plan—or help their partner rework the plan—to correct it. They can then revise the paper accordingly. Word processors make easy work of this sort of cut-and-paste revising for those students who have access to them.

If we have a class that finds identifying extraneous material particularly difficult, we might try an in-class exercise. We can type two or three extraneous sentences or phrases into a couple of paragraphs taken from a professional essay and, using the overhead projector or duplicated handouts, have the class work together to spot the intruders.

Diagnosing and Remedying Problems of Coherence

Student problems with coherence stem almost entirely from the inability of some writers to put themselves in their reader's place and write their work from a reader's point of view. These problems are associated with writers who have what they want to say so clear in their own minds that they do not realize they have left out material needed to allow readers to make sense of their ideas. These problems also stem from writers being so involved with the order in which a set of ideas came to them that they do not realize these ideas would be clearer to their readers ordered in another way.

Thus, coherence problems lend themselves especially well to peer-group work, where a writer can witness his work through the eyes of outside readers. To find and revise away their own problems of coherence, students need to learn to act as readers of their own writing. They need to ask themselves: Is this point really clear? Does it follow unmistakeably from the idea above? Is something missing?

GLOBAL COHERENCE PROBLEMS. That which gives the paper unity will also contribute to its coherence. There is an orderliness inherent in the tight-knit development of organizing idea and topic sentences I described earlier. Beyond that, coherence is achieved through the logical ordering of the sentences within the paragraph segments and through the creation of smooth transitions between these sentences and the segments.

We can advise our students that the best way to test for smooth transitions is to read their papers aloud to themselves or to a sympathetic listener. Abrupt endings and jerky transitions become immediately apparent in an oral rendition. To test for the logical quality of the ordering is more difficult. But working closely with a structural plan can be helpful in diagnosing overall structural difficulties. And scholars have provided tools for discovering problems on the paragraph level.

PARAGRAPH COHERENCE PROBLEMS. Though detailed teaching of paragraph structure can be distracting for students when they are doing their writing, they can often put this knowledge to good use when they revise. In particular, it can be helpful for diagnosing structural problems within the paragraph.

Scholars such as Francis Christensen and Alton Becker have conducted research to determine exactly what makes for coherent paragraphs. To further their research, each scholar has developed an apparatus of analysis. As our students revise, they may find one or the other apparatus useful to diagnose a coherence problem that they sense within one of their paragraphs, but are unable to point to precisely.

TRI Method. Alton Becker's approach to the paragraph is relatively simple.[10] He sees it in terms of the statement of a (T)opic, a (R)estriction on or a development of that topic, and an (I)llustration of the topic. More informally, his schema is known as TRI. Here is how he would analyze a typical paragraph, in this case one taken from Charles Slack's "If I'm So Smart, How Come I Flunk All the Time?"

(T)	"With few exceptions, our students acted like dummies," said Homme, "even though we knew they were ahead of the rest in knowledge.
(R)	They were so used to playing the class idiot that they didn't know how to show what they knew.
(I)	Their eyes wandered, they appeared absentminded or even belligerent. One or two read magazines hidden under their desks, thinking, most likely, that they already knew the classwork. They rarely volunteered and often had to have questions repeated because they weren't listening. (*Eye*, Jan. 1969)

Although most good paragraphs fit the TRI structure, Becker's system also allows for an occasional TIRI, ITR, TRIT, or even IRT. Furthermore, Becker enhances the usability of his system by adding the symbols Q(uestion) and A(nswer) along with P(roblem) and S(olution). In another paragraph from the Slack article, the symbols work in this way:

(Q)	Were the experiments a success?
(A)(T)	The scientists said Yes but the students said No.
(I)	When grades were measured using standardized tests under strict laboratory conditions, marks went up more than one year on the average. Meanwhile, back at the school, the students were still barely passing, at best.

(T)   "The experiment was fine for the scientists. They proved their theory on paper and made a name for themselves, but most of us were still flunking in class," remarked one seventeen year old.

Christensen's Method.   Sometimes students need a more precise guide than the TRI method to help them recognize the source of a particularly troubling problem in paragraph coherence. Then Francis Christensen's more complex method may serve them better.[11] Christensen's research, like Becker's, led him to focus on the topic sentence, which Christensen defines as

> the sentence on which the others depend, . . . the sentence whose assertion is supported or whose meaning is explicated or whose parts are detailed by the sentences added to it. (79–80)

Except for paragraphs that begin with transitional material, Christensen found that paragraphs generally open with a topic sentence. The topic sentence is then developed in two possible ways: by sentences that are either coordinate with it or subordinate to it. By "coordinate" sentences, Christensen means sentences that explain or restate the matter in the topic sentence. By "subordinate" sentences, he means those that exemplify, modify, or develop the topic material. He believes that each of the rest of the sentences in a good paragraph is also developed in either of the two ways—in relation either to the topic sentence or to the sentence immediately before it.

Christensen suggests a paragraph analysis, with parallel structures indented in a parallel way, that permits students to understand this structure visually. Christensen always numbers the topic sentence as "1." He assigns coordinate sentences the same number, and subordinate sentences one number less than the sentences to which they are subordinate. As an example of his method, I have analyzed the following paragraph from Perry Turner's "What Killed Arthur Dimmesdale:"

1. Nobody likes to miss the point, and soon after Kahn published his conclusions, scholars were hastening to concur.
  2. Barbara Storms, for instance, a University of Chicago student of literature, rejoiced over Khan's reading:
    3. "Gone is the heavy symbolic or allegorical structure put forward so often by literary scholars.
    3. The reader is left with the kernel of a possible truth rather than the chaff of rhetoric that only leads to more questions."
  2. Virginia McCormick, an English teacher at Allen High School in Allentown, Pennsylvania, took a less heady but no less approving tone:
    3. [T]here is no reason," she declared, "that both theories—Dimmesdale's death as a result of a guilty conscience and his death as a result of herbal poisoning—cannot co-exist." (*Science*, 1985)

For a paragraph to be truly coherent, every statement must be either coordinate with or subordinate to the topic sentence or with or to the statement preceding it. If a sentence does not fit in this way, it is clearly out of place—either in the sequence in which it occurs or in the particular paragraph segment as a whole. Christensen's system of analysis thus offers a practical method for discovering the exact source of problems students may sense in the coherence of their—or their partners'—paragraphs.

PROBLEMS OF LINKAGE.   Structural coherence of the sort we have been discussing is basic to the coherence of expository essays. But sometimes a student can check his or her paper thoroughly, conclude that it is structurally sound, and yet find that it still does not read as smoothly and coherently as he or she would like. The problem then might very well be a lack of appropriate linkage between ideas. Besides an underlying coherence, writers have to give their readers surface clues to help them connect their ideas together so that they can be understood. They can give these clues by using two basic methods: repetition and transitional devices.

Repetition for Clarity.   Our students have probably never stopped to consider that all sentences in the context of a paragraph or an essay ought to consist of old material and new material. Repeating old material is necessary to provide continuity of thought and to prevent confusion. New material is needed to develop ideas and to avoid monotony. If we ask them to check it out, the realization usually strikes them with surprise. Almost any professional paragraph will do. Even in a paragraph as commonplace as the one preceding this, the paragraph headed *Problems of Linkage*, for example, this principle holds true. Something Old, Something New.

ILLUSTRATIVE MODEL

Something Old, Something New

OLD, LINKING MATERIAL	NEW IDEAS
Structural coherence of the sort we have been discussing is basic to the coherence of expository essays.	
	But sometimes a student can check his or her paper thoroughly, conclude that it is structurally sound, *and yet* find that it still does not read as smoothly and coherently as he or she would like.
The problem *then*	might very well be a lack of appropriate linkage between ideas.

continued	
Besides an underlying coherence,	writers have to give their readers surface clues to help them connect their ideas together so that they can be understood.
They can give these clues by using	two basic methods: repetition and transitional devices.

Clearly, student writers can achieve better coherence by grounding each sentence in matter that reinforces what the reader already knows.

- Sometimes writers can achieve this reinforcement by an exact repetition of words or phrases (for example, the repetition of "coherence" and "coherently" in the sample paragraph).
- Sometimes they want to repeat the idea, but would rather change the wording to avoid monotony (as I did by interchanging "linkage" and "connect[ion]" in the example).
- Sometimes the repetition is better handled by substituting an appropriate pronoun (for instance, "it" for "paper" and "them" for "readers").

We can encourage our students, whichever method of repetition they use, to think of the idea to be repeated as a colored thread that they weave through the tapestry of their essay, both to create the pattern for their ideas and to hold those ideas together. In checking over their own paper—or a partner's paper—for coherence, they need to make sure that these important threads are in place.

PROBLEMS OF TRANSITION.   Faulty or nonexistent transition also results in writing that lacks coherence. If our students are to respond helpfully to each other's papers and to revise successfully themselves, they will need a comfortable understanding of transitional devices. The English language is rich in these words and phrases that not only help writers tie ideas together, but also point the reader to the particular relationships that hold among a writer's ideas. Experienced writers rely heavily on them. The brief paragraph on "Problems of Linkage" in the box on Combining Old and New Material just examined, for instance (though it certainly was *not* composed as an exemplary paragraph), offers a number of instances of these devices: "But" suggests a mild contradiction of what went before. "And yet" conveys that despite the obstacles raised, the concept expressed remains true. "Then" implies that what follows depends on the truth of what preceded. "Besides" indicates an addition to the earlier idea. And "so that" expresses a causal relationship.

The Transitional Words and Phrases Student Guidelines offers a partial list of such devices and the general relationship to which each points. It could be helpful to our students.

STUDENT GUIDELINES

Transitional Words and Phrases

Phrases of sequence: first, second, third . . . ; first, then; after, afterward, since, before, when, whenever, until, as soon as, as long as, while, in (in 1923, in the summer, and so on), at (Christmastime, at the end of term, and so on), finally

Phrases of affirmation: in fact, actually, indeed, certainly

Phrases of negation: nevertheless, on the contrary, notwithstanding, on the other hand, despite, still, however, but, yet, conversely

Phrases of concession: although, though, granted that, no doubt, to be sure, whereas, of course, doubtless, certainly

Phrases of illustration: for example, for instance, to illustrate, in particular, specifically

Phrases of addition: and, also, moreover, or (nor), furthermore, next, again, too, second (third, and so on), another, finally

Phrases of qualification: frequently, often, usually, in general, occasionally, provided, in case, unless, when, since, because, for, if

Phrases of summation: therefore, thus, in conclusion, to sum up, so, consequently, accordingly, all in all, in short, on the whole, in other words, then.

Transitional Devices for Appropriate Linkage.   Our students need to learn how to use devices such as these to help tie their work together and make it more coherent. Perhaps even more to the point, they should also understand the damage that faulty use of these transitional words and phrases can do to their writing. We need to teach inexperienced students that such transitional phrases cannot easily be interchanged since they point to very specific relationships. One way to do this is to give them a multiple-choice demonstration with humorous consequences. We might, for instance, ask them to examine the following on the chalkboard or screen and decide on the appropriate transition:

> Jane held the smoking gun in her hand;
>   *furthermore,* she was not the murderer.
>   *consequently,* she was not the murderer.
>   *nevertheless,* she was not the murderer.

When they figure out that only one of these equally useful transitional words keeps the sentence from being ridiculous, they may well resolve to save their work from equally disastrous results. We can suggest that if they have any question whether the transitional words they choose lend their sentences precisely the meaning they intend, they should ask someone else to read through the passage.

Coherence and Sentence Combining. Coherence problems are clearly stylistic as well as structural. If we feel our students need more practice than they get in their revising activities, I recommend open sentence-combining exercises.[12] (See Chapter 7.) To turn sentence kernels into a coherent paragraph, they will be compelled to make decisions about using repetition and transitional devices appropriately.

Diagnosing and Remedying Problems of Emphasis

Because even the simplest composition contains a number of ideas competing for a reader's attention, it is important that writers give the most significant of these ideas the most emphasis. Establishing the appropriate emphasis is central to stylistic considerations; but emphasis, for good or for ill, is also established in the very structure of a composition. There are two main ways to achieve emphasis structurally: by the proportion of the work devoted to an idea and by where an idea is placed in the essay.

EMPHASIS BY PROPORTION. To achieve a quantitative sort of emphasis, it is a good rule of thumb to assign the space in a composition roughly in proportion to the importance of each idea:

> The greater the importance of an idea to the overall point, and to convincing the reader to accept that point as worthy of consideration, the more space that should be devoted to it.

This principle may seem obvious, but unfortunately it is one our students sometimes disregard.

The Writer's Fatigue Problem. Too often, inexperienced writers begin their compositions with enthusiasm and cover the early points fully, only to find themselves running out of steam with only the energy to summarize their final points briefly. Unfortunately, this mode of writing creates papers that often do not reflect their authors' intentions. If, for example, a writer organizes an essay's ideas in the usually effective order of least to most important, the most important ideas, occurring later, will be the ones slighted should a decline in energy set in. The results are particularly disastrous when the problem occurs in an essay based upon the "although clause" structure, where the other side is explicated first with the writer's point of view following and refuting it. The effect of writers' fatigue here is to emphasize the "although" side at the expense of the writer's own.

There are three good revision strategies we can offer our student when writers' fatigue is the problem:

1. When the early part of her draft pleases her, she can leave it pretty much as written, and (perhaps having fortified herself with a nap or an apple) rewrite the final section(s) with the same care and spirit with which she began.
2. If the early part seems wordy or overdone, he can cut it down and do less rewriting with the later parts. This alternative needs a caveat, though. Often when the first portions are too profuse, the latter portions tend to be too scanty.
3. A third alternative is to shift the controlling idea itself to match the emphasis that the writing has taken. If the student now finds the "although" position more interesting than her original controlling idea—and since writers tend to discover their thoughts by writing, this reversal is not as rare as one would think—she can vary her stance. In this case, she needs first to write a new introduction and beginning section(s) and then to revise what she had written earlier to serve as the main focus of the paper.

Since all these alternatives involve fairly extensive revision, we should probably warn our students that whenever they are writing and sense fatigue creeping over them, they should stop, rest, and refresh themselves before continuing.

EMPHASIS BY POSITION.   Another way to put emphasis on certain ideas is to give them a prominent position in the paper. Beginnings and endings are the sections that readers are most impressed with and remember longest. They are the parts, therefore, that make the best showcase for a writer's most important ideas.

When students check over their paper (or a partner's paper) for revision, they should make sure that the controlling idea is either stated outright or prepared for early in their paper and that it is given a resounding declaration toward the end. They should also check the supporting paragraphs so that no idea of importance is permitted to get lost in midparagraph or midsentence. They also will need to be sure that all points of any prominence have at least a sentence or two of their own, and that these important ideas are positioned at the beginning or end of the paragraph. Students should also check for a shift of emphasis at the close. They should, for example, watch that no "By the way, I forgot to mention earlier . . ." or "On the other hand . . ." sort of material is included in the conclusion.

Checklist

We can help our students revise for structure by providing them with a good checklist and, at least in the beginning, requiring its use. The Student Guidelines can easily be modified to fit the special needs of our own students.

STUDENT GUIDELINES

Revising for Structure

Key: Keep your organizing idea in mind. Try to achieve:

UNITY

1. Check to see that every paragraph and every sentence contributes to supporting the organizing idea.
2. Be sure that the sentences in each paragraph support the paragraph's topic sentence.

COHERENCE

1. Read your essay carefully to see if your ideas come across clearly and if they follow one another in a reasonable manner. If you are not completely certain, ask someone else to examine your paper with these points in mind.
2. If your rereading uncovers coherence problems in the presentation of your major ideas, return to your outline and shift its points about until you discover a logical ordering. Then reorder the sections of your paper to fit it. Do not hesitate to "cut and paste."
3. If your rereading discovers problems of coherence within your paragraphs, reorganize the offending paragraphs. Discard any intruding material. If you have difficulty locating the specific problem, try the TRI or the Christensen method of analysis.
4. If your ideas are logically placed and yet your paragraphs still do not seem to hang together properly, examine your linkage systems.
   • Check to see if there is enough repetition to guide the reader through the pattern of your ideas.
   • Check to see that your transitional words and phrases relate your ideas to each other appropriately.

EMPHASIS

1. Make sure that the amount of space you have allotted to each idea coincides with its importance.
2. Be especially careful that your "although" material does not overpower your own point.
3. Make sure that you have placed discussion of your major points at the end and/or at the beginning of your essay and that you have not buried them in midparagraph or midsentence.

Revision Teaching Strategies

FULL-CLASS TEACHING.   Some revision strategies can be taught to the class as a whole. For example, David Wallace and John Hayes taught students to revise globally in an eight-minute presentation. By using overhead transparencies to illustrate how an expert writer and a novice writer revised a similar text, they were able to show the students how

> the novice began to make changes immediately [but] . . . limited himself to eliminating spelling, wordiness, and grammar errors, [while] the expert writer . . . read through the entire text to identify major problems and then focused on improving the whole text. . . . [In] also address[ing] global issues, [he] added an initial purpose statement, select[ed] and delet[ed] information for the specified audience, reorganiz[ed] the text, and provid[ed] explicit cues to the new overall organization. (59)

Students who heard this presentation produced both statistically significantly more global revision and better papers.

Such minilectures delivered before a test or an in-class essay assignment can work in our classrooms too. The key to their success lies in the students' perceiving that this knowledge will serve an immediate and personal need. And surely this is the appropriate context for all our work with the unity, coherence, and emphasis revising strategies if we want to engage our students' minds with this material.

Returning Themes.   Deriving comparable gain from a discussion of returned themes is much less likely. For although I heartily recommend sharing good papers with the class because it is an enjoyable experience for everyone and promotes author confidence, little carryover to the next assignment takes place. Reading bad examples of student writing is seriously detrimental to student morale, and in any case is seldom useful. Ordinarily, most students see discussion of completed assignments as an autopsy on ideas now dead and suppurating. Full-class discussion of revising techniques will work when—and only when—we can bring each student to feel that the information to be gained applies to him or her personally and that he or she can put it to immediate use.

APPLYING THE KNOWLEDGE.   Unfortunately, there is often a gap between knowing and applying what one knows. And this gap is particularly pronounced when we are talking about revision skills. The problem is that if our students are diligent in writing their papers—and most of the time, most of them are—the papers will reflect the best the students can manage at the time. An inexperienced writer who has already made his paper as good as he is capable of doing at the time will be hard put to improve it without some help. Rereading may turn up surface errors or infelicities that he can spot and correct. But, as research has confirmed, inexperienced writers—even when encouraged to revise—do not know how to make major changes without intervention.[13] Just as novice tennis players will make mistakes and, if not shown differently, will continue to make them and thus reinforce their errors each time they hit the ball, so writers, without corrective intervention, will make the same mistakes repeatedly.

INTERVENTION.   Intervention can come in a variety of shapes and sizes. It can come as an outside reader: a parent, a sibling, a friend, or a roommate. In the academic setting, we can provide the intervention by setting up student partnerships or peer groups, or by arranging one-on-one conferences with a tutor or with the teacher. The pedagogical goal of all this intervention is not so much to make the product, the composition, something the student can be proud of—though surely that is not an insignificant outcome—but rather to help students internalize the process so that, as experienced writers, they can provide their *own* intervention.

Peer-group intervention (which we will discuss later in this chapter) offers the possibility of an intimacy, unlikely in a full-class situation, in which trust can develop and a noninjuring frankness can be encouraged. Since the groups meet simultaneously, they also have the advantage of providing all students at once with an opportunity to have their papers discussed and to be themselves active discussants. And students can learn to revise successfully in these groups. Nevertheless, the most effective way to reach the student and produce that "Aha" revision experience is a one-on-one meeting in the student–teacher conference.

HOLDING STUDENT–TEACHER CONFERENCES

Advantages

Scholars, researchers, and teachers endorse this form of intervention over other forms. They do so for a number of reasons:

1. *Conferences individualize teaching.* "It is an incomparable means of individualizing the teaching-learning relationship," as Jan Turbill phrases it. According to Roger Garrison, "A class doesn't have writing problems; only individuals have problems saying what they mean." In Donald Murray's words, "Each student in the class is facing his own problems at his own pace."

2. *Conferences provide the support immediately needed.* In conference, each student is given help in figuring out explicitly what she needs to do with the particular problem at hand. As Charles Cooper explains: "Writers are not helped by being told in advance what to avoid. They need to write, to get immediate supportive, helpful response to what they have written, and then to write again."

3. *Conferences demonstrate the actual impact of writing on a reader.* As Muriel Harris notes, "Since the writing teacher reacts as a reader, students can see

that writing is primarily an act of communication in which the needs of
the reader are crucial considerations."

4. *Conferences provide expertise.* When the teacher is a conferee, the student
   gains not only a reader, but a reader experienced in reacting to student
   texts, a reader knowledgeable about structure and style and sensitive to
   student needs, a reader able to offer the kind of guidance not elsewhere
   available to the student, as Lester Fisher and Donald Murray point out.[14]

RESEARCH CONFIRMS EFFECTIVENESS.   The usefulness of student–
teacher conferences is also confirmed by much research. It demonstrates, for
instance, that conferences help underachievers at the elementary, junior high,
and high school levels work up to their potential: and as J. P. Shaver and D.
Nuhn discovered, this learning growth continues as much as two years later.
Conferences also are more successful than other pedagogical techniques with
college freshmen who need remedial work, as studies by D. G. Sutton and
D. S. Arnold and by Allan Gates confirm. Conferences also help nonremedial
college freshmen in both two-year and four-year programs, according to the
research of Myrna Smith and Barbara Bretcko and of Mildred Fritts. The
Smith-Bretcko study is interesting in that only the first two of six conferences
showed statistically significant improvement. Only one study of conferencing
that I have come across fails to show improvement in the conferenced students over the control group (it was conducted by Judith Budz and Terry
Grabar), but here the results were not statistically significant.[15]

Moreover, research shows that students feel themselves growing in their
writing skills through conferences with their teachers. Even the students in
the Budz and Grabar study were "unanimously favorable" to conferencing.
And "the great majority" of the students from the University of New Hampshire writing program that Thomas Carnicelli surveyed "felt they had learned
a great deal from . . . the conference method." Perhaps most spectacularly,
every one of the 1,800 students he surveyed found conferences more useful
than classes.[16]

HOW A CONFERENCE WORKS.   The writing conference between an
insightful composition teacher and a receptive student can be a most remarkable occurrence. The student comes in with an essay in which she has tried
to get across her ideas. She may have a vague feeling that she hasn't quite
done so, but for the life of her she can't figure out why. The student has a
blind spot where the effective communicating of her ideas is concerned. Her
habitual way of structuring her perspective, as cognitive psychologists say,
prevents her both from understanding the reason why her paper doesn't quite
work and from being able to improve it. The teacher has the opportunity to
remove the blind spot, to turn on the electric bulb and help the student to a
new perspective. By leading her to understand how she might "fix up" the
current paper, the teacher can subtly indicate a new way of structuring
thought which, with reinforcement and practice, should free the student to

write better essays in the future. That moment when the lightbulb goes on, as we all know, is what teaching is all about. The individual student–teacher conference is the best way there is—some say the only way—to achieve such moments in the teaching of composition.

Conducting the Conference

Since a conference is a very personal mode of teaching, each of us will handle ours in a somewhat different way. There are, however, a number of techniques that teachers have found helpful. And though we each modify our use of these techniques to fit our own personality and our own approach, the principles upon which they are based have an underlying validity. Carnicelli's expression of these principles is, I believe, particularly helpful. He derives the "essential tasks that a conference teacher must perform" from the student comments he collected in his survey. According to Carnicelli, in a conference the teacher should:

- Read the paper carefully.
- Offer encouragement.
- Ask the right questions. Carnicelli suggests:

   "What's your purpose in this paper?"
   "What parts of your paper do you like the most?"
   "What parts of your paper did you have trouble with?"

- Evaluate the paper: "[T]he teacher's task is not to force students to write in a certain way, but to persuade students to adopt certain values, [the common criteria of good writing,] by demonstrating their usefulness and validity" (116).
- Make specific suggestions for revising the paper.
- Listen to the student (105–111).[17]

What follows here is another, more detailed, set of conferencing procedures—procedures completely compatible with Carnicelli's suggested tasks. These procedures have been tested and proved by experience to provide a way by which a teacher might guide a student from the first hesitant beginnings of a conference through to a productive conclusion.

DISPELLING ANXIETY. When a student approaches the conference room or desk, he naturally experiences apprehension, for he knows that his paper, his surrogate self, is to be held up to close scrutiny at what appears to him to be an awesome bar of judgment. Such anxiety, of course, deters learning; therefore, we must try our hardest to dispel it.

Even if the two or three interviews preceding the arrival of this student have demanded our most intense concentration, we should make every effort to turn our complete attention to the newcomer. We are naturally glad to see him, and we need to let him know that we are. We can show our pleasure in any way with which we are comfortable: a smile, a cordial greeting, perhaps a compliment or a moment of friendly chitchat about the weather or the news. Even if the rest of the conference is going to eschew the personal and be confined fairly strictly to what is on the written page and the thoughts that lie behind it, it is important to establish a warm and accepting ambience right from the start. The student is a person, not a disembodied intellect; and only when the person is comfortable can the intellect function at its best.

We should seat our student where the two of us can read his paper together. Sitting on either side of a corner desk or table probably gives both of us the best access to the paper under consideration. Sitting opposite decidedly weakens the opportunity for mutual endeavor, and adds an authoritarian symbolism that is counterproductive.[18] When we are sure our student is comfortable, the conference proper can begin.

READING, REACTING, AND COMMENTING ON THE GOOD POINTS. Some teachers prefer to read the paper for the first time with a student in the conference. With this method, students can see an actual reader responding to their work. They can witness at firsthand our delight in some passages, and perhaps our confusion at others. New teachers may need time to feel comfortable with this method, but it *is* feasible—especially with brief papers—and it is time-saving.

Other instructors elect to annotate the paper before the conference and then give it a quick glance or two as a reminder at conference time. Inexperienced teachers often feel more secure with this method. But in choosing we must exercise caution. Having analyzed the student's paper and formed our own ideas about it ahead of time, we need to take special care not to dominate the conference.

Others of us prefer taking a first overview of the essay at the conference before working with it and its author. Using this method, we might skim the essay, taking particular note of its central idea and the way it is developed. We should not spend too long at this reading, however; we will want to spare students the painful suspense that can develop when the wait for a teacher's reaction is drawn out.

Emphasize Content. Whatever method we choose, our first response should be to the content of the essay, to what the student is saying. Barbara Fassler [Walvoord] proffers an analogy to a teacher's reception of a student's paper that gives real insight into the feelings of the student writer:

> When a child brings you a drawing, you do not begin by succinctly pointing out its faults. You begin by reacting to what it is meant to be: "Ah! a tree! Is that the same tree you climbed yesterday in the park?" A student's paper, like a child's drawing, is a gift, a self revelation, a communication.[19]

So it is. When we make our first response, we must, as Fisher and Murray insist, "establish ourselves as respectful, receptive readers" (170). And when we give our first evaluative impressions, we should find a way to say something both favorable and honest about the work. In those rare instances in which the particular composition we are examining is a total disaster, we might remind our student of the merits of an earlier paper or of a wise comment she made in class. Since a certain amount of self-confidence is a necessity for the production of good writing, we must find some sincere way to assure our student that she has the potential to write a really fine paper, a paper we both can be proud of.

DECIDING ON A SINGLE PROBLEM AREA.   We might begin by asking our student what area he believes to be the greatest source of his paper's difficulties. Almost always, if the student is not actually stymied or too shy to voice an opinion, he will hit upon some aspect of the major problem.

We might share our views with him, discuss the problem together, and come to some mutual understanding about our approach to revision. It is important that we direct our revision work toward one major area, because it is almost impossible for a student to address a whole proliferation of problems together. Furthermore, if we try to correct all the faults at once, our student may become so overwhelmed by the amount of revision to be accomplished — and by the magnitude of his ineptness — that he may quietly give up before he begins. In fact, if Carol Laque and Phyllis Sherwood are right, the entire success of the conference method may well "depend upon the instructor's ability to focus on the major problem of the paper." They suggest considering the paper with a sequence of priorities in mind and selecting for concentration that problem area which has the highest degree of priority in the sequence. The sequence Laque and Sherwood recommend is, with only a couple of small modifications, that which has been implied in the present work.[20] For them, too, considerations of structure precede considerations of style:

1. [Central Idea or] Thesis
2. Organization
3. Development
4. Voice
5. Sentence Structure
6. Diction
7. Punctuation
8. Spelling

First Things First.   Why should we focus the emphasis of our dialogue in this manner? Let's consider the flawed paper as a patient who is troubled by both typhoid and acne. If we, as physicians, begin by treating the acne, the patient might very well die of typhoid fever before we get the acne cleared up. Should we begin by treating the typhoid, however, the acne might well be on its way to complete recovery by the time the patient is cured of his typhoid. This result is even more likely when we consider that the hormonal imbalance brought on by the more serious illness may very well be an underlying cause of the surface affliction.

Though perhaps farfetched, the analogy of taking care of the minor ill in the process of curing the major one turns out to be quite exact. Laque and Sherwood cite a number of examples of student papers rewritten in order to correct structural flaws that eliminated most of their mechanical errors in the process. I also have often noted that the quality of sentence structure and diction in the papers of my students directly reflects the clarity of their understanding and expression of their ideas. But even in cases where the mechanical errors are more deeply rooted and cannot be eliminated so patly, first things still must come first. Students who can express their central points clearly and back them up logically can still be understood, can still get their ideas across, even when their syntax or spelling leaves a good bit to be desired.[21]

GOING OVER THE PAPER TOGETHER.   The next step (sometimes the first step) might be a thorough reading of the paper by teacher and student together. While we read, we might be searching for manifestations of the basic problem and for ways to solve it. The entire task should be student-oriented. The conference is not meant to be a time when a teacher evaluates a student's work with the student in attendance, but rather a time when the student figures out the ways she can improve her work, aided by the teacher's helpful guidance. After all, the paper is the student's and all the ideas must come from her. Before she can rewrite, she has to come to a clear understanding of the difficulties for herself. The teacher's duty, then, is to elicit the student's ideas when they do not come forth spontaneously and to ask the kinds of questions that will help her discover both difficulties and remedies for herself.

CONSTRUCTING A PLAN OF ACTION.   After we have gone over our student's paper and discussed it thoroughly with him, we are ready to help him make a plan of action from which he will rewrite his essay. Notwithstanding the necessary centricity of the student in the analysis of his paper, we must not be afraid to offer real and substantial aid in directing him toward his rewriting, especially in the beginning assignments. We must help him find a way to express his ideas effectively. He should leave the conference not only with a precise idea of how he will construct his revised paper and the confidence to do it well, but also with a concrete written plan to serve as his tool in revision.

As much of the input into the written plan as possible should be the student's own and certainly all of the ideas should be his but if we have to help structure the plan for a conference or two, we must not feel we are interfering with the student's learning. In fact, it has been my experience that after a couple of assignments have been conferred over, controlling ideas revised, and structural plans constructed — with teacher help where needed — and revised compositions rewritten from these plans, even the less able students are well on their way to being able to construct a clearly organized paper completely on their own.

Handling Structural Problems in the Conference

Most conferences on early expository papers will be concerned with high-priority structural problems. We will see papers that have no controlling ideas at all or that express controlling ideas that do not reflect the structure of the rest of the paper or that do not reflect what the student wants to say. Or the expressed controlling idea might say what the student has in mind but not be supported by the rest of the paper. Or the problem may be some combination of these possibilities.

DIAGNOSIS. Whatever the difficulty, the solution can come only after a careful diagnosis; and this diagnosis is not easily made. We must exercise an earnest concentration both in analyzing the paper and in questioning the student to discover what the student wishes to get across and what the paper does in fact say. We also need concentrated deliberation to discover possibilities for reconciling the differences between what is meant and what is said in an orderly and persuasive way.

To this end, when we go through the essay with our student, we might observe the controlling idea and its relationship to the structure, asking the questions that will help us discover any discrepancies between the two or between the stated and implied controlling idea. If the paper seems fairly well organized, we might work out its underlying structural plan with its author, get the plan jotted down, and then help our student find ways to modify it so that the revised paper will structure the ideas more effectively. If the organization is obscure, we might instead ask the student to jot down the separate ideas the paper contains as we go along, with the goal of relating them to one another and eventually constructing a workable organization based on these relationships.

Helping Students Discover their Point. If our student's ideas are not spelled out clearly in the paper, we might question her about them so they can be recorded accurately. When the paper has no discernible controlling idea, the accumulation of ideas jotted down from the paper or from our questions can be used as a sort of inventory from which the student might discover where she wants to focus her ideas. When the existing focus is inadequate, these notes might be used in a similar way to modify the controlling idea so that it fits the content of the essay more accurately.

Where there are information gaps in an essay — that is, where there are not enough retrievable ideas to flesh out or even to bring into being that which the student clearly wants to get across — we must question him in a sensitive way, listen carefully to his answers, and make sure the salient points are recorded. Occasionally, we will meet an essay that contains almost no retrievable material relevant to the subject. In these instances, most of the inventory of ideas recorded will have to be based upon this sort of interrogation.

A Sample Conference

It is very difficult to convey the method of conducting this sort of conference through a mere explication of procedures because every conference raises different problems and requires different solutions. So much of the way we handle the encounter is subjective, even intuitive. For this reason, I include here excerpts from a transcription of a taped student–teacher conference. This transcription is in no way meant to be taken as a model of "The Perfect Conference." Rather, I offer it as a sample of the kind of conference techniques that can work to help students produce revisions appreciably better than their original efforts and which thus contribute to their growth.

A CONFERENCE

Steve wrote the following essay as an in-class theme during the first week of a composition course:

> It is extremely hard to find one book that means the most to me. After reading literally thousands, they are all sort of equally equal. But after sifting through, the Book most important to me would turn out to be, in reality, four books. I realize this sounds strange, but the book that has helped to shape my life so far is J. R. R. Tolkien's immortal trilogy and its Preface, The Hobbit.
>
> It really isn't the Book itself, but the effects of having read the book that means a lot to me. After reading The Lord of the Rings in fourth grade, essentially the first books I can remember enjoying, the very word "Reading" took on a new meaning. It wasn't a dull word connoting Drudgery. It was an exciting word, full of New Things and Fantastic Ideas. Since then, I have been reading no-stop, and I now read about a book a day. I almost exhausted the Walnut Hills High School Library, and I have read every book at home. And I love every word.
>
> But that is not the only reason The Lord of the Rings is so important to me. After reading the trilogy, I started talking about it, and writing letters to people and I don't know what all else. Eventually, I had a small (3 letters) correspondence with Dr. Tolkien himself, and a couple of other more voluminous correspondences with some of his cohorts and other various people around the world. My interest in Linguistics stems from this as does my Wargaming fever. From one of these contacts, Dr. P. E. I. Bonewits of U. Cal. Berkeley, I received a

continued

copy of "Dungeons and Dragons," the premier fantasy wargame, and, after playing it a number of times and many others like it, I designed a number of games and I am now reaping good profits from the sale of these games.

As if that isn't enough, my entire group of friends revolves around Wargaming, and I count that a direct result of Tolkiens books.

So, I suppose you could say that almost my entire life has been affected by a book that has almost nothing to do with reality (or "reality as we know it" as a few of my colleagues would say.)

After some friendly preliminaries, the conference began in earnest:

Teacher: What do you see as the source of the difficulty?

Steve: Um . . . Not defining the one thing, the one idea and really sticking to it. But just throwing out lots of ideas and not defining the main one and . . .

Teacher: And? . . . But that's it.

Steve: Yeh. (Chuckle) Exactly.

Teacher: Actually, it does define an idea. I mean, it does and it doesn't

Steve: It does?

Teacher: Yeh. You had it focused. And obviously that's an important thing. And you know how to write to a point. And here you had an in-class theme with no time to really gather your thoughts. But you didn't forget. Look here: (Reads aloud through first paragraph) . . . "The book that has helped to shape my life so far is J. R. R. Tolkien's immortal trilogy and its Preface, The Hobbit." So the point is "Helped to shape my life."

Steve: Yuh.

Teacher: The question was "Importance to me" and you switched it over to "helped to shape my life." And you tried in each paragraph to get back to how this has shaped your life. I suspect . . . I suspect the reason the paper doesn't completely satisfy is that "It helped to shape my life" . . .

Steve: Is so . . .

Teacher: Is so . . . —and although each one of these paragraphs does somehow attempt to prove it—it's such a large thing—I mean, to SHAPE A LIFE! (Mutual laughter)

Steve: That's quite a lot, isn't it? (More mutual chuckling)

Teacher: So, I think . . . If we could narrow the scope of your controlling idea. "Helped to shape your life . . . (Pondering)

Steve: (Pondering, a few false starts) I'm really not sure.

Teacher: Well, what we could do . . . is go through and read your paper . . . and use it as if it were an inventory of your ideas.

Steve: Mmm. Hmm. (Quiet assent)

Teacher: And get them all down and then sort them out and then look at them and try to see what your essay really has said. And you have said a lot of good things. It really isn't a bad paper at all. Especially under the circumstances . . . the first day . . . an in-class theme. No, it's really quite good. Lots of boyish charm (Mutual laughter) in there. But it does get away from you sometimes.

Steve: Yeh, it does.

Teacher: (Pause. Skims quickly through the first paragraph and then reads from the beginning of the second paragraph): "It really isn't the Book itself, but the effects of having read the book that means a lot to me."

Steve: Not too good. Not real clear.

Teacher: Not really. So what you are trying to say there . . . is . . . that there is nothing really important to you within the book, but just what the book led you to do?

Steve: Yes.

Teacher: (Musing) That isn't true. . . . That can't be true. Do you think it's true?

Steve: I think so, yeh.

Teacher: I mean there must be something in the book that made you . . . want to correspond with its author and the rest. . . .

Steve: Well. . . .

Teacher: There's got to be. If we could maybe isolate that . . . that might be . . .

Steve: That (uh) might be it. . . . We just might . . . stumble on the point. At least . . .

Teacher: Right. (Mutual chuckles)

Steve: But I'm not sure . . .

Teacher: What do you think it was that attracted you to it so much?

Steve: Its all the weird things that happen in it. All the elves and fairies and hobbits and dwarfs, and stuff like that.

Teacher: What else?

Steve: Oh, the medieval setting. I've always been interested in that.

Teacher: So you liked books with medieval atmosphere, but Tolkien did it best? Is that it?

Steve: And it was the first book I read that wasn't about anything here, that took you totally away from this world and created a world for itself, a fantasy world, that's what it is.

Teacher: The first book?

Steve: Yea. Probably the first. I like fantasy books. You know, they make up a world and try to stick to it—one with its own laws, and logical possibilities and things like that.

Teacher: Had you read *Alice in Wonderland?*

Steve: Yuh, but that was different.

Teacher: It was fantasy too, so maybe there's something in the difference.

Steve: I don't know. Possibly it's that I didn't take *Alice in Wonderland* seroiusly. But I do take Tolkien seriously.

Teacher: Why is that, do you think?

[Discussion of Alice as fantasy and satire omitted.]

Steve: Maybe it's that *Alice* is too much fantasy. And it's different from the other. Tolkien's stuff is serious fantasy.

Teacher: You say serious. Is it like C. S. Lewis's fantasies where there's philosophy and religion in it?

Steve: No. Not at all. It's like . . . It's an adventure story . . . similar to a western, only it's a miniworld where magic works, and there's dragons and weird things flying around—things like you see in your sleep. And then the good guy with the white hat, Tolkien makes him a little, tiny, odd sort of fellow with hair on his feet, who eats a lot. And then he makes the guy who looks over him—you know, there is always somebody there who is powerful and mysterious—and he makes him a magician. And the bad guy who is always trying to take over, he makes him a wizard, a wizard that doesn't even have a body, just evil and bad. And . . . that's Tolkien.

Teacher: So there's something in this that's primeval—like good versus evil.

Steve: Oh yuh . . . That's the whole thing. The good versus evil. That's . . . the whole thing. I'm really into the wargame thing. And that is what it's about. You see, there are three sides you can possibly be: Good and Evil and Neutral. . . . Though, of course, there are also shades of grey. But ultimately it's the forces of good versus the forces of evil. That's what it's all about.

[Discussion of the epic and its similarity to the primeval aspects of "serious fantasy" omitted.]

Teacher: So the wargames part. There's your "serious," isn't it? That's what you mean by "serious?" "A fantasy that is serious?"

Steve: Yes. In *Alice in Wonderland*, there is no conflict there except maybe Alice and the Queen. Always hollering, "Off with her head. Off with her head." (Mutual chuckles) Not a serious conflict anyway. [Discussion of the conflict of reason versus unreason in *Alice* omitted.]

Steve: But Tolkien is serious fantasy.

Teacher: I think now you have really hit what it is you find in Tolkien.

Steve: Mmmm mhmm. (Quiet assent)

Teacher: So what is beginning to take form is what brought you to this attraction. Do you want to show that first? And then maybe show how your tremendous attraction for this has shaped your life.

Steve: Mmm mhmm. (Quiet assent)

Teacher: And maybe that's what's wrong here in the essay—that this essential linking point is missing.

Steve: Yuh. (With enthusiasm)

Teacher: What it is about these books . . .

Steve: Mmm hmmm.

Teacher: Maybe that is it. . . . Well, let's go through your essay and see. [Teacher and student now read through the paper together, the teacher pausing along the way to comment on such passages as "The very word 'reading' took on new meaning. It wasn't a dull word connoting Drudgery. It was an exciting word, full of new things and exciting ideas."]

Teacher: This passage is vague as it stands, but if you had already put into your paper the sort of things we have just talked about, this sentence would have had real meaning.

Steve: Yup.

Teacher: You would have already explained it.

Steve: (Chuckle)

Teacher: [Most of the teacher's comments were on substance, but occasionally she remarked on grammar points, spelling, and the like.] This error in syntax will straighten itself out when you rewrite. Let's skip it for now.

Thus, they went through the paper, marking down salient points as they reached them. And when they were finished, their worksheet looked something like the one in Figure 5–1.

Figure 5–1. Conference Worksheet

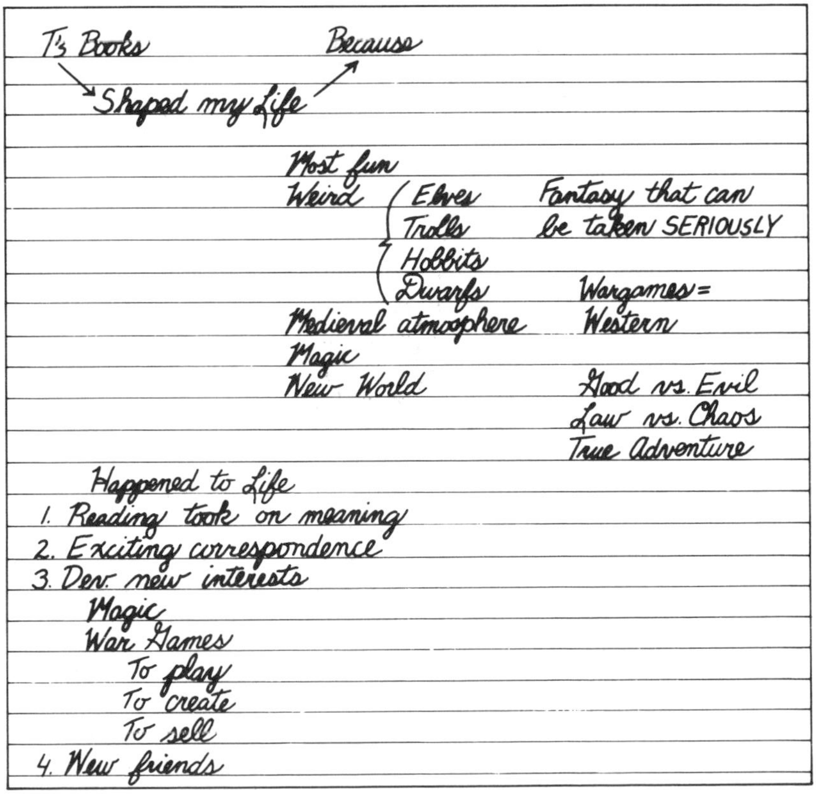
T's Books
Because
Shaped my Life
Most fun
Weird
Elves
Trolls
Hobbits
Dwarfs
Fantasy that can be taken SERIOUSLY
Medieval atmosphere
Magic
New World
Wargames = Western
Good vs. Evil
Law vs. Chaos
True Adventure
Happened to Life
1. Reading took on meaning
2. Exciting correspondence
3. Dev. new interests
Magic
War Games
To play
To create
To sell
4. New friends

Working together, Steve and his teacher played with these ideas until they came up with the following working thesis and structural plan:

Working Thesis: Because Tolkien's books gave me my first contact with the world of serious fantasy, they have shaped my life.
1. Introduction
2. Tolkien's books = World of serious fantasy
   • Fantasy world
   • Serious
3. Results
   • Reading took on meaning
   • Entered into exciting correspondences
     – Tolkien
     – Bonewits
     – Others
   • Developed new interests
     – Magic
     – Wargames
        Playing the games
        Creating and inventing new games
        Publishing and selling new games (receiving royalties)
   • Built friendships around new interests
4. Conclusion

Surveying their handiwork, Steve and his teacher agreed that he would be able to write a richer, more meaningful essay working from this outline. And the conference came to its end.

The Value of Conferencing.   In the give and take of conferences like this one and in the private struggle and hard work of the follow-up rewriting, our students learn how to write. Sometimes during these conferences and often in the rewritten papers, we can catch a glimpse of learning in progress, a glimpse of that which gives our profession its meaning and its joy.

Conferencing Problems: The Problem of Teacher Time

Regardless of the potential for learning inherent in the student–teacher revision conference, the method is not without problems. The two most troublesome difficulties are the problems of teacher time and of student dependency.

Conferences are time-consuming. There is no getting around that fact. We English teachers are notoriously overworked: on top of our heavy teaching schedules, we have a constant influx of papers to respond to. Our students learn by writing; and if they write, we must read. The problem is especially difficult for high school teachers in those districts that insist that English instructors teach up to six periods a day. And for the many students dependent on bus schedules, out-of-class conferencing is all but impossible.

Nevertheless, student–teacher conferencing can be so significant to a student's growth that, in my opinion, we should explore every possibility within our own situation to provide this opportunity. Fortunately, there are a number of strategies teachers have discovered and used successfully to minimize the time strain — strategies we can try or modify to fit our own needs.

THE COLD-TURKEY OPTION.   To eliminate long hours of preliminary paper grading, some teachers read a paper for the first time during a conference with its author. It takes fifteen minutes or so whether we grade a paper thoroughly or meet with a student about it; but conferencing time is far more productive for student revision, as a considerable body of research attests.[22] Conferencing in this way does not eliminate paper marking entirely. But grading the final draft, revised after the conference, is a much easier chore because the paper is now familiar and because we need not include directions for revision.

Furthermore, letting students watch us respond to their papers has inherent advantages (see page 162). As Muriel Harris writes, "Whatever happens in this unrehearsed setting, writers have the opportunity to witness readers reading their prose (*Teaching One-to-One* 43).

Conferencing can even save grading time for those of us who are more comfortable collecting and viewing student papers ahead of time. It is not necessary to mark a student's paper thoroughly before a conference. All we need to do is glance at it to get some ideas and perhaps jot down a thought or two as a reminder before the conference.

CONFERENCING AMID A WRITING WORKSHOP.   A number of teachers, both in the schools and at the college level, have enjoyed particular success in teaching writing — and have made time demands manageable — by turning their composition classrooms into writing workshops. They hold brief conferences throughout the class period while their students work individually on their own writing projects at their own pace. All instruction is individually tailored, except for brief minilessons — as Nancie Atwell calls them.[23]

With all this diverse activity, how can chaos be kept at bay? Donald Graves suggests beginning each class period with a "status-of-the-class" group conference to find out exactly what each student will be doing that day. When attendance is called, the students tell what topic they're working on, what draft, whether they will be conferencing with a fellow student, or whether they would like to meet with the teacher.[24] Nancie Atwell recommends keeping track of this information on weekly status forms (91).

In the least structured versions of the writer's workshop, such as those of Graves and Atwell, the teacher serves as facilitator or as coach. In more structured versions, such as those advocated by Roger Garrison and Thomas Carnicelli (see notes 14 and 16), the teacher plays the role of editor. In these versions, the teacher designs student projects and assignments and meets with students in three- to five-minute conferences throughout the class period to help them solve the specific writing problems that occur in the course of composition.

Individualized Writing Plus Class and Conference. Donald Murray, who describes his method in detail in "The Listening Eye, Reflections on the Writing Conference," uses a variation of the class-as-workshop strategy. Students work at their own pace on their own writing projects and come into faculty offices for regularly scheduled fifteen- to twenty-minute conferences. In most variations of this procedure, academic classes are also provided.[25]

Individualized Writing Saves Teacher Time. Individualized-writing-conference strategies seem to have been successful both in terms of student satisfaction and of improved papers. Many instructors also consider them to be the most time-efficient of any composition pedagogy. Murray, for example, writes almost apologetically about how easy his method is — and how well it works:

> Each year I teach less and less, and my students seem to learn more. I guess what I've learned to do is to stay out of their way and not to interfere with their learning. ("Listening Eye" 16)

And Carnicelli argues persuasively that — even for the instructor with "outrageous teaching conditions," with five composition sections and 175 students — workshop teaching is the most time-efficient way to teach composition:

> A teacher who is willing to give up classes and written comments on student papers — no great losses educationally — can teach effectively by individual conference. . . . Conference teaching is a practical option, not an impossible ideal. (111)

Too Much of a Good Thing? The major criticism raised against the workshop-conferencing method is that it may be too much of a good thing. Although this technique individualizes, it does not take differences in learning styles into account. It does not work for every student or for every assignment. It also can raise the problems of student dependence we will consider below. The good news is that workshop conferencing can also work when combined with other strategies. We might, for instance, use it two weeks at a time for writing units. Or, as teachers in some college freshman composition programs do, we might devote a day or two of every week's classroom time to this sort of learning.

Conferencing Problems: The Problem of Student Dependency

What is potentially finest in the conference method is the opportunity it offers for the growth of a student's individual, independent thought. Paradoxically, its greatest danger is the possibility of our inadvertent stifling of that independence. In every conference there is always the risk that we, as teachers, can become intrusive. Even when we are well aware of this risk, it is often really difficult to hold back and not intrude. All the personality, character, and intellectual traits that made us choose to be English teachers — as well as all our training in composition and language — push us to get involved personally with the student's paper and to help the student make it as good as *we* can make it. But if we are not careful in our enthusiasm, we can take over a student's thinking.

Our intrusion can produce a confused student and a confused paper. We know exactly how we would rewrite the paper ("Here, let me show you"). And we pressure the student to rewrite her paper in ways foreign to her thinking and to use ideas she doesn't quite grasp. Thomas Carnicelli in his most helpful article, "The Writing Conference," includes a transcript of just such a conference. His analysis provides insight into why such conferences fail:

> [The teacher] heard the student's idea . . . [and] acknowledged it — but she was not alert to the possibilities in it. The student brought it up repeatedly and was eager to supply specific details. These were strong "clues" that the subject had potential. The teacher didn't hear them. Nor did she seem to hear how unresponsive the student was to [her] idea throughout most of the conference. The teacher kept on pushing that idea until she ended up virtually forcing it on the student. The revised draft is the worst of both worlds. (129)

Yet even if we mold the student's thinking adequately and the paper is a success, we still have not achieved our pedagogical goal: the learning experience has been ours — not our student's.

Even the most skilled of us fall into this pattern from time to time — it is so very hard not to overhelp. How do we avoid it? By deliberately concentrating on listening to the student. What is his agenda for the conference? What is her purpose in the paper?

To forestall this problem, Murray adopts a deliberately nondirective stance. Here are some useful questions he has worked out:

> What did you learn from this piece of writing?
>
> What do you intend to do in the next draft?
>
> What surprised you in the draft?
>
> What do you like best in the piece of writing?
>
> What questions do you have of me? ("Listening Eye" 16.)

THE TEACHER AS CRUTCH.   Sometimes the better job we do with each interview, the greater the danger that we will build up a dependency in our student, especially if conferencing becomes routine. It's important to supply a crutch—while it is much needed. But when the broken bone heals, the patient should begin to walk on his own. He may return to the crutch for a particularly difficult effort, but a good doctor gradually weans him from it. As Muriel Harris puts it, "The teacher's goal is to work him—or herself out of a job, that is, to make the student independent" (*Teaching One-to-One*, 28).

LIMITED CONFERENCING: A PRACTICABLE SOLUTION.   The skills that are best taught in conference—and, indeed, are difficult to teach in any other way—are understanding expository focus and structure and learning how to manipulate them effectively, persuasively. It has been my experience that most students gain this knowledge—and it *is* breakthrough "Now-I-know-how-to-write" knowledge—in reworking their first or second conferenced, expository papers. Smith and Bretcko's findings that only the first two in a series of six mandatory conferences lead to statistically significant improvement in a student's revision skill tend to confirm these observations (See note 15).

If some student–teacher conferencing is essential, but too much can be damaging and, in any case, does not fit the time many of us have available, then limited conferencing would seem to be a solution. Where should we draw the line? I would recommend mandatory conferences for the first expository paper at least, and for the first two if we can possibly manage it. After that, peer-response intervention and/or workshop quickie-conference intervention should be sufficient. Of course, we should always give students the option to request fuller conferences when they need help with a writing problem they find particularly troubling.

Managing Limited Conferences.   Limited conferencing poses few difficulties on the college level. Composition instructors are expected to confer with their students; office space and hours are available for the purpose. We can jog class assignment dates so as not to be overburdened at any one time. If we pass out appointment schedules for our students to sign when papers come due, and if we let students know how serious we are about the importance of keeping appointments, conferences can proceed in an efficient manner.

Mandatory conferences for entire sets of papers speeds grading time since they will need little or no notation. And though we must read all papers in later sets, we can save a bit of time on them by making only cursory notation on those papers we feel need conferencing.

High school teachers are, on the whole, more circumscribed. Although some of us teach at schools run on modular schedules where students are permitted more freedom of movement more on the college model, most of us are bound by rigid schedules that make it very difficult to see most of our students any time during the school day except in our own class period and at that time only in the company of all the others. How then can we arrange conferences? Before- and afterschool preparation periods are a good time to schedule individual meetings with our students. Some schools, understanding the special burden carried by writing teachers, wisely provide us with extra work periods; others at least assign us monitoring duties in small study halls where conferences are feasible. We are limited, of course, to meeting during these periods only with those students who are free at those times. But we can turn an occasional class period into a "Reading Time" and schedule conferences for those students who cannot come to us at other times. Through a combination of these methods, and by limiting the number of mandatory conferences, we should be able to give each of our students the conference attention they need.

"Reading Time."   Reading periods are helpful for conferencing. If we sit as far from the readers as we can, speak very quietly, and avoid confidential discussion, we can make good use of this time. By working efficiently, we probably can schedule four 10–12 minute conferences per period—time enough to fit in students whose schedules do not otherwise jibe with ours. Where little or no outside-class conferencing time is available, we might schedule a "Reading Week" and confer with most of an entire class during this time.

In planning these reading days, we need not feel that we will be "wasting" the time of the nonconferees. We can provide interesting library materials and give the nonconferring students an opportunity to become reacquainted with the pure pleasure of reading. With the new emphasis on literacy and reading response theory, much has been written recently praising the classroom reading approach. Daniel Sheridan, for example, writes persuasively about "bringing reading into the classroom." He recommends alternating assigned reading with response discussion and concludes that once we have met the goal of "a room full of human readers,"

> we will have shown students that "literature" and "reading" are not two different things and that the classroom is a place for literature to happen."

Abraham Bernstein some years ago tried out free-reading time with several of his classes, including one made up primarily of poor readers. He concluded that reading days were not only essential for his purposes at his desk, but that they contributed markedly to the growth of the readers.[26] Free-reading periods or partial periods, then, would seem both to benefit our students and to provide us time for quiet conferences.

The strategies suggested in this chapter should make conferencing practicable and keep it from becoming a burden on our time. But even if limited conferencing represents an increase in teacher time, our reward is a tremendous increase in the effectiveness of our teaching.

TEACHING PEER REVISION

If we decide to limit our conferences with students, we need to provide an alternative intervention to spur effective revision. The most effective alternative is the peer-response group. Peer review, which can take place in small groups of three to five students or, often more successfully, in pairs, goes a long way toward solving the two major problems that can beset conferencing: it can counteract student dependence upon the teacher, and it can also cut down on our out-of-class work time.

Effective peer-response groups, however, are not easily achieved. Their success is dependent upon a good deal of thoughtful preparation. What we need to do, as James Moffett phrases it, "[is] to teach the students to teach each other." [27]

Building Sensitivity, Instilling Trust

Ask any effective teacher of the peer-group method what single effort contributes most to the success of this procedure and you will invariably hear the answer "Building trust." Unless an empathetic trust exists between students, a student might respond to another paper in a way that can cause pain and inflict damage on the writer's fragile self-confidence. Conversely, in order to protect each other from such damage—and to protect themselves from their classmate's possible rejection—a nontrusting student is reluctant to respond to a fellow student's paper beyond offering a few indeterminate compliments. As Sarah Freedman discovered in her research, "Students [go] to great lengths to avoid evaluating each other and to maintain smooth social relations with their peers." [28] Freedom to express our minds openly depends upon our assurance of safety from the danger of being ridiculed for our thoughts. Simply put, in a composition class it is essential that we trust one another.

ESTABLISHING AN ACCEPTING, OPEN ENVIRONMENT. How do we build that trust? We will have gone a large part of the way when we create a warm, accepting, and open atmosphere in our classroom.

Because everybody is especially vulnerable where our own writing is concerned, we must do everything we can to establish in our composition course the sort of supportive ambience that assures every member that the aim of the class is always the improvement of each student's writing and never his or her humiliation. Since this is a mutual purpose, we should create an atmosphere of "All for one and one for all" and never permit even a hint of student against student, clique against clique, or teacher against student. The entire class should come to recognize the vulnerability of every individual writer and learn to couch criticism in tactful terms. Students should never lose sight of the fact that it is a piece of writing that is under scrutiny, not the worth of its author. Of course, our standards should be high; excellence should be our mutual goal. But human nature being what it is, excellence cannot be achieved at the expense of the ego. In establishing an accepting atmosphere, we are also working toward openness and frankness of communication.

Teacher Commitment. How is such an atmosphere achieved? Often it comes from the force of the teacher's personality since, within their own classrooms, teachers are powerful role models. When we are unequivocably committed to the goal, we can communicate this commitment in our every contact with students, as individuals and as a class; and they will respond in kind. We can encourage every instance of behavior that contributes to this goal and immediately squelch behavior that detracts from it. As role models, we ourselves can do our best to be open, frank, and fair, yet sensitive to each student's needs; nor need we be afraid to reveal glimpses of our own vulnerability.

TEACHING TACTFUL, CONSTRUCTIVE RESPONSE. In addition, we might also teach our students the techniques of constructive criticism. We might teach them that as an audience for the papers of their fellow students, their role is, in Mary Elizabeth Fowler's words, "not simply to point out flaws" (or, I might add, always to say "That's very good"), but to "assist the writer in clarifying his thinking."[29]

Whole-Class Response. Our own modeling of tactful, constructive response in conference is, of course, helpful, but by itself not sufficient. Students need experiential practice before they are ready to take on the responsibility of reacting to a fellow student's paper on their own. We can begin by reading some papers to the class as a whole and encouraging appropriate response.

Actually, if we start our composition program with a series or two of student–teacher conferences (see pages 175–76), we will want to read to the class—or have the student authors themselves read—the really excellent post-conference papers. Sharing first-rate work is always desirable. The author gains an appreciative audience and a chance to communicate the ideas that were the impetus for the work. Besides the pleasure of hearing the paper itself, the audience gains knowledge of what "good" means in the immediate student context. We can also use these paper-publishing times to begin to build in the constructive response skills students will need for effective peer revision. We might, for example, ask the student audience—after they have made their appreciative noises—to tell specifically why they like the paper, to identify as precisely as they can what makes the paper good.

Students preparing for peer-response work, however, will also need to hear some earlier drafts that will benefit from their criticism. This can be a salutary experience if the atmosphere is warm and accepting, *and* if we choose fairly good, easily improvable papers.

We can encourage the listening students to base their comments on responses to questions such as these: What exactly do they like about the theme just read? In what ways could it be improved? What technique was particularly effective? What technique was a good idea in their opinion, but did not quite work out in practice? Where in the paper do they tend to get confused? What point needs clarifying? What point needs further exemplification? Comments and questions derived in this way can lead to a lively discussion, from which the writer of the paper under consideration can emerge a good deal more knowledgeable about ways to achieve rhetorical effectiveness in writing, the tender ego of authorship scarcely bruised.

An alternative method recommended by Stephen and Susan Tchudi, among others, is to have the class, working from an overhead projection, analyze a suitable paper from last year's class.[30]

Peer-Group Preparation

To begin the actual peer-group work, we are fortunate in having available *Sharing and Responding*, workbook for Pat Belanoff's and Peter Elbow's *Writing with Power*.[31] The manual is filled with practicable ideas and useful exercises for establishing a successful peer-group program. Elbow and Belanoff recommend a set of sequential directions to the group:

1. No Responding: Sharing. The writer reads a paper aloud; the listeners listen carefully, but "receive it without comment."
2. Descriptive Responding: Sayback. After the paper is read, the listeners "sum up in a sentence or two what [they] feel the writer is *getting at*," by "pointing, summarizing, [telling] what's almost said or implied, [and noting] the center of gravity."
3. Analytic Responding. The reader[s] ask the writer to provide, in writing or orally, the essay's main point and how it has been supported, to give the assumptions it is based upon, and to explain the writer's relationship with the essay's audience. Then the writer asks the reader[s] to pretend they believe everything in the essay and tell why; immediately afterward, they are to pretend they doubt everything and give their reasons for their doubt. Finally, after the paper has been worked on, each reader — or the writer — writes a descriptive outline of the paper, first of the work as a whole and then paragraph by paragraph, summarizing in a sentence what the section is *saying* and then what it is *doing* — "how it is functioning in the strategy of the whole essay, what it is trying to accomplish with to its readers."
4. Reader-Based Responding: Movies of the Reader's Mind. At this stage the writer "gets readers simply to tell what happens inside their heads as they read the writing."
5. Criterion-Based or Judgment-Based Responding. Working from a set of appropriate criteria for imaginative or expository writing (a sample provided by Elbow and Belanoff, 53–54), reader[s] — or the writer — evaluates the essay quality by quality, being sure to point to specific passages to back these judgments and to describe honestly particular mind-movies that explain the judgments.

If some students are still having difficulty with constructive responses, we might single out an able group to model peer discussion for the class.

Providing Students with Substantive Response Tools

Peer-response groups need more than interpersonal skills to make the strategy work successfully. They also need a good deal of substantive knowledge about composition; they need to experience the sort of practical information discussed on page 148ff. Classroom instruction, exercises, theme writing, and especially conferencing and rewriting not only help our students learn to write, but also supply them with concepts and vocabulary invaluable for peer response. Peer revision is more likely to succeed when students are comfortable with the basic rhetorical concepts.

INDEPENDENT PEER REVIEW. Experienced, knowledgeable, or especially able or mature students need little else than background in the basic concepts. For them the primary value of peer response may lie in the opportunity it offers for growth in independent thinking. As Anne J. Herrington and Deborah Cadman explain:

> The primary concern when initiating peer review is not to teach students how to critique written drafts—that's secondary; it is first to create a classroom environment where we give students the gift of having some responsibility— some authority for their own learning.[32]

Proficient students need less teacher guidance and "the gift of having some responsibility" is best implemented with the least such guidance. In leading relatively unstructured peer groups, we can provide students with highly specific assignments but leave the peer groups to respond to the assignments, for the most part, without specific cues or structure. With this strategy, teachers hope to develop what Herrington and Cadman call the "active reciprocal decision-making" (184) that leads to gains in both confidence and competence whether students accept the suggestions of their fellows or whether, having considered them thoughtfully, they reject them.

When the strategy works, it results in growth, not only in independent thought but also in writing capability. Herrington and Cadman, having analysed peer reviewing in Sylvia Forman's anthropology research course, for instance, found the unstructured peer-review strategy successful with these college junior and senior anthropology majors:

> Students can give sound advice to their peers even on matters they are having difficulty with in their own writing. [And] writers can profit both from the response they receive about their own drafts and from reading the drafts of others. (185)

In another study of advanced writers successfully using peer review, F. Bender found them gaining in independent thinking as they also profited from "incorporating explicit peer revision cues that were compatible with their own views."[33]

STRUCTURED PEER REVIEW.   Peer-review groups can also offer less-advanced students the opportunity to grow in independence, but ordinarily only when these students work their way through carefully structured responding tasks. George Hillocks's meta-analysis of all relevant research between 1962 and 1982 determined that peer-group composition work

> is most effective when the tasks are carefully structured (i.e. when the cues are clear . . .) but not so effective when the tasks are largely unstructured. (*Research in Written Composition* 237)

Peer revision works best when we provide assignments that are detailed and explicit and fill-in-the-blank forms with plenty of space for student response. Let me describe as an example one highly structured program that functions well.

George Shoemaker of Washington Court House High School in Ohio leads one of the most successful peer-group programs I know of.[34] Peer-group revision is the heart of his classes' composition study. Shoemaker intensively introduces each writing assignment (which is often associated with the class's current reading). He then hands out printed, detailed instructions for the assignment. Students are expected to write at least three drafts of a major assignment, and each draft is reviewed at a peer conference. For each assignment Shoemaker hands out three forms to be filled in by each of the three readers to help them guide the required conferences. Shoemaker creates differing forms for each assignment, with the sets growing in complexity as the term advances. But, in general, the first conference works on overall structure, focus, and clarity; the second reviews the overall problems discussed in the first and moves on to concentrate on section, paragraph, and sentence structure, and on coherence; and the third helps the writer edit for style and mechanics. When writers turn in their final drafts of an assignment, they also include all preliminary drafts and revision forms.

Shoemaker holds composition workshops on a regular basis. On workshop days students work individually or in peer groups and the teacher is also available for miniconferences. The Peer Review Student Guidelines offers condensed excerpts from some of Shoemaker's sample assignment and conference sheets.

STUDENT GUIDELINE

Peer Review Sample Sheets

SAMPLE ASSIGNMENT
Audience: Your choice.
Purpose: To argue that Mark Twain's *Huckleberry Finn*, despite recent attacks, does indeed have redeeming social features.
Follow the following writing process:

1. Prewrite: Show evidence of preplanning and thought.
2. Drafting: Complete first draft of the paper.
3. Revising: Complete 3 peer conferences and revisions.
4. Editing: Complete a final check of your paper, using the self-check list.
5. Publishing: Submit paper to teacher for evaluation.

PEER REVIEW CONFERENCE #1
1. What does the author need to do to let you *know more clearly* exactly what he/she is trying to say?
2. What does the author need to do to help you understand the *importance* or meaning of his/her subject?
3. In what portions are *more supporting details* needed?
4. In what portions should *unnecessary or unimportant details be removed?*
5. In what sections does the author *need to make his/her meaning clearer?* (Where do you say, "I don't quite understand this?")
6. Which sections need to be *moved to a different position* in the paper?

PEER REVIEW CONFERENCE #2
 I. Leftovers from Conference #1.
    [Brief repeat of first conference questions.]
 II. Closer Examination
    A. Which sections/paragraphs/sentences should be reworded to make them more effective?
    B. Which sections/paragraphs/sentences should be reworded to make them more effective? [Consider the author's purpose and audience carefully in making this judgment.]

PEER REVIEW CONFERENCE #3
1. Are there any run-on sentences?
2. Are there any sentence fragments?
3. Are any of the sentence structures awkward?
4. Is the paper divided into paragraphs correctly and indented?
5. Does the author use proper verb tense and agreement?

continued
6. Is the paper punctuated correctly?
7. Is the spelling correct?

Check for the following. The work:

is inspired ___	shows strong voice (personality) ___	is well organized ___
is clear ___	shows control of topic ___	is fluent, smooth ___
is coherent ___	shows skillful word choice ___	is profound ___
is vivid ___	involves reader with topic ___	has few errors ___
	explores more than one angle ___	

Evaluative Research

A good deal of research has been done on the effectiveness of peer-response groups. George Hillocks's meta-analysis suggested, as I mentioned earlier, that peer-group composition work functions most effectively when "tasks are carefully structured." Later research, however, on peer-revision groups taking part in carefully cued activies offers a mixed verdict. For example, when peer-motivated revision was compared to self-revision using the same evaluating forms, C. E. Harris found peer response led to significant improvement; A. M. O'Donnell's study found no statistically significant difference; and P. W. Swift found both methods supported "modest improvement" in the quality of student work.[35]

USING PEER GROUPS EFFECTIVELY. What can we conclude from such variety in scholarly research? Assuming that the research itself is valid, we can, I think, infer that the variation stems from individual differences in teachers and students. Peer-response groups are tricky to manage, and some students respond better to group work than others do. In addition, this strategy fits better into some instructors' repertoires than in others, sparking some strong evaluative opinions.[36]

Differences beyond class and instructor fit can be attributed, I think, to differences in the amount of training various instructors offer their peer groups and the fact that peer response is more effective in dealing with some revision problems than with others.

Wise use of peer-response groups, then, means that we allow sufficient time for training our student responders, that we select tasks for them appropriate to the training and to group work, and that we provide them with clear directions specifically defining those tasks.

Provide Training and Specific Direction. Students need a good deal of understanding to make peer response work. Since our own conferences can supply part of that understanding, conferencing should probably precede its use. In addition, we should provide specific training in both the social and academic skills necessary to make peer-response groups work to enhance revision. See pages 177–79 for specific training ideas. And when our students set about their peer-response work, we should be sure to supply them with carefully thought-out specifications for the tasks they are to undertake, keyed to the concepts and the vocabulary of the training sessions.

Use Peer Groups Selectively.   Peer response is a strategy we should use with discrimination. At least in the beginning, we should put the groups to work primarily on those tasks they can handle best. What are these tasks?

- Peer groups excel in finding and praising especially good passages in one another's work.
- They can also demonstrate to the writer what they do not understand and can sometimes help him to determine why they don't.
- With training they can show which points need more support and can sometimes suggest where that support might come from.
- They are also good at spotting errors. Both skilled and unskilled writers find and correct far more errors on someone else's paper than on their own, as Glynda Hull's research, for instance, confirms.[37]

Peer groups are less effective in helping students make needed structural changes. Student readers know when they are confused by a paper, of course, but they have a great deal of trouble suggesting anything beyond surface changes to remedy their confusion. They can learn to spot a paper that lacks focus, but they find it extremely difficult to help a fellow student discover the central focus of her ideas and even harder to help her subordinate the supporting ideas to that focus. It may be just as well not to expect these groups, in reacting to structure, to go much beyond helping the writer identify her controlling idea, at least at first.

Rewriting, Editing, Proofreading

The revising phase of the writing process consists of three distinct practices: rewriting—performing global, usually structural revision, what Faigley and Witte call "revisions that affect the meaning of the text" ("Analyzing Revision" 401); editing—making changes, usually stylistic, within the paragraph and sentence, and in word choice; and proofing—correcting errors and infelicities. I have concentrated on teaching rewriting in this chapter, for that is the heart of the process of revision. Look to Chapters 6 and 7 on teaching style for a more thorough discussion of editing, and to Chapter 8 on handling writing problems for speakers of nonstandard dialects for discussion of proofreading and error correction.

IDEAS FOR DISCUSSION OR ESSAY

1. Analyze the conference excerpted here in light of the ideas discussed in this chapter. Explain the psychological and pedagogical mechanics of the

conference as you see them. Where do you feel the teacher is doing a good job and why? Where and how would you have handled the situation differently?

2. In recent years peer-response groups have been the focus of a good deal of research and a much-discussed strategy in the scholarly literature. Read at least two articles on the subject and, in conjunction with the material presented here, develop your views on one phase of the issue in a one- or two-page essay.

3. The most important and the most difficult task a teacher has in helping a student revise the structure of an essay is to discover what structure could better serve the author's purposes. I have recommended eliciting from the essay its present structure—that is to say, its controlling idea and structural plan—studying them carefully, and then helping the student construct a better plan. We can work with a pre-essay or accompanying student-made structural plans in the same way.

   The following are three first-draft plans written by students in a class in the teaching of composition. Study each one carefully and then construct revised plans suggesting the revisions you would recommend if these plans were written by their students. (Hint: The organizing idea controls the structure. Where inconsistencies occur, one or the other must change.)

4. Structural plans of the final papers, revised after conferences, follow. Are your plans similar to theirs? If they are not, which do you think would result in the more effective paper? Why?

ORIGINAL THESES AND OUTLINES

Sample A
Organizing Idea: The benefits of behavioral modification supercede all forms of discipline or all methods of teaching.
  I. Introduction
 II. Description of behavioral modification
     A. Definition
     B. Techniques
        1. Praise and ignore
        2. Soft reprimand
        3. Token reinforcement
III. Academic
     A. Research study
     B. Benefits
 IV. Emotional results
  V. Conclusion

Sample B
Organizing Idea: Although the teacher has an obligation to try to teach the black speaker standard English, he must have an accepting attitude toward the nonstandard speaker.
1. Introduction

2. Show differences in BE and SE, giving some examples
    • Copula
    • Possession
    • Double negative
3. Materials available
    • Reading
        Langvater experiment
        Dialect-based reader
    • Writing soundscript
    • B & B written in BE
4. How to change attitudes
    • Argument for teaching S.E.
    • Rosenthal study
    • Isenbarger study
    • Agee study
5. Conclusion

Sample C
Organizing Idea: The self-discipline in the Montessori classrooms is superior to imposed discipline seen in traditional classrooms.
— Introduction
— Body
1. Definitions
    • Liberty
    • Discipline
2. Examples of the discipline in both Montessori and traditional classrooms
3. Results of both methods in regard to learning
    — Conclusion: Summary

REVISED ORGANIZING IDEAS AND STRUCTURAL PLANS

Sample A
Organizing Idea: A current classroom problem is a lack of teaching method that contributes both to academic skills and emotional development. Behavior modification offers a solution to this problem.
  I. Introduction
 II. Description of behavior modification
III. Academic problems
    A. Presentation of problems
    B. Solution through behavioral modification techniques
IV. Emotional problems
    A. Presentation of problems
    B. Solution through behavioral modification techniques
    V. Conclusion

Sample B
Organizing Idea: Although the teacher has an obligation to try and teach the Black English [BE] speaker Standard English [SE], the teacher must have an accepting attitude toward the language of the nonstandard speaker.

1. Introduction: SE must be taught
   - Different theories on how to treat black nonstandard speakers
   - Definitions of SE and BE
   - Why SE must be taught (although clause)
   - Statement of organizing idea
2. Argument for accepting BE
   - Intellectual argument: BE is a real language
     * Historical theory
     * Examples of its systemization
   - Pedagogic argument: Emotional effect on student
     * Rosenthal study
     * Agee study
     * Isenbarger study
3. Methods of accepting BE in the classroom
   - Don't correct verbally
   - Reading
     * Langvater experiment
     * Dialect-based reader
   - Writing
4. Conclusion (reemphasis on importance of accepting attitude)

Sample C
Organizing Idea: The self-discipline in the Montessori classrooms is superior to the imposed discipline often seen in traditional classrooms.
— Introduction
— Definition of "discipline"
   1. Traditional definition: discipline vs. liberty
   2. Montessori definition: discipline = liberty
      — Examples of discipline problems and approaches
   1. In traditional classrooms
      Problems
      Results
   2. In Montessori classrooms
      Problems
      Results
      — Conclusion

NOTES

1. Lester Faigley and Stephen Witte, "Analyzing Revision," *CCC* 32 (1981): 410; Nancy Sommers, "Revision Strategies of Student Writers and Experienced Adult Writers," *CCC* 31 (1980); Stephen Witte, "Pre-Text and Composing," *CCC* 38 (1987): 397–425; and Muriel Harris, "Composing Behaviors of One- and Multi-Draft Writers," *CE* 51 (Feb 1989) 188.

2. Barbara Hansen, "Rewriting Is a Waste of Time," *CE* 39 (1978): 956–60, found no statistically significant improvement in the work of students who were required to revise (without intervention) and those who merely kept correction sheets. R. J. Bracewell, M. Scardamalia, and C. Bereiter, in a series of experiments described in George Hillocks, Jr., *Research on Written Composition: New Directions for Teaching*

(NCRE and ERIC, 1987), 44–48, showed that 4th and 8th graders were able to pick out sentences that needed revision but, with no intervention, were unable to revise the sentences so that they became appreciably better or change them in ways that improved the work as a whole. In fact, 8th grade revisions were judged to worsen the compositions. See also Joan Henley, "A Revisionist View of Revision," *Washington English Journal* 8, #2 (1986): 5–7, who makes similar observations in her classroom. See also Linda Flower and John Hayes et al, "Detection, Diagnosis, and the Strategies of Revision," *CCC* 36 (1986): 16–55.

3. Hansen also found that intensive discussion of revision and revision exercises were as effective as rewriting (without intervention) in improving writing ability (960).

4. See especially David L. Wallace and John R. Hayes, "Redefining Revision for Freshmen," *RTE* 25 (1991): 54–64. See also J. Fitzgerald and L. R. Markham, "Teaching Children about Revision in Writing." *Cognition and Instruction* 4 (1987): 3–24; V. L. B. Olson, "The Effects of Revision Instruction and Peer Response Groups on Revision Behaviors, Quality of Writing, and Attitude toward Writing of Sixth-Grade Students." *DAI* 47 (1986): 12A; and Hansen.

5. Faigley and Witte, for instance, establish that most writers—even those who are experienced—do most of their revision between the first and second drafts ("Analyzing Revision," 407). And even Sommers, whose research demonstrates the importance of recursive revision, conducted this research in terms of separate drafts; see her "Revision Strategies."

6. George Hillocks, Jr. "The Interaction of Instruction, Teacher Comment, and Revision in Teaching the Composing Process," *RTE* 16 (1982): 261–78; Louise Bridwell, "Revising Strategies in Twelfth Grade Students' Transactional Writing," *RTE* 14 (1980): 216; and C. Effros, "An Experimental Study of the Effects of Guided Revision and Delayed Grades in Writing Proficiency of College Freshmen," Final Report (New Haven: Yale U, 1973), ED 079-764.

7. Matthew Doherty, "The Missing Link: Rewriting," *EJ* 54 (1965): 848.

8. John J. Ruszkiewicz, "The Great Commandment," in *Training the New Teacher of College Composition*, Charles W. Bridges, et al. eds. (Urbana: NCTE, 1980), 83.

9. Donald Murray, *A Writer Teaches Writing: A Practical Method of Teaching Composition* (Boston: Houghton, 1968), 11.

10. Alton Becker and Richard E. Young, "Toward a Modern Theory of Rhetoric: A Tagmemic Contribution," *HER* 35 (1965): 466.

11. Francis Christensen, "Generative Rhetoric of the Paragraph," in *Notes toward a New Rhetoric: Nine Essays for Teachers*, 2nd ed. (New York: Harper, 1978), 79–80.

12. Stephen Witte and Lester Faigley make a similar suggestion in "Coherence, Cohesion, and Writing Quality," *CCC* 33 (1981): 201.

13. Hillocks *Research*, 42–49. See also note #2.

14. Jan Turbill, *No Better Way to Teach Writing* (Rosebery, New South Wales, Australia: Primary English Teaching Assn., 1982), 34; Roger Garrison, "One-to-One: Tutorial Instruction in Freshman Composition," *New Directions for Community Colleges* 2 (1974): 56; Murray, *Writer Teaches*, 16; Charles Cooper, "Responding to Student Writing," in *The Writing Processes of Students*, ed. W. Petty and P. J. Price (Buffalo: SUNY at Buffalo, Dept. of Curriculum and Instruction, 1975) 39; Muriel Harris, *Teaching One-to-One: The Writing Conference.* (Urbana: NCTE, 1986), 5; Lester Fisher and Donald Murray, "Perhaps the Professor Should Cut Class," *CE* 35 (1973): 169.

15. J. P. Shaver and D. Nuhn, "The Effectiveness of Tutoring Underachievers in Reading and Writing," *JER* 65 (1971, #3): 107–12; D. G. Sutton and D. S. Arnold,

"The Effects of Two Methods of Compensatory Freshman English," *RTE* (1974): 241–49; Allan Gates, "A Study of the Effects of Work Undertaken in an Independent Learning Center by Marginal Students at Marshalltown Community College." *DAI* 37 (1977): 7002A; Myrna Smith and Barbara Bretcko, *Research on Individual Composition Conferences*, (Urbana: ERIC, 1974): ED 091 709; Mildred Fritts, "The Effects of Individual Teacher Conferences on the Writing Achievement and Self-Concept of Developmental Junior College Writing Students," *DAI* 37 (1977): 4185A. ED138 988; Judith Budz and Terry Grabar, "Tutorial versus Classroom in Freshman English," *CE* 37 (1976): 654–56.

See also Doris I. Smith, "Effects of Class Size and Individualized Instruction in the Writing of High-School Juniors," *DAI*, 1 (1974), 2844A (Florida State U), which compares individualized, small-group, and full-class instruction, and determines that these techniques improved student writing in the order given; James R. Bradshaw, "An Experimental Study Comparing a Traditional Teacher Lecture Method with an Individualized Method of Instruction Business Report Writing," *DAI* 35 (1974): 3382A (Brigham Young U); Roy C. Maize, "Two Methods of Teaching English Composition to Retarded College Freshmen," *JEP* 45 (1954): 22–28; and James J. Lynch, "The Conference Method in Teaching English Composition in Junior-Senior High School," *Bulletin of the National Association of High-School Principals*, 46 (1962): 119–20. All are detailed studies that offer strong support for individualized composition instruction.

16. Thomas Carnicelli, "The Writing Conference: A One-to-One Conversation," in *Eight Approaches to Teaching Composition*, eds. Timothy Donovan and Ben McClelland (Urbana: NCTE, 1980), 102, 105.

17. See also Rosemary Arbur, "The Student-Teacher Conference," *CCC* 28 (1977): 338–42. She derives a similar list from therapeutic social-work conferences— here somewhat abbreviated:

1. *Engagement:* putting the student at ease, conveying acceptance, and identifying the purpose of the meeting
2. *Problem Exploration:* leading the student from a sense that "everything" is "wrong" with the paper to a focus on what specific problems should be worked on.
3. *Problem Identification:* isolating as specifically as possible the most serious problem at hand
4. *Agreement to Work on a Problem Together*
5. *Task Assignment:* what the student must do
6. *Solution:* the stage reached when the problem is eliminated
7. *Termination.*

18. Greg C. Sieminski, in "Couching Our Cutting with Compassion," *CCC* 42 (1992): 211–17, suggests conferencing side-by-side on an office sofa, but I am not sure I endorse his suggestion. The sofa works well in relaxing some students, but has just the opposite effect on others whose comfort zone is more spacious.

19. Barbara Fassler, "The Red Pen Revisited: Teaching Composition through Student Conferences," *CE* 38 (1976): 188.

20. Carol Laque and Phyllis Sherwood, *A Laboratory Approach to Writing* (Urbana: NCTE, 1977), 41. I have taken the liberty of reversing the order of "diction" and "punctuation" and of "voice" and "sentence structure" on the list (18) to make it correspond more closely to the emphasis of this volume.

21. I do not recommend reinforcing obvious spelling or punctuation errors by ignoring them altogether when annotating or correcting a paper; but they are better ignored than permitted to become the focus of a teacher-student conference when the paper also exhibits the more fundamental flaws. For the Laque and Sherwood examples, see especially 101–02 and 106.

22. See especially Nancy Sommers, "Responding to Student Writing," *CCC* 32 (1982): 148–56 and Mary F. Hayes and Donald Daiker, "Using Protocol Analysis in Evaluating Responses to Student Writing," *Freshman English News* 13 (no. 2) (1984): 1–4. See also John V. Knapp, "Contract/Conference Evaluations of Freshman Composition," *CE* 37 (1976): 650; Lois McAllister, "Tell Me What You Had in Mind," *EJ* 59 (1970): 231–34; Fassler, 192; and Fisher and Murray, 172.

23. Nancy Atwell, *In the Middle: Writing, Reading, and Learning with Adolescents* (Portsmouth: Boynton, 1987), 91.

24. Donald Graves, *Writing: Teachers and Children at Work* (Portsmith: Heinemann, 1983), 302.

25. Donald Murray, "Listening Eye," *CE* 41 (1979): 13–18.

26. Donald Sheridan, "Changing Business as Usual: Reader Response in the Classroom," *CE* 53 (1991): 813; Abraham Bernstein, *Teaching English in High School* (New York: Random House, 1966), 121–24.

27. James Moffett, *Teaching the Universe of Discourse* (Boston: Houghton, 1968), 196.

28. Sarah Freedman, et al. *Response to Student Writing*, (Urbana: NCTE, 1987), 15.

29. Mary Elizabeth Fowler, *Teaching Language, Composition, and Literature* (New York: McGraw Hill, 1965), 11.

30. Stephen Tchudi and Susan Tchudi, *The English/Language Arts Handbook: Classroom Strategies for Teachers* (Portsmouth: Boynton, 1991), 150.

31. Peter Elbow and Pat Belanoff, *Starting and Responding* (New York: Random House, 1989.

32. Anne J. Herrington and Deborah Cadman, "Peer Review and Revising in an Anthropology Course: Lessons for Learning," *CCC* 42 (1991): 197.

33. F. Bender, "A Study of Teacher and Peer Comments in the Revising Process of College Writers." *DAI* 51 (1990): 02A.

34. In 1990 two classes of Shoemaker's were part of a composition research project. The papers of these college-bound juniors, who studied writing by the method described, improved significantly more than those of comparable groups who were taught according to a variety of methods.

35. Hillocks, *Research*, 237; Harris, *Effective Strategies in Peer Evaluation of Writing* ERIC No. ED 272 897; O'Donnell, et al. *Written Communication* 4 (1987): 90–99; P. W. Swift, "The Effect of Peer Review with Self-Evaluation on Freshman Writing Performance, Retention, and Attitude at Bronard Community College. *DAI* 47 (1986): 10A.

36. Many instructors are especially pleased with the positive attitudes that are engendered by peer-response groups. And this evaluation is backed by the research, for instance, of M. V. H. McManus, "A Study of Peer-Response Groups in a Tenth-Grade Writing Class," *DAI* 47 (1986): 08A and of J. Katstra et al., "The Effects of Peer Evaluation, Attitude Toward Writing, and Writing Fluency of Ninth-Grade Students," *JER* 80 [1987]: 168–172.

On the other hand, Linda Flowers and Sarah Freedman have both found that even the positive social interactions within peer groups can be counterproductive to the kind of evaluative efforts helpful to student revision. Freedman reports that in unstructured situations, students spent most of their group time "telling one another jokes or talking about weekend plans, friends, or hair-coloring" (22). And even providing "dittoed response sheets specifically designed to prompt evaluation," did not greatly improve the final result:

> Although the sheets kept students to task and did prompt problem solving, much of their thinking, it seems, was directed to solving the puzzle of how to fill out the teachers' sheets while avoiding an evaluative response. (15)

In analyzing Freedman's data, Linda Flower concludes in "Cognition, Context, and Theory Building," *CCC* 40 (1989): 285, that "It seems naive to assume that the cognitive processes we desire will naturally follow from the social situations we engineer." (285)

Fisher and Murray are also critical: They report that in peer response groups, "some students don't read students' writing sensitively and critically, some students can't yet understand what the writer is talking about, some students are bored and pay little attention, and some students have progressed far beyond the kind of writing and the problems faced by the writer" (10).

37. Glynda Hull, "The Editing Process in Writing: A Performance Study of More Skilled and Less Skilled College Writers," *RTE* 21 (1987): 8.

Section B

Teaching Expository Style

Style, in its finest sense, is the last acquirement of the educated mind; it is also the most useful.

— Alfred North Whitehead

□ □ □   **6**

Teaching Audience and Voice: Help from the Art of Rhetoric

Pleasing audiences is part of a writer's skill. Creating voices is how it's done.
— Dona J. Hickey

Rhetoric enables writers and speakers to design messages for particular audiences and purposes.
— Erika Lindemann.

□ □ □

Thus far we have concentrated upon ways to teach focus and structure in expository writing because the lack of this knowledge is at the heart of the writing problem for so many of our students. But point and organization are not the only factors involved in the production of effective and persuasive expository prose. Besides gaining an understanding of structure—the ways of organizing their ideas—our students need to learn something about style, the ways of expressing their ideas. In teaching students about style, contemporary teachers have the considerable benefit of being able to derive pedagogical strategies both from the ancient art of rhetoric and from the modern science of linguistics. In this chapter and in Chapters 7 and 8 we will explore some of the possibilities offered by each of these sources.

STYLE

A Theory of Style

Style is the way something—an idea, a fact, a concept, or a thought—is expressed. Because style must be conceived in terms of both expression and the thing expressed, theorists have been troubled by the question of whether style and content are separable entities or whether they are one.[1] This question obscures the truth of the matter, however, for style is demonstrably neither identical to meaning nor separable from it. Take, for example, the sentence "The girl was reluctant to leave." The explicit meaning, which has something to do with a girl's feelings about leaving, is clearly not the style of the sentence. Just as clearly, the style, a plain indicative statement in the active voice with an infinitive complement and so on, is not coextensive with the meaning.

Nevertheless, the style of this sentence does have something important to do with its meaning, for style unquestionably contributes to meaning, as comparing our example sentence with another of similar content but quite different style reveals:

1. The girl was reluctant to leave.

2. She just didn't want to go nohow.

The denotative meanings of these two sentences are, for all practical purposes, identical, but the connotative meanings differ widely. The girl and her feelings may be the same, but the way she is observed and reported, and consequently the way she will be perceived by the reader, are entirely at variance. Though the style of neither sentence accounts for its meaning, the difference in the styles of the two sentences accounts for the difference in their meanings. Content provides a passage with its explicit or denotative meaning; style, the way the content is expressed, provides the implicit or connotative meaning. Style is thus an integral contributor to the essential meaning of a passage of speech or writing.

TONE. Defined in this way, style not only encompasses surface features such as those exemplified above, but also tonal qualities. For tone is also "the way content is expressed." Barbara Wenner, for instance, explains tone for her students at the University of Cincinnati with two letters from credit card companies received by a widow of her acquaintance on the day after her husband's funeral:

1. We are requesting that the charge cards in your possession be cut in half and mailed immediately in the enclosed envelope. If you have already disposed of the cards, sign the bottom of this letter to that effect and mail it to us. If your account is past due, send a check or money order immediately.

2. We received notice that your husband has died. Please accept our sympathy. If you would like to have the charge-card account put in your name, all you need to do is send us James's card, cut in half, or a written statement that his card has been destroyed. After we receive this notification, we will make the necessary changes.

Both letters are the same in content, but they differ so markedly in tone that one brought the widow additional grief and even rage while the other appeared to her to present but a minor problem, soon to be rectified. Wenner's students have no difficulty guessing which company got the widow's future business. Style thus also encompasses the rhetorical relationship between writer and reader often referred to as tone.

EVALUATING STYLE.   Because style is part of meaning, it can be evaluated only in terms of how well it contributes to the intended meaning of the whole. In other words, bad style occurs when there is an incongruity between the connotative and the denotative meanings. The greater the congruity between the implicit and the explicit meanings, the better the style. The second letter from the credit card company was clearly written in better style than the first because in keeping the widow's goodwill, it better served the company's purpose.

But style cannot be evaluated out of context. Though "She just didn't want to go nohow" would be unseemly and incorrect as a serious statement by an author who was attempting an essay in standard English, and thus could clearly be judged bad style in that context, it might be very good style when coming from the mouth of a mountaineer narrator in a passage where "The girl was reluctant to leave" would sound pretentious and inappropriate.

PEDAGOGAL USES.   The theory of style outlined here, which was originally developed by W. K. Wimsatt, Jr., and Monroe C. Beardsley,[2] offers a rich pedagogical context to the teacher of composition for a number of reasons. It is an explanation of style that makes good sense to students. With it we can demonstrate to our students that they can vary their meaning and the impression their words create by varying the way they express their thought, and they can learn to judge what effect certain variations are likely to have. With this theory, we can also help our students improve their style by showing them how to weed out of their writing the stylistic errors that are created when the way they phrase their ideas is at variance with their intended meaning. It also provides a good theoretical background for teaching both the linguistic approach to style and the approach of traditional rhetoric.

The Rhetorical Stance

Rhetorical style is that which seeks to persuade. Traditional rhetoric considers style in terms of a tripartite persuasive relationship of speaker (or author), subject, and audience (readers), in which the author tries to express himself or herself in such a way that the audience is persuaded to accept the author's view of the subject. This relationship is often signified by a device known as the rhetorical triangle, represented here in Figure 6 1.

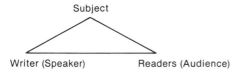

Figure 6–1.

ARISTOTLE'S DEFINITION.   Aristotle first codified this relationship, and his explanation provides the basis for the whole discipline of rhetoric even to the present day:

> Let Rhetoric be defined as the faculty of discovering in the particular case what are the available means of persuasion. . . . Of the means of persuasion . . . there are three kinds. The first kind reside in the character (ethos) of the speaker. The second consist in producing a certain attitude (pathos) in the hearer; the third appertain to the argument proper, in so far as it actually or seemingly demonstrates.[3]

WAYNE BOOTH'S VERSION.   The definition of contemporary rhetorician and teacher Wayne Booth is surprisingly close to Aristotle's, though undoubtedly our students would find its language easier to work with:

> Rhetoric is the art of finding and employing the most effective means of persuasion. . . . [It can be] thought of as the art of "putting it across."
>
> What makes the differences between effective communication and mere wasted effort . . . is something I shall call the rhetorical stance, a stance which depends on discovering and maintaining in any writing situation a proper balance among the three elements that are at work in any communicative effort, the available arguments about the subject itself, the interests and peculiarities of the audience, and the voice, the implied character, of the speaker.[4]

Teaching our students to master what Booth calls "the rhetorical stance" is perhaps our major goal in the teaching of expository style.

This goal is not easily achieved. When we focus our students' attention on style, we run the danger of encouraging excess. In stressing the various elements of style, we can inadvertently lead our students into the corruptions inherent in too strong a concentration upon a single element. Booth warns of the perversions resulting from imbalance:

> The first perversion . . . the pedantic stance, springs from ignoring the audience or overreliance on the pure subject. The second, which might be called the advertiser's stance, comes from undervaluing the subject and overvaluing pure effect: how to win friends and influence people. . . . [And the third]

perversion of the rhetorician's balance [is] . . . what might be called the entertainer's stance—the willingness to sacrifice substance to personality and charm. (144–45)

BALANCE.   Balance is what is important. For our students to find the balance appropriate for each bit of writing they undertake, they will need to understand something of the possibilities for persuasion inherent individually in subject matter, in themselves as the controlling voice, and in appeals to their audience. We can help them find this understanding by providing experience with each of these rhetorical approaches.

THE AUDIENCE AND THE APPEAL TO EMOTION

With the present scholarly interest in reader-response theory, the audience corner of the rhetorical triangle (See Figure 6–1) has assumed a current dominance. Articles are written on the subject in professional journals, and many composition textbooks insist that students define their projected audience before beginning their prewriting activities. But, except in business-writing classes, where the connection between the nature of the person one is writing to persuade and one's purpose for writing is crystal clear, students tend to ignore audience when they write.[5] They see no practical reason to factor it into their considerations—probably because of the special problems the classroom situation brings to the relationship of writers and their audience.

Audience Problems in the Classroom

Wayne Booth tells the story of the graduate student who was bright and articulate in class, but whose papers were invariably "pretentious, dull and disorganized" and sometimes also "obscure" (139). But one day, incensed over Booth's interpretation of a literary work, he dashed off to his teacher a lively, stimulating, and convincing response. Booth attributes the remarkable improvement in his student's writing to the student's having found a genuine rhetorical purpose and a genuine audience.

Most of us have had similar enough experiences to have been made aware of the difficulty of not having an actual audience in the classroom. Though not all our students are troubled by it, the problem of audience is inherent in the academic situation where most writing is necessarily done for practice rather than in response to an authentic need to communicate with somebody, its natural purpose in the "real world."

SIMULATING AN AUDIENCE.   How can we combat this problem? One solution that many teachers find useful from time to time is to give assignments simulating various writer–reader situations. For example, a student can pretend to be one of Chaucer's pilgrims and write a letter to a friend or relative describing the journey to Canterbury and characterizing two or three fellow pilgrims. Or, as Richard Larson suggests, "instead of asking routinely for an 'analysis' of Lady Macbeth, urge the student to reply to someone who thinks the Lady was a foolish, misguided but loyal wife who was only trying to encourage her husband to better himself."[6]

Writing and then answering letters to "Dear Abby" or Ann Landers, a popular activity, especially for our younger or less able students, comes closer to creating a "real" situation.[7] Whether in assuming their first roles of "Confused in Connecticut," "Perplexed in the Poconos," or "Muddled in Middletown," or in playing their later parts as "Abby" or "Ann," students must, of necessity, be aware of the reader who they are asking or to whom they are giving needed advice or welcome humor.

FINDING AN ACTUAL AUDIENCE. As enjoyable as these exercises can be for our students, insofar as they remain artificial, "Let's pretend" devices, they do not directly address the problem of finding a genuine audience for classroom writing. A few actual audiences are available to our students, however. From time to time, they may, for instance, write letters to actual people in response to genuine issues.

Letters to the Editor or to Officials. When our students are excited about a topic—a new rule on campus or a matter of local or national politics, for example—we can let them discuss the controversy in class and then assign them to write a letter to an official who could make a difference. Or we can have students bring in an article or editorial that aroused their interest from a newspaper or magazine and, after discussion, ask them to respond in a letter to the editor of the publication. After students work over these letters for rhetorical effectiveness, they can send them off to their real-world correspondents.

Such assignments prepare our students for participatory citizenship. They give them a chance to approach the media with a healthy skepticism, to think through a situation seriously, and to have a sense of being able to make their voices heard. And in trying to make their letters persuasive, they can learn a good deal about audience analysis. In particular, they can learn to ask themselves: What is my *real* purpose here? Do I want simply to blow off some righteously indignant steam? Or do I want to persuade my reader? The true lesson in writing these letters may well have something to do with catching more flies with honey than with vinegar.

WRITING FOR POSSIBLE PUBLICATION. Many of us create audience awareness in our students by suggesting they write their expository articles for the readership of an appropriate magazine or journal. Although this approach also involves some pretense, it always holds out the tantalizing possibility of realization.

In using this approach, we should help our students become familiar with widely varying periodical audiences by encouraging them to browse through a variety of different magazines or journals in the library or in the classroom. In the discussion following this activity, we might first ask our students to identify by age, socioeconomic class, sex, or special interest the audiences toward whom various periodicals are directed. Then we might help them to discover some of the ways the authors of articles published in these periodicals direct their writing toward the needs, desires, expectations, and interests of these target audiences. For classes that are particularly stimulated by such discussions, we might bring in copies of *Writer's Market* or *Writer's Digest* so that they might share the professional view of these matters.[8]

MAKING USE OF THE NATURAL CLASSROOM AUDIENCE. Despite the value of such exercises, the truth is that, whatever the assignment, teacher and classmates are a student writer's only original readership. Nevertheless, since the classroom contains a known, living audience, it offers opportunities that even professional writers can envy. Frederick Crews, for instance, who both teaches and writes professionally, sees the composition class as far more advantageous in this respect than "the normal situation of every essay-writer" where

> you know that your prose is expected to make contact with a reader's feelings . . . but you don't have a clear idea of who this reader is. . . . You have to assume a nonexistent relationship and keep on writing. It's almost like composing love letters "to whom it may concern" and mailing them off to "Occupant" or "Boxholder."[9]

In the writing class, on the other hand, students can get to know the teacher and classmates who will read their papers, and almost as in conversation or with letter writing, they can discover their readers' response. Our task as teachers, then, is to enhance our students' sense of their actual audience. We can let them share their work with one another in full-class sessions or in small groups. In addition, we can make sure our written or personal comments to our students respond to the substance of what they have said in their compositions rather than just to their technical successes and failures.

STUDENTS AS THEIR OWN FIRST AUDIENCE. When students image their fellow students—or even the readers of a certain periodical—as their readers, they are taking a giant step toward setting up the most useful audience of all: the self as reader. How do they image their classmates or, say, *Newsweek* readers as their audience? The very best way to do so is to try their writing out on themselves. If, for instance, they were reading the draft they have just written as an article in *Newsweek* or if it were given to them as the work of a fellow-student, how would they respond? Would this draft answer the questions it raises in their own minds as readers? As readers themselves, do they find it clear? Might they be offended by anything in the tone?

Mature and experienced writers become their own best critical audience. One of the most important tasks we have as writing teachers is to help our students develop effective self-reader skills.[10]

The Audience and Controversy

Since the purpose of all good expository writing is to persuade the reader— the audience—one could say that, to some extent, all good expository writing is controversial. Aristotle and the other classical rhetoricians certainly saw it that way and regarded their audience as worthy antagonists who needed convincing. Even so, all expository writing is not equally controversial. We need to stress this point to our students because the degree of controversiality determines to an important extent the writer's relationship with the reader.

To determine just how controversial their topic is, students should ask themselves just how far their readers are likely to agree with their point of view on it. They should be able to place this degree of agreement somewhere along the continuum shown in Figure 6–2. The amount of agreement our students expect from their readers should help them decide to what extent they will want to emphasize their "although" material. The more controversial their point, the more care—and usually the more space—they will need to devote to handling it.

Thus, in helping students plan their papers, it is useful to focus on the "although clause" of their working thesis. They should examine it to see how much controversiality it implies. For even though "although clauses" are by definition contrary, they can express or imply any position along the Controversy Continuum.

TEACHING READER APPROACHES FOR NONCONTROVERSIAL TOPICS. Many "although clauses" suggest that their theses are not particularly controversial. Reports of original research, for example, often imply that

Figure 6–2. The Controversy Continuum

(u) Total agreement	(v) General agreement, but reservations about certain specifics	(w) Complete neutrality or lack of opinion based on ignorance of the issue	(x) Disagreement in part (the rest agreed to or passed over because of ignorance of specifics)

| (y) Total disagreement without emotional involvement | (z) Total hostile disagreement | | |

"although the thesis idea is newly discovered. . . .." A similarly noncontroversial "although clause" might hint that "Although this material is well known, I have a new angle, approach, or interpretation to bring to it." Such "although clauses" might even suggest that "Although I am sure you will agree with me once I tell you or remind you of the conditions. . . .." Such "although clauses" do not put readers in an adversary position. And because writers can expect easy reader acquiescence from basically noncontroversial topics, our students need not give particular emphasis to the "although" material in such essays.

The Invisible "Although Clause."   Some noncontroversial essays barely mention this material. Often in critical analyses, for example, the underlying "although clause" suggests that the author has not yet read a completely satisfying interpretation of the work at hand; but though this foundational idea is clearly implied, the author never mentions it explicitly in the essay, but goes directly into her own interpretation. Our students can learn to follow suit.

The Review of the Literature "Although Clause."   Or students may find it useful to base their introduction on their "although" material, even in noncontroversial writing since it can justify their purpose for writing. Scholarly papers often take this approach. Since their usual purpose is to respond to prior work or the results of previous research on the topic, many scholars begin theirs with a survey of earlier accepted opinion—technically called "a review of the literature." This review functions as an "although clause" to the paper's working thesis because the paper's purpose is to react to this material in some new way. When teaching this sort of writing, we can show enough professional examples for students to understand how they might follow this conventional usage themselves.

TEACHING READER APPROACHES FOR CONTROVERSIAL TOPICS.   Our students confront a strikingly different challenge from their readers when their theses are openly controversial. With controversial theses, they face the problem of winning over their readers from attitudes of disagreement ranging from indifference to hostility. The greater the disagreement, the greater care our students will need to take with the "although" material expressing that disagreement, and the greater the attention they will need to pay to the feelings and needs of their readers.

Two Approaches.   Aristotle's advice that we must regard our readers as worthy opponents is often useful. Frequently, as our students determine their point and define its support, they will want to think of their readers as intelligent skeptics with "show me" attitudes.

But this approach alone may not always be the most effective one when our students are concerned with convincing readers of the value of what they have to say. Carl Rogers, a contemporary psychologist, has added modern psychological insights to Aristotle's ancient ones on the question of writer–

reader relationships. Rogers advises us to reach readers through those areas where agreement might be worked out, to try for some commonality of ideas as a start. He writes:

> Mutual communication . . . leads to a situation in which I see how the problem appears to you, as well as to me, and you see how it appears to me as well as to you.[11]

In other words, Rogers recommends that writers put themselves in their readers' place. His advice is similar to the folk wisdom of Native Americans that suggests "walking a mile in the other person's moccasins."

In Their Disagreeing Readers' Moccasins. In order to help our students put themselves in the place of those readers who strongly disagree with their point, we might ask them to try to remember how they had felt when they had read or heard something that challenged their most deeply held opinions. In the course of discussing such memories students should recall that the feelings such challenges aroused were not comfortable. Chances are they will also remember how easily an opponent of some idea they valued could overstep the line and make them feel defensive—or angry.

In Their Uncommitted Readers' Mocassins. It may be easier for our students to put themselves in the place of their uncommitted readers. If we begin discussion of the last time they were reading or listening to a partisan presentation of controversial material about which they had not yet made up their mind, they will surely recollect their desire to weigh matters for themselves and not be unduly influenced by the writer or speaker. They may even remember finding themselves in sympathy with the side they considered the underdog—that is, with the side the writer or speaker opposed, the side that could not argue back.

If these memories of themselves as a committed or uncommitted audience are at all vivid, students will realize that they cannot expect to ignore the views opposed to their point and hope that their readers will be unaware of their existence. They will know that these views are bound to be passing through the minds of those readers who are acquainted with the controversy, and they can be fairly certain that those who have not yet learned of it will be raising some of the issues in their minds as they present their case. And this thinking should lead students to two important conclusions about handling the "although" material:

1. When urging a controversial thesis, writers cannot afford to disregard or give only fleeting attention to the ideas of the opposition. Discussion of such material usually needs to expand beyond an introductory sentence or two.
2. It is to the writer's advantage to deal with these views fairly. Because their readers expect the other side to get a fair hearing, name-calling, sarcasm, snide remarks, or an abusive or superior tone will assuredly backfire.

Fair, Not Neutral.   In speaking strongly for fairness, however, we must take care not to give the illusion that we are advocating neutrality. We need to explain—and exemplify—the reality that presenting all positions equally leaves readers confused and dissatisfied. Even more convincing to students should be our argument that fairness itself demands that readers learn where writers stand. Fairness requires writers to identify their own position and to present the other side's arguments in terms of their position without distorting the views of either side. Thus, though it is to our students' rhetorical advantage to present the opposition viewpoint fairly, they should not hesitate to present their own opinions from their partisan point of view.

Roger's Strategies.   From Carl Rogers's thoughtful consideration of the negotiation at the heart of successful psychiatric counseling we can draw highly teachable persuasive strategies:

First, students should learn to root points of controversy in as broad a base of agreement as they can manage. Their readers are far more likely to give serious consideration to their differing viewpoint when writers show their own basic goodwill and their eagerness for their readers' goodwill by conceding to their side whatever points they can honestly concede. Good examples abound; for instance, William Raspberry's opening to his op-ed essay, "Children of Two-Career Families":

> Maybe you have to be crazy to argue with two Harvard psychiatrists—particularly two such insightful psychiatrists as Barrie Greiff and Preston Hunter.
>
> So before I register my small objection to their article in the May–June issue of *Harvard Magazine*, let me say that nearly everything these two doctors have to say about the strains and stresses of dual-career families makes sense to me.

And students need to put themselves in their readers' shoes and anticipate their response. In trying to think as their readers might think, they should be able to anticipate their questions and supply answers, to foresee their objections and quiet them.

Our students may find the Student Guidelines useful whenever they handle controversial topics.

STUDENT GUIDELINES

Strategies for Arguing Your Controversial Point Persuasively

1. Define the opposition material fairly.
2. Set forth your own position.
3. Concede what can be conceded.

continued
4. Raise and answer possible objections — that is, argue what must be argued.
5. Present your own case.

NOTE: Points 1 and 2 and points 4 and 5 may be handled in reversed order, depending upon circumstances.

Teaching Techniques for Influencing the Reader's Feelings

Classically, the audience corner of the Rhetorical Triangle (see Figure 6–1) is also the emotional corner. Student writers need to learn "to make contact with a reader's feelings," to use Crews's expression (3). To do so, it is not as important for our students to project any particular reader for their writing as it is for them to be convinced that, if their writing is to be meaningful at all, they must aim it at *some* reader. Whatever becomes of their writing, it will not be processed by a machine; it will be read by a reader who is as human as they are themselves, a real human being who can be both pleased and offended.

TEACHING STUDENTS TO AVOID STIRRING NEGATIVE FEELINGS. It is probably best to start out with complete frankness and set forth two important initial precepts:

- Don't bore your reader.
- Don't annoy or offend your reader.

Don't Bore Readers. Should a student respond to the first precept with "But what if the reader is just your teacher?" we can answer, with a grin, "As far as I'm concerned, it is particularly important that you do not bore your teacher." Some students find it hard to imagine a teacher being bored by student essays, but they respond very well to the hint — especially if we also emphasize how much we enjoy reading their papers when they are lively and interesting.

How can our students keep their work from boring their readers? They can write in a lively, natural style; they can include wit or humor where appropriate; they can eliminate wordiness, unconscious repetition, and all "padding"; and they can avoid monotony of diction or syntax. To avoid monotony of syntax, they should try to vary the length and structure of their sentences. To avoid monotonous diction, they should avoid repetitive vocabulary patterns and, where possible, clichés. Many teachers have found sentence-combining exercises (see Chapter 7) useful in teaching these skills.

Our emphasis on the avoidance of a boring style can be overdone quite easily, however. Keeping in mind that all the world is new to youth, we must be careful not to label as "cliché" an image or phrase our student has just freshly discovered or perhaps even reinvented. We must also take care that we do not place too much stock on mere liveliness, lest we risk the response exemplified by one of Booth's colleague's students, who complained, "I soon learned that all I had to do to get an A was imitate Thurber" (145).

Don't Offend Readers' Taste.   Teaching the second precept, about not annoying the reader, requires tact. The saying "One man's meat is another man's poison" is no less true because it is too often quoted. Our students' problem as writers is increased because in most cases they do not know their projected readers well enough to be sure of their taste. They certainly cannot count on any clear uniformity of taste. We need to convince them, therefore, that they are better off to avoid any language that large numbers of their potential readers would find offensive.

   Cultural Slurs.   Foremost among this language are slurs against racial, religious, or national groups or against any other group that has been subject to stereotyping. Not for rhetorical reasons alone is it important for us to stress that no group has a monopoly on any characteristic, either good or bad, nor to remind our students that it is not only false, but also boring to imply that it does. We must, of course, also make clear that we are not suggesting it is wrong to take issue with the opinions shared by a particular group. Students can, for instance, express strong disapproval of the terrorist tactics of the Palestinian Humaas organization without implying that "All Arabs are. . . ."

   Gender Slurs.   We will not, of course, be able to take up every sort of stereotypical thinking individually. But we certainly should not omit discussing stereotypes about women since more than half the population is involved. We need not dwell on the obvious boorishness of using such terms as "broad" or "chick," or of suggesting either of the contradictory notions that all women are weak and helpless or all women are domineering nags. Our students have difficulty with the dated sexist thinking rooted in the language itself. Here it is possible for them to offend quite unawares. They may find the following hints helpful:

STUDENT GUIDELINES

To Avoid Sexist Language

1. Use plurals wherever possible to avoid having to choose a sex-marked pronoun. For example, if you write "Judges should come to *their* decisions fairly," you avoid the awkward "A judge should come to *his or her* decisions fairly."
2. Avoid the use of expressions such as "lady doctor." These carry the insulting implication that a professional who is a woman is somehow less of a professional than a man is since it assumes that the occupational term by itself

continued
refers exclusively to men. When you write simply "Susan is an engineer," there is no lack of clarity.
3. Choose the more general term, not the male term. For example, use "humankind" rather than "mankind" and "person" instead of "man" (as in "We had a six-person stage crew" or "a five-member chess team").

Profanity and Obscenity. Another sensitive topic. On the one hand, we ask our students to speak in their own voices, and their informal voices often include such language. On the other hand, we ask students to think of their readers, and a sizable group of readers are offended by this language—including some of us ourselves. The answer, I believe, lies in suggesting that our students give careful thought to the sensibilities of the particular readers intended for a specific essay and to their purpose in the work. Unless writers feel certain that they cannot achieve the desired effect without using an expression many consider profane or obscene, they would probably be wise to delete it before the final draft.

Don't Annoy Readers by Carelessness. Students who habitually neglect to proofread their work find it difficult to understand the degree of annoyance such carelessness evokes. We have all known teachers who consider the submission of a smudged, untidy first draft or a paper full of easily corrected mechanical errors a personal affront. We have likewise all met or heard of businesspeople who do not hire an otherwise qualified applicant whose letter of application contains misspelled words and nonstandard usage or punctuation. Whether or not this sort of carelessness bothers us personally, we owe it to our students to let them understand the impression it leaves on some readers.

Avoid Inappropriate Jargon. Another annoyance to their readers we can caution our students to avoid is the use of "gobbledygook," with all its meaningless jargon, showy overcomplexity of syntax, and excessive nominalization. Though some of our students at first may not recognize this as a problem and others may even find themselves somewhat impressed by it, we can attack the problem with humor. We can ask our students to translate into plain English such blatant examples of gobbledygook as business-writing consultant's Albert Joseph's favorite: "Management has become cognizant of the necessity of eliminating undesirable vegetation surrounding the periphery of the facility" (Please kill the weeds around the building).[12]

We and our students will have little trouble, unfortunately, collecting similar examples we run into in our daily lives.

TEACHING STUDENTS TO PROMOTE READERS' POSITIVE FEELINGS. Once our students have come to understand these negative precepts, we can begin to show them methods by which they can influence their readers' feelings in positive ways. The premise fundamental to all work in this area is that it is possible to vary the emotional impact of prose by controlling the emotional intensity of the diction, the intensity and quantity of the imagery, and the degree of rhythmic quality of the syntax. If our students can become aware of the connotative possibilities of the words and images they can use and of the various syntactical patterns they can employ, they can learn to control the emotional content of their writing, intensifying it for climaxes and perhaps conclusions, neutralizing it for matter-of-fact presentations.

TEACHING THE USE OF PRECISE DICTION. English may be the best language in the world to employ for emotional impact because it is remarkably cosmopolitan in its vocabulary. The language we speak today originated in the combination of a Germanic Old English with a Romance Norman-French tongue, the mixture including also a fair-sized proportion of words borrowed directly from Latin and a generous smattering of Old Danish and other Scandinavian languages, plus a few Celtic remainders. Voraciously eclectic, English has continued to enlarge its word horde by borrowing vocabulary from a wide variety of languages ever since.

Probably the best way to introduce our students to the extraordinary semantic richness of the English language, therefore, is to start them thinking about synonyms, for there is scarcely a concept for which there are not at least two or three forms of English expression. That with which we think, for example, is variously called *mind* (Old English derivation), *reason* (Old French), *intellect* (Latin), or even *psyche* (Greek).

Denotative Precision. This multiplicity of synonyms does not fully account for the richness of the language, however. More important is the variety of nuances and shades of meaning offered by these synonyms. We can explain to our students that competing words of identical meaning do not exist long in a language together: either one word becomes dominant and drives the other out of use or their meanings differentiate enough so that both are needed to give a full range of expression for the concept. Thus, though synonyms can substitute for one another in certain contexts, they are never totally interchangeable. If, for instance, our students wanted to write about publicizing something, they would have a wide range of synonyms from which to choose, including *broadcast* (Old English), *publish* (Old French), *propagate* (Latin), *spread* (Old English), *promulgate* (Latin), *disseminate* (Latin). Which they would choose would depend a great deal upon the nature of the material they wished to publicize. They might, for instance, *broadcast* a game, but not *promulgate* it; they might *promulgate* a doctrine, but not *spread* it; and although they might *spread* fertilizer, they would surely not *propagate* it. (The more incongruous we can make the examples, the clearer we can demonstrate our point). Examples such as these demonstrate that even a series of synonyms can offer a wide variety of denotative meanings.

Connotative Precision. Connotative nuances also abound. True to the usual pattern in English, the words within this group derived from Anglo-Saxon (Old English) sources have an aura of greater informality than do the others, expecially those derived directly from the Latin. Even these words do not suggest the colloquiality of other synonyms of *publicize*—such as *ballyhoo* or *hawk about*—and even the Latinate words are less formal or less sublime (in Longinus's sense) than the biblically allusive *give tongue*.

Furthermore, synonyms do not have equivalent emotional weight or moral value. We might ask our students what is likely to be more important: that which is *promulgated* or that which is *bandied about?* Which is more likely to be believed? Or even more likely to be true? The semantic abundance of English thus permits writers

1. To express thoughts precisely and exactly
2. To control levels of formality or informality
3. To control the level of subjectivity or objectivity so as to imply the exact value intended.

STUDENT EXERCISES

Synonyms

If our students should need practice to solidify their understanding of these concepts, we might have them bring in lists of synonyms from which they can compose sentences illustrating the varying shades of denotative and connotative meanings we have been discussing with them. We might ask them to arrange some of these lists in an order ranging in value from highly positive through neutrality to extremely negative, as for example:

sagacious		fragrance
astute		bouquet
discerning		aroma
knowing		scent
shrewd	or	redolence
canny		rankness
cunning		putrescence
sly		stench
slick		stink

We might also ask them to arrange their lists according to emotional intensity:

dishabille
disarray

continued

continued
disorder
messiness
dirtiness
sloppiness
squalor

As a further exercise, we might ask students to write contrasting evaluative descriptions of the same interior setting or landscape, or to write
letters of recommendation from contrasting perspectives for an individual with a set of given characteristics. Such letters might contain, for
example, such sentences as these, listed in Brown and Zoellner's student rhetoric:

- Jerry Caldwell establishes rapport with his superiors very easily.
- Caldwell possesses the important capacity to see things from the perspective
  of his superiors.
- One cannot help but remark how quickly Caldwell establishes a congenial
  intimacy with his superiors.
- Caldwell doesn't consciously intend to adjust his view to those of his superi-
  ors—it just seems to fall out that way, with a consistency truly remarkable.
- Jerry Caldwell, one soon notes, has the happy faculty of always getting along
  with the people it pays to get along with.
- Jerry Caldwell, frankly, is a nasty little toady.[13]

A Word of Warning.   In teaching such exercises, we introduce our students to the wonders of the thesaurus, and some become enamored. Unfortunately, for some students such love can turn into comic valentines. Dissatisfied with the "commonness" of words that they know well and can use
without self-consciousness, they comb the thesaurus for more exotic synonyms. They seem unaware that interchanging synonyms without regard to
connotation or nuance can lead to such downright embarrassing sentences as
these from my students' papers:

- The nurse was *interminably* helpful.
- She was well known for her *soporific* conversational style.
- The graduate's father glowed with paternal *superciliousness.*

We may need to teach such students explicitly to use the thesaurus to gain
precision in their diction or to spur the memory when the elusive word is
just on the "tip of their tongue," but not to find a more impressive term—
especially one foreign to their natural vocabulary.

TEACHING STRONG VERBS AND VIVID NOUNS.   To help our students achieve the spare, clean style of writing that most of us admire, we
need to teach them to prefer strong verbs and vivid nouns and to go lightly

on adjectives, adverbs, and especially qualifiers. We can give them examples of passages such as this from a George Will magazine essay:

> When other kids' teams *were girding* for Homeric battles at the top of the league, my heroes [the Chicago Cubs] *had wilted* like salted slugs. (*Newsweek*, July 11, 1977)

If the students don't immediately see the effectiveness of such verbs, we could have them substitute a form of *be* or of a copulative verb such as *seem*, *appear*, or *become* that also need adjectival or nominative completion. For example, we might suggest:

> FAULTY   When other kids' teams *were getting ready* for Homeric battles . . . , my heroes *became* like salted slugs.

Furthermore, we can use such examples to show them that when nouns are strong, writing is not improved — and can be seriously diminished — by the addition of modifiers. Try for instance, converting this sentence from an essay by William Raspberry:

> This sense of uselessness, I am convinced, lies behind the shocking statistics on teen-age pregnancy, youthful homicide and suicide, crime, alcoholism, and drug abuse.

With modifiers added it could read:

> FAULTY   This *futile* sense of *utter* uselessness, I am *firmly* convinced, lies *dangerously* behind the shocking statistics on *aimless* teenage pregnancy, *malevolent* youthful homicide and *pathetic* suicide, *miserable* crime, *wasteful* alcoholism, and *deplorable* drug abuse.

Though every modifier in this revision is completely appropriate to its context, our students should have no difficulty in noting that the overkill lends a ludicrous, almost ironic, tone, even to a subject as serious as Raspberry's.

Similarly, we can add an infusion of *very*'s and *really*'s to almost any passage to show how these intensifiers often tend to diminish rather than magnify their subjects. "Serious warfare" appears more serious, for instance, than "really serious warfare."

Without deprecating the usefulness of copulative verbs, which, after all, predominate in English usage, or even of well-chosen modifiers, which good writers often put to vigorous use, we can still suggest that our students — especially in their revising — make their nouns and verbs as explicit and vivid as they can.

TEACHING FIGURES OF SPEECH: "FLOWERS OF RHETORIC."   In addition to touching the feelings of their audience semantically, ancient rhetoricians also approached their audiences through a complete repertoire of figures of speech which, as expanded and redefined during the Renaissance, came to be called "the flowers of rhetoric." Although many of the more elaborate figures are no longer a part of contemporary prose, some thirty to forty figures of the more than two hundred eventually categorized still maintain more than historical interest for us and our students. These include irony, the rhetorical question, inversion, and a wide variety of metaphor, repetition, and parallelism. For especially able students and those with a strong interest in language or history, a study of such figures can prove fascinating. A number of excellent references are available to help construct an enrichment unit or special study project for these students.[14]

For most of our students, however, rhetorical figures exert a practical rather than a scholarly appeal. For them, these figures — like points of grammar — are better studied when a perceived need arises — that is, when students understand how they can use them to enhance their writing.

Rhetorical-Figure Exercises.　We can, for example, point out especially serendipitous uses of rhetorical questions or inversions or parallelism in our student's work. Or we can give collaborative study groups professional examples of these techniques and ask them to point out places where such figures might enrich their members' papers.

To make this exercise useful, students will need to understand how these figures work — that is, why they are effective. They should have little difficulty in figuring out that by being different from the ordinary run of prose figures of speech call attention to themselves and thereby lend emphasis to the substance they express. Every appearance signals the sensitive reader to alertness, flashing the unconscious mind a "Watch now. This stuff is important" message. Beyond that, students should also be able to see a reason for the power of particular figures.

Rhetorical Questions.　For instance, they might point out that the rhetorical question not only catches a reader's eye because it is different from the rest of the prose, but also engages the reader's mind because, though it expects no overt answer, it is directed to the reader personally. Shana Alexander's is typical of the use of such questions our students can find:

> How is it that China can eliminate the house fly, and we can't even clean up Central Park? ("Getting Old in Kids' Country," *Newsweek*, December 11, 1972)

Irony.　Though irony often is not easy for our students, we can help them understand that in writing ironically, in saying or implying the opposite of what they believe to be true, they are using an effective way to get their readers to identify with them and their point of view. They should be able to see that writing ironically requires their readers to understand their actual intentions, and thus through its use they create a sly bond of conspiracy. It is as if they give a broad wink to their readers and flatter them by saying: "Those of you who are in the know will realize I am joking. I don't dare say how dreadful I think this matter is, but with *your* intelligence you will understand the strong criticism hidden in my words."

Effective examples should help clarify. Show them, for instance, a typical Walter Williams' sentence, such as this:

> It is fairly certain that societal love cannot explain the assimilation of past disadvantaged groups. (Heritage Syndicate, May 1980)

With our help, students should be able to see that Williams expects his shrewd readers to understand that he is very far from being only "*fairly* certain" and that he has no faith at all in the reliability of "societal love."

Inversion. Again, in the figure of inversion, students should be able to point to the curious emotional quality produced by inverting the syntax, as it does, for instance, in this passage from Joyce's *Portrait of the Artist as a Young Man:*

> But her long fair hair was girlish: and girlish and touched with the wonder of mortal beauty her face. (Modern Library edition, 299.)

This material comes alive for our students when we teach it as a way of enhancing particular essays.

Creating Rhetorical Figures. After our students clearly understand what is at work in these figures, they can go on to try creating their own. For the most part, they will experience rapid success. But sometimes they will run into problems. Irony, for example, can be a bit tricky. Students usually need some help in understanding the risks of being either too broad or too subtle. We need to counsel them that if their irony is too broad and sarcastic ("The cafeteria food here is just g-r-r-reat!," for instance), they are in danger of having their readers accuse them of being unfair or simplistic. But if, on the other hand, they are too subtle and do not give adequate clues to their real meaning, their readers may very well take them seriously and think they mean just the opposite of what they intend.

On the whole, however, once students begin to find themselves comfortable with figures such as these, our main task may well be to caution restraint. Some students become especially attached to inversion, for instance, and use it liberally throughout even their most mundane essays—sometimes to ludicrous effect—as in these two examples taken from my students' papers:

> The two teams continued to play the football game, though down fell the rain until deteriorated were the conditions.

> Teachers place too great an emphasis on grades. Due to the constant pressure, haggard and worn appear the students.

We thus may need to convince our students that since figures of speech gain their ability to affect an audience through their contrast with the norm, they lose their power through inappropriate use or overuse.

Further Discussion of Rhetorical Figures. Although all the "flowers of rhetoric" can enhance expository prose, some are more familiarly associated with poetry or narration and thus can be profitably first approached in such study. In fact, I have adopted that method in this text. Here metaphorical tropes and schemes involving repetition of sound (alliteration, assonance, consonance, and the like) are discussed with the teaching of poetry writing in Chapter 12 and the rhetorical embellishment provided by the use of anecdote, dialogue, characterization, realistic detail, and irony is included in Chapter 11 on teaching narrative writing.

THE WRITER, THE WRITER'S VOICE, AND THE "ETHICAL" APPEAL

The author's voice speaking through a piece of writing is extraordinarily influential on readers—often more influential than the readers are themselves aware. A recent computer analysis of the results of the grading of a typical group of experienced English teachers involved in an assessment project showed that voice was the single most important feature distinguishing the papers they graded "A" from the papers they graded "B"—much, I should add, to the teachers' own surprise.[15] Because of the tremendous rhetorical influence of the writer's voice, it is important that we help our students to a consciousness of their voice—their speaking selves—in their writing.

As teachers we have two main tasks in shaping this awareness: we have to help our students find their own writing voice, and we have to help them learn to vary this voice to fit the writing circumstances, the audience, and the subject of the occasion.

Helping Students Discover Voice

Before we can accomplish these tasks, our students must become aware of the speaking voice present in *all* writing and must learn to listen for it both when they read and when they write.

RECOGNIZING FICTIONAL VOICES.   Probably the best place to start a study of written voice is with first-person novels or short stories where the voice of the narrator is most insistent. Those of us who teach an integrated literature-composition curriculum might use as matter for discussion whatever first-person piece of fiction the class happens to be studying. The rest of us could duplicate pertinent passages from *Robinson Crusoe* or *Moll Flanders, David Copperfield* or *Great Expectations, Huckleberry Finn* or *Tom Sawyer, Augie March, To Kill a Mockingbird, My Name Is Ascher Lev, Invisible Man,* or *Catcher in the Rye,* or passages from short stories written by Joseph Conrad, William Faulkner, Ernest Hemingway, Phillip Roth, Grace Paley, or Flannery or Frank O'Connor.

After students have "listened" carefully to the narrator's "speaking voice," we can ask them to articulate their impressions of that character. Most students who have not given serious thought to voice or point of view before are surprised to discover how much they can infer about the background and character of the narrator from a passage whose subject matter contains no such directly stated information.

We should, of course, insist that students keep strictly to the text as they develop arguments to support their judgments. If they think Moll Flanders is mercenary, for instance, what words convey that impression to them? What phrases and devices make them conclude that Huck Finn is illiterate, or that he is morally naive but basically decent? Often our students will find themselves in agreement on their general impressions, though they might cite quite different aspects of the chosen passages as evidence for their conclusions. Even when they disagree, they will learn much through discussing the textual evidence supporting their conflicting impressions.

IDENTIFYING NONFICTIONAL AUTHORIAL VOICES. When our students have demonstrated a certain ease in interpreting character from the voice of fictional narrators, we might have them attempt the more subtle discrimination of the projected character and personality of speakers in expository prose. What character does John Steinbeck project in *Travels with Charlie*, for instance? How does it differ from that projected by the voice of John Hershey in *Hiroshima?* Or from that of Germaine Greer in *The Female Eunuch?* As different as these individual voices are, can they be distinguished together as the work of twentieth-century writers from the voices of the nineteenth-century essayists Charles Lamb or William Hazlitt? Or from Richard Steele or Dr. Johnson of the eighteenth century? Sir Thomas Browne of the seventeenth or Francis Bacon of the sixteenth? Nor should we neglect contemporary writers, the journalists and editorialists familiar to our students from newspapers and popular magazines. We might also include some examples of student writing.

How Writers Imply Character through Voice. We will want our students to be concerned also about the "how" of authorial voice. How, for instance, does Steinbeck's language convey the notion of a traveler who is friendly and concerned about people? How does Hershey make us believe that he was objective and nonjudgmental when he investigated the events at Hiroshima? What is there about the work of Sir Thomas Browne that convinces us that we are in contact with a man of a curious and interested turn of mind? What is there about the way Suzy has written her theme that makes us believe she is confident (or hesitant) about the opinions she expresses? If our discussion of these points is very specific, our students will come to understand the tonal effect that semantic, syntactical, and even grammatical variation can achieve. Discovering authorial purpose, however, is the central issue in any discussion of expository voice.

UNDERSTANDING AND CONTROLLING VOICE. Our goal throughout this whole discussion is to accustom our students to listening for the narrator's voice in everything they read and to arrive at judgments concerning the speaker in a conscious, rather than a purely visceral, way. In pursuing this goal, we must train our students to analyze the author's voice, perhaps the most important clue to a writer's intent. This skill is valuable. It is a tool that enhances the understanding—and the pleasure—our students take in their reading. It is also a consciousness essential to the informed citizens of a free society. Furthermore, our students must gain this consciousness before they can learn to control the voice in their own writing.

Cicero's Exercise.   Once they gain this consciousness, we might encourage our better students to try to imitate the style—and especially the voice—of some of the authors they study, as rhetoric students have been doing from Cicero's day almost to our own. We might assign a paragraph on a simple descriptive topic—perhaps "The First Snowfall," "The Cafeteria," or "The Big Game"—and have them try to capture the voice and the tone of two or three authors of widely diverging styles.

Walker Gibson's Exercise.   Although Cicero's exercise is truly relished by our most capable students, many of a more average bent find it difficult indeed—too difficult, in fact, unless some specifications for diction and sentence structure are included. Walker Gibson has constructed a three-step exercise with just this sort of specification. He begins with the following assignment:

> Write me a few sentences in which you describe the circumstances of your birth and early life, as if you were beginning some sort of autobiography. Just a few sentences. Ten minutes.[16]

In the second step, Gibson presents his class with the introductory paragraphs from Charles Dickens's *David Copperfield* and Saul Bellow's *Augie March* and leads his students in the sort of comparative analytical discussion described above until they are not only able to characterize the two narrators (old-fashioned, British, witty, easy, urbane, for example, as opposed to modern, American, serious, tense, independent), but can point to the syntactic semantic features of both samples through which these characterizations have been achieved.

In the final step, Gibson asks his students to apply their knowledge of these specified features to their own autobiographical paragraphs, rewriting them first in an imitation of David's voice and again in an imitation of Augie's. The exact assignment changes, of course, with the features different classes discover, but Gibson offers a typical set of directions:

> In their [Dickens's imitation, students should] put half of their verbs in the passive voice, more than half of their statement in subordinate clauses, place some subordination ahead of subject-verb structure in their sentences, and use no contractions. Their [Bellow] rewriting, of course, would proceed contrariwise; use no passive verbs, little subordination after subject-verb, interrupt the syntax with a dash or two, and include a few contractions. (309)

In adapting this exercise, we might switch the subject-authors to two equally diverse contemporary essayists. And we might wish to ask our students to complete the assignment by including a brief commentary in which they would set down their conclusions as to which of the two imitations was most like their own style of writing, which felt more natural to them, and which of their three autobiographical openings they thought the most effective. The paragraphs and the commentary should provoke lively discussion. Gibson's exercise can thus provide our students with a transition from the theoretical consideration of other people's styles to a practical delineation of their own.

Helping Students Find Their Own Voice

The conclusion that almost inevitably arises from discussions such as those described above is that there is no such thing as an absence of voice in written composition, that all writing reflects its author (or narrator), and that all writing is to some degree personalized. But when we come to asking students to apply this knowledge to their own writing, some of them may at first be reluctant. Children of a mechanistic age, they have somehow enshrined depersonalization in their system of values. In particular, they may insist that a personal voice destroys the "objectivity" they believe essential to expository writing, and they may fear that a personal voice could entice them into using the "I" many believe they have been forever forbidden.

RECOGNIZING THE VOICE OF A MACHINE. To counteract this misperception we might find (or write) one of those jargon-filled paragraphs awkward with the typical nominalizations that help a writer avoid the first person. We could, for instance, ask students to note the voice in this passage:

> The possibility existed for the implementation of the increase in productivity. The findings of the survey have been announced and have resulted in concern that increased market availability would have implications of a weakening in demand and a softening in price.

Under this gobbledygook, there is, of course, a voice. But, as our students themselves will recognize, that voice is scarcely human: it is the voice of a machine. Having experienced such horrors, they may well come round to Sheridan Baker's opinion:

> Good writing should have voice, and that voice should be unmistakeably your own.[17]

FINDING ONE'S OWN VOICE. How can our students find their own voice and become comfortable with it? There is much we can do to help them on their way. The following exercises offer students the progressive opportunity to recognize the nuances in the sound of their own voices, to include these nuances in their written work, and to learn to employ them to rhetorical advantage.

1. **Tape-recorded impromptu speeches.** We can offer our students the chance to listen to their own voices in impromptu speeches, which we record. They can pull a student-suggested topic for a minute speech from a container. Or for a slightly longer speech, students can choose their topic from a list of current questions we have prepared.

   We can make verbatim transcriptions of a student's oral style in this way, which can be read aloud so the class can try to recognize authors by their characteristic tone.

2. **Oral and written voice.** Students can be asked to make an oral presentation of a paper, as Leo Hamalian suggests, first giving its purpose and essence spontaneously and then reading it aloud.[18] Classmates can be encouraged to compare the two renditions to see if the student's voice rings through the written work. If the audience finds naturalness or conviction lacking, students can be asked to revise their work to include more of the quality of their spoken voice.

Helping Students to Vary Their Voice

Through discussions and exercises such as these, our students can gain a sense of the author's voice speaking to the reader of a written composition; they can become aware of the special sound of their own voice when they become that author; and they can come to understand the persuasiveness which comes when that voice conveys conviction, when their voice "rings true." From such understandings, they will probably conclude that they must learn to express *themselves* in their writing.

When they have made such a judgment, they will be faced with the question central to the authorial corner of the rhetorical triad (see Figure 6–1): Which self should I express in my writing? For our students, like all human beings, are a composite of many different selves and have many different stances in which they face the world. A single one of our students might be, in Bruce Lockerbie's words,

> a member of a family, a member of a school society, citizen of a community, citizen of a nation . . . an athlete, a musician, a scholar, a lover, [who from time to time adopts the stance of] a crazy teen-ager on a discotheque floor, a cloistered pedant afflicted with polysyllablism, a finger-jabbing evangelist, a folksy acquaintance dropped in for a chat.[19]

Which self, then, should students express in a given composition? Our answer is clear: (1) The appropriate self—the self that expresses itself with the degree of formality (and informality), the degree of expertise, and the degree of subjectivity (or objectivity) most appropriate to the particular subject and most agreeable to the particular audience, along with; (2) His or her "better" self.

HELPING STUDENTS FIND THEIR APPROPRIATE VOICE. Students will want to know how to find the voice to express the self appropriate to the subject and to the audience. We can assure them that, for the most part, they already understand instinctively what are the appropriate tones and that they regularly employ them as occasions arise in their ordinary lives. To convince our students of their natural expertise, we might assign an exercise in which they address messages on a single specified topic to (1) their best friend, (2) their employer, and (3) their date. They might, for example, explain to each why they cannot keep an appointment—perhaps because the agreed-upon time will be their only opportunity to make up a failed examination.

Degree of Formality.   In the discussion that follows the writing of these notes, we should lead our students to consider just how the notes differ. They should have little trouble recognizing that the notes vary in their degree of formality depending upon the degree of intimacy and the individual quality of the particular relationships. The note to the friend, for instance, might be an approximation of the student's conversational style, while that to the employer might show a greater care for the conventions of standard syntax and might even be phrased in a more Latinate vocabulary.

Degree of Subjectivity.   We might also introduce another element that controls variation in voice, the degree of subjectivity or objectivity with which the writer considers the topic. To demonstrate the workings of subjectivity-objectivity, we might suggest some controversial issue of current interest and perhaps give students twenty minutes or so of class time to jot down a paragraph attacking the issue from each of these perspectives.

Afterward, when they are looking at their papers and now taking the time to think through what they had done naturally and instinctively under tight time pressure, our students will probably first point to the matter-of-fact quality of the objective style and the more emotional quality of the subjective. We might then try to elicit ways they went about achieving these effects. They would probably discover in their subjective paragraph, for example, a more highly charged vocabulary, a greater use of personal pronouns, and perhaps a more rhythmic quality to the sentences than the more connotatively neutral diction of their objective stance. In the paragraph written with an objective approach, they would find shorter, less complex sentences.

When should writers be subjective and personal and when should they adopt an objective stance? The personal note, without question, requires a subjective tone, and the description of the scholarly contents of an academic course, almost as certainly, requires an objective one. But what of topics that may be viewed in either way—as, for example, capital punishment or abortion rights? Here writers have to make conscious decisions in choosing between their subjective or their objective voice.

Objective or Impassioned Persona?   The most effective writers usually rely upon a combination of both. We might suggest to our students that in argumentative writing, such as that required by the topics mentioned above, they might gain authority over their material by approaching it in the stance of an "Objective Observer," who stands off at a distance and, like Dragnet's Sergeant Friday, gives "Just the facts, ma'am, just the facts." Their readers will appreciate their insistence upon the unembellished facts and may be drawn to their interpretation of them.

On the other hand, the righteous indignation of an "Impassioned Advocate" speaking out for justice carries a moral authority. If our students can demonstrate with the objective facts that their indignation is indeed justified, they can wear their advocacy like a banner, and still be able to carry their readers with them.

Which Voice Is the Best? Clearly, the one most appropriate to the writer's purpose in the specific instance. As I argued at the beginning of this chapter, that style is best in which the author's purpose and the way it is put into words are most at one. We need to urge our students to consider their relationship to their readers to capture the appropriate tone for the particular piece of writing and to maintain this tone consistently.

Ethos: Helping Students Discover the Voice of Their "Better" Self

The most persuasive voice of all is the voice of the writer's "better" self. Aristotle thought that the most persuasive speaker was at root a good person whose speech could convince his audience of that goodness; for an audience is much moved by what it perceives to be the *ethos*, the ethical character, of the speaker. And Aristotle's precepts are still of value to our students today. Edward P. J. Corbett writes:

> The [personal] appeal can be the most effective kind of appeal; even the cleverest and soundest appeal to the reason could fall on deaf ears if the audience reacted unfavorably to the speaker's character.[20]

The personal characteristics most affecting to an audience, according to Aristotle, are (1) good sense, (2) high moral integrity, and (3) good feelings toward others—especially, perhaps, good feelings toward the members of the audience. To explore these ideas, we can have students work in groups and read through a series of essays. The task of each group would be to determine how professional authors project (or do *not* project) these three ethical qualities. Having shared their ideas in full-class discussion, students can then derive ways of doing it themselves.

THE VOICE OF GOOD SENSE. How can our students persuade their readers that they have good sense and intellectual authority? They need, first, to be able to show whatever special expertise they might have. How can they show it? Competent handling of the material clearly demonstrates command of the subject. And this is particularly true when students have to write on a subject where they have had little previous understanding. We need to convince them that study is the only answer in such situations. But we can assure them that when they master a subject well enough to be able to speak knowledgeably about it, they will be able to write on it convincingly.

THE VOICE OF INTEGRITY. For readers to give credence to a piece of writing, they need to trust the author. How can our students project the necessary strength of character? One essential way is through absolute precision in their use of source material. We need to insist that if they quote as much as a brief phrase from another writer, they must designate it as a quotation and credit its author. If they borrow even part of an idea, they must never neglect to credit its source. We need to remind our students that unless they as writers tell their readers otherwise, those readers have the right to believe that every word and every idea are original with the author. Should a writer give readers reason to suspect differently, their faith in the writer and in what he or she writes will be severely shaken.

Another means of giving moral authority to their work is to treat the opposition fairly—though in the still-partisan way discussed earlier.

THE VOICE OF GOOD FEELINGS TOWARD OTHERS. An author projects good feelings toward readers especially by letting them understand that they share each others' values. (See discussion of the Rogerian approach to readers, pages 202–5.) Where writers must part company with the values of their readers, they must understand that they are doing so and tactfully prepare for this departure.

We might also tell our students that though the voice speaking from the composition should be knowledgeable and certainly should not betray ignorance of the subject, in deference to the readers it also should not show off or seem to brag. It should speak in a genuinely confident tone with neither arrogance nor false modesty. It should be rooted in solid values and speak in tones neither prissy nor licentious. Never blasé or bored, the writer's voice should reflect a sincere interest and concern for the subject without becoming gushy or resorting to florid prose. And writers should take special care not to offend.

Answering Our Students. Although our discussion of voice and the projection of the writer's image has the authority of a continuing tradition more than two thousand years old, we must not be surprised if some of our students regard it with distaste. They may protest that the presentation suggested would be studied and calculated, and therefore manipulative and essentially false. To counter such objections we need to remind our students, first of all, that we have agreed that the voice projected, whatever its modulation, must be truly their own or the work will not carry conviction. We are suggesting only that they use the voice of their better self. As Toby Fulwiler writes:

> There is something that I stand for, some set of beliefs and ideas that characterize me—that, too, is part of voice.[21]

Furthermore, not subterfuge, but awareness of the relevant elements of a situation, is involved in our students' finding the appropriate voice for a specific occasion.

We can also approach our students on the pragmatic level. We can argue that since their writing, like all writing, will have a voice that will necessarily make some impression, good or bad, upon the reader, surely they should want to make it a good one. Teachers, like all readers, unconsciously evaluate the writer's character from the voice projected as they read. Teacher Eugene H. Smith had the opportunity to bring this assessment to the conscious level when he was asked by a colleague to respond to a student theme. In his analysis he wrote, in part:

> I sense a mechanical, unimaginative quality in this voice. The assignment was probably approached in a businesslike way, probably with an unspoken, "O.K., he wants me to answer some questions. The answers are pretty obvious. I'll crank 'em out by the numbers, and there's one more silly assignment done. What's next?"[22]

If we read these comments to our students, they may exchange sheepish glances with one another, for they will probably be surprised at how clearly underlying attitudes speak through a writer's prose. We might follow up Smith's analysis by bringing in similar examples of student themes (though, of course, not those written by members of the class before us) and ask the class to detect underlying attitudes just as Smith did. Such a discussion should help motivate most of our students to take a real interest in the tone projected by their writing voice.

REVISING FOR VOICE AND TONE. Even those students who still do not feel really comfortable in consciously going about creating a favorable image will probably be able to see the merit of revising their first drafts to eliminate negative tonal impressions. We should recommend this sort of revision enthusiastically; for when our students go back and reread their first drafts, they become their own best audience. If sufficient time has elapsed, they can even experience their own work in a frame of mind akin to the way their readers will experience it. Thus they may be able to be affected in a similar way by inconsistencies of voice and lapses of tone.

Avoid an Offensive Tone. Tone is the sound of the writer's voice talking to the reader. No matter how cogent a writer's argument, readers will not be persuaded if they find the tone offensive. A class discussion about offensive tone should probably elicit the conclusion that what is offensive in writing tone is similar to the tones that most people find irritating in conversation and that conversations make us uncomfortable when they make us feel inadequate.

We can have students list what makes them personally uncomfortable. Using these lists as a basis for further discussion should evince that, in writing as in conversation, it is better to avoid an overbearing tone or a show-off manner. A sneering tone does not prompt readers to share in the disapproval the writer expresses. It rather leads them to believe that the writer (or speaker) is mean-spirited, not to be trusted on this point, and probably not very sound in general. Students will probably also decide that a gushy tone does not convince readers that the subject deserves such effusions, but rather that the writer (or speaker) is insincere and, again, not to be trusted.

They may also note that conversationalists—and readers—tend similarly to shy away from an angry tone. Satire scholar David Worcestor offers a particularly telling explanation for why tones that seem overemotional tend to backfire:

> It is acute discomfort to be present where a man has fallen into a furious passion. If you are in such a situation, and the object of your acquaintance's rage has no connection with you, you will experience an instinctive craving to turn the painful situation into a ludicrous one. This is done by withdrawing all sympathy from the blusterer and by taking a more relativistic view of him as a lobster-faced baboon in a fit.[23]

We may need to help students to curb expression of their righteous indignation for these pragmatic reasons, and instead deliberately to adopt a more persuasive moderate tone.

Revising Tone. Students—indeed all writers—find tone a particularly difficult element to check for themselves. Peer-response groups or partners can be helpful here. But we need to remind students worried about tone to consider asking their response partner to read their essays aloud to them. When writers read aloud their own work, the group (or partner) may hear only the tone meant, rather than the one that the paper actually imparts.

More often than not, students will be able to correct the flaw by omitting a word or two or by substituting words of a less inflammatory character. Should the problem go deeper and the questionable tone pervade the entire essay, students may want to reword the whole piece so that it reflects a more reasoned point of view. Group revision should convince our students that there is much persuasive force in restraint.

In revising their papers, students should find the Voice and Tone Student Guidelines helpful.

STUDENT GUIDELINES

Voice and Tone

1. *Degree of formality (or informality):* Are the voice and tone appropriate to the formality of the occasion? Of the subject? Of the relationship between the

continued

continued

  writer and the readers? Does this degree of formality remain consistent
  throughout the composition? If not, where are the inconsistencies?

2. *Degree of expertise:* Is the degree of simplicity (or difficulty) of vocabulary
   and syntax appropriate to the knowledge or ignorance of the readers? Does
   the modesty or confidence in the tone of address reflect the relative expertise
   of writer and reader appropriately? Do these items remain consistent
   throughout? If not, where do violations occur?

3. *Degree of subjectivity (or objectivity):* Is the degree of subjectivity of the tone
   and voice appropriate to the occasion? The subject? The readers? If I have
   chosen the approach of the "Objective Observer" or the "Impassioned Advocate" (or a stance in-between), do I retain it consistently throughout? If not,
   where are the inconsistencies?

4. *"Better" self:* Do I put my best foot forward? Do I let my genuine interest
   in, or enthusiasm for, the subject show? Are my own integrity, high values,
   and concern for others implicit throughout? Do I approach my audience as
   a respected friend rather than as an adversary?

5. *Possible lapses:* Does the voice in my paper ever become even momentarily
   peevish? Sneering? Sardonic? Falsely modest? Arrogant? Overbearing?
   Blasé? Cynical? Unconfident? Defensive? If so, where are the lapses?

Personal Pronouns

We really should not leave a discussion of the relationship of writers to their
readers without some mention of the rather tricky problems of personal pronouns. Students are surprisingly misinformed in this area. Somehow a large
number of them have come to believe they have received a solemn edict:
"Thou shalt not use 'I' or 'You' in thy writing." Even when a teacher points
out to them that people can scarcely be expected to write compositions about
their own experiences or ideas without using "I," many students respond
"Ye— —es, that would seem sensible, but you're still not s'posed to use 'em."
Thus, even though some of these students suspect that the prohibition is all
palpable nonsense, they still invent all sorts of circumlocutions and lean heavily on passive constructions in order to avoid the first-person singular.

  Throughout our course, therefore, we will need to assure and *re*assure
our students that these pronouns need not be neglected in written discourse.
In fact, as James Hoetker and Gordon Brossell discovered in their research,
essays written in the first person received significantly higher holistic scores
than those written in the third person.[24]

  Particularly when we are concentrating on style, we might want to point
out the purposes pronouns can serve, the rhetorical effects they can produce.

FIRST PERSON: *I.*   In a single-author work, "I" is the writer's voice speaking to the reader, and our students should learn to feel comfortable using it
whenever they want to communicate directly with the reader. The need for

this sort of communication will, of course, arise far more frequently in a subjective than in an objective work. When "I" is also the subject of the work or a participating observer—as in essays on "The Things I Did Last Summer," "My Brother," or "My Religious Beliefs"—the writer will naturally use "I" very often. In a research paper or in other such objective work, some writers will use the "I" infrequently, others perhaps not at all. Nevertheless, our students should understand that there is no prohibition on the use of "I," even in this more objective sort of work.

Since "I" in itself indicates subjectivity, its use brings the writer into closer communication with the reader and creates a warmer, more personal tone, which can also be persuasive. When writers want to put the force of their own conviction and/or moral character behind their words, as for instance when they present themselves in or near the role of the "Impassioned Advocate," they will find the first-person singular effective. "I" also gives writers a method of distinguishing their personal opinion from the factual matter surrounding it or from the views of others being reported.

When Is Too Much? The use of the first-person singular can be overdone, of course. Although "I" phrases, such as "I believe" or "I think," act as qualifiers, like "perhaps," which can add a scholarly hesitancy or a becoming modesty to an assertion, too many such expressions point to a hesitancy or a lack of confidence in the statements they qualify. And since the reader is perfectly aware that the writing *is* the writer's beliefs or thoughts, some teachers discourage this usage.

In addition, such common student "I" phrases as "In this paper I am going to prove . . .," though not really incorrect, are awkward skaffolding that should be dismantled or, at least, discouraged in the final draft. (See discussion in Chapter 4.) Then, too, as in conversation, an excessive use of the first person, especially when used repeatedly at the beginning of sentences, can suggest an unpleasant egocentrism.

FIRST PERSON: *WE*. Much of what has already been said about "I" applies equally to "we." When there are multiple authors, "we" is the voice of the composition, and in such works "we" can also be the subject. "We" can also be the subject of single-author works, as in essays concerning "my brother and me" or "the girls in the club." Like the first-person singular, the first-person plural should be used in these cases as the exigencies of the narrative demand or when the authors want to communicate with the reader. The effects of the plural form employed in these ways are much like those of the singular.

"We" also has other uses and creates other effects. "We" permits authors to include their readership in whatever they wish to say. It is the natural pronoun in works where the writer is a member of the group addressed, as, for example, in the present book where "we" are all teachers (or prospective teachers) of composition. It can also be used in a larger sense to take the readers into the writer's confidence, to include them in the writer's sentiments, as, for instance, in "We cannot help but conclude from these examples. . . ." This usage can be effective in reinforcing the author–reader relationship, for in its use it says "We—that is, you, dear reader, and I—have just discussed. . . ."

When Is Too Much?   There are also rhetorical dangers in the overuse of the first-person plural. When "we" is used too frequently where "I" is really meant as a substitute for the authorial "I" phrases—as, for example, in "We will soon explain this point," it can create the overbearing quality of a royal imperative. And as effective as the cozy "You-and-I-dear-reader 'we' " may be, when used to excess it can take on the tone of saccharine condescension sometimes associated with the less-skilled kindergarten teacher or pediatric nurse.

SECOND PERSON: *YOU*.   We will probably need to be more careful in advising our students on the use of this pronoun, for the word is used in two different senses: the "you" of address, as in "you, dear reader," and the impersonal "you," used colloquially to signify "one." The colloquial impersonal "you" is gaining in acceptance. It imparts a currently much admired informal, vernacular quality to the prose in which it appears. If this implication is the writer's intention, all is well. But if the writer intends the more formal approach of standard written English, then the informal "you" is incongruous, the connotative and denotative meanings conflict, and according to our definition, bad style is created.

On the other hand, addressing the reader directly with "you" can be an effective device when appropriately used. It can give a conversational, folksy tone, as in the works of Henry Fielding, or it can lend a personal imperative in works calling upon their readers for action.

THE SUBJECT AND THE APPEAL TO REASON

In explaining the elements of the Rhetorical Triad, ancient rhetoricians identified the speaker (or writer) with an appeal to ethics—that is, an appeal based upon the speaker's character—identified the audience (or readers) with an appeal to emotion—their feelings—and identified the subject itself with an appeal to reason. In order to make the style of the composition appeal to reason, these rhetoricians had the speaker (or writer) discover the logic inherent in the subject matter and then structure the composition or arrange it accordingly to this logical pattern. This advice is as valid for our students today as it was for the youth who followed the peripatetic philosopher about the garden of ancient Athens. Contemporary methods for teaching composition according to this advice are outlined earlier in this book in Chapters 2 through 5.

Balance

As central as a reasoned presentation of subject matter is to the creation of good expository prose, we must be careful not to stress it to the exclusion of the other elements of the Rhetorical Triad, for when the style of a work reflects only the subject, forgetting the speaker and audience, a curious sort of academese is produced, redolent of empty pedantry. Booth says this kind of writing is "written not for readers, but for bibliographies," and that it "soils our scholarly journals" (142). Ken Macrorie excoriates such writing and calls it "Engfish."[25]

We must strive to help our students achieve rhetorical balance, lest we help turn them into Engfishers.

IDEAS FOR DISCUSSION OR ESSAY

1. How do you define style? Are you attracted to one of the three theories outlined by Milic? (See note 2.) Do you believe style to be an aspect of a writer's personality? Do you think that it is inseparable from meaning, that style and meaning are essentially one? Do you consider style to be a way of adorning, of embellishing, meaning? Or do you favor the Wimsatt-Beardsley theory detailed in this chapter? Write your own definition of style and tell how, in terms of your theory, good style can be distinguished from bad style and how, using your theory, students may be helped to improve their writing style.

2. Discuss Booth's paragraph on stylistic perversions (pages 197–98), a passage often acclaimed as a succinct analysis of the causes of bad writing. Exemplify each perversion with a sample from professional or student writing, or create your own examples.

3. Do you share Booth and Macrorie's concern that in neglecting voice and audience teachers often encourage students to write in a style that has no value outside of the educational setting? Basing your arguments on your experience in your own student days, defend or dispute their contention.

4. Try out for yourself some exercises that Dona J. Hickey includes in *Developing a Written Voice* (31–53) and I have summarized below. Hickey designed these exercises to give insight into stylistic features of the written voice by severely constraining the writer:

   a. Write a half-page paragraph using
      • No sentence of more than ten words
      • No word of more than one syllable.
   b. In writing and sharing these paragraphs, what can you conclude about the power of short sentences? About monosyllabic words? About colloquial speech patterns? About how personal assumptions concerning the constraints determine both topic and style?

    c. Write an extended paragraph or two, about a page in all, with
- No sentence of more than eighteen words
- No words of more than two syllables, with at least half of only one
- Each sentence at least four words shorter or longer than the one before it
- At least half the sentences ending in a consonant sound.

    d. In writing and sharing these paragraphs, what can you conclude about varying sentence length? About the most important part of the sentence? About coherence? About word choice?

5. A number of exercises for students have been included in this chapter. Work through two or three yourself and write an evaluation of their effectiveness.

NOTES

The part opening epigraph is from Alfred North Whitehead, *The Aims of Education* (1929).

    Chapter 6 opening epigraphs are from Dona J. Hickey, *Developing a Written Voice* (Mountain View, Ca.: Mayfield, 1993) 192–93; and Erica Lindemann, *A Rhetoric for Writing Teachers*, 2nd ed. (New York: Oxford UP, 1987), 32.

    1. Louis T. Milic persuasively argues that all theories of style can be comprehended under three theories: psychological monism—that is, the style is the man—Crocean aesthetic monism—form and content are inseparable—and rhetorical dualism—style is an adornment of meaning. Milic grants a strain of truth to all three theories, but insists that only dualism is pedagogically viable for the teaching of composition. In "Theories of Style and Their Implication for the Teaching of Composition," *CCC* 26 (1965): 66–69, 126.

    2. In the much anthologized articles: Monroe C. Beardsley, "Style and Good Style," *Reflections on High School English*, ed. Gary Tate (Tulsa: U of Tulsa P, 1966), 91–105, and W. K. Wimsatt, "Style as Meaning," *Introduction to The Prose Style of Samuel Johnson* (New Haven: Yale UP, 1941).

    3. Aristotle, *Selected Works*, Trans. Lane Cooper (New York: D. Appleton, 1932), 7, 8–9.

    4. Wayne Booth, "The Rhetorical Stance," *CCC* 14 (1963): 139, 141.

    5. The surprisingly little research that has been done on the effectiveness of prewriting audience definition has failed to show qualitative improvement in student papers where this was required. For confirmation, see George Hillocks, Jr. *Research in Written Composition: New Directions for Teaching*, (Urbana: NCRE and ERIC, 1986), 84–91. See also H. E. Nugent, "The Role of Audience Awareness in the Writing of College Freshmen," *DAI* 41 (1979): 3279-A; and Gordon Brossell, "Rhetorical Specification in Essay Examination Topics," *CE* 45 (1983): 165–173, who writes:

> There is almost no experimental research evidence to support the idea that full rhetorical specification assures essay examination topics that will elicit the writer's best writing. (165)

    Duane H. Roen concurs in 'The Effects of Audience Awareness on Drafting and Revising," *RTE* 22 (1988): 75–88, though he suggests that "audience analysis is a particularly valuable revising activity" (83).

6. Richard L. Larson, "Teaching Before We Judge: Planning Assignments in Composition," *Teaching High School Composition*, eds. Gary Tate and Edward P. J. Corbett (New York; Oxford UP, 1970), 215.

7. For a full description and an elaboration of this exercise, see Albert C. Yodr, "Dear Ann: I have a Problem" in *Writing Exercises from "The Exercise Exchange,"* ed. Littleton Long (Urbana: NCTE, 1976): 97–98.

8. Hugh Rank in "Audience-Directed Writing: Magazines and Personae," *EJ*, 1970): 405–8, gives a detailed account of a similar series of lessons.

9. Frederick Crews, *Random House Handbook* (New York: Random House, 1974), 3.

10. Peter Elbow in "Closing My Eyes as I Speak: An Argument for Ignoring Audience," *CE* 49 (1987): 50–69, points out that students sometimes need to "learn to turn off audience awareness and write in the desert island mode—to turn off the babble of outside voices in the head and listen better to quiet inner voices. . . . to forget about other readers [and] be one's own reader" (65).

11. Carl Rogers, "Communication: Its Blocking, Its Facilitation," in *On Becoming a Person* (Boston: Houghton, 1961), 336.

12. Albert Joseph, *Put It in Writing* (Cleveland: Industrial Writing Institute, 1977), 22.

13. Clarence A. Brown and Robert Zoellner, *The Strategy of Composition: A Rhetoric with Readings* (New York: Ronald, 1968), 297–98. Some other exercises on synonyms are included in Thomas W. Wilcox's "Synonymy and Tone," in Long, *Writing Exercises*, 37–40.

14. Among them, Hickey, *Developing a Voice*, Chapter 4, especially 77–106, where she defines and exemplifies a good number of the most useful tropes and schemes; Edward P. J. Corbett, *Classical Rhetoric for the Modern Student*, 2nd ed. (New York: Oxford UP, 1990), who offers a thorough-going analysis of the way these devices serve to affect an audience; and Richard L. Graves, "A Primer for Teaching Style," *CCC* 25 (1974): 282–85, who outlines exercises through which the classic figures of speech might be taught.

15. During a workshop in connection with Wilmington College's Early English Composition Assessment Project, sponsored by an Ohio State Board of Regents grant, 1990–91.

16. Walker Gibson. "An Exercise in Prose Style," *Rhetoric: Theories for Application*, ed. Robert W. Gorrell (New York: Oxford UP, 1970), 306.

17. Sheridan Baker, *The Practical Stylist* (New York: Harper, 1986), 6.

18. Leo Hamalian, "The Visible Voice: An Approach to Writing," *EJ* 59 (1970): 229.

19. Bruce Lockerbie, "The Speaking Voice Approach Joins the Rhetoric Parade," *EJ* 56 (1967): 414.

20. Corbett (1965), 80.

21. Toby Fulwiler, *College Writing*, (Glenview, Ill.: Scott, 1988), 164.

22. The essay which prompted these comments is quoted in full along with Smith's complete analysis in "Composition Evaluation: A Problem of Voice," *EJ* 56 (1967): 1190.

23. David Worcestor, *The Art of Satire* (Cambridge: Harvard UP, 1940), 17–18.

24. James Hoetker and Gordon Brossell, "The Effects of Systematic Variations in Essay Topics on the Writing Performance of College Freshmen," *CCC* 40 (1989).

25. Ken Macrorie, *Uptaught* (New York: Hayden, 1970).

Teaching Grammar and Syntax: Help from the Science of Linguistics

> When I want to free myself from a particularly obnoxious person at a cocktail party, all I have to do is tell him I'm a grammarian. . . When I like the person and want to continue the conversation, I say I'm a linguist.
>
> —Max Morenberg

□ □ □

Linguistics is the systematic study of language. This study has been approached from a striking diversity of outlooks. Late in the nineteenth century the Grimm brothers of fairy-tale fame, along with like-minded colleagues, opened the door to modern scientific study of the history of language by discovering the interconnectedness of the languages making up the Indo-European family of languages. Since their time, anthropological linguists, regional-dialect linguists, and other historical linguists have built upon the foundations of their work. In recent years, and especially since the emergence of the computer as a research tool, linguistic research has focused upon attempts to discover workable models capable of explaining the complex processes involved in the generation of language: psycholinguists have been working on theories to explain the developmental growth of language capacity from infancy onward, while linguistic grammarians have worked on theories to explain exactly how human thought is formulated into actual speech.

Despite the obvious interrelatedness of linguistics and language arts, until quite recently the body of linguistic knowledge has been little more than tangential to the teaching of writing.[1] But now linguistics is also assuming pedagogic importance. For example, linguistics offers the insights we need to help our nonstandard-dialect-speaking students (this topic is discussed in Chapter 8). Moreover, linguistic understandings can help us make the study of grammar more relevant to student writing, and also form the theoretical background for sentence-combining exercises, the single most effective way to teach writing style. These topics will be the focus of Chapter 7.

THE GRAMMAR CONTROVERSY

How should we teach our students English syntax? Should we teach grammar at all? The answers are far from simple. For thoughtful and comprehensive discussions of the problem in terms of the research, see recent books by Rei R. Noguchi, George Hillocks, Jr., and Constance Weaver.[2] See also Teaching Grammar: A Summary of the Research, below.

Problems with Traditional Grammar Pedagogy

A solid body of scholarly research has demonstrated that knowledge of grammar will not, of itself, improve writing style. Over the years a wide variety of studies have compared the growth in writing skills of classes taught formal grammar—traditional, structural, or transformational—with those involved in reading or writing programs including only incidental instruction in grammar, or in some cases no grammar instruction at all. Almost without exception these studies have shown no significant improvement in the postcourse tests of the grammar-treated groups. In fact, occasionally, where the grammar lessons replaced time spent teaching composition directly, the grammar classes registered less gain. These results seem to hold whether the research was conducted at the grade school, high school, or college level, and whether the length of the experiment was as little as a few weeks or as much as three years.

These studies not only show no special improvement in student writing, but sometimes also, and quite remarkably, no particular elimination of the very errors that the lessons were designed to correct. Papers written by students after a course in traditional grammar were no more free of errors in grammar than those written by comparable students who had not taken the course. Nor did the students who were taught grammar do better on objective grammar tests. And though students who studied transformational grammar were able to show their mastery of the subject on objective tests, they did no better on sentence-combining tests than did their counterparts who had never heard of transformational-generative grammar.

Researchers have been almost unanimous in their conclusions.

TEACHING GRAMMAR: A SUMMARY OF THE RESEARCH

Early research in the teaching of grammar was concerned mainly with ways to improve students' grammar, to eliminate error from their speech and writing. Most of these studies compared the scores on objective grammar tests of classes that received intensive grammar instruction with comparable classes that did not. The invariable result was that there was no significant difference in the scores. Among these studies are the following, which differ in methods employed in the control groups and type of error emphasized, but not in their conclusion about the inefficacy of traditional grammar training as a remedy for error.

Teaching Traditional Grammar Useless for the Elimination of Errors

Ash, I. O. "An Experimental Evaluation of the Stylistic Approach in Teaching Written Composition in the Junior High School." *Journal of Experimental Education* 4 (1935): 54–62.

Asker, W. "Does Knowledge of Formal Grammar Function?" *School and Society* 17 (1923): 109–11.

Boraas, J. "Formal English Grammar and the Practical Mastery of English." Ph.D. diss., University of Minnesota, 1917.

Briggs, T. H. "Formal English Grammar as a Discipline." *Teachers of College Record* 14 (1913): 1–93.

Bowden, S. P. "The Effects of Formal, Traditional Grammar Study on the Writing Ability of Secondary School Students." *DAI* 40 (1979), 1389-A.

Butterfield, Clair J. "The Effect of a Knowledge of Certain Grammatical Elements on the Acquisition and Retention of Related Punctuation Skills." Ph.D. diss., University of Iowa, 1945.

Catherwood, Catherine. "A Study of Relationships between a Knowledge of Rules and Ability to Correct Grammatical Errors and between Identification of Sentences and Knowledge of Subject and Predicate." M.A. thesis, University of Minnesota.

Clark. J. D. "A Four-Year Study of Freshman English." *EJ* 24 (1935): 410.

Crawford, C. C., and Madie M. Royer. "Oral Drill versus Grammar Study." *Elementary School Journal* 36 (1935): 116–19.

Cutright, Prudence. "A Comparison of Methods of Securing Correct Language Usage." *Elementary School Journal* 34 (1934): 681–90.

Frogner, Ellen. "Grammar Approach versus Thought Approach in Teaching Sentence Structure." *EJ* 28 (1939): 518–26.

Greene, H. A. "Direct versus Formal Methods in Elementary English." *Elementary English* 24 (1947): 273–85.

Harris, R. J. "An Experimental Inquiry into the Functions and Value of Formal Grammar in the Teaching of English, with Special Reference to the

continued
  Teaching of Correct Written English to Children aged Twelve to Four-
  teen." Ph.D. diss., University of London, 1962.
Hoyt, F. S. "The Place of Grammar in the Elementary Curriculum." *Teachers
  College Record* 7 (1906): 1–34.
Karp, M. "An Individual Method and a Group Method of Teaching College
  Freshmen the Mechanics of English Composition. *Journal of Experimen-
  tal Education* 11 (1942): 9–15.
Milligan, J. P. "An Evaluation of Two Methods of Teaching Written Sentence
  Structure." *Elementary English Review* 16 (1939): 91–92, 106.
Rapeer, L. "The Problem of Formal Grammar in Elementary Education." *Jour-
  nal of Educational Psychology* 4 (1913): 125–37.
Robinson, Aurelia D. "An Investigative Study of Two Methods of Teaching
  Grammar: Conventional Instruction and Programmed Instruction." *DA*,
  33 (1973), 6779A.
Segal, D., and Nora R. Barr. "Relation of Achievement in Formal Grammar to
  Achievement in Applied Grammar. *Journal of Educational Research* 14
  (1926): 401–2.
Steward, J. "The Effect of Diagramming on Certain Skills in English Composi-
  tion." Ph.D. diss., University of Iowa, 1941.
Symonds, P. M. "Practice versus Grammar in the Learning of Correct Usage."
  Journal of Educational Psychology 22 (1931): 81–95.
Werner, P. C., and W. S. Guiler. "Individual versus Group Instruction in
  Grammatical Usage." *Journal of Educational Psychology* 24 (1933): 140–51.

More recent studies have concentrated less upon the simple correction
of error and more upon the production of more mature sentences and
of overall good writing. Here the results have been less clear-cut. Nevertheless, a pattern seems to emerge.

Teaching Traditional Grammar or Linguistic Grammars Useless for the Improvement of Student Writing

Elley, W. B., et al. "The Role of Grammar in a Secondary English Curricu-
  lum." *Research in the Teaching of English* 10 (1976): 5–17.
Fry, D.J.W. "The Effects of Transformational Grammar upon the Writing
  Performance of Students of Low Socio-Economic Backgrounds." *DAI*
  32 (1972): 4835-A.
Harter, M. T. "A Study of the Effects of Transformational Grammar on the
  Writing Skills of Seventh Graders." *DAI* 39 (1978) 2794-A.
Kennedy, L. D., and A. D. Larson. "The Influence of Structural and of Tradi-
  tional Grammatical Instruction upon Language Perception and Writing
  Ability." *Illinois School Research* 5 (1969): 31–36.
O'Donnell, Roy C. "The Correlation of Awareness of Structural Relationship
  in English and Ability in Written Composition." *Journal of Educational
  Research* 57 (1964): 464–67.
Sullivan, J. L. "A Study of the Relative Merits of Traditional Grammar,
  Generative-Transformational Grammar, or No Grammar in an Ap-

continued

continued
proach to Writing in Communication One at Colorado State College."
DA 29 (1969): 2686-A.

White, Robert H. "The Effect of Structural Linguistics in Improving English
Composition Compared to that of Prescriptive Grammar or the Absence
of Grammar Instruction." Ph.D. diss., University of Arizona, 1965. [Seventh Graders]

Whitehead, C. E., Jr. "The Effect of Grammar-Diagramming on Student
Writing Skills." DA 26 (1966): 3710. [High school students]

Modern Grammar Training May Contribute to Development of Sentence Complexity (weakly indicated)

Bateman, D. R., and F. J. Zidonis. *The Effect of a Study of Transformational Grammar on the Writing of Ninth and Tenth Graders: NCTE Research Report #6.* Urbana, Ill.: NCTE 1966. [But the study has been discredited; see James Moffett, *Teaching the Universe of Discourse* (New York: Houghton Mifflin, 1968), 165.]

Davis, M. W. "A Comparative Analysis of Sentences Written by Eighth Grade Students Instructed in Transformational-Generative Grammar and Traditional Grammar." *DA* 28 (1967): 213-A. [Some improvement in sentence formation in the generative group. Writing not considered.]

Gale, I. F. "An Experimental Study of Two Fifth-Grade Language-Arts Programs: An Analysis of the Writing of Children Taught Linguistic Grammars Compared to Those Taught Traditional Grammar." *DA* 28 (1968): 4156-A. [No overall writing differences found; some improvement in syntactic complexity in the linguistic group.]

Goddin, M.A.P. "A Comparison of the Effect on Student Achievement of a Generative Approach and a Traditional Approach to the Teaching of English Grammar at Grades Three and Seven." *DAI* 29 (1969): 3522-A. [Some improvement in sentence formation in the generative group. Writing not considered.]

Mellon, John C. *Transformational Sentence-Combining: A Method for Enhancing the Development of Syntactic Fluency in English Composition: NCTE Research Report No. 10.* Urbana, Ill.: NCTE, 1969. [But the results were duplicated and even surpassed by an identical sentence-combining study which omitted the grammar work; see Frank O'Hare, *Sentence Combining: Improving Student Writing Without Formal Grammar Instruction: NCTE Research Report No. 15.* Urbana, Ill.: NCTE, 1973.]

Morgan, G. D. "A Study of the Writing Maturity of Students in a Linguistically-Based Composition Program at the Intermediate Level." *DAI* 31 (1971): 3178-A. [No overall writing differences found; some improvement in syntactic complexity in the linguistic group.]

Thompson, C. L., and M. Middleton. "Transformational Grammar and Inductive Teaching as Determinants of Structurally Complex Writing." *California Journal of Educational Research* 24 (1973): 28–41.

White, Robert H. "The Effect of Structural Linguistics in Improving English Composition Compared to that of Prescriptive Grammar or the Absence of Grammar Instruction." Ph.D. diss., University of Arizona, 1964.

continued

[White's measure was holistic evaluation rather than sentence maturity or complexity.]

Incidental, On-the-Spot Grammar Training at Least as Effective as Any Formal Grammar Instruction

Elley, W. B., et al. "The Role of Grammar in the Secondary School English Curriculum," *Research in the Teaching of English* 10 (1976): 5–17. [This careful, large, New Zealand study found that, after three years of research, its 248-166 students receiving traditional grammar, much-disliked transformational grammar, and no grammar (incidental) instruction all made equal progress on written essays, holistically evaluated, and even on writing mechanics.]

Harris, R. J. "An Experimental Inquiry into the Functions and Value of Formal Grammar in the Teaching of English, with Special Reference to the Teaching of Correct Written English to Children Aged Twelve to Fourteen." Ph.D. diss., University of London, 1962. [Students with incidental grammar instruction not only had far fewer errors than those taught traditional grammar in a formal course, but also produced more mature writing.]

Lynn, William J. "Contrastive Approaches: An Experiment in Pedagogical Technique." *College English* 38 (1976): 144–52. [Incidental instruction in conjunction with a modified traditional grammar program produced better student essays than did a (much disliked) structural-grammar course or a freewriting program, originally favored by the instructor.]

UNDERSTANDING THE DATA. There is little surprise for most of us in these results. We have all known students who could get 100 percent on every fill-in-the-blanks grammar quiz, but who found it almost impossible to write acceptable English prose. The transference simply does not take place; nor, perhaps, should we expect it to. Knowledge of the theoretical description of a process and the skill that actuates it are two vastly different things. Peter Rosenbaum lends support to such a conclusion when he writes that we might as well expect instruction in the Newtonian description of the mechanics of the forward pass to make the quarterback a good passer as expect instruction in grammar to "improve performance in the literate skills."[3]

Why Teach Grammar at All?

Why, then, should we take time to teach grammar to our students? The evidence against the usefulness of a course in formal grammar would seem to be conclusive, yet we must be careful not to misinterpret this evidence to mean that grammar should not under any circumstances be taught.

**IMPORTANCE OF INCIDENTAL PERTINENT GRAMMAR INSTRUC-
TION.** In fact, the best of the recent research tends to indicate that student
writing skill improves most when a composition program is augmented by
incidental grammar training given whenever the need arises. The quarterback
may not need a graduate course in quantum mechanics to improve his throwing (though, of course, he might wish to undertake the study for other reasons), but his forward pass might well be helped if his coach calls his attention to some relevant points about direction, velocity, and the dynamics of
motion during practice. So it seems also to be with the study of grammar.

THE GRAMMAR GAP. Unfortunately, however, there is a real problem
in relying totally upon the incidental teaching of grammar, as some school
systems have tended to do in the years since the results of the research have
become known. This sort of makeshift treatment, if it persists throughout a
student's school years, tends to leave a gap in the student's education which
many of them perceive as a genuine intellectual need. Grammar appears high
on lists of responses to surveys questioning college freshmen about what they
feel should have been given greater emphasis in their high school English
classes.[4]

In an informal way I have confirmed this report. One semester not long
ago, when I was simultaneously teaching courses in both freshmen composition and high-school English teaching methods, I asked the freshmen to give
the prospective teachers the benefit of their recent experience in the high-
school English classroom by writing to them their views on what ought (and
ought not) to be taught there. An overwhelming percentage suggested more
grammar instruction, a choice that surprised me immensely, but which was
anticipated by the section of student teachers, whose personal high school
experience had been more recent than mine.

In particular, students express their sense of inadequacy in their grammar
training during work on writing style. They complain about lack of enough
grammar background to give them sufficient understanding of syntactic
structure or the necessary vocabulary to work effectively in this area.

TOWARD A SOLUTION. The facts, then, are these:

1. However justifiable a course in formal grammar may be on intellectual or
   humanistic grounds, it does not, of itself, enhance the growth of writing
   ability in students.
2. An incidental, fill-the-need approach to grammar seems to contribute far
   more substantially to the development of these skills.
3. But total reliance upon the incidental method leaves students with a bothersome gap in their intellectual development, particularly as it concerns
   their writing style.

The pedagogical solution to this apparent paradox is to limit our writing-
related teaching of grammar to stylistic areas, where it can succeed. As Noguchi writes:

> The inability of formal grammar to contribute anything useful to content and organization explains why grammar cannot serve as a comprehensive approach to writing. . . . Formal instruction in grammar has potentially the most to offer in the area of style. (12)

In most of our classrooms, there are two times when stylistic considerations come to the fore: when we teach *editing*, the last step in the revising stage of the composing process, and when we teach writing style as a discrete skill. Strategies for helping our students obtain the grammatical knowledge they need at these two junctures will be the focus of the remainder of this chapter.

TEACHING STYLISTIC REVISION AND EDITING

If their knowledge of grammar is to carry over and lead to improved writing skills, students must make a conscious connection between the two. Perhaps the time that students perceive the connection most acutely is when they need to do the editing that creates the final stylistic surface of their papers. After students have completed the global rewriting of their papers (discussed in Chapter 5), most of the stylistic infelicities — even errors in syntax, diction, and usage — tend to straighten themselves out as the writer's ideas unmuddle. But, as we know all too well, some problems inevitably remain. Some of these problems can be attributed to hasty or careless proofreading, but more of them stem from lack of knowledge. For grammar training to be of use, students must perceive acquiring such knowledge as an answer to a current writing problem and also must be motivated to acquire it.

Motivating Incidental Grammar Study

The best way I know to induce students to care about errors and other surface stylistic problems is not to record the grade on their papers until all surface emendations are made. We can write encouraging comments on our students' final drafts and even give the paper a grade so that they can savor the success of their composition. But when the official grading is postponed and they cannot enjoy the material fruits of their labor until they clean up the surface problems, they are eager to learn whatever it takes to make satisfactory emendations. When students are required to correct errors circled on their papers and don't know how to correct them, or when they have seen a notation such as *frag.* written in the margin for the umpteenth time and don't want to have to see it again, or when they tire of asking their study group "Is it right this way or that way?" and need some knowledge to be able to figure it out for themselves, our students can't help but acknowledge the gaps in their learning and will be ready to study whatever grammar is relevant to mastering these errors.

DELAY RECORDING THE GRADE. Why not just indicate the errors and awkwardnesses and expect students to correct them on the next theme?

Considerable research confirms what every teacher has observed: unless revision is required, all such indications of ours are ignored.[5]

Suggested Logistics.   How explicit should we be in our notation of student error? Simply encircling or pointing out most errors is ordinarily best. This strategy puts the action directly in the student's court. The student has to figure out what is wrong. When an error is due to carelessness, haste, or—as is more often the case—a vagueness in the student's familiarity with the problem, the hint on the paper is enough to set the student's thinking right, and the physical act of correction reinforces the perhaps hazy knowledge. When students aren't sure how to make the correction, the nonspecificity of our notation makes them aware of their lack of understanding and forces them to look it up or to ask us or their collaborative revision group for assistance.

Having made their corrections, should students recopy their essays? Though some students prefer to send in clear copy, most consider such activity busy work—as, I must confess, do I. My strong preference is for corrections to be made directly on the text itself. Such a plan not only saves student time, but also our own since it does not require us to reread the entire paper. Of course, when the paper has been created on a word processor, errors are most conveniently removed at the machine.

HOW MUCH GRAMMAR SHOULD WE TEACH?   However relevant the grammar lessons, we still need to make them brief, pleasurable, and few enough that they don't get tedious. As Hillocks writes, "We need to learn how to teach standard usage and mechanics . . . with *minimal* grammar" (248–49). It's true, though surely "paradoxical," as Noguchi puts it, that "maximizing the benefits of grammar instruction to writing requires teaching less, not more, grammar" (16). But limiting our teaching in this way means being highly selective in lessons we choose to teach.

WHAT PORTIONS OF GRAMMAR SHOULD WE TEACH?   Some of our lessons will, of course, develop spontaneously out of a class's immediate need. We should have sufficient reference and exercise materials about and be flexible enough to be able to answer students' questions on whatever grammatical gap in their understanding they want clarified.

Individual Problems.   When such gaps in knowledge are idiosyncratic to individual students, we can individualize their learning. It is a good idea to have a variety of reliable exercise sheets available to give these students an opportunity to practice their particular problems.

Group Problems.   More often than not, however, we will find a good number of students making the same stylistic mistakes. And we can predict these errors with some degree of confidence. Only twenty forms of error, for example, accounted for 91.5 percent of all the errors in the three thousand student papers Andrea A. Lunsford and Robert J. Connors analyzed in their massive study.[6] They include:

1.	No comma after introductories	11.5%
2.	Vague pronoun reference	9.8%
3.	No comma in compound sentence	8.6%
4.	Wrong word	7.8%
5.	No comma in nonrestrictives	6.5%
6.	Wrong/missing inflected ends	5.9%
7.	Wrong/missing preposition	5.5%
8.	Comma splice	5.5%
9.	Possessive apostrophe error	5.1%
10.	Tense shift	5.1%
11.	Unnecessary shift in person	4.7%
12.	Sentence fragment	4.2%
13.	Wrong tense or verb form	3.3%
14.	Subject-verb agreement	3.2%
15.	Lack of comma in series	2.7%
16.	Pronoun agreement error	2.6%
17.	Unnecessary commas with restrictives	2.4%
18.	Run on, fused sentence	2.4%
19.	Dangling, misplaced modifier	2.0%
20.	Its/it's error	1.0%

We can fairly well count on these stylistic problems cropping up in our students' papers, but trying to address all of them would surely backfire. The list is too long. To sharpen it, we should consider not only the errors students make, but in particular the errors they make that are most distracting to readers.

MOST DISTRACTING PROBLEMS: MECHANICAL ERRORS. Professor Maxine Hairston from the University of Texas surveyed members of the business and professional community to discover how her correspondents felt about lapses from standard written English and which errors they found most offensive. They found some errors bothersome indeed; particular mistakes they singled out are listed in the Student Guidelines in the order in which they ranked them.[7]

STUDENT GUIDELINES

Reader-Annoyance Error List

EXTREMELY SERIOUS LAPSES FROM THE STANDARD:
Nonstandard verb forms. For example: *he done, we was, he don't.*
Double negatives. For example: *He hasn't got none.*

continued

continued

Fragmented sentences. For example: *When she went home.*

Pronoun objects used as subjects. For example: *Him and Jones are going.*

Run-on sentences. For example: *He loved his job he never took holidays.*

Capitalization fault, especially failure to capitalize proper names referring to people and places

Comma error: Intrusion between the verb and complement of the sentence. For example: *Cox cannot predict, that street crime will diminish.*

SERIOUS LAPSES FROM THE STANDARD:

Parallelism fault. For example: *The politician's tour included munching on such ethnic delights as pizza, bagels, and gyros and some adorable Chinese-American babies whom he kissed.*

Subject-verb disagreement. For example: *The box of stamps were on the desk.*

Adjectives used as adverbs. For example: *He treats his men bad.*

Comma error: Not setting off interrupters such as *however* with commas.

Pronoun subjects used as objects. For example: *The Army sent my husband and I to Japan.*

Sit and *set* usage confused. For example: *Sit your papers down and set back in that chair and relax.*

Hairston's research also distinguished "Lapses that seem to matter very little" and "Lapses that do not seem to matter"; these lapses need not matter much to us either. Her list of "Moderately Serious Lapses," however, should give us some concern. It includes tense shifting, dangling modifiers, quotation mark omission, *this* and *these* confusion (*these kind*), comma error (omission in a series), faulty word choice, *which* ambiguously used, pronoun object errors *(That is her)*, and *affect* and *effect* confusion.

Interpreting the Hairston Survey. However we may feel about the relative unimportance of mechanics to the substance, structure, and overall style of student writing, we cannot get around the fact, confirmed by the Hairston survey, that for a large proportion of readers errors in mechanics present an almost impenetrable block between themselves and the writer's message. It's not that readers cannot understand error-marred writing; ordinarily they can. But research such as Hairston's has shown that certain lapses from Standard English cause readers to form such negative judgments about the competence of the writer that they disregard the merits of the content. Since we naturally want to help our students protect themselves from such built-in disadvantage, it makes good sense to concentrate our deliberately limited grammar study on remedying those errors that readers most scorn.

If we examine the results of Professor Hairston's survey, we find that almost all the lapses that most offended her readers fall into two categories: *nonstandard-dialect usage* and *errors of the sentence*. Nonstandard dialect issues, though not so pervasive on the Lunsford/Connors list, are especially troubling to readers. They call for a special and particularly sensitive pedagogy, however; so let's postpone discussion of them until Chapter 8. As for specific sentence errors, the Hairston and Lunsford/Connors lists coincide remarkably. Many students have serious problems with the sentence fragments, run-on sentences, and sentence-confusing comma placement that many readers find so bothersome. If our own students are typical in this way, we should offer them appropriately timed study of the grammar directly related to these problems.

Learning to Correct Errors of the Sentence

Why do students have so much difficulty with the mechanics of writing sentences? Since most of them have no such trouble with their speech, the problem may well lie in the distinction between oral and written sentence formation. As Robert DeBeaugrande writes:

> Because talk does not identify or mark off units with formal means, unskilled student writers often blur sentence boundaries and produce fragments and splices.[8]

Students are not sure where written sentences begin and end or even, apart from using an initial capital and a final period, how to punctuate them. What should we do about this problem? Scholars and teachers disagree on this issue. Some argue that these skills depend on knowledge of the essence and boundaries of the English sentence and therefore we should teach this knowledge directly. Others, including Noguchi, DeBeaugrande, and Weaver, argue that to teach students the syntax of the sentence is to burden them with the sort of grammar study that research proves ineffective. They maintain that sufficient knowledge to overcome errors of the sentence can be conveyed behaviorly without explicit grammar instruction. As Weaver writes:

> Students *do* need to develop a good intuitive sense of grammar, but they can do this best through *indirect* rather than direct instruction. Instead of formally teaching them grammar, we need to give them plenty of structured and unstructured opportunities to deal with language directly.[9]

TESTING FOR SENTENCES. When students write their papers, many simply record their speech in written form. In editing their papers, they will come across "sentences" about which they are unsure, or their collaborative group will point them out, or we will have marked them for them. How are they to find out whether these expressions are sentences or not? DeBeaugrande suggests taking the "sentence" in question and "mak[ing] up a "yes/

no" question about the statement made in [it] (i.e., a question that could be sensibly answered with Yes or No)" (363). True sentences can be transformed in this way. Fragments cannot be. And run-ons or comma splices can make two such questions. Note for example, how a sentence from this paragraph undergoes this transformation:

> True sentences can be transformed in this way.
> Can true sentences be transformed in this way? ["Yes" or "No"]

The test works even with complex sentences, though with more difficulty; for instance:

> When students write their papers, many simply record their speech in written form.
> Do many students simply record their speech in written form when they write their papers? ["Yes" or "No"]

But fragments, such as this paragraph's opening "when" clause would be if it had been punctuated as a sentence, cannot be made into a question answerable by yes or no:

> When students write their papers.
> When do students write their papers? [No "Yes" or "No" answer possible]

Evaluation.   Some critics find methods of this sort circuitous. Such tests are designed to eliminate the necessity for teaching grammar, yet they are dependent upon some knowledge of grammar. This one, for instance, requires considerable language ability to be useful for complex sentences, and, in fact, was proposed by Weaver as a test for independent clauses. But "independent clause" is in itself a complex syntactic concept, one that surely must be explained before we can ask our students to test for it.

Nevertheless, Weaver reports success with this method, and so does Noguchi, who uses it in a more complex variation (75–78).

HELPING STUDENTS AVOID RUN-ON AND COMMA-SPLICED SENTENCES.

Why do so many of our students have problems with run-ons and comma splices? Only part of the difficulty derives from not knowing the boundaries of the sentence (independent clause); the larger part derives from mistaken notions of how to punctuate compound sentences. But once students have mastered a sense of an independent clause (partly, perhaps, through exercises such as that outlined above), the punctuation should not be hard to learn: there are so very few options.

Writers can choose to (1) put two related independent clauses into two separate sentences; or (2) join them in one sentence—ending the first with a semicolon and the second with a period; or (3) join them together in one sentence by concluding the first with a comma and beginning the second with a coordinate conjunction such as *and* or *but*. In teaching this material, we would not necessarily have to use this vocabulary. We might instead ask students to suggest two brief and related sentences, and then, working on the chalkboard, make them aware of their options for combining them. As for example:

> Jack and Jill went up the hill. They wanted to fetch a pail of water.
> Jack and Jill went up the hill; they wanted to fetch a pail of water.
> Jack and Jill went up the hill, and they wanted to fetch a pail of water.

Karnofel's Acronym Exercise. Ninth-grade teacher Jeff Karnofel has developed an exercise with which he has actually overcome the run-on sentence and comma-splice problems in his classes. He catches his students' attention by placing the following initials in a squared off corner of his chalkboard:

1. S.S.
2. S;s.
3. S, [ABSONFY] s.
4. S; [A C], s.
Ø S, s.

The initials remain an enigma while the class goes about its usual activities, and not until the students plead for demystification—often a day or two later—does Karnofel reveal the secret:

> 1. Sentence. Sentence.
> 2. Sentence; sentence.
> 3. Sentence, [and, but, so, or, nor, for, yet] sentence.
> 4. Sentence; [adverbial connective: Ex: therefore], sentence.

> But connecting sentences with just commas is FORBIDDEN.

For the next couple of weeks students find next to the original initials on the chalkboard a changing paragraph-writing exercise. A typical assignment might be: 1, 1, 3, 4, 2, 3 or 2, 3, 1, 4, 1, requiring the students to create a paragraph by using each of the compound sentence forms in the order prescribed. Karnofel sometimes suggests the content: "Describe your room at home" or "What did you notice on the way to school today?" And sometimes he leaves the content to his students. But in every case he assures them that the format they follow is just for practice and has no connection with the way writers construct paragraphs in the real world.

Karnofel says his students enjoy the writing exercises and related discussion, and rarely have problems punctuating compound sentences again.

Gliserman's However Poem Exercise. Martin Gliserman similarly uses formatted sentences to teach punctuation.[10] He is especially interested in the semicolon and creative imagery to teach its use. In suggesting a poetic format for what Karnofel calls his "#4 sentence," Gliserman also teaches an appropriate use for adverbial connectives;

Structure 1. is made of something;
however, Structure 2. is made of something else.

Glisterman's example:

Shacks are made of wet feathers;
however, gas stations are made of tooth-picks.

HELPING STUDENTS AVOID UNINTENTIONAL FRAGMENTS.
Sentence fragments are more difficult to work with in the classroom. Although they are frequently mentioned as one of the most bothersome of writing errors, they are not always erroneous. Professional writers frequently include them for stylistic purposes, particularly to suggest informality or to create emphasis. For example, Lewis Thomas uses a fragment to write about atomic bombs:

I cannot think that way [in terms of the immortality of the earth] any more. *Not while those things are still in place, aimed everywhere, ready for launching.*

And Charles W. Slack includes one in his essay on some educational research:

When grades still failed to rise, the scientists felt there might be some truth in what the young team members were saying. *Not that teachers were to blame, necessarily.*[11]

And though it would be both dishonest and patronizing to deny the effectiveness of the occasional chosen fragment, we certainly need to teach our students to recognize them and to discourage their use.

Gliserman/Weaver Fragment Exercise.   Gliserman and Weaver both endorse the boxed Three-Step Exercise, which I have exemplified with my own samples.

STUDENT EXERCISE

Fragments

Step 1. Turn each of the following sentences into five fragments:
   Example: We will vote on Tuesday.

- voting on Tuesday
- when we vote on Tuesday
- that we will vote on Tuesday
- Tuesday, which will be voting day
- for us to vote on Tuesday

continued
Step 2. Turn each fragment into a complete sentence.
   Examples:

   • Voting on Tuesday was a new experience for the new resident who was
     used to voting on Mondays.
   • When we vote on Tuesday, we should be sure of our candidate.
   • Mary said that we will vote on Tuesday.

   Step 3. Some of the following are sentences; some are fragments.
Turn each of the fragments into complete sentences.

To make this exercise effective, we should probably keep the exercise sentences short in Step 1 and not offer more than three at a time. In writing the items for Step 3, a good ratio would be three complete sentences to seven fragments of all varieties. Complex sentences should be included.

This exercise should help our students understand the essence of a fragment because it allows them to deal with fragments creatively from every angle. My one reservation about it is that it does require fragment making, and to that extent it reinforces error in the mind of the inexperienced writer.

HELPING STUDENTS AVOID SENTENCE-OBSTRUCTING COMMAS. Many of our students are unclear about the function of commas. Some have a vague notion that a comma signifies in writing what a pause does in oral speech. These students say a sentence aloud, place commas at every possible pause, and hope for the best. Students have developed this oral-test rule for comma placement, I am convinced, because they have neither the patience nor the folly to memorize the twenty to thirty diverse rules for commas typical of many school texts and college handbooks.

But, for whatever reason they occur, scattershot commas are truly bothersome to readers, as the Hairston study confirms. Readers find unnecessary commas especially intrusive because a comma interrupts the flow of the text. A single purposeless comma placed between a subject and its verb or a verb and its object can make a sentence almost incomprehensible:

   FAULTY   • She and her friends, knew that he would come.
   FAULTY   • She and her friends knew, that he would come.

To help our students avoid annoying their readers in this way, we need to bring some logic and unity to comma teaching; fortunately, the subject lends itself to both.

The Purpose of Syntactical Commas.   The purpose of commas within the sentence, that is, paired syntactical commas, is to prevent interruptions from interfering with the readers' understanding of the central subject-verb-object flow in the sentence[12]—and that may be why a single interrupting comma is so very disturbing. A pair of commas ensure that all interrupting material is separated off.

The Overall, Umbrella, Never-Fail, Handy-Dandy Comma Rule.   We don't need a special comma rule for every interrupting grammatical construction. It doesn't matter if the interrupters are parenthetical remarks, interjections, transitional words and phrases, appositives, nonessential relative clauses, adverbial clauses or phrases, or participial and other sorts of explanatory phrases. Nor do our students have to learn all their names and definitions. One rule covers all:

> Surround nonessential sentence-interrupters with commas.

All students need to do is to be able to recognize interrupters, the words, phrases, or clauses that interrupt the sentence.

How can we get our students to recognize this material? We might tell them that if they can pick it up by its commas and remove it from the sentence, and the sentence continues to make good sense, they can be sure they have a genuine interrupter (figure 7–1). A useful oral test for true interrupters is to see if the words in question can be meaningfully spoken in gossipy tones, parenthetically, behind the hand. We should go over a good number of interrupters of all varieties using these tests until our students are familiar and comfortable with the concept.

When they are editing, students who recognize interrupting material will know to *surround* it with commas, remembering to mark it off *on both sides* by commas. Of course, someone will ask, "What shall we do if what we are calling 'interrupting material' doesn't really interrupt, but occurs at the beginning or the end of a sentence [or of an independent clause]?" This is the kind of question best turned back on the student: "What do *you* think one should do?" Provide the student with an example ("Nonetheless [ ] Jill

Figure 7–1.

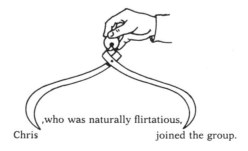

Chris ,who was naturally flirtatious, joined the group.

climbed the hill again," for instance), and most students will have no difficulty in seeing that only one comma is needed when other punctuation (here
the preceding period) supplies the other half of the pair.

The Student Guidelines offer a variety of useful examples of comma-
separated interrupting material.

STUDENT GUIDELINES

Examples Using Commas to Set Off Interrupting Material

1. Even the civilization of Sumer, *the birthplace of written language*, declined
   and vanished.
2. *Nevertheless*, artifacts of this civilization, *having survived the centuries*, can still
   be found in museums.
3. The Oriental Museum at the University of Chicago, *for example*, has an impressive collection; *unfortunately*, it is little-known.
4. May the class take a field trip to Chicago, *Professor Marx?*
5. Professor Marx, *who had long believed in the benefits of field trips*, booked reservations for his group on the first bus heading for Chicago.
6. Alison and Craig, *when the field trip was over*, went home.
7. *When the field trip was over*, Alison and Craig went home.

Pedagogical Dividends from Studying the Comma Rule. Teaching
the Umbrella Comma Rule opens the way for discussion of two other interesting questions. When students look at adjective clauses such as the "who"
clause in #5, they are bound to raise the issue of the distinction between
nonessential relative clauses, such as this one, which require commas because
of the material's semiparenthetical nature, and essential relative clauses,
which do not.

Study of syntactic comma usage also helps clarify questions about the
curious punctuation of adverb clauses. Students will easily understand the
parenthetical nature of adverb clauses when they occur in examples like #6.
And these examples help clarify the necessity for a comma after an introductory adverb clause in instances such as #7. But such examples inevitably bring
up the question of no comma preceding a concluding adverb clause. The
notion of interrupters may help students to understand why the final adverb
clause is regarded as "natural" in that place and not an interrupter at all. The
following Student Guidelines address the question explicitly.

STUDENT GUIDELINES

Using Commas to Set Off Introductory
Adverbial Material

1. *When you begin a sentence with an adverb clause*, add a comma before you begin your main clause.
2. You need not use a comma *when the adverb clause concludes your sentence.*
3. *In the case of a number of prepositional phrases at the beginning of your sentence,* you have the option to clarify with a comma.

INCIDENTAL GRAMMAR LESSONS CAN SUCCEED. Teaching succinct grammar lessons such as these help our students solve editing problems as they occur. By keeping these lessons brief, interesting, and—especially—relevant to the problem at hand, we should be able to help our students make the difficult transference from exercise to editing skill.

TEACHING STYLE AS A SKILL

The Need to Teach Grammar Systematically

Sometimes we have no choice. A board-mandated curriculum requires systematic grammar study. Mindful of the problems inherent in such study, how should we proceed? If syntactic knowledge is not to be compartmentalized in our students' minds—or forgotten as soon as learned—students must be motivated to learn it. A pedagogical solution to this apparent paradox is to teach a modified, functional approach to grammar at times of perceived stylistic need. We can make a full grammar review relevant to our students' writing by teaching it as an aid for studying and practicing style.

HIDDEN BENEFITS. I would also argue, despite all the research demonstrating the futility of teaching grammar systematically, that there can be educational advantages to introducing our stylistic work in this manner. The piecemeal and individualized grammar study we have just discussed, however—as useful as it is—sometimes fails to satisfy students and they consequently develop a longing for a scheme to tie it all together. Incidental grammar learning is fine, but it is hit and miss. The human mind craves unity, and takes comfort in explanation that offers a sense of completeness. And so sometimes our students—especially the scholars among them—feel a desire to have some systematic knowledge of the language they speak, quite apart from the gains this knowledge may or may not promote in their writing skills.

But if we can make the lessons unified enough to satisfy our students intellectually, pleasurable enough to engage their minds, and relevant enough to improving their writing style to motivate their concentration, our grammar teaching should enrich our students.

TO INTRODUCE SENTENCE COMBINING. An especially good time for a grammar review is the beginning of our work with sentence combining. Even in the first sentence-combining discussion, students perceive the need for a common vocabulary to make their ideas clear to one another. I certainly do not mean to imply that students' successful completion of a program of sentence combining is dependent upon their thorough knowledge of formal grammar. Freedom from the necessity of intensive grammar training is, in fact, one of the advantages of using sentence combining rather than the more traditional kinds of linguistic exercises. But, if our students are to communicate successfully with one another about the various kinds of *phrases*, *clauses*, and *sentences* in their papers, it is essential that teacher and students share a common understanding of the concepts signified by those terms. And so it is best to open the study of sentence combining with a brief, but systematic, review of the necessary nomenclature.

How Should We Teach Grammar?

It is easier to say how we must not teach it — for, traditionally, grammar has been badly taught more often than not.

STUDENTS SHOULD DISCOVER PATTERN AND UNITY. We must not, for example, fall into the practice of the many handbooks that provide what seems to be an endless list of unrelated rules. I have seen handbooks with more than twenty pages of comma rules, for instance, when one handy, overall umbrella rule, as we have seen, will take care of most problematic syntactic situations. We should instead teach a few well-integrated grammatical principles.

Conjunction Principle. For example, we can suggest to our students that syntax permits us to express our ideas and to join them together in various ways. The first and second major classes of words (nouns, verbs) express the ideas; the third and fourth major classes (adjectives and adverbs) describe these ideas; and the fifth class (various conjunctions, including prepositions) joins everything together. Students will readily understand the notion of connection or conjoining as an important function of language. And once they are looking for unity, they will be able to see that the coordinating conjunctions are related to the subordinating conjunctions, the adverbial connectors, and even to prepositions in their connecting or conjoining function.

DEFINITIONS SHOULD CORRESPOND TO FUNCTION. We should also not follow another practice of many traditional handbooks, passing on standard definitions that provide no useful information, "A phrase is a group of words," for instance. Even more important for our credibility, we should not offer definitions that contradict what students instinctively know about their language.

Noun Definitions. Some nouns, for example, may be "the name of a person, place, or thing," but many are not. Students who learn this common definition have a great deal of trouble recognizing abstract concepts, such as *honesty* or *love*, as nouns and thus, more importantly, cannot figure out how they function as subjects or objects in clauses or phrases.

Sentence Definitions. Even less true is the common definition that "A sentence is a complete thought." A complete thought does not have to be confined in a sentence. This nonsentence, for instance, is surely a complete thought:

> Last night's dream with all its brilliant color, with all its dizzying madness, with all its provoking symbolism—over and over in her mind.

Nor does a sentence have to convey a complete thought—or any thought at all, for that matter—to be a sentence:

> Twas brillig and the slithy toves did gyre and gimbol in the wabe. (Lewis Carroll.)

Students will dutifully memorize and parrot back these definitions, but they will not be able to use them in any meaningful way because, as definitions, they are essentially meaningless.

Isn't it better to teach our students functional definitions that will be true wherever they choose to apply them? For instance, shouldn't we rather have them think of the essence of a sentence as

> Something doing or being.

Or more often

> Something doing or being something.

Using traditional vocabulary, a good functional definition of a sentence is

> A subject verbing, or A subject verbing an object.

or even

> A subject predicating.

This definition, however, as our brighter students will no doubt point out, applies as well to a clause as it does to a sentence. Of course, sentences always have a subject and a verb, but dependent clauses also have both of these and phrases often one or the other. To make the definition both true and usable for our students, we will have to add enough so that they can distinguish a sentence from a nonsentence:

> A sentence has subject, verb, and usually an objective element, often with their various modifiers, and *nothing attached to keep it from standing on its own.*

TERMINOLOGY. What kind of vocabulary should we employ? Should we, like the traditionalists, say *noun* and *verb?* Or should we use *Class I word* and *Class II word,* as do the structural grammarians? Should we refer to *subject* and *predicate?* Or should it be the *noun phrase* and the *verb phrase* of the transformational-generative linguists? The answer must depend upon the background of our students, for what I propose here is just a review and a systemization of a subject with which our students should already have some degree of familiarity from their grade school days. If they are already grounded in structural or transformational terminology, well and good; we should build upon what they know. However, if they already have some understanding of traditional terms—the much more likely probability—we should not impose a strange new nomenclature upon them. In employing traditional terms, however, we need not discard the many helpful insights that have come from linguistic research, such as those demonstrated in the examples above.

Teaching a Functional Approach to Grammar

Contemporary grammarians and linguists have yet to reach a consensus on the appropriateness and exact meaning of grammatical terminology; no two textbooks agree completely—though they all agree on the importance of a functional definition. The accompanying Student Guidelines has the merit of teachable definitions: it incorporates the sort of logic appreciated by students without departing in any fundamental way from current expert opinion. In so doing it offers a useful set of terminology with each term functionally defined.

STUDENT GUIDELINES

Working Definitions of Major Parts of Syntax

A. PARTS OF SPEECH
Parts of speech are words that function in a sentence as subject, verb, complement, or their modifiers.

NOUNS AND PRONOUNS function as subjects or objects. For further identification, nouns can be made plural (usually by the addition of a final *s,* and most of them can be tested for nounhood by

continued

continued

placing a *the* or an *a(n)* in front: the *boy*, a *propensity*. Gerunds (an -*ing* form of a verb) would thus be considered nouns (the *singing*, a *shouting*). Pronouns stand in for nouns, and (as we might point out to our students) pronouns should only be used in such a way that the specific noun referred to is abundantly clear.

VERBS express the doing or being of the subject. They change their spelling or take on an auxiliary or helping verb (*be, have*, and the like) to mark the time of their action or being (*run, ran, will run, is running, was running, has run, had run; rest, rested, will rest, is resting, was resting, has rested, had rested*). When expressing present time, verbs also change spelling (usually by adding or removing an *s*) to indicate the number (single or plural) and person (first, second, or third): *I rest, you rest, he/she/it rests, they rest*. Verbs may be tested for verbness by placing a *to* or a *they* in front: to *buy*, or they *relegate*.

ADJECTIVES describe or modify subjects and objects, that is, nouns. In a sentence they occur either before the noun they describe or in its complement position. Words thus may be checked for adjectivity by trying them in these slots: "the *silly* noun is *contentious*." Present participles (an -*ing* form of a verb) and past participles (usually the -*ed* form of a verb) should thus be considered adjectives (the *sleeping* girl, the *announced* lecture). Determiners, including the articles (*the, a, an*), demonstrative pronouns (*this, that, those*, and the like), and possessive pronouns (*my, her, his*, and the like) function as adjectives and therefore are most logically considered special kinds of adjectives.

ADVERBS describe or modify the verb and, by telling when or where or how or how often the subject acts or is, they mark the sentence for time, place, manner, or frequency. The largest single group of adverbs is formed by adding -*ly* to adjectives (*quickly, softly, prettily*). Adverbs are not easily identified by slots because, unlike the three other major parts of speech, they are characterized by mobility within the sentence. (For example: "The birds fly *quickly*." "*Quickly*, the birds fly." "The birds *quickly* fly." All are grammatical English constructions.) Intensifiers, such as *very, most, quite, somewhat*, and *fairly*, which modify adjectives and adverbs, have usually been considered adverbs as well — though the logical connection is tenuous.

FUNCTION WORDS serve primarily to shape the sentence and hold it together. They include coordinating and subordinating conjunctions (*and, but, or*, and so on, and *because, when, although* and the like); adverbial connectors (*therefore, however, nevertheless*, and so on); prepositions, which link their object (a noun and its modifiers) to the sentence (*under, over, around, in, out, above, to, from*, and the like); and question words, which shape a sentence into a question (*who, why, how*, and so on). Function words occasionally also serve

continued

to interrupt the sentence, as do the interjections (*ouch! wow! oh dear*, and the like)

B. PHRASES

Phrases are groups of words that have no subject and verb of their own and function much as do the single-word parts of speech.

PREPOSITIONAL PHRASES act as adjectives and describe nouns, or act as adverbs and modify verbs or tell where or when or how. Each consists of a preposition and its objects with its modifiers. Examples: The woman *with the bright red bikini* (adjectival) swam *in the pool* (adverbial).

PARTICIPIAL PHRASES are dominated by a present participle (*-ing* form of a verb) or a past participle (*-ed* form of a verb) and function as adjectives. Examples: Mary, *dancing gaily* (present participial phrase) *and dressed all in red* (past participial phrase), began to sing.

ADVERBIAL PHRASES (truncated adverb clauses) are participial phrases headed by adverbial subordinating conjunctions that function much as adverbs do. Examples: *while sitting by the road* (present participle); *when drenched with rain* (past participle).

ABSOLUTE PHRASES are participial or prepositional phrases that include their own subjects. Instead of modifying only individual words, absolute constructions often modify whole clauses. Examples: The man hobbled, *his cane in his hand* (subject + prepositional phrase). The man hobbled, *his cane dangling from his arm* (subject + present participial phrase). She looked into the distance, *eyes misted over* (subject + past participial phrase).

APPOSITIVE PHRASES consist of a noun and its modifiers and modify a noun or a noun phrase by equating themselves with it. An appositive phrase might be considered a relative clause from which the relative pronoun and verb *to be* have been omitted. Examples: The book case, [which was] *a dark mahogony structure,* . . . ; Joe Dandelion, (who was) *my uncle.* . . .

INFINITIVE PHRASES are phrases dominated by *to* + a verb and can serve, much as nouns do, as subjects of sentences or clauses and as complements to verbs: Examples: *To laugh* is good for the soul (subject). Goldilocks began *to cry* (complement). Infinitive phrases can also be used as adjectives: The crowd applauded her efforts *to sing* (modifying the noun *efforts*). Infinitive phrases can serve as adverbs as well: Joe hurried *in order to be on time* (modifying the verb *hurried*).

GERUND PHRASES are phrases dominated by a gerund (an *-ing* form of a verb) and serve as nouns. Example: *Laughing heartily* is good for the soul.

continued

continued
C. CLAUSES
All clauses, like sentences, consist of a subject and a predicate.

MAIN CLAUSES (independent clauses) could stand on their own as a sentence.

SUBORDINATE CLAUSES (dependent clauses) are prevented from independence by the presence (usually) of an initial subordinating conjunction or relative pronoun.

ADVERB CLAUSES are clauses headed by an adverbial subordinating conjunction that function as adverbs. They can serve as part of a complement or, followed by a comma, they can precede the main clause. Example: *When the ball was over*, Mary stopped dancing.

NOUN CLAUSES are headed by a subordinating conjunction, such as *that* or *where*, and serve as subjects or objects of sentences or as objects of prepositions. Examples: She told me *that she was happy* (as object). *That she was happy* was all too apparent (as subject). He was afraid of *what he could not understand* (as object of preposition).

ADJECTIVE (OR RELATIVE) CLAUSES are headed by a relative pronoun and act as adjectives. These clauses either give parenthetical information about a noun that does not restrict or change the noun's meaning or they can provide essential identification that restricts the meaning of the noun. Examples: The pencil, *which was old and broken*, lay among the others (nonrestrictive and therefore set off by commas). He chose the pencil *which was old and broken* (restrictive).

D. SENTENCES
A sentence is a subject verbing.

A SIMPLE SENTENCE has but one clause, a main clause.

A COMPLEX SENTENCE has a main clause and one or more subordinate clauses.

A COMPOUND SENTENCE has two or more main clauses.

A COMPOUND-COMPLEX SENTENCE has two or more main clauses and at least one subordinate clause.

A PERIODIC SENTENCE builds up phrases and subordinate clauses to a climactic presentation of its main clause at the end. Example:

To transfer admiration from the thing possessed to its possessor; to conceive that the mere possession of material wealth makes of its possessor a proper object of worship; to feel abject before another who is wealthier — such emotions do not so much as enter the American mind. — Hillaire Belloc.

A CUMULATIVE SENTENCE follows its main clause with a series of modifying phrases and clauses. Example:

continued

> It is with the coming of man that a vast hole seems to open in nature, a vast black whirlpool spinning faster and faster, consuming flesh, stones, soil, minerals, sucking down the lightning, wrenching power from the atom, until the ancient sounds of nature are drowned out in the cacophony of something which is loose and knocking at the world's heart, something demonic and no longer planned—escaped, it may be—spewed out of nature, contending in a final giant's game against its master.—Loren Eiseley

Teaching Syntax

THE SENTENCE.   The best place to begin is the sentence. It is particularly appropriate if we plan to use this review to embark on a study of sentence combining. Students easily understand if they are about to begin *sentence* combining, they ought to be fairly certain of what exactly a sentence is.

Depending upon the level on which we are teaching, we might ask our students what they think a sentence is. (For a discussion on the definition of the sentence, see pages 250–51.) We might ask each of them to give a sentence. Or we might ask them to say the longest or the shortest sentence they know. In any case, we ought to end with the recitation of very short sentences and put some of them on the board. Our list should include such minimal sentences as:

> The girl picked the daisy.
> The squirrel climbed the tree.
> Bats hit balls.

Some students will claim that three words is as short a sentence as one can get. But they will inevitably be challenged by those who remember the possibility of others even shorter:

> Birds fly.
> Flowers bloom.
> Babies coo.

To which list the class cynic is sure to add:

> Garbage stinks.

If everyone is agreed that these all are indeed sentences and that the latter are sentences cut to the bare bone, then we have sufficient data to determine what a sentence is essentially. We thus can ask our students: What is the sentence in essence? What does it need, what must it have, to be a sentence? Our students will find the answer:

A sentence is something doing or being.

It is a subject and its verb (or "simple predicate"—though I have found *predicate* an almost meaningless term for most students).

A sentence is a subject verbing.

That's all it actually takes to make a sentence, we can say, but most sentences go a bit farther and are instead *something doing or being something*, a subject, a verb, and an object or quality to complete the verb (complement). That's really all there is to it, we can assure our students. Everything else is based on that simple formula:

subject-verb-[complement].

CLAUSES AND PHRASES.   Clauses and phrases, for example, can be explained in these terms. Like sentences, clauses are defined by the presence of subject and verb. An independent (main) clause is of itself a sentence, though within a larger structure. Given initial capital and terminal punctuation, it could stand alone. A dependent (subordinate) clause, though also possessing subject and verb, cannot stand alone because it is encumbered with a (usually initial) word (a subordinating conjunction or a relative pronoun) that attaches it to its main clause and signals its dependent relationship. The sentence

The wind blows

for instance, could serve as a main clause;

That the wind blows,
When the wind blows, and
[The wind] *which blows*

are subordinate clauses. Phrases are distinguished from clauses by the absence of a subject and its verb.

PARTS OF SPEECH.   The subject-verb-[complement] configuration is also at the root of our understanding of the function of the parts of speech. *Nouns* and *pronouns* are words that serve as subjects or objects of sentences, clauses, and phrases, the *pronouns* used when appropriate as stand-ins for particular nouns. *Verbs* are the words that indicate what the subject does or is, and when. *Adjectives* describe or modify subjects or objects (nouns). *Adverbs* describe or modify the verb, and by telling when or where or how or how often the subject acts or is, adverbs mark the sentence for time, place, manner, or frequency. *Function words*, such as *coordinating* and *subordinating conjunctions*, *connectors*, *prepositions*, and *question makers*, serve to shape the sentence and hold it together.

SUBORDINATE STRUCTURES FUNCTION AS PARTS OF SPEECH. Phrases and subordinate clauses function in the sentence in ways identical to the single-word parts of speech.

Prepositional phrases, for instance, can serve as adjectives or adverbs depending upon whether they describe a noun (The child *with the ribbon*) or a verb (played *in the garden*). *Participial phrases* act as adjectives because they modify nouns (the ship, *sailing swiftly, managed by its crew*). *Infinitive phrases* usually behave as nouns and serve as subjects ("*To err* is human") or as complements (He learned *to swim*).

The three kinds of subordinate clauses are distinguished by whether they operate as nouns (subject: "*Where e'er I fly* is Hell"; complement: She said *that she could fix it*), as adjectives (The girl *who was intelligent* . . .), or as adverbs (The band stopped playing when the dance was over).

A Teaching Strategy: Aardvarks or Armadillos

Though this sort of explanation, and the working definitions upon which it is based, is to a degree oversimplified, it is logical and neat and students appreciate its comprehensiveness. It is, nevertheless, concentrated and demanding—not at all amenable to the lecture method. We will need to find a way to engage our students' interest when teaching this material. One good way is a chalkboard exercise that, if the terms are amusingly chosen, can give the class as much enjoyment as learning.

DISCOVERING THE LIMITS OF THE SIMPLE SENTENCE. We might start by asking our students to help discover what a simple sentence is capable of being. They began the grammar study by setting its minimal boundaries. Now they will have to push the simple sentence to its maximum contours to find out just how much they can add to it before it becomes complex or compound. As our students add each modifier to the base (subject-verb-complement) to create their model sentence, we can pause for discussion of each of the various parts of speech, kinds of phrases, and—later—kinds of clauses they employ. But first they will need to choose their minimal subject-verb-object.

One class worked out their sentences after having selected as their base sentence:

"Armadillos eat."

They then quickly added the complement "oatmeal cookies":

Armadillos eat oatmeal cookies.

With adjectives added to both subject and complement, their sentence read:

Clumsy armadillos eat *burnt* oatmeal cookies.

The class then annexed an adverb:

> Clumsy armadillos *slowly* eat burnt oatmeal cookies.

In adding adjectival phrases, the class chose a prepositional phrase for the subject and a participial phrase for the complement:

> Clumsy armadillos *with growling stomachs* slowly eat burnt oatmeal cookies *dipped in pastelike catsup.*

Next they attached an adverb phrase, making their new sentence read:

> Clumsy armadillos with growling stomachs slowly eat burnt oatmeal cookies dipped in pastelike catsup *while falling off a cliff.*

When their sentence had reached this length—and it looked even longer spread across a large blackboard, many of the students had difficulty believing that "all this" could still be merely a simple sentence. The teacher assured them that indeed it was, that the number of words and phrases added did not matter, and that the length of the sentence was immaterial: a sentence remains *simple* as long as it contains only one clause, that is to say, only one subject and its predicate. "What if we add another subject," one of the students wanted to know, "would we still have a simple sentence?" After some hesitancy, the class agreed that they would, that they would then have merely a simple sentence with a compound subject. And so they added another subject:

> *Little lemmings and* clumsy armadillos with growling stomachs slowly eat burnt oatmeal cookies dipped in pastelike catsup while falling off a cliff.

Could they compound the verb as well? Yes, indeed:

> Little lemmings and clumsy armadillos with growling stomachs slowly eat burnt oatmeal cookies dipped in pastelike catsup *and play stud poker* while falling off a cliff.

MAKING A SENTENCE COMPOUND. Well, what could they do to make their sentence a compound sentence? "Add another main clause, of course," a number of them murmured, and so they produced:

> Little lemmings and clumsy armadillos with growling stomachs slowly eat burnt oatmeal cookies dipped in pastelike catsup and play studpoker while falling off a cliff, *but they are silly beasts.*

UNDERSTANDING THE COMPLEX SENTENCE. How could the class turn this sentence (to which by now they were beginning to become really attached) into a *complex* sentence? Many of the students were amazed to learn that their entire concoction of lemmings and armadillos and catsup and poker and cliffs could be turned into a dependent clause—and thus no sentence at all—by the addition of a single word—actually by the addition of any number of single words—a fact they soon realized as they considered which adverbial conjunction to add: "Since little lemmings . . . ," "When little lemmings . . . ," "After little lemmings . . . ," "Although little lemmings . . . ," "Until little lemmings. . . ." The class finally settled upon the following for their complex sentence with an *adverb clause:*

> *Because little lemmings and clumsy armadillos with growling stomachs slowly eat burnt oatmeal cookies dipped in pastelike catsup and play stud poked while falling off a cliff,* they are silly beasts.

For their complex sentence with *noun clause* they created:

> *That little lemmings and clumsy armadillos with growling stomachs slowly eat burnt oatmeal cookies dipped in pastelike catsup and play stud poker while falling off of cliffs* means they are silly beasts.

For their complex sentence with an *adjective (relative) clause*, they produced:

> Little lemmings and armadillos *which are clumsy and have growling stomachs* slowly eat burnt oatmeal cookies dipped in pastelike catsup and play stud-poker while falling off of cliffs.

As for their compound-complex sentence, the class simply concluded their relative-clause sentence with a semicolon and followed it with "they are silly beasts":

> Little lemmings and armadillos which are clumsy and have growling stomachs slowly eat burnt oatmeal cookies dipped in pastelike catsup and play stud poker while falling off of cliffs; they are silly beasts.

We can make sure an exercise such as this prompts learning as well as laughter if we take care to go slowly enough so that all questions are answered and at every addition all students fully understand the syntactical significance of the new structure.

PUNCTUATING THE SENTENCE. This exercise also affords our students the opportunity to catch up on some points of punctuation that may be puzzling them. When, for instance, should the semicolon be used? Why do we need to use a comma to separate an adverb clause from the main clause when it is placed at the beginning of a sentence, but not when it appears at the end? How does one really know when to set off a relative clause with commas? What makes the construction nonrestrictive, the material parenthetical? (In the armadillo example, the class engaged in a mildly heated debate over whether to enclose "which are clumsy and have growling stomachs" in commas and thus have it parenthetically express a truth about all armadillos or whether to leave off the commas and make the clause act restrictively to distinguish these armadillos from all the other oatmeal-cookie eaters.)

Transference. A review such as this helps our students feel more at home with the operation of parts of speech, phrases, and clauses, and the workings of punctuation. If we can give it a relevant spin, it can also provide useful background for other writing projects and can be used to prepare the way for sentence combining.

TEACHING SENTENCE COMBINING AS STYLISTIC CHOICE

If we want our students to become conscious of writing style and actually to improve their own, I cannot recommend any pedagogy more enthusiastically than sentence-combining exercises. Research shows that sentence combining improves the overall style of the writing of most students who practice it.[13] As Charles Cooper, best known for his thorough reviews of composition research, writes of sentence combining: "No other single teaching approach has ever consistently been shown to have a beneficial effect on syntactic maturity and writing quality."[14]

Sentence Combining Theoretically Considered

Sentence combining is derived directly from transformational-generative grammar theory.[15] Transformational-generative grammarians liken the linguistic knowledge stored in the human brain to a model of the grammar of a language—English, for instance. This model is a computerlike device that transforms thought into sentence kernels and these kernels into our spoken or written expression. English kernels are simple, indicative sentences (S) consisting of subject and predicate, which linguists call noun phrase (NP) and verb phrase (VP). The equation for a sentence is:

$$S \rightarrow NP + VP$$

The sentence-combining approach assumes that all the sentences we actually speak or write are derived from these simple basic sentences.

According to this theory, our minds combine these minimal sentences in complex ways to create an infinite number of possible sentences. In this view, the sentence "A troubled Hamlet gazed thoughtfully at the skull" represents the surface structure of a deep-language structure that originated in these three "kernels" or basic sentences:

- Hamlet gazed at the skull.
- Hamlet is troubled.
- Hamlet's gaze is thoughtful.

These same kernels could also produce:

- Hamlet, who was troubled, gazed at the skull thoughtfully.
- Thoughtfully, a troubled Hamlet gazed at the skull.

- The skull was gazed at thoughtfully by a troubled Hamlet.
- Hamlet, who was troubled, gazed thoughtfully at the skull.

Sentence-combining exercises provide sets of such kernels and thus offer a way to duplicate consciously the unconscious sentence-forming process. Through them students can be led to perceive their stylistic options and make their choices according to the criterion of rhetorical effectiveness.

Why Are Sentence-Combining Exercises So Effective?

STYLE. These exercises permit students to experience and experiment with style consciously. The exercise provides content in the form of sentence kernels; the student is asked only to manipulate the kernels to achieve the most effective style. Because the exercises assign stylistic manipulation within a fixed content, they effectively separate style from meaning. They permit students to distinguish what is said from how it is said.

INTELLECTUAL CREATIVITY. Sentence-combining exercises succeed because they permit students to manipulate language creatively. As William Strong suggests, they let students construct written discourse rather than tear it down. Instead of learning to analyze or diagram sentences, they learn to build and create them. And, unlike most traditional grammar problems, sentence-combining exercises challenge students enough to afford them the enjoyment of intellectual stimulation. If students learn new syntactic possibilities and experiment with these options (see the section on cued exercises, 270–73), they will have the opportunity to get on intimate terms with the sort of sentences mature authors write, to play with them and thus make them their own. This practice, in Strong's words, "trains a kid to hold longer and longer discourse in his head—to embed and subordinate at greater depth as a means of expressing thought."[16]

COMFORT. Perhaps the most important reason these exercises work for our students is that they offer not only a structured opportunity for practice but a psychologically secure vehicle for that practice. Sentence combining gives the student a chance to practice, to experiment, and to make mistakes— all without the anguish usually associated with learning to write. Because the content of the compositions is part of the "given," students somehow do not experience the sort of ego involvement that usually makes learning to write so difficult. Although some such anxiety is inevitable in learning any activity, especially when there is a comparative discussion of the work, sentence combining reduces this discomfort to the impersonal level of, say, the math class. The fundamental reason underlying the success of these exercises is that they give students a chance to struggle with all the intricacies of writing style in as nonthreatening a context as we can possibly make.[17]

Introducing Students to Sentence Combining

The best way for students to understand sentence combining is to combine sentences. Having offered a brief explanation and demonstrated some examples on the board, we need to turn our students loose with a short set of sentence kernels and see what they can make of them. To show the abundance and variety of possible combinations, consider handing out the following Student Exercise[18] and sending some students to the board to try it, while others work at their seats.

STUDENT EXERCISE

Introduction to Sentence Combining

Make effective sentences out this set of simple kernels:

- The game was over.
- The crowd was excited.
- The crowd left the stadium.
- The crowd filled the streets.
- The streets were narrow.

The most direct combination of these kernels gives you:

> The game was over, and the excited crowd left the stadium and filled the narrow streets.

But whether this is the most pleasing or most suitable sentence these kernels can yield, you can't know until you experiment with other options. In order to explore these options, you should feel free to experiment in the following ways:

- To combine the kernels in any order that sounds good to you
- To add appropriate function words (for instance, *after* as in "After the game," or "after-game crowds"; or *because*, as "because the game was over"; *as*, as in "As they left the stadium"; *who*, as in "who had left"; or *which*, as in "which are narrow."
- To change the form of words (for instance, *excited* to *excitedly* or to *excitement*; *filled* to *filling* or to *were filled*.
- Not to combine at all—that is, occasionally to let a kernel sentence stand as is. "The game was over," for instance, might make an impressive conclusion standing alone.
- To add or to delete a detail, as, for instance, the addition of *exceedingly* to "narrow" or *always* to "filled."

---

continued

Don't hesitate to be creative. The more kinds of sentence structure you can learn to use comfortably, the richer your writing will become.

Students will be impressed by the number of different combinations that these few kernels produce and will enjoy comparing the results of their efforts.

We might try another brief set or two of such kernels to acclimate students to the sentence-combining process and to help them begin to formulate some evaluative criteria. The Paris at Sundown Exercise works well in this regard.

STUDENT EXERCISE

Paris at Sundown

1. The sun sank down.
2. It sank over the river Seine.
3. A girl sat at a sidewalk cafe.
4. The girl was American.
5. The girl finished her coffee.
6. She finished idly.
7. The girl watched the passersby.
8. She watched eagerly.

EVALUATING SENTENCES. Having discovered the abundance of possibilities in combining even the simplest set of kernels, our students may already understand that there can be no single "right" way to combine them and that there is *no* single "correct answer" to any sentence-combining puzzle.

Still, they have probably also determined that some ways are better than others, and they may be wondering if there aren't some objective criteria to help them distinguish the best combinations. Clearly there are criteria, but these are rather subjective. And that is why they need to compare their work with that of other students and discuss the results. Through discussion, our students will be able to develop a surer sense of what is effective with their readers and thus become more confident about their own judgment. In arriving at some preliminary conclusions, students can not go far wrong in relying on these three standards:

- Clarity and directness of meaning
- Rhythmic appeal
- Intended emphasis

Necessity for Context. Soon, however, we will want to move our students to longer exercises, to sets of kernels that they can develop into paragraphs. For as useful as criteria such as the three noted above can be, they take on real meaning only in terms of a specific writing situation. In fact, most evaluating questions can only be answered with "It depends." Is a long sentence better or worse than a short sentence? It depends. Is it better to begin a sentence with a phrase or a clause? It depends. Is it better to put dependant clauses at the beginning or at the end of sentences? Again, it depends.

What it depends upon is where the sentence in question fits into its paragraph, what its purpose is within the paragraph, and what its relationship is to the other sentences in that paragraph. For instance, a composition filled with brief sentences of the subject-verb-object variety would surely give the impression of immature writing, rather like that of a first reader:

> Here is a dog.
> His name is Spot.
> Run, Spot, run.

But such sentences can also provide an impressive note of contrast after a series of longer and more complicated sentences.

Purpose, balance, and variety *within the larger context* are the important considerations. For good sentences build upon one another. Their rhythms and their meanings flow from one to the other. Furthermore, a phrasing that would make a good topic sentence for a paragraph might well be inappropriate for a supporting sentence. And certainly a sentence that is meant to serve as a transition should have a different phrasing from one that is intended to be climactic.

The answer to what makes a good sentence, then, is largely dependent upon the purpose of that sentence within the context of a whole composition. And for this reason, the most effective sentence-combining exercises we can give our students will offer them the opportunity to choose their options within the context of paragraphs and short essays.

Leading Sentence-Combining Discussion

The heart of a sentence-combining program is the discussion evoked by comparative consideration of the paragraphs and essays the students have constructed from lists of kernels in the assigned exercises.

CLASSROOM LOGISTICS. Students should have access to at least three or four written versions of each exercise besides their own. Therefore, we will need to assign four or five students, alternating with each exercise, to share their work with their classmates. They can copy their work on the board (an effective, though cumbersome and time-consuming procedure) or make transparencies or sufficient photocopies.

It is important that the compositions be available not only to the eyes, but also the ears of the students. Reading aloud whole compositions and individual sentences should, in one way or another, be a part of each lesson's activities, and students should be encouraged to try out alternative structures aloud during the composing process as well.

Teacher Preparation. Though it is useful for us to come prepared to help our students understand certain points which, by our own working of the exercise, we realize are especially appropriate to it, lecturing simply does not work with sentence combining. Here, the student papers are, in every sense, the text, and the students themselves, the commentators. Our duty is mainly to ask the kind of questions that will direct our students' attention to the wide variety of syntactical options available to them in each rhetorical situation and that will help them formulate their own rhetorical guidelines for evaluating the relative merits of each option within the particular context.

TEACHING ASSUMPTIONS. Implicit in our discussion leadership or participation might be some assumptions:

1. As native speakers, our students are experts and already have all the linguistic equipment they will need to make their judgments intelligently. (Those who are not native speakers of English can learn from the ingrained knowledge of their classmates.)
2. Students learn better in a positive environment. Because we want to emphasize strengths rather than weaknesses, "Why do you think this version is better?" is a better question than "Why do you think this version is worse?"
3. Our primary goal is to encourage syntactical and stylistic experimentation. This goal takes precedence over our goal of promoting correctness. This assumption must guide us as we encounter error, especially the error (such as the dangling modifier) that often comes about from the manipulation of unaccustomed forms.
4. In the beginning sessions, demonstrating a variety of options is more important to our students' learning than closely evaluating and making judgments.
5. Finally, since as few as five or six kernels can be combined into a very large number of quite grammatical constructions, there is rarely a single correct answer. Sound and logic provide us with helpful evaluative guides, but even experts disagree about what is best.

DISCUSSION QUESTIONS. What sort of questions should we ask? They will vary, of course, with the subject matter and with our particular purpose for the day, but we will want to have in our repertoire a generous supply of questions such as those in the Evaluative Questions Student Guidelines and in the Sample Questions on the pizza exercise. A good way to start our inquiry is with an overall view of the featured compositions as wholes. We might then want to look at the parts of the essays more closely: the introductions, the midsections, the conclusions. Or we might want to delve into why the versions differ. Or we might want to consider why and how one version is more pleasing than another.

Sentence-combining discussion works well in a full-class setting, and I would certainly recommend beginning in this way. In later lessons, after the activity is firmly established, we may wish to vary the procedure, and have collaborative learning groups discuss the combined paragraphs or essays. Small groups permit every student's work to be considered in greater detail. The Evaluative Questions Student Guidelines should also prove useful as group discussion guides.

STUDENT GUIDELINES

Evaluative Questions for Collaborative Learning Groups

OVERALL IMPRESSION
1. Which of the versions do you think is the best? Why?
2. Which versions seem to handle the material most creatively? Have any of them changed or added to the original wording? If so, do the changes make an improvement? Why? Or why not?
3. Which versions offer the most variety in sentence structure? Which have tried the most unusual or interesting structures?
4. Which is the most rhythmically effective version? How is this effectiveness achieved?
5. Are any of the versions weak in coherence or in unity? How might these flaws be corrected?
6. In what major ways do the versions differ?

PURPOSE AND POINT
1. Do all the versions seem to have the same purpose? If not, how do they differ? If yes, what is that purpose?
2. Do the differences in style reflect a difference in purpose? Or simply different approaches to the same purpose?
3. How well do the various stylistic strategies serve their purpose? (If you think, for instance that the point of "Pizza Parlor" is to focus on the pizza and the reactions it evokes, which version best gives that emphasis?)

continued
4. How might some versions be changed to communicate their points more effectively?

AN EXAMPLE. These questions are useful in general. But we will also
need to help our students examine their work in close detail—part by part,
perhaps sentence by sentence. No general guide can account for the variations. Our questions must apply to the specific problem the students have
tackled and the particular solutions they have come up with. The following
sample questions apply to The Pizza Parlor Exercise (from my *Writing Effectively*) and to the four paragraphs students created from it that are reproduced here.

STUDENT EXERCISE

The Pizza Parlor

Combine the following kernels into strong sentences making up an effective paragraph. The kernels are grouped to help you decide upon the
size of individual sentences, but you may disregard these groupings if
you wish.

1. Sam is the pizza chef.
2. The pizza chef removes the pizza.
3. The pizza is hot.
4. The pizza is steamy.
5. He removes it from the oven.
6. The oven is oversized.
7. He removes it deftly.

8. The cheese is yellow.
9. The cheese bubbles.
10. It bubbles over the tomato sauce.
11. It bubbles over the pepperoni.
12. The pizza cools.
13. The waitress eyes the pizza.
14. She eyes it with hunger.
15. She eyes it with envy.
16. The waitress inhales the odors.
17. The odors are delicious.

continued

continued
18. The pizza is ready (finally).
19. The waitress delivers the pizza.
20. She delivers it with resignation.
21. She delivers it to the customers.
22. The customers are eager.
23. The customers are accepting.

ILLUSTRATIVE MODELS

The Pizza Parlor

Using these twenty-three kernels, students created the following sample paragraphs:

A. Sam, who is the pizza chef, removes the pizza deftly from the oversized oven. The pizza is hot and steamy. The cheese is yellow, and it bubbles over the tomato sauce and over the pepperoni. As the pizza cools, the waitress eyes it with hungry envy. She also inhales the delicious odors. When the pizza is finally ready, the waitress delivers it with resignation. The customers accept it with eagerness.

B. Sam, the pizza chef, deftly removed the hot, steamy pizza from the oversized oven. The yellow pizza cheese bubbled over the tomato sauce and the pepperoni. While the pizza cooled, the waitress, hungrily eyeing it with envy, inhaled the delicious odors; and when it was finally ready, she delivered it with resignation to the eager, accepting customers.

C. The hot, steaming pizza is deftly removed from the oversized oven by Sam, the pizza chef. The cheese bubbles over the tomato sauce and pepperoni. Hungrily, the waitress enviously eyes it, inhaling the delicious odors, while it cools. Finally it is ready, and she resignedly delivers it to the eagerly accepting customers.

D. Yellow cheese bubbles over tomato and pepperoni as Sam, the pizza chef, deftly removes the hot and steamy pizza from the oversized oven. Hungrily the waitress eyes the cooling pizza, and enviously she inhales the delicious odors. With resignation she delivers the pizza to the customers, who accept it eagerly.

SAMPLE QUESTIONS TO HELP STUDENTS ANALYZE PART BY PART. The following questions applying specifically to the sample student Pizza Parlor paragraphs typify those we might want to ask in any comparable lesson.

1. *Which begins best?* Do you prefer the Sam openings (A and B) or the pizza openings (C and D)? If you like the Sam openings, how do you feel about the "who" clause in version A? Does it add desirable emphasis? Or does it detract from a concise, direct approach? If you think the initial emphasis belongs on the pizza itself, do you like the passive method in C? Or do you prefer the way the D version manages to focus upon the appetizing "bubbling yellow cheese" by subordinating Sam to a dependent clause placed later in the sentence?

2. *Which version has the most effective conclusion?* Do you like the conclusive ring of the brief final sentence in A? How do you feel about the directness in A's use of "accept" as an active verb and about the final parallelism A achieves with

   . . . delivers it with resignation.
   . . . accept it with eagerness

Do you prefer that ending to B's ending where the waitress delivers the pizza

   . . . with resignation to the eager, accepting customers

or to C where she delivers it:

   . . . resignedly to the eager, accepting customers?

Do you find "resignedly" or "with resignation" the more effective term in this context? Or do you prefer D altogether, where the first phrase of the final sentence, "With resignation," parallels the "hungrily" and "enviously" beginnings of the preceding clauses? And how effective do you find D's concluding "who" clause?

   With resignation she delivers the pizza to the customers, *who accept it eagerly.*

3. *What about the use of verbs?* Does turning the opening sentence passive in C help to advance the meaning? Or does it make it vaguely indirect or awkward? Does changing the verb tense to the past in B seem to improve or detract from the paragraph?

4. *What about the length and complexity of the sentences?* Do you find the third sentence in B too long and complex? If so, where would you suggest breaking it up? How could it be better phrased? A has a number of very brief sentences. Are they effectively employed? Would some be more productively combined? If so, which ones? And how? Or is there already sufficient variety in length and structure?

5. *How do the paragraphs stack up in a close analysis of stylistic features?* Let's compare the different handling of these two important kernels:

> She eyes it with hunger.
> She eyes it with envy.

A handles the situation in a single striking phrase: "hungry envy." Do you find this phrase impressive? Why? How do you feel about C's surrounding the waitress with adverbs:

> *Hungrily* the waitress *enviously* eyes it.

Do you think this construction is excessive or awkward? If so, how would you suggest revising it? Do you prefer the alternative construction in B?

> The waitress hungrily eyes it with envy?

Do you find the parallelism of the treatment in D especially effective?

> Hungrily, the waitress eyes the cooling pizza.
> Enviously, she inhales the delicious odors.

Note that D is a bit creative with the text. Do you feel that the changes and additions offer improvements?

Helping Students Expand Their Repertoire of Stylistic Options

Sentence-combining exercises are at their most useful when used in such freewheeling ways to construct and discuss paragraphs and essays. These are called "cueless" or "contextual" exercises. Sentence combining, however, can also be used successfully to study the specifics of style. After all, the grammar of a language, defined broadly as linguists do, contains a large—though limited—number of options. But many students confine themselves to only a few. Sentence-combining exercises can be used to introduce students to unfamiliar syntax, to give them enough practice using it to make them comfortable with it, and to let them try out a variety of syntactic options for expressing the same idea.

CUED EXERCISES FOR REVIEWING SYNTACTIC CHOICE. Our students are often unaware that they have choices of expression. Usually they write the first phrasing that comes to mind and assume that it is the only way. We need to show them that ordinarily they have multiple options. For instance, English gives us a good number of ways of expressing the adjectival, noun-describing function. A variety of these are summarized in the Choosing Adjective Clauses Student Guidelines.

STUDENT GUIDELINES

Choosing Adjective Clauses and Phrases

The adjectival function consists of modifying, describing, and developing the nouns that serve as the subjects and objects of sentences — and of clauses and phrases. The adjectival function not only is important, but also allows varied approaches to expression — though this fact is not generally known to inexperienced writers. Such writers tend to restrict their use of adjectival modifiers to two positions, either using them as adjective complements:

- The baritone is *plump*.
- The baritone is *lusty*.

or sandwiching them in between the article and its noun:

- The *plump* baritone
- The *lusty* baritone
- The *singing* baritone (participial adjective)
- The *red-bearded* baritone (participial adjective)

Two other positions for adjective placement are equally appropriate, though less frequently employed. These positions are directly before or directly following the noun and its article:

- *Plump and lusty*, the baritone . . .
- The baritone, *plump and lusty*, . . .

Yet another way of describing the baritone would be to do so through the use of an adjective clause:

- The baritone, *who is plump and red-bearded*, . . .
- The baritone, *who was singing happily*, . . .
- The baritone, *who was a lusty singer*, . . .

Or you might prefer to employ a prepositional phrase:

- The baritone, *in his red beard*, . . .
- *With his lusty singing voice*, the baritone . . .

Another alternative is to use an appositive. Nounlike in form and adjectival in function, the appositive is a descriptive phrase that stands as an equivalent to the noun described:

- The baritone, *a lusty singer*, . . .
- *A plump and red-bearded man*, the baritone . . .

continued

continued

One of the most useful of all adjectival modifiers is the participial phrase, a phrase denoting the *-ing* or *-ed* form of a verb and used adjectivally immediately preceding or immediately following the word described:

- *Singing lustily*, the baritone . . .
- The baritone, *singing lustily*, . . .
- *Red-bearded and bronzed by the sun*, the baritone [sang lustily].
- [We saw] the baritone, *red-bearded and bronzed by the sun*.

Uses of Cued Exercises. Cued sentence-combining exercises — those with specific syntactic directions — give students an opportunity for practice with specific syntactic options. Take for example, the following adjective construction problem.

- The earthquake set the dishes rattling in the cupboard.
- The earthquake registered 6 on the Richter scale.

This exercise could be cued in a number of ways. On the one hand, we can use these exercises to introduce students to the uses of syntactical constructions that are unknown or, at least, unfamiliar to them. We might, for example, ask our students to "Make these kernels into a single sentence using at least one adjective clause." With these directions, we would expect such answers as:

- The earthquake, *which registered 6 on the Richter scale*, set the dishes rattling in the cupboard.
- The earthquake, *which set the dishes rattling in the cupboard*, registered 6 on the Richter scale.

Or we might suggest that they "Make these kernels into a single sentence using at least one participle phrase." With this cue, we would expect answers such as:

- The earthquake, *registering 6 on the Richter scale*, set the dishes rattling in the cupboard.
- *Having set the dishes rattling in the cupboard*, the earthquake still only registered 6 on the Richter scale.

Or we might ask our students to "Combine the kernels using an appositive." Here we would expect:

The earthquake, *a true dishes-rattler*, registered 6 on the Richter scale.

On the other hand, we might cue students to select their own adjective construction and their solutions could include any of these or others.

Limitations of Cued Exercises.   Despite the real benefits to be derived from using cued or "signaled" exercises, we should not rely too narrowly on them, for the method has some important limitations. First, these problems, isolated as each of them is, without any relationship to a larger whole or an overall significance, offer no context in which to weigh options. Except for an occasional free-choice assignment (as in the last suggestion above), they offer no opportunity for the students to ask the important questions of rhetoric: Which phrasing is more effective in this context? Which is most conducive to persuading the audience of the truth of my point?

Furthermore, having students form complex statements out of context also leaves them vulnerable to becoming enamored of certain constructions and to using them indiscriminately without any regard for appropriateness. James Moffett warns against just this risk:

> It is very dangerous to separate a learning action from the motive that one expects will engender the action in authentic practice. . . . If [a student] learns to coil and embed constructions as an extraneously motivated intellectual feat, he may write his own sentences without regard for the needs of the whole discourse in which they occur and which alone can provide the proper context for them.[19]

In addition, cued problems have cued solutions, and once the new concept is mastered, these exercises can become as sterile and unprofitable as more traditional grammar exercises.

CREATIVE ALTERNATIVES.   To maintain student creativity, we might add to each set of cued "Combining Kernels" exercises a few "Compose Your Own." For instance, in introducing our students to the noun clause, an interesting construction that is likely to be unfamiliar to many of them, we might offer a combination of exercises, such as the Combining Kernels Exercise.

STUDENT EXERCISE

Combining Noun Clauses

COMBINING KERNALS
Combine the following sets of sentence kernels into effective sentences containing at least one noun clause.
Sample Problem:

- Leslie had copied from René's paper.
- René was very angry about this.

continued

continued
A Sample Solution

- René was very angry that Leslie had copied from his paper.

1. National Guardsman PFC Alfred Amos wondered this:
- Was his battalion going to train at Camp Grayling in Michigan?
2. The Burger Doodle waitress sweetly informed her customer something about the menu.
- Escargot is not on the menu.
3. The society matron lost all her money.
- This fact did not keep her from putting on aristocratic airs.
4. She would never go hungry again.
- Scarlett O'Hara swore this to herself.
5. Maria forgot to tell me something about the party.
- Where is the party going to be?
6. Two objects cannot occupy the same space.
- This is a law of physics that cannot be refuted.

Compose Your Own.
   Create effective sentences by adding at least one noun clause to each of these sentences.

1. Alice had a dream that . . .
2. Napoleon wondered whether . . .
3. Edison explained how . . .
4. . . . is a well-known fact.

Adding inventive problems such as the "Compose Your Owns" helps solve the creativity difficulties of cued sentence-combining exercises. The more serious context criticisms about a lack of context can also be overcome by making contextual paragraph or essay exercises the focus of our sentence-combining program.

RECOMMENDED SENTENCE-COMBINING TEXTS. The best books to look to for effective sentence-combining exercises are William Strong's *Sentence Combining: A Composing Book* and *Sentence Combining and Paragraph Building*. For more-advanced levels, Donald Daiker, Andrew Kerek, and Max Morenberg's, *The Writer's Options: Combining to Composing* is excellent. You might also find useful exercises in Chapters 2, 5, and 8 of my composition text, *Writing Effectively*.[20]

IDEAS FOR DISCUSSION OR ESSAY

1. Try some of the Sample Exercises. Try, for instance, to write "Pizza" first from the waiter's point of view and then from the customer's.

2. Write your own sentence-combining problems. (One good way is to find an interesting essay in a magazine and reduce a paragraph or two to kernels.) Perhaps exchange them with your fellow students and try them out together. Or, if you are observing in a classroom or doing student teaching, try them on your own students.

3. This chapter touches upon some excellent topics for research: for example, the relative merits of the various grammars—traditional, structural, transformational-generative, and so on—for teaching writing; comparison of sentence combining with other methods for teaching style; and whether grammar should be taught in the composition class, what kind, and how much. Follow up an area of research that interests you and incorporate it into a brief research paper.

NOTES

The chapter-opening epigraph is from Max Morenberg, *Doing Grammar* (New York: Oxford UP, 1991), vii.

1. As Joseph M. Williams points out in "Non-Linguistic Linguistics and the Teaching of Style," *The Territory of Language: Linguistics, Stylistics, and the Teaching of Composition* (Carbondale: Southern Illinois UP, 1986).

2. Rei R. Noguchi, *Grammar and the Teaching of Writing: Limits and Possibilities* (Urbana: NCTE, 1991): Chapter 1, "The Limits of Grammar in Writing Improvement," 1–16; George Hillocks, Jr. *Research on Written Composition: New Directions for Teaching* (Urbana: NCRE and ERIC, 1986): Chapter 5, "Grammar and the Manipulation of Syntax," 133–61; and Constance Weaver, *Grammar for Teachers: Perspectives and Definitions* (Urbana: NCTE, 1979): 3–6, 88–90.

3. Peter Rosenbaum, "On the Role of Linguistics in the Teaching of English," *HER* 35 (1965): 341–42.

4. See, for example, Sallibelle Royster, "A Backward Glance at High School Composition," *EJ* 56 (1967): 1187–88.

5. See especially Mary F. Hayes and Donald A. Daiker, "Using Practical Analysis in Evaluating Responses to Student Writing," *Freshman English News* 13 (1984): 1–4, 10; and C. H. Knoblauch and Lil Brannon, "Teacher Commentary on Student Writing: The State of the Art," *Freshman English News* 10 (1981): 1–4.

6. Andrea A. Lumsford and Robert J. Connors, "Frequency of Formal Errors in Current College Writing, or Ma and Pa Kettle Do Research," *CCC* 39 (1988): 395–409.

7. Maxine Hairston. *Successful Writing: A Rhetoric for Advanced Composition* (New York: Norton, 1981), 245. In quoting Hairston's list, I have adjusted the wording of some items to make them more accessible and have supplied examples where they were lacking.

8. Robert DeBeaugrande. "Forward to the Basics; Getting Down to Grammar," *CCC* 35 (1984): 362.

9. Weaver, *Grammar for Teachers*, 5.

10. Martin Gliserman, "An Act of Theft: Teaching Grammar," *CE* 39 (1978): 791–800.

11. Lewis Thomas, "Late Night Thoughts On Listening to Mahler's Ninth Sym-

phony," in a book of the same title (New York: Viking Penguin, 1982); Charles W. Slack. "If I'm So Smart, How Come I Flunk All the Time?" *Eye* (January 1969).

12. Most of our students come from their early education with a fairly good understanding of commas of address, and commas in dates and series, and work with compound sentences, already discussed, should teach students the use of the conjunctive comma. It is the placement of the syntactic comma, the structural comma within the sentence, that is so troubling to our students.

13. This improvement was impressively demonstrated by a carefully controlled study with Miami University freshmen in 1976 by Max Morenberg, Donald Daiker, and Andrew Kerek. See especially their "Sentence Combining at the College Level: An Experimental Study," *RTE* 12 (1978): 245–50.

The Miami study demonstrated the value of sentence combining both for syntactic maturity and for improvement of writing style. Earlier studies that show acceleration in the growth of students' syntactic maturity include: James W. Ney, "Applied Linguistics in the Seventh Grade," *EJ* 55 (1966): 895–97, 902; Donna Kay Raub, "The Audio-Lingual Drill Technique: An Approach to Teaching Composition," M.A. thesis, George Peabody College for Teachers, 1966; Barbara D. Miller and James W. Ney, "The Effect of Systematic Oral Exercises on the Writing of Fourth-Grade Students," *RTE* 2 (1968): 44–61; John C. Mellon, *Transformational Sentence-Combining: A Method for Enhancing the Development of Syntactic Fluency in English Composition: NCTE Research Report No. 10* (Urbana: NCTE, 1969); Kellogg W. Hunt and Roy O'Donnell, *An Elementary School Curriculum to Develop Better Writing Skills*, United States Office of Education Project No. 8-9093 (Tallahassee, Fla.: Florida State U, 1970); Anne Oberchain, "Effectiveness of the Precise Essay Question in Programming the Sequential Development of Written Composition Skills and the Simultaneous Development of Critical Reading Skills," Master's thesis; George Washington U 1971; M. R. Vitale et al., "Effect of Sentence-Combining Exercises Upon Several Restricted Written Composition Tasks," *JEP* 62, No. 6 (1971): 521–25; Kenneth David Fischer, "An Investigation to Determine if Selected Exercises in Sentence-Combining Can Improve Reading and Writing," Ed.D. diss. Indiana U, 1973; Frank O'Hare, *Sentence Combining: Improving Student Writing Without Formal Grammar Instruction* (Urbana: NCTE, 1973); David Perron, "An Exploratory Approach to Extending the Syntactic Development of Fourth-Grade Students Through the Use of Sentence-Combining Methods," Diss. Indiana U, 1974; Warren E. Combs, "Some Further Effects and Implications of Sentence-Combining Exercises for the Secondary Language Arts Curriculum," Diss. U of Minnesota, 1975, and "Further Effects of Sentence-Combining Practice on Writing Ability," *RTE* 10 (1976): 137–49; Elray L. Pedersen, "Improving Syntactic and Conceptual Fluency in the Writing of Language Arts Students Through Extended Practice in Sentence-Combining," Diss. U of Minnesota, 1976.

More importantly, the following studies indicate an improvement in writing quality as well: The O'Hare, Combs, and Pederson studies (above) and Maureen A. Sullivan, "Parallel Sentence-Combining Studies in Grades Nine and Eleven," in *Sentence Combining and the Teaching of Writing: Selected Papers from the Miami University Conference, Oxford, Ohio October 27–28, 1978*, eds. Donald Daiker, Andrew Kerek, and Max Morenberg (Akron: Dept. of English, U of Akron, 1979).

For the most useful evaluative discussion of sentence-combining research, See Hillocks, *Research*, 141–151.

14. Charles Cooper, "Research Roundup: Oral and Written Composition," *EJ* 64 (1975): 72.

15. It's ironic to note—though it makes not a whit of difference—that the sentence-embedding transformations originated by Noam Chomsky in the *Syntactic Structures* in the 1950s, upon which sentence-combining was originally predicated, were discredited by Chomsky in his *Aspects of the Theory of Syntax* in 1965. See Williams, "Non Linguistic Linguistics," 174.

16. William Strong, "Sentence Combining: Back to Basics and Beyond," *EJ* 65 (1976): 56.

17. A word on the pedagogical history of sentence combining. After the publicity accompanying Kellog Hunt's and especially Frank O'Hare's work, teachers at all levels began trying these exercises. And after the first edition of William Strong's excellent high-school text offered a usable collections of contextual exercises, they became an important part of the composition program in many schools. With the Daiker, Kerek, and Morenberg research confirming evidence of the value of this teaching strategy and the publication of their college text, the popularity of sentence combining reached fad proportions—unfortunately.

Some advocated turning entire composition programs over to this one method; others said that there was no writing problem it could not solve. But because sentence combining failed to cure acne, or because those who had devoted their whole program to it tired of it, or simply because it was time for the next fad, sentence combining suddenly lost its luster, and now it is seldom mentioned.

But sentence combining exercises remain as they always have been—though not a panacea, still a first-rate way to teach writing style.

18. This and the other exercises in this portion of the chapter are taken from my *Writing Effectively*, 2nd ed. (New York: Harper, 1989), upon which I have relied heavily throughout this chapter.

19. James Moffett: *Teaching the Universe of Discourse* (Boston: Houghton, 1968), 171.

20. William Strong, *Sentence Combining and Paragraph Building* (New York: Random House, 1981) and *Sentence Combining: A Composing Book*, 2nd ed., (New York: Random House, 1982); Donald Daiker, Andrew Kerek, and Max Morenberg, and Jeffrey Sommers, *The Writer's Options: Combining to Composing*, 5th ed., (New York: Harper, 1994).

□ □ □ **8**

Stylistic Problems from Nonstandard Dialects

Writing teachers may not be able to avoid the notion that Standard American English is a prestige dialect, and perhaps they should not, but they should confront the fact head-on, encouraging students to learn to master it for their own benefit.
— Victor Raskin and Irwin Weiser

□ □ □

Many students who do not speak the standard English dialect have special problems with style, problems of such severity that they can even interfere with the students' ability to acquire the more fundamental writing skills. These students need the sort of training already outlined in this text—indeed, they may need a more intensive grounding in this training than do their other classmates. However, in order to make this training accessible to them and in order to make their prose style communicative to their readers, they need in addition to gain command of Standard American English (SAE), the dialect of the American academic world and of formal written English.

Students who must learn English as a second language have similar problems; in fact, some of the techniques for gaining command of the standard dialect were developed from methods pioneered in ESL (English as a Second Language) teaching programs. But the latter group of students are not handicapped by linguistic interference, the conflicting signals sent out by two dialects within the same language. Nor are these students troubled as much by the qualms about disloyalty and difficulties of identity that inevitably face speakers of a nonstandard dialect as they attempt to acquire the standard dialect. It is to these special difficulties that nonstandard speakers encounter when learning to write that this chapter is addressed.

STANDARD AND NONSTANDARD AMERICAN–ENGLISH DIALECTS

Knowledge of SAE is important for our students because, informally, it is the major dialect spoken by educated Americans and, formally, it is the English of formal American prose. It differs in a number of ways from other American dialects—for instance, those spoken by some people of Appalachian, Puerto Rican, Mexican, Native American, or Chinese heritage—and from that of many people living in exclusively African-American or working-class white neighborhoods.

Other American Dialects

Though the standard dialect is useful in the general American society beyond the particular linguistic communities, it is not intrinsically "better"—more beautiful, more efficient, more inherently communicative—than any of the other dialects. Studies in comparative linguistics have overturned some important misconceptions about the relative value of various languages and dialects. Linguistic data gathered in all parts of the world have shown conclusively that not only do all peoples everywhere have complex languages, but that neither the elaborateness, efficiency, nor aesthetic quality of these languages has anything whatever to do with the people's degree of civilization, intelligence, or moral character. One noted linguistic anthropologist, Edward Sapir, writes:

> We know of no people that is not possessed of a fully developed language. The lowliest South African Bushman speaks in the forms of a rich symbolic system that is in essence perfectly comparable to the speech of a cultivated Frenchman.[1]

Comparative value judgments in the world of language are thus simply irrelevant from the scientific viewpoint and can amount to little more than a personal preference that is usually based on "I like what I'm used to."

AFRICAN-AMERICAN VERNACULAR.   Linguistic techniques have also been applied to the analysis of dialects, and particular attention has been paid to the African-American Vernaculars.[2] This research shows that far from being degenerative or ungrammatical versions of the standard dialect, these dialects are fully grammatical, syntactically rigid languages in their own right, sharing a similar vocabulary with SAE, but operating from different rules of grammar in a number of important features.

African-American Vernacular still carries features of the West African languages that shaped its formation. It includes, for example, the "habitual" tense of the African languages, which is not designated in SAE. It is expressed in African-American Vernacular by "be" ("He be coming," "Mama be working"). African-American Vernacular also shares the West African avoidance of a double signification of plurality ("two dog"), a feature also characteristic of many Chinese-American English dialects. African-American Vernacular, like the Appalachian dialect, also retains features of the sixteenth- and seventeenth-century English spoken in colonial America and immortalized in the King James Bible. Among these features are the repeated subject ("The boy, he . . ." as in "Thy rod and thy staff, they . . .") and the reinforced negative ("Nobody don't . . ."), commonplace in Shakespeare's plays.

IMPORTANCE OF STANDARD AMERICAN ENGLISH. SAE is thus no more traditional nor grammatical than the other American dialects. But by virtue of its identity as *the* written language, it has become the universal dialect, the dialect spoken on television, the dialect in which government and commerce and education are transacted. Moreover, SAE is not the hidebound, Latinate language that some authority considers "correct": it is the dialect educated Americans actually speak, and in its more formal version, it is the dialect they really write.

The Pedagogical Controversy

Meeting in collision in our classrooms, then, are SAE, the dialect of education and business, and many native American students to whom it is a foreign dialect. Our task is to teach all of our students to write. What are we to do about students to whom the language, the very vehicle of their writing, is unfamiliar, but who are equipped with an otherwise serviceable language of their own?

THE STANDARD-DIALECT-ONLY APPROACH. Until rather recently, many teachers felt the only proper response to nonstandard usage was to stamp it out, obliterate it, get rid of it forever. They did not pass by an opportunity to bully or cajole their students out of speaking the dialect of their homes and neighborhoods; and they covered their students' papers with corrections, couched, I'm afraid, in what was often an incomprehensible symbolism for their students.

For far too long, students unaccustomed to the standard dialect were prodded into learning it by shame and ridicule. Teachers openly conveyed the impression that their own dialect was "Right and Good" and that of the students—their parents, friends, and community—was somehow wrong and illiterate. These teachers seemed unaware of their students' pain and the blocks to learning they were setting up by creating a sense of disloyalty.

Approach Evaluated. On the one hand, such teaching simply did not work. A great proportion of the corrections merely went unheeded, and the rest, misunderstood, contributed through the process of analogy to the creation of yet more errors. On the other hand, this approach took a sorry toll in student distrust of teachers and of education and, more damaging yet, in negative student self-image. Not unnaturally, the students felt that when their language was rejected, they themselves were rejected; and when their writing failed, they themselves failed.

THE HOME-DIALECT-ONLY APPROACH. Teachers sensitive to the practical limitation and moral degradation of the Standard-English-only approach understood the necessity for reform. The NCTE, for example, published a position paper in 1974 on the rights of students to their own dialect. It "affirm[ed] the student's right to his own language—the dialect of his nurture in which he finds his identity and style" and suggested that the training of teachers be changed to "enable them to support this goal of diversity."[3] Some school boards and other governmental bodies mandated "students' rights to their own language" by law. New York City, for instance, ruled out rote attempts to train the student ear to SAE cadences and some Michigan teachers were taken to court for teaching SAE usage.

The home-dialect-only approach is also influential in many classrooms. There nonstandard dialect speakers are encouraged to write *all* their papers in their own dialect. Teachers, not considering nonstandard usage as error, make no attempt to teach students to edit with standard forms. Those who are uncomfortable with nonstandard dialect in academic papers or expository themes confine their assignments to journal writing and personal narrative.

Approach Evaluated. Unquestionably, the abuses of the standard dialect approach need to be acknowledged and eliminated. It is important to reassure students of their linguistic worth and make them aware of the beauties of their own dialect. From a practical viewpoint, students with weak self-image do not learn well. And surely, abasement of students under any pretext is morally intolerable.

But in making these necessary reforms, some in our profession have managed to throw out the proverbial baby with the bath water. In throwing out linguistic harassment, some ideologically committed teachers have also thrown out access to the current power system by denying knowledge of the standard dialect to those who need it most. For though the standard dialect offers no aesthetic or intellectual advantages to its users, its use does bestow undeniable social, political, and economic advantages. And when we leave our students ignorant of its effective use, we cut off their access to the doorways, not only of power, but of simple economic security.

Despite the compassion that animates this approach, we would do our students an irremedial injustice should we follow it completely and thus deny them access to the educated version of their native language. The basic orality of the nonstandard varieties of English often results in writing filled with what standard speakers generally regard as errors and which—as Mina Shaughnessy carefully documents[4]—they find highly distracting, distracting to the point that they are unable, or unwilling, to ferret out the meaning the writing attempts to convey.

Often these "error"-distracted readers are people upon whom the student's future depends. The views of one of Joseph Harris's students is interesting in this respect. Ron, a factory worker from central Pennsylvania, appreciated the opportunity offered by a students' "right in their own language" approach, but upon reflection, rejected it:

> As I look back over my writings for this course, I see a growing acceptance of the freedom to write as I please, which is allowing me to almost enjoy writing (I can't believe it). So I tried this approach in another class I am taking. . . . The first paper . . . came back with a D−. . . . My view is, if they open the pen I will run as far as I can, but I won't break out because I have a bad habit, it's called eating.[5]

Ours is still very far from "the best of all possible worlds," but it is the only one we have. And while we work to improve it, our students must deal with the large number of its citizens who, considering their own the best of all possible dialects, judge those who have not learned to handle it not as different, but as stupid, and stigmatize them accordingly. Well might we say that these people's ignorance is their own problem and not ours; but, realistically, it is our students who must bear the stigma.

Bidialectism

We are thus faced with a serious pedagogical problem: how to teach the standard dialect without impugning nonstandard dialects and those who speak them. Sylvia, a African-American young woman from Philadelphia and another of Harris's students, puts the dilemma in clear, personal terms:

> I understand the relevance and importance of learning to use "public language," but . . . I am also afraid of losing my "private identity"—that part of me that my parents, my relatives, and my friends know and understand. However, on the other hand, within me, there is an intense desire to grow and become a part of the "public world"—a world that exists outside of the secure and private world of my parents, relatives, and friends. If I want to belong, I must learn the "public language" too. (19)

We are fortunate that this dilemma has a feasible answer: bidialectism. In educating nonstandard speaking students, we must not try to take away their home dialect. But we also must not deny them the opportunity to write as educated people write. No, we should help our students add to what they have by assisting them to achieve written fluency in another exceedingly useful dialect as well. We should aim at making our students bidialectic, just as the Spanish, French, or German teachers aim at making them bilingual. Later on, if our students do not choose to make use of this knowledge, that will be their decision, but we will have done our part in providing the wherewithal for choice. Sabina Thorne Johnson points up our responsibility:

> For minority students, the acquisition [of Standard English] provides a linguistic freedom of choice, whereas the perpetuation of dialect furthers separatism in the form of linguistic ghettoizing . . . if individual students wish to volunteer in a linguistic revolution, then that should be their choice after they have acquired an alternative means of expression; it should not be their instructor's, as it would be were he to provide no alternative to their dialect.[6]

Knowledge is empowering; ignorance is limiting. By helping our students to fluency in the standard dialect, we empower them to join the established system if that is their desire or, should they choose to oppose the established system, such fluency empowers them to oppose it on far better terms.

MOTIVATING OUR STUDENTS

The factors that make the teaching of the standard dialect controversial also contribute to making its learning difficult to motivate. The intrinsic arduousness of this study, however, makes effective motivation especially important. For our students to be eager to write SAE, we will have to convince them that the skill will be valuable enough to them to make it worth the time and effort they will be required to spend, but also to reassure them that in learning SAE they will not be giving up something even more precious to them—their own identity.

We must therefore adopt a dual motivational strategy and work with it on the first day and from time to time throughout the term. We will need both to urge the advantages of learning SAE and also to reinforce our students' sense of the validity of their home dialect.

Teaching the Advantages of Using Standard American English

There are two strong motives that we can suggest to our students to help provide them with the determination to learn to write SAE. The first is their need to communicate in writing, and the second—and more important—is their need to succeed in a world where nonstandard dialect is a negative social and economic marker.

THE COMMUNICATION MOTIVE. We might explain that the various nonstandard American-English dialects are primarily oral with writing conventions still undeveloped.[7] Therefore, when our student-speakers of these dialects write, they have not only to transliterate the sounds of their oral speech, but to invent their own spelling, punctuation, and so on, as they go along. Without agreed-upon conventions for guidance, their message often becomes difficult to understand.

We might let our students discover the truth of this observation for themselves by giving them copies of a student paragraph that demonstrates the erratic punctuation typical of the writing of an untrained nonstandard speaker. Even if the paragraph is written in the vernacular of a student's own dialect, he or she will probably experience a good deal of trouble trying to read it aloud coherently.

Yet, we can assure them, if they are willing to put forth considerable effort, the communications gap can be overcome and they really will be able to succeed in learning enough to make a substantial difference in the clarity and acceptability of their writing.

THE SOCIAL, POLITICAL, AND ECONOMIC MOTIVE. The other major motive for our students learning to write in SAE offers many of them an even stronger inducement for study, for it is based upon the social, political, and economic advantages of a ready command of the standard dialect. Since no dialect is inherently "better" than any other, we will have to be completely frank with our students about the reality of these advantages in society as it is now constituted. As much as we might wish the situation to be otherwise, it is a fact that ordinarily the formal student paper not written in SAE will not get an A; the letter lacking standard writing conventions will not win the applicant the job; the report not couched in SAE will not result in a promotion.

Those who have succeeded in becoming genuinely bidialectic often express their appreciation for their teachers' candor, especially on this sensitive topic. They say that they are particularly grateful for having the linguistic situation put before them in terms of the practical realities of the present world. We can, I think, trust their statements and bring a similar frankness to our students.

Reinforcing Students' Sense of the Validity of Their Home Dialects

We need, nevertheless, to recognize the sensitivity of the issue and exercise care and discretion in dealing with it. We must keep in mind that in emphasizing the social, political, and economic implications of SAE, we may be inadvertently contributing to what is perhaps the most deep-rooted and difficult learning problem the nonstandard-dialect student must face; for we may be arousing fears of disloyalty and self-betrayal. Some of our students will feel that they are being disloyal to their family, friends, neighborhood, and all who have nurtured them in their early years, whenever they attempt to master the standard dialect. In those instances where our students perceive the standard dialect as the language of the oppressors, they may feel they are going over to the enemy in learning it themselves. Students who are troubled by this problem not only feel like traitors to their cultural or racial group, and to their families, but also, in a fundamental sense, like traitors to themselves. They are afraid that in studying the new dialect they are somehow rejecting the old and thereby surrendering their own identity.

Because the actual process of mastering a dialect akin to one's own is a learning situation of extraordinary difficulty demanding extraordinary commitment on the part of the learner, such feelings may not only be destructive psychologically, but also destructive of successful intellectual accomplishment. Not all of our students will experience these sentiments, and those who do will not have them all the time. Nevertheless, we can expect such attitudes to inhibit the work of many of our students intermittently throughout the entire program.

We should therefore strive throughout all our teaching to support our students' sense of the authenticity of their native dialect, to stress its usefulness both for creativity and for communication within their own linguistic community. If we do so, we will also be helping to strengthen our students' image of themselves as prospectively successful learners.

DIALECT CONFIDENCE-BUILDING STRATEGIES. There are a number of ways we can achieve this end. The value of these methods depends upon the age and sophistication of our students, upon the particular social outlook they bring to the classroom, and upon the amount of teaching time we can afford to spend.

Emphasize the Equity of All English Dialects. One method is to attack the problem directly. SAE is important because it is the dialect of written English, we assert; but at the same time we must make clear that this importance does not make it intrinsically superior to any other dialect, nor does it make the people who speak it inherently more worthwhile, or even more articulate.

We might ask our students to name a person or two from among their nonstandard- and from among their standard-dialect-speaking acquaintances who express themselves especially well and are exciting to listen to, and then to think of some from both groups whose speech is dull and inexpressive. Our point is thus demonstrated: the value of a particular dialect lies in the speaker and not in the language spoken.

Show the Grammaticality of All Dialects. We can also assure our students that SAE itself is not linguistically better than the other English dialects. It is important for those students who have been told that their dialect was "ungrammatical" to discover the actual grammar of their own dialect. We might point out to these students the ways in which their dialect marks tense, for instance, or number. In making the comparison between SAE and the other varieties, our students can experience a certain sense of pride when they discover that a feature of their dialect appears more versatile or more efficient than that feature in SAE. For example, speakers of African-American Vernacular are usually delighted to find out that their dialect can indicate a tense that is absent in SAE, and Chinese-American English speakers—and others whose language is less inflected than SAE—note the redundancies of the standard dialect with satisfaction.

Teach Some Appropriate Historical Linguistics.   If it is at all possible, it is a good idea to plan time for our students to learn about the origin of language and languages, about the ways they are constantly changing, about how linguistic communities are formed, and about how dialects develop. We might give particular emphasis to studying the formation of our students' own dialects. Students find it helpful to know the origin of features of their dialects that diverge from the standard: of Spanish characteristics in Chicano or Puerto Rican dialects, for instance, of West African features in African-American Vernacular, or of reminiscences of Elizabethan English in Appalachian English.

From time to time, some teachers like to have their students teach them interesting or colorful phrases from their own dialect. They thus create a reverse learning situation that many students especially enjoy. And, of course, this new information can be shared with the class.

Though it is most important for students to be familiar with the background of their own dialect, it is also helpful for them to gain some understanding of the formation of other American English dialects. This knowledge not only tends to reduce whatever prejudice our students might be harboring for another group, but it also helps put their own dialect in the broader perspective of a wide spectrum of nonstandard dialects.

Interdialectical Exercises.   Exercises requiring interdialectical paraphrasing offer a way of emphasizing the multiplicity and variety of English vernaculars. They are also useful in developing our students' ability to translate nonstandard English into the current standard for written English.[8] Our students might translate passages from *Huck Finn* into its more formal SAE equivalent or passages from *David Copperfield* into its less formal, more contemporary SAE equivalent. African-American students particularly enjoy making translations from Alice Childress's *A Hero Ain't Nothing but a Sandwich*.

Translating rock lyrics to standard dialect is a variation of interdialectical interpretation that students especially relish, according to Gloria Flaherty, who has used the idea at both the junior high and high school levels. Students bring in their favorite rock lyrics in nonstandard dialect. Excluding those with violent themes, Flaherty duplicates them for the class. Then she has her students translate them into the standard dialect and share their efforts.

We might make use of any interest students show in heroics or knights in armor to have them work with interlineal transcriptions of brief passages from the Old English *Beowulf* or the Middle English *Sir Gawain and the Green Knight*. A group with religious interests might want to try putting one of the various early renditions of the biblical psalms into a modern dialect. Or, if they are required to read Chaucer or Shakespeare, students might enjoy trying their hand at writing SAE equivalents of short passages from these works. Although such exercises may seem far afield, they all demonstrate the ubiquitousness and respectability of English dialects that vary from the standard, and they lessen any opprobrium students might feel in converting their own dialect to SAE. And, of course, they provide practice in making such conversions.

Face Linguistic Bigotry Candidly.　　At some point we might also need to confront the question of linguistic prejudice directly. We might explain that all people naturally grow up talking the language that they are brought up with. (Students usually enjoy the story of the visitor to Japan who came home raving about how brilliant all the Japanese children are: "Why, Japanese is the hardest language you could ever imagine—yet even four-year-old babies over there can speak it fluently!") With human nature being what it is, each person is not only more comfortable speaking the dialect he or she grew up with, but is also firmly convinced that that dialect is the best and that those who don't speak it are outsiders who cannot quite be trusted.

Show How Linguistic Bigotry Transcends Race.　　Sometimes our students of color think of the issue of standard and nonstandard dialects in a racial context. Learning about the racial diversity of American nonstandard dialects is helpful for these students. They are also interested in learning about exact parallels of their situation that contain no racial overtones—for example, that of the Swiss students in German-speaking Switzerland. Swiss is an oral dialect of German, nonstandard and subject to all the scorn that word implies. Ironically, Swiss is called "Low German," and its speakers must learn to read, write, and speak Standard German from the time they enter their Swiss school.

Another example may be found in Shaw's *Pygmalion* (or *My Fair Lady*). The most penetrating analysis available of the social and economic implications of standard and nonstandard dialects, these plays deal with speakers of Cockney and Standard British English, who are all of the same race. Either play is interesting to teach in a unit on language and dialects; in fact, the New York City Board of Education prescribes such study in its program.[9]

TEACHING APPROPRIATENESS OF DIALECT USAGE.　　If we adopt a rhetorical, persuasive-purpose, approach, we can reinforce the value of our students' home dialects and at the same time help them delineate the appropriate occasions for the substitution of SAE. We can discuss the use of the various levels of standard and nonstandard dialects in terms of the purpose of the particular discourse, to whom it is addressed (whom it is meant to persuade), and whether it will be written or spoken.

In such a discussion, our students should readily be able to see that SAE would be truly inappropriate for nonstandard speakers in certain situations—for example, in going to visit one's grandparents, in leading playground groups in the home neighborhood, or in going out with friends, especially friends who share the dialect. In other situations, SAE is more suitable or, depending upon the rhetorical context, more advantageous.

We must insist, I think, that SAE is the appropriate dialect for expository writing situations, and especially for academic writing. At the same time, we should be careful to show how very effective nonstandard dialect can be in fiction. Here is the time to dig out short stories and novels written by Mark Twain, Frank O'Connor, Eudora Welty, Claude Brown, Alice Walker, Richard Wright, and other such masters of dialect. We can encourage our students to follow models such as the works of these or comparable authors and write a short story or a poem in their own home dialect. And home dialect is, of course, completely appropriate for personal narrative and journal writing.

Responding to Home-Dialect Writing.   How should we respond to non-standardisms in our students' writing? Those in formal writing are useful for diagnosis and remedial work; we can work with them in ways discussed later in the chapter. Those that are a part of home-dialect dialogue in some short stories or of the authorial voice in some personal narrative are appropriate to these genres and can be encouraged; but since nonstandard dialects have no written conventions, we probably should insist on student authors following standard capitalization, punctuation, and—where possible—spelling conventions, for the sake of clarity.

"Errors" in informal work such as journals or notes to us require a thoughtful, tactful approach. Red penciling or calling obvious attention to them betrays the freedom of these genres. Yet ignoring them altogether reinforces their inappropriate use in the classroom. A good solution to the dilemma is to model standard English forms as we reply to what our students have written. For example, a student might write:

> Your cool I really liked doing those rock songs.

Rather than noting the run-on and circling the *your*, we might reply in words that provide a pattern of the conventional forms in question:

> Thanks for the compliment. I think you're a good student, and I'm glad you enjoyed the rock-song exercise.[10]

Special Motivation

Motivating strategies such as these should provide, in Mina Shaughnessy's words, "a respect for one's own linguistic aptitude and a confidence that the act of mastering a second variety of English is neither a disloyal nor a destructive act, but in fact a claim upon a wider culture" (186). If they have worked, then our students will have developed a commitment to this learning that should sustain them through the difficult beginnings of study.

But useful as they are, these strategies cannot entirely solve the deep-seated, study-interrupting problems that are especially common among nonstandard-dialect-speaking students. These students need the same sort of "we know you can do it" reassurance, discussed in Chapter 1, that all our students do. But they may need a special dose of it. For the great majority of them are not really at home in the academic world. Most students who have not acquired the rudiments of the standard dialect before we meet them, having spent a good number of years in a school environment dominated by it, come to us with a sense of failure.

Often they do not so much express this sense through a lack of self-confidence as through a matter-of-fact certainty that they cannot succeed in school, especially not in writing. The following paragraph, for instance, captures the typical nuances. It was written by a high school senior for a first-day sample on a nonspecified topic.

> I don't like writing very much, as you can tell by the way I started off my paragraph. I never did like writing because I can't spell to good or I don't have anything to write about. I am glad that we don't get graded on it, or I will get a very bad grade. As you can see I started off a lot of sentences, I don't, I never or, I am which is not very good English I don't think.[11]

Sometimes hostility accompanies this certainty of failure, but more often it is expressed in a latent distrust.

HAVE STUDENTS EXPERIENCE SUCCESS.   In order to counteract this self-defeating attitude, we must construct the program in such a way that our students can experience both success and the awareness of having succeeded. In other words, we must build upon what our students already know, add new material in small doses, and test frequently to determine if they are digesting these small doses. With this method, each student daily experiences a series of small successes. Lyn Brendel of Beavercreek High School in Ohio, for example, has developed a confidence-building method of grading. She counts the correct responses instead of the errors. For instance, when a class working on run-on sentences writes a paragraph, she marks a C[orrect] for every properly formed sentence and rewards students who earn the most C's.

The feeling of success is reinforced in the next lesson which should build upon and hark back to the one before. If students have not "caught on" to the new material, they can discover the lack immediately and seek help. We must make sure that there is no stigma attached to not accomplishing the small unit, that missing the mark is not considered failure but only a temporary setback or, possibly, an opportunity to diagnose and get a firmer grip on the source of the problem.

We're on Their Side.   As for the distrust, we have to recognize that it exists and seize every opportunity to convince our students that teaching is not an adversary proceeding. Or if they must view it in that way, then they should learn that we—teacher and student—are on the same side, battling against wily ignorance which is the source of our mutual problem. We must somehow lead our students to understand that when they succeed, we are as happy as they are, that we are with them all the way.

Programming for Success

Though successful programs for nonstandard-dialect students have much in common with successful writing programs in general, they differ from them in two important, perhaps paradoxical, emphases: these programs need to be more highly structured and more individualized.

HIGHLY STRUCTURED PROGRAMMING. Nonstandard-speaking students need a more rigidly structured program than their fellow students, according to the literature and to the instructors I have interviewed who have worked most successfully with these students. This fact may be difficult for some of us to accept. "Something there is" in a humanist, to paraphrase Robert Frost, "that does not love" rigidity or standardization in teaching. Yet when we talk to teachers who have made writing programs for these special students work, they tell us that experience has changed their minds in this respect. James L. Fenner, for instance, writes:

> For the teacher with some respect for creative work, the whole idea of producing compositions by formula may be anathema; . . . such a formula [may even] appear unduly restricting if not downright insulting. . . . Nevertheless for the [nonstandard-speaking] student . . . some such crutch may be necessary, if he is to succeed. . . . I hold with those who believe that creative work, whether in writing or elsewhere, is the one supremely noble activity and achievement of mankind. And I hold with those who insist that students can, should, and must be given opportunities to exercise the creative energies they may possess. But my reverence for this important work does not prevent me from finding merit in [such highly structured] teaching.[12]

Students, such as many of our nonstandard speakers, who are not at home in an academic environment, are usually more comfortable with and thrive better in a program, and with materials, that impose a fairly rigid external structure—at least until they can internalize that structure and develop the necessary discipline within themselves.

INDIVIDUALIZED PROGRAMMING AND ATTENTION. The trick is to base highly specified, precisely formatted assignments in individualized instruction, whose relevance to the ongoing writing is clearly apparent. Individualized instruction is particularly important for our nonstandard-speaking students. They must be allowed sufficient time to "catch on" at each stage of learning. Yet though these students vary substantially in their rates of progress, they still do best when their learning momentum is not interrupted, either to wait for the slower students or to keep up with the swifter. They thus need a curriculum individualized enough to permit them to proceed at their own speed.

These students also need a large measure of personal attention. Many need a personal approach to assimilate the unfamiliar language of academic material. And because of these students' feelings about failure, they also need more frequent reassurance that they are on the right track as they go along, and firmer guidance to make sure they do not wander too far from it.

With a combination of individualized and structured teaching strategies we can provide our nonstandard-speaking students with a writing program in which they may experience success in both composing and editing.

TEACHING THE EDITING PROCESS

The editing process is the point in learning to write where nonstandard-dialect students are at their greatest disadvantage and where they need special assistance, for the writing difficulties that are peculiarly theirs are basically stylistic.

Compose First, Edit Later

These surface problems need to be dealt with through the editing process, during the rewriting time. This point is important to emphasize because it is so frequently ignored. Far too often these students attempt to edit as they compose, to "get it right the first time," and in so doing, they effectively stifle creative thought. What is more, their overwhelming concern for immediate correctness often results in truncated papers or errors of hypercorrectness (for example, the placing of 's on all available plural nouns and present-tense verbs). These students' obsession with correctness is ruinous to both the heart and surface of their work, and it is thus essential that we free them to make mistakes.[13]

We can do so by insisting upon their separating composing from editing. We should lead them to understand that while they are composing their first drafts, even while they work with these drafts to make them coherent and effectively structured, they are not to give conscious attention to surface correctness. We can assure them that they will have plenty of opportunity to work on surface problems after they have expressed and ordered their ideas and that, in fact, much awkward expression and the errors it entails are actually eliminated during the structural improvement of their essays. Not only should we not expect perfect first drafts, but we might confide the truth many teachers have noticed: that an increasing discrepancy between the first and final drafts usually signifies improvement in a student's writing.

So Many Errors, So Little Time

We should thus approach the surface problems of syntax, usage, punctuation, spelling, and diction only after we have helped our students achieve coherent, well-structured first drafts. Yet, even so, our task at first may appear overwhelming. Their papers still may seem to be filled with departures from the formal writing conventions of SAE. There are so many errors!

How are we to teach our students to edit out the errors in the current draft and not make them again in the next? We will need to approach our students individually, diagnose their problems, and then help them understand the why of the problems so that they can recognize them in the future and conquer them. We will also need to prescribe specific exercises to give practice in dealing with the diagnosed problems. But since the prescribed exercises will take the students into unknown territory, we will also need to provide quick feedback so that this experience will not simply reinforce harmful habits. These strategies can work, but they all take our time.

VARYING RESOURCES. All of us teach with time constraints, but some situations provide more helpful resources than others. The optimum approach for each of us will vary with the resources available to us. It will depend on whether we are blessed with classroom computers or easy access to a well-equipped skills lab, or whether we have paraprofessional help or trained peer tutors, or whether we are completely on our own. I suggest the following three approaches because of the varying limitations of our teaching situations. They can be used alone or in combination, depending upon how much time is available for personalized instruction for each student.

CLASSROOM METHODS

Personalized Studies. The first procedure involves a personal diagnosis for each student based upon the first draft of a written assignment. Then with close tutorial supervision, the student completes exercises (best adapted from the student's own writing) that lead to the solving of the diagnosed problems and the eventual satisfactory completion of the assignment. (See pages 309–12 for an example of this strategy.)

This method is ideal because it is tailored specifically to the individual needs of the student. If it is at all possible, each student should experience it at least once or twice during the course, even under the less-than-ideal conditions of a crowded classroom.

Individual Work within Classwide Assignments. A second method starts with a classwide diagnosis of writing problems. The curriculum is then keyed to the problems diagnosed. Students work at their own individual rates through a sequence of exercises which they share with a group similarly diagnosed or with all of their classmates. At frequent intervals students discuss their work with the teacher or a tutor. The work is personalized to the extent that students will be given extra material to help with points they find difficult, or they may skip material they already know.

Classwide Diagnosis and Prescription. In yet a third method, a class curriculum is set up after a classwide diagnosis of writing problems, and the class works together to try to master each problem with the help of class discussion and student board work. All students work at the same time on the same theme or paragraph assignment and on the same set of exercises, preparing them for that assignment or helping them edit it after the first draft, but the teacher (or tutor) stays in close touch with the work of each student and may vary the exercises in number and in difficulty to meet individual needs.

Diagnosis of Individual Problems

Each of the procedures begins with diagnosis. We should start with a careful analysis of a sample or samples of a student's writing. Diagnostic tests can also be useful, but they are most effective as a supplementary tool. After we have discovered the pattern of deviation from SAE employed by this particular speaker of this particular dialect, and determined something of the rationale behind this specific pattern of departure, we might use printed tests or exercises to define the particulars and the extent of the pattern. For example, if we uncover a pattern of difficulty with past and present tenses of irregular verbs, we can find out which verbs need work through printed tests.

The best work on error diagnosis is still the pioneering work of Mina Shaughnessy, who based her approach upon her analysis of thousands of papers from open-admission students at City University of New York. The following discussion relies substantially upon her conclusions.[14]

UNDERSTANDING THE DIAGNOSTIC DATA. Researchers and teachers following Shaughnessy have developed diagnostic strategies that can divide the problem into manageable units. First, we will need to separate the genuine errors, those violations of rules the students are unsure or unaware of, from transcribing errors, those mistakes caused by the students' inexactitude in getting down what they want to say or by their inability to proofread effectively. Since the latter sort of errors are perceptual rather than conceptual, they are more easily controlled.

Finding Perceptual Errors. The perceptual errors may be discovered through comparing the students' vocalized rendition of the essay with their written version. Tape-recording equipment is particularly useful in this respect, because it permits the students themselves to make the comparison and find at least some of the discrepancies on their own. We also need to teach the class proofreading skills and stress their importance. But we will need to make each student, individually, aware of—and thus watchful for—the structures he is most likely to mistranscribe.

Diagnosing Conceptual Errors. Even after the perceptual mistakes are discounted, a discouragingly large number of errors are likely to remain. When we examine a student's work more carefully, however, we generally find that she tends to use the same nonstandard construction repeatedly (though often not consistently). Most of the individual errors can, in fact, be systematized into a few important problem areas. As David Bartholomae writes:

> Through a perception of such patterns, one can discover that errors are not random, but products of systematic decision-making—that is, evidence that there is a grammar to students ungrammaticality.[15]

If we encourage our students themselves to take important responsibility in the diagnostic process, noting the pattern in their habitual mistakes and with our help collecting their errors under appropriate categories in their notebooks, we will be helping them to the motivation and intellectual comprehension they will need to become bidialectic.

Prescription for Individual Solutions

After we and our students have analyzed their departures from standard written English, we need to prescribe means of helping them not only to edit the errors from the text in question, but to be able to keep them from recurring in future texts.

We know that nonstandard speakers respond well to highly structured work, and so our prescriptions will lean heavily on written exercises, quick feedback exercises from software or self-help manuals such as Joseph C. Blumenthal's *English 2200, 2600,* and *3200* (Harcourt Brace), and oral drill. Nevertheless, the extensive use of these materials is problematic to many of us.

EXERCISES.   The research that shows the lack of connection between grammar courses and improved writing (see Chapter 7) holds as much validity for students who speak nonstandard English as it does for those who speak the standard dialect. Students learn pretty much what we teach them; if we demonstrate that our chief aim is for them to succeed at their workbook exercises, then motivated students will become adept at doing exercises. The transference of such skills to the act of writing is certainly as little likely from those unfamiliar with written English as from those who are accustomed to it.

Yet these students do need to achieve an ease in handling standard syntactical patterns; and since they did not grow up with it, they must of necessity acquire this fluency in an artificial way. To have genuine command of the language, they will need practice and repeated experience with various standard constructions, and this need suggests the usefulness of structured exercises. But these exercises are valuable only to the extent

1. that the students realize the connection between working the particular exercise and gaining a skill or knowledge that will help them attack a particular problem they perceive in their writing and
2. that the exercises permit the students actually to write—to construct phrases, sentences, even paragraphs of their own.

Exercises in Context.   When we encourage our students to do exercises, we must make sure that they understand the way the particular exercise fits into the larger context of their writing. Though it is never easy, there are a number of ways we might try to make the relationship explicit. The best way is for us to help the students discover the most distracting problems in their own work, motivate them to overcome these problems, and then prescribe a series of exercises with which they can attack the problem.

Student-Constructed Exercises.   The most individualized of all exercises are those that students construct themselves. For example, if students are having problems with the *-ed* form of verbs, we might have them write a few sentences describing the steps Fred takes when he shops for groceries (or any topic that elicits statements in the present tense) and then, after checking over their verbs, ask our students to rewrite the sentences assuming that Fred had gone on his shopping trip yesterday. Similarly, if the problem were subject-verb agreement, we might have our students write a brief paragraph with a dual subject (two sisters going to a football game, for instance) and then have them tell the same story about a single person.

If we are unable to individualize the work to this extent, we might prescribe standardized exercises in the same individualized way. Exercises like those exemplified here and others based upon the same principle are available in a most helpful booklet, *Write Me a Ream*, by Linda Ann Kunz and Robert R. Viscount.[16] Other good exercises treating the same problems appear in workbooks and printed exercise sheets, as well as in computer programs, videotapes, and filmstrips, for those of us who have access to this equipment.

Variety.   When we prescribe exercises for particular writing problems, it is good to have a large variety of approaches available. Not only do people learn in different ways, but a skill is often more effectively reinforced when approached by diversified means. If exercises are prescribed to fit specific difficulties students themselves have come to recognize in their writing, such practice can be a valuable tool in their learning to write.

WORKBOOKS.   Writing courses that center to any large extent upon a workbook or a particular sequence of exercises, however, have a greater problem establishing the necessary transference. Nevertheless, such sequences offer a logical and stable structure that provides students with the security and discipline so important to them.

Though adopting such standardized material homogenizes the curriculum for a whole class of students who may speak a number of differing dialects, such uniformity may not be as limiting as it would at first seem. Recent studies have shown that speakers of a wide variety of nonstandard American dialects hold most of the nonstandard features of their dialect in common,[17] and teachers can tailor a workbook program to cover the writing problems relevant to their students' differing needs. Actually, our students differ more in their rates of progress than they do in their writing problems, and a workbook that offers programmed instruction in the hands of a teacher who will provide tutorial help can permit all students to work at their own best rate.

Tailoring Workbook Assignments.   Teachers who choose this sort of program not only must find materials that give their students a chance to create their own phrases and sentences—that is, the opportunity to think through the problems in their own words and in their own way—but also must be very sure to coordinate the exercises with the writing assignments. If the focus of this week's activities is to be on pronominal agreement, for instance, then the subject should be covered in class discussion, in the workbook or exercises, in sentence-combining study, and in the work associated with the writing assignments; and the whole unit should be grounded in the agreement problems discovered in earlier student writing.

Teachers who use this approach report that even when they have taken all possible precautions, the application of workbook knowledge to actual writing does not come to most students immediately. But if the connection is continually demonstrated, after a few weeks the students suddenly begin to understand, and there is what seems like an overnight improvement both in student motivation and in their writing.[18]

ORAL WORK.   Perhaps the most effective pedagogical tool for teaching the standard dialect to those who do not speak it natively is oral drill. After all, it is the ear that needs training. Nonstandard speakers do not make usage errors in written English to be perverse, but because "he don't" sounds better to them than "he doesn't" and "I seen" seems more natural that "I saw." If those of us who were reared in the standard dialect want to understand just how hard it is to make these adjustments, we should think how difficult it would be for us if we were chastised every time we said "he doesn't" and were forced to say "I seen." Oral exercises, such as reading aloud, dictation, patterned conversation (for younger students), and language-lab work provide a method of training the "ear" of those students whose native dialect sets up such troublesome interference with some of the conventions of SAE that they are left without a reliable internal guide.

Despite its usefulness, oral drill has generated strong opposition from those who say that in making their ears respond naturally to standard usage, students will lose something of their own dialect. These objectors argue that it is almost impossible to be completely bidialectic. And, despite the millions of Americans who have contentedly and successfully learned to shift registers, their contention has more than a little truth to it. Nevertheless, I still recommend exercises that train the ear because that is the only way to become truly conversant in a new dialect or language. And becoming bidialectic is of crucial importance for our students for all the reasons detailed at the beginning of this chapter.[19]

Rote Exercises.   The most effective means of training the ear is through oral rote exercises. They can be implemented in the following manner: Individual diagnosis more than likely will reveal groups of students with the same nonstandard locutions. In fact, some problems may well be shared by an entire class. Groups gather to work on their mutual problem. They write brief sentences in standard English that include the specified usage. Everyone makes a copy. A leader reads the sentences one at a time and the group responds in unison. The exercise is repeated again and again over time. When the whole class is involved, the rote exercise makes a good opening or closing for class. Eventually, the standard usage will start to sound natural.

Individualized Oral Exercises. Laurel Eckels, who directs the Skills Center at Wilmington College, uses an individualized version of the rote exercise. Using a diagnostic instrument, she has the students discover their nonstandard usages. (The exercise would work with any usage problem, but Eckels generally limits it to irregular verbs.) Her students make up sentences using the standard replacement for each nonstandard expression discovered. After their sentences have been checked for errors, the students tape them in their own voices. Then they play and replay the tapes.

The exercise is almost universally successful. Yet, even with highly motivated students like the prospective teachers Eckels works with, it takes about six weeks before they begin to distinguish between standard and nonstandard usage in the conversations around them.

School Dialect. Should we "correct" our students when they slip nonstandard usage into their classroom participation? There is no general agreement on this issue. Some teachers would rather not make their students self-conscious about their classroom speech and prefer to confine their remedying to written work. Others, believing that their students need to be orally bilingual, find a way to approach their students' speech tactfully.

If we choose to work with students' classroom remarks, it is even more important to lay down the fundamental value of acceptance of all dialects outlined earlier in this chapter and to reinforce this value throughout the semester. Once the principle of appropriateness of dialect is established, we might draw a distinction between "home talk" and "school talk" and suggest that SAE is the appropriate dialect for school. Only then—and only if our students are agreeable to the idea—might we gently follow a "I didn't have no homework last night" with "How would you say that in 'school talk,' Bill?"[20]

A Sequence of Pedagogical Priorities

With each student having so much ground to cover, how can we determine where to begin? Our priorities should be based, first, upon the amount of reader distraction a particular breach of standard writing convention causes and, second, upon the degree of interrelationship between the features. Maxine Hairston's study (See Chapter 7) and Mina Shaughnessy's findings suggest the following order of priorities:[21]

1. HANDWRITING. Though poor handwriting is not a problem that will seriously affect many of our students, when handwriting is genuinely illegible it can be such a disabling handicap that it must be our primary concern. We must see that students suffering from this handicap get proper tutoring and practice in the skill, and if it is at all feasible, that they learn to use the word processor or programmed typewriter.

2. ERRORS OF THE SENTENCE. After illegible handwriting, the errors that readers find most disconcerting of all are the basic sentence faults, especially run-on sentences, fragments, and the erroneous punctuation and misplaced capitalization that accompanies them. Study of the sentence represents a particularly economical expenditure of our time and effort, for this study encompasses a number of the more important problems. (See pages 304–9.)

3. SUBJECT-VERB AGREEMENT AND OTHER "S" PROBLEMS. Though recognized by readers as quite a different problem from sentence errors, subject-verb agreement difficulties do interrelate with them and may be studied in sequence. The problem with *s*, which is partially based upon the tendency of speakers of a number of nonstandard dialects to simplify a final consonant cluster *(speaks)*, and also includes difficulties with the possessive *('s* and *s')* forms, is very much complicated by a tendency toward random hypercorrection.

4. VERB-TENSE DIFFICULTIES. Verb-tense problems are rooted in nonstandard vocalization and vary with the dialect, but readers report them all as highly disconcerting when transferred to writing. For example:

- Tendency to drop part or all of the final consonant cluster—especially when it eliminates both the third-person-singular present-tense *s* and the *-ed* in the past tense, thus making the past tense equivalent to the present *(walk[s], walk[ed])*.
- Inflectional problems with such common irregular verbs as *have, do, go, see,* and *give.*
- African-American Vernacular use of *be* to signify a non-SAE tense and omission of *be* in their formation of the present progressive ("She be going." "She going.").

5. DOUBLE NEGATIVE, "AIN'T," AND OTHER SUCH NONSTAN-DARD USAGES. Speakers of dialects influenced by languages (such as Spanish) that include double negation habitually double negatives in their English speech as do speakers of dialects deeply rooted in older English, who also regularly use *ain't* as the negative form of *be*. Some employ the negative inversion ("Can't nobody help") in their speech as well.

This usage, however, is largely oral because students seem to have been made aware of the nonstandard quality of such locutions. But since this is widely considered a particularly distinctive marker of nonstandard English, it is an important problem to work on where it does persist in a student's writing.

6. PRONOUN AND PRONOUN AGREEMENT. A number of American English dialects include pronoun usages which, if they transfer over into our students' writing, are highly distracting to the reader. Among them:

- Confusion of subject/object forms (for instance, the Native American and Creole "Him going")
- Confusion of gender ("Mary walk and then he turn" of some African-American Vernaculars or the Spanish-American English "The building, she . . .")
- Pronominal apposition ("John's father, he . . ." of African-American Vernacular, Spanish-American, and other dialects).[22]

7. SPELLING. The most important tool for chronically poor spellers is the word processor's spell-checker. Once they learn how to use it, they can eliminate a great number of errors. Unfortunately, this device will not help with misspellings that reflect actual—though unintended—words. It will not, for example, distinguish between *two, too,* and *to.* Most such words are amenable to a few easily learned rules ("*I* before *e,* except after *c* . . .", for instance) and the few remaining can be kept on a personal list of habitually misspelled words and deliberately memorized. Once each week we can get the poor spellers together in pairs to test each other. And missed words can be collected in a class list for a class spelling test of our own.[23]

The preceding priorities in teaching editing by no means exhausts the kinds of errors our nonstandard-dialect students will make while they are learning to write, but it fairly well covers what Virginia F. Allen calls "those features that truly distinguish Standard English from nonstandard usage," where readers are more likely to become distracted or take offense, and where, as Allen rightfully contends, "teachers and students need to concentrate their energies" (356).

TEACHING THE COMPOSING PROCESS

I have included this chapter on helping nonstandard-speaking students with their writing problems in the section on Style because the greater part of the problems particular to these students are surface stylistic problems. Nevertheless, these students also tend to have some difficulties with composing, and thus a few comments on this subject may also be appropriate.

Composing Problems of Nonstandard-Dialect Speakers

The differences in composing skills are not so much in kind as in amount. Many of our nonstandard-dialect students—especially those from oral cultures—may be at an early stage in their thinking about writing. In teaching the composing process to nonstandard speakers, as in all teaching, we must start where the students are.

VERBALIZERS. Some may be at the stage of writing that James Moffett labels "written verbalization."[24] For students at this stage, writing is an external expression of their thinking. We can recognize this stage by the lack of coherence in the papers, especially by the large number of skipped words and sudden turns of thought. They will say, "Oh, but *I* know what I mean."

Teaching Strategies. Students who write undigested thought of this sort need continual reminders that they are writing to be read. And so they need to put themselves in their readers' shoes. The following exercises are useful reminders of the plight of a confused reader:

1. *Board Work:* Several students go to the board and try to draw a design (usually a geometric figure) to the written specifications of a fellow student, as he or she reads it to them.
2. *Process Paper Assignment:* The student must write a paper telling how to do something so well his or her partner can actually do it.
3. *Descriptive Assignment:* The student must describe an object or a scene so accurately that her or his partner can draw exactly what the student had in mind.
4. *Riddle:* What is this kitchen object? The student reads his or her riddle aloud. The other students guess what it is. When they guess wrong, they have to suggest details to be added that will limit the description to the object the writer has in mind.[25]

VOCALIZERS. Students at Moffett's "vocalization" stage employ in their writing the same tactics they use in their conversation and, in fact, think of composition as written speech.

Teaching Strategies. We might praise such writers for the fresh spontaneity which written speech sometimes achieves. But vocalizers also need to know that, since their readers do not have the conversational advantage of being able to respond to them or ask questions directly, they need to provide their readers with the necessary background and transitions to make their ideas completely understood.

Because these students think of writing in terms of conversation, Mina Shaughnessy's formulation of composing principles in terms of a projected conversation between reader and writer may clarify these ideas for them:

Listener	**Writer's Response**
1. What's your point?	Thesis statement
2. I don't quite get your meaning.	Restatement in different words
3. Prove it to me	Illustration, evidence, agrument (273)

Composing Assignments

Nonstandard-dialect-speaking students seem to thrive best when the procedure they are to follow is laid out formally in a series of required steps. Perhaps because one of their chief difficulties is that they do not perceive composing as a series of steps at all, these students have no conception of prewriting or rewriting. For many, "You tell us what to write, and we'll write it" is their whole approach to composition.

THOUGHTFULLY SEGMENTED ASSIGNMENTS. If we can break down the unmanageable single command "Write!" into a series of assignments, we can provide our students with a way to proceed. Let us therefore consider making each writing assignment we give these students call for a set of writings rather than a single paper. Here are some suggestions:

- We might ask our students to begin by paraphrasing the assignment into words that clearly state their understanding of exactly what they are to do and then to record these words at the top of a page.
- Finding a specific topic from all the possibilities offered by the assignment should be our students' second step, the results of which they might record under the first.
- On the same page there may be room for our students to jot down their inventory of ideas, a highly important third step.
- On another sheet, they might record their efforts to coordinate and subordinate their inventory of ideas into categories.
- On yet another page, they might write a working-thesis statement (which they drew out of the inventory and the categories) and a structural plan of arguments to support it.[26]

Only after our students have completed and recorded this preliminary work should we permit them to begin writing their "first draft," a term we must, I think, insist upon because it so clearly emphasizes the transitional quality of this stage of their writing project.

If editing exercises are needed, our students might include them in their set of writings too, along with any intermediate drafts which they may need, or choose, to compose.

MODEL STRUCTURAL PLANS. During the crucial organizing step, many teachers provide for their nonstandard-dialect students additional imitative and formulaic guidance. They give their students sample paragraphs or essays coordinating with the assignment, which are transcribed in an outline pattern with, for example, the topic sentence of the paragraph marked, supporting statements numbered, and supporting material for each of these statements indicated. They then supply the student with a blank copy of the formulaic pattern and suggest that the students complete it with their own material.

A Warning. In making use of such patterned formats, we must be very careful to insist that they are only sample patterns of the many possible writing patterns. When we ask students to fill in the blanks or follow a format, we must be sure they understand that they will only be practicing, only doing exercises.

We might want to use the infamous "Five Paragraph Theme" as such an exercise—and many teachers have found it to be a truly illuminating one for their students. The reason for its infamy is that over the years it has somehow developed a mystique that transcends its exercise essence until many students actually assume it to be the only appropriate format for an expository or persuasive essay. A glance at any essay anthology should immediately disabuse them of the idea, but many cling to it tenaciously nonetheless.

Because of the persistence of such notions, we must take special care to dispel all such rigidity from our students' minds. For example, we might accompany a five-paragraph-theme exercise assignment with a demonstration of professional essays of varying structures.

EXPLICITLY DETAILED ASSIGNMENTS. Another, less elaborate, way to guide and support our students is to provide them with definitively detailed assignments. Laurel Eckels uses this sort of assignment to prepare students in her remedial classes for the essay tests and in-class themes they are bound to encounter in their academic careers.

For one effective example, Eckels shows her students the videotape, "Tools of Exploitation" (from *The Africans: A Triple Heritage* [Films, Inc., 1986]) and bases the following essay question on it:

> Define *exploitation* as it is explained in the videotape; and support your definition with specific examples from Africa in the past and in the present.

Such assignments explicitly direct students in organizing the content of their writing, telling them what to put where. They leave them nothing to struggle with except the basic thinking behind the problem, the most important place to put their energies. And, at the same time, explicitly directed assignments provide students experience with appropriate and useful ways of structuring that thinking.

HIGHLY STRUCTURED, BUT NOT SIMPLISTIC ASSIGNMENTS. Note the seriousness and, to a degree, complexity of Eckels's assignment underneath its carefully structured surface. Because many nonstandard-speaking students need a more structured approach to the academic conventions, some assume that they are capable of dealing only with simplified ideas—or even that they find such assignments preferable. We would make a serious mistake in acceding to this assumption. Mike Rose reminds us of the fallacy in such thinking:

> Certainly it is a sound motivation and learning principle to begin with the simple—let the student experience success—and then move toward the more complex. No argument. But we should not assume that the successful completion of an assignment the student might well perceive as being simple, even juvenile, is going to make him feel better about himself or his writing.[27]

To help students master the formal aspects of a writing lesson, we sometimes assign simplistic topics, such as "What I Think about TV" or "My Dog Spot." But when students respond to such conceptually empty topics, some of them just turn off their minds. And even when students master the formal aspects of the lesson in such an assignment, there is little transference when they are faced with more complex discourse structures, as some preliminary research demonstrates.[28]

Problems with Personal Narrative. Some advocate limiting assignments to personal narratives in an effort to make writing as easy as possible for nonstandard-dialect speakers. But as effective as such topics can be (see also pages 403, 409ff), this exclusivity would be a mistake. Research shows that students do not prefer simpler, more familiar topics. When given an opportunity to express their choice, most select the more difficult academic-type topic over an easier, more personal one. Most students, but, in particular, weaker writers, favor topics that they perceive as "real," topics they believe relevant to their educational or vocational ambitions.[29]

And personal narrative topics sometimes have an additional weakness. The value systems of some of the cultures from which our nonstandard speakers come can cause these students to become uncomfortable when asked to write on such topics.

The best assignments are unquestionably those that best motivate. But research shows that the accepted opinion on what really motivates may be mistaken. As Rose writes:

> Current work on achievement motivation has shown it to be a highly complex cognitive-affective phenomenon that includes such dimensions as perception of the difficulty of a task and perception of the role of luck or skill in completing the task. Add to these perceptions psychodynamic variables such as the degree of comfort with the content of a task, and it is no longer clear that simple and personal topics are most motivating. (115)

SAMPLE LESSON STRATEGIES

Space is not available here to suggest lesson plans for an entire program for nonstandard-dialect students, but I would like to offer an outline for a sample unit of study for two different postdiagnostic approaches to this special writing program: one, a class-unit approach designed to treat problems widely diagnosed throughout the student population—in this case, a unit on "Eliminating Sentence Faults," and the other, a personally prescriptive, step-by-step approach aimed at the revision of an individual essay.

TEACHING STRATEGIES

Exercises and Activities for Eliminating Sentence Faults

I. IDENTIFYING SENTENCES

A. *Written identification of sentences and fragments.* We might ditto off a list of sentences and fragments from student papers, making quite sure we include some long fragments and some short sentences. After the students correctly identify them as either fragments or sentences, we can talk over their choices briefly, but ask them to hold their papers for further discussion.

B. *Aural identification of sentence capitalization and punctuation.* Having discussed the end punctuation and initial capitalization of the sentence, we might dictate a not-too-complex paragraph for our students to transcribe. We should caution our students to listen carefully for sentences, and we must read slowly enough for them to do so. Students also need time at the end of the exercise to make sure that every sentence ends in a period (or question mark), that everything that does end in a period is a sentence, and that every sentence begins with a capital letter. Because some students tend to capitalize promiscuously, they should also check that the words at the beginning of sentences are the only words capitalized (except for the proper nouns, which we might specify). Afterward, students might proofread one another's papers and review the exercise, but again hold the papers for further discussion.

C. *Inductive discovery of what makes a sentence.* After we are all agreed on the answers for exercises A and B, we might ask our students to try to explain the basis for our decision. Why do we think that some items are sentences while others are not? What do all that we call sentences have in common? Are these shared features missing from all the items we call fragments? Although some students may readily bring up the terms "subject" and "verb," we must not cut off discussion too early, but encourage questions and comments until we are sure that the terms have some real meaning for all of the students. At that time, they might go back to exercises A and B and encircle the subjects and underline the verbs.

II. GAINING A SENSE OF THE SENTENCE

The value of our students getting a feel for sentences cannot be overestimated. As Mina Shaughnessy writes:

continued

The perception of the sentence as a structure rather than a string of words is probably the most important insight a student can gain from the study of grammar. . . . What becomes clear . . . is that the sentence is not simply a subject and verb but rather a base containing a subject and verb to which all other information can be attached, either directly to the base itself or indirectly to words that are attached to that base. (133)

A. *Building a sense of the sentence.* Class participation in building a sentence by attaching various modifiers onto a subject-verb base (as the class did in building their armadillo sentence in Chapter 7) can convey a feeling for what a sentence is, and thus makes a good exercise for nonstandard-dialect students. I would, however, suggest that we not burden these students with the technical nomenclature used in the Chapter 7 version of the exercise, but rather take our clues for terminology from them and use the terms they suggest or are comfortable with.

B. *Sentence combining.* The combining of kernels into sentences can also convey a sense of the sentence and is thus an especially important exercise for these students. But their work with sentence combining should differ somewhat from the ideas suggested in Chapter 7. Before becoming involved with the comparative rhetorical effectiveness of various combinations, these students need to play with sentences to gain an understanding of what sort of embeddings, combinings, and modifications are possible within the sentence.

C. *Student-made kernels.* Using sentence kernels made by students is a variation of sentence combining that can give students a feeling of even more intimate control of the elements of a sentence. For this exercise, the class divides into two groups. Each group makes up its own series of sentence kernels and then combines them into a more complex sentence. When they have finished their task to their own satisfaction, they give their kernels to the other group. Both the work and the discussion which accompanies it can be helpful.

A variation that Gloria Flaherty uses has students write their kernels in their home dialect and make their sentences in SAE.

D. *Dictation.* Aural exercises reinforce the written work. With each repetition of dictation exercises, the number of fragments, run-ons, and excess capitals on our students' papers should decrease markedly.

III. GETTING THE SUBJECTS AND VERBS TO AGREE

Now, while our students' attention is focused on the subject and the verb as the base of a sentence, may be a good time to bring up the necessity for their agreement in number, a conspicuous convention of SAE that is not present in many nonstandard dialects. This convention

continued

continued

causes students a great deal of trouble because the letter *s*, practically the lone survivor of the once elaborate English inflectional system, is now used to mark, rather contrarily, both plural nouns and single (present-tense) verbs—not to mention the singular possessive. We must, I think, own up to the difficulty and let our students know that we too see the irony of the situation. We might even capitalize on the mnemonic possibilities inherent in the very curiousness of the circumstances. Thus, we can set up the rule:

> In a clause or sentence, only one—either the subject or the verb—may be in its *s* form.

A. *Playing with subject-verb homonyms.* The only way to know which, the subject or the verb, should have the *s* is to think in terms of the number of subjects (one or more) involved in what the writer wants to say. To direct student attention to the question of singularity or plurality of their subjects—and again to play on the whimsy inherent in the situation—we might ask our students to make two sets of sentences: one set using words like *fires, matches, stitches, tires, glances, dances, lights, whistles, throws* as subjects, and another set in which the same words serve as verbs.

B. *Dictation.* Oral work can be particularly important in working with subject-verb agreement, because a major reason for some students' erratic placement of the *s* in their writing is that they are not conscious of it orally in their own speech or in the speech of others. The passages we choose to read aloud should be rich in the problem construction. In addition, if some of our students are letting their difficulty with the possessive (*'s, s'*) or such contractions as *it's* add to their confusion on this issues, then including some examples of these troublesome forms within the dictation might be a good way to approach the confusion.

C. *Answering questions.* Students who have a problem with agreement will need a great deal of practice to gain command of SAE construction. Correct-the-error exercises tend to reinforce, as much as they change, thinking; and the usual workbook multiple-choice exercises/problems, though somewhat helpful for improving proofreading skills, have little effect upon the development of fluency. A better approach is to give assignments that require students to formulate the answers to questions that involve the specified usage.

Mina Shaughnessy suggests the following exercise as diagnostic, but used either in its written form or as oral drill, it is helpful in developing an "ear" for the standard constructions.

> Directions: Ask the student to answer each question with a full sentence.
>   1. Do students usually get to class on time?
>   Yes, students usually get to class on time.

continued

> 2. Does Jerline usually get to class on time?
>   Yes, Jerline usually gets to class on time.
> 3. Does Henry seem unfriendly to you lately?
>   Yes, Henry seems unfriendly to me lately. (139)

D. *Composing stories with single and multiple heroes.* After our students have developed some fluency in handling single and plural subjects in sentences written in the present tense, we might have them compose as a class a little anecdote about a group of alligators or avocados — or students — doing something in the present (like going to the mall, for example). As the students compose their story, we must record it privately, reading it back from time to time to assure continuity. After the story is finished, we should read it back to the class as a dictation. When the students exchange their papers to proofread, we should caution them to take special care that the subjects and verbs are in order.

Then, as the culmination of the exercise, the students should rewrite their story individually — but this time using a single hero.

IV. GRASPING THE SUBORDINATING AND COORDINATING POSSIBILITIES OF THE SENTENCE

With their understanding of the nature of subjects and verbs reinforced, our students should be ready for a closer and more specific study of the possibilities of the English sentence. The aim of this further study is for students to become comfortable writing the constructions they already handle well in their speech. They need confidence in their ability to handle these constructions and a knowledge of the conventions that govern their putting them into writing. Sentence combining can provide a good foundation for this sort of study, and dictation exercises can reinforce this learning.

A. *Coordinating sentences, linking them together.* Using student-made sentence kernels or signaled sentence-combining exercises for compound sentences, we might introduce our students to the two major ways to link sentences together: by an *and* (or *but, or, for, so,* or *yet*) with a comma closing the first clause and preceding the *and,* or by a semicolon (without conjunction) closing the first clause and separating it from its partner clause. When our students have worked with the sentence-combining exercises long enough to understand the nature of the compound sentence (a term which, if unfamiliar, we might choose not to mention at all), we might bring up the problem of run-on sentences (including comma splices). We might ask them to reason from examples and try to think why readers find this particular disregard for convention so distracting. Inductive discovery of the confusion caused by these errors should

continued

continued

motivate the students to try to avoid them in their own work. These new concepts might also be profitably reinforced by dictation exercises.

B. *Subordinating ideas in subordinate clauses, embedding them into the main sentence.* Nonstandard-dialect students, like all speakers of English beyond early childhood, routinely use subordinate constructions in their speech. But we need to get our students to think in a more concrete way about these constructions. To use them appropriately, students need to understand how the structure reflects the subordinating of the less important to the more important idea in the sentence.

The same sort of structured sentence-combining work we used for compound sentences should also serve to reinforce our student's instinctive knowledge about subordination. We should probably not, however, refer to these constructions by their technical names, but rather by their introductory words—for example, "*who-which* describers," "*although* or *if* or *when* clauses," or "*that* clauses."

A variety of sentence-combining exercises are effective for this study. In addition to providing our students with exercises in which a kernel for a main clause and a kernel for a specified subordinate clause are given, we can also offer main clauses with the direction to add, for instance, an "*even though* clause" to it, or give them a series of compound sentences and suggest that at least some of them would make better sense by subordinating (or embedding) one of the clauses in the other. Accompanying oral exercises should include all of the subordinate clause constructions.

C. *Subordinating phrases, embedding them in the sentence.* Most of our students use prepositional phrases easily in their speech and, except for occasional semantic problems, have little difficulty using them appropriately in their writing. On the other hand, appositives and both the present and past participial phrases (which we might term "*-ing* and *-ed* phrases") are rarely a part of these students' habitual speech, though most do have some familiarity with them from their reading. Nevertheless, once students understand these constructions, they see their usefulness and adopt them into their writing with surprising ease.

D. *How and when to use the comma with subordinate constructions.* If we present the comma rule with an emphasis on its logic, students accept it as sensible. It seems "right" to them that

> *Subordinate material must be enclosed in commas when it is extra, parenthetical, not essential to the basic subject-verb-complement meaning of the clause.*[30]

Students can learn to visualize the concept when we tell them to think of the commas as little handles with which they can pull the extra (parenthetical-like) material within them right out of the sen-

continued

tence. This metaphor also helps to explain why, except for introductory or concluding phrases and clauses, there must always be two commas; with the two handles, there is no impediment placed between a subject and its verb.

V. THE WRITING ASSIGNMENT: THE SUMMARIZING AND CULMINATING PROJECT

After we assign supplementary oral and written exercises as individually needed, our students should have developed enough feeling for the syntax of the sentence and knowledge of its appropriate punctuation to permit them to edit their writing in these respects with some proficiency. In editing their next writing assignment, therefore, we should ask them to pay special attention to initial capitalization, end punctuation, subject-verb agreement, and the elimination of run-on sentences and unintentional fragments. They might then submit their draft to a partner or student group for proofreading in these areas. When the compositions are read and discussed in class, in addition to our usual praise of good ideas, good organization, and good writing, we might also single out for commendation those papers that are not marred by sentence errors.

Individualized Study. The following outline is based on notes made by Diane Menendez describing her tutorial work with a nonstandard-dialect-speaking student, Jamala, in the University of Cincinnati Writing Laboratory, which she directed. The student's teacher sent her to the writing lab for remedial help. The assignment was a brief essay on "My Ambition."

TEACHING STRATEGIES

A Sample Tutorial

STEP 1.
Diagnosis. The skipped words and poorly designated sentences made Jamala's theme almost incoherent and revealed her to be at the Moffett's stage of "inner verbalization," that is, verbalized thought.

STEP 2.
In an attempt to move Jamala along to "outer verbalization," the stage of written speech, and to produce a document that more nearly mir-

continued

continued

rored what she wanted to say, the tutor asked Jamala to talk her theme into a tape recorder and then to make a careful attempt to transcribe it word for word. With a little help, the written theme became a total transcription of the tape.

Result: With most of the omitted words restored, the sentences fell more or less into place, and the work became coherent.

STEP 3.

The tutor read the essay aloud, pausing as she went along to react to its meaning:

> "Oh, you like to cook. . . ."
> "And you like to go marketing. . . ."
> "Here you start talking about going to the movies. But I'm getting confused. I was hoping to find out what you especially like to cook. . . ."

Result: Jamala herself recognized the lack of focus and realized that she must find some way of tying her ideas together to help the reader.

STEP 4.

Because the theme as it stood did not offer enough ideas for the student to put into order, the tutor took an elementary structure from the work—"I like to . . . ," I would like to . . . ," "I would like to be . . ."—and asked Jamala to generate twenty-five sentences with those beginnings.

Result: The resulting sentences elicited more ideas and produced a working vocabulary for the theme (at the same time giving the student much needed practice in the formation of complete written sentences).

STEP 5.

After going over these sentences together with her tutor, Jamala decided that the dominant idea they seemed to disclose was that the things she really liked to do best were all part of homemaking. Taking this idea as her working thesis, she discarded the ideas that did not fit with it and organized the others into rudimentary clusters associated by some common idea, such as cooking.

Result: When the ideas representing the clusters were put in an appropriate order, they produced a plan for her discourse, a road map from which Jamala could construct her theme.

STEP 6.

Jamala wrote a full draft of the paper.

Result: The paper now made good rhetorical sense, though it still exhibited an abundance of surface problems.

continued

STEP 7.

Diagnosis Again: Jamala wanted to get her stylistic problems under control as well. The tutor, having made a copy of the theme for herself, asked Jamala to read it aloud to her so that she would be able to distinguish those errors that were only a matter of transcription and were corrected in Jamala's normal speech from those errors that were the result of genuine ignorance of the conventions of standard written English. The tutor charted these genuine errors on a diagnostic sheet.

Result: An analysis of the misspelled words revealed a heavy concentration of the wrong choice of vowel to indicate the *schwa* sound. The most stigmatizing syntactical problems were a lack of agreement between subjects and their verbs and the lack of sentence end-punctuation.

STEP 8.

The tutor took Jamala into her confidence throughout the whole diagnostic procedure and, having explained the importance of subject and verb agreement to clear and effective writing, found her well motivated to try some exercises aimed at solving the problem. In these exercises, Jamala

a. identified the subject and verb of every sentence in her paper;
b. wrote these subjects and verbs down on a separate page;
c. studied them for identifying characteristics (how one knows a subject from a verb) and learned what function they serve in the sentence;
d. learned about subject-verb agreement and, using the words listed from her paper as a vocabulary, constructed a series of correct sentences; and
e. studied the work and formulated rules to guide her in the future. (Her first rule was: "I need to look back and check all my 'to be' verbs and make sure I write 'am.' ")

Result. Jamala prepared a page that will be the beginning of her own grammar handbook to which she can turn for reference. The rules, which she wrote at the top of the page, can be changed and adapted as her learning increases.

STEP 9.

Having learned about the function of subject and verb in the sentence, Jamala was able to recall some earlier training in end-punctuation; and her work here, which was mainly review, went quickly. The tutor also did not want to take too much time on this first paper with the spelling problem. So, having explained the difficulty inherent in the use of the *schwa* in modern English, she asked Jamala to prepare a spelling page on the misspelled *schwa* words for her handbook, using the dictionary, and to see if she could come up with a rule for this page too.

continued

continued
STEP 10.
Jamala made all the surface corrections discussed here on the last draft of her theme and wrote a final copy. In order to make sure that her final draft had been written down as she had conceived it, Jamala asked to read it again on tape and then check it for omissions.

IDEAS FOR DISCUSSION OR ESSAY

1. For those who are unfamiliar with the special problems encountered in teaching writing to nonstandard-dialect-speaking students, a field trip to a writing laboratory or composition classroom that specializes in teaching these students is highly recommended. An analysis of insights gained on the field trip would make an interesting essay or a provocative discussion.
2. The controversy over teaching the standard dialect makes an excellent topic for debate. Read the literature on the subject and prepare formal arguments supporting one of the three major positions:

   Resolved: Standard American English is the only correct English, and teachers have an obligation to help their students eliminate error.

   Resolved: Every person has the right to his or her own language, and schools and colleges have no business tampering with it.

   Resolved: Teachers should attempt to encourage their nonstandard speakers to be bidialectic, at least in their writing.

3. Write an analysis of either the Sentence Faults unit or the Sample Tutorial.

NOTES

The epigraph is from Victor Raskin and Irwin Weiser, *Language and Writing: Applications of Linguistics to Rhetoric and Composition* (Norwood, NJ: Ablex, 1987).

1. Edward Sapir, *Language* (New York: Harcourt, 1921), 22.
2. Although the term Black English Vernacular (BEV) has been used technically to distinguish African-American dialects for a number of years and, in fact, is still in use (See, for example, Geneva Smitherman's "Black English, Diverging or Converging?: The View of the National Assessment of Educational Progress," *Language and Education* 6 [1992]: 47–61), the term currently preferred seems to be "African-American Vernacular."
3. In 1971 the officers of the CCCC created this resolution, which was adopted by the Executive Council in November 1972 and by the membership at the annual meeting in Anaheim, California in March 1974. Embodied in a paperback *Students Write to Their Own Language*, Special Issue of *CCC* 25 (1974), it is still available for sale from the NCTE.
4. Mina Shaughnessy, *Errors and Expectations: A Guide for the Teacher of Basic Writing* (New York: Oxford UP, 1977).

5. Quoted in Joseph Harris, "The Idea of Community in the Study of Writing," *CCC* 40 (1989): 18.

6. Sabina Thorne Johnson, "Remedial English: The Anglocentric Albatross?" *CE* 33 (1972): 671. For another convincing polemic for bidialectism, see Dorothy Z. Seymour, "Black Children, Black Speech," *Commonweal*, (Nov. 19, 1971): 175–78.

In using the term *revolution*, Johnson does not write metaphorically. The opposition to bidialectism is primarily political—Marxist and revolutionary. As James Sledd argues in "Doublespeak: Dialectology in the Service of Big Brother" *CE* 33 (1972):

> If [bidialectism, which Sledd calls] doublespeak were to succeed, the restive communities of the poor and ignorant would be tamed; for potential revolutionaries would be transformed into the subservient, scrambling, anxious underlings who constitute the lower middle class in a technological society. (448)

For another expression of the anti-bidialectal point of view, see Wayne O'Neil, "The Politics of Bidialectalism," *CE* 33 (1972): 433–38.

7. Though nonstandard dialects still lack conventions for written transcription, they are rich in literary conventions, a field currently being accorded a good deal of scholarly attentions. See, for example: Henry Louis Gates, *The Signifying Monkey: A Theory of Afro-American Literary Criticism* (New York: Oxford UP, 1988) and *Figures in Black: Words, Signs, and the "Racial" Self* (New York: Oxford, 1987); Martin Bernal, *Black Athena* (New Brunswick, NJ: Rutgers UP, 1987); Gayle Addison, Jr. *The Black Aesthetic* (New York: Doubleday, 1972); Ramon Saldivar, *Chicano Narrative: The Dialectics of Difference* (Madison: U of Wisconsin P, 1990); Paula Gunn Allen, *The Sacred Hoop* (Boston: Beacon, 1992); and Sidney Larson, "Native American Aesthetics," *MELUS* 17 (1991–92): 53–67.

8. A number of the following suggestions were derived from the ideas of Sabina Johnson and her associates, "Remedial English," 675–76, from the *New York Board of Education, Nonstandard Dialect*, (Champaigne: NCTE, 1967): 19; and from Gloria Flaherty, formerly of Stebbins High School in Dayton, Ohio and now at Wilmington College.

9. Board of Education, New York, New York, *Nonstandard Dialect*, 19.

10. The example is suggested by Gloria Flaherty who used this technique successfully with her high school students and now teaches it in her language arts methods classes.

11. Collected by Sandra Wittstein, Wilberforce University, when she was Director of the Writing Laboratory, Hughes High School, Cincinnati.

12. James L. Fenner, "Can Average Students Write?" *EJ* 56 (1967): 735, 738. See also, for instance, Vernon E. Lattin, "A Program for Basic Writing," *CE* 40 (1978): 314–15.

13. See especially Sondra Perl, "The Composing Processes of Unskilled College Writers," *RTE* 13 (1979): 317–36.

14. For a good summary and analysis of Shaughnessy's work, see David Bartholomae, "Released into Language: Errors, Expectations, and the Legacy of Mina Shaughnessy," in *The Territory of Language: Linguistics, Stylistics, and the Teaching of Composition*, ed. Donald A. McQuade (Carbondale: U of Illinois P, 1986), 65–88.

15. Bartholomae, 74.

16. Linda Ann Kurz and Robert R. Viscount, *Write Me a Ream* (New York: Columbia Teachers' College P, 1973).

17. Among them: Marilyn S. Sternglass, "Close Similarities in Dialect Features of Black and White College Students in Remedial Composition Classes," *Teachers of*

English to Speakers of Other Languages Quarterly, 8 (1974): 271–83; "Dialect Features in the Compositions of Black and White College Students: The Same or Different?" *CCC* 25 (1974): 259–63; and Samuel A. Kirschner and S. Howard Poteet, "Nonstandard English Usage in the Writing of Black, White, and Hispanic Remedial English Students in an Urban Community College," *RTE* 7 (1973): 351–55.

18. This phenomenon is attested to by Linda White and Pauline Smolen, who note its occurrence every quarter in their skills-centered English for Effective Communication course at University College, University of Cincinnati. It is also confirmed by Helen Mills, "Language and Composition: Three Mastery Learning Courses in One Classroom," *Journal of Basic Writing* (Fall, Winter 1976): 56–68; see also Shaughnessy, 275–79.

19. Diane E. Bartley and Robert L. Politzer in their *Practice-Centered Teacher Training: Standard English for Speakers of Nonstandard Dialects, Language and the Teacher: A Series in Applied Linguistics,* Vol. 27 (Philadelphia: Center for Curriculum Development, 1972) offer a thorough scholarly study of the linguistic background of the various nonstandard dialects as well as a comprehensive set of highly teachable oral exercises and drills. Other oral work is outlined in the New York Board of Education's *Nonstandard Dialect* and in Ruth I. Golden's now rather dated *Improving Patterns of Language Usage* (Detroit: Wayne State UP, 1960).

Virginia Allen's "Teaching English as a Second Dialect," [Columbia] *Teachers College Record,* 68 (1967): 355–70, provides motivational strategies as well as a few oral drills and exercises; San-su C. Lin gives an overview of a basically oral program and describes her implementation of it in "A Developmental English Program for the Culturally Disadvantaged," *CCC* (1965): 272–76; and Joseph Collignon describes an oral reading program in "Why Leroy Can't Write," *CE* 39 (1978): 852–59.

20. The concept of discrete discourse communities may be of relevance here. For a variety of opinion, see especially David Bartholomae, "Inventing the University" in *When a Writer Can't Write,* ed. Mike Rose (New York: Guilford, 1985) 134–65; Stanley Fish, *Is There a Text in this Class?—The Authority of Interpretative Communities* (Cambridge: Harvard UP, 1980); and J. Harris, "The Idea of Community."

21. See Shaughnessy, 131. Her findings coincide with Constance Brown's determination of those errors which most clearly predict failure (in Johnson, *Remedial English,* 681–82) and with the intuitive conclusions of Basic English teachers.

22. Priority pronoun work for nonstandard-speaking students should not be confused with much of the work on pronouns emphasized in traditional grammar classes—such as the appropriate use of *who* and *whom* or the singular referent to *everyone* or *anybody*. These usages are currently undergoing change in SAE and consequently should be of low teaching priority, especially for these students.

23. We sometimes neglect to help our students with their spelling, partly because we despair of even making a dent in the problem, and partly because we tend to underestimate its importance. We must not neglect it, however, since the following attitude of one construction company president is both typical and widespread: "I won't hire a man who can't spell, not even to drive a truck. If he can't spell, he can't read. If he can't read, I won't trust him around my equipment." As quoted by Jane McClellan, "A Clinic for Misspellers," *CE* 40 (1978): 324, a practical article on teaching remedial spelling.

24. James Moffett, "I, You and It," *CCC* 16 (1965): 244, and *Teaching the Universe of Discourse* (Boston: Houghton, 1968): 33. Some of Linda Flower's discussion of "writer-based" writing may also be relevant. See "Writer-Based Prose: A Cognitive Basis for Problems in Writing," *CE* 41 (1979): 19–37.

25. This strategy was developed by Ellen Layne, William Howard Taft High School, Cincinnati.

26. Pauline Smolin leads the student through a process similar to this in her useful workbook, *How to Write a Well-Organized Paragraph* (Self-published, 1978).

27. Mike Rose, "Remedial Writing Courses: A Critique and a Proposal," *CE* (1983): 115.

28. Brooke Nielson, "Writing as a Second Language: Psycholinguistic Processes in Composing," Diss., U of California at San Diego, 1979. Cited by Rose, 115.

29. Bernard Weiner, "Achievement Motivation, Attribution Theory, and the Educational Process," *RER* 42 (1972): 203–15.

30. The omission of the standard terms here is deliberate. As Shaughnessy notes, restrictive-nonrestrictive terminology "is confusing to many because the prefix *non* seems to suggest 'no'—that is, no commas—whereas it is the non-restrictive clause that requires commas" (30).

Section C

Teaching Special Kinds of Expository Essays

These distinguish academic writing. . . . the goals of self-directed critical inquiry, of using writing to think through genuine problems and issues, and of writing to an imagined community of peers.

—Linda Flower

Teaching the Research Paper

PROBLEMS IN TEACHING THE RESEARCH PAPER

A Tale

A jeans-clad figure sits hunched up over his notebook in the library. Concentrating intensely, he pushes an unruly lock of hair out of his eyes and takes a firmer grip on his pencil. Several thick books with dark covers and small print lie open before him, and he works with each in turn. "P.Q. Snerd, The Vanishing Aardvark," he copies dutifully at the top of a page from a loose-leaf notebook and adds the name of the publishing house, its city, and a date. "Pgs. 86–93" finishes the heading.

He turns to page 86, glances at it, and begins to scribble rapidly. Skipping articles, conjunctions, and transitional phrases, and occasionally abbreviating or omitting a lengthy construction or a cumbersome argument, he reproduces—more or less—what Snerd has written. From time to time he will insert a phrase or a comment of his own; not infrequently, he will attempt to paraphrase a sentence, always carefully preserving its essential structure or its distinctive wording. When he has filled a loose-leaf page from the chapter by Snerd, he turns to a book by Smith and fills two more pages in the same way. He repeats the process with the works of Jones and Brown and, feeling shyly satisfied with his good day's work, he packs up his notebook and wends his weary way home.

The days pass, filled with the joys and woes of adolescent life, and suddenly the due date for his paper is very close. Although by this time there is no possible way for him to separate his own words from those of Snerd, Smith, Jones, or Brown, he turns eagerly to his "notes," for he knows that from them his paper must come.

SAD ENDINGS. This story of the beginning of a research paper has only two possible endings, and both of them are sad. In one ending, the student reads over his "notes" and rather likes them. "Not bad at all," he thinks. With dispatch he then corrects them for spelling and punctuation as best he can, affixes the appropriate footnotes, and voila! the first draft. All that is needed now is to write transitional sentences connecting the sources to one another, to copy these pages neatly, and to turn in his research paper. Such is the source of many a neophyte's research papers whose footnotes are sequential, source by source, and whose lines of argument are similarly sequential.

In the other ending to the story, the student reads over his "notes" and falls in love: "Snerd really has it. He is totally right. He says just what I have always thought!" (or "He says just what I want to say.") But what to do? The teacher insists that at least four sources be cited. The answer, of course, is to use Snerd as the base of the paper and fit in little bits of Smith and Jones and Brown where it seems most natural. Papers of the second sort tend to be better papers because they are capable of exhibiting a single structure instead of four. However, in their inadvertent plagiarism and their lack of purposeful thought, they are, no less than in the first case, "an expense of spirit" and "a waste of shame."

Objections to Teaching the Research Paper Considered

Because this story is not fantasy but a reality that produces a deluge of high school and undergraduate research papers every year, many thoughtful and knowledgeable teachers believe that the research paper should not be required short of graduate school.

THE RESEARCH PAPER: A VALID GENRE? Richard L. Larson might not even require research paper teaching in graduate school. In a much anthologized article, Larson goes so far as to question whether the generic research paper actually exists at all. He writes:

> I am not aware of any kind or form of discourse, or any aim, identified by any student of rhetoric or any theorist of language or any investigator of discourse theory, that is distinguished primarily—or to any extent—by the presence of the fruits of "research" in its typical examples.[1]

Professor Larson has, as always, my deep respect, but he is wrong about the research paper: it does exist generically. In teaching the form to college-bound high school seniors or to college freshmen, I have often tried to coordinate their English-class efforts with their work in their other courses. To give my college students practical assistance with their assignments in other disciplines, I have read many scholarly journal articles suggested by my colleagues in the physical, biological, and social sciences and from the humanities. I discovered that these articles, intended as models for the assigned student papers, have an inherent similarity, whatever the discipline:

- All are expository in form, structured so as to support their central point most persuasively.
- All have the conventional introduction, body, and conclusion. Instead of the conventional introduction discussed in this text, scientific articles—physical, biological, and social—typically open with an abstract. But the abstract, though perhaps more of a summary than the usual humanities scholarly paper introduction, like it, conventionally sets up the problem, the procedures, and the thesis.
- All credit those who originate the ideas discussed through a mandatory, conventionalized system of documentation. (The new MLA system even brings similarity to documentation across the disciplines.)
- Scientific research articles—physical biological, and social—are of two kinds, reviews of literature and reports of experiments, and both kinds are similar to humanities papers.
  - Scientific reviews of literature are not distinctive from humanities library papers. They set up the literature in terms of the authors' varying perspectives on the issue under consideration and show why the arguments supporting the reviewer's point of view are more persuasive.
  - Articles that report experiments differ from humanities papers in content, but are similar to them in structure. Almost uniformly, they begin with a review of pertinent literature to show why the research is needed; this "review" is comparable to the "although clause" format. They then set up their hypothesis, which is comparable to the tentative statement of a controlling idea. They describe the procedures by which the researchers tested the hypothesis and give the resulting data; this material provides their support. Then they analyze their findings and come to a conclusion, just as humanities papers do.

There is no question but that there is a well-defined genre for academic discourse. It is the way scholars communicate with one another.

IS IT MORALLY RIGHT TO TEACH ACADEMIC DISCOURSE? In the 1980s scholarly journals rang with the denunciations of idealists who believe that teaching any sort of academic discourse is immoral, either for political reasons (because it accedes to the demands of a powerful, repressive system), or for sociological reasons (because it denies students the power of their own self-expressive voice), or for both.[2]

The problem with this point of view is that in an idealistic attempt to empower disadvantaged students psychologically to rebel against the establishment that oppresses them, those who refuse to teach academic discourse deny their students the power to join it, should they so wish—a power they themselves enjoy. Peter Elbow, himself an idealist, addresses this issue directly:

> Discourse carries power. This is especially important for weak or poorly prepared students—particularly students from poorer classes or those who are

the first in their families to come to college. Not to help them with academic discourse is simply to leave a power vacuum and thereby reward privileged students who have already learned academic discourse at home or in school.[2]

If by their own free choice students choose to conform to the conventions of the academy, we do not have the right to deny them. We either believe in freedom or we do not.

RESEARCH PAPERS IN HIGH SCHOOL? IN FRESHMAN COMP?

More fundamentally, objections have been raised to the main reason for including the research paper in the high school or in the freshman composition program: to serve the non-English disciplines and the students who will need to write to their specifications. Glen A. Love and Michael Payne, for example, suggest that research papers are not assigned in the lower undergraduate levels as often as is commonly supposed, and they add that many departments prefer to offer their own course in bibliography or in methods of research for the upper-level and graduate students who are required to write them.[4]

Many who would not agree with this observation nevertheless question the value of the usual high school or college freshman unit. Thomas Taylor, for instance, argues that the conventions of high school research papers, as commonly taught, are so different from those required in college courses that they make the latter more difficult to learn. He also feels that these conventions can encourage inadvertent plagiarism. Surveys of college faculty opinion tend to confirm this point of view. Many of the correspondents in an National Counsel of Teachers of English survey, for example, agree with James Haman from Georgia Tech that too often the high school research paper becomes "a river of quoted brilliance dammed occasionally by a student-produced sand-bar."[5]

Objections Considered.   Such arguments are persuasive. Anyone who has ever had to work with the students of an incompetent teacher can attest to the tremendous difficulty of reteaching a subject that has been learned erroneously and can thus well understand and even sympathize with those who condemn the composition-class research paper on these grounds.

On the other hand, opposing this position is the grateful testimony of the many graduates who managed to master the basics of the research paper in high school or in freshman composition. Ollie T. Dickie, for instance, reports:

> My pupils who go on to college often tell me that the one research paper they have done puts them well in the lead in a class where some of the students have never turned the first stone of research.[6]

How many teachers have among their cherished possessions letters such as the following from a young woman currently serving as rare-book librarian at one of our largest state universities?

After looking carefully at the name and address on your request, I came to the conclusion that this must be the same Mrs. N. who had taught English at M. High School. I was in your AP senior class and have many good memories of that experience. A massive term paper project (with term paper partners and faculty advisors) still stands out in my mind as a rewarding project which proved very helpful for college term papers. . . .

This positive testimony is reinforced by the plaintive voices of those who earnestly wish that they might have had the research experience. Edna McQuire, in surveying her classes of college freshmen for their retrospective views on their high school English classes, discovered that the missed experience most strongly regretted was learning the research paper. These students' intuitive response is given confirmation by research such as Brooke Nielson's, who found a pronounced drop in proficiency when her sample writers shifted registers from informal to academic discourse.[7]

TEACH IT WELL. It is not difficult to understand why students want to study the research paper. Most colleges still offer many courses in which it is required. In fact, in some courses the term paper and the final are the only requirements. Furthermore, in large lecture courses paper and final sometimes offer students their only direct contact with the professor. Very rarely does any writing instruction accompany such a paper assignment. The assumption is that the students will enter the course knowing how to write a research paper or at least possessing a degree of proficiency in research techniques.

What is clear, then, is not that we should avoid teaching the research paper, but that we should avoid teaching it badly. Every college-bound high school student and every college freshman should be given the opportunity to learn the skills necessary for the construction of a scholarly research paper.

MECHANICS OF TEACHING THE RESEARCH PAPER

Because our primary purpose throughout the research project will be to teach methodology rather than any specific set of facts, it will not be necessary, nor even desirable, for the finished product to be of any great length. Four or five typewritten pages (1,000–1,200 words), in most cases, are enough room for students to do justice to a limited subject, and at the same time to allow them constantly to "see it steadily and to see it whole." Equally important, the finished product will not be so lengthy that it prevents the teacher from giving it attention commensurate with the effort put into it.

Scheduling

Making the completion of even a brief research paper a rewarding experience necessitates a certain disruption of routine. Regular theme assignments and heavy reading homework, for instance, should certainly be suspended during the weeks the class is involved in the project. Although language work, discussion based upon short readings, and in-class themes may be continued, the teacher will find that the students' hearts are not with other work while their enthusiasm is centered upon their research.

Since working on a research paper is such an all-consuming activity, it would seem advantageous to limit the time scheduled for the project as much as possible. Nevertheless, it is very difficult to accomplish the work in a period of less than four to six weeks. Even if we convert our class into a workshop or a writing laboratory, or we meet in the library for the duration of the project, four weeks seem to be a necessary minimum time frame. I have experimented with a three-week schedule for freshmen on a quarter term, only to be besieged toward the end with requests for deadline extensions.

Table 9–1 Research Paper Schedule

Time Frame	Activity
Week 1 — Monday	Class discussion defining and describing the scholarly research paper. Suggestions for and aid in selecting the topic to be researched.
Week 1 — Wednesday	Deadline for formulating the research problem and (with a little luck) hypothesis. Conferences with students experiencing difficulties.
Week 1 — Friday	Instruction in note taking.
Week 2 — Wednesday	First examination of note cards.
Week 3 — Monday	Second examination of note cards, with particular attention to the cards of those whose earlier cards were poorly written.
Week 3 — Wednesday	Deadline for formulating a thesis. Conferences with students experiencing difficulty.
Week 3 — Friday	Instruction in organizing the paper; methods of forming structural plans.
Week 4 — Monday–Friday	Conferences on individual working theses and structural plans, a requirement at this stage.
Week 4 — Friday	Approved structural plan due. Instruction in writing the paper from note cards and plans.
Week 5 — Monday	First draft of paper submitted to partner. (A useful addition to the research paper project is the pairing of students, generally on the basis of ability, for the purpose of proofreading one another's work and exchanging advice. For those students who are learning the skills of critical analysis, such a plan also offers the opportunity to put these skills to practical use by writing a critique of the partner's paper as part of the assignment.)
Week 5 — Friday	First draft (and critique) returned to partner.
Week 6 — Monday	All papers due.

Marilyn Schauer Samuels has developed a successful minicourse on the research paper which she teaches in an intensive fifteen-day period during a college intercession; but even in these circumstances, with students expected to spend five to six hours a day in class or in the library, study materials are sent out two weeks before class begins, and the students are required to have chosen their topics by the first day.[8]

Planning ahead is particularly important for such a long-term project. Table 9–1 offers a serviceable five-week schedule, which can be easily modified to fit a variety of circumstances — for example, the opportunity to work on the project on a daily or a four-day-a-week basis, or for a Tuesday–Thursday class calendar. This schedule serves both as an example of the necessary planning and as a foundation for the remainder of this discussion. A procedure such as that outlined in Table 9–1 breaks up the work into sequential steps. At each step, there are precautions that may be taken and techniques that may be used to anticipate, and therefore avoid, the inadvertent plagiarism, oversubjectivity, pointlessness, and other problems that beset the unwary student. A more detailed explanation of these steps may point up some of these techniques.

INTRODUCING THE RESEARCH PAPER

In introducing the research paper, it is wise to be explicit about the exact nature of the paper because most of our students know very little about research papers and some are remarkably misinformed.

Defining

We can tell them that research papers are the ways scholars talk to each other. As such, they are highly conventionalized, with conventions familiar to scholars all over the world. We might begin with a definition such as this:

> The scholarly research paper is a specialized form of expository writing in which an attempt is made to add to the world's accumulated scholarship by formulating some definite statement about, or based upon, a careful study of already existing ideas or data on a particular topic (or optionally on ideas developed experimentally by the researcher).

Our students will want us to go back over the definition more slowly to explain its parts. Let's begin with that which is most familiar.

A SPECIALIZED FORM OF EXPOSITORY WRITING. When we tell them that a research paper is a kind of expository writing, we are grounding this unfamiliar kind of paper in something they are already familiar with. They will know from this description that the purpose and form of their research paper will be like that of all expository writing.

As in all expository writing, the writer's purpose is to develop a point; but in a research paper, this point is always explicitly stated as a thesis. And, in a far more conventionalized, often mandatory way, writers are expected to set out their thesis in the introduction, support it logically in the body, and restate it most convincingly in the conclusion. Actually, a research paper is expository writing intensified and conventionalized.

A CAREFUL STUDY OF ALREADY EXISTING IDEAS OR DATA.
How, then, does the research paper differ from the sort of expository essays our students are by now used to writing? We can explain that in their research papers, they will not be talking only from their own personal knowledge, but will instead be basing their work and their conclusions upon "a careful study of already existing ideas or data." Because these already existing ideas are the creation and possession of the minds of other people, our students will have to be very careful to acknowledge this fact. They will have to make a real distinction between the ideas they have discovered while doing research and their own comments and conclusions based upon these ideas, or their own conclusions will not be valid.

To assist writers in making this essential acknowledgment and in clarifying these necessary distinctions, scholars have developed an apparatus for documentation. Footnotes, bibliographies, and the like may thus be presented as a sort of shorthand to make scholarly work easier. Even those students who had conceived of the documentation apparatus as an evil trap designed exclusively to catch the unwary student can see a certain fairness and sense in it all.

AN ATTEMPT TO ADD TO THE WORLD'S ACCUMULATED SCHOLARSHIP.
This part of the definition still undiscussed, the goal of research, may at first strike our students as a little far-fetched. After all, how can *their* papers advance scholarship? We can answer that by finding out what has been said on a topic and by taking it one step further, or at least by assessing it from a new and individual point of view, their work *can* contribute to the scholarly accumulation. Although the notion of themselves as burgeoning scholars is one most of our students have seldom entertained, I have discovered that when they think about it, they rather like the idea, and many identify with it with enthusiasm.

This concept also helps explain and reinforce the notion that a research project is a project of discovery. It helps students understand that in undertaking it they seek to discover something new, to form their opinion on the basis of something they do not yet know.

The idea adds a meaningfulness and a seriousness of purpose that is needed to sustain the weary student through several weeks of hard and tiring work, and is also needed in some cases, I'm afraid, to forestall a cynical retreat into plagiarism.

Besides, this concept has the further advantage of expressing the simple truth that research is what scholars do. The conventions of research help scholars to communicate with one another. Although the chances are slight that our own students will produce those few among the novice research papers each year that form the kernel of later dissertations and scholarly articles, still, by initiating them into the methods of research, we are giving them the key to the world of scholarship. In introducing the section on the research paper in his rhetoric text, Hans Guth quotes Frederick Schepman:

> Usually we are content to gather knowledge carelessly, taking life as it comes, reading as institutions decree and our tastes decide. Research, however, leads to a different kind of knowledge, for the researcher gathers knowledge systematically. And because research is conducted systematically, it results in knowledge that is not merely personal but also public—at its best, man's knowledge.[9]

Helping Students Choose Topics

Although the methodology our students will learn will remain much the same whatever subject they work with, the topic is of crucial importance to the students themselves, for their attitude toward it will strongly influence the success of their projects. There are a number of considerations to bear in mind when we make our decision about the kind of topics we will offer our students:

1. Most important, the topic must be interesting enough to our students for them to be eager to spend four to six weeks in its company. It must be a subject they are eager to look into, but one that they will approach with no already unshakeable convictions.
2. The topic must be strictly limited to fit the time to be spent, the length of the proposed manuscript, and especially the capabilities of the individual student. For although students' papers will incorporate ideas from sources uncovered in the research process, students must be able to think through the project entirely by themselves.
3. It must be a topic for which adequate source material, especially primary source material, is available. It is sometimes difficult for students to grasp the differences between primary and secondary sources, and thus they tend to underestimate the importance of reliance upon the former. But they usually begin to understand when we explain that primary source material is "right from the horse's mouth."

   Primary source material is always the most direct, most relevant material; but what it is, specifically, depends upon the topic under consideration. Hofstadter's famous article about Lincoln, for example, would be a secondary source if it were approached for its factual material to document a paper about Lincoln's life. The same article would be primary material when used for a paper comparing, for instance, various theories concerning Lincoln's motivation. Since students will be weighing the evidence and coming to their own conclusions, it is important for them to read as much as possible of the writing of those directly concerned with the problem being studied, and far less necessary at this early stage of their development for them to have access to predigested opinion.

4. The topic selected for investigation should appear fruitful for yielding a possible thesis. In fact, it is not at all a bad idea for students to consider adopting a particular hypothesis—even at this early stage in the project—so long as they are truly aware that for the present their idea is *only* a hypothesis and that they may need to relinquish it should it prove inappropriate as a thesis.

TOPICS RELEVANT TO STUDENTS' PERSONAL LIVES. Within guidelines such as these, we can arrive at our decision about the subject matter for the research project. Students find topics interesting when they are in some way relevant to their own lives, either to their personal lives or to their intellectual lives. In recent years a number of successful plans for projects have been developed that give students the opportunity to do scholarly research on subjects pertaining directly to their personal lives.

Research to Answer Questions of Vital Personal Interest. Mary Ellen Grasso, for instance, conducts a program in which brief daily sharing of human-interest items from newspapers and magazines leads her students to choose a topic for their research papers from the "important questions they have on their mind that they would like to have answered."[10] Among the questions her students have investigated are:

- Every other member of my family is divorced, including my parents. What are my chances of remaining married?
- I am Jewish and I never heard of Tay-Sachs disease before. How can I find out whether [my three boys] are carriers?
- What can be done about people who are afraid to fly in planes?
- Are there any new treatments for alcoholics?
- What help is there for the rape victim? (84)

Although some of Grasso's students choose to investigate problems peripheral to their lives, such as "How we can save the baby seals from being slaughtered," most of them select topics that touch on their own lives in very intimate ways. Through the individual conferences that accompany the project or in the classwide oral sharing with which it concludes, Grasso found that "some students were moved to action" in the world outside the classroom, and that all of them "gain[ed] confidence in their ability as student researchers and composition students." Because "they answered their own questions . . . , they [were] interested in finding out the information for themselves, not just for the instructor" (86).

Investigating Career Possibilities. A more specific version of the life-centered research paper is an assignment designed to help students make career decisions. Alice S. Horning implements one such project successfully. Her students begin their research with self-exploration as they work through a battery of instruments including Donald Super's Career Development Inventory, the Myers-Briggs Type Indicator, and computer-based guidance systems such as SIGI+. They then research a particular career by conducting interviews and doing library readings. The final step is to write a brief research paper applying what they have discovered about their own talents and predilections to what they have learned about the requirements, challenges, and rewards of a specific career. Their task in this paper is "to argue that a particular career either is or is not a good choice for them."[11]

Life-centered topics have great appeal—especially for the student whose education orientation tends to be pragmatic and vocational. They offer a meaningful way to teach research to students who have few scholarly interests or ambitions. Nevertheless, we should not disparage more traditional topics. We would seriously underestimate our students if we assumed that they cannot also find real excitement in the world of the intellect.

TOPICS RELEVANT TO STUDENTS' INTELLECTUAL LIVES. The greatest spur to scholarly research is intellectual curiosity. Since students share this quality with scholars, they too can learn to participate with eagerness in the great quest to find out, to understand, to know.

The Researcher as Detective.　　Research offers much the same excitement as the detective story; in fact, the two have often been compared. One of my favorite mystery novels is Josephine Tey's *Daughter of Time*, in which her detective-scholar unravels the historical mystery of who killed the little princes in the Tower. *Daughter of Time* is at once a suspenseful thriller and a convincing scholarly defense of King Richard III. W. Keith Krause has worked out a research project that also combines detection and research. He has his students delve into newspaper accounts of famous crimes, weigh the evidence, and solve the mystery. Susan Glick suggests asking students to "solve the mystery" by explicating a letter or two from the published correspondence between two historic personages. But whatever the area of investigation, the best academically oriented research-paper topics should offer much the same challenge as detective fiction, and should therefore share the same appeal.[12]

Literary Research.　　Nowhere is the conception of the research paper as a detective mystery more useful than in the class where this paper is integrated into the literature program. Students can get really involved in such questions as, "Why didn't Hamlet kill the king?" or "Was Lord Jim's final act a truly heroic deed or just another foolish romantic gesture?"

Without some idea of this sort, inexperienced research paper writers often become trapped in the snares of dull summarization. Biographical papers, in particular, tend to bog down in life summaries. The biographer as detective, however, can pursue some mystery in the subject's life or character, for example, "Who was Shakespeare's dark lady?" or "What in Edgar Allan Poe's life or character accounts for the morbidity of so many of his stories?"

Multipurpose Literary Research.   The whole-language approach can be useful in teaching the research paper. After the class reads a literary work together, we can ask them to research an aspect of it that intrigues them. We might choose historical fiction as the seminal work because of its richness and variety. Stephen Vincent Benét's *John Brown's Body*, for example, from which the sample research paper presented later in this chapter is derived, can generate any number of topics. The student author of the sample paper, for instance, was struck by the line "Each side claims to act in strict accordance with the will of God" and decided to investigate how a single work, the Bible, could be used to justify the opposing moral positions of both North and South. A more literary-minded student could become interested by the form of the poetic novel and choose to find out how *John Brown's Body* compared with others of that genre. A history buff might decide to check into the accuracy of Benét's depiction of the battle scenes.

Robert Penn Warren's *All the King's Men* lends itself to similar treatment. Being a roman à clef, it also offers a chance to conduct research on the degree of accuracy of the various characterizations. Sherwood Anderson's play *Abe Lincoln in Illinois* can also be approached in this way, as Carlisle L. Rast suggests.[13] *Beowulf*, an entirely different sort of work, also provides a fruitful starting point for a variety of kinds of research. It raises such intriguing mysteries as "How do Grendel and Grendel's mother compare with the other monsters of folklore?" "Is *Beowulf* a Christian or a pagan work?" and "What are the parallels between the poem *Beowulf* and the exciting relics of the Sutton Hoo excavations?"

Language Research.   In recent years there has also been a trend toward combining the research paper with the study of language or linguistics. Although students can find much that is fascinating in this field, we must be wary lest they become inextricably embroiled in the highly technical language of this highly technical discipline. Rather than encouraging our students to try to discover their own answer to such questions as "Whether transformational or structural grammar offers the more valid approach," I would recommend that we suggest the investigation of such topics as "How do scientists think language began?" "Can animals really be taught to use language?" or "What do scientists believe to be the origin of African American English?"

Toni-Lee Capossela has had success with a language research project based on Peter Farb's *Word Play*.[14] Students begin by doing sociolinguistic field research to test one of Farb's theses, choosing such controversial topics as "verbal dueling, slang, Black English, diglossa, sexist language, linguistic chauvinism, taboo, obscenity, and euphemism." Then, as Capossela explains it,

> Sometimes field research merely affirms Farb's thesis, but more frequently students find themselves qualifying, updating, modifying, extending, or contradicting him. When this happens, they attempt to account for the discrepancy. Have the rules changed [since 1973]? Is this an example of different

rules in different communities? Did Farb oversimplify in the interests of brevity? . . . Students re-formulate Farb's thesis to make it more accurate. (77)

Then they do library research to support their own hypothesis with the work
of other sociolinguists.

Interdisciplinary Research Projects.   Some of the most successful research projects are team efforts. In a school or college that requires a core
curriculum or one in which all the students of a given composition teacher
are also enrolled in another course, a research paper can be taught in the
two courses simultaneously. The assignment can be made, for instance, in
an American history course, a problems in democracy course, or a Western
civilization core, with the paper worked out in the composition class according to the factual specifications of the other discipline. Students can become excited about such cooperative ventures because, unlike many of the
papers we assign, this one is not perceived as "practice": it feels like "the
real thing."

The second-reader approach is another kind of interdisciplinary project
that works especially well with classes of a scholarly bent. Students choose to
investigate a problem that has been puzzling them from any field, providing
they can find a second reader for the paper for any subject outside of their
composition teacher's areas of competence. During one such project some
high school seniors produced interesting papers on such wide-ranging topics
as genetics, orchestral instrumentation, and isometrics, while other students
asked the originating teacher for special help with literary problems, and still
others took the opportunity to get help and joint credit for a paper required
in their sociology course. Students and cooperating teachers alike were enthusiastic about the project.

Similarly, if we are teaching college freshman, we can give our students
the opportunity of completing research papers assigned in their other classes
under our supervision — with, of course, the cooperation of the other instructors.[15]

Casebooks.   Finally, in thinking of sources for research papers, we should
give some consideration to casebooks. Casebooks consisting of a series of
documents and articles are available as source material on a number of historical and political topics. Current-topics examples include the *Opposing Viewpoints* series, books of essays written by knowledgable people who present
arguments on both sides of such controversial issues as "The Middle East,"
"Latin America and U.S. Foreign Policy," and "Immigration," and the *CQ
Researcher*, published weekly by the *Congressional Quarterly*, each issue of
which offers historic and current background information and views on a
single topic such as "Are term limits a bad idea?" or "Can teens balance
school and jobs?" Or we can make our own casebooks by assembling articles
representing a variety of points of view on a question currently in the news.

Such works as the *Norton Critical Editions* serve much the same purpose for literary research.

Casebooks can provide an important service to those of us whose students do not have access to good libraries, for they offer them the opportunity to consult primary sources. Because casebooks give the teacher total control over the sources, they can also be helpful in curtailing any temptation to practice deliberate plagiarism, where, sadly, this practice may have become entrenched. Since the casebook user does not need to learn library skills, assignment of a casebook research paper also provides a simpler project for our less-able students. Yet despite the advantages of the casebook approach in these circumstances, it does put a significant check upon our students' investigations and also denies them one of the more important benefits of the research project: the opportunity to learn how to use the resources of the library.

TEACHING NOTE-TAKING TECHNIQUES

Let me say it right out: not only is the taking of appropriate notes the key to a successful research paper, but failure to understand this skill will almost certainly guarantee disaster.

Introducing Note Taking

When we introduce note taking to our students, we need to be sure they grasp its function fully. Most students understand the obvious function of note cards as a means of separating out from bulky and unwieldly works pertinent bits of information and recording them in a more serviceable form.

PURPOSE OF NOTE CARDS.   But few see ahead to the cards' ultimate use. Well-taken notes not only permit students to recall their readings, they help them to formulate conclusions and organize their ideas. And later, when they write their papers, they help them to support their ideas clearly and accurately.

Few students are aware of the fundamental importance of the note cards to the final organizing process or to the making of a clear-cut division between that which is "mine" and that which is "thine." Consider the untutored young man in the story that opened this chapter:

- First, by not copying down direct quotations, he blurred the distinctions between what the author actually wrote and his own interpolations; he thus forever destroyed the possibility of either quoting accurately or of commenting without plagiarism.
- Second, by not separating out individual ideas or chains of thought but keeping an author's work together as a whole, the hapless student has not

only made his notes all but useless for the purposes of organizing his paper, but he has almost assured himself of a thematic development plagiarized from one (or a series) of his authors.

He might have avoided all his problems by mastering the note-taking procedures that scholars use.

Fail-Safe Note-Taking Procedures

One is tempted to think that note-taking techniques are personal and idiosyncratic. But my discussions with published scholars here and abroad uncovered a surprising uniformity of basic strategies. Perhaps that is not so surprising, all things considered. After all, all scholars want to take care of this frankly tedious task in the quickest, most expeditious way. And they want a method that will simultaneously record others' ideas while providing a vehicle for formulating their own.

Because of the vital importance of the note-taking process to the success of the entire project, I believe that even the most liberal among us is justified in insisting that our students follow the scholarly note-taking procedure:

TEACHING STRATEGIES

Teaching Scholarly Note-Taking

1. *Notes must be written on cards and limited to one idea to a card.*
2. *Heading Summary.* Each card must be headed by a brief summary of its contents. If the cards are to be valuable as organizational tools, each must be labeled in such a way that the nature of its contents can be comprehended at a glance. The heading on a working card should therefore be a closely specified subject: "Lincoln's early opinions on child-labor restrictions," for example, might fill a top line.
3. *Author, Page Identification.* Each card should be identified by author's last name and page number. A subheading such as "Catton, 38" is quickly managed and takes little space. It not only documents the source, but reinforces the student's sense of recording the voice of a real human, to whom the words belong.
4. *Bibliography Card.* The subhead—surely sufficient identification for the notation—refers to a second set of cards containing all the essential bibliographical information.

   We might suggest that it is a good idea (the human memory being what it is) for students to make a bibliography card, including the library code number, for every usable book as soon as it comes into their possession. Figures 9–1 and 9–2 show samples of the two types of notecards.

continued

Catton, Bruce
This Hallowed Ground
prepublication excerpt in
American Heritage 7 (October 1956) 30-65.

Figure 9–1. Sample Bibliography Card

Cultural differences in the Union Armies
Catton, p. 42
There were times . . . when it seemed that the Union soldiers
disliked each other more than they disliked the Confederates.
. . . The easterners gaped at the westerners, especially at
Sherman's men, considered them undisciplined and
abominably unmilitary in appearance, and remarked that
except for the color of their uniforms they look exactly
like Rebels. S's men in turn, . . . hooted and jeered
at the men fr. the Army of the Potomac and made
remarks about "kid gloves and paper collars" –
to which the easterners replied w/ disdainful
comments about "backwoodsmen."
Me: Were the real cultural distinctions – Urban (E) vs.
Rural (W. & S.) ?

Figure 9–2. Sample Note Card

continued

continued

5. *Quotation Card.* Most notes should be direct quotations of significant single points. (See Figure 9–2.)

   Why? First, because quoting, even using appropriate ellipses and brackets, is far easier than true paraphrasing—and much easier to teach; moreover, most of us will not have taught paraphrasing by note-taking time. Second, because having the author's own words available is a time-saving advantage when it is time to write because writers have no way of knowing until that time what use they will want to make of the note then.

   And third, if we are going to insist—and I believe we must—upon the students never quoting so much as a phrase without so indicating, we must show them how to lay the groundwork for this scrupulousness in their note-taking techniques.

6. *Fact-List Card.* The other most useful note is the list, an enumeration of items of strictly factual material. Even here, our students must understand that any directly quoted phrase must be so signified.

   By arbitrarily limiting the types of acceptable notes, we can help steer our students clear of the perilous semicopying, semiparaphrasing technique that the untutored student so frequently adopts and from which inadvertent plagiarism almost inevitably stems.

7. *Summary Card.* A third kind of permissible card is the summary card, but it should be used with care. When students read an article or chapter they believe to be relevant to their study though not important enough to quote, they might find it useful to summarize the author's point briefly *in their own words*, adding a note of their own about the author's bias or focus.

8. *Personal Comment.* If note taking is to serve a cognitive purpose as well as a purely stenographic one, note cards should also be vehicles for recording the student's thoughts. When students are struck by an idea while doing their research, they should jot it down on the card with the material that inspired it. Students should also note if a quotation reinforces, contradicts, or exemplifies material in another note. This practice helps them put related cards together when it is time to write.

   Personal comments should be labeled explicitly as the student's own, as, for instance, Figure 9–2 demonstrates. We should strongly encourage student commentary because it forces them to think about what they are reading and recording.[16]

9. Students will find it helpful to arrange the cards by topic, rather than by author, for storage. This alignment will permit them to discover their own configuration of ideas.

Insistence upon these techniques makes teacher checking of the cards obligatory, but with careful sampling this task may be quickly accomplished. Our students may complain of our rigidity, but we can assure them that these conventions were contrived to make their work faster and easier. Once they accustom themselves to them, they will agree.

The Photocopying Option.   If students have access to photocopying, they may prefer to use this technology instead of note cards. With a little ingenuity they can transfer note-card efficiency to this more convenient mode. But they will have to be prepared to handle new problems. If they photocopy a new sheet for each separate idea, they will still be able to work with individual ideas and sort them into separate files; and if they highlight relevant material or encircle it, they can separate the relevant from the irrelevant on each page. As with note cards, they should label each sheet with the author's name and the source's page number (if obscured), as well as with an identifying summary of the highlighted or encircled point. All related sheets should be stored in a single folder.

TEACHING NOTE-TAKING TECHNIQUES.   As serviceable as these note-taking techniques are, our students will still need some instruction and some practice before they will be able to make them work for them.

What to Note.   Inexperienced students sometimes have no idea at all about what material is appropriate to record. They don't even appreciate the value of primary source material. The problem stems from their inability to imagine their finished paper. To help them, we need to provide sample research papers from other years or from textbooks, and show them exactly how the writers used their sources for quotation and paraphrase to support their points. Then we might hand out a brief article rich in primary sources on a particular topic and ask the students to suggest passages that would be appropriate to record.

While students are recording these passages on cards, we might also take the opportunity to teach them how to trim their quotations by substituting ellipses for the unneeded material.

How to Weigh the Material.   Another problem some students have is distinguishing between fact and opinion. They have little sense of the author behind what they read and sometimes even harbor the feeling that anything they see in print is automatically true. This gullibility diminishes the quality of their research.

If our students are experiencing this problem, we can devise exercises to help them. We can provide them with passages of expository prose that demonstrate an obvious bias and ask them to identify the viewpoint and, in a sentence or two, to summarize what the author is trying to get across. With practice, they should eventually become able to determine what is fact and what is opinion. For example, students should have little difficulty pointing out the emotionally charged language that shows the author's slant in a recent "objective" article in a popular newsmagazine:

> Insulted by the *paltry* European offer, U.S. representatives *openly* considered walking out—*imperiling* $1.5 trillion in commerce within all 15 of the GATT's trade areas (emphasis mine).

Aware of the bias, what can readers believe in this sentence? Because the article is from a usually reliable periodical, they can probably count on the accuracy of the figures. And discounting the heavily charged "paltry" and "imperiling," but weighing in the implications of "openly," they are probably also safe in assuming that the delegates did contemplate leaving, though they did not actually leave. Perhaps they were restrained by concern for the consequences, as the use of "imperiling" implies.[17]

When to Make a Card.   The decision of whether to make a bibliography card is not a difficult one. We can tell our students that any time a work looks even a bit promising it is a good idea to get down the essential information so they can locate it again. But whether to write a note card is a more complex matter. There are two methods, and neither is completely satisfactory. Students can take down everything that touches their topic to any significant degree and risk ending up with a sizable batch of cards they will never use. Or they can limit their note taking to points they can foresee using in their papers and risk passing up ideas they will have to frantically search for later. Students must find their own balance. I recommend taking few notes until they settle on their research question, but I also suggest that after they define their hypothesis, erring on the side of too many notes will probably save them time and effort in the long run.

Private Notation.   Students should be free to use on their cards whatever abbreviations and symbols that are meaningful to them, for the cards are their private tools and are meant for their own use. They are certainly not meant to make an elegant showing for the teacher.

One kind of symbolization, however, should be discouraged: some students number or letter the cards based upon a single work consecutively and keep them together as a single unit. This practice has the same deleterious effect as copying all of the material from one author on a single page of loose-leaf paper.

STUDENT NOTE TAKING.   Many students derive a sense of security from having access to a concrete list of what to do and how to do it. The following Student Guidelines could serve in this capacity.

STUDENT GUIDELINES

Note Taking

1. *Bibliography cards.* Whenever a book or article seems to be even a remotely possible source, make a bibliography card for it, jotting down all the pertinent information—including the library call number.

continued

2. *Topic label.* Upon finding an idea, a single idea, that bears on the topic, identify it on the top line of an index card by summarizing the passage that contains it in a few words ("Reporters emotional observing Gilmore's execution"), or condense the author's point into a phrase ("Capital punishment = revenge"), or simply give it a label ("Statistics in support").

3. *Source identification.* Identify the source by recording the author's last name and the page number on the card (on the second line, in a top corner, or following the quotation). This abbreviated identification will lead at footnote time to the full information on the bibliography card.

4. *Content: Direct quotation.* Find the sentences or phrases that convey the essence of the idea and quote the author word for word on the card. Delete extraneous material, such as "as we said earlier" or "let us examine the facts," and even material important to the author's argument but not closely related to your concerns, and replace such material with ellipses (. . .).

5. *Personal notation.* If the quoted material inspires some thoughts of your own, skip a line and jot them down, making sure to add your initials or some other sign (me: . . .) to indicate whose thoughts they are.

6. *Content: Lists of facts.* If the passage under consideration is important only because of the facts or statistics it contains, instead of quoting the passage directly, number the facts and list them in a logical and orderly way. If this listing involves the use of any authorial phraseology, indicate it with quotation marks.

7. *Storage.* Keep the cards arranged by topic. This arrangement will rarely coincide with an author's organization.

RULES TO REMEMBER

• Only one idea to a note card.
• Always maintain a 100 percent clear-cut demarcation between any wording of the author's and any wording of your own.

If time allows at all, we should probably check our students' note cards twice: first, preliminarily, to make sure they have caught on to the idea, and a second time to make sure their cards will be adequate for them to use to write good papers. If we have an insecure class that needs prompt feedback, we might consider giving a letter grade (or perhaps a check, check-plus, or check-minus) on the second inspection.

HELPING STUDENTS WRITE THEIR RESEARCH PAPERS

Teaching Research Theses and Structural Plans

As our students do their research, they should be testing out their hypotheses in their minds, adding to them, modifying them, finding evidence and arguments to support them or discarding them and looking for more plausible hypotheses. Those students whose research has confirmed their hypothesis, or modified it, or even reversed it will have no trouble formulating their theses; for their hypotheses (or the negation of their hypotheses) become their theses. Nor do those students who began their research with a specific inquiry and have found the answer to that inquiry have problems with their theses, because their answers become their theses.

NOTE CARDS: A CONCRETE INVENTORY OF IDEAS. For those who do not come to their theses spontaneously, the research project offers an opportunity for a concrete exemplification of the methods of organizing-idea and structural-plan formulation we have been teaching and they have been practicing right along. The notion of an inventory of ideas becomes concrete when students begin working with their cards. They can relate their ideas to one another in a physical way by arranging and rearranging their cards into small stacks representing categories of ideas, or topics, or arguments. Eventually a meaningful arrangement should take shape, and from this arrangement our students can derive their working theses (see Chapter 2). If our students have been diligent about recording their thoughts about the notes and the relationship between the notes during note taking, this process becomes much easier.

THESIS PROBLEMS. Ordinarily, students will have little difficulty in finding a thesis for their research papers, but there are one or two problems that arise with some frequency. Some students, particularly those whose preliminary hypotheses have not worked out as anticipated, have the tendency to propose self-evident or purely descriptive theses. Although a thesis certainly need not be blatantly controversial, still a less than exciting paper will result from an attempt to argue that "George Washington was the first president of the United States" or that "The Grand Canyon is an impressive sight." Perhaps more to the point, the resulting summation of George Washington's life, even if extended for twenty pages, is not really a research paper, nor is the resulting description of the Grand Canyon, no matter how exquisitely detailed.

Must Have a Point. Students who experience this problem need to have us point out to them again that a research paper, like all good expository prose, must present a point. A good way to avoid bland, self-evident papers is to require the working theses to be phrased with the inclusion of an "although clause" or its equivalent. (See Chapters 2 and 6.)

Point Need Not Be Overtly Controversial. While we are emphasizing the controversial aspect of the thesis statement, however, we must be careful not to give the impression that a highly contentious paper is required. After such discussion, students sometimes need to be discouraged from writing personally evaluative theses or hortative tracts. There are so many interesting nonsubjective statements a writer could make about socialism, *Paradise Lost*, or Buddha that surely it is not necessary for the point of a paper to amount to "I think it is good" or "I think it is bad." We should help guide our students' thinking into more fruitful channels.

For examples of working theses from some successful student research papers, see those heading each of the structural plans included in the Illustrated Models.

STRUCTURAL PLANS.   Construction of a structural plan is the most vital step in the writing of a research paper, for it is at this point that the student must think through the totality of the reading and the ideas inspired by that reading and come to grips with the problem of organizing them into a lucid entity. Reviewing the methods for constructing a serviceable plan is useful here. We can show our students how to group and regroup their notecards until the topics fall into natural subdivisions of the five or six major points of what will become the paper. Then we can help them arrange these groups, or points, into the best possible order for the presentation of the theses. Because of the individual character of the problems encountered and the crucial nature of this step in the project, it is highly desirable to schedule a workshop day for discussion and approval of the preliminary structural plans.

You may find it helpful to examine some theses and structural plans from which students have created successful research papers. See the Sample Structural Plans.

ILLUSTRATIVE MODELS

Sample Structural Plans

RESEARCH PAPER ON A SCIENTIFIC TOPIC
Thesis: Schizophrenia is caused by a chemical imbalance in the brain and thus should be treated chemically, not by psychotherapy.

1. Introduction. "Although clause": Until recently schizophrenia was treated through psychotherapy alone,
   Leading to ⟶ Thesis
2. Presentation of research that shows schizophrenia to be the result of chemical imbalance in the brain.
   Farley's research
   Potkin's research
   Fisher's research
   Terensius and Kline's research
3. Possible cause for this imbalance
   Diet
   Virus
   Genetic causes

continued

---

continued
4. Failure of the psychoanalytic approach
5. Recommendation: Drug therapy should replace psychotherapy for schizophrenia

Research Paper on a Historical Subject

[The paper developed from this plan may be found on pages 363–69.]

Thesis: During the Civil War the Bible became the South's main justification for slavery and the North's foremost weapon against it.

1. Introduction: Setting up the paradox
2. Antislavery use of Bible
   • Influenced the leaders
   • Quoted at abolitionist meetings
   • Quoted in abolitionist literature
3. Proslavery use of Bible
   • Biblical passages used as justification
   • Biblical history used as justification
     — The Patriarchs
     — The Mosaic Law
4. Abolitionist rebuttal
   • Interpretation of cited passages

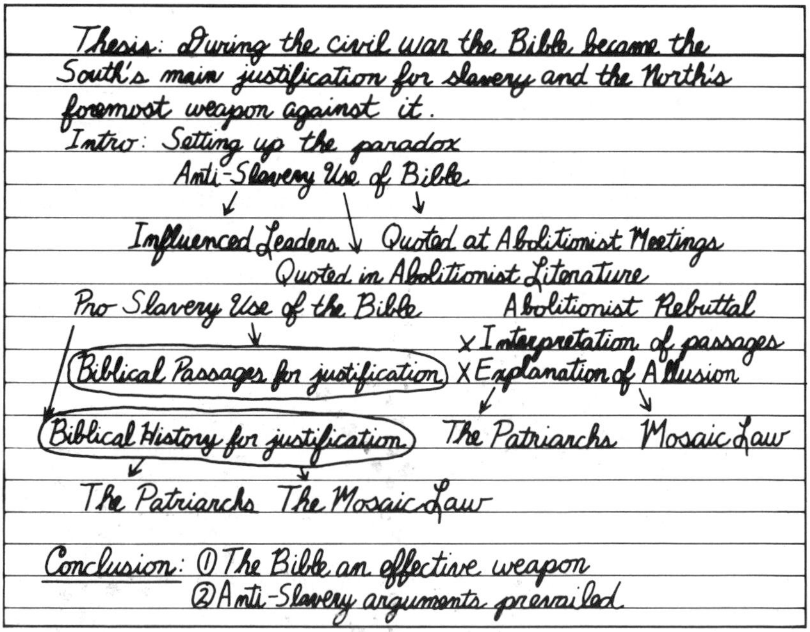

Figure 9–3.

continued
- Explanation of allusions to biblical history
    - The Patriarchs
    - The Mosaic Law
5. Conclusion
    - The Bible was an effective weapon
    - The antislavery arguments prevailed

Research Paper on a Literary Topic

Thesis: None of the major theories suggested by literary scholars completely answers the central critical question in Shakespeare's *Hamlet*, the question of why Hamlet delays in killing the king. Yet a combination of these theories can offer a plausible explanation.

I. Introduction—stressing the variety of critical answers to the question (Leading to)→ Thesis
II. Detailed presentation of the most plausible theories.
   A. Theory of melancholia (A. C. Bradley)
      1. Explanation
      2. Facts in the play it accounts for
      3. Facts in the play it does not explain
   B. Oedipal theory (S. Freud. Olivier and Mel Gibson's movie interpretations)
      1. Explanation
      2. Facts in the play it accounts for
      3. Facts in the play it does not explain
   C. Theory of practical impossibility (G. B. Harrison)
      1. Explanation
      2. Facts in the play it accounts for
      3. Facts in the play it does not explain
III. My theory. A combination of II A, II B, & II C.
   A. Explanation
      1. Hamlet's delay in Acts I, II, & III.
      Caused by Hamlet's melancholic (II A) and, to some extent, oedipal (II B) preoccupation with the possibilities of his mother's guilt.
      2. Hamlet's delay in Acts IV & V.
      Caused by lack of practical opportunity (II C) until Hamlet actually does the deed.
   B. How this theory accounts for the facts in this play
   C. How it avoids the problems of the other theories
IV. Conclusion

Helping Students Create Their Research Papers

It is possible for students to experience something almost akin to pleasure in the actual writing of their papers, for there is a sort of delight to be found in combining the fruits of research efforts—the well-organized structural plan, the well-coordinated note cards—in an almost puzzle-building way and watching the whole project consequently fall into shape. Still, we may need to explain to our students how they might go about this process. We can tell them that they will write the introduction, approaching and then setting forth their theses. Then we can show how, working point by point down the structural plan, they can read through the pertinent cards from the stack, which has been arranged to coordinate with the structural plan, and write each section.

USING NOTE-CARD SUPPORT. There are two major ways students can make use of the material on their cards. The fact that they have the exact words of the author permits both options.

Making the Material Their Own. On the one hand, our students can read over the cards associated with a particular point, digest the information they contain until it becomes part of their own thinking, and—putting the cards completely aside—make their point about the subject in their own way. Our students probably should write the greater part of their paper in this fashion.

Quoting or Paraphrasing. On the other hand, many times paraphrasing or quoting the material on their cards directly is the right choice. Students should quote (or paraphrase) when the author's words (or their version of them) are in themselves proof of whatever their passage is asserting. All primary source material can be quoted (or paraphrased) for this purpose—whether it is a statistical chart for a scientific paper, a literary passage for a critical analysis, an expert opinion when students want to weigh scholarly views, or even the words of the person-on-the-street when students need mass opinion.

Teaching Quoting and Paraphrasing

The two lessons we teach that will be most crucial to our students' writing successful research papers are note taking (discussed above) and how to support their points with quotation and paraphrase. Almost all students will need practice in

- Introducing their quotations or paraphrases in their own words
- Gracefully indicating the source of the words or ideas
- How to paraphrase
- Determining when to quote and when to paraphrase.

Let's go over each of these places of potential student difficulty.

INTRODUCING IN THEIR OWN WORDS. Some students—sometimes very able students—seriously misunderstand the nature of a research paper and produce a sort of patchwork quilt of cleverly fitted quotations. To prevent such disasters, we need to emphasize the idea that although a research paper must be based upon a solid groundwork of scholarly opinion, it cannot be simply a pastiche of the ideas of others; the student as author must at all times remain fully in control.

"But how can I really be in charge of my paper when I hardly knew anything about the subject until after I started to research it?" our students sometimes ask. We can answer, "But your thesis is your own, isn't it? Your point of view is your own. Your approach is your own. And the way you are putting together your sources to reflect that point of view and to prove that thesis is all your own, too. Therefore, you must remain firmly in the driver's seat."

Where Not to Quote. These students will be eager for practical advice on how to exercise and demonstrate this control. We can tell them that since the thesis is all their own, the introduction and the conclusion should also be all their own, with quotations—if indeed any are used in these sections—employed only for stylistic effect. And since the development and structure is their own, all topic sentences should likewise be their own, and likewise be free of quotation.

In fact, we might point out to our students that their control should be so absolute that *their finished papers should still make good sense even if all quotations and paraphrased passages were removed*—though admittedly they might lack something in the way of exemplification and color.

Distinguishing the Writer's Voice. Wherever the students decide to use quoted or paraphrased material, they should never simply insert it to speak for itself; they should rather introduce it in their own voice. They themselves should make the relevant point and then bring in the author of the quotation or paraphrase to back it up. A paper cannot simply burst into quotation as a bird bursts into song. Even when the paper is read aloud so that quotation marks have no significance, a listener should be able to understand that a new voice is speaking, and, for the most part, should be told whose voice it is; for instance, through introductions such as, "as Smith writes."

The quotations themselves should be shaped to fit the context of the paper. Writers, in the driver's seat, should mold quotations appropriately into their syntax; and we can show them how to use ellipses and brackets to do so. For example:

> The power and force of the Old Testament were so much a part of [William Lloyd] Garrison that many associated the two together. Ernest Sutherland Bates likens him to "a fiery Hebrew prophet" and Wendell Phillips in his beautiful eulogy said that Garrison was "Taught of God . . . God endowed, and God-sent to arouse a nation." (Sample Research paper, page 364)

We might also provide practice for our students in this skill.

When quotations and paraphrased material are handled in this way, a paper can achieve clarity, and even more important, the author will maintain control.

INTRODUCING THEIR SOURCE.   It is important that students not only make their point or subpoint in their own words, but also introduce the author of their supporting material (whether quoted or paraphrased) by name. Wherever their voice — or their ideas — gives way to another's, students need to signal the change to their readers by such phrases as "according to Snerd" or "as Jones puts it."

Mentioning the name of the person from whom students took the material not only clarifies the distinction between their voice and that of their sources, it also lends the authority of their source to their argument. Additionally, by eliminating the need to identify the source, it makes their parenthetical documentation less intrusive. (See page 356.)

Some Introducing Hints.   The first time students mention an author or informant, they should give her or his full name. At this first mention, they might also want to add an identifying tag such as "Jane S. Doe, professor of literature at Johns Hopkins University" or "John Q. Doe, agronomist with the U.S. Department of the Interior." In this first reference it is also often useful to mention the name of the work from which they are quoting: "According to Leslie L. Pickle in *Poltergeists for Fun and Profit,* . . ." or "In *Poltergeists for Fun and Profit,* Leslie L. Pickle points out, . . ." In later references, citing the last name alone is sufficient: "Doe argues that . . ." or "As Pickle explains, . . ."

HOW TO PARAPHRASE.   Students find paraphrasing a difficult skill to master. "Paraphrasing" is in itself a misleading term. Students often misconceive it to mean a sort of "semi"-phrasing, indicating that they should retain the essential phraseology of a passage while changing it a little. Yet, in changing the words of a passage themselves, students often get a proprietary feeling for it and consequently no longer see a necessity for crediting the original author. Guided practice in the art of interpretive rephrasing of passages is thus often important. Famous passages make a good vehicle for this practice. Katherine Burton uses the final sentence of Lincoln's Gettysburg Address in her teaching. Among the paraphrases produced by her students are the following, which can serve as examples of the approach:

> Lincoln never forgot that the nation, much as it had accomplished by its own efforts in a terrible struggle, was still a nation under God, that it should not be cocksure and irreligious, but even in its high idealism must remember that it was only under God that its high hopes were to be fulfilled.

> The conception of democratic government which Lincoln set forth was of a people's government of, by, and for the people, as his rhetorical phrases made so emphatic.

As Lincoln implied in the conclusion to his Gettysburg Address, American democracy was the one great free government of the nineteenth century. If democracy failed here, it perished from the whole earth, he said in his final words.[18]

DECIDING WHEN TO QUOTE AND WHEN TO PARAPHRASE. How writers support their points is such an individual decision that we don't really dare impose our private tastes upon our students. We need rather to be sure they understand the difference between quoting and paraphrasing and are comfortable with either or with mixed strategies. Here are some examples taken—along with their documentation—from the student paper included in this chapter.

The first example shows the Abolitionists' dependence upon the Bible to reinforce their antislavery arguments. Note that the student makes the point first in her own words in both versions.

Use of Quotation

The Bible was the backbone of the Abolitionist cause. "Take away the Bible," William Lloyd Garrison said, "and our warfare with oppression and infidelity, intemperance and impurity, is removed—we have no authority to speak and no courage to act" (qtd. in Nelson 177).

Use of Paraphrase

The Bible was the backbone of the Abolitionist cause. William Lloyd Garrison felt that if the Bible could not be used, then they would lose their best authority and would no longer have either the justification or the spirit to continue. (Nelson 177).

In the next example she uses quotation and paraphrase to express the religious rationale of the slaveholders:

Use of Quotation

There was . . . a widespread belief [in the South] that [slavery] was somehow good for the slaves. The Reverend Phillip Schaff considered slavery as "a wholesome training school for the Negro taking him from the lowest state of heathenism and barbarism to some degree of Christian civilization" (qtd. in Cole 256).

Use of Paraphrase

There was a widespread belief in the South that slavery was somehow good for the slaves. Reverend Phillip Schaff, for instance, thought that slavery was a means of educating the slave in civilization and in Christianity (Cole 256).

Students will find the Using Quotation and Paraphrase Student Guidelines helpful.

STUDENT GUIDELINES

Using Quotation and Paraphrase

1. POINT. Introduce your point in your own words. Use the quotation or paraphrase for support only. Never simply insert it to speak for itself. *Your paper should be able to make coherent sense with all quotations and paraphrases omitted.*
2. PERTINENCE. Use a quotation or a paraphrase only when your point could not be supported as well without it. Remember that too many quotations can produce a patchwork-quilt effect.
3. BREVITY. Trim your quotations as closely as possible, leaving only the phrasing that is completely relevant to your point. Carefully shape the quotation to fit *your* context, but be accurate and true to the author's original meaning.
4. IDENTIFICATION. Give the quotation a source. Either name its author specifically ("William Garrison," "Reverend Phillip Schaff," "John Brown") or in general ("a famous New England poet"). Even when the paper is read aloud (so that quotation marks have no significance), a listener should be able to understand that a new voice is speaking, and for the most part, should be told whose voice it is.

THE MECHANICS OF QUOTATION.   When we introduce the conventions for transcribing quoted material, some of our students will complain that there are altogether too many purposeless rules. To them we can explain frankly that the purpose of these conventions is to make the quoted material instantly recognizable and to make the text as a whole easier to read. Some students, on the other hand, will express their eagerness for the security of a list of rules. The rules most likely to prove useful to all the students are listed in the Student Guidelines.

STUDENT GUIDELINES

Conventions for Using Quotations

PLACEMENT
1. Brief quotations should be enclosed in quotation marks:

   The power and force of the Old Testament were so much a part of Garrison that many associated the two together. Bates likens him to "a fiery

continued

Hebrew prophet"( ) and Wendell Phillips said that Garrison was "Taught of God . . . God endowed, and God-sent to arouse a nation" ( ).

2. A quotation that extends over three lines should be indented and blocked off. (You do not need to use quotation marks when you use this form. The indentation itself says "quoted material.") For instance:

Wendell Phillips, like so many of his time, used Bible language and imagery in the remarkable oratory of his Abolitionist addresses. Take, for example, this excerpt from his "Dangers from Slavery" speech:

> Then the wicked will walk on every side for the vilest of men will be exalted, and America, become the mock and scorn and hissing of the nations, will go down to worse shame than was ever heaped upon Sodom; for the lust of wealth, land and power, she will also have committed the crime against nature. ( )

3. Poetry should be indented and quoted in lines, just as written on the original page:

The prose of *The Liberator* is interspersed with poetry, most of which has more passion than art:
> God is a God of mercy, and would see
> The prison-doors unbarr'd—the bondmen free!
> He is a God of Truth, with purer eyes
> Than to behold the oppressor's sacrifice! ( )

4. Brief portions of poetry (three lines or less) may be included within the text, but you should indicate the line divisions by slashes:

According to Stephen Vincent Benét's Bible-reading slave-trader, "It's down there, Mister, / Down there in black and white" ( ).

PUNCTUATION
Punctuate your quotations according to the following rules:

5. Carefully copy the author's punctuation (and spelling and wording) within the quotation.

6. When you trim the quotation to meet the requirements of your own introductory sentences and the point that you are making, substitute three periods (. . .) for any omitted words. Any additions or changes in wording that you have to make so that the quotation will fit the demands of your own text should be included in brackets [ ]. For example, the italicized portion of the following passage from page 31 of Professor Scholar's book would read ambiguously if quoted out of context:

> George Washington was the first president of the United States. *He was the father of his country.*

To quote it so your readers would be sure about your subject and be aware you had changed the wording, you would enclose your own words in brackets:

continued

continued

>   According to Professor Scholar, "[George Washington] was the father of his country" (31).

7. A quotation within a quotation is indicated by single quotation marks (that is, an apostrophe):

>   Professor Researcher points out that "Edison tested the first record player with 'Mary Had a Little Lamb' " (21).

   Double quotation is awkward, however, so avoid it if you can.

8. You have your choice of a variety of punctuation for introducing your quotation.
   a. You can make the quotation an integral part of the sentence by using no additional punctuation:

   >   Thus both sides claimed to act "in strict accordance with the will of God" ( ).

   b. You can introduce the quotation informally with a comma:

   >   According to F. C. Stifler, "The great Lincoln was nurtured on the Bible as few men ever have been" ( ).

   c. Or you can introduce it more formally with a colon:

   >   Lincoln's actions on slavery, as on all important issues, were governed by his creed: "What doth the Lord require of thee, but do justly, to love mercy, and to walk humbly with thy God?" ( ).

   d. You can use commas to interrupt the quotation by inserting its identifying tag:

   >   "Take away the Bible," William Lloyd Garrison said, "and our war-fare with oppression . . . is removed" ( ).

   e. Or you can use a comma to put the identifying tag at the end:

   >   The prophets were particularly outspoken on the subject. "Woe unto him . . . who useth his neighbor's services without wages," Jeremiah wrote (22:13).

9. All punctuation that is part of a quotation itself goes *within* the quotation marks:

>   Kahn wondered: "What killed Arthur Dimmesdale?"

   Periods and commas always go *within* the quotation marks — sometimes illogically:

>   Our national anthem is "The Star-Spangled Banner."

10. *An Exception:* Parenthetical references follow the quotation marks and precede the punctuation as in the examples above. Only when a quotation is separately blocked (as, for example, in 2 above), do the parentheses stand outside the sentence.

Putting the Rules into Practice

Guidelines can only suggest what students should do. How they will put these suggestions into practice has to be determined by their individual purposes in creating the paragraphs of their own paper and by the specific context of each of their points and subpoints. We will need something more experiential to teach our students how to handle these complexities. If we immerse them in a close simulation of the actual process, they can work out strategies that will be personally useful to them.

QUOTING AND PARAPHRASING DISCOVERY EXERCISE. We can give our students a set of facts that closely approximate a portion of an assignment, and by letting them work through the decision-making process, we can help them see how their options would vary with their purpose. For intellectually curious students, consider using the Medieval Peasant Exercise, derived from Eileen Power's "The Peasant Bodo" chapter in her *Medieval People*.

STUDENT EXERCISE

Medieval Peasant Research Paper

Your thesis is:

Although wars and kings have long been the mainstay of history books, the everyday life of common people is at least as historically significant. Take, for example, the medieval peasant.

Your outline is:

   I. Introduction: Although . . . ⟶ Thesis
  II. Sources of current knowledge about med. peasants
     A. Estate Book of Abbey St Germain, 811–26.
     B. Charlemagne, *Instructions to Stewards*, 8??
     C. Aelfric, *Colloquium*
     D. Others
 III. What we can know about:
     A. Feudal relationships
        1. Peasant tenant privileges
        2. Peasant feudal obligations
           a. Rents
           b. Taxes
           c. Labor

continued

continued

B. Peasant–church relationships
   1.
   2.
   3.
   4.
C. Important events in peasant life
   1.
   2.
   3.

IV. Conclusion

Your present task is: Write the section for point III. A. 2. c. Your point here is: Contemporary sources show how hard the medieval peasants worked to fulfill their feudal obligations.

Your note cards on this point include Figures 9–4 to 9–7.

Estate obligations of plowmen
Abbey St. Germain Estate Book, 78
Me: Each tenant owed the manse labor of:
1. field work – about 3 days a week specified unit of seasonal plowing.
Ex: "Winter: Sow 4 perches. Spring: 2"
2. labor services – so many weekly (Ex: 2 plowings) at steward's demand.
3. handwork – spec. weekly number, as needed, of repairs, gathering, carrying, wood-chopping, ale-making, etc.

Figure 9–4. Estate obligations of plowmen

continued

Obligations of other workers
Charlemagne, 45
[Each steward should have in his district]
good workmen, namely, blacksmiths, silversmiths,
shoemakers, turners, carpenters, swordmakers, fishermen,
foilers, soapmakers, men who know how to make beer,
cider, & all other kinds of beverages, bakers to make
pastry for table, netmakers who know how to make
nets for hunting, fowling, fishing . . .

Figure 9–5. Obligations of other workers

Peasant women worked too.
Charlemagne, 43, 49.
"Women . . . are to give at the proper time the materials,
i.e. linen, wool, vermilion, wool combs, soap, grease,
vessels, and other objects that are necessary . . . And
let our women's quarters be well looked after,
furnished w/rooms w/stoves & cellars, & let them be
surrounded by a good hedge, & let the doors be strong,
so the women can do our work properly."

Figure 9–6. Peasant women worked too

continued

continued

Imaginary dialogue w/ Anglo-Saxon man
Aelfric, 95.
"Well, ploughman, how do you do your work? Oh,
sir, I work very hard. I go out in the dawning,
driving the oxen to the field & I yoke them to the
plough. Be the winter never so stark, I dare not stay
at home for fear of my lord; but every day I must
plough a full acre or more, after having yoked the
oxen & fastened the share to the plough. [My] boy, who
drives the oxen with a goad, is hoarse from cold &
shouting."

Figure 9—7. Imaginary dialogue w/ Anglo-Saxon man

Teaching the Exercise. Students may need a little time to identify with the simulation, but they will soon grasp the need to develop a topic sentence embodying the suggested point. Chances are they will work out a topic sentence pretty much like this:

> Topic sentence: According to contemporary sources, medieval peasants worked exceedingly hard; for they not only had to get their own living but also fulfill their feudal obligations.

In considering how they would combine the information on these cards to make their point, we can help them work out the idea that their decision must depend upon the degree of emphasis they want to put on this particular idea. The greater the emphasis they want to give to the point, the more specific they should be in their supporting evidence.

If they want to use it in a rather minimal way, to make their point and get on to other ideas more important to their argument, they could support their topic sentence by simply combining their sources and summarizing (see Example A). If the section is to be somewhat significant to the paper as a whole, they might cite and paraphrase from the more relevant sources (see Example B.) But if the point is one they truly want to emphasize, they might decide to support their point not only by paraphrasing but also by quoting directly (as in Example C).

This might be a good place to break into work groups, each with the task of composing a paragraph with one of the suggested emphases. It is important to conclude by sharing and comparing their examples. The following samples are the best of one class's work:

ILLUSTRATIVE MODEL

Sample Supporting Paragraphs

Minimally Emphatic Support (Summary of Source Material)

Example A: *According to contemporary sources, medieval peasants worked exceedingly hard; for they not only had to get their own living but also to fulfill their feudal obligations.* Plowmen had to plow and keep up the estate on which they were tenants. Skilled craftsmen had to furnish the estate with shoes, fish, swords, and everything the landholders needed for themselves or for gifts to the king. And the women were confined to their own quarters so as not to be distracted from weaving cloth and making pottery for the estate.*

> *The material in this paragraph was derived from Abbey St. Germain 78, Charlemagne 43, 45, 49, and Aelfric 95.
> [A footnote is needed here because the multiple sources make parenthetical documentation cumbersome. Italics indicate the topic sentence.]

Semiemphatic Support (Paraphrase of Sources)

Example B: *According to contemporary sources, medieval peasants worked exceedingly hard; for they not only had to get their own living but also to fulfill their feudal obligations.* Estate books such as that of the Abbey de St. Germain specify the exact amount of fieldwork, labor service, and handwork required for each farming peasant (78). Charlemagne's instructions to his stewards give us some notion of the product demands made upon blacksmiths, carpenters, swordmakers, and other skilled craftsmen (45), as well as those made upon peasant women (43, 49). Even fiction, such as the Anglo-Saxon Aelfric's "Dialogue with a Ploughman," confirms the peasants' heavy burden of toil.

Emphatic Support (Including Quotation of Sources)

Example C: *According to contemporary sources, medieval peasants worked exceedingly hard, for they not only had to get their own living but also to fulfill their feudal obligations.* Estate books such as that of the Abbey de St. Germain specify the exact amount of fieldwork, labor service, and handwork required for each farming peasant (78). Charlemagne's "Instructions" to his stewards give us some notion of the product demands made upon blacksmiths, carpenters, swordmakers, and other skilled craftsmen (45). The "Instructions" also evidence the particularly burdensome requirements placed upon women, who were to "be surrounded by a good hedge and . . . doors [that were] strong so that [they] can do our work properly" (49). Even fiction, such as the Anglo-Saxon Aelfric's "Dialogue with a Ploughman," confirm the peasants' heavy burden of toil:

> "O sir, I work very hard. I go out in the dawning, driving the oxen to the field and I yoke them to the plough. Be the winter never so stark, I dare not stay at home for fear of my lord; but every day I must plough a full acre or more" (95)

Our students will probably also need some individual practice. We might try assigning exercises such as #4 or #5 in the Ideas for Discussion or Essay at the end of this chapter. These exercises offer another opportunity for interim feedback if that is desired.

As students become more experienced in research writing, they will begin to develop a surer intuition about what approach to take and how to handle it.

TEACHING STUDENTS ABOUT DOCUMENTATION

Documentation is important to the validity of a research paper, for it not only gives credit where credit is due, but it adds the powerfully persuasive force of authority to the writer's arguments. By documenting an idea, a writer is saying "This is not simply my belief; it is the opinion of expert So-and-So" or "It is borne out by the facts she has presented or the study she has made."

Teaching What to Document

The question of what should be credited is not always easy to answer. Too many text interruptions can be distracting and can leave the impression of a stuffy, fuddy-duddy sort of mind. But too few can amount to plagiarism. As our students become more experienced in research, they will develop a feel for what should and what should not be credited. Until they develop this natural sureness, we can advise them to avoid the greater of the two evils. In other words: When in doubt, document. The Student Guidelines gives them sound advice upon which to base their decisions.

STUDENT GUIDELINES

What to Document

1. All quotations MUST be credited.
2. All paraphrases MUST be credited.
3. Material that is not directly quoted or paraphrased from your source should be credited whenever it is, in any way, exclusive to its author. You do not need to credit it if it is common knowledge. The test should not be "Did I know this information before?" but rather "Can this information be found in an encyclopedia or in almost any book on the subject?" For example, you may not personally know the birthday of Tsar Nicholas II of Russia, but there would nevertheless be no reason to document such a fact because it is available in any number of sources. Information that needs documentation includes:

   • Interpretations
   • Opinions

continued
  • Challengeable data, including:
  • Statistics
  • Results of surveys
  • Results of studies

Remember that the results of research are only as good as the people who did the work. Your reader has the right to know who they are.

Teaching How to Document with Ease

Despite its importance, the very idea of documentation can arouse feelings of panic in inexperienced writers. But, as it is with unfamiliar dogs, the bibliographical bark is much worse than its bite. The social and physical sciences long ago streamlined their systems.[19] And now, with the conventions newly established by the authoritative Modern Language Association (MLA), the documentation hound has been defanged in the humanities as well. The essential information can now be communicated without seriously inconveniencing either writer or reader—a situation to which we English teachers can offer a fervent "Hoorah!"

This essential information is actually rather compact. The MLA System of Documentation Student Guidelines summarize all the basic conventions.

STUDENT GUIDELINES

The MLA System of Documentation

To use the MLA system, you as writer should:

• Present your bibliographical information in full in a List of Works Cited at the conclusion of your paper.
• Provide information specific to the individual reference (page numbers, for example) in parentheses within the text itself:
     . . . ," according to Professor Smith (367).
  When you do not identify your source directly in your text, you also include within the parentheses the author's last name or whatever information your reader will need to find the appropriate entry in the List of Works Cited:
     . . . ," as scholars have found (Smith 367).
• Resort to footnotes only when the material within the parentheses (several author's names, for example) becomes so lengthy and cumbersome that it disrupts the reading of your text.

And that's really all there is to it. But although the MLA System of Documentation Student Guidelines accurately reflect the basic conventions, our students will surely have questions about how to use the system in specific situations. Let me try to suggest answers to some of the more frequently asked questions.

WHAT GOES BETWEEN SOURCE PARENTHESES? To distract the reader as little as possible, parentheses interrupting the text should contain as little as possible. Since there is no need to duplicate information, we can recommend that our students identify their sources in the text itself. As they introduce quotations or paraphrases, they should ordinarily mention the author(s) name(s). In the absence of a known author, they can cite the title — or a clearly recognizable shortened version of the title. To further decrease distraction, *The MLA Style Manual* suggests that the page number or numbers stand alone within the parenthesis: (173) — without an abbreviated *p.* or *pp.* or further punctuation, for instance.

With the work clearly identified, the usual citation for both books and articles can be a single, uncluttered page number within parentheses directly following the cited material or at the first natural pause after it. All other parenthetical references are variations on this standard notation. The list of examples in the Models for Parenthetical Documentation Student Guidelines can provide students models for handling a variety of documentation situations.

STUDENT GUIDELINES

Models for Parenthetical Documentation

All citations refer to the List of Works Cited on pages 360–61.
When you cite the author's name in your text:.

E. B. White also makes this point (100–101).

When you do not identify your source in the text:

This point has been made before (White 100–101).

When you refer to a passage quoted in another work:

Jemshed Khan argues that Chillingworth poisoned Dimmesdale with atropine from herbs gathered in the forest (qtd. in Turner 82).

When you cite an author who has more than one work listed in your List of Works Cited, distinguish the work in the text or by including an (abbreviated) title as well as the author's name in the parenthetical note:

In *Successful Writing: A Rhetoric for Advanced Composition,* Maxine Hairston reports on her research which showed that successful business professionals

continued

> "seem to believe . . . writers should observe the conventions of standard English" (245).
> A recent survey shows that the "men and women who occupy positions of responsibility in the business and professional world . . . seem to believe that writers should observe the conventions of standard English" (Hairston, *Successful Writing* 245).

When you refer to a work listed by title in your List of Works Cited, include a (abbreviated) title. But if you abbreviate, remember to begin with the word that begins the entry in your List of Works Cited so your reader can locate the full reference easily.

Dictionary or encyclopedia references are alphabetically listed and need no page numbers.

> According to the editors of *Funk and Wagnall's Encyclopedia*, though barber and surgeon were once one, by the time of the Rennaisance "the surgical practice of the barber was restricted to bloodletting and toothpulling" ("Barber").

When you refer to a passage in a multivolume work, include the volume number and separate it from the page number with a colon:

> God is a God of mercy, and would see
> The prison-doors unbarr'd—the bondmen free.
> (*Old South Leaflets* 4:6)

When you cite a classic work of literature, available in many editions, the page number of your particular copy is of less value to your reader than the canto, chapter, act, scene, or line of the work. The conventional citation is the division number first and then the line, separated by a period:

> *When your reference is to a Biblical passage*, cite chapter and verse:

> All through the Bible, the principles of freedom and equality are stressed: "Have we not all one father? Hath not one God created us?" (Malachi 18.8).

When your reference is to a verse play, cite Act, scene, and line. Use Roman numerals for the Act and scene:

> When Hamlet learns who murdered his father he exclaims, "O my prophetic soul!" (I.v.40).

When your reference is to a long poem, cite book or canto and line:

> At the end of Milton's *Paradise Lost*, Adam and Eve, "with wandering steps and slow, / Through Eden take their solitary way" (12.648–49).

When your reference is to a work of prose, begin the entry with the page number of your edition followed by a semicolon:

> In Dickens' *Great Expectations* Pip has to learn not to consider his relatives "coarse and common" (139; ch. 18).

continued

continued

> Despite her insanity, Blanche Dubois makes her final exit with dignity,
> saying: "I have always depended on the kindness of strangers" (Williams,
> *Streetcar*, 142; sc. 11.).

And finally, when you refer to a work as a whole, mention the author's
name and you need not interrupt your text with any citation at all:

> Achtert and Gibaldi carefully edited the new *MLA Style Manual.*

WHEN SHOULD FOOTNOTES (OR ENDNOTES) BE USED? Just as
our students are heaving a sigh of relief that parenthetical documentation has
relieved them from ever having to write a footnote, we will have to tell them
that important as in-text notation is, it cannot replace footnotes altogether.
Readers are distracted when parenthetical notation becomes too lengthy.
When they need to provide a quantity of information that interferes with
easy reading comprehension, they should use a foot- or endnote.

Students usually find using the MLA's suggestion of notes at the end of
the paper, just preceding the List of Works Cited, much the easier procedure. The content of the notes will, of course, be the same in either case.

The Student Guidelines lists situations when these notes are appropriate.

STUDENT GUIDELINES

Models for Foot or End Notation

*When you want to call your readers' attention to sources beyond those you refer
to in the text:*

3. See also Bloom, 38–44, and O'Brien, 109–117.
4. Snerd strenuously disagrees; see 98–99.

When you base a paragraph on multiple sources (as in *Medieval Peasant*,
Support Example A.)

5. The material in the above paragraph was derived from Abbey St. Germain 78; Charlemagne 43, 45, 49; and Aelfric 95.

*When you have referenced a secondary source and want to provide the origi-
nal source:*

6. Jemshed Khan, "The Scarlet Letter—A Rash Conclusion?" *New England
Journal of Medicine* 311 (August 9, 1984): 416 (qtd. in Turner 82).

continued
Those rare occasions when you need to use footnotes to comment upon the text: Though it is ordinarily wisest to omit comments you cannot work into the text, sometimes you need to add a point to clarify an idea or to define a troublesome concept. And once in a great while you might make an "It is interesting to note in this connection . . ." note. (See the Sample Research Paper, pages 368).

HOW DO YOU MAKE A LIST OF WORKS CITED? If our students have made their bibliography cards carefully, they should have no trouble at all constructing their Lists of Works Cited. All they will need to do is alphabetize their cards by author (or title where there is no author) and copy the information in list form. The author's name is written last name first to make the alphabetizing clearer. The rest of the entry is indented under that name. The MLA suggested format is summarized in the Models for Entries in List of Works Cited Student Guidelines. We might call attention especially to the recommended punctuation and order of items.

STUDENT GUIDELINES

Models for Entries in List of Works Cited

Please note: The models suggest a sequence appropriate for all entries. Naturally most entries will not contain the entire list.

A BOOK OF ANTHOLOGY
Author's Last Name, First Name. "Name of Article [if anthology]." *Title of Book.* Ed.[itor's] or Trans.[lator's] Name. 3rd ed. Place of Publication: Publisher [Unless published before 1900], Date. [Volume]: 3: [pages] 3–33. [Volume and pages included only when your reference is limited to a specific article or section, e.g., "Introduction."]

MAGAZINE OR JOURNAL ARTICLE
Author's Last Name, First Name. "Name of Article." *Title of Journal,* [Volume] 3 (1933): [pages] 30–33.

The List of Works Cited Student Guidelines offer an alphabetized list of works cited to demonstrate the MLA conventions for a wide variety of bibliographical entries our students may have cause to use.

STUDENT GUIDELINES

List of Works Cited

Article in Alphabetized Familiar Reference Work
(Note absence of publication information)
"Barber." *Funk & Wagnalls Standard Reference Encyclopedia.* 1967 ed.

Book with a Single Author
Dickens, Charles. *Great Expectations.* New York: Washington Square, 1963.

Anonymous Book or Pamphlet
Education Directory: Higher Education 1967–68. Part 3. Washington, D.C.: Government Printing Office, 1968.

Anonymous Newspaper Article
"Fossils Strengthen Evolutionary Link between Dinosaurs, Birds." *Richmond NewsLeader*, Aug. 14, 1986: A2.

Multiple Works of One Author
Hairston, Maxine. *Contemporary Composition.* 4th ed. Boston: Houghton Miflin, 1986.
– – –. *Successful Writing: A Rhetoric for Advanced Composition.* New York: Norton, 1981.

Work Preceding 1900. (Publisher Unnamed.)
Old South Leaflets. Eds. Directors of the Old South Works. 8 vols. Boston: 1896–1900.

Separately Published Work in Anthology
Shakespeare, William. *Hamlet. The Complete Works of William Shakespeare.* Eds. Hardin Craig and David Bevington. Glenview: Scott, Foresman, 1973. 899–943.

Reprinted Article
Turner, Perry. "What Killed Arthur Dimmesdale?" *Science 85* (Oct. 1985): 81–82. Rpt. in *Writing Effectively.* Beth S. Neman. New York: Harper, 1988.

continued
Work with More Than Three Editors
Williams, Tennessee. *The Glass Menagerie. An Introduction to Literature.* Eds.
Sylvan Barnet et al. 6th ed. Boston: Little, Brown, 1977. 889–949.

Article in Anthology
White, E. B. "The Distant Music of the Hounds." *The Second Tree from the
Corner.* New York: Harper, 1949. 131–33.

Preliminary Research Experiences

The research project we have been discussing is a complex venture in expository writing and research techniques that can challenge the abilities of college
freshmen, as well as college-bound juniors and seniors. Such a project need
not spring fully grown like Athena from her father's head, however. It can,
and I believe it should, be prepared for by preliminary programs presented
earlier in a student's career. If students lack this earlier preparation, a preliminary program can lead directly into the research paper itself.

EARLY EXPERIENCE WITH QUOTED MATERIAL. Research habits
are inculcated, for good or for evil, whenever students are given their first
"look it up" assignment, sometimes as early as the fifth or sixth grade, almost
always by the junior-high years. Those tedious "reports," great portions of
which have been inadvertently plagiarized from *Compton's Encyclopedia* or
World Book can be eliminated altogether—along with the deplorable habits
they breed—if we would insist right from the beginning upon documented
direct quotation.

Even the youngest and least able students are able to read up on a subject
in the classroom or school library and pick out the three (or four or five)
sentences they find most interesting or the points they see as most important.
They can copy down these sentences from their books, magazines, or ency-
clopedias, carefully noting the source and, if available, the author. On the
day the "reports" are to be given, the students can read their sentences aloud,
telling the source of each, and conclude with a few words presenting their
own impressions or conclusions on their chosen subject. They should also be
prepared from their reading to answer questions from their classmates or to
discuss the subject informally with them.

Older or more experienced students, as they copy their sentences, can
learn to change the features that would make the passages difficult to understand out of context. They should, for instance, change an unclear "he" to
"George Washington" or an unclear "it" to "the aardvark" and eliminate
such unnecessary material as "As we mentioned earlier."

THE LIMITED RESEARCH PAPER. A limited research paper offers an intermediary research experience for the academically inclined; for the immature, the less able, and the nonacademically oriented, it presents an opportunity for the sort of intense thinking that is beneficial to all, but narrowed to a process within their scope. As the subject matter, we might propose a controversial topic of interest to the students and provide articles expressing divergent points of view. The articles could be from sports, auto, rock music, or more conventional magazines. Having read an article or two, the student could adopt a point of view: for example, a particular band or automobile is — or is not — effective. Using this judgment as a topic sentence, they are to write a persuasive paragraph or a brief essay, supporting their point of view with quotations from the article.

Within this truly narrowed scope, students can learn not only argument and support, but also the appropriate way to use quotations and how to document their sources. Somewhat more advanced students could also learn the more difficult skill of paraphrasing.

Limited Sources: Contained Thesis. In "The Beginning Research Paper," Carlisle Rast outlines a procedure for a somewhat more complex, but still well limited, research paper that might serve as a model for such papers (70–71). After teaching Robert Sherwood's *Abe Lincoln in Illinois*, Rast poses the question of the historical accuracy of Sherwood's interpretation of the various characters. Then assembling a collection of history books, he suggests that his students find out for themselves by checking what three historians have to say about a particular character.

The scope is thus narrowed to a well-defined topic, which is not only limited in itself, but which can easily be found by a quick check of the index of a book. Note cards and documentation are required, but limiting the research to three sources simplifies matters a great deal. And although the students are given the essential decision-making power, the format of their theses is predetermined. Besides being a truly meaningful culminating activity for the study of a literary work, such a project gives valuable research practice to those who will need these skills later on and a good intellectual workout to those for whom this will be their only research experience.

A SAMPLE RESEARCH PAPER

The following student paper was selected for inclusion because it exemplifies not only the development of a thesis and basic documentation common to all such papers, but also a number of the perplexing little points that often arise when we teach the research paper. For instance, the paper deals with the developmental problems of deriving a nonliterary paper from a literary work and of combining primary and secondary source material, as well as such documentation questions as how to credit secondarily quoted material, how to refer to a work that will be quoted frequently throughout, how to label precisely material derived from a large, diffuse source, and how to manage informational notes.

THE INFLUENCE OF THE BIBLE ON THE SLAVERY QUESTION

> The will of God prevails. No doubt, no doubt—
> Yet, in great contest, each side claims to act
> In strict accordance with the will of God.
> Both may, one must be wrong. (Benét 213)

During the Civil War the Bible became the South's main justification for slavery and the North's foremost weapon against the institution. Thus both sides claimed to act "in strict accordance with the will of God." This was entirely possible for them to do, in all sincerity. There are ample grounds in the Bible upon which to base either a violently anti-slavery or a strongly pro-slavery point of view, for the Bible is in some ways a very contradictory book. With differing interpretations, the Bible can be made to prove many viewpoints. Both of the opposing sides in the slavery controversy realized the effectiveness of the Bible and put it to constant use.

The Bible was the backbone of the Abolitionist cause. "Take away the Bible," William Lloyd Garrison said, "and our warfare with oppression and infidelity, intemperance and impurity, is removed—we have no authority to speak and no courage to act" (qtd. in Nelson, 177). The powerful leaders of the North were so thoroughly steeped in the Bible from the days of their childhood that it naturally had a large influence upon their lives. According to F. C. Stifler, "The great Lincoln was nurtured on the Bible as few men every have been" (42).[1] His actions on the slavery question, as on all important issues, were governed by his creed: "What doth the Lord require of thee, but to do justly, to love mercy, and to walk humbly with thy God" (Micah 6.8).

The spirit of John Brown, which legend tells us walked the night and could not rest until the last slave was free (Benét), was a direct product of the Bible, for this first and most ardent of the Abolitionists followed the Scriptures to the point of fanaticism. He studied the Bible with such zeal that his speech and writing acquired the flavor of the Old Testament. He was known throughout the land as a "Terrible Saint" or "God's angry man" (Madison 41, 43). Wendell Phillips, too, was influenced by the Holy Book. He believed that the Bible was the "final authority on human bondage"; he even went so far on these grounds as to curse the Constitution because it condoned slavery (Madison, 64). Phillips, like so many others of his time, used Bible language and imagery in the remarkable oratory of his Abolitionist

(cont'd)

(cont'd)
addresses. For example, this excerpt from his "Dangers from Slavery"
speech:

> Then the wicked will walk on every side for the vilest of men
> will be exalted, and America, become the mock and scorn and
> hissing of the nations, will go down to worse shame than was
> ever heaped upon Sodom; for the lust for wealth, land, and
> power, she will also have committed the crime against nature
> (Old SL 5:15).

Perhaps William Lloyd Garrison did more with the Bible to further his
cause than any other Abolitionist, both in his fiery speeches and in
the Liberator, his daring newspaper. Even his first anti-slavery address was marked by constant Biblical allusion:

> Thus saith the Lord God of the Africans, Let this people go, that
> they may serve me; I ask them to proclaim liberty to the cap-
> tives, and the opening of the prison to them that are bound;—
> to light up a flame of philanthropy that shall burn till all of
> Africa be redeemed from the night of moral death and the song
> of deliverance be heard throughout her borders (Old SL 8:10).

The power and force of the Old Testament were so much a part of
Garrison that many associated the two together. Bates likens him to
"a fiery Hebrew prophet" (454), and Wendell Phillips in his beautiful
eulogy said that Garrison was "Taught of God . . . God endowed, and
God-sent to arouse a nation" (Old SL 4:7). Thus, the influence of the
Bible was extended into the minds of the leaders of the Abolition
movement, and their voices carried it to the people.

There were many ways in which the people received the spirit of
Abolition, and in most of these the Bible played a major role. There
were monthly prayer meetings. Songbooks and hymnals filled with
Biblical phraseology appeared by the score. Time and time again the
techniques of a religious revival and a Fourth of July rally were inter-
mingled (Nelson 176). Abolitionist propaganda was also spread
through poetry and novels, and again the Bible influence was very
apparent. The most stirring novel of the era, Uncle Tom's Cabin, was
written by Harriet Beecher Stowe, members of whose family had been
ministers for generations, and who, consequently, was brought up on
the Bible.[2] The famous New England poets, who lashed out so strongly
against slavery, did so with an enormous fund of Scriptural knowledge
as background. Whittier, for example, according to Nelson, "wrote biblically as naturally as he breathed." In 285 of his poems are 816 passages drawn from the Bible (176). For instance, as the controversy
was coming to a head, he wrote:

(cont'd)

> He flung aside his silver flute,
> Snatched up Isaiah's stormy lyre,
> Loosened old anger spent and mute,
> Startled the iron string with fire (qtd. in Nelson 176).

Lesser poets, too, drew from this unending source:

> Though hearts be torn asunder,
> For freedom we will fight:
> Our blood may seal the victory
> But God will shield the right![3]

The publication that most aroused the ire of the pro-slavery enthusiasts and the admiration of the Abolitionists was William Lloyd
Garrison's Liberator. It was a newspaper composed of a series of anti-
slavery essays and poems. Throughout there are many Bible references and some of the writing style is reminiscent of the Hebrew Bible. The prose is interspersed with poetry, most of which has more
strength than style:

> God is a God of mercy, and would see
> The prison-doors unbarr'd—the bondmen free!
> He is a God of truth, with purer eyes
> Than to behold the oppressor's sacrifice![4]

Thus by words and actions the Abolitionist movement advanced in the
North with the Bible as the cornerstone of the whole effort.

Until so much anti-slavery sentiment had been aroused in the
North, the Southerners had looked upon slavery as a necessary evil.
They condoned it because they believed it an economic necessity, but
were mildly apologetic toward the institution on moral grounds. There
was, however, a widespread belief that it was somehow good for the
slaves. The Reverend Phillip Schaff considered slavery "a wholesome
training school for the Negro—taking him from the lowest state of
heathenism and barbarism to some degree of Christian civilization"
(qtd. in Cole 256). There was also a feeling that God had willed the
superiority of the white race. After much reflection, Alexander Stevens
came to this conclusion. He said:

> A proper subordination of the inferior to the superior race was
> the natural and normal condition of the former in relation to
> the latter. . . . The assignment of that position in the struc-
> ture of society to the African race amongst us was the best for
> both races and in accordance with the ordinance of the Cre-
> ator. (199)

More often, however, this belief was confined to a much vaguer feeling
as expressed by Benét in his description of Mary-Lou Wingate:

(cont'd)

(cont'd)

> In heaven, of course, we should all be equal,
> But until we came to that golden sequel,
> Gentility must keep to gentility
> Where God and breeding had made things stable,
> While the rest of the cosmos deserved civility
> But dined in its boots at the second-table. (162)

Perhaps the South would have continued to apologize for slavery, but for the denunciations of the Abolitionists; for few had ever before considered it in the light of a "scriptural blessing," as historian Lloyd terms it (164). But after the severe attacks of Garrison and the others, the South, on the defensive, thoroughly investigated the matter.

Elaborate proofs were prepared justifying slavery on Biblical grounds. These were completed by intensive research and were intricately planned. The Old Testament justification of slavery fell into two principal arguments. The first: that from the beginning the Negro race had been condemned to servitude; and the second: that God Himself had expressly sanctioned the institution of slavery. The proof of the first argument was found in Noah's angry prophecy to Canaan, Ham's son:

> Cursed be Canaan: a servant of servants shall he be unto his brethren (Genesis 11.25–28).

Because legend tells that Ham was the founder of the dark races, this point became quite influential. Even Benét's Bible-reading slave-trader used this as his excuse for his infamous work. The poem reads:

> He touched the Bible. "And it's down there, Mister,
> Down there in black and white—the sons of Ham—
> Bondservants—sweat of their brows." His voice trailed off
> Into texts. "I tell you, Mister," he said fiercely,
> "The pay's good pay, but it's the Lord's work, too.
> We're spreading the Lord's seed—spreading his seed—" (15).

The second argument was put into a syllogism by Arthur Young Lloyd:

- Whatever God has sanctioned among any people cannot be in itself a sin.
- God did expressly sanction slavery among the Hebrews.
- Therefore, slavery cannot be in itself a sin (189).

All that was needed to complete the argument was concrete Biblical evidence of the two premises. Passages were found and pointed out in detail by the Southern clergy. Several quotations were always cited proving the existence of slavery in patriarchal times. Among the ones most often quoted were the commandment to Abraham concerning circumcision, which particularly specifies, "he that is bought with thy money" (Genesis 6:9), and the advice of the angel to Hagar, Sarah's runaway servant: "Return to thy mistress and submit thyself under

(cont'd)

her hands" (Genesis 11:13). The complicated proofs continued by placing emphasis on the Mosaic law. Frequently stated were the long passages regulating the conduct toward "bondservants" (Leviticus 25:44–46; Exodus 21:2–6, 20–21). But perhaps repeated with most regularity was this one quotation, which stressed the property idea:

> And ye shall take them for a possession; they shall be your bondsmen forever: but over your brethren, the children of Israel, ye shall not rule one over another with rigor. (Leviticus 25.42–43)

Thus, with no mention of the later sections of the Hebrew Bible, the arguments for the Old Testament justification of slavery were complete. Now firmly convinced that slavery was consistent with the will of God, the South sent out its challenge: "You cannot abolish slavery, for God is pledged to sustain it!"

The North accepted the challenge and answered the South's every argument with clear-cut logic. Their first point was that the pro-slavery evidence pertaining to the Mosaic law was really inconclusive because it related exclusively to the "regulation of the Hebrew social system" (Drisler 3). William Jay said, "It is wholly immaterial whether the Jews held slaves or not, since it is admitted by all that if they did, they acted by virtue of a special and express permission from God, while it is equally admitted that no such permission has been given to us" (626). Several technical denials were made to the "Cursed be Canaan" argument. It was pointed out that there is no reason to believe that Noah's curse extended to the other children of Ham (Drisler 3). Furthermore, the Hebrew Bible speaks of a vast Canaanite family in which there were both Negroes and whites (Gasparin 104).

The North's most conclusive arguments, however, were not defensive. In the later sections of the Bible there are many passages which actually forbid slavery; but even within the five books of Moses several quotations may be found which prohibit slavery and slave trade as well. Among these are:

> And he that stealeth a man and selleth him or if he be found in his hand, he shall surely be put to death. (Exodus 21.16)

and

> Thou shalt not deliver unto his master a bondman that is escaped from his master unto thee. (Deuteronomy 23.16–17)

The prophets were particularly outspoken on the subject. "Woe unto him . . . that useth his neighbor's services without wages," Jeremiah wrote (22:13). And all through the Bible, time and time again, the principles of freedom and equality are stressed:

> Have we not all one father? Hath not one God created us? (Malachi 18.8)

(cont'd)

(cont'd)

Thus the North argued that there is little to be gained in following literally all of the ancient laws set down in the Bible for a specific people in a particular set of circumstances, but that the ideas expounded in the Scriptures are just and right.

The Bible thus proved to be an excellent weapon, not only because of its variety in interpretations, but because of its widespread appeal. As we have seen, the Bible arguments influenced all men from the very lowliest to the greatest leaders of the time in both sections of our country. As for the right of the matter, from our modern perspective, the Northern Biblical arguments would seem to have had the clear logical and moral superiority; and, as we know, they prevailed.

NOTES

1. Stifler cites an interesting conversation that Lincoln once had with an agnostic friend: "You are wrong, Mr. Speed; take all of this book on reason that you can and the rest on faith, and you will, I am sure, live and die a happier and better man" (42).

2. From an autobiographic passage by Harriet Beecher Stowe (qtd. in Nelson 178).

3. Lucy Larcom, "The Nineteenth of April" (Bugle Echoes 38).

4. "The Salvation," stanzas 10, 12. The Liberator, Jan. 1, 1832 (Old SL 4:6).

LIST OF WORKS CITED

Primary Sources

Benét, Stephen Vincent. John Brown's Body. Garden City, N.Y.: Doubleday, 1928.

Holy Bible. Authorized King James Version. Cleveland: World Publishing Company, 1955.

Bugle Echoes: A Collection of Poems of the Civil War, Both Northern and Southern. Ed. Francis F. Browne. New York, 1886.

Drisler, Henry. Criticism of John H. Hopkin's "Bible View of Slavery." New York, 1863.

Gasparin, Agenor Etienne. The Uprising of a Great People. New York, 1862.

Jay, William. Miscellaneous Writings on Slavery. Boston, 1853.

Old South Leaflets. Eds. Directors of the Old South Work. Boston: 1896–1908.

Stephens, Alexander H. Recollections of Alexander H. Stephens. Ed. Myrta Lockett Avary. New York: Doubleday, 1910.

Secondary Sources

Bates, Ernest Sutherland. American Faith. New York: Norton, 1940.

Cole, Arthur Charles. A History of American Life: The Irrepressible Conflict, 1850–1865. Vol. 7. New York: Macmillan, 1934.

(cont'd)

Lloyd, Arthur Young. <u>The Slavery Controversy</u>. Chapel Hill: U of N. Carolina P. 1939.

Madison, Charles A. <u>Critics and Crusaders</u>. New York: Holt, 1947.

Nelson, Lawrence Emerson. <u>Our Roving Bible</u>. New York: Abington-Cokesbury, 1945.

Stifler, Francis Carr. <u>The Bible Speaks</u>. New York: Duell, Sloan & Pierce, 1946.

IDEAS FOR DISCUSSION OR ESSAY

1. Discussion of teaching the research paper brings to the fore the painful subject of plagiarism. Bearing in mind that to bring up the topic with our students before there has been any violation will appear to signal a lack of trust, but that failing to indicate our feelings to our students ahead of time will be considered a breach of fairness should violations occur, how do you think the problem should be handled? Should we accept the teaching of the research paper as an opportunity to help guide our students toward standards of honesty? Or should we hope for the best and treat any deliberate plagiarism that might arise as a very private matter?

2. Discuss the comparative merits of life-centered and academically oriented research papers.

3. Do you find the student paper included here overdocumented? If you do, do you feel that it is nevertheless better to have too many source indicators than not enough, especially in the paper of an inexperienced student? Or would you suggest that she make some changes in her use of her sources? How?

4. According to the text, when a student research paper fails, the problem is likely to be faulty notetaking or faulty use of sources to support the points. The following two exercise simulations provide practice in quoting and paraphrasing and in exercising rhetorical judgment. Do them yourself and give your evaluation of them.

   a. To practice the technique of quoting effectively, let's say that you are working on a passage about the ancient Etruscan attitude toward death for a research paper. Quote the following note card—or portion of it—as you would for such a passage. Follow the quotation with the parenthetical reference: (466). Remember to identify your author and be sure to introduce your quotation with a statement of your own.

   b. To try out the strategy of paraphrasing, rewrite the Etruscan passage for the same supposed paper by paraphrasing the material (or a portion of it). In order to paraphrase, restate the author's point in other words. If you need to use any of the original phrasing, be sure to enclose those portions in quotation marks. Ordinarily, you will be introducing your

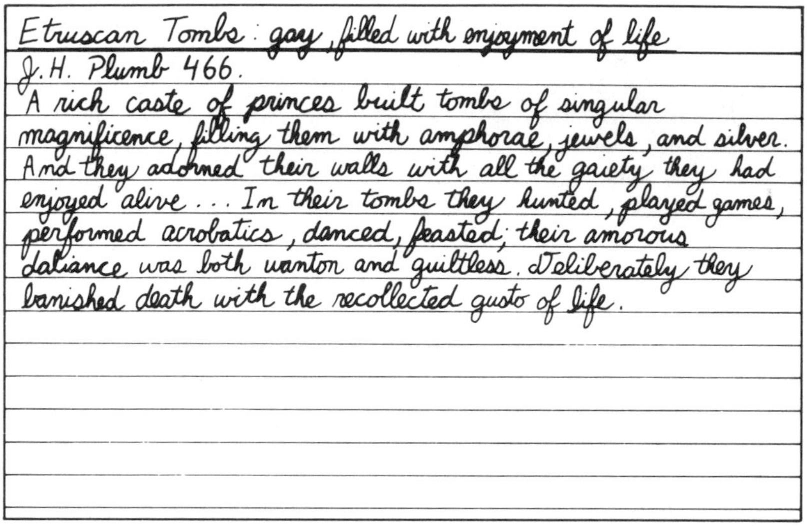

Etruscan Tombs : gay, filled with enjoyment of life
J. H. Plumb 466.
"A rich caste of princes built tombs of singular
magnificence, filling them with amphorae, jewels, and silver.
And they adorned their walls with all the gaiety they had
enjoyed alive . . . In their tombs they hunted, played games,
performed acrobatics, danced, feasted; their amorous
dalliance was both wanton and guiltless. Deliberately they
banished death with the recollected gusto of life.

Figure 9–8.

material with such phrases as "The author said *that.* . . ." (See examples on page 345.) Remember to include the parenthetical reference: (466).

   c. Which version of your Etruscan passage (the quoted or the paraphrased one) do you think is most effective? Why? Would you prefer a mixed version combining both quotation and paraphrase?

5. This final exercise provides the opportunity to practice putting together a typical research paper segment.

   Imagine that you have collected the following note cards from 1970s magazine articles for a section of your research paper on American fads of the seventies. Write a paragraph making use of the information they contain. You may quote and/or paraphrase or omit material as you choose (see p. 353). Be sure to make your own points and mention the authors by name. You might take the following as your topic sentence:

   Topic Sentence: In the seventies fads were all-pervasive, self-preoccupied, and sometimes less than wholesome.

6. Look into the research or the expert commentary on any topic bearing on the teaching of composition which has intrigued your interest in the discussion thus far or into the material which will be covered later in the course on a related subject that interests you; then write a scholarly research paper following the procedures outlined in this chapter.

Interest in partic. fad is short-lived
Tucker 000.
Today, the question often is not, "What do you do?" but "What are you into?" Macramé one week, astrology the next, health food, philosophy, history, jogging, movies, EST — we fly from "commitment" to "commitment" like bees among flowers because it is easier to buy a new toy than to repair an old one.

Figure 9–9.

The "Me" Fad
Goodman 470.
The new therapies — from the isolation tank on — offer us ways to "get into ourselves." Those who aren't "doing their own thing" or "finding themselves" are "getting in touch with their feelings."... The range of the new therapies is characterized by a frenzied search inward.

Figure 9–10.

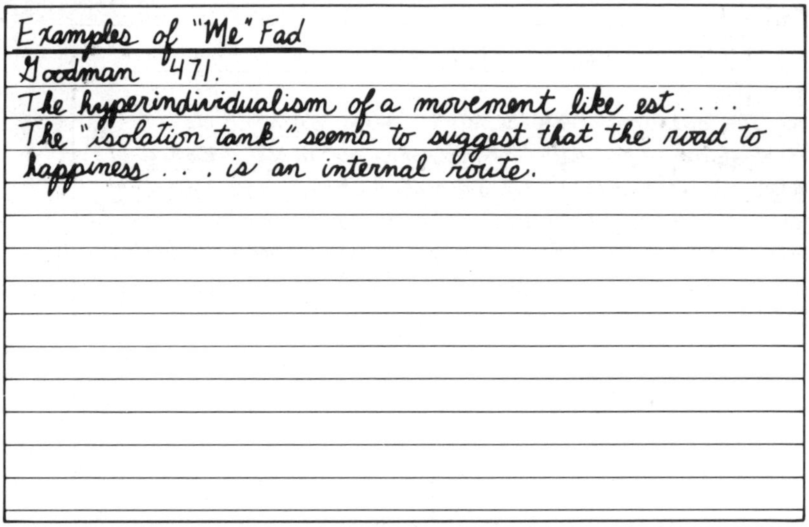

Examples of "Me" Fad
Goodman '471.
The hyperindividualism of a movement like est. . . .
The "isolation tank" seems to suggest that the road to
happiness . . . is an internal route.

Figure 9–11.

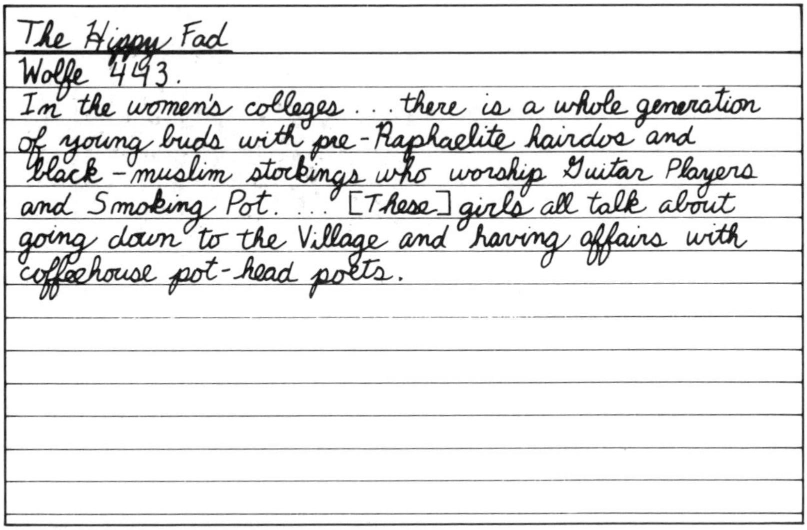

The Hippy Fad
Wolfe 4193.
In the women's colleges . . . there is a whole generation
of young buds with pre-Raphaelite hairdos and
black-muslim stockings who worship Guitar Players
and Smoking Pot. . . . [These] girls all talk about
going down to the Village and having affairs with
coffeehouse pot-head poets.

Figure 9–12.

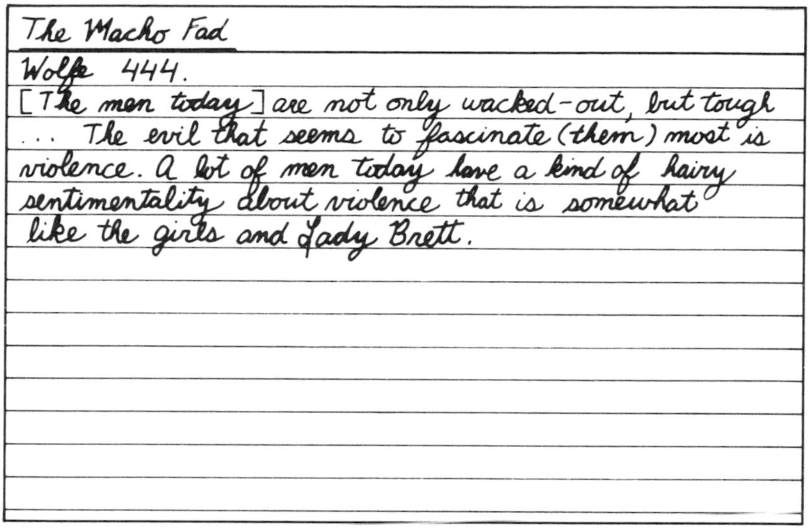

The Macho Fad

Wolfe 444.

[The men today] are not only wacked-out, but tough ... The evil that seems to fascinate (them) most is violence. A lot of men today love a kind of hairy sentimentality about violence that is somewhat like the girls and Lady Brett.

Figure 9–13.

NOTES

The part opening epigraph is from Linda Flowers, "Negotiating Academic Discourse," *Reading-to-Write Report* No. 10, Technical Report no. 29, (Berkeley: Center for the Study of Writing at U of California at Berkeley and Carnegie Mellon U).

1. Richard L. Larson, " 'The Research Paper' in the Writing Course: A Non-Form of Writing," *CE* 44 (1982): 811–16.

2. For arguments supporting restricting student academic writing for political and social reasons, see, for example, a number of the essays in *Profession 88*, Phyllis Franklin, ed. (New York: MLA, 1988) and, more recently, Patricia Bizzell, "Beyond Anti-Foundationalism to Rhetorical Authority: Problems Defining 'Cultural Literacy'," 52 *CE* (1990): 661–82. For an impassioned refutation of these views, see Sandra Stotsky, "Writing as Moral and Civic Thinking," 54 *CE* (1992): 794–808, especially page 797.

3. Peter Elbow, "Reflections on Academic Discourse: How it Relates to Freshmen and Colleagues," *CE* 53 (1991): 135.

See also Mike Rose, "Remedial Writing Courses: A Critique and a Proposal," *CE* 45 (1983): 110, where he suggests that "students must, early on, begin wrestling with academically oriented topics that help them develop into more critical thinkers, that provide them with some of the tools of the examined life, and that, practically, will assist them in the courses they take." And see Linda Flower, "Negotiating Academic Discourse."

4. Glen A. Love and Michael Payne, "The Research Paper: Does it Belong in High School?" *EJ* 56 (1967): 739.

5. Thomas Taylor, "Let's Get Rid of Research Papers," *EJ* 54 (1965): 126–27; and James Haman, quoted in "What the Colleges Expect: A Report of the NCTE Committee on High School-College Articulation," *EJ* 50 (1961). See also Robert M. Gorrell, "Freshman Composition," in *The College of Teaching English*, ed. John C.

Gerber (New York: Appleton, 1965): 108–9; and Beth Neman, "A Handbook for the Teaching of the Research Paper," *EJ* 56 (1967): 262.

6. Ollie T. Dickie, "Turning the First Stone of Research," *EJ* 43 (1959): 42.

7. Edna McQuire, "College Freshmen on Writing in High School," *EJ* 51 (1962): 256; Brooke Neilson, "Writing as a Second Language: Psycholingiustic Processes in Composing," Diss., U of California at San Diego, 1979.

8. For the details of the procedure of this course, see Marilyn Schauer Samuels' article "A Mini-Course in the Research Paper," *CE* 38 (1976): 189–93.

9. Frederick Schepman quoted in Hans P. Guth, *Words and Ideas: A Handbook for College Writing* (Belmont: Wadsworth, 1969): 293.

10. Mary Ellen Grasso, "The Research Paper: Life Centered," *CE* 40 (1978): 83–86. See also Colleen Marshall, "A System for Teaching College Freshmen to Write a Research Paper," *CE* 40 (1978): 87–89; and Anne C. Coon, "Using Ethical Questions to Develop Autonomy in Student Researchers," *CCC* 40 (Feb 1989): 85–89.

11. Alice S. Horning, "Advising Undecided Students through Research Writing," *CCC* 42 (1991): 75–79. For a similar project, see Elaine Blatt and Jane Bergman, "Career Research—A Multi-Discipline Approach," *Community College Frontiers* 7 (1978): 15–19.

12. W. Keith Krause, *Murder, Mischief, and Mayhem: A Process for Creative Research Papers* (Urbana: NCTE, 1978); Susan Glick, from a private letter, September 1979. For more advanced students, the six chapters of Part III of Marilyn Lutzker's *Research Projects for College Students: What to Write Across the Curriculum* (Westport: Greenwood, 1988) provide a wide variety of ideas for topics employing primary source material, as well as valuable information on how students can locate that material.

13. Carlisle L. Rast, "The Beginning Research Paper," *EJ* 50 (1961): 469–71.

14. Toni-Lee Capossela, "Students as Sociolinguists: Getting Real Research from Freshman Writers," *CCC* 42 (1991): 75–79. Peter Farb's *Word Play: What Happens When People Talk* (New York: Knopf, 1974) is a scholarly book written in lay language and filled with fascinating and controversial ideas about the interplay of language and human behavior.

15. Or, if we ourselves have special knowledge of another discipline, we might take the research project as an opportunity to share our interest with our students. Sandy Johnson, for instance, uses her special knowledge of the arts to direct a research project on American artists, architects, and composers, which culminates in audio and visual oral reports in addition to research papers. "Sight, Sound and the Research Paper," *EJ* 58 (1969): 1031–63.

16. Carolyn Boiarsky of Peoria Community College teaches her students to search their summary cards (#7) and personal comments (#8) for ideas for topic sentences once they begin to write.

17. For another, somewhat different exercise in interpretation, see David Kerner, "Jigsaw Puzzle in Exposition," *Writing Exercises from "The Exercise Exchange,"* ed. Littleton Long (Urbana: NCTE, 1976), 124–28.

18. Katherine Burton, "Citing Borrowed Material," in *Writing Exercises*, 122.

19. The social and biological sciences, for the most part, use the American Psychological Association (APA) system of documentation, and the physical sciences use numerical systems such as that of the American Chemical Society (ACS). Complete style guides are available for each of these. Condensed versions for students may be found in my *Writing Effectively*. When doing interdisciplinary papers, it is wise to use the documentation system favored by that discipline.

□ □ □ **10**

Teaching the Rhetorical Analysis

"I am convinced that reading, speaking
and writing are part of a whole. Learning to read without involvement with
writing and speaking is like learning music without ever singing or playing. It
can be done. But it won't be done well.
And it won't be any fun."
— William Raspberry

□ □ □

The rhetorical analysis (also called *critical* analysis or *literary* analysis)[1] is a
specialized form of expository writing, just as is the research paper, discussed
in Chapter 9. It is specialized both in subject matter, which is limited to
works of literature or other art forms, and in approach, which is almost exclusively analytical and interpretative. It is, nevertheless, important to remind
our students that every rhetorical analysis is an expository essay, and everything they have learned about expository writing holds true for it as well.

THE NATURE OF RHETORICAL ANALYSES

In defining the rhetorical analysis, we will probably first have to dispel a
misconception or two. Thus, we may need to insist that a rhetorical analysis
(or book report, as it is known in many schools) is *not* a plot summary. Nor
is a rhetorical analysis simply an evaluation ("I liked it because it was interesting"; "To me, Faulkner is a pretty good writer"). No. What our students
should expect to write, rather, is an interpretation of the work (or works).
And they should expect to do so in terms of the way the author chooses to
get his or her meaning across.

The Interpretative Essence

We need to teach that interpretation is expected whatever kind of literature or art our students deal with and whatever the approach they select or are assigned, for rhetorical analysis assignments come in many varieties. Students may be surprised to learn, for example, that a rhetorical analysis would be expected from all of the following assignments:

- Write a book report on the novel you have just read.
- Critically analyze Coleridge's "The Rhyme of the Ancient Mariner."
- Tell how Kate Chopin's "The Story of an Hour" fits in with contemporary feminist concepts.
- Comment on Shakespeare's use of imagery in *Macbeth*.
- Write a paper demonstrating just how effectively you believe George Will is in getting across his point in his latest essay.
- Compare Wright's treatment of his protagonist in *Native Son* with Ellison's in *Invisible Man*.

Whatever the assignment, the heart of our students' rhetorical analyses will be their answer to the two major analytical questions:

1. What is the author trying to say—or make the reader feel or understand? [meaning]
2. How does he or she go about saying it? [method]

The emphasis students place on their answer to each of these questions will vary, but the presence of both is unavoidable, for they are the essence of rhetorical analysis.

The Reading–Writing Connection

How are our students to find their answer to these questions? By thoughtfully reading the work. In writing their analyses they will almost precisely reverse their reading and interpretative processes.

The rhetorical analysis is a particularly useful kind of writing for our students to learn because, more than any other, it links writing with reading and thus has a special import for a whole-language approach to teaching English.

WHOLE LANGUAGE TEACHING: COMBINED CURRICULUM. All the components of the language arts curriculum become more significant when we teach them from a whole language approach. Pragmatic necessity motivates vocabulary work based on reading assignments, and spelling work based on vocabulary work, and grammar and usage that come out of writing problems—from writing assignments related to student reading. Reading and writing form a particularly happy marriage, for they are actually two sides of the same coin. Everything we read was once written; and no significance attaches to something written until it is read.

In earlier chapters I suggest referring students to professionally written essays so that through reading essays, stories, and poems from the point of view of their craftsmanship, students become more skilled in writing these genres (see Chapters 11 and 12 for a discussion of teaching students to write stories and poems). The principle also works well in reverse. In trying to write essays, stories, and poems, students develop understandings of the writer's craft and thereby develop their reading comprehension skills. Thus before we can teach our students how to write rhetorical analyses, we need to teach ways to respond to literature.

READING-RESPONSE PEDAGOGY. Whenever we teach a work of literature, we must first consider our student readers. As Louise Rosenblatt and other theorists have demonstrated, reading is necessarily an interactive transaction between reader and text; meaning is created at the point where the words of the text interact with the experience the reader brings to it.[2] And here is where we too must begin.

When we ask our students for their reactions to the reading we have assigned or that we have done orally together, and we take these reactions seriously in class discussion, encouraging students to follow their private lines of thought and to debate their ideas with one another, we not only promote a healthy interaction of reader and reading matter, but we also foster the self-confidence that leads to deeper thought. There is great value in the response papers that come out of such activity.[3] Journal writing assignments provide much the same opportunity. And in no literature lesson should we ignore personal reader response.

But if we are going to ask our students to write analytically, they will have to begin to think like authors themselves. Those who only see a rhetorical work as a vehicle for the reader's pleasure and knowledge must also learn to understand that it is also a medium of communication between author and reader.

READING TO FIND THE AUTHOR'S PURPOSE. Our students will need to realize that a work of literature is a creation of an author for a particular reason or set of reasons. In it the author offers, and sometimes even urges, his or her point of view on the subject at hand. Once students learn to read literature in this way, they can view their own writing as a means of communicating *their* ideas. The method through which this understanding can take place is called "close reading," a procedure that should be at the heart of a combined language-arts program.

Close reading involves a concentrated, phrase-by-phrase reading of a passage or a work in a concerted effort to discover what the author is trying to say and how he or she goes about saying it. We need to train our students to ask themselves these questions again and again as they go along.

Interpretive Validity. Teaching students to read for the author's purpose or meaning should in *no* way imply that writing has a single meaning that we teachers know and our students don't. There are, of course, a variety of valid interpretations for every work, and we should be sure our students are aware that we know this to be true. We should, indeed, value and explore each idea our students seriously offer. But we should also help them learn to test their ideas for validity. For though all interpretations should be respected, they are not equally valid.

I have found the following is a good rule of thumb for determining the validity of an interpretation:

> The validity of any interpretation is determined by the proportion of elements within the work that it takes into account—and the number of elements that do not fit the theory.

This concept is not immediately easy for all students to understand; but once they catch on, they are delighted with it. Working them through an example makes it clear. For instance, if students have formed a tentative interpretation of Robert Browning's "My Last Duchess" centered on the Duchess's unfaithfulness, they might weigh it by this rule to determine its validity. In doing so, they would discover that such a theory fits well with the intent of the Duke's argument, and it would account for the Duke's anger. But, on the other hand, they would note that it does not conform to his description of her childlike ways, nor to her close supervision and confinement implied in the poem. And it leaves out completely the telling details Browning plants that point to the Duke's obsessive possessiveness, such as those contained in the lines: "No one puts aside the curtain I have drawn for you but I" and

> . . . Notice Neptune though,
> Taming a seahorse, thought a rarity,
> Which Claus of Innsbruck cast in bronze for me.

Weighing their tentative interpretation in this way should develop enough of the students' skepticism to make them reexamine the Duke's character and motives, and perhaps decide to craft a theory that takes more elements of the poem into account and leaves fewer out. This process gives students a method for working out their own interpretations with their classmates; it provides them with a measuring tool for testing out the interpretations they come up with; and it confers a certain security—the security of believing that our teacherly judgments are not wholly arbitrary and, at the same time, offering a technique through which they can challenge these judgments.[4]

Freedom of Response. Reading to discover what an author is trying to communicate in no way negates a student's own response; rather it focuses it. We need to make it clear that in suggesting that students try to understand their author's meaning, we are not asking them to identify with the author, nor to accept what that author has written as true. Once students figure out for themselves what the author is saying, they are free to react to it however they choose. In fact, one of the most significant benefits of close reading is the healthy skepticism it tends to nourish in our students.

TEACHING CLOSE READING

Close reading begins with a concentrated phrase-by-phrase reading of a passage or a work. We can train our students to read closely by doing it aloud together with them. They may also want to take notes as they go along. Elaine Maimon suggests that they copy down selected passages in order to "get inside the author's rhythms and style."[5] In any case, they should ask about or look up any word or reference they don't fully comprehend, and be sure that they understand it clearly before they are ready to pull their impressions together.

Purpose: To Become Conscious of the Author.

The purpose of close reading is not only to understand the author's meaning fully. It is also to discover what the author does to affect a reader's thinking and emotions. Close readers need to consider the rhetorical work as a "presentation of an author's way of looking at life," as Cleanth Brooks and his colleagues put it, and to recognize that their job is to discover what way of "looking at life" is being presented.[6] To do so, they must ask themselves continually: What is the author attempting here? Why would the author include this passage? Why did the author create this effect?

READING LITERALLY.   Reading for the author's intent does not mean that students should search their imaginations for hidden meanings and arcane symbolisms as they sometimes believe. We need to convince them that, actually, quite the contrary is true—at least at the start. Close reading is first of all a reading for *literal* meaning.

Our students should ask themselves the following questions as they read. What do the words really say? What do they explicitly mean? What does the syntax literally convey? Only after they have established the literal meaning, should they begin to think about hidden themes or symbolic significance. Of course, readers must delve beneath the surface in order to discover what the author is trying to get at, but we can reassure them that all the clues they need to construct a valid interpretation are present right there in the words themselves.

ANTENNAE.   Our task is to show our students how to look for the clues. As we read together, we should continually be asking questions of our students, calling their attention to emerging patterns, encouraging them to discover some for themselves. How can they learn to do these things?

We might tell them that they have to develop the sensitivity of their antennae! Strangely enough, as bizarre as this image seems, students of all ages seem to be delighted with it. What is more, they find this image of themselves as readers with long antennae sprouting from their heads and groping about for insight surprisingly useful.

My notion is that the large, red lightbulbs on the ends of my students' antennae light up when they come across anything in their reading that seems odd or out of place or, paradoxically, patterned or familiar. Thus, their antennae will flash (and often their hands will go up) when they discover such strange similes, so different from what one expects, as "like a patient etherized upon a table" in Eliot's ". . . Prufrock," and also when they find images, ideas, or phrases, such as "There will be time" from the same poem, repeated until they become expected, single colored threads patterning the tapestry. Repetition, parallels, metaphors, intriguing openings, interesting conclusions—anything that calls attention to itself as out of the ordinary should light up the antennae bulbs and signal such questions as:

- I wonder why the author put that there? Used that construction? Emphasized that point?
- How does this point fit into the work as a whole? Into the author's purpose as a whole?

Purpose: To Become Conscious of Their Own Reactions

Our students will also need to develop a sensitivity to their own reactions as they read and a habit of looking for the author's purpose behind an unusual personal response:

- Why do I respond to that situation, character, image, or whatever in that way?
- Does the author intend me to feel this way?
- What did she do to provoke this response?"

RECIPROCAL INTERPRETATION. By exploring in this way the methods an author uses to influence a reader's relationship with the material, our students should be able to arrive at a tentative interpretation of the work. Close reading is thus double-edged. Our students study the author's methods to understand the meaning; and once they have established a tentative meaning, they look for methods that will support or argue for their interpretation of it. The Close Reading Student Guidelines should be helpful in both searches.

STUDENT GUIDELINES

Close Reading

1. *Clues from the overall structure.* Start with the overall structure. How is the work organized? What are the beginning, middle, and end? How does the gross structure contribute to the creation of the overall impression you have decided is the author's purpose?
2. *Clues from the individual parts.* Examine the work part by part. Which parts do you see as most important in contributing to the author's purpose? How do they do so? How do they fit into the whole? Are there portions that do not seem to contribute to, or perhaps seem even to contradict, your interpretation? Can the discrepancies be reconciled? If not, can your interpretation be adjusted to fit the new elements?
3. *Clues from substructures, motifs, patterns.* Within the overall structure, are there any secondary structures or motifs? Are there unusual elements within the work, ideas or stylistic constructions that catch your attention? Why do you think the author included them? Do they form a pattern? How do they contribute to the author's purpose? To your interpretation?

PREPARING STUDENTS TO WRITE THEIR RHETORICAL ANALYSES

First the reading; and then the writing. By the time our students are ready to write their first rhetorical analyses, chances are they have already successfully written other expository essays. The best way to help them over their new project jitters is to remind them of this fact and to assure them that since analyses are also expository papers, they already know, in general, how to structure them.

Finding Their Organizing Idea

The analysis, like all expository essays, is best structured about a controlling idea. Once our students have a good notion of their author's point or theme, they are well on their way to the working thesis of their own paper. The organizing idea in almost all rhetorical analyses includes, or at least touches on, the analyzed author's theme or point. On the other hand, the two are far from identical. Students are often, understandably, confused on this issue, and so we must take care to teach them how to distinguish their author's purpose from their own.

SEPARATING AUTHOR'S PURPOSE FROM WRITER'S.   The distinction rests on the single significant structural difference between ordinary expository essays and rhetorical analyses. In the usual expository essay, writers express and support their own ideas. But rhetorical analyses are a special kind of expository essay; in them writers interpret, analyze, and comment upon the ideas of another author.

Students must realize that no matter how heartily they may agree with their author's view of life, their point can never be identical with their author's. The typical working thesis of a rhetorical analysis is basically interpretative. For example:

> In "Accepting the Unacceptable" Meg Greenfield persuasively argues that the United States' response to terrorism is not only ineffectual, but actually damaging.

By contrast, the following working thesis on the same topic would NOT do for a *rhetorical analysis* of Meg Greenfield's article, even though it might lead to a good enough essay on a similar subject:

> The United States' response to terrorism is not only ineffectual, but actually damaging.

The boxed Student Guidelines suggest some practical ways to help our students avoid such difficulties:

STUDENT GUIDELINES

How to Separate Your Author's Purpose
From Your Own

1. Get in the habit of speaking in terms of the author, "William Raspberry argues . . . ," "Lewis Thomas uses his Mahler symphony metaphor to . . . ," "Kate Chopin develops the character of Mrs. Mallard for. . . .t"
2. Keep close to the work itself. When you leave it to make comparisons with external experience or other works, be sure that your purpose remains interpretative.
3. Quotations can keep you on the track. Use them freely—though keep them brief. Document them appropriately.
   A well-chosen excerpt can supply irrefutable proof for the point you are making. Furthermore, if you include (in moderation) the words of an author who writes with wit and charm, you cannot help but enhance the effect of your own style.

Developing their Support

As with all expository essays, writers of rhetorical analyses must support their organizing ideas. They gather their support from their close reading. Writing a rhetorical analysis is the inverse of the close reading process. Interpreting is inductive. The reader assembles the evidence and finds a plausible interpretation that fits it. Expository writings—and rhetorical analyses *are* expository—on the other hand, are deductive: A writer begins with an organizing idea and supports it with appropriate evidence. In a rhetorical analysis, the writer begins with an interpretation of a rhetorical work and supports it with the evidence uncovered by close reading.

To argue that the author intends a particular meaning or effect, our students will have to figure out how the author tries to bring the reader to understand, experience, or (in the case of the essay) acquiesce in his or her meaning. All of our classroom work in each of the genres should help students develop the intellectual tools to do this figuring out; but when they are ready to write their first analyses, they may find some additional guidance useful. The boxed-Student Guidelines for Close Reading above can be equally useful in turning interpretative clues into support.

LOOKING FOR SPECIFIC SUPPORTING DETAILS. To make the general questions in the Student Guidelines even more useful, we should teach our students how to phrase them in terms of the specifics of the genre and the literary work they are considering. How is the conflict approached in each of the important scenes? What pattern of imagery do you see your author building through her use of such and such metaphors? How far are we supposed to trust what Huck, for instance, says—how much is meant to be taken as dramatic irony? For inexperienced students, we might even want to prepare a set of study questions specific to the assigned work. Analyses of this sort should yield sufficient material to support our students' organizing ideas effectively.

Helping Students Solve the Technical Problems

Two final remarks on stylistic conventions, which though minor are sometimes troublesome to our students.

USE PRESENT TENSE. First, rhetorical analyses, in order to prevent awkwardness, are conventionally written in the present tense. In most circumstances, therefore, "As Jane Austin writes in this passage" is preferable to "As Jane Austin wrote."

WHEN TO SUMMARIZE. The second troublesome convention is the matter of how much summarizing of the literary work students should include, how familiar with the work they should assume their readers to be.

We can suggest that a good rule to follow is to assume that their readers have read the work, but several years ago. Using this rule of thumb, they should summarize whatever material is necessary to make their points clear, but only as much as the demands of their own organizing idea and arguments require.

Students should find the boxed Guidelines on Rhetorical Analysis Conventions useful.

STUDENT GUIDELINES

The Conventions of Rhetorical Analysis

1. **Style for Authorial Inclusion**
   - It is conventional to use the present tense for rhetorical analysis. Write "Shakespeare *develops* his theme by . . ." not "Shakespeare *developed* his theme by. . . ."
   - It is conventional to credit the author with conscious manipulation of strategy as, for example: "Shakespeare develops his theme by. . . ."
   - And although you need not hesitate to say "I" where appropriate, your name standing as the author of the essay is usually sufficient identification for matters of opinion. Therefore, avoid writing "*I think* Shakespeare develops his theme by. . . ." And do not hesitate to write "Shakespeare develops his theme. . . ."

2. **Conventions for Summary**
   - *Always identify the work (or works) you will be analyzing by title and by author in your introduction.*
   - *In order to orient your readers, be sure to include somewhere early in your paper a brief summary of the basic points or plot of your work—if only a sentence or two in length.*
   - *Never introduce a point without giving enough background from the work to make the point comprehensible to your readers. Never attempt to explicate a passage without quoting the passage.*
   - *On the other hand, do not get caught up in retelling the story, in rearguing the article. Keep your attention focused upon your purpose of developing your own* rhetorical thesis.

TEACHING STUDENTS HOW TO INCLUDE
EVALUATIVE RESPONSES IN ANALYSES

The question of whether we should teach students to include a personal or evaluative response in their rhetorical analyses is a difficult one. On the one hand, there are strong arguments for us not to encourage this practice. Evaluative responses are not a traditional requirement for rhetorical analyses. Many inexperienced writers are uncomfortable including such comments, while others, who tend to confuse simple response writing, such as journal entries, with analyses, are baffled by what they consider subtle distinctions.

On the other hand, if we discourage these responses, we discourage thought. We want our students not simply to interpret what they read, but to react to their interpretations. Furthermore, even in introductory classes, we often have students with the skill to respond to their reading in rather sophisticated ways. And some could grow in their ability to write rhetorical analyses by learning to derive their evaluative responses from current critical theory. No single rule of thumb can provide a universal answer; but we can perhaps agree on separate approaches to meet the needs of our very diverse student populations.

Evaluative Strategies for Our Inexperienced Writers

Inexperienced or less skilled students need to know that evaluative comments are not required for a well-written rhetorical analysis. And, in fact, unnecessary personal evaluations can give a rhetorical essay a less than professional tone. Such comments as the vague "I liked it because it was interesting" or the obvious "I think Faulkner is a pretty good writer" are better left unsaid.

And yet an aptly observed and firmly based evaluative remark can make student analyses more effective and is an option they should consider if they have an opinion on the work that they feel they can support.

EVALUATIVE GUIDELINES. To help inexperienced writers structure evaluative responses within their rhetorical analyses, we might offer the following suggestions—but with the caution that though these rules are useful, they are not infallible:

- Do not mingle your evaluative comments with analysis and interpretation. The concluding paragraphs are an especially appropriate place for evaluative material.
- Base your evaluation firmly upon your analytical and interpretative findings.
- Evaluate the work on how well the author succeeds in doing what he or she has set out to do. To insure that your personal comments are appropriate to the genre, phrase them in terms of meeting the author's purpose.

It may be difficult for students to understand the difference between appropriate and inappropriate evaluative comments, but an example should make the point clear. We might suggest that in writing a rhetorical analysis of *The Scarlet Letter*, for instance, it would be appropriate to comment (if they believed it to be so) that Hawthorne could make a stronger symbolic statement with Pearl if she seemed more like a real little girl. On the other hand, it would not be conventional to the analysis genre to comment (no matter how truly) that they do not care for stories about Puritan life.

Critical Theory for Our More Sophisticated Students

Some of our students may not be satisfied simply to interpret a literary work. Once they discover the author's intended meaning, they may want to go on and use that meaning to make some statement of their own. Some of these students may be interested in social issues, deeply involved with feminism or the plight of the poor, for instance. Others may have a curiosity—or, at least, an arousable interest—in cultural history or the psychology or political motivation of authors or their characters. Surely, we want to encourage these students to pursue interests such as these. Critical theory can supply a method.

CRITICAL THEORY AND RHETORICAL ANALYSIS.   Strategies based on current critical theory offer an intriguing supplement to the techniques for writing rhetorical analyses already suggested. They would not, however, displace them. For ever since the dominance of the New Criticism movement, all rhetorical analysis begins with a close reading of the text to determine the author's intended meaning.[7] Determining the meaning authors intend and where they are coming from in working toward fulfilling their purpose is especially suited, it seems to me, to the various postmodern critical points of view. The essentially rhetorical approach of close reading and rhetorical analysis—"What's the author up to now?"—promotes the skeptical, "show me" reading that postmodern critics demand.

Furthermore, the rhetorical analytical process described in this chapter is arguably an all but indispensable complement to postmodern criticism. Starting out with whatever solidity the actual words of a text can provide should be particularly compelling in the face of the postmodern view of a secular world where there is no external Truth for author and reader to share, but only shifting sets of culturally or psychologically based premises—a view, as Lester Faigley explains where the "key assumption" is

> that there is nothing outside contingent discourses to which a discourse of values can be grounded—no eternal truths, no universal human experience, no universal human rights, no overriding narrative of human progress.[8]

But if to the postmodern reader no human author is capable of complete objectivity or complete truth (though I can't help thinking that only very naive readers *ever* had this expectation), then, more than ever, readers need to analyze critically what they read in the traditional "what is the author trying to say" fashion—if they are to make any use of the work at all. Once readers grasp the author's ideas, however tenuously, and ferret out the assumptions that underlie them, they will be able to make use of these ideas or dispute them according to the approach adopted and their own value system.

Thus, the rhetorical analytical process is a productive strategic component within a whole array of postmodern critical techniques. And, conversely, postmodern critical approaches can be a useful supplement to the rhetorical analytical strategies of our most able students. Such study will help them add to the traditional, "*What* is the author trying to say?" a further highly interesting query, "*Why* is the author trying to say it?"

CRITICAL THEORY AND PEDAGOGICAL STRATEGIES. Some of the currently popular theoretical approaches offer strategies that broaden readers' scope of analysis. Freudian criticism, for example, furnishes a psychoanalytical framework from which to probe the subconscious motivation of author or characters; Marxist criticism sets up an analytical structure based on class conflict and means of economic production to determine the empowering principles of the material economy and class structure of the society from which the author speaks; new historicism provides methods for determining the social interaction and perceptions of reality held by the culture from which—or about which—the author writes.

Other theoretical approaches supply means for determining if the value system of the author under study coincides with the reader's own. Feminist criticism, for instance, offers techniques for discovering if what an author is saying is based on assumptions of male dominance; Afro-American criticism provides strategies for determining if it is based on racist assumptions; Marxist criticism suggests strategies for isolating societal wrongs. All these offer bases for supporting an evaluation of a literary work and might be useful for our students to explore.[9]

CLASSROOM METHODS. There are two approaches we might use to encourage such exploration. One emphasizes what Gilbert Ryle calls *knowing that* and the other *knowing how*—though the difference is only in emphasis.[10] In following the *knowing that* approach, we would teach a unit on critical theory. To work with a *knowing how* emphasis, we would integrate background on critical theory into the reading/writing curriculum.

An Enrichment Unit for Gifted Scholars. A class of particularly able students might find a unit on critical theory challenging and intriguing. We might use a coordinated set of handouts or a textbook to provide a focus for a critical study. Charles Bressler's *Literary Criticism: An Introduction to Theory and Practice* (1994) is an intelligent, well-organized textbook that surveys critical theory from Plato to Derrida and explains it clearly enough for students to understand. Besides a highly selective bibliography, every chapter includes a sample student analytical essay with questions for discussion. We might also use the student essays to exemplify or model writing assignments for our own students.

A unit on critical theory could provide welcome enrichment for gifted students in a general classroom as well. While their classmates were still struggling with writing rhetorical analyses, we might give those who had already mastered the essential skills an opportunity to learn a variety of critical theories and to put this knowledge to use systematically in future assignments.

Integrating Critical Theory into Combined Language Arts Study. Alternatively, we might teach critical theory in conjunction with our work with literature and critical analysis. We could teach the various critical approaches as they seem appropriate to the works being read and written about. Rather than teaching our students a unit with its emphasis on *knowing that* certain philosophers have devised certain critical theories, we might help them in *knowing how* to use such theories as they do their close reading and draft their rhetorical analyses.

Knowledge of current critical theories would provide our more able students with a means to channel their evaluative responses. Students could use the theoretical approach they favored to support a positive evaluation of their interpretation of a work or to underpin a negative evaluation, showing why the author is mistaken, wrongheaded, or duped. If students wished, they might use their personal evaluation as a springboard for discussion of social issues. They might, for instance, use a critical approach to disagree with their author's point of view in such a way as to promote their own social agenda — say, feminist, socialist, anti-racist. . . . Or, having acknowledged the author's intentions, students might analyze the work instead as evidence for the value system and thought of its time and place.

Teaching the Review, An Evaluative Rhetorical Analysis

A review (or *critique* as it is sometimes called) is a rhetorical analysis whose purpose is to provide the reader with a guide to the book, essay, drama, musical performance, or other artistic work it discusses. In rhetorical analyses, evaluative passages are optional, as we have seen, but reviews require evaluation. In fact, often the organizational idea itself may be judgmental:

- This movie is well worth seeing because . . . .
- The world of literature is little enriched by this author's first novel because . . . .

Like all rhetorical analyses, a review is concerned with what the author is trying to say and how he or she goes about saying it, but in the review, as the sample theses indicate, the analytic function backs up the evaluative.

HOW MUCH TO SUMMARIZE. Another literary convention students need to be concerned with in writing reviews is how much of the work to summarize. Oddly enough, a reviewer's summary of a work needs to be both more complete and more limited than in other rhetorical analyses. It needs to be more complete because the purpose of the review is to acquaint readers with the work. But on the other hand, reviewers must be careful not to give away so much that readers will no longer need (or want) to experience the work for themselves.

Analyses of Particular Kinds of Literature

In this chapter we have discussed teaching the general conventions of the rhetorical analysis. But to write a good rhetorical analysis of a work, our students need to have not only general understandings, but also knowledge of the techniques and strategies specific to the kind of art or literary genre they are dealing with. The rest of this chapter and the two that follow, Chapters 11 and 12, offer strategies specific to teaching rhetorical analyses of expository, narrative, and poetic literature respectively and exemplify pedagogically the general principles suggested here.

Rhetorical analyses are also concerned to a fairly significant extent with the conventions of the genre of the work being studied. The following section on teaching expository rhetorical analysis takes into account the conventions of expository writing that are considered in the earlier chapters of this text. I have postponed discussing teaching narrative rhetorical analysis and poetic rhetorical analysis until the creative writing chapters, 11 and 12, which cover in detail the conventions associated with the narrative and poetic genres.

TEACHING RHETORICAL ANALYSES OF EXPOSITORY WRITING

Expository writing may be the easiest kind of writing for our students to approach analytically. It is the genre they know best in an academic sense because we work so hard with it in the classroom. To compose a rhetorical analysis of an essay, they only have to reverse their thinking from the writer's point of view to that of the reader, from how they can get across what they have to say to how another author has done so. The territory then should already be familiar.

Finding the Author's Meaning

Furthermore, only in expository writing do authors express their meaning directly. Most of the time, as we have seen, authors state their central idea in an explicit sentence or two, and where they do not, they imply it so clearly that readers should have no difficulty in formulating it for themselves. But, perhaps because the point of an expository essay is so easily determined, finding the author's meaning is not as central to analysis of expository prose as it is to analysis of other kinds of creative expression. Our students' task in writing an analysis of expository prose is more likely to concern itself with determining the author's way of viewing the point and discovering the means by which he or she attempts to persuade them to consider this point of view.

Determining the Author's Viewpoint

Students need practice both in uncovering authors' meanings and discovering their attitude toward what they saying. We can give them this practice either through whole class analysis of an essay or by having students discuss it in small groups and then compare their findings when the class meets together as a whole. Study questions such as the following should be helpful:

- To discover your author's approach, you need to think a bit about the tone of the piece. How literally does your author intend her or his words?
- What connotations do the words convey?
- What value judgments are implied?
- Is your author always speaking to you in a straightforward way or is there some irony (see pages 437–40) in the tone?
- Read between the lines. Is your author trying to communicate something that is not written on the paper?

Detecting irony may be the most difficult reading task of all. Helping our students work through examples such as this passage from Lewis Thomas's essay on atomic stockpiling is a useful strategy.

> The man on television, Sunday midday, middle-aged and solid, nice-looking chap, all the facts at his fingertips, more dependable looking than most high-school principals, is talking about civilian defense. . . . It can make an enormous difference, he is saying. Instead of the outright death of eighty million American citizens in twenty minutes, he says, we can, by careful planning, get that number down to only forty million, maybe even twenty.[11]

Discussion should bring out that though Thomas describes the man on TV as solid and dependable, experienced readers can catch the hints that Thomas believes him to be unsound. We then can elicit the specific details that let us know Thomas is talking about appearance only ("more dependable *looking*; repetition of "he *says*," for instance) and those details that help us recognize the irony Thomas places on "enormous difference." Our most perceptive students can lead their fellows to understand that, unlike the TV speaker, Thomas believes that twenty million and eighty million dead are equally horrifying. Exercises such as this can convince our students that many sophisticated writers, like Thomas, never spell out their ideas in words, but make their point by implication only. They'll know that preparing to write a rhetorical analysis means catching all such implications.

Discovering the Author's Methods

Once our students are clear in their understanding of their author's organizing idea and of his or her approach to that idea, they will be ready to begin looking for the techniques the author uses to persuade readers of the truth of that way of thinking. Many of these techniques are discussed in detail in Chapter 6 on expository rhetorical style. The accompanying Student Guidelines, arranged in the order traditional with rhetoricians since the days of Aristotle, summarizes the rhetorical strategies our students should find most helpful to review.

STUDENT GUIDELINES

Rhetorical Strategies Available to Composers of Expository Writing

I. Appeal to Ethical Sense
   A. Presentation of the author as a good person, a likable person, a believable person
   B. Presentation of the author as a knowledgeable person, personally experienced in this area and/or well studied in it
   C. Presentation of the author as a fair-minded, reasonable, understanding person
   D. Presentation of the author somewhere on the scale of objective observer— — —impassioned advocate
II. Appeal to Reason
   A. Clear, coherent presentation of thesis
   B. Clear, though less forceful presentation of (or allusion to) the opposing point of view ("although clause" usually preceding thesis presentation)
   C. Logically consistent presentation of supporting material ("arguments")
   D. Supporting material ("arguments") that are internally logical and consistent
   E. "Arguments" based upon fact, statistics, authority, logic
III. Appeal to Emotion
   A. Devices associated with poetry
      1. Imagery
         a. Metaphor, simile, symbol, connotative language
         b. Personification, hyperbole, and allusion
      2. Rhythmic, emotion heightening language
      3. Repetition and variation

continued

continued
   B. Devices associated with fiction
      1. Narrative, anecdote
      2. Dramatization dialogue
      3. Characterization
      4. Specific detail
      5. Irony
   C. Devices of sentence structure
      1. Parallelism
      2. Balance and antithesis
      3. Periodic sentences
      4. Cumulative sentences

Writing Their Rhetorical Analyses

Once our students have developed their reading, interpreting, and analyzing skills, they will be ready to apply them to an assigned (or self-chosen) essay and write their analysis of it. What process should they follow? Clearly, they should pursue a close variation of the procedure they usually take whenever they undertake to write an expository essay.

THE WRITING PROCESS. They should read the target essay with great care—perhaps underlining the significant passages and annotating the margins. They should give it good deal of thought, possibly discuss it with others, in order to reach a solid interpretation of what their author is saying and what his or her purpose is in writing it. To find their own approach, they might try free-writing or any other heuristics they've had some success with. These efforts should result in the students finding a usable working thesis, from which to derive a tentative organizational plan. And then they write, revise, perhaps rewrite, proofread and complete.

A Preliminary Exercise. Students might be helped by first walking through the whole rhetorical-analysis writing process together. One useful strategy is for students to close-read an essay together as a class or in their study groups, then work it through the prewriting process until they discover an organizing idea and a structural plan they think would structure an effective paper. The boxed Goodman essay could be well-suited for this exercise, because students could compare their analysis ideas with those of a student who completed the assignment successfully. Afterward, by reading and discussing Anna's paper, they could bring the exercise to completion without actually writing a joint paper.

THE TARGET ESSAY

The Cult of Impotence
by Ellen Goodman

1. If they ever dig down through layers of future generations, looking for artifacts that tell something about mid seventies America, let's hope they find John Lilly's isolation tank. It will tell them a great deal.

2. The California physician and psychoanalyst has designed an enclosed tank, with 10 inches of water heated to precisely 93 degrees and room for exactly one person. Why? As he told *People*, "Lying on your back, you can breathe quite comfortably and safely, freed from sight, sound, people and the universe outside. That way you can enter the universe within you."

3. Think what Greta Garbo could have done with that. Think what we do with it—"free" ourselves from other people and the environment, enter the "universe within."

4. The "isolation tank" is as good a symbol as any of a time when we are making a positive value out of our sense of impotence in the world, and a cult out of the fragmentation of society and missed connections of our personal lives. Over the last few years—driven by events more complex than the labels "Vietnam" and "Watergate"—we have turned inward, to the search for personal solutions. We are no longer convinced of the possibility of social change or even the capacity to "do good." Every change reverberates.

5. We have discovered that when you cure typhoid you get overpopulation and when you raise the standard of living you destroy the environment. It is no wonder that we "work on" an area that seems more within our control and power: ourselves.

6. This self-centering is not only a retreat from the world, but a by-product of the current condition of our lives. The newest definition of American individualism is aloneness.

7. In the years since 1960, the number of "primaries"—people living alone—has risen by 87 percent while the number of families has risen only by 23 percent. Fifteen million of us live alone. Fifty million of us

continued

continued

are single, widowed or divorced. At least partially in response to this, the new therapies—from the isolation tank on—offer us ways to "get into ourselves." Those who aren't "doing their own thing" or "finding themselves" are "getting in touch with their feelings." The West Coast greeting, "What are you into?" is most aptly answered with one word: myself.

8. In the hyperindividualism of a movement like est, we are trained to be self-reliant, totally responsible to and for our own lives. The range of the new therapies is characterized by a frenzied search inward. The "isolation tank" seems to suggest that the road to happiness, peace, fulfillment, understanding, is an internal route. As Dr. Lilly says, "If you are able to retire deep inside yourself, you can find the quiet place which nobody can penetrate. This way you can isolate yourself in your deep inner core."

9. But then where are you? Then what? The impulses to more self-awareness, self-exploration are positive ones—but not if they lead to a dead end of navel-gazing, a permanent retreat from others and the problems of the world. At a time when we seem in almost perilous need of personal connection and social solutions, the tendency toward the isolation-tank psychology can be a sad perversion of the old American individualism.

10. I am reminded of a brief exchange Peter Marin had with a man "into" mysticism, and which he repeated in a piece written for *Harper's* last year. He wrote:

> "He was telling me about his sense of another reality. 'I know there is something outside of me,' he said, 'I can feel it. I know it is there. But what is it?'
>
> " 'It may not be a mystery,' I said, 'Perhaps it is the world.' "

ILLUSTRATIVE MODEL

Working Thesis and Structural Plan

Thesis: G. persuades that although the "universe within" may appear delightful, it actually is only a (rather selfish) way to hide from reality.

1. Introduction——→ Thesis
2. How G. wins readers by joining in their attraction to "individualism": . tone . logic . content
3. How G. retains readers even when she turns and attacks extreme "individualism": . tone . logic . content
4. Conclusion. [Use final anecdote]

RHETORICAL ANALYSIS OF GOODMAN'S
CULT OF IMPOTENCE
By Anna Adams

Self-awareness was the trend word for the seventies. More than a fashion fad, "finding yourself" or "getting into yourself" had become a way of life. Individualism was taken to the point of isolation. In adopting John Lilly's isolation tank as the perfect symbol for the *me* decade, Ellen Goodman points out that American individualism meant aloneness—replacing reality with the "universe within" (2). In the isolation tank Goodman found a symbol which not only summed up the beliefs of the me generation, but also expressed what was wrong with the entire value system. In "Cult of Impotence," Goodman persuades the reader that although the "universe within" may appear to be delightful on the surface, retreating into oneself is nothing more than a way to hide from reality.

The heart of Goodman's persuasiveness is the tone of the article. With her open manner and friendly voice, Goodman shows she understands the attractiveness of individualism as well as its dangers. Goodman includes the reader in her "we" from the very beginning:

Think what *we* do with it—"free" *ourselves* from other people and the environment, and enter the "universe within." (3. Emphasis mine.)

Almost involuntarily, the reader pauses and imagines a life free of the demands of other people and other things. Consciousness only of oneself and one's own needs could almost be a paradise.

continued

continued

Goodman then offers explanations for why Americans felt the need to find the "inner self" in the seventies. With Vietnam and Watergate, Americans were confused and afraid. It appeared as though the world itself was out of control. Everything that people tried to do to improve life—cure diseases, raise living conditions—ended in disaster—overpopulation, environment destruction. Disgusted and bemused, the me generation turned to the only thing that could be controlled—the Self. The reader is swept along with Goodman not only by the friendly conversational quality of her tone, but by her logical offering of explanations as to why the "universe within" is needed. Again, the reader finds herself understanding and sympathizing with the *me* generation and its need to "find itself."

However, Goodman does not praise this value system, but rather criticizes it. And, although she, too, seems to place a high value on being one's own person, Goodman is able to convince the reader that retreating into oneself is not the answer.

Goodman's argument seems objective because of her use of specifics. She is not someone speaking from emotion. She uses exact facts in describing the isolation tank, for example: It holds "10 inches of water heated to precisely 93 degrees." In addition, she uses statistics to emphasize the degree of isolation and aloneness of our population. "In the years since 1960, the number of primaries . . . has risen 87%. Fifteen million of us are single, widowed, or divorced" (7).

After reading these impressive statistics, the reader is forced to modify her image of self freedom. It can no longer only mean being able to control oneself and one's world. It takes on the new meaning of a terrible loneliness. The reader sees herself isolated, lonely, and limited—limited only to that which is inside her. And, as Goodman points out, "But then, where are you?" (9) Goodman can then openly express here contempt for the "universe within." After all the time one spends "finding" herself, she only finds herself "at a dead-end of naval gazing" (9). At this point, Goodman forcefully restates her thesis:

> At a time when we seem in most perilous need of personal connections and social solutions, the tendency toward the isolation-tank psychology can be a sad perversion of the old American individualism. (9)

Goodman then reinforces her point by putting her arm around the reader and relating an anecdote that sums up the entire argument: "I know there is something outside of me . . . I can feel it. I know it is there. But what is it?" To this Goodman has only to reply, "Perhaps it is the world" (10), and the reader must agree.

Assignments

Our students should now have composed a fairly lucid first draft of a rhetorical analysis. But we must not be disappointed if we find some students retrogressing in their work, either structurally or syntactically. In attempting this new kind of paper, they are, to a certain extent, entering a new discourse community where the rules are unfamiliar. Under these circumstances, as we have seen, students may return to earlier stages and have all sorts of difficulties with skills they had seemed to have long mastered. As one of my students said one day under such circumstances: "When I tried the new assignment, I went back to being all flooped up!"

The answer, of course, is conferencing (of one kind or another—see Chapter 5) and then a chance to revise without penalty. That should do the trick; and in the next paper they should be back to speed—or even better.

When our students become proficient at writing rhetorical analyses of professional essays, we might want to have them try out their analysis skills on one another's papers.

For more work with rhetorical analyses, see Chapters 11 and 12.

IDEAS FOR DISCUSSION OR ESSAY

1. Where do you stand on the place of personal or evaluative response in rhetorical analysis?
2. Define your position on the value of teaching current critical theory to students learning rhetorical analysis.
3. Close read, analyze, and discuss Ellen Goodman's essay or a comparable one.
4. Write a review or critique of Anna's paper (or that of one of your classmates'—see Number 5).
5. Write a rhetorical analysis of an "Op Ed" syndicated essay from one of this week's newspapers or from one of the weekly news magazines.

NOTES

The chapter opening epigraph is from William Raspberry, "Good Writing and Jazz: Lost Arts" (*Washington Post* Writers Group: June, 1994).

1. I favor the term *rhetorical analysis* over the others because, for the uninitiated, *critical* has negative connotations and *literary* is restricted to creative writing. More significantly, perhaps, *rhetorical* alone conveys the definitive assumption underlying analysis of a written work that, since *all* writing is inherently persuasive, the aim of analysis is to get at the author's purpose, to interpret what he/she says.

2. See especially Louise M. Rosenblatt, "Towards a Transactional Theory of Reading," *Journal of Reading Behaviour* 1 (1969): 31–47.

3. This strategy resembles David Bleich's three-step reading process: 1) "symbolization": individual interpretation; 2) "resymbolization": written response to the reading; 3) "negotiation": interpretive classroom give and take. Bleich's is an effective pedagogical technique—though rightly open to Steven Mailloux's charge of philo-

sophical inconsistency with his subjective reader-response theory, from which it supposedly was derived. Bleich, *Readings and Feelings: An Introduction to Subjective Criticism* (New York: Oxford UP, 1975); Mailloux, *Interpretive Conventions: The Reader in the Study of American Fiction* (Ithaca: Cornell UP, 1982); 32–37.

4. Throughout the entire section on *Interpretive Validity* I have been directly addressing the arguments put forth by the deconstructionist followers of Jacques Derrida. For an advocate's explication of their exceedingly complex theory, see Sharon Crowley's *A Teacher's Introduction to Deconstruction* (Urbana: NCTE, 1989).

My problem with deconstructionism is that it is pedagogically sterile. However intriguing it may be linguistically and philosophically, and however useful scholars have found it as a gad-fly to sting the intellectual complacency of some of their fellows or as a goad to stimulate their own thinking, it can only undermine a writing program because it does not acknowledge the communicative function of writing nor the possibility of authorial purpose. As Derrida's NCTE explicator, Crowley summarizes:

> Derrida's work raises doubts about the status of writing as a vehicle for "communication" . . . . [since] the meaning we derive from reading is located as much in the process of reading, and in the social and cultural contexts which surround our reading, as it is in the "text itself" (16).

Furthermore, in Crowley's words, "a deconstructive pedagogy . . . would . . . reject the notion of [authorial] intention altogether" (36).

Derrida himself, as well as Stanley Fish and Richard Rorty, scholars also considered post-structuralists, have disavowed the potentially extreme consequences of their theories. Derrida states:

> Deconstructing academic and political discourse doesn't mean simply destroying the norms or pushing these norms to utter chaos. I'm not in favor simply of disorder. . . . If deconstruction is only a pretense to ignore minimal requirements of knowledge of the tradition, it could be a bad thing.

Derrida is quoted by Dinesh D'Souza in "Pied Pipers of Relativism Reverse Course," *The Wall Street Journal* (July 27, 1993), who sums up the current position of the three scholars:

> We may have our doubts about the universality of standards, they seem to conclude, but this is no justification for jettisoning the classics, or for placing ignorance and knowledge on an equal plane.

5. Elaine Maimon, *Writing in the Arts and Sciences* (Cambridge, Mass: Winthrop, 1981). Gloria Flaherty suggests (in private correspondence) taking these notes in a "double-entry" journal, with a column for facts on the left and another for reflection on the right.

6. Cleanth Brooks, Robert Penn Warren, and John Thibout Purser, *An Approach to Literature*, 4th ed., (New York: Appleton, 1964): 4. If we choose to teach writing as communication, these author-critic-teachers, now undergoing a positive critical reassessment, offer an especially teachable approach.

7. Even deconstructionists begin with a close analysis of a text. And even though some of them claim that every text is so much in flux that no meaning can be established, in fact, their close reading, in every example I have read, yields what most readers would agree is a good approximation of the author's intended meaning—

before the author goes on to suggest that the text in question, like all others, yields no determinable meaning. For a typical example, see Gary Peller, "Reason and the Mob: The Politics of Representation," *Tikkun* (July/August 1987).

8. Lester Faigley, *Fragments of Rationality: Postmodernity and the Subject of Composition* (Pittsburgh: U of Pittsburgh P, 1992), 8.

9. A number of useful texts defining and commenting upon the various postmodern critical approaches have been written especially to provide background for English teachers. In addition to Crowley's *A Teacher's Introduction* [see note 3 and Faigley's *Fragments* [see note 8], they include: *Conversations: Contemporary Critical Theory and the Teaching of Literature*, eds. Charles Moran and Elizabeth F. Penfield (Urbana: NCTE, 1990). And Charles E. Bressler, *Literary Criticism: An Introduction to Theory and Practice* (Englewood Cliffs: Prentice, 1994), which, though designed for students, may prove the most accessible text for teachers as well — especially for those of us to whom current theoretical criticism is unfamiliar.

10. Gilbert Ryle, *The Concept of Mind* (New York: Barnes and Noble, 1949) in Erika Lindemann, *A Rhetoric for Writing Teachers*, 2nd ed. (New York: Oxford UP), 8.

11. Lewis Thomas, *Late Night Thoughts on Listening to Mahler's Ninth Symphony* (New York: Viking Penguin, 1982).

Part III

TEACHING CREATIVE WRITING

'Tis wise to learn; 'tis God-like to create.

—John Godfrey Saxe

□ □ □

☐ ☐ ☐ **11**

Teaching Narrative Writing

Draw your chair up close to the edge of
the precipice and I'll tell you a story.
— F. Scott Fitzgerald

☐ ☐ ☐

Teachers look at creative writing in two quite different ways. In talking about teaching creative writing either we mean teaching our students to express themselves creatively, that is, in a lively style, rich with experiential detail, which in some way reflects their honest selves; *or* we mean helping them to create for themselves the stories, poems, plays, satires, and personal essays of which our literature is composed. Most of the literature on the subject stresses one or the other: expression or artifact, imagination or imitation. But the truth is that a creative writing program ignores at its peril either part of the creative writing experience. Both elements are essential. Our goal should be to help our students achieve lively, honest writing that is shaped and disciplined by the conventions of the various literary forms.

TEACHING CREATIVE WRITING AS VIVID SELF-EXPRESSION

Many of our students write in a stiff and cumbersome style, full of vague generalities and devoid of individuality or spirit. Many of them are so fearful of "getting it wrong," of "not doing it right," that they become pen-tied and can scarcely write at all. In order to write creatively and well, these students need to discover a direct line between what is in their minds and hearts and what goes on their paper; they need access to their own observations, thoughts, and feelings, and enough relaxation of their defenses to get at least some of it in writing.

Providing Freedom

To help our students achieve these goals, we need to provide them with the freedom to be honest, with permission to take risks and make mistakes, and with the certain knowledge that they cannot lose our good opinion by exploring a point of view with which we disagree or by proffering an expression we do not think felicitous. We must let our students know that they need not feel threatened by the permanence of written expression, for in our class they can always change their minds, always revise and rewrite. We must create an ambience in our classrooms that supports the efforts of each student and assures each one that our affection and respect is in no way dependent upon where they place their commas or their modifiers, or upon our view of the fantasies that pass through their minds. And we must make sure that this caring atmosphere continues when the students discuss each other's work. Our students should offer their honest reactions concerning their fellows' work, but they should never forget that they are not criticizing disembodied abstractions but rather the private thoughts of human beings very much like themselves.[1]

HOW DEMANDING SHOULD WE BE? We should also give serious thought to the level of the standards we impose, to the strictness of the criticism we offer. Chances are slight indeed that among the "mute, inglorious" students in our classroom there is a future Milton or that even a few of them will become professional writers of a more mundane sort. There is little justification, therefore, for us to demand the sort of professional standards that would be a helpful spur in a workshop intended for novice authors.

On the other hand, there is intolerable condescension as well as dishonesty in the opposite assumption that since our students are young, inexperienced, and for the most part untutored, they are not capable of producing anything of real merit, and thus we should respond to any kind of creative effort as if it were a masterpiece. Our best course is, therefore, the middle ground. We should give an abundance of praise for whatever is praiseworthy, provide friendly criticism where major problems are within our students' present capacity to remedy, but maintain a neutral silence on the rest. As students grow in their writing capacity, we can raise our standards by commenting upon a wider variety of flaws. But if we hold to Browning's idea that a man's reach must always exceed his grasp, we will push most of our students to a state of frustration.

The trick of a good writing coach is to have a shrewd understanding of just where every student's "grasp" lies, of what he or she can attain just now, and set our standard for his or her work just there. Ken Macrorie calls this technique "moving" the students "from success to success."[2] And it can be done. I have rarely taught a student who did not create at least one paper during the course of a term of which he or she could realistically be proud.

Freedom-Creating Strategies

Many teachers find that when they have achieved a classroom atmosphere that combines honesty and genuine respect, frankness and tact, and an awareness of both human vulnerability and of human capacity for achievement, they have achieved a situation in which openness can be attained and creative endeavor can thrive. Other teachers feel that simply creating such an atmosphere is not sufficient; they want to incorporate creative freedom into class assignments.

FREEWRITING. Freewriting is the mainstay of the writing programs of such well-known instructors as Ken Macrorie and Peter Elbow.[3] It is an exercise in writing whose only restriction is that the writing does not cease until the time set aside for it runs out. Freewriting is never graded, nor necessarily even read by the teacher (after the first trial or two), except by student request. (See pages 66–70 for a fuller description of ways of implementing this technique and especially of its use as a prewriting tool and a heuristic for invention.)

Advantages. Each exercise should be saved and savored by its author throughout the term and can in this way become a phrase-bank or an idea source for the student. Furthermore, freewriting helps students:

- Relieve writing block. It helps to loosen up the compulsive perfectionist. Because its rules forbid proofreading and insist on forging ahead at all costs, students who are hamstrung by the desire never to make a mistake are forced, at the very least, to set down their ideas.
- Explore thought. Freewriting can also aid in unblocking the mental channels of those who cannot write a word because they cannot bring themselves to think about a subject. After a little practice, students can use this exercise to explore the contents of their own minds, to find subjects or ideas of interest to them. When they focus their freewriting on a single subject, students can learn to explore their ideas on that subject and begin to channel them in fruitful ways, gaining important experience for their more formal compositions.
- Release their imaginations. Almost every writer occasionally produces some pure gems of expression, retrievable for future use, out of the general babble of unrestrained and undigested thought.
- Develop their authentic voices. An even more important carryover is the development of the student's own personal voice, which naturally cannot be denied when the rules are sincerely followed, and, after the habitual exercise freewriting affords, often manages to transfer to planned work as well.

In the Classroom. The success of freewriting exercises is largely dependent upon the personal style of the teacher and, to a lesser extent, upon the attitude of the students. Some teachers who are comfortable with the approach experience remarkably good results by beginning each period with a regular ten-minute freewriting time, sometimes completely free and sometimes focused. But others do not find it worthy of the time spent upon it. We might want to try out the exercise a time or two to see how our students respond and how it meshes with our own teaching style before deciding whether to include freewriting in our regular curricula. But as a treatment for individuals or classes with severe "writer's-block" problems, a series of freewriting sessions offers an excellent prescription.

JOURNAL KEEPING. Another activity that many teachers have found helpful in providing students with a sharper awareness of their own thinking is the keeping of journals. The student journal is not meant to be a diarylike collection of true (or fantasy) confessions, but rather a private idea and impression storage cupboard from which our students can take nourishment when they sit down to write.

For Free Personal Impressions. We might ask our students to record each day in their journals at least one impression that stirred them or at least one idea that gave them pause; we might also ask that with each entry they leave enough space to add further thoughts relating to it later on. Their journal is the place to record quotations that seem striking to them as well as commentary explaining the nature of the appeal. It is the place to try out the interesting expressions or odd metaphors that come into their heads. It is the place to attempt close visual description of a person or place that attracts or repels them, and to add sound, odor, taste, and tactile impressions to the description. In their journals, our students can try to pin down and explore a momentary or recurring feeling they have experienced, a dream they have had, an insight they have gained. There they can record subjects that have puzzled or excited or disturbed them.

To Respond to Set Stimuli. Sometimes, especially at the beginning of a class journal experience we can give our students class time for journal jotting. We might, in fact, use student journals for a daily freewriting. Occasionally we might even set up an experience for a journal entry. We might, for instance, bring in a recording of music that has moved us (Stephen Judy suggests that Stravinsky or Bartok works well[4]), or a painting or poster or set of photos capable of generating interest, and ask our students to free-associate about them in their journals. We might bring in a newspaper clipping for our students' response to an issue of current interest.

Or we might bring in an object and ask them to write a full description. We might suggest that they turn their heads in one direction and write down everything they can see, or we might ask them to close their eyes and listen to and record everything they hear. We might go outside and sit on the lawn and try the same exercises.

To Respond to Academic Experiences. Students enjoy writing journal responses to the movies or TV shows they see or the speakers they hear. Journal responses also provide appropriate ways for students to react to assigned readings. Journals work particularly well in a poetry unit, for instance. Linda Welshimer Wagner has her students respond to short passages of prose or poetry on controversial subjects—reacting to both the subject and to the style of the author.[5]

Our Response to Journal Responses. Periodically—say, every two or three weeks—we should probably ask our students to turn in their journals.[6] Sharing students' private thoughts is a real privilege, so we should always treat their journal entries in that spirit. To preserve privacy, for instance, we may suggest their stapling together any pages they would rather we would not see—though few students take advantage of this option.

It is also important for our students to know that though we will read their journals with great interest, we will never grade them. Teachers who use journal assignments most effectively make their responses to the entries something of a running conversation with their correspondent. The most successful teacher notations are personal replies to the ideas the student expresses. Encouraging comments on students' creative experiments are also helpful. Our response should not be that of a correcting authority, but of a person truly interested in what they have to say. No red pencil here. The closest we should come to correcting errors is to model the conventional construction in our response. (See, for example, page 288.)

Though journals should not be graded, we need to demonstrate their curricular importance in a material way. Some teachers do so by lowering a student's overall average for incomplete work and raising it for especially energetic journal keeping. Teachers using a point system assign a hefty percentage of points for a completed set of entries with proportionate subtractions if assignments are missing.

Perhaps because the threat of grades is removed and students don't feel they have to try so hard to "get it right," perhaps because a journal offers a uniquely unbridled opportunity for thinking through and expressing what students really want to say, the writing in their journals often has more energy and voice than students' usual work, and they really seem to enjoy their journal keeping.

STORY WORKSHOP CREATIVITY EXERCISES. In introducing a unit on creative writing, some teachers choose to go beyond freewriting and journal keeping to other projects designed to stimulate students' inherent creativity. Those devised by John Schultz for his Story Workshop are some of the more interesting of these projects. The essence of the Story Workshop method is the arousal of a general creative atmosphere through a set of imagination-provoking speaking and listening exercises. For example, Schultz uses round-robin association word games that place the emphasis on "the surprise word, the unplanned word, the word not prepared or ready before your turn, the felt word, the word welling up." When Schultz senses a "state of imaginative seeing" in a group of students, he leads them into writing.[7]

Observation-Enhancement Activities

For our student writers to render character and setting with the kind of detail that achieves the illusion of an exact and particularized reality, they need to cultivate the habit of precise observation. To promote this skill, teachers have developed activities and assignments designed to sharpen the students' awareness and promote more precise definition in their responses. George Hillocks, Jr., for example, in *Observing and Writing*, offers an imaginative and highly teachable sequential set of exercises.[8] (See also pages 133–35 for a discussion of similar exercises suggested for expository writing.)

In implementing such exercises, we can encourage our students to observe more precisely than they are ordinarily accustomed to, to record their observations with an accuracy not often expected of them, and eventually to become discriminating in the selection and patterning of their observations.

OBSERVING PRECISELY. We can give students an opportunity to employ all of their senses in making these observations. How? Provide them with substances having a variety of odors (for example, vanilla, benzol, damp soil, menthol, lavender, lilac, ammonia, cloves, cinnamon), or objects with a variety of tactile forms or surfaces (for example, polyethylene, sandpaper, steel wool, nylon hosiery, carpeting), or bits of food with a variety of tastes, or a tape recording of a number of widely differing sounds. When we deny the students use of their sense of sight (by using blindfolds, curtains, dark containers, and so on), they are forced to employ the underused senses of touch, smell, and hearing as they explore the samples.

RECORDING ACCURATELY. Students then describe the substance or sound clearly enough for another to identify it, or at least precisely enough to understand the tester's experience with it. In writing up these exercises, our students will come to understand that though the English words specifically describing an odor or a taste, for instance, are limited (there are after all, only four actual tastes: sweet, sour, bitter, and salt), the sensations from all the senses can be described in terms of the other senses ("a heavy odor," "a sweet smell") and the unknown can be likened to the known: "It feels like . . . ," "it tastes like. . . ."

Even greater accuracy can be demanded from recordings of visual observations. Students may be asked to describe a shell, for example, so accurately that their classmates can pick it out of a group of similar shells (Hillocks, 10) or to describe a geometric figure so precisely that their classmates can use the description to draw a similar figure.[9] In a more difficult exercise, students reach into a bag to discover an unfamiliar object (calipers, a micrometer, a hand drill, a small stuffed animal), which they describe for their partners to draw (Hillocks, 8). In every case, when the description or drawing is compared with the real object, our students should be able, as Hillocks writes, to "discover where they went wrong, and try to come to an understanding of what aspects of the communication process were most difficult" (8).

INTERPRETING INTELLIGENTLY. After our students have become accustomed to focusing their attention on the details that their senses reveal to them and have become fairly adept at describing these impressions, they sometimes—in their eagerness to please us—run the risk of providing too much of a good thing and fill their papers with long lists of undiscriminated sensory data. At this point they need practice in narrowing down the myriad sense signals that come to them in every situation to the few telling details that will convey their overall impression of the thing described. Hillocks suggests a visual-observation exercise that is helpful in this regard:

> Students work . . . with a set of . . . pictures of, for example, city street scenes, railroad scenes, mountain villages, marketplaces. The pictures in each set should be similar but capable of evoking clearly different impressions— one picture might be the impression of gloom, another of poverty, another of brisk business-like people going about their affairs. . . . Each student writes a description of the scene . . . mak[ing] use of the details in the picture to convey the impression that the student feels it conveys. . . . When students have completed their descriptions, the teacher collects . . . and redistributes [them]. . . . The reader selects the picture described from among all the other pictures, studies the picture and the composition, and writes some comments about the writer's effectiveness, pointing out particularly strong use of detail and suggesting changes or additions that might be useful. (17–18)

A Writing Assignment. As a culminating exercise for a program of planned observation, we might ask our students to go to a place rich in characteristic sounds, sights, smells, and tactile impressions such as the cafeteria, the ocean or other natural setting, the bus station, or a busy downtown corner, and come to some understanding of the mood that this place invokes in them. Their composition should be a compilation of this sensory data arranged in such a way that the reader will share their impression and sense their mood.

When our students can manage this sort of an assignment with some degree of skill, they are well on their way toward creating a theme for a personal narrative or a short story.

TEACHING THE PERSONAL NARRATIVE

Personal narratives are the most popular assignment in many English classrooms, and yet the genre is not clearly defined. Roughly speaking, they come in three general varieties.

Types of Personal Narratives

PERSONAL ESSAYS. More, perhaps, than any other genre, personal essays embody the spirit of creative self-expression. They are not structured in any definitive way. These essays are authorial musings on a theme or a set of ideas: college life, for example, in James Thurber's "University Days," the excitement of the circus in Thomas Wolfe's "Circus at Dawn," memories of youth in Jesse Stuart's "If I Were Seventeen Again." These essays depend upon a theme for unity, but within that theme authors are free to ramble. In a sort of organization by chain of consciousness, they can link their ideas to one another using only the gossamer threads of association that bind thought to thought.

Or essayists can choose a structure that is a little more rigid. They can organize their musings around a rough chronological or geographic scheme, as John Steinbeck does in *Travels with Charlie*, or around a series of contrasts, as E. B. White does in "Walden." Often a personal essay will take the form of the narration of an experience and the savoring of the feelings and thoughts that the experience calls up — but in these kinds of essays the essayist comes close to being a fiction writer.

AUTOBIOGRAPHICAL SHORT STORIES. The most common personal narratives are, for all practical purposes, short stories with an autobiographical narrator. With student authors, these narratives often take the form of initiation stories in which the experience related results in a sudden maturing insight for the central figure, a first sure glimpse of the reality of the adult world. Since these narratives are so closely linked to stories, we can help our students understand how to exploit the conventions of the short story to make the most effective use of their basically factual material. (See pages 413–48 for suggestions on teaching the short story.)

EXPOSITORY-STRUCTURED PERSONAL NARRATIVES. Another type of personal narrative is closely related to the expository essay: it makes some point about the author's life, interests, beliefs, or goals, and, using this point as the organizing idea, supports and illustrates it with factual material from the author's life. This sort of essay can be a highly effective way for students to explicate their personal philosophy or explore their plans and goals.

Many high schools ask their juniors and seniors to write brief autobiographies to help the guidance counselor in assisting them toward their college or career goals or to provide practice for the autobiographical statement required with many college applications. We should urge our students to write thesis-centered personal narratives when this sort of autobiography is called for.

Leading into the Personal Narrative

The freewriting, journal-keeping, and creativity and observation exercises described here are all useful in helping to ready our students for any of these kinds of personal-narrative writing. In addition, teachers have developed projects specifically directed toward personal-narrative writing.

SELF-DEFINITION ACTIVITIES. Harvey S. Wiener, for instance, suggests an effective program with a self-defining personal narrative as its culminating project. He begins with the reading of Walt Whitman's poem "There Was a Child Went Forth" with its emphasis upon images that define the self ("Look'd upon, that object he became"). His students then create individual collages, each of which attempts to answer the question "What Am I?" by means of visual imagery. The project concludes in the writing of brief personal narratives that answer the question "What Am I?" by using intense verbal imagery.[10]

A similar activity is the creation of a "Who's Who in the − −th Grade," to which the students contribute brief paragraphs explaining one unusual thing about themselves.[11]

READINGS AND MOVIES. Students identify with characters in the books and stories they read and the movies they see. Teachers can encourage that identification to spur invention for personal-narrative writing. Lyn Brendel, for example, assigns stories or movies involving a character who is changed by a particular event or series of events and then suggests that her students write about a similar situation that happened to them. If a fictional character is changed by dialogue, then the students might write about what somebody said to them—or what they said to somebody—and how it changed them. If the change in the fictional character is caused by an action that, for instance, reveals the human flaws in an idolized adult, then Brendel's students write about an adult action that may have disillusioned them in a significant way. She asks her students to avoid writing about recent events in their lives, suggesting that they choose something that happened at least two years earlier. She feels that the passage of time gives them a more reliable perspective on emotional events—and protects them from revealing confidences they might later regret.[12]

To help her students with organization, Brendel offers them an optional three-part structure for narratives of this variety: (1) my original feelings or situation; (2) the event that caused the change; (3) my current feelings or situation.

Symbolic Meaning. Finding and writing about a symbol important in their own lives is another effective writing task relating personal-narrative writing to student reading. Lyn Brendel has developed an assignment of this type using Hawthorne's *Scarlet Letter*. After she and her students have discussed the symbolism in the novel, she asks her students to find an object or possession of their own that has great emotional, physical, or even financial value for them, to write about how they acquired the object, and to point out where its value for them comes from. Almost invariably students derive the object's value from the details of its acquisition.[13]

The Writing Process

A writing-workshop class structure seems to be admirably suited to writing personal narratives. Nancie Atwell's seminal work, *In the Middle: Writing, Reading, and Learning with Adolescents*,[14] offers an abundance of ideas on organizing and teaching a class in this way. Among the variety of effective methods teachers have derived from Atwell's work is the personal-narrative writing process Melissa Snyder uses with her classes at Clinton-Massie County High School in Ohio, described below.

SETTING UP THE PROCESS. To get the class started in a personal-narrative direction, we might model thinking of things to write about. Snyder, for example, starts by telling her students mildly humorous, everyday stories about her children: "My daughter seems obsessed with video movies and is always acting them out. Last night. . . ." Having gotten our students intrigued and laughing, we can suggest that they jot down at least three such ideas about things that have happened to them. Then we might say something like "Since it has helped me to share my ideas with you, I want you to share your ideas with a partner." Shortly after the partners' conversations become really animated, we might ask them to choose one idea and start writing.

There are always a few laggards. But we can tell them, "Don't worry about how to start or how long the final essay should be. It doesn't matter. We're just going to get our ideas down." It also helps to sit down and write with our students, concentrating so intensely that we wave off interrupters. Soon everyone will be writing with equal intensity.

TURNING FREEWRITING INTO FIRST DRAFT. The next day we could put our own draft on the overhead projector and ask, "How can I turn this into a real narrative?" We can try out whatever suggestions we receive and, again modeling, show our own method of what Melissa Snyder calls "hacking out" a structured work from the freewriting. We might then ask for comments.

To get our students started, we might put some directions, such as these suggested by Snyder, on the board.

- Wade through the beginning writing until you find where your narrative really starts.
- Find the best part of your narrative, your favorite part, or the main idea and circle it. (Maybe have your neighbor help you choose.)
- Take that as the beginning of your new draft.

When our students begin writing, we can go around the room and speak to them individually—or they can bring their papers up to us for miniconferences. We might ask them such questions as:

- What do you think of this paper?
- What do like the best about it?
- What do you think is not so good?
- How can you make that like the best? [15]

TURNING FIRST DRAFTS INTO A FINAL DRAFT. The next day we might offer a ten-minute period of direct instruction at the beginning of the hour to begin giving stylistic revising hints. We might put two sentences on the board: a dull statement describing a situation and another such description filled with vivid detail, and ask students which one they like best and why. We could also put on the board a pair of sentences that similarly displays the advantages of dialogue, for example:

- My friend and I wanted to go to a movie.
- "Hey Jan, let's go to a movie."

Depending on how the drafts are going, we might, alternatively, present a minilesson on beginnings or descriptive writing. Or we might discuss staying in focus, concentrating on purpose, not digressing. In this regard we might ask: "Why are you telling this? What do you want readers to understand?"

With this combination of minilessons, teacher–student conferencing, peer-group or partner discussion, and straight writing workshop, our students should complete satisfying narratives. Finished work should be shared orally and then published by bulletin board or class magazine.

Reading Narrative Models

Probably the most important part of preparing our students to write the personal narrative, is having them read good essays in this genre. Students need to ponder the various ideas and listen to the diverse voices of a good number of writers before they dare to express their own ideas in their own voices in this the most individual of all writing styles. The combined curriculum ideas discussed below thus apply to reading/writing personal narratives as well as to short stories.

TEACHING THE SHORT STORY

The focus of this chapter is teaching students to write creative narratives, but reading stories and essays (and poems) with an eye to their craftsmanship is essential for those attempting to write in these forms. As Edward P. J. Corbett argues, it is the "internalization of structures [which takes place when literary works are studied and imitated] that unlocks our powers and sets us free to be creative, original, and ultimately effective [writers]." [16]

Conversely, the craft of literature cannot really be fully understood unless students attempt to write something in the genres for themselves. Edith

Wharton dismisses in an offhand way "those who have never thought of fiction as the art of composition," and William J. O'Malley writes that just as "a man does not begin to savor the interplay of voices in a chorus until he has directed one . . . [he] does not begin to savor the words, the rhythm, the details, the metaphors, the structure or the experience which they were chosen to communicate until he has tried to wrestle his own experience into words."[17]

Whole Language Teaching—The Combined Curriculum

The language arts are one. Though we may separate them occasionally for intensive individual study, we forget their essential unity at our pedagogical peril, as many successful teachers who have adopted a whole language approach have determined.

And, as I point out in Chapter 10, a combined curriculum works particularly well with reading and writing. Since writing presupposes a reader and reading implies a writer, essentially they cannot be uncoupled. If we want students really to experience a kind of writing, they need to read it, write about it, and write some examples of their own.

READING TO WRITE.   More specifically, when we teach a unit on fiction, our students need to read stories, critically analyze at least one, and write at least one for themselves.

To do so, they need to become aware of their own reaction to what they read. (Please see Chapter 10, page 377, where reader response pedagogy is discussed in detail.) They also need to master the close-reading skills. (Please see Chapter 10, pages 379–81, where teaching close reading is discussed in detail.)

Students need to achieve an author-centered view of literature. They need to be able to sensitize their antenae (see page 379) and discover their answers to "What is the author trying to say?" "How does he or she go about saying it?" Once students understand literature as "the presentation of an author's way of looking at life," as Cleanth Brooks and his associates define it,[18] they can begin to view their own writing as works through which they also can make some statement of their own. And once they understand the conventions of narration and specifically of the short story, they can begin to plan their own stories.

Teaching Creative Writing Within a Literary Context

In the combined curriculum, a unit on the short story should culminate in the students' writing short stories of their own. There are two approaches to this writing assignment. One way is to ask our students to work throughout the unit on creating a final short story, with preliminary assignments part and parcel of the final goal.[19] The other approach is to lead up to the writing of a final short story with a series of writing assignments, each exploring one of the component elements of the art of fiction. Whichever approach we adopt, the creation of an original short story should be assigned right at the beginning lest our students use up their energy, enthusiasm, and ideas on their preliminary work. Throughout the entire unit the cumulating short stories should be enthusiastically planned for and discussed.

But where to begin? Whichever approach we choose, it might be a good idea to start by responding to that major student grumble that our subject is so elusive students can't get a solid grasp on it before it slips and slithers away. We can counter this complaint by agreeing together to some definitions.

DEFINING NARRATIVE WRITING. In expository writing authors convey their ideas about the world to the reader by stating them more or less directly, we might remind our students. But in narrative writing, authors convey their ideas more subtly—by telling a story. "Sure, and we're going to write a short story, we know that; but what exactly are we supposed to write?" is a typical response. Though we may be living in post-structural times, we have very few post-structural students. Most of them—with an assignment to be tended to—want the security of a more formalized definition. Brooks and his coauthors suggest one of the most pedagogically useful ones:

> A narrative tells of a significant conflict, usually involving human beings, that is resolved in such a way as to imply a comment on human values, feelings, or attitudes. (Closely adapted from Brooks *et al.* 9.)

This definition is serviceable in the classroom because it defines the elements of fiction in terms with which our students will already be knowledgeable. They will easily be able to find within it the familiar character, plot, and theme; but even more helpful, this definition also shows how the three traditional elements relate to one another to form the integral whole that is the story (or novel). To paraphrase in more customary terms,

> the constituents of narrative writing are a *plot* involving *characters* that will be resolved to bring out a *theme*.

Mode of Procedure. There are two basic ways to teach these elements, the unified and the segmented approaches:

- In the unified approach, we present each story as a whole and teach the various components of fiction as they are needed to help our students understand the story.
- With the segmented approach, we make an arbitrary decision about the order in which we would like to teach the elements of fiction. Then, assigning stories where a particular element seems more prominent or more easily grasped, we can explain and emphasize the elements one at a time, returning to earlier stories for further exemplification where appropriate.

Because every good story illustrates its author's skillful integration of all the elements of fiction, both approaches have some problems. With the unified approach, we need to interrupt the first stories too often with explanations; and with the segmented approach, we have to delay a full appreciation of the early stories until later knowledge makes full analysis meaningful.

There is merit in both approaches, but the segmented approach lends itself better to the linear presentation necessitated by a book, and therefore I have organized this chapter's discussion in that way. And though I have used a variety of illustrations to exemplify strategies for the elements of fiction, I will rely especially on examples from Kate Chopin's brief masterpiece, "The Story of an Hour." I include a copy here for your convenience.

THE STORY OF AN HOUR

Kate Chopin

Knowing that Mrs. Mallard was afflicted with a heart trouble, great care was taken to break to her as gently as possible the news of her husband's death.

It was her sister Josephine who told her, in broken sentences, veiled hints that revealed in half concealing. Her husband's friend Richards was there, too, near her. It was he who had been in the newspaper office when intelligence of the railroad disaster was received, with Brently Mallard's name leading the list of "killed." He had only taken the time to assure himself of its truth by a second telegram, and had hastened to forestall any less careful, less tender friend in bearing the sad message.

She did not hear the story as many women have heard the same, with a paralyzed inability to accept its significance. She wept at once, with sudden, wild abandonment, in her sister's arms. When the storm of grief had spent itself, she went away to her room alone. She would have no one follow her.

There stood, facing the open window, a comfortable, roomy arm-chair. Into this she sank, pressed down by a physical exhaustion that haunted her body and seemed to reach into her soul.

She could see in the open square before her house the tops of trees that were all aquiver with the new spring life. The delicious breath of rain was in the air. In the street below a peddler was crying his wares. The

continued

notes of a distant song which someone was singing reached her faintly, and countless sparrows were twittering in the eaves.

There were patches of blue sky showing here and there through the clouds that had met and piled above the others in the west facing her window.

She sat with her head thrown back upon the cushion of the chair quite motionless, except when a sob came up into her throat and shook her, as a child who has cried itself to sleep continues to sob in its dreams.

She was young, with a fair, calm face, whose lines bespoke repression and even a certain strength. But now there was a dull stare in her eyes, whose gaze was fixed away off yonder on one of those patches of blue sky. It was not a glance of reflection, but rather indicated a suspension of intelligent thought.

There was something coming to her and she was waiting for it, fearfully. What was it? She did not know; it was too subtle and elusive to name. But she felt it, creeping out of the sky, reaching toward her through the sounds, the scents, the color that filled the air.

Now her bosom rose and fell tumultuously. She was beginning to recognize this thing that was approaching to possess her, and she was striving to beat it back with her will—as powerless as her two white slender hands would have been.

When she abandoned herself, a little whispered word escaped her slightly parted lips. She said it over and over under her breath: "Free, free, free!" The vacant stare and the look of terror that had followed it went from her eyes. They stayed keen and bright. Her pulses beat fast, and the coursing blood warmed and relaxed every inch of her body.

She did not stop to ask if it were not a monstrous joy that held her. A clear and exalted perception enabled her to dismiss the suggestion as trivial.

She knew that she would weep again when she saw the kind, tender hands folded in death; the face that had never looked save with love upon her, fixed and gray and dead. But she saw beyond that bitter moment a long procession of years to come that would belong to her absolutely. And she opened and spread her arms out to them in welcome.

There would be no one to live for during those coming years; she would live for herself. There would be no powerful will bending her in

continued

continued

that blind persistence with which men and women believe they have a right to impose a private will upon a fellow-creature. A kind intention or a cruel intention made the act seem no less a crime as she looked upon it in that brief moment of illumination.

And yet she had loved him—sometimes. Often she had not. What did it matter! What could love, the unsolved mystery, count for in face of this possession of self-assertion which she suddenly recognized as the strongest impulse of her being.

"Free! Body and soul free!" she kept whispering.

Josephine was kneeling before the closed door with her lips to the key-hole, imploring for admission. "Louise, open the door! I beg; open the door—you will make yourself ill. What are you doing, Louise? For heaven's sake open the door."

"Go away. I am not making myself ill." No; she was drinking in a very elixir of life through that open window.

Her fancy was running riot along those days ahead of her. Spring days, and summer days, and all sorts of days that would be her own. She breathed a quick prayer that life might be long. It was only yesterday she had thought with a shudder that life might be long.

She arose at length and opened the door to her sister's importunities. There was a feverish triumph in her eyes, and she carried herself unwittingly like a goddess of Victory. She clasped her sister's waist, and together they descended the stairs. Richards stood waiting for them at the bottom.

Someone was opening the front door with a latchkey. It was Brently Mallard who entered, a little travel-stained, composedly carrying his gripsack and umbrella. He had been far from the scene of the accident, and did not even know there had been one. He stood amazed at Josephine's piercing cry; at Richards' quick motion to screen him from the view of his wife.

But Richards was too late.

When the doctors came, they said she had died of heart disease—of joy that kills.

Teaching Conflict and Plot

In identifying fiction as a "narrative . . . of a significant conflict" our definition centers on conflict, that is, the struggle between two (or more) antagonists. Narrative writing without conflict is simply an unfocused relation of a series of events.

CONFLICT.　One of our students' most important tasks when they read or are about to write a story, therefore, is to identify its conflict as precisely as possible. To do so, they must discover who the *actual* antagonists are. Specifically, they need to determine that the story is based upon the struggle between John and Jim over Molly's affections or between Galileo and the church over doctrinal issues. Categorical generalizations, which some students suggest, such as a conflict between Man and Man, or between Man and Institution, offer little aid in approaching a story and—at the start—such abstractions as honesty versus guile, or science versus religion, are also not especially helpful guides for interpretation.

Conflict in Chopin's Story.　When faced with a complex story, determining the central conflict may be difficult; but our students must come to a decision in order to understand the story. In "The Story of an Hour," for instance, most students will easily agree that the conflict takes place within Mrs. Mallard, the central character. But they may well be divided on the nature of the conflict. Is it her own spirit opposed to her internalization of the will of society as represented by her sister, Josephine, and her husband's friend, Richards? Or is her inner antagonist her husband, Brently? Both are valid readings. And much of the way our students eventually interpret the story will be based upon the specific way each makes his or her conflict determination.

CHRONOLOGY AND CLIMAX.　Students unused to thinking in terms of conflict will wonder about its relationship to the more familiar term, *plot*.

> Plot may be considered the way that a conflict is worked out in time.

The plot of any particular story is a *chronology* of the incidents which set up, intensify, and then resolve the conflict.

Time Lines.　Our students can often think through a plot more clearly if they diagram it as a time line. A time line can be a useful way to understand the underlying structure of the stories read and can be especially helpful when students are working with stories that may originally appear formless to them. Because fiction is art, not life, the conflicts within it must have a beginning, a middle, and an end; the time line gives them this emphasis. Students should realize, however, that beginnings, middles, and ends need not represent the actual chronology of events. Some stories begin near the end of the action and tell most of their tale in flashbacks. Others begin *in medias res* and work their way in both directions. Some, like *Catch 22* or *Lord Jim*, have highly irregular time sequences.

Time lines can also play an important role in planning the construction of our students' own stories. For once they conceive of a conflict which interests them, a time line can help them work out how it will be entered into, how complicated, and how resolved; it can then also help them decide what incidents to dramatize along the way and whether to tell their tale strictly chronologically or through a disjointed time sequence. The time line in Figure 10–1 is typical. In the sample time line, the word *situation* stands for the given, the way things are after the introductory passages of the work and before complications in the conflict set in. Each X marks an incident in the conflict, a dramatic episode in the development of the action. The curved line represents the pattern of emotional intensity.

The notion of *climax* is a concept about which experts disagree: some see it as the moment of greatest emotional intensity, others as the point where the outcome becomes inevitable. Where these points in the action do not coincide, our students must decide where the climactic point really occurs. As for the *denouement*, most stories have some kind of postclimax conclusion to round them off and return readers to their own world again.

Climax in Chopin's Story. Where do our students place the climax in "Story of an Hour"? For them, the moment of greatest emotional tension may or may not coincide with the final revelation. Their choice depends upon how much emphasis they feel Kate Chopin puts upon her heroine's death. Does she show that Mrs. Mallard cannot come to terms with the demands that society and her husband place upon her freedom and succumbs to them in death in a final climactic scene? Or does Chopin make a climax of Mrs. Mallard's triumphal moment of understanding the central importance of personal freedom? If so, then does Chopin mean us to take her heroine's death, interrupting only what will once again be a freedomless life, as the denouement rather than the climax of her story? Again a crucial interpretative question.

Depending on their individual interpretations, students could work out the plot of "Story of an Hour" along either of the plot lines presented in Figure 10–2.

FORESHADOWING. Thinking through the plot in this way is also helpful for planning foreshadowing, the half-hidden hints or portents of things to

Figure 10–1. Plot as a Time Line

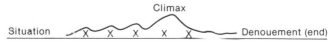

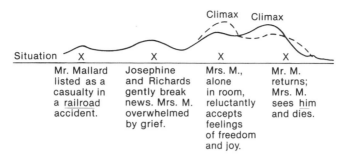

Figure 10–2.

come, which authors like Thomas Hardy use so effectively to emphasize fate and inevitability and O. Henry and Saki use to secure the ironic overtones of their surprise endings. When creatively used, foreshadowing is also a highly effective way of building suspense.

Foreshadowing is important because a plot must be plausible. Though authors are, of course, the creative force behind their narratives, our students may be surprised to learn that they are far from completely free. Authors make a bargain with their readers: in exchange for what Coleridge calls "the willing suspension of disbelief," the author promises to keep the work within the laws of probability and cause and effect—even though life itself is not always so careful and so neat.

Once a character is developed in a particular way, once options have been chosen or events have transpired, their natural consequences must be followed through. One good method I have used to bring home to students the importance of consistent plotting is by reciting an old Russian folk riddle:

Riddle: What is green, hangs from the ceiling, and sings?
Answer: A herring.
  Reply: But a herring isn't green, it doesn't hang from the ceiling, and it doesn't sing.
Answer: That's just to make it harder.

Students see immediately that the riddle is vastly unfair, and understand that, except perhaps to make an absurdist comment on life, its rationale has no place in the art of fiction. Quite simply, authors are bound by what they write. Each incident in the plot must plausibly follow from what has gone before. If authors set up a situation that can produce only green, singing, ceiling-hanging effects, then—if they are to keep faith with their readers—whatever they choose to follow from it will have to be green, singing, and hanging from the ceiling—even a herring in the next scene will have to be verdant, musical, and fond of heights.

Foreshadowing in Chopin's Story. Every event, therefore, must be foreshadowed, prepared for. Take an example from "The Story of an Hour." People do not usually fall over dead when they hear bad news—as dramatically moving or rhetorically convenient as such sudden demises may be for authors. But Kate Chopin carefully foreshadows her heroine's death, and so we accept it. She tells us in the very first line that "Mrs. Mallard was afflicted with a heart trouble" to such an extent that "great care" needed to be taken in telling her about her husband's death. She also lets us know that Mrs. Mallard was not one of those people who first greet news "with a paralyzed inability to accept its significance," but rather one who gives herself immediately "with sudden wild abandonment" to a storm of grief. With this foreshadowing, in addition to all the emotional strain the reader knows Mrs. Mallard has undergone within the hour, as our students will agree, her death does not seem improbable.

REVERSAL. Not only must writers observe the laws of cause and effect, but even if they choose to create what Aristotle calls "reversal"—a surprising (or ironic) turning of events—the possibilities for this reversal must be inherent in the story all along. And though one may not be able to predict the outcome early in the story, in order to satisfy the readers, the reversal must be completely plausible when it is understood retrospectively.

We should make sure that our student authors are well acquainted with reversal. Aristotle, for one, considered it essential to a well-formed plot. This sudden turnabout in a major character's thinking or fortunes gives tension to a story much as the "although clause" gives tension to an essay. And like the "although clause," it may be implied rather than explicit.

Reversal in Chopin's Story. Again "Story of an Hour" provides good examples. To the original situation, Brently Mallard's reported death, Mrs. Mallard reacts with a quick, intense grief for her loss. In the second episode, she experiences a reversal of emotion and her grief turns to joy with the realization of her new freedom. In the final episode, the situation itself has reversed and Mr. Mallard appears. Mrs. Mallard again experiences a sudden intense grief, this time at the loss of her newfound freedom. Her heart cannot stand the reversal, and she dies. Kate Chopin's story is classic in its plotting.

STUDENT EXERCISES

Practice With Plotting Techniques

ACTION PHOTOS

The Stilled-Frame Photo Exercise, is a good way to introduce the study of plot. Using it, we show our students an action photograph, police

continued

officers capturing robbers, for instance, a tense moment on the basket-ball court, or a quarrel on a neighborhood street, and ask them to think of the photograph as a single frame in a sequence of movie or television film, that is, as a single scene in a continuing action.[20] Class discussion should focus on speculations about what might have gone before; what might have followed; and what specifically in the picture itself provides the clues. After the discussion, students should choose one from a group of such photographs and, using it as the base for one incident in a time line, work out a full plot sequence. The exercise might also include a brief summary of the clues in the picture that prompted the suggested plot.

PARTNER PLOTTING

Another plot exercise students especially enjoy is the Partner Plot. Con-centrating particularly on plot and plot devices (such as foreshadowing), students working in groups construct an action tale up to, but not in-cluding, the climax. They set up the conflict, give the events that lay the groundwork for the outcome, but stop just before the turning point.

Then, promising not to tell what they have in mind, they exchange papers with their partner group. Students become adept at setting and picking up one another's clues. And part of the fun of the exercise is reading the combined stories together as a class when all the students match wits in supplying each other with plausible and effective endings.

Teaching Characterization

The second narrative element is the characters involved in the conflict. Writ-ers of fiction—and that includes our students as they write their own sto-ries—face two major problems in portraying their fictional characters: mak-ing them clear to the reader and also making them believable. In reading closely, our students will want to find out as much as they can about each of the characters in the stories. They can judge the characters by what the au-thor tells about them and by what they do. They can also try to understand them by what they say and what other characters say about them—although they should be reminded that not everything a fictional character says will turn out to be true.

CHARACTERIZING BY DIRECT DESCRIPTION, DIALOGUE, AND BEHAVIOR. We can ask our students to work with stories they have read,[21] and inductively discover the ways by which professional authors make their characters clear to their readers. Direct description is the technique that will probably attract their attention first. They should easily find passages for illustration, such as the following richly insightful description of the bride-groom on the train in Stephen Crane's "The Bride Comes to Yellow Sky":

The man's face was reddened from many days in the wind and sun, and a direct result of his new black clothes was that his brick-colored hands were constantly performing in a most conscious fashion. From time to time he looked down respectfully at his attire. He sat with a hand on each knee, like a man waiting in a barber's shop. The glances he devoted to other passengers were furtive and shy.

Vivid as such direct description can be, the insights it embodies seem actually to come alive in dialogue, as our students will be able to point out:

"Ever been in a parlor car before?" he asked, smiling with delight.
"No," she answered, "I never was. It's fine, ain't it?"
"Great! And then after a while we'll go forward to the diner, and get a big layout. Finest meal in the world. Charge a dollar."
"Oh, do they?" cried the bride. "Charge a dollar? Why, that's too much—for us—ain't it, Jack?"
"Not this trip, anyhow," he answered bravely. "We're going to go do the whole thing."

Authors also characterize by noting typical behavior, as, for example, in this excerpt from James Thurber's "The Secret Life of Walter Mitty":

"Why don't you wear your gloves? Have you lost your gloves?" Walter Mitty reached in a pocket and brought out the gloves. He put them on, but after she had turned and gone into the building and he had driven on to a red light, he took them off again. "Pick it up, brother," snapped a cop as the light changed, and Mitty hastily pulled on his gloves and lurched ahead.

Reliable Characterizations.   Even our very young and most literarily unsophisticated students may feel themselves to be on fairly firm ground in interpreting (and reproducing) characterizations developed in these three ways, for in description they have the author's word for the truth of the portrayal, and in dialogue and action they have their own observations as their guide. If they decide that the bridegroom is a hard-working man, unaccustomed to luxury and not quite comfortable with it, but good-natured and eager to "do right" by his bride, or that Mitty is a henpecked, submissive man, whose rebelliousness is kept well beneath the surface, they have good evidence in the quoted passages for these conclusions.

CHARACTERIZATION THROUGH WORDS OF OTHER CHARACTERS OR SELF.   As our students go on to evaluate characterizations garnered through the thoughts and speech of other characters, we will have to urge them always to filter these characterizations through what they know of the reliability and motivation of the speaker. For example, the views of an emotionally unbalanced character with a grudge may be a useful vehicle for readers to derive impressions of the speaker, but they can tell little or nothing from these views about the person referred to, who may or may not be as described.

Questionable Characterization. This need for filtering impressions is a difficult concept for many of our students when they first encounter it, and if they are unable to come up with any immediate instances, we might bring to their attention some broad illustrations of unreliable narrators. The narrator in Robert Browning's "My Last Duchess" clearly exemplifies the notion, as do a number of the narrators in Edgar Allan Poe's short stories. We might, for example, ask our students to tell what sort of a man Fortunato is from the narrator's description in Poe's "The Cask of Amontillado." When they think about it, they will see that they really have no way of knowing:

> The thousand injuries of Fortunato I had borne as I best could, but when he ventured upon insult, I vowed revenge. You, who so well know the nature of my soul, will not suppose, however, that I gave utterance to a threat. At length I would be avenged; this was a point definitely settled—but the very definiteness with which it was resolved precluded the idea of risk. I must not only punish, but punish with impunity. A wrong is unredressed when retribution overtakes its redresser. It is equally unredressed when the avenger fails to make himself felt as such to him who has done the wrong.

Readers must exercise the same caution when approaching characterization by self-revelation. When a character thinks, all we know is that the material mentioned is what that character believes to be true. When a character speaks, all we can say for certain is that what he has spoken is what he wants his listener to understand. On the other hand, we can tell our students, characters in books, like people we know, have a way of telling us more about themselves than they themselves are aware of. Though the opening paragraph from "The Cask of Amontillado," for example, tells us very little about Fortunato, it tells us a good deal about the speaker. From its content, the reader can infer that the speaker is not only revengeful, but also cold and calculating. By permitting an underlying hysteria to creep into the tone, Poe helps the reader further realize that the speaker is also quite mad.

But unless we want to engender a whole anthology of mad narrators (who do seem to captivate the adolescent imagination), we must encourage our students to discover other examples too. They should look for instances where the author seems to wink at the reader while a character is speaking and to whisper conspiratorially, "Better discount what this character says about himself or herself and form your own judgments from the way it's said."

Students must learn to take all sorts of factors into account. Granny's delirious condition throughout most of Katherine Anne Porter's "The Jilting of Granny Weatherall," for instance, must be considered in assessing the validity of her perceptions; Huck Finn's lack of education, and especially his ignorance of the value of his own moral standards, must be weighed against what the reader understands of his basic honesty and good sense in evaluating his judgments; and the reader's acceptance of all the utterances of child characters, charming though they may be, must be qualified in terms of the childishness of their outlook and the limitation of their experience. Our students must also learn to question the words of all speakers who talk about themselves, for even otherwise reliable characters share the very human tendency of justifying themselves in their speech or thought in ways not always strictly in accord with the truth. Flannery O'Connor reminds us of this tendency in these lines from "Good Country People":

> [Mrs. Hopewell] said, stiffening slightly, "I keep my Bible by my bedside." This was not the truth. It was in the attic somewhere.

CHARACTERS IN CHOPIN'S STORY.   What do we know of the characters in Kate Chopin's story? We know that Josephine and Richards are kind, considerate people, who can be counted upon even in an emergency to do the right thing. They broke the sad news to Mrs. Mallard in a kind, capable way, and Josephine was lovingly there for her sister when she needed her. On the other hand, beyond the obvious concern for Mrs. Mallard's health, is there not just a touch of what might be a habitual condescension in Josephine's "imploring" into her sister's keyhole:

> "Louise, open the door! I beg; open the door—you will make yourself ill. What are you doing Louise? For heaven's sake open the door."

Is there not just a trace here of a stronger personality dominating a weaker one—for her own good?

We know of Brently Mallard only from his wife, who comes to believe that she has been wronged by him. Yet even in her perhaps prejudiced eyes he is a "tender" and "loving" man with only "kind intentions." It is clear that Chopin wants to underscore Mallard's basic kindness to make the issue of his dominant will more clear-cut. Though we do not see any example of this dominance, we know from his wife's private thoughts that she, at least, believed that she suffered from it. What is the nature of what Mrs. Mallard refers to as a "powerful will bending her in blind persistence"? Perhaps Josephine's speech gives us echoes of it.

And how does Chopin want us to regard her central character? She tells us that Mrs. Mallard is "repressed" and yet "strong." She shows us that she is one who experiences powerful emotions with "wild abandonment." Still, we see the reluctance with which Mrs. Mallard accepts the unconventional insight that comes to her:

> She was beginning to recognize this thing that was approaching to possess her, and she was striving to beat it back with her will.

In Mrs. Mallard, Chopin shows us a woman who has the courage to be completely honest with herself. And yet, what about her moral character? Does Chopin want us to regard her feelings about her loss of her husband as "a monstrous joy"? Or are we to sympathize with them?

STUDENT EXERCISE

Characterization

Students appreciate opportunities to practice the various modes of characterization. For direct physical description to convey a sense of reality and to imply the personality or character of the person described, the description must be on the one hand, exact and specific, and on the other hand, vivid and appropriate. Teachers have created exercises to develop both sets of qualities.

WORD PORTRAITS
Alfred L. Crabb, Jr., has had success with word portraits. In the first step of his exercise, he shows his class the portrait of an expressive face (for example, an opaque projection of a *Time* cover). He then requests descriptions of specific features and collects them on the board. He next asks how the portrait might be put into writing:

> Different ways of describing a single feature will permit discussion of which is the most effective. Problems in organization arise: Is it better to give overall impressions first, beginning with outstanding features, or is it better to work from top to bottom? Should everything about the eyes be told at the same time, or is some of the material unnecessary, or should the wrinkles be handled with the other facial wrinkles?[22]

As a preliminary to their individual work, each member of the class then attempts a descriptive paragraph about this portrait. For the main exercise, each student is asked to write on a separate portrait. When the papers are read in class, the pictures that inspired them should also be shared.

CREATING DIALOGUE
An exercise in creating dialogue that junior high students especially enjoy is giving speech to comic-strip characters by appropriately filling in blanked-out balloons in some of their favorite strips.[23]

To help students achieve good characterization through dialogue, where the voices must ring both true in general and true to their speakers' current emotional states is more difficult. Hillocks has developed a role-playing exercise where appropriate gestures and facial expressions must also be considered. Students working with partners are first asked to act out an encounter between two characters and then to write it up as dialogue. The students are given a list of specified characterizations and situations from which they may choose or use as inspiration to

continued

continued

invent a similar one of their own. Among the situations Hillocks suggests is the following:

Characters: Two boys
1. A teenage boy lacks confidence and experience to be a member of a local team.
2. The second boy of the same age is captain of the team and has great self-confidence. His main objective is that his team should win.

Situation: The first boy wishes to be a member of the team but does not know how to ask. He approaches the second boy shyly. (20)

CHARACTERIZING BY GESTURE

A character in a story is most effectively depicted by voice or action, but such characterization seems to be difficult for the nonprofessional writer to achieve. Hillocks suggests using physical pantomime to develop this skill in our students. Sitting in a circle so that they can see one another, students first try to make their hands suggest the varying traits of evil, anger, helplessness, greed, guilt; to make their feet appear "restless, embarrassed, impatient, or angry"; and to make their posture show "confidence, fear, fatigue, discouragement, cheerfulness" (18).

Then individual students pantomime such situations as "a middle-aged person, impatient and becoming more and more angry after waiting in a doctor's office for two hours" or "a very young child, guilty and frightened, waiting in a principal's office after throwing a rock through a school window" (19), while their classmates try to guess the situation. The students follow up the pantomiming by writing a description of a character in a particular emotional state under certain circumstances, relying primarily upon specific details of his or her actions to carry the information.

CHARACTERIZING SCHOOLMATES

Another exercise that invariably arouses student enthusiasm is the assignment of character sketches of a classmate, teacher, or some other person known to at least a number of the students. These character sketches are to concentrate upon mannerisms and tone of speech and the sound and accent of the spoken voice, although they may also include references to characteristic ways of walking, standing, studying, behaving. During the period between the day the exercise is assigned and the day the brief composition is written, students greatly expand their habits of observation. When the sketches are read (I recommend teacher perusal of them first to weed out the rare—but possible—insulting or injurious paper), student recognition of the subjects of well-written papers is gleeful and insightful.

Teaching Point of View

Closely related to strategies of characterization is the matter of point of view, an element of fiction whose importance cannot be overestimated. As Percy Lubbock writes:

> The whole intricate question of method, in the craft of fiction, I take to be governed by the question of the point-of-view—the question of the relation in which the narrator stands to the story.[24]

Perhaps the most crucial question our students can ask when they are trying to gain insight into a story is "From whose point of view are we seeing the action?"

Yet, despite its significance, point of view is a concept that some students find difficult to grasp. It is thus best approached inductively. We can present our students with a passage from a story or novel (it is wisest to choose from those they have already read) and ask them to identify the person from whose point of view it is written. Whose voice is speaking here? we might ask. To some the question will seem tautological: Who else could be talking but the author?

OMNISCIENT AUTHOR-NARRATOR. So to begin where the least sophisticated of our students are, we can start with passages where the author truly is the speaker and addresses the reader in his or her own voice, as does Fielding, for example, in *Tom Jones:*

> As we determined, when we first sat down to write this history, to flatter no man, but to guide our pen throughout by the directions of truth, we are obliged to bring our hero on the stage in a much more disadvantageous manner than we could wish; and to declare honestly, even at his first appearance, that it was the universal opinion of all Mr. Allworthy's family that he [Tom] was certainly born to be hanged. Indeed, I am sorry to say there was too much reason for this conjecture.

Fielding is the quintessential omniscient narrator. Though insisting he is bound by "truth," the tale is his to tell and he can tell it any way he pleases, commenting wherever he chooses in his own voice upon the various ramifications of the story and even, as in the example, upon his mode of writing. He can see into the minds of all his characters and can reveal their thoughts. He is not only fully aware of all that has already occurred, but he is equally cognizant of what is to come, and can even tantalize the reader with this knowledge.

Authorial Considerations. All authors, of course, are capable of this sort of omniscience. But they can choose to limit what they say—even what they see—to suit their narrative or rhetorical purposes. Even the truly omniscient narrator is under no obligation to tell all he knows, as Fielding openly confesses:

Whether Partridge was innocent or not will perhaps appear here after; but if the historic Muse hath entrusted me with any secrets, I will by no means be guilty of discovering them till she shall give me leave.

SEMIOBJECTIVE AUTHOR-NARRATOR.   Stories narrated by their authors range in degree of objectivity from the intimacy of the "Dear reader, I will tell you all" approach of Fielding and Kurt Vonnegut to the almost uninterrupted dialogue of Ernest Hemingway's Nick Adams stories. "In between" we can help our students discover the author, such as Thomas Hardy in "The Three Strangers," who though commenting and speculating almost as freely as Fielding, limits authorial commentary to those external details that a perceptive observer, had one been present, might note: "The sad wan light revealed the lonely pedestrian to be a man of supple frame."

A wide variety and range of such authorial points of view, from the personally managerial to the almost solely dramatic, can be exemplified in almost any sizable collection of stories. The particular illustrations are insignificant. What is important is that our students have the opportunity to trace the handling of point of view through enough examples to be able to distinguish the author's voice from the dramatized portions of the story and to become conscious of its various connotations and nuances.

PROTAGONIST NARRATOR (FIRST PERSON).   When our students have developed some familiarity with the author's voice, we should call their attention to stories in which the dominant voice is not supposed to be that of the author at all, but rather the voice of one of his characters. We might explain that to bring the reader closer to the action, an author can choose to speak from the mouth of a participant in that action. It is as if the author has crept inside the character's head and speaks with his voice and sees with his eyes.

Students find the first-person protagonist the easiest to distinguish of all the points of view. Given a passage from anywhere in Frank O'Connor's "First Confession," for instance, students will readily be able to see that the child, Jackie, is telling the story:

> But when Father came in later Nora said in a shocked voice: "Oh, Dadda, do you know what Jackie did at dinner time?" Then, of course, it all came out; Father gave me a flaking; Mother interfered, and for days after that he didn't speak to me and Mother barely spoke to Nora. And all because of that old woman! God knows, I was heart-scalded.

The voice in any passage from Ralph Ellison's *Invisible Man* (chapters of which are often anthologized as short stories) can also be quickly recognized as that of the protagonist, who—in a genuine tribute to the novelist's art— students persist in identifying with that of Ellison himself:

> "I got my money on the big boy." Hearing this, I almost cropped my guard. I was confused: Should I try to win against the voice out there? Would not

this go against my speech, and was not this a moment for humility, for nonre-
sistance? A blow to my head as I danced about sent my right eye popping like
a jack-in-the-box and settled my dilemma. The room went red as I fell. It was
a dream fall, my body languid and fastidious as to where to land, until the
floor became impatient and smashed up to meet me.

When asked to listen carefully to the voice and to describe the speaker
more precisely, our students should be able to tell that the mature diction
("dilemma," "languid," "fastidious," and so on) indicates that the Ellison passage is written in retrospect by the protagonist after he has reached his maturity, while such expressions as "gave me a flaking" and "heart-scalded," sweet
with brogue, reveal the voice of an Irish child in the O'Connor passage.

Authorial Considerations.   Though the total immersion of the reader in
a character's subjective consciousness is a very powerful way to tell a story, it
presents the author with genuine problems. For, in adopting this point of
view, the writer relinquishes a fair measure of control. Not only must she
give up her identity as a separate controlling intelligence, but she must also
eliminate from the story any information, however vital, that her narrator
would not be in position to know, as well as that information (such as his
own appearance) that he would be unlikely to talk about. We can put the
problem to our students and ask them to use their reading and their ingenuity as guides to figure out ways an author might get around these difficulties.

Dramatic Irony.   Some truly insightful students might suggest the technique of dramatic irony, though it is unlikely they would use the term. With
our help, they may be able to point out that there is very often a discrepancy
between what the character-narrator thinks is true and what the author believes, and wants the reader to realize, actually is true.

Many of the widely anthologized Poe stories are helpful in bringing students to understand this point because even a truly unsophisticated reader
realizes that "there is something wrong" with his characteristically mad narrators.

Our students should also be able to see that the author's opinions are
never quite the same as those of a child narrator either and, in fact, that a
great deal of the charm of such stories lies in this very discrepancy. They
should be able to imagine O'Connor chuckling with his readers over Jackie's
childish perceptions in "First Confession," and also to see that authors like
O'Connor rely upon our mature, educated understanding to see through the
childish chatter and grasp the poignancy of the point they are making
through their narrators.

This understanding is more difficult for our students to acquire when the
voice that speaks to them in the story is less clearly differentiated from the
author's own. Nevertheless, if we lead them to look closely at such passages
as the one quoted from *Invisible Man*, they can begin to comprehend the
more subtle dramatic irony they contain. In that passage, Ellison wants us

to share the retrospective understanding of his now-experienced protagonist (understanding denied to him at the time of the incident) of the moral monstrosity of the men who wielded the power in that community and of the folly of trying to win their praise or gain their respect.

By working with examples such as these, we can help our students understand that dramatic irony is a highly effective way for an author to project his or her own views, despite—and through—the differing perspective of a character.

OVER THE SHOULDER OF THE PROTAGONIST (THIRD-PERSON NARRATOR). By studying their sample short stories carefully, some of our students may make the discovery that in some of the stories a compromise seems to have been effected between the author's voice and a character's point of view. In such stories, though the narrator remains on the outside and all of the characters are spoken of in the third person, they may notice that the reader is privy to the thoughts of one of the characters, that all the perceptions in the story seem to be those of the same character, and that even the narrating voice seems to take on the colorations of this character's speech.

Authorial Advantages. Though thus retaining the advantages of an intimate acquaintance with the mind of the protagonist, authors of these kinds of stories distance themselves enough through the use of the third-person pronoun to provide objective descriptions of the narrating character as well as to give, where necessary, details of the plot that may be beyond this character's ken.

Examples of this sort of treatment abound, for its use is the most common point of view written into stories today. The stories of James Joyce offer particularly clear-cut illustrations. Here, for instance, are the opening lines from "A Little Cloud":

> Eight years before he had seen his friend off at the North Wall and wished him godspeed. Gallaher had got on. You could tell that at once by his travelled air, his well-cut tweed suit, and fearless accent. Few fellows had talents like his and fewer still could remain unspoiled by such success. Gallaher's heart was in the right place and he had deserved to win. It was something to have a friend like that.

Figuring It Out. But though the point of view seems clear to those of us who are experienced readers, it will not be so to a number of our students. With this in mind, we might ask them: Who is saying these words? Whose voice is that? How can you tell? How does the narrator reveal himself in these words?

If, after consideration, some students are still unable to reply with any degree of certitude, are unable to say in this instance, for example, that the speaker is Gallaher's friend, a man who tends to think in clichés ("heart in the right place," "unspoiled by success," "deserves to win"), and who is more impressed by Gallaher's success than the facts will perhaps warrant, then they can turn back to the text and look for further evidence. In this particular story the next lines supply the answer: these are clearly the thoughts of the protagonist, Little Chandler.

> Little Chandler's thoughts ever since lunchtime had been of his meeting with Gallaher, of Gallaher's invitation and of the great city of London where Gallaher lived.

But all stories are not so explicit, and our students may still be unsure. They may wonder how the reader, when faced with third-person material, can determine whether authors are speaking for themselves or whether they are sitting on a character's shoulder, so to speak, writing through the character's consciousness. A close comparative study of the first and second paragraphs of "A Little Cloud"—or of other such contrasting paragraphs—should help students learn how to distinguish the difference. In the second paragraph Joyce asserts the authorial privilege, not abrogated by use of the third-person narrator, of supplying necessary information beyond the understanding of the central character:

> He was called Little Chandler because, though he was but slightly under the average stature, he gave one the idea of being a little man. His hands were white and small, his frame was fragile, his voice was quiet and his manners were refined. He took the greatest care of his fair silken hair and moustache and used perfume discreetly on his handkerchief. The half-moons of his nails were perfect and when he smiled you caught a glimpse of a row of childish white teeth.

We might help our students pick out the specific words and phrases that account for the sharp contrast revealed in the style and tone of these passages between the mind of Little Chandler and the mind of James Joyce.

Working in this way to identify the person from whose point of view a story is told provides our students with practice in listening for the speaking voice that should serve them well in their reading—and in their writing.

SUBORDINATE OR PERIPHERAL NARRATOR (FIRST OR THIRD PERSON).
Another alternative available to the author who wants both the intimacy of the character narrator and the distance to comment on the situation is to narrate the story from the point of view of a secondary character or even from that of a casual observer.

Our students can find examples of stories narrated from the point of view of these subordinate characters written in both the first and the third persons: Marlowe in Joseph Conrad's *Lord Jim*, for instance; the doctor in Somerset Maugham's "Rain"; a townsperson in William Faulkner's "A Rose for Miss Emily" and in Robert Penn Warren's "The Patented Gate and the Mean Hamburger." As our students make such discoveries, we should encourage them to try to figure out in each case why the author did not choose to tell the tale personally or to narrate the story through the eyes of the protagonist.

Why did he choose to use this particular character for his spokesperson? Would our students choose to use this viewpoint if they were writing the story?

VARIETY OF POINTS OF VIEW. Authors present their stories from points of view that range all the way from the complete subjectivity of one character's perspective to an objectivity that goes beyond the author's view to the strict dramatization of action and dialogue of a play or one of Hemingway's dialogue-centered tales. Our students should have no difficulty in realizing that a reader's job is to interpret the story in terms of this point of view. They should find the Point of View Student Guidelines useful in interpreting their reading and especially in preplanning their own stories.

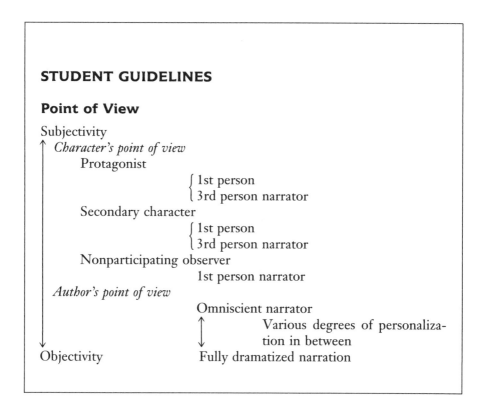

STUDENT GUIDELINES

Point of View

Subjectivity

↑ *Character's point of view*
      Protagonist
             { 1st person
             { 3rd person narrator
      Secondary character
             { 1st person
             { 3rd person narrator
      Nonparticipating observer
                1st person narrator
Author's point of view
              Omniscient narrator
                ↑   Various degrees of personaliza-
                ↓   tion in between
↓ Objectivity   Fully dramatized narration

Such a schematized survey of points of view still does not cover every possibility, however. Many novels and a good number of short stories are told in the third person from multiple points of view. Nevertheless, because this way of writing is extremely difficult for the inexperienced writer to bring off successfully, we should, I think, discourage our students from attempting it, at least in their first ventures into the writing of fiction.

Point of View in Chopin's Story.   "From what point of view is Chopin's 'The Story of an Hour' written?" is the sort of question we might well ask our students. Having acquired some understanding of this idea, most will agree that it begins in the author's own voice:

> Knowing that Mrs. Mallard was afflicted with a heart trouble, great care was taken to break to her as gently as possible the news of her husband's death.

And they will also see that the narration continues in this fairly objective manner until Mrs. Mallard goes to her room alone.

At that point, our most discerning students may suggest that Mrs. Mallard's point of view takes over. Chopin continues using the third-person "she" because with it she can get outside her heroine and provide the reader with external description of her character. But from this time until close to the end of the story, we are not only privy to Mrs. Mallard's thoughts but the narrating voice even takes on the colorations of Mrs. Mallard's own:

> There would be no one to live for during those coming years; she would live for herself. . . . And yet she had loved him—sometimes. Often she had not. What did it matter!

The Crucial Point-of-View Question.   How reliable a narrator is Mrs. Mallard? How close are her views to Chopin's own? This is perhaps the central critical question of the story, and the way our students answer it will, to an important extent, determine their interpretation of the story.

STUDENT EXERCISE

Point of View

In order to understand better the nature and possibilities of point of view, we might want to ask our students to try an exercise or two in which they would take an old familiar story, such as "The Three Bears," "The Tortoise and the Hare," or "Little Red Riding Hood," and explore it from a variety of points of view.[25]

How does the story differ when it is told by Baby Bear? Father Bear? or Goldilocks? Our students could experience the way Aesop's tale becomes two quite different stories when it is told from the turtle's and from the hare's points of view. Similarly, they might learn that Little Red Riding Hood sees the world in a far different way than does the wolf. Whatever story they pick, they cannot help but discover for themselves the tremendous thematic and structural impact of point of view.

Teaching Theme

Questions such as those that students ask about the value system from which Chopin wants her readers to view Mrs. Mallard lead directly to a consideration of the theme, the "what the author is trying to say" that is the heart of a story. Although the theme does not exactly summarize a work's entire meaning the way a thesis does, it is the idea that informs every part of a story and gives it its reason for being. Few student short stories are originally inspired by a thematic idea, but all the good ones evolve such an idea as their authors approach their plot and their characters.

If we can say that fiction begins in conflict, we might add that it ends in theme. And the theme comes directly out of the resolution of the conflict. As Brooks and his colleagues put it in our definition:

> Fiction is a narrative . . . of a significant conflict that is resolved in such a way as to imply a comment on human values, feelings or attitudes.

Students easily accept the importance of theme, but because some may have difficulty conceiving of it as anything other than the "moral of the story," they often need help in uncovering it.

DETERMINING A THEME.   How do our students find a story's theme? If thinking over the story does not intuitively bring a theme to mind, Brooks and company's definition points to one good method: since a narrative work consists of "a significant conflict that is resolved in such a way as to imply a comment on human values, feelings or attitudes," they should be able to find that comment—the theme—by *identifying the conflict* and *noting how it is resolved*. The procedure outlined in the Discovering a Theme Student Guidelines has proved helpful to more than one student who didn't get an instinctive sense of theme from the reading.

STUDENT GUIDELINES

Discovering a Theme

1. Precisely identify the conflict in your story. (Do not pick a general conflict, such as "man against nature." Focus on something specific, such as "Joe versus the Antarctic.")
2. Ask yourself: What is the outcome of the conflict? Who wins?
3. Generalize on your answers to (1) and (2) and formulate a tentative theme.
4. Test out your tentative theme to see if it is consistent with all the significant features of the story that you noted in your close reading. Ask yourself: Is this what all the elements of the story seem to be aimed at? Is this what the author is really trying to say?

FINDING THEME IN CHOPIN'S STORY.   About the only way to show our students how to determine their notion of a story's theme—and thus their interpretation of the story—is to walk through the discovery process with them. The following analysis of "The Story of an Hour" summarizes one class's experience with the interpretative process during a guided class discussion.

Working Through the Discovering a Theme Guidelines.   General speculation on a theme did not prove fruitful, so we turned to the strategy outlined in the Student Guidelines. Working through them, this class had two distinct ideas of the conflict and thus arrived at two separate thematic possibilities:

Possible Theme A

1. Conflict: Mrs. Mallard versus (an internalized) Josephine and Richards, or more specifically, Mrs. Mallard's view on marriage versus the conventional views.
2. Resolution: Conventional views win. No sooner does Mrs. Mallard come to terms with her joyous feelings of freedom from being a wife than she is faced with the continuation of that state. No longer able to face continuing in that role on society's terms, she dies.
3. Generalization (and tentative theme): It is impossible (some said, It is unnatural) for women to try to strive for lives of "self-assertion."

Possible Theme B

1. Conflict: Mrs. Mallard versus Louise Mallard.
2. Resolution: Louise wins—at the loss of her life.
3. Generalization (and tentative theme): Freedom of will is the most important value; it alone makes life meaningful or even worthwhile.

Both of these tentative themes—as different as they are—seem to be based on valid interpretations of the story, depending upon how the evidence is read. The question turns on Kate Chopin's use of irony.

Teaching Irony

Irony may be the most difficult concept we teach. Understanding that what is said is the opposite of what is meant takes intellectual maturity and a sophisticated insight. Though some of our students readily understand simple sarcasm—and even use it comfortably—verbal irony must be broadly drawn for their comprehension and most are very literal-minded about anything on the printed page.

THREE KINDS OF IRONY.   Another reason so many of our students find irony hard to fathom is that there are at least three quite different—though related—idea systems that go by this name, and it is sometimes hard for them to grasp the underlying unity of the concept. That unity is inherent in the definition Wynkyn de Worde formulated in the sixteenth century, which still captures the essence of the term's meaning and appeals to students because of its brevity and quaintness:

> "Ironye," Wynkyn wrote, is "that which sayeth one thing but giveth to understand ye contrarye."

All three of the literary uses of irony can be approached in these terms:

- In verbal irony, the *speaker* means the contrary of what he says (or writes).
- In dramatic irony, the *author* means something contrary to what the speaker says.
- In circumstantial irony (or irony of fate), *fate* sees that events turn out contrary to human expectations—often almost as if in mockery of these expectations.

In the course of the discussion in this chapter, I have already had occasion to mention each of these kinds of irony. Although irony is not an essential feature of fiction (as it is of satire, for instance), many authors find it a highly effective tool for, as our definition phrases it, "imply[ing their] comment on human values, feelings and attitudes" in the writing of their stories. And though it is a sophisticated tool, some of our students may want to learn how to employ it with profit.

Verbal Irony.   Verbal irony is intended irony. We can explain it to our students by suggesting remarks they might make where they intend the listener to understand the opposite of what they actually say—for example, "I'm just bubbling over with satisfaction after that really gourmet treat we just had in the lunchroom!" In works of fiction, they can recognize it most easily in the comments of an author-narrator who, like Fielding or Saki or Flannery O'Connor, is of an ironic turn of mind. In "Good Country People," for instance, they will find Flannery O'Connor including such ironic comments as:

> Mrs. Hopewell had no bad qualities of her own but she was able to use other people's in such a constructive way that she never felt the lack.

But though students may not find it as easily recognizable, verbal irony also occurs in the speech of characters who are portrayed as having an ironic turn of mind, as, for example, Hulga in "Good Country People." When her mother effusively responds to their rural visitor's self-negations by protesting, "Why, good country people are the salt of the earth!," Hulga retorts, "Get rid of the salt of the earth, and let's eat."

Some of our students may also share this frame of mind. Although we may have to caution them to avoid the "smart-alecky" tone that youthful excesses in the use of irony often entail, we might help them work their ironic attitude effectively into the fabric of their stories.

Dramatic Irony. Dramatic irony is a more subtle concept than verbal irony and is consequently more difficult for our students to understand. Here the irony is not intended by the speaker. A homey example again may serve to clarify the concept for them. One that works fairly well is a telephone monologue that we might dramatize for the class between, let's say, Harry and his friend Agatha:

> Hello, Agatha? Well, this is Harry. And I just had to call you and find out if you had heard the news about that dreadful old gossip, Mabel Jane. . . . I never heard of such a gossip! Talk. Talk. Talk. But what she has to gossip about I'll never know. Everybody knows that her nephew ran off and married that no-good Collins woman up in Sturgeon Creek. . . . Yes, and her daughter's not supposed to be everything she should be; and there are definite rumors about her brother's business too. . . .

The question is, of course, who is really the gossip? Our students easily see how Harry, all unknowingly, convicts himself with every word he says.

In dramatic irony the irony of the situation is not understood by the speaker, only by the listener, part of whose pleasure comes from recognizing the ignorance of the speaker. In literature, the author and the reader share the secret knowledge; it is as if the author winks at the reader behind the character's back. In "Good Country People" again, for example, Flannery O'Connor wants her readers to smile at the series of clichés which fill Hulga's mother's speech whenever she feels the need to say something philosophical or profound:

> "Why!" she cried, "good country people are the salt of the earth! Besides we all have different ways of doing, it takes all kinds to make the world go 'round. That's life."

Dramatic irony can also be used for tragic effect or to heighten suspense. Familiar examples work well here too. Many of our students know the crypt scene in *Romeo and Juliet*, where the audience understands that Juliet is only unconscious, but Romeo thinks she is dead. Most have felt the power of the dramatic irony in that scene, power that almost makes them want to call out, "Don't kill yourself, Romeo! She's alive! Only wait. She's really alive!" Most have also seen war movies on television where the little bride is happily sweeping her apartment, preparing for the homecoming of her pilot husband, whose plane the audience has just seen shot down.

In both cases, the author has made the audience or reader privy to a truth that the character does not know. Romeo's heartbroken cry, "Thou womb of death / gorged with the dearest morsel of the earth, / . . . I'll cram thee with more food," and the little bride's cheerful murmur, "Soon my darling will be coming home," are thus infused with a dramatic irony that is understood by the audience and works its emotional pull upon them.

Circumstantial Irony/Irony of Fate. This emotional pull is not unrelated to that which the reader (or audience) experiences in the presence of circumstantial irony or the irony of fate. This irony has provided an important theme in literature from the days of Sophocles, for since the dawn of civilization human beings have often viewed themselves as helpless creatures whose ambition to exert some control over their own destiny is at first encouraged and then almost playfully thwarted by what seems to be the whimsical powers of the universe.

The irony of fate comes into play when the outcome of a situation in life or in literature is not only contrary to what was planned for and expected, but seems almost to be in mockery of the appropriate outcome. Many O. Henry stories provide good teaching examples of circumstantial irony because—though sometimes simplistically handled—it is always clear-cut. An especially good choice is "The Gift of the Magi," familiar to most of our students from its traditional Christmas performance on television. We can recall the story with them and elicit the details of the ironic conclusion, where the wife has sold her one treasure, her hair, to buy a chain for her husband's one treasure, his watch, which he likewise has sold to buy a decorative comb to adorn her (now lost) hair.

Whatever illustrations we choose, however, we should bring our students to realize the versatility of this theme. Though it can be tragic, as in *Oedipus Rex*, and poignant, as in "The Gift of the Magi," it also has the humorous possibilities demonstrated in "The Ransom of Red Chief," where the kidnappers are so harried by the antics of a kidnapped child that they are willing to pay the parents to take him back. If we can help our students develop the knack of viewing situations within their own experience in this way, we are giving them a glimpse of an important source of the raw material of fiction.

IRONY IN CHOPIN'S STORY.   Kate Chopin uses no *verbal irony* in "The Story of an Hour." Neither she in her own voice nor any of her characters when they speak say anything that is the opposite of what they mean. Chopin does, however, use both of the other kinds of irony to quite remarkable effect.

Circumstantial Irony.   Irony of fate is deeply ingrained in Chopin's story. There is a grim ironic laughter behind every reversal of the plot. The analyzing class found it, for example, in the fact that Mrs. Mallard should experience her husband's death—for which she has already mourned—with joy. And they discovered even more when, after that forbidden joy, her husband turns out to be alive. The fateful chortle is there again when, after Mrs. Mallard has exchanged a fear of a long life for a wish for it, her original death wish is granted.

Dramatic Irony.   As for dramatic irony, it is this which gives the final sentence its bite and its pathos:

> When the doctors came, they said she had died of heart disease—of joy that kills.

The doctors thought that Mrs. Mallard's feeling upon seeing her husband alive was a joy so sudden and profound that her heart could not stand the strain. The class saw clearly that Chopin has given her readers to understand quite the opposite. And yet on second thought, they could see in a final irony of fate that it may well have been joy that killed Louise Mallard—though not the joy the doctors had understood. For had she not experienced the joy of freedom, its loss would not have affected her.

Interpreting Chopin's Story. Which of the two proposed themes the students favored depended primarily on whether they interpreted Chopin's use of Mrs. Mallard's point of view ironically or not. If they read her character ironically, then they found dramatic irony in passages such as this:

> She did not stop to ask if it were not a monstrous joy that held her. A clear and exalted perception enabled her to dismiss the suggestion as trivial.

These students see Mrs. Mallard's joy as monstrous, her feelings toward her kind husband as lacking in gratitude, and her ennobling of the idea of self-assertion as selfish and egotistical. Other students identified Chopin's views closely with those of her heroine. Then found no irony in her use of the phrase "clear and exalted perception," but saw it rather as Chopin's way of overriding any tendency of the reader to echo Mrs. Mallard's fear that hers might be "a monstrous joy."

STUDENT EXERCISES

Theme

We should encourage our students to keep the notion of an underlying meaning in mind as they explore the material for their own short stories and plan their approach to it. But inexperienced minds have problems with subtlety, and the notion of theme can seem thoroughly subtle and illusive to many of our students. They have little trouble writing fables or narrative homilies where the whole purpose of the narrative is to point to a moral, but they do not understand how to work in thematic ideas that are expressed indirectly through a resolved conflict. They need some preparatory experience with nonverbal material to wean them from "the moral of my story is . . ." mode of thinking.

THEMATIC COLLAGES

In this exercise, students begin by stating their views on an issue of human behavior that is important to them. They might, for instance,

continued

continued

write "loving parents provide children the freedom they need to grow" or "Loving parents provide the structure and control their children need, and secretly appreciate." Having decided on their issue and formulated a statement expressing their perspective on it, they make a collage to illustrate it.

At the conclusion of the project, the students present their collages to the class. Their explanations and their classmates responses should lead to a discussion on theme, one enlightening to all.

THEME DISCOVERY OUTLINES
The theme discovery questions, answered in reverse order, can provide training in the concept of theme. Students begin with a statement of their point of view on an issue—it could even be the issue they used for their collage. Then, working with the Discovering a Theme Student Guidelines (see page 436), they invent a conflict involving characters and suggest a resolution for it that would imply their viewpoint on human behavior.

Students who are particularly successful with this exercise may want to base their short story on it.

TEACHING SHORT STORY WRITING

From the very beginning of our study of fiction, our students should understand that they will be writing a short story themselves, so that during all the reading and discussing and exercises that go on throughout the study they will be preparing themselves for this work. The short story is the one writing task that students are almost invariably enthusiastic and excited about. By providing them with a little direction, we can channel this enthusiasm to motivate the sometimes difficult literary study that must precede their writing in a combined curriculum.

Gaining the Appropriate Understandings

As our students read stories and discuss them, they begin to get a feel for plot, character, point of view, theme, irony—the narrative elements. Exercises can also be helpful.

WRITING EXERCISES. Exercises, such as those included in this text, provide students with opportunities for experiential contact with each of the narrative elements and a chance to discover their nature for themselves. Each of these exercises also provides a preliminary writing encounter, a chance to try out each of the narrative elements in their own writing.

Teaching Verisimilitude

But even after our students have developed a good grasp of the elements included in the definition of fiction we have been working with, they will still need some understanding of how to make their stories believable. For though fiction is not really a "slice of life," as it has often been called, it cannot provide the insights into living that are among its greatest values unless it purports to be true, unless—at least while reading—the reader can believe that the actions have happened and the characters are real people. Much of our work with student writers should be designed to help them achieve this verisimilitude.

Credibility is achieved mainly in three ways: through concrete detail, through a creditable narrator, and through consistency of plot and character.

SPECIFIC CONCRETE DETAIL. The technique students find easiest to master is specific detail. They can see through their reading how a generous use of concrete detail embeds a piece of writing in reality. Such explicit information as times and dates and places convinces the reader of the work's truth. When readers learn, for instance, that the lottery described in Shirley Jackson's "The Lottery" took place on the morning of June 27th (which was "clear and sunny"), how can they doubt its existence? And who could dispute the reality of a tale that begins as factually as Ambrose Bierce's masterpiece of horror, "The Boarded Window":

> In 1830, only a few miles away from what is now the great city Cincinnati, lay an immense and almost unbroken forest.

Our students can learn to collect—or invent—such details and use them to make their own writing convincing.

Vivid Sense Details. Description can be made concrete not only by using such explicit references, but also by including sensory impressions. If our students have participated in observation activities such as Hillocks suggests (see page 408), they will have developed their sensitivity to these impressions. We need then only call their attention to the effective use authors, such as William Sansom, can make of these sensory details. For example, a reader cannot help but believe in the reality of a setting described with this vivid specificity:

> He walked on. No twigs snapped, everything too old, rotten, wet. Beneath the trees a thick undergrowth of elder and nettles had grown: he had to snake his way through—once he stopped suddenly, holding his breath: a statue, an eyeless youth in Greek drapery, was watching him from the thicket; mossed and in half-shadow, it stood still as life. He coughed—no echo—and went on.

Sensory details, like these from "The Ballroom," both establish credibility and help create and sustain a mood.

A CREDIBLE NARRATOR. Another technique for promoting verisimilitude is the use of a credible narrator. Actually, any first-person narrator contributes to the believability of a work of fiction because, by simply telling her own story, the narrator bears witness to its truth: "I know this happened because I was there." If the accents of the narrator ring true, then the story rings true.

If the narrator is not the protagonist, it is helpful if he is a knowledgeable observer. We believe Joseph Conrad's Marlowe because he tells us about the sea and he clearly knows the sea and even more because he tells us about the minds of men and we are convinced that he is a keen and shrewd observer of his fellow man.

The Skeptical Narrator. The stranger and less believable the tale, the more necessary to establish belief by means of a trustworthy narrator. Students who are interested in writing a story dealing with the supernatural are well advised to develop their tale through the eyes of a skeptic, for when that skeptic stops protesting and becomes convinced, one's reader is often convinced too. Shakespeare employs this principle in *Hamlet* where the skeptical Horatio is brought in to witness the appearance of Hamlet's father's ghost. Poe uses a similarly skeptical narrator to the same effect in "The Fall of the House of Usher."

CONSISTENCY OF PLOT. The third technique through which credibility may be sustained is consistency both in plot and in character. Our students must understand that fiction must be logical. Though life is capable of taking strange turns and can include wonderous coincidences, a work of fiction, if it is to be believable, does not have that luxury.

Action must spring logically and consistently from the characteristics of the participants as they have been developed in the story; turns of plot must be capable of logical cause-and-effect analyses. If our students want to surprise their readers, they must build that surprise out of what is inherently possible in the plot and psychologically realistic in the characters. Though the culminating action need not be revealed until the end, inexorable forces set in motion by elements in the plot or the characters should seem, at least in retrospect, to have made the conclusion inevitable.

There is a good reason that truth is stranger than fiction: readers insist that the strangeness of fiction be made consistent with what their logic and common sense tells them about the way things happen in the world.

CONSISTENCY OF CHARACTER. In addition to projecting their characters clearly, writers need to make them believable. When characterizing by description, our students need to include the sort of vivid, concrete sensory details that make us visualize, and believe in, Mrs. Mallard.

Credible Dialogue. Dialogue also must ring true. It should sound the way people actually talk. We should encourage our students to read passages of dialogue aloud as they compose. What is said, and the tone in which it is said, should be consistent with the nature of the characters as they have been depicted throughout the story.

Psychological Verisimilitude. To achieve psychological verisimilitude, the behavior, thought, and speech of the characters should be of the sort that might be expected from the characters, given the characteristics with which their authors have endowed them, and should seem logically to stem from these traits. The behavior, thought, and speech of a character should also be consistent both internally with each other and externally with the varying judgments that have been expressed about the character by others in the story.

Finding a Topic

The subject matter for the story does not seem to trouble most students, many of whom, oddly enough, seem to have a story already in their heads waiting to be written. We need to caution them, however, that most successful stories deal with situations and characters with whom their authors are familiar. This statement does not mean that our students should be confined to writing about themselves, but it should suggest that they will write better stories if they set their work in a milieu that they thoroughly understand and if they people it with characters who are like people they know. If they want to try fantasy or science fiction or a tale with a historical setting, not only should they be certain that they can fully realize the time and place imaginatively, but they should make sure that the characters who inhabit that distant place or time or who experience strange occurrences are enough like themselves, or those they know intimately, in thought and emotions, that they can be fully understood and realistically portrayed.

STIMULATING STUDENT IMAGINATIONS. For those students who just cannot think of a story to write, there are stimuli we can employ to quicken their creative imaginations.

With Storytelling Pictures. Narrative pictures, such as old *Saturday Evening Post* covers, which can be brought to class and pinned on the board or placed in the chalk tray to permit the students to "live with them" for a while, are often helpful in igniting the spark that turns into a story. Many public libraries have files of such illustrations, and they are also available in art books that can be passed around or studied in groups. Especially useful are the beautiful *Norman Rockwell and the Saturday Evening Post* art book and Mahonri Young's *American Realists: Homer to Hopper*.[26]

A quite different art book that is especially successful in stimulating junior high imaginations is Chris Von Allsburg's *The Mysteries of Harris Burdick*,[27] a collection of rather bizarre drawings with witty subtitles. A student teacher recently used it to spark ninth-grade Halloween tales, much to her students' delight.

With Objects and Sights. We might have our students bring in objects or pictures of objects that interest them and have them try to imagine a story around one of these objects. We might also have them observe the world about them with special care. Who knows? Inspiration for a story may be lurking in a face they might see on a bus, or in a conversation they might overhear at the self-service laundry.

With Other Works of Literature.   Some teachers also have had success in making set story assignments where plot or theme is derived from another literary work. Laurence Perrine, for instance, summarizes in three or four sentences the plots of stories his students have not yet read and asks them to create their own short stories based upon one of these plots. As a follow-up, Perrine suggests that the students read the original story and make a list of the differences in point of view, characterization, theme, or any other feature that contributes to the effectiveness of a story.[28]

Donald J. Dunning recommends that his students choose a work in another genre and use its plot as the basis for a short story, "chang[ing] the time and place to the present and the setting around you" and "limit[ing] the time to a few vital minutes in their main character's life, even if this means starting the story close to the climax." The poem "La Belle Dame Sans Merci" and some of Aesop's fables have worked well for his students.[29]

Writing Their Short Stories

Once our students have gotten their story ideas, they should be able to begin writing. After all, they should have a good idea of the genre, having read and discussed a number of effective short stories in class and having had the background experience of earlier reading as well as TV drama and movie viewing. Our students should now be able to relate this knowledge to their new understandings gained through their classroom experience with point of view, plot, character, and theme. And this knowledge should provide the essential underpinnings for their own writing.

The Hints for Writing Student Guidelines should help our students plan their writing. Students have found such a checklist useful both in composing and in revising their short stories.

STUDENT GUIDELINES

Hints for Writing a Short Story

    I. Have the story (and how it's going to turn out) fully in mind.
   II. Decide:
       A. What will be the basic conflict?
       B. From whose point of view will it be told?
          1. A major character (first or third person)

continued

      2. A minor character (probably first-person narrator)
      3. You, the author. How objective will your viewpoints be? Omniscient? Strictly objective? Something in between?
    C. Where will it begin?
      1. Will some or all be told in retrospect?
      2. Do you want to plunge right in — *in medias res?*
      3. Would you rather build up from an introduction?
III. Exposition — How will you handle it?
    A. First-person narrator simply telling the situation
    B. The author's remarks
    C. Dialogue
    D. Some extra device, such as newspaper article, radio, someone telling someone else the story for one reason or another, and so on
    E. A combination of any of these
IV. Plot — Plan it carefully (you might wish to outline it briefly).
    A. Remember it consists of:
      1. Situation given through exposition (see III)
      2. Complications
      3. Climax
      4. Conclusion
    B. Be sure to dramatize important incidents — not simply narrate them.

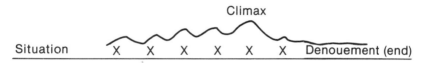

    C. Try to foreshadow subtly what is to come. (Leave hints that will take on meaning later.) This is particularly important if you decide to try a surprise ending.
  V. Characters — at least one or two should be developed rather fully. We should be able to know them. They may be developed through:
    A. Self-revelations (self-narrative, dialogue)
    B. Narrative or dialogue of other characters
    C. Descriptive detail provided by the author
    D. Action
 VI. Setting — Can you make it work for you?
    A. Plan how you will identify time and/or place. (You can do it subtly if you wish.)
    B. Are you trying to create a mood or atmosphere? Setting is a good way to provide it.
    C. Use of concrete detail here will help lend verisimilitude to your story.
    D. If the setting is to play a major role in the action, be sure it is adequately described.
VII. Final Checklist
    A. Does your story say what you want it to say? (Theme)
    B. Have you used SPECIFIC detail throughout?

continued

continued

C. Does the dialogue (if any) ring true?

D. Does the plot hold a reader's interest throughout and increase in excitement up to the climax?

TEACHING RHETORICAL ANALYSIS OF NARRATIVE WRITING

Unless our approach in teaching a combined curriculum is exclusively focused upon the teaching of creative writing, we will want to assign the writing of rhetorical analyses (or book reports, as younger students may be more comfortable calling them), for this assignment gives our students the opportunity for a more intimate acquaintance with a literary work than can be achieved in any other way.

Chapter 10 details strategies that teachers have used successfully in teaching students to write rhetorical analyses. Please see pages 375–99 for effective techniques to help students master the conventions and general principles of rhetorical analysis. In addition, perhaps, you might find useful the following summary of the process in terms of working with short stories.

Applying Analytical Principles to Short Stories

CLOSE READING. Specifically, to analyze a short story rhetorically, our students first should give it a thorough close reading with the goal of discovering their author's meaning and method—their answer to the rhetorical questions: What is the author trying to say? How does he or she go about saying it? Extending their antennae, they should note that which is different—striking, unusual—and that which is the same—repetition, parallels, patterning—and figure out why the author chose to include these features of plot, character, point of view, or style.

INTERPRETATION. THE STORY'S THEME. Through this process, each student should find an interpretation emerging, just as it did when we worked through the Chopin story. And from their interpretations will come their notions of theme. If the theme is not immediately apparent to the students, they can work through the Discovering a Theme Student Guidelines on page 436, and surely they will catch a glimpse of what they think the author tries to say.

Once they have at least a working-model idea of the author's meaning in the story, they can begin to plan out their papers.

STRUCTURE. Our students should probably not find the task of organizing their rhetorical analyses too forbidding, for this writing is a subgenre of expository writing, and they can follow the same procedures that they should already be comfortable with. To heighten their security, we might even provide novice students with a general structure for critical analysis—though, of course, cautioning them that the pattern is very general indeed and that they are free to modify as they choose:

1. An introduction leading into an organizing idea that sets forth our student's interpretation of what the author has to say,
2. A body supporting the organizing idea (interpretation) by demonstrating how the author has gone about saying it, and—optionally—
3. A conclusion that includes the students' own reactions to the author's theme or their evaluation of how well the author succeeded in expressing it or the ways in which she or he has fallen short of the goal.

CONTROLLING IDEA. The prototypical working thesis for a critical analysis is: "Our Author in 'This Story' suggests such and such an idea." We may find such a formulation useful because it helps students bear in mind the distinction between the author's theme and their own and because it reminds them that every rhetorical analysis of a narrative work necessarily includes the writer's interpretation of the author's meaning, the story's theme.

Nevertheless, students also need to know that though in a majority of analyses, interpretation of theme is a major part of the idea controlling the structure of the analysis, this is not always the case; other organizing ideas are frequently appropriate and, depending upon the assignment (see page 376), sometimes required. Those students who have been introduced to theoretical criticism, for example, (See pages 386–88) might choose to develop a working thesis from their specialized reading; they might even choose to work from an evaluative point of view.

SUPPORT. Where can our students find the support they need to make their interpretation persuasive? Why, in the very ideas that suggested it to them—the ideas they derived from their close reading. Since writing a rhetorical analysis is, in this sense, close reading in reverse, we might refer students having difficulty finding their support to tools such as the Close Reading Student Guidelines, page 381.

AN OPTIONAL EVALUATIVE OR PERSONAL RESPONSE. See the discussion in Chapter 10, pages 384–89.

A Rhetorical Analysis of Chopin's Story

How does this approach work in actual practice? Let's return to the Kate Chopin example and see how the points discovered in close reading might be used to support a students' point in rhetorical analysis. Recall that students differed in their interpretations, in the ideas they felt Chopin was trying to get across thematically in "The Story of an Hour."

Theme A: It is impossible (alternative theme—it is unnatural) for women to try to strive for lives of "self assertion."

Theme B: Freedom of will is the most important value; it alone makes life meaningful or even worthwhile.

SUPPORTING THEME A. Those students who see Mrs. Mallard's joy as monstrous could support their interpretation by concentrating upon the hysterical quality of such phrases as "feverish triumph in her eyes" and "approaching to possess her." With this interpretation, they might conclude that Chopin wants the reader almost to relish the irony implicit in Mrs. Mallard's final descent of the stairs "like a goddess of Victory."

SUPPORTING THEME B. On the other hand, those students who identify Kate Chopin's views closely with those of her heroine, could support their interpretation by emphasizing Chopin's use of spring imagery and noting her attaching to it the symbolism of both life and freedom:

> She could see in the open square before her house the tops of trees that were all aquiver with the new spring life. . . . She felt [something coming to her] creeping out of the sky, reaching toward her through the sounds, the scents, the color that filled the air. . . . "Free, free, free." . . . She was drinking in the very elixir of life through that open window.

These students might also attach symbolic importance to the way that Chopin at the beginning of the story equates her heroine with her married state by pointedly calling her (alone among the characters) by her married title: *Mrs.* Mallard. Readers do not even learn her given name until after her belief in her husband's death has set her free to be an individual person of her own.

In further support of this interpretation, students could also stress the power of Chopin's insight into a woman's soul. They might back up this view by artful quotation of portions of the story that point out the psychological truth of Mrs. Mallard's experience. First the grief. Then the dazed state. And then the gradual release of the old feelings and the reluctant acceptance of the new freedom. Finally, the passionate embrace of a true sense of self.

Placing the Climax. With this interpretation, the ecstasy of that "brief moment of illumination" becomes the climax of the story, overshadowing even the ironies of the final scene. For students who see the story in this way believe that the knowledge that comes to Mrs. Mallard in that moment is in itself the theme of the work: that "to impose a private will upon a fellow-creature" is "a crime"; and that it is no less a crime whether it proceeds from "a kind intention or a cruel intention."

Viewed in this light, the final scene becomes yet another way for Chopin to reinforce the importance of Louise Mallard's insight. This scene, so interpreted, dramatically demonstrates that after such a realization, life with her husband on the same basis is no longer possible for Louise Mallard. Reading the story this way adds a final irony, for it makes the doctors righter than they knew when they spoke of the "joy that kills."

STRUCTURING A RHETORICAL ANALYSIS OF CHOPIN'S STORY. A number of differing valid rhetorical analyses could be written for "The Story of an Hour"—as they could for all good short stories. The following is a workable outline for a rhetorical analysis of Chopin's story based upon thematic interpretation B sketched above:

> *Working Thesis:* In "The Story of an Hour" Kate Chopin uses a complex system of plot reversals and multiple ironies to convey powerfully to her readers the idea that a life of submission to the will of another—even if the other is a kind and loving person—is not a life that is worth living.

    I. Introduction
   II. Brief summary of plot in terms of its reversals and ironies
  III. Chopin's stress on the importance of Mrs. M's moment of insight
      A. Creditability of Mrs. M.'s point of view
      B. Her relationship to Richards, Josephine, and Mr. M.
      C. Symbolic building to the moment: spring and life-renewing imagery
      D. Psychological truth of Mrs. M.'s experience
      E. Symbolic use of title: *Mrs.* first and individual name, *Louise*, afterward
  IV. The nature of Mrs. M.'s insight
   V. Conclusion: The importance of the insight (and final ironies)

A SHORT STORY UNIT

It is sometimes difficult to organize the content of a coordinated unit. The boxed Teaching Strategies outlines a short-story unit which, as modified appropriately, has been used successfully in teaching eleventh grade, twelfth grade, and college freshman students to learn to read and write the modern short story.

TEACHING STRATEGIES

A Short Story Unit Plan

1. Point of View and Character
   a. Required reading
      Faulkner, "The Two Soldiers"*
      Harte, "The Outcast of Poker Flats"
   b. Discussion of stories in terms of their characterization with emphasis on the importance of the spoken voice—dialogue or narration—as well as

  *Sample stories selected from a typical survey of American literature text; they are all widely anthologized.

continued

continued
description and action in character development. Also concentration on point of view (in the technical sense).

    c. Paper: A character sketch of a classmate using his speaking voice and enough specific detail to make him recognizable when the unidentified themes are read aloud.

2. Plot
    a. Required reading
       O'Henry, "The Cop and the Anthem"
       Hawthorne, "The Ambitious Guest"
    b. Discussion of stories in terms of plot construction: situation, complications, climax and conclusion, with emphasis upon how a conflict builds to a climax and is resolved in the conclusion. Work on techniques of exposition and foreshadowing and the creation of suspense.
    c. Paper: One-half a short story giving the situation, presenting the characters, but stopping before the climax. Half-stories to be traded and finished by a classmate. (Each student thus writes two half-stories.)

3. Theme
    a. Required reading
       Benet, "The Devel and Daniel Webster"
       Hemingway, "The Old Man at the Bridge"
    b. Discussion of stories in terms of their theme, working with the previously discussed stories in this respect as well as this week's reading. Particular attention paid to irony and social criticism.
    c. Paper: A rhetorical analysis of a story that had not been discussed in class.

       Students are advised to determine the theme of the story and its emotional impact and to consider the techniques through which they are achieved. Stories from which they are to choose are:
           Steinbeck, "Flight"
           Thurber, "The Secret Life of Walter Mitty"
           Crane, "The Bride Comes to Yellow Star"
           London, "To Build a Fire"

4. Style
    a. Required reading
       Bierce, "The Boarded Window"
       Cather, "The Sculptor's Funeral"
       Jackson, "The Lottery"
    b. Discussion of stories in terms of stylistic techniques, emphasizing such devices as specific and exact detail to achieve verisimilitude, the use of observation and the five senses in descriptive passages, the importance of subtlety, the surprise ending and how it is achieved.
    c. Paper
       A short story making use of the techniques discussed throughout the unit. (*Saturday Evening Post* covers and other narrative-illustrative art on display throughout the week to help in inspiring ideas)

Outside reading: A collection of short stories by a well-known (and well-regarded) author of the students' choice.

continued

Unit examination:
  I. (The major question) A rhetorical analysis of story hitherto unknown to the students, but one in which there is a well-defined ironic theme, clear and appealing characterization through selectively detailed description and dialogue, and clever use of a restricted point of view to achieve a surprise ending. Suggestions:
     For younger students, O. Henry's "Witches' Loaves,"
     For older students: William Carlos Williams's "The Use of Force" or, if still unread, Kate Chopin's "The Story of an Hour."
 II. The comparison of the use of point of view in two specific required stories, of irony in two others, and of social comment or criticism in yet two more.
III. The identification and brief characterization of six (out of nine) characters from the required reading.

HELPING STUDENTS TO REVIEW PERFORMANCES

With videotapes easily available and many local theaters giving student groups very attractive pricing, more and more of us are including dramatic performances in our teaching of narrative literature to our students' great gain. Since drama tells a story, everything said here about teaching narrative literature applies to it equally well. Like all narrative literature, a play or a movie consists of characters involved in a plot in order to present a theme.

Special Features of Performed Drama

But drama is meant for the stage. And analyzing performed literature differs from analyzing their literary versions in two important respects. First, the question "What is the author trying to say" about a performed drama or a movie is not nearly as important as "What is the acting company, or the director or producer, trying to say?" Although the author's story and theme are fundamental to any production, what we really want our students to get at in their analyses is the meaning of the entire theatrical experience, and that involves the way the author's material is interpreted in actual performance.

Second, the methods by which the author and, in this case, the director and the company "go about saying it" must also be expanded to include not only the techniques of story-telling discussed ealier but also the techniques that go into producing the particular sounds, motion, spectacle of the production.

A thorough discussion of these elements is beyond the scope of this work, but the Analysis of a Performance Student Guidelines should help us to plan our pre- or post-performance class discussion. And our students should find it useful when they prepare to write a rhetorical analysis of a particular performance.

STUDENT GUIDELINES

To Analyze a Performance

BACKGROUND

1. If the work is of an identifiable genre (Theatre of the Absurd, Restoration Comedy, Senecan Tragedy, or other type), what are the characteristics of this form? What are the authors of the works of this kind trying to accomplish by them? Is there anything you should know about the traditional staging or costuming or musical accompaniment of such drama? How closely does your particular production follow the traditions of the genre? In what ways does it depart from them and why?

2. If the play is written in or set in another time or another place, are there historical, geographical, philosophical, or social facts that would shed light on the performance? Does this presentation try to suggest that other time or place? If so, how? To what extent? If not, why not?

3. If you are familiar with the work in written form, how closely does your production follow the script? How does this performance handle those ambiguous elements that must be interpreted anew with each production. (If you are watching *Macbeth*, for example, does the director have the Banquo actor appear as Banquo's ghost at Macbeth's feast or is the ghost to be taken as only a figment of Macbeth's overwrought imagination?)

4. If your production is based upon a drama (or story) that is one of a series, or has a strong autobiographical flavor, are there any essential facts that you should know about your author's life or works? (I would urge you to use such material cautiously, however, and to concentrate your analysis upon the performance itself.)

ACTION AND CHARACTERS AND THEME

All of the suggestions about analyzing narrative literature are pertinent here. In addition, the following questions may be helpful:

1. How are the acts divided? How are the scenes arranged? Is there any particular pattern in the scenes or sub-scenes? How are subplots handled? What is the function of each scene in the overall pattern?

2. By what gestures, intonations, and attitudes does each actor characterize the character he or she portrays? Is there any interaction between particular characters that is especially telling? How personally or how distantly do the actors relate to the audience? If there are asides, soliloquys, or direct audience address, how are they handled? How does the audience respond to them? Do the comic characters encourage the audience to laugh *at* or *with* them? How much empathy do the noncomic characters elicit? How closely is the audience expected to identify with the protagonists (central characters)? What emotions—sympathy? antipathy? indifference?—do they arouse?

continued

3. If the drama is a tragedy or if it has tragic overtones, what is the basis for the tragedy? Is it caused by a flawed hero? A flawed society? Fate? Some combination of these causes? How does the audience feel at the close of the tragedy? Does a *catharsis* (the washing away of the tragic emotions) take place? Despite the downfall of the leading character(s), is there anything hopeful about the ending (the return of order, for instance)? How is this hope conveyed?

SETTING AND STAGE-BUSINESS

1. Can you find any motifs or symbolic representations in the dialogue, props, or, perhaps, in a repeated action of one of the characters? What does this motif or symbol seem to mean the first time it appears? Does it take on additional meaning as it is repeated? If so, what?
2. What is the nature of the sets and scenery? Are they realistic or do they merely suggest the place? Is there a symbolic quality about them? If so, what are they meant to express? How does the lighting contribute to the background of the drama? Do any special lighting effects stand out in your memory? What is their significance?
3. How do the costumes affect the mood of the production? Do they help characterize individual characters? If so, how?
4. If there is any particular stage business beyond that which would normally accompany the dialogue, what is its significance? If you have noticed any special patterning in the positioning of the actors upon the stage, what meaning can you give it?

EVALUATIVE QUESTIONS
1. How did the audience respond to the play? Were they attentive? Were they fidgety—coughing, fanning, whispering together? Did they laugh in the appropriate places? Were they hushed in the appropriate places? Did they respond warmly and appreciatively at the close?
2. Did you find the action plausible? Did it seem to be true to the laws of logic and of cause and effect? Did the characters seem to act in ways that were psychologically consistent with what you were given of their characters? In short, were you able to suspend your disbelief?
3. Was the production a unified and satisfying experience for you? Why or why not?

Special Features of Movies

All of the discussion that applies to helping our students respond to stage drama applies to motion pictures as well. But film drama adds an extra dimension: the eye of the camera, and that can make a big difference. For example, when we teach point of view, we demonstrate that dialogue—that is, dramatic narration—is the most objective point of view of all, leaving readers almost free to make their own interpretation. But in movies, the eye of the camera augments the interpretive control of director and actors common to all performances and provides a highly controlled point of view, directing the viewers' ideas and guiding their thoughts while it focuses their attention. Thus, in order to analyze movies, our students must be conscious of where the camera is directing their attention. We should also suggest that they try to understand why.

To plan discussion about a viewed movie or for writing a rhetorical analysis of a movie, the Movie Analysis Student Guidelines should augment the Performance Analysis Guidelines in a helpful way.

STUDENT GUIDELINES

To Analyze a Movie

In addition to the analysis questions for all performances (pages 454–55), after viewing a movie, ask yourself:

- Why that distant shot? Why that close-up?
- Why this particular juxtaposition of images? of scenes? of characters?
- Why a darkening or a lightening?
- Why the concentration on this curious object?
- Why, for example, is the camera concentrating with such emphasis on the mouth (or the teeth) of the speaker?
- Why is it not focusing on the speaker at all?
- Where is it directing our attention instead?
- Are the listener's reactions more important?
- Is there something in the setting to which the speaker's words are supposed to relate?
- Why is this scene hazy? Why is this one so extra sharp in its contrasts?
- Why is that part of the scene out of focus?

IDEAS FOR DISCUSSION OR ESSAY

1. Try out the strategy suggested on page 436 for finding an author's theme when it remains illusive; Choose a piece of narrative writing and identify the parties to the conflict upon which its plot is founded. Who wins the conflict? Suggest a tentative theme by generalizing from the conflict and its resolution.
2. In narrative works that you are familiar with, find examples of (a) verbal irony, (b) dramatic irony, and (c) irony of fate. How would you explain to a class how each example contributes to its author's purpose in the work as a whole.

3. How would you explain point of view to a class? It might be useful to bring in an example of narrative writing in which a character narrates the story and another, such as "The Story of an Hour," which, though told in the author's own voice, is written from a character's point of view.
4. Many teachers believe that modeling writing with our students helps our teaching in a number of ways. Therefore,
   a. Making use of whatever hints or suggestions offered in this chapter that you find helpful, write a short story of some 750–1500 words.
   b. Making use of whatever hints and suggestions offered in this chapter that you find helpful, rhetorically analyze a short story you find intriguing or a movie or play you have recently seen.
5. Did writing a short story yourself help you understand and interpret the story you rhetorically analyzed? Or, if you reversed the order, did writing the rhetorical analysis help in writing your short story? Keeping your own experience in this respect in mind, discuss the merits of the combined curriculum.

NOTES

The chapter-opening epigraph is from F. Scott Fitzgerald, *Notebooks.*

1. Some practical ideas for achieving an open and caring classroom of this sort are suggested earlier in this text. See especially Chapters 1 and 6.

2. Ken Macrorie, *Uptaught* (Rochelle Park, NJ: Hayden, 1970), 48.

3. Ken Macrorie, *Telling Writing* (Rochelle Park, NJ: Hayden, 1980) and *Uptaught*; Peter Elbow, *Writing Without Teachers* (London: Oxford UP, 1973). Free writing was supported early by Michael Southwell, "Free Writing in Composition Classes," *CE* 38 (1977): 676–81; Joan M. Putz, "Persuasion + Protection = Potency: A TA Approach to English 101," *CE* 36 (1975): 571–77; and Jean Pumphrey, "Teaching English Composition as a Creative Art," *CE* 34 (1973): 666–73. This strategy is now generally accepted, at least as a useful invention heuristic, and is recommended in most composition textbooks.

4. Stephen Judy, *Explorations in the Teaching of Secondary English: A Source Book for Experimental Teaching* (New York: Dodd, 1975): 80.

5. Linda Welshimer Wagner, "Practice Without Pain," *EJ* 37 (1968): 221–22.

6. Gloria Flaherty (formerly of Stebbins High School English Department, Dayton, Ohio; currently on the faculty of Wilmington College) suggests putting classes on alternative schedules for journal collection dates, so that we only have one set of journals to respond to at once.

7. John Schultz, "Story Workshop: Writing from Start to Finish" in *Research on Composing: Points of Departure*, ed. Charles R. Coopper and Lee Odell (Urbana: NCTE, 1978), 151–187; quotation from 155.

8. George Hillocks, Jr. *Observing and Writing* (Urbana: ERIC and NCTE, 1975).

9. See T. J. Ray, "Describing Geometric Forms for Feedback," in *Writing Exercises from the Exercise Exchange*, ed. Littleton Long (Urbana: NCTE, 1976), 111–14; and Robert Clueth and Lee Ahlborn, *Effective English Prose: Writing for Meaning/Reading for Style* (Syracuse: Singer, 1965), 5.

10. Harvey S. Wiener, "Media Compositions: Preludes to Writing," *CE* 35 (1974): 566–74.

11. As described in Edward J. Gordon and Edward S. Noyes, eds. *Essays on the Teaching of English: Reports of the Yale Conferences on the Teaching of English* (New York: Appleton, 1960), 85.

12. For a change caused by dialogue, Lynn Brendel, who teaches at Beaver Creek High School in Ohio, often uses Carson McCullough's "Sucker," where the protagonist is changed by his cousin's angry outburst, and the cousin himself, who can never take back his hasty words, is also changed. For change caused by disillusionment, Brendel suggests Robert Cormier's "Mine on Thursdays," where the daughter's observation of her father's behavior from the rocket-ride above him changes their relationship forever.

Gordon and Noyes describe a similar successful assignment used at James Hillhouse High School in New Haven (117–21).

13. Symbolic items motivating typical essays have included a student-writer's late father's gift of his mother's pearl necklace, not to be warn until her thirteenth birthday, and a musical instrument, only given to another student-writer after years of hard practice.

14. Nancie Atwell, *In the Middle: Writing, Reading, and Learning with Adolescents* (Portsmouth: Heinemann, 1987).

15. Melissa Snyder's questions are derived roughly from Don Murray. See especially his "Listening Eye: Reflections on the Writing Conference," *CE* 41 (1979): 13–18.

16. Edward P. J. Corbett, "The Theory and Practice of Imitation and Classical Rhetoric," *CCC* (1971): 249–50.

17. Edith Warton, in the preface to *Ethan Frome*, as quoted by Charles Murphy, "The Teaching of Fiction as Composition," *EJ* 55 (1966): 33; and William J. O'Malley, "Literary Craftmanship: The Integration of Literature and Composition," *EJ* 52 (1963): 248.

Mimi Schwartz, in "Wearing the Shoe on the Other Foot: Teacher as Student Writer," *CCC* 40 (1989): 203–215, confirms O'Malley from her personal experience. She writes:

> Writing literature . . . made me a more careful and appreciative reader. I study the craft far more than before to see how others have solved my problems. . . . I began considering the options the writer chose to take or not to take. Did I agree with them? . . . Was there another [ending] I would have liked better? I felt less docile, more like an active partner in the text.
>
> I've introduced this kind of reader response . . . into my classes. . . . Instead of asking "What is the purpose of this digression?" I ask, "If R. were in your writing group, would you advise him to leave this section in or take it out?" The consensus was "Leave it in!" and the reasons were far more insightful than if I assumed a priori that the digression was good, and they'd better figure out why.

18. Cleanth Brooks, Robert Penn Warren, and John Thibout Purser, *An Approach to Literature*, 4th ed., (New York: Appleton, 1964): 4.

19. Mary Hiatt, for instance, in "Teaching the Writing of the Short Story," *EJ* 54 (1965): 810, argues strongly for this approach.

20. This concept is suggested by Fred E. H. Schroeder in "How Not to Assign 'What-Did-You-Do-Last-Summer': A Cumulative Course in Writing Personal Narratives," *EJ* 57 (1968): 81.

21. The stories used for exemplification in this chapter are all widely anthologized and are available in the texts and paperbacks used in our schools and colleges.

22. Alfred L. Crabb, Jr., "Describing a Face," in *Writing Exercises*, 101.

23. Suggested by Sally Bork for "*EJ* Work-Shop: Composition Starters," *EJ* 62 (1973): 1284.

24. Percy Lubbock, "The Craft of Fiction: Picture, Drama, and Point of View," in *Approaches to the Novel*, ed. Robert Scholes (San Francisco: Chandler, 1961), 103.

25. Margaret B. Fleming uses this strategy with her classes at the University of Arizona.

26. *Norman Rockwell and the Saturday Evening Post*, ed. Norman Rockwell (Philadelphia: Rittenhouse, 1976); if not available, try Arthur Guptill, *Norman Rockwell, Illustrator* (New York: Watson-Guptill, 1946, 1975). Try also Mahonri Young, *American Realists* (New York: Watson-Guptill, 1977).

27. Chris Van Allsburg, *The Mysteries of Harris Burdick* (Boston: Houghton, 1984).

28. Lawrence Perrine, "Getting a Short Story Under Way," in *Writing Exercises*, 40–42.

29. Donald J. Dunning, "A Derivative Approach to Creative Writing," *EJ* 54 (1965): 845–47.

□ □ □ **12**

Teaching Poetry Writing

For a good poet's made as well as born.
— Ben Jonson

□ □ □

EXPERIENCING POETRY

A number of times throughout this book I have discussed the misconceptions our students are likely to bring to various subjects of study. When approaching the subject of poetry, however, I am very much afraid that frequently the misconceptions brought to this study may also be our own.

Attitudes

Many of us share what is perhaps the largest and most dangerous misconception of all: that our students do not like, that they even hate, poetry. Granted, there is much in our culture pushing our students toward this stance. The heroes who are glorified in our schools and colleges and in the culture at large are far more likely to be athletes than poets—and what is worse, the culture seems to enforce a dichotomy between the two. American folklore and its manifestation on television and in the movies constantly throw out snide little hints and signals that there is something suspect, something a bit sissified, about a fondness for poetry, to the extent that any athlete worth his boxing gloves or her tennis racquet really ought to steer clear of that silly rhyming stuff. Our students cannot help but be influenced by such hints and signals.

But we as their teachers should understand that this seeming abhorrence of poetry on the part of our students is really just a pose. Almost all little children, before these cultural signals begin to influence them, respond with delight to the sort of poems and rhymes they hear on "Barney & Friends" and "Sesame Street" or at Mommy or Daddy's knee. Tots all over the world play chanting and singing games, and mothers of all cultures croon poems and lullabies to their babies. The appeal seems to be archetypal, tied up in some way with the fundamental nature of humanity. Advertisers exploit poetry's appeal when they use jingles to sell their products. Memory experts depend on it to train the memory, and the many professional lecturers who punctuate their talks with appropriate lines of verse use this appeal to ingratiate themselves with their audiences. If we enter into our classwork in poetry with an underlying faith in this universal appeal and with a positive assumption about every student's potential to write satisfying poems and every student's capacity to enjoy them, we will almost surely discover that the time we spend with poetry will be for many of our students among their most enjoyable classroom moments.

Getting Started

The very best way I have found to introduce this study is with a Poetry Jamboree. For the reasons mentioned, we often face a backlog of prejudice against poetry at the start; but, in this instance, a head-on discussion of the problem is not the most effective means of dealing with it. Such a discussion, by forcing a participant to defend a position, must necessarily harden the participant in that position; it can turn what starts out as a mere stance into what may become a firmly held conviction. Furthermore, as the discussion turns us into advocates for poetry, it undermines the all-important influence of our perhaps unspoken, but firmly held, assumption of its universal appeal. Since the prejudice against poetry is, for the most part, only skin-deep, it can be overcome more easily than we might imagine.

POETRY JAMBOREE. We can demonstrate to our students the truth of our assumption that poems can give them pleasure by simply providing them the opportunity to experience that pleasure for themselves in a Poetry Jamboree—a free and joyous reading of favorite poems.

Sharing Joy. Our assumption is, of course, that everyone has favorite poems (and the truth is that almost everyone does—though in many cases this fact is a closely guarded secret). If some students seem puzzled by our suggestion that they bring to the next class meeting a poem they really like (and a second choice in case their first is selected by someone else), we can help spur ideas by asking them to think over all the poems they have read or heard somewhere that they still remember. We might suggest that they try to recall poems and rhymes they were especially fond of as little children or lyrics of songs they like that are good enough to stand on their own without the music. We must make plenty of books available to our students to stir their memories or from which those who really have no earlier poetry experience can discover something that appeals. We must also make sure that we bring a number of anthologies to the Jamboree so that we can help our students find poems they can describe, but whose author or title they cannot recall, and so that we can add some favorites of our own to the program.

Dealing with Bigotry.   But what do we say to the student who actually comes right out and complains, "But I don't like poetry"? Probably the best approach is to put a new perspective on the statement, making irrelevant any consideration of the particular qualities of the poetic genre, by treating the statement as an example of the sheer prejudice it is. We might reply that we find it a highly bigoted statement and just as silly as if the student had said, "I just *lo-oo-oove* all poetry." This student is certainly entitled to hate some poems, we might add—maybe even many poems—but generalizing about all poems, even those he's never read, is pure bigotry and certainly not worthy of his usual open-minded self.

If we have established a warm relationship with the individual and the class, and if we speak with a certain whimsy, the complainer is usually not offended and the subject rarely comes up again, except perhaps in a joking way. For the Poetry Jamboree almost never fails to attract even this student to at least a couple of the poems, as our students' favorites work their magic over us all.

Leading the Jamboree.   The Poetry Jamboree itself is just for fun. It must be held in a relaxed atmosphere. Even if it has been our custom to have our students sit in the traditional rows, for this session we really should ask them to pull their desks into a circle so that everyone can see each other and respond to each other. Though we might encourage the students to read their own selections, we should not insist if they are reluctant, but instead read the poems for them ourselves or give them to especially strong student readers.

We should respond freely to the poems and encourage our students to do so as well. We might react with such comments as "Oh, that's a good one," or "I've always loved that poem," or "Frost is one of my favorites too," or "Wherever did you find that poem? I've never heard it before. Awfully good isn't it?" or "That poem is funny and touching at the same time." Before very long, our students will be following suit and talking informally to one another about what they like and don't like and why.

If a question of interpretation comes up—and it well might, for often a student will say, "I like it all right, I guess, but just what does it mean?"— then we should refer the question to the student who chose the poem. If this student is reluctant to hazard an interpretation, we might then help the class to figure it out; but we should not attempt to analyze or "study" these poems. During the Jamboree we will want simply to savor them together.

Very often students will ask for a second day of Jamboree. Because this activity is so close to our real purpose in teaching poetry, if we can possibly spare another day, surely we should give it to them.

WHAT IS A POEM?   Our students have been exposed to a variety of poems during the Jamboree. The usual session will ordinarily include such diverse examples as Frost's "Stopping by Woods," Benét's "The Mountain

Whippoorwill," Langston Hughes's "A Dream Deferred," E. B. Browning's "How Do I Love Thee?," or Bob Dylan's "Blowin' in the Wind"; Paul Simon's "The Sounds of Silence," the Beatles' "Eleanor Rigby," Holme's "Old Ironsides," Lewis Carroll's "Jabberwocky" and "You Are Old Father William," (and sometimes Edward Lear's "The Owl and the Pussy-cat"); a favorite bit from Kahili's "The Prophet," Poe's "The Raven" and "Annabel Lee," U2's "Mysterious Ways," and Alfred Noyes's "The Highwayman;" Sandburg's "The Fog," Gwendolyn Brooks's "We Real Cool," Thayer's "Casey at the Bat," Shakespeare's "When Icicles Hang by the Wall," and always something by the perenially popular Robert Service, usually "The Spell of the Yukon" or "The Cremation of Sam McGee."

Definitions. Confronted with such diversity, the question, "What is a poem?" arises. We might ask our students to discuss the question or we might ask them to think for a moment and then jot down their definitions. In response to such an assignment, one class of high-school juniors conceived of a number of definitions, the best of which are included here:

- A poem should be the words you write down or think or say to represent the feelings you experienced when you thought or heard or saw or did something.
- A poem is a piece of a man's soul transformed into words.
- A poem is a combination of emotion and creative imagination. It embodies beautiful thought, feeling, or action.
- A poem is a way of expressing one's feelings in a sort of rhythmical form.
- A poem is a composition written in verse form which conveys the poet's feelings and thoughts about some particular subject.
- A poem is a thought scribbled down with a meaning.

Discussion. This class's response to these rather characteristic definitions was also typical. A number of the students were impressed with the poetic quality of some of the definitions and praised them highly. But one or two took issue with this evaluation and argued that although they too thought these definitions pretty, they didn't think they fitted lots of poems they knew. When pressed for a "for instance," they suggested that they didn't think "The Cremation of Sam McGee" "embodied" such a "beautiful thought" or that "Jabberwocky" expressed much "of the soul of the writer" or even that it had all that much "meaning." Some students claimed that poems like "Jabberwocky" or "McGee" weren't really poetry at all. But most maintained that they were and insisted that any good definition couldn't leave them out. When the teacher intervened to ask just what qualities that set poetry off from prose could be found in all—or almost all—poems, a heated discussion followed.

Conclusions. The result of this class's discussion is the conclusion we might expect any of our classes to come up with: the only qualities that really seem to differentiate all poetry from prose are

1. a sound that is more rhythmic and
2. a use of language more imaginative
   than is ordinarily found in prose writing.

Teaching Goals

Time spent simply enjoying poems is a good beginning for any study of poetry, and any such study can probably profit from a discussion of what poetry is all about. But before we can take our class beyond such introductory work, we will have to make a firm decision about our goals in teaching poetry and, in particular, about how much literary content we feel will be important for our students to learn.

CHOICES.   Do we want simply to expose them to the elements of poetry in order to give them an opportunity for self-expression through that medium, or do we want our students to have more formal knowledge of these elements in order to be able to manipulate them more consciously in creating their own poems and to be able to read poetry with a keener understanding?

If our purpose is the former, we might want to consider developing a program from the ideas Kenneth Koch worked out in his highly successful experiments in teaching the untutored elderly and young children to write poems (discussed below); if our chief aim is the latter, then we would want to work through the close reading of a number of good poems and include a systematic consideration of the imagery and the sound of poetry. Or we could develop our own mixture of approaches.

Though the close-reading approach is more traditionally compatible with an intensive study of literature, both approaches are possible within the combined curriculum. On the one hand, Koch introduces into his program the reading of such poems as Blake's "Tyger" and Donne's "Valediction: Forbidding Mourning" to stimulate his students' own poetic efforts. On the other hand, some teachers of highly technical poetry-writing courses, such as Edward Profitt,[1] have found Koch's assignments useful exercises in their teaching. Yet despite some compatibility of this sort, the two approaches are fundamentally diverse and will be considered separately here.

A CREATIVE-EXPRESSION APPROACH TO POETRY WRITING

Kenneth Koch, a recognized poet, while teaching adult courses for aspiring poets, became convinced of the value of creative experience to the life of just about anyone and consequently accepted the challenge to teach poetry writing to those members of our population who would seem farthest removed from this craft: schoolchildren—including those in classes for nonreaders— and residents of nursing homes, who, as it happened, had had almost no formal education. The story of his remarkable success—and the enthusiastic poems that are "the proof of the pudding"—is recorded in *Wishes, Lies and Dreams: Teaching Children to Write Poetry, Rose, Where Did You Get That Red? Teaching Great Poetry to Children,* and *I Never Told Anybody: Teaching Poetry Writing in Nursing Homes.*[2]

Koch's results have been duplicated by other teachers in similar situations, and his strategies and techniques also have been adapted to fit the needs of the high school or college classroom, again with considerable success. We might consider adapting some of his ideas for our own use.

Strategies and Principles

Some of Koch's most effective teaching strategies evolved from his struggle to provide his students with legitimate poetic forms that did not involve meter and rhyme. Koch has nothing against the teaching of meter and rhyme (*I Never Told* 29), but he did not wish to overwhelm his students with the technical aspects of meter and discovered that rhyme in the hands of those who are unsophisticated in literature is counterproductive:

> Unfortunately, for inexperienced writers rhyme tends to destroy or at best to dull the qualities one hopes that form will help create. When our students used it, their work was quite inferior to what they otherwise wrote. (*I Never Told* 28)

A REPETITIVE BASE. The "alchemy" he found "to change prose to poetry" was repetition, repetition and listing of all kinds:

- Repetition of a word (Put the name of the color in every line or so)
- Repetition of a phrase (Start every line or so with the words, "I never told anybody"—or "I, the Ocean")
- Repetition or listing of a certain kind of content (in every line or so put a different thing the music reminds you of)
- Repetition of a rhetorical device (in every line or so make a different comparison) (*I Never Told* 26).

The use of repetition gave even those of Koch's students who dictated their verses "a sense of writing in lines." In addition, this "formal organizing principle" provided

> what they wrote some of the disconnectedness and surprising juxtapositions of poetry, as well as providing it with a structure. . . . It organized memories and feelings in a way that, by putting them in a new order showed new things about them, and which could cause the writer, coming on them this way by surprise, to be moved by them and to communicate that emotion in what was said. . . . With repetition and listing the students could get more of poetry's content and form without losing anything good that was naturally theirs, in language or in what they had to say. (*I Never Told* 26–27)

BOLD THEMES.   Besides providing his students with a form for each session, Koch also gave them a somewhat arbitrary theme. The bolder the theme, he discovered, the more evocative. The rather daring ideas of "Being the Ocean" or "Talking to the Moon" worked especially well with Koch's older students. As for the children, he encouraged them "to be free and even crazy in what they wrote":

> The trouble with a child not being crazy is that he will instead be conventional; and it is a truth of poetry that a conventional image, for example, is not, as far as its effect is concerned, an image at all. (*Wishes* 17)

MOTIVATING GOOD STUDENT POETRY.   The assignments that seemed to work best were not only bold, but also involved typically poetic elements: *wishes, comparisons, noises, lies,* and *colors* (*I Never Told* 24). All of the successful ideas were about "feelings, impressions and associations." They all involved the thinking about or calling up from memory of "small things, particular details, especially those connected with feeling and sensation" (*I Never Told* 24).

Sense Stimuli.   These topics might be inspired by direct sensory stimuli: seeing and enjoying the perfume of a bouquet of fresh spring flowers, holding a small white mouse, listening to stirring music, touching sand and seaweed and listening to sea shells, crunching autumn leaves, listening to the wind or a train whistle.

Poetic Stimuli.   They might also be derived from themes already handled by the great poets: quiet and quiet things and moments from William Carlos Williams's "The White Horse," questions and answers about the origin of things from Blake's "Tyger" ("Rose, where did you get that red?"). All these topics call for the expression of intense and intimate feelings, but only indirectly.

Narrow and Specific Stimuli.   Koch is convinced—and I think, rightly—that asking directly for students' feelings on "Life" or "Love" or any of the other "big" subjects stifles thought and freezes imagination. Twice he attempted such topics with his elderly students—when he asked them to write about the Great Depression and about growing older—and both times the students wrote generalizations and platitudes. Similarly, a grade school teacher of his acquaintance reported about her unsuccessful attempt to have her students write poems beginning each line with "Love is. . . ." Koch points out that this topic also had the additional problem of being phrased for children in terms foreign to their natural speech.

Naturally Phrased Stimulus Words.   All successful topics that encourage repetition of particular words must be phrased in a way consistent with the poet's speech. For example, Koch is convinced that the popular assignments in which he asked the children to begin every other line with "I seem to be

. . ." and the following line with "But really I am . . ." would never have worked if he had used the adult wording of "My seeming self" and "My true self." In the same way, the teacher does not ask a child to "imagine" or "pretend" something, but rather to "think about" it or "be" it. Even for adults, "being" something—the ocean, a white mouse—is far more conducive to the making of good poems than is simply describing the object.

The Teaching Process

In each of Koch's lessons, there are three distinct stages.

INTRODUCTORY STAGE. First is the introductory stage, where the teacher introduces the thematic and structural idea and where his or her own enthusiasm for the project spills over to the students and helps to create the mood of excitement out of which good poems can come.

The introductory period is anything but a passive time. During it the sensory stimuli are experienced, the thematic poems are read, and association games are often played—as, for example, "Close your eyes and tell me what color this sound is. What color is England? France? Spain? Monday? Saturday? The number fourteen hundred?" (*I Never Told* 215).

Modeling. Especially in the beginning, students need some kind of model for their poems; they also need assurance that they can really produce poetry. For his child students, Koch used the poems of other children as models to emulate; for his elderly students, some stanzas from poets like D. H. Lawrence, Walt Whitman, and W. C. Williams with their "combination of prosiness, talky quality, repetition, and lyricism" served as models of the sort of poems they might be expected to produce (*I Never Told* 8).

Collaborating. Also, especially in the beginning, a class may need the additional stimulation of creating a collaborative poem, where each participating student supplies a separate line. Wishes ("I wish . . .") and childhood ("I remember . . ."), for example, are good topics for collaborative efforts.

THE WRITING STAGE. While the students are writing their poems, the teacher gives individual support and guidance. Sometimes the assignment has to be explained on an individual basis; sometimes students get stuck and need to be encouraged to continue; sometimes they need the teacher to make a few suggestions and to prompt the strength of will to begin again:

> I was useful in the classroom [Koch writes] for getting the children in a good mood to write and then for keeping them going. And they were useful to each other in creating a humming and buzzing creative ambiance. (*I Never Told* 31–32)

THE READING STAGE. After the poems are finished, the teacher reads them all aloud and responds to them as one poet to another: "This line moves me," "This image is especially exciting." And always, poetry is taught as an art, the poem as a creative artifact. Koch believes that the teacher must

> always pay attention to the text, and especially to the esthetic qualities of the text, rather than to the person who wrote it. That is, saying, "This line is beautiful. I like the way it repeats the word green," rather than, "How wonderful that you could write that." (*I Never Told* 44)

Through this reading aloud, the creative excitement is maintained, and the learning of the entire experience is reinforced.

A Creative Challenge

Koch's method of teaching poetry writing thus offers many exciting possibilities, both as a program of its own and, as will be seen, as a useful source of interesting assignments in conjunction with a poetry program having a more literary focus.

TEACHING IMAGERY WITH A LITERARY FOCUS

Another way to approach teaching students to write poems is the more traditional analytic way. With this method, students glean knowledge of the basic techniques of poetry writing by studying recognized works to discover the ways their authors achieve effectiveness and power. In this approach, the students' attention is directed especially toward the two elements that set poetry apart: rhythm, the sound of poetry, and imagery, poetry's special language.

Imagery: The Language of Poetry

Knowledge of imagery, which can give students a feeling for metaphor and a sense of the exciting possibilities and color offered by the variety of metaphoric structures traditional to poetry written in English, greatly enhances our students' potential as skillful writers and readers of poems. Yet many of us hesitate to impart such knowledge because of the abuses that too often occur in its teaching.

What is needed is a way to explain the language of poetry that neither involves the memorization of a long, diffuse list of rhetorical figures nor results in students thinking that the be-all and end-all of poetry interpretation is the identification and labeling of metaphor (the "Lookee, there's a simile!" syndrome).

Fortunately, neither of these problems is insurmountable. There is a logic and order in the metaphoric system of English poetry that can be made clear to our students, and it can be taught with such emphasis on function and meaning that the pursuit of mere nomenclature can be understood for the silliness it is.

THE OBJECTIVE CORRELATIVE.   T. S. Eliot's notion of the objective correlative, though he phrases it a bit awkwardly, offers the clearest and most teachable description of the function of imagery. He writes:

> The only way of expressing emotion in the form of art is by finding an objective correlative; in other words, a set of objects, a situation, a chain of events which shall be the formula of that particular emotion; such that when the external facts, which must terminate in sensory experience, are given, the emotion is immediately evoked.[3]

At first our students will probably find Eliot's phraseology difficult to comprehend, but we can assure them that the passage is worth their concentration because the objective correlative is the key to the entire metaphoric system. Once they have grasped its meaning, the whole concept of metaphor will fall into place.

WHEN WORDS DON'T WORK.   We can begin by explicating carefully. We might tell our students that Eliot says (and we agree) that we can't express emotion in words directly; we simply do not have the words. By way of demonstration, we might ask our students to convey how they feel when they have a stomach ache and are nauseous. Undoubtedly, we will be answered by facial grimaces, hands clutching throat or abdomen, and a chorus of moans and gargles sounding like "Yuccch" or "Gwrrrk." If we say, "But you're not using words! Put your feeling into words," some will respond, "We can't. We just can't. There are no words." Others might try a semimedical description: "There is a constricted feeling in my throat . . ." but will probably be booed down by those who feel that that sort of language is very far from what they are feeling. And others may start sputtering, "It's like . . . It's like. . . ."

"IT'S LIKE . . ."   At this point we might choose to sum it all up in words something like these: "You see, Eliot's right. There are no real words for feelings (except the strictly technical, which will not serve); so in order to communicate our feelings to others in writing, where we can't use the grimaces and gestures and sounds you just used to convey your meaning so vividly, we will have to find something more substantial to compare it to, something our readers can understand. The thing 'it's like' that some of us were groping for is what Eliot calls the *objective correlative*, something objective to correlate to and thus to explain the subjective feeling we couldn't find words for."

That Indescribable Feeling.   Here someone is probably going to ask, "But what exactly is an objective correlative?" And we can explain that it is as Eliot tells us: a "set of objects, a situation, a chain of events" that an author sets up as a comparison, a substitution, for an indescribable feeling, in hopes that the readers' memories of these objects, situations, or events will be similar enough to that of the author to evoke something like the appropriate indescribable feeling in them.

Nausea.   In suggesting examples, it is probably a good idea to go back to the sick, nauseous feeling with which we began. Thus we might point to stanza 4 in "The Highwayman," where Noyes aims at conveying just such a feeling:

> And dark in the dark old inn-yard, a stable-wicket creaked
> Where Tim the osler listened; his face was white and peaked;
> His eyes were hollows of madness, his hair like mouldy hay
> But he loved the landlord's daughter,
> The landlord's red-lipped daughter,
> Dumb as a dog he listened, and he heard the robber say—

In setting up the evil stablehand with all his sick fantasies as the betrayer of the dashing highwayman, Noyes wants the image of Tim the osler literally to turn the reader's stomach. So how does he do it? We might single out the "mouldy hay" simile, and ask our students what sort of impression it evokes. If in response we are again confronted with the same sort of grimaces and gestures originally called forth by the nausea exercise—and it is very likely we will be, then our students will be able to see the connection and understand the objective correlative in a personalized, visceral way.

Love.   Of course, imagery is not always negative. Sometimes poets want to convey a highly positive emotion, like love. How do they do that?

> O, my luve is like a red, red rose,
> That's newly sprung in June.
> O my luve is like the melodie
> That's sweetly played in tune.

Robert Burns could be sure we would take his meaning because, like mouldy hay, roses and sweet melodies are rooted in almost universal "sensory experience" and evoke similar impressions in all of us. It might not be a bad idea at this point for us to ask our students which of their senses are called into action by the images of "mouldy hay," "red, red roses," and "melodies sweetly played," and what impressions are evoked from them. As our students compare impressions, they should also begin to understand that as their experiences vary, their response to each metaphor will also vary. To this extent, each of us takes a poet's words and creates a poem for ourselves, similar to— but not identical with—the poem other readers create with the words, or indeed that which the author himself had in mind.

Comparison.   The language of poetry thus often speaks of one thing in terms of something else meaningful to the reader or listener in order to convey the elusive feeling or complex idea attached to the first item through the concrete sensory means of the second. In this way, imagery consists of the objective correlatives of the author's otherwise inexpressible emotions or ideas. Comparison is thus the basis of all imagery.

The needs of some classes will be satisfied with this knowledge alone, plus whatever further exemplification is necessary to clarify it and reinforce it; but other classes may want to delve more deeply into the technical aspects of the metaphoric system in order to understand more fully the workings of metaphor. In these classes we should go further and explain that we talk about an image in terms of its form and/or its content.

Images of Form

We might tell them that images are distinguished by form according to the explicitness of the relationship between the objective correlative (the "O.C.," as students are more comfortable calling it) and the indescribable feeling or idea that it conveys. There are four main categories of form into which almost all images might be placed: metaphor, simile, connotative language, and symbol.

METAPHOR. Probably the most important of the images of form is metaphor, a term used throughout this chapter in its generic sense as a synonym for any sort of an image, but which, when used technically, means the kind of image in which the O.C. is equated with its idea or feeling. For example, when Noyes writes "his eyes were hollows of madness," he means that "his eyes" (or rather the feeling Noyes wants to convey about his eyes) = "hollows of madness."

With true metaphor, we can always find an equals sign—even when it is not directly indicated by the copulative verb. For instance, in Carl Sandburg's "The fog came in on little cat feet," fog = cat, while in "The ship ploughed the waves," the equation is between the way the ship went through the waves and ("equals") the ploughing of a field.

Extended Metaphor. Metaphors gain power when they are extended or elaborated upon, that is, when qualities related to the indescribable idea or feeling are spoken of in terms of qualities related to the O.C. For instance, in Noyes's line "The moon was a ghostly galleon, tossed upon cloudy seas" (moon = ship and clouds = sea), there is a double metaphoric relationship.

Metaphoric Series. Metaphors can be used to create a powerful cumulative effect when they are arranged in a series:

Life's but a walking shadow, a poor player	[Life = a shadow]
That struts and frets his hour upon the stage	[Life = an actor]
And then is heard no more: it is a tale	[Life = an idiot's tale]
Told by an Idiot, full of sound and fury,	
Signifying nothing. (Shakespeare)	

SIMILE. A more explicit relationship between indescribable feeling and the O.C. is found in the simile, where the presence of "like" or "as" explicitly signals the comparison:

My luve is *like a* red, red rose . . .
My luve is *like* a melodie / That's sweetly played in tune (Burns)

His hair like mouldy hay.
Dumb *as a* dog, he listened. (Noyes)

Our throats were tight *as* tourniquets. (Shapiro)

The holy time was quiet *as* a nun / Breathless with adoration.
(Wordsworth)

CONNOTATIVE LANGUAGE. A third form of imagery, connotative language, is a little more difficult for our students to understand, for here the comparison is merely implied in the language. Examples from "The Highwayman" can be helpful again. We might explain the difference between connotation and denotation and then offer our students these lines:

> But he loved the Landlord's daughter,
> The Landlord's red-lipped daughter,

Then if we ask them what they think Bess the Landlord's daughter was like, we are likely to get some rather embarrassed smiles. If we persist and ask further, "Is she pretty? Is she sexy?," the smiles are sure to increase. "Well, then, how do we know? If we stick to the denotative meaning of the words, all we find out is that the blood vessels near her oral orifice are close to the surface. What is there about the word 'red' and the word 'lip' that makes you smile so knowingly?"

Our students should then have little trouble seeing that both "red" and "lip" have in addition to their denotative meaning sensual connotations that are so descriptive that Noyes, having only two syllables in which to sum up his heroine, chose these two.

SYMBOLISM. In symbolism the O.C. has at the same time both a literal and a figurative (sometimes more than one figurative) meaning. Robert Frost's "Fire and Ice" is a good place to begin a discussion of symbolism, because, unlike most symbolic usages, this poem provides its own explication. In speculating whether the world will end in fire or ice, Frost clearly intends "fire" to mean conflagration and "ice" to signify glacial cold; but in musing over the implications of the question, he takes the trouble to point out explicitly that by "fire" he also intends "desire," and by "ice," "hate."

Our students having understood the concept of symbolism where it is so clear-cut may then sense the power it exerts in its more ambiguous manifestations; and they may then be ready to explore the enigmatic beauties of such poems as William Blake's "The Sick Rose" or Samuel Taylor Coleridge's "Kubla Khan." Our students' understanding of the ways words can be endowed with symbolic connotation without sacrificing their literal meanings should be helpful to them when they write their own poems.

IN SUMMARY.   In metaphor, the O.C. is *equated* to the idea or feeling. In simile, the relationship is a little more distant. The O.C. is shown rather to be *similar* to the subject. The writer uses the words "like" or "as" to convey this similarity. With connotative language, the comparison is only implied by the connotations of the words used to express the ideas. And in symbolism, the O.C. has both a literal and a symbolic meaning—that is, at one time the O.C. both means itself and stands for something else, just as the American eagle is both a bird and a symbol of American strength and freedom. Our students should find the Student Guidelines helpful in illustrating how each of these forms work.

STUDENT GUIDELINES

Imagery of Form

Definition: Imagery is comparison. The image centers on an objective correlative (O.C.) to which the writer compares an indescribable idea or feeling to evoke a similar idea or feeling in the reader.

Forms of Images	Subject	Comparison	Objective Correlative
METAPHOR:		=	*O.C.*
Example:	Tim's eyes	"were"	"hollows of madness"
SIMILE:		*like (as)*	*O.C.*
Examples:	Tim's hair	"like"	"mouldy hay"
	Tim's listening	"dumb as"	"a dog"
CONNOTATIVE LANGUAGE:		*implies*	*O.C.*
Example:	Landlord's daughter's sensual attractiveness	implied by	"red-lipped"
SYMBOL:		=	*itself*
		AND *stands for*	O.C.
Example:	Tim, the osler	=	the stablehand, a character in the poem
		AND *stands for*	stealthy, unseen evil

Images of Content

Every image is formed as a metaphor, a simile, connotative language, or a symbol. But images can also be classified in terms of their content, of the particular relationship between their O.C.'s and the indescribable feelings or ideas they express. Understanding how some of the imagery of content works can be helpful to our student poets, not only in their interaction with the poems they read, but also in their own writing.

HYPERBOLE.   If, for example, the emotion they want to express is inexpressible because it is so big, so vast, so overwhelming that any regular image would be an understatement and only an exaggeration will do, then they can turn to hyperbole to express their feelings. For instance, Burns sets forth the extent of a lover's faithfulness through hyperbole:

> And I will luve thee still, my dear,
> Till a' the seas gang dry!
> Till a' the seas gang dry, my dear,
> And the rocks melt wi' the sun!

And Benét uses it to extol the excellence of an expert fiddler:

> He could fiddle all the bugs off a sweet-potato vine
> He could fiddle down a possum from a mile-high tree;
> He could fiddle up a whale from the bottom of the sea.

Both of these examples of hyperbole are metaphors in form. Burns's faithfulness *equals* the staying power of the seas, and Benét's fiddler's playing is so good that it *equals* the power it takes to get the bugs to leave a vine or a whale to leave the sea. Not all hyperboles, however, are phrased as metaphor. "Vast as the ocean is my love," for instance, is clearly a simile.

PERSONIFICATION.   If poets want to add human appeal to the nonhuman indescribable idea they are trying to get across, they might well choose to personify their O.C. and endow it with human characteristics. Personification, another kind of content imagery, comes in two varieties.

Personification of Abstractions.   One variety turns abstract concepts into human beings, like the characters in the old morality plays: Faith, Hope, and Charity, and Evil Deeds. Older poetry is full of such personifications; for example, those that people Milton's "L'Allegro" and "Il Penseroso":

> *Sport* that wrinkled *Care* derides
> And *Laughter* holding both *his* sides.

And though abstract personifications are rarer in modern poetry, they are still employed, as, for instance, in this line of W. H. Auden: "There's *Wrath* who has learnt every trick of guerilla warfare."

Humanized Nonhumans. Our students, however, will probably feel more comfortable themselves using the sort of personification that ascribes human characteristics to the nonhuman. Such metaphors give these verses of Tennyson and Walt Whitman, for instance, their power:

> He [The Eagle] clasped the crag with crooked *hands*.

> Smile, O voluptuous cool-breathed earth.

ALLUSION. Another way poets—including our own students—can expand the emotional universe of a poem is to tint their O.C. with the unmistakable color of another piece of literature. By alluding to another world, the poet can include it within its own. For example, by quoting part of the line "[I am] dying, Egypt, dying," from the final act of *Antony and Cleopatra*, Louis MacNeice reminds us of the almost unbearable feelings of waste most of us experience at the destruction of the gloriously gaudy universe Shakespeare creates in that play. In this way, MacNeice incorporates these feelings into our response to his "Song" ("The Sunlight on the Garden").

Ironic Allusion. Sometimes allusion can also be used for ironic effect. T. S. Eliot, for instance, rounds off a sordid passage in "The Wasteland," lamenting the absence even of "empty bottles, sandwich papers, . . . cardboard boxes, cigarette ends" from the banks of the Thames, with reminiscences of poems particularly rich in cultural meaning and traditional beauty. By integrating into his verse the moving first line of the psalm "By the Waters of Babylon I Sat Down and Wept" and the compelling refrain from Spencer's "Prothalamium," "Sweet Thames, run softly till I end my song," Eliot develops an ironic contrast that emphasizes the sordid rootlessness of modern life and accentuates the poem's sense of despair.

SYNESTHESIA. Sometimes poets find sensory impressions connected to only one of the five senses inadequate to convey the complexity of their emotion, and so, for their O.C.'s, they resort to stretching or bending sensory experience beyond the limits of a single sense in an imagery called synesthesia, after the psychological malady in which the victim "hears" color and "sees" sound.

Synesthetic metaphors are often particularly striking and effective. MacNeice, for instance, uses them throughout his "Song" to comment upon human helplessness in the face of the inexorable passing of time. His poem opens:

> The sunlight on the garden
> Hardens and grows cold.
> We cannot cage the minute
> Within its nets of gold.

And Dylan Thomas, who often employs synesthesia, uses it in "Do Not Go Gentle" to get across the wild bravado of some youth: "Wild men who caught and sang the sun in flight."

PARADOX. In advanced classes or in those with a special interest in poetry, we might also want to share the exciting possibilities of the poetic use of the paradox, a figure where a normally incomprehensible mystery, such as the nature of God or of love or of indomitable human striving, is expressed in an O.C. that appears to be a total contradiction, but which makes sense within the logic of the poem. In "Do Not Go Gentle," for instance, Dylan Thomas uses the oxymoron, a paradox in a phrase, to suggest the insight with which thoughtful men approach death—"Grave men, near death, who see with *blinding sight*"—and again to urge his father to be fierce in fighting off death a while longer:

> And you, my father, there on the sad height,
> *Curse, bless* me now with your fierce tears, I pray.

John Donne uses paradoxical imagery throughout his sonnet "Batter My Heart" to beg God for a mystical experience that will force his reason to bend to God's will. Concluding with one of the most striking metaphors in all literature, he expresses the paradoxical purity of such a forcing and the paradoxical freedom the pious find in exact obedience to the will of God:

> Take me to you, imprison me, for I,
> Except you enthrall me, never shall be free,
> Nor ever chaste, except you ravish me

METONYMY. Because it is often employed to striking effect, we might want to add metonymy (a term now widely used also to indicate synecdoche) to our students cache of useful metaphors of content. In these images, a part (or something closely related) stands for the whole. For example, in these lines from A. E. Houseman, "the leather" = a football:

> Is football still aplaying
> Along the river shore
> With lads to chase *the leather*
> Now I stand up no more?

STUDENT GUIDELINES

Imagery

All imagery is basically comparison, the finding of the most precise literary notation to serve as the objective correlative (O.C.) for the emotion or idea to be evoked.

OF FORM
1. Metaphor. When the O.C. is *equated* with the compared item.

continued

> "To see the cherry hung with snow." (Houseman)
> (cherry blossom = snow)

2. Simile. When the comparison is pointed to explicitly by *like* or *as*.

> "Apple blossoms look *like* snow." (John Farrar)

3. Connotative language. When the comparison is *implied* by the connotations of the words employed.

> "I met a traveler from an antique land." (Shelley)

4. Symbol. When the O.C. has at least two layers of meaning.

> "And miles to go before I *sleep*" (Frost)
> means both a lengthy distance to cover before
> bedtime and much to do before death.

OF CONTENT

1. Hyperbole. When the O.C. is wildly exaggerated (implying a superlative emotional coloring).

> "He fiddled all the bugs off the sweet-potato vine." (Benét)

> "Forever and a day." (Longfellow)

2. Personification. When the O.C. is human or has human characteristics.

> "And Laughter holding both his sides." (Milton)

> "He [the eagle] clasped the crag with crooked hands." (Tennyson)

3. Allusion. When the O.C. refers to a literary source (taking on the emotional coloration of the source).

> "No, I am not Prince Hamlet, nor was meant to be." (Eliot)

4. Synesthesia. When the imagery involves a confusion of the senses.

> "Moulten golden notes
> And all in tune.
> What a liquid ditty floats" (Poe)

5. Paradox (and oxymoron). When the O.C. expresses a seeming contradiction.

> "And if some lover, such as we,
> Have heard this *dialogue of one*." (Donne)

6. Metonymy (including synecdoche). When the O.C. is the part that stands for the whole or is closely related to it.

> "Your smile had caught fire at Orly"
> (Smile = the person killed in the air-crash)

> "The hippocratic eye will see / In nakedness, anatomy." (Graves)
> (The hippocratic eye = the whole doctor)

Exercises in Imagery

Many teachers assign exercises or the writing of brief poems to solidify their students' knowledge of the various kinds of figurative language.

ANIMAL METAPHORS. Because the distinction between the abstract and the concrete is so essential to students' understanding of imagery, Charles Rathbone asks his students to express such abstract concepts as "anticipation," "honor," "love," "defeat," "death," "kindness," "envy," and "joy" in terms of animal metaphor. He begins by providing his own example: "Anticipation is a twitching poodle."[4]

FRESH SIMILES. Baird Shuman offers an exercise in simile to the participants of his Poet's Workshops that helps them strive for more interesting imagery. He tells his students:

> Anyone can say that something is as red as apple, but to say that something is as red as a winter sunset or as a drunkard's nose or as a cardinal's hat is to use a fresher image.[5]

And he asks them to find five "fresh images" for such similes as "As yellow as. . . ," "As green as. . . ," "Quieter than. . . ," "Rougher than. . . ," "As stubborn as. . . ," and "Richer than . . ." (1269).

CLASSMATES IN IMAGES. Don M. Wolfe has his students describe their schoolroom and their classmates in terms of metaphor or simile. When they have all written such images as "Joe's crewcut sticks up like the bristles of a brush" or "Helen's eyes are milky blue," the class shares them and evaluates them on the basis of "Which are the fresh, the original [images] that you have not heard in conversation or read in a book?"[6]

DAILY LIFE IN IMAGES. Rathbone suggests another exercise in which students create "similes, metaphors, or personifications" to express their feelings about some of the following topics: "Garbage cans," "a cats' tail," "fried onions," "chewing gum under a counter," "spring rain," "a freshly polished fender," "fresh dittos," and "finger tips after washing dishes" (854).

IMAGE POEMS. The difficulty with assigning the writing of poems before students learn about rhythm and the sound of poetry is that the poems produced are likely to be quite formless. Teachers find that Kenneth Koch's poem topics, with their unity of theme and their emphasis on repetition, satisfy the need for form before meter or formal rhythm is taught.

Koch's ideas also invite discovery and practice of the various kinds of imagery. For example, "I am the sea" or "If I were the snow" or "I am a white mouse" are actually exercises in personification; his lesson on "lies" produces some wonderful hyperboles; and his color poems (what color is that sound? that feeling?) stimulate synesthetic images. Koch includes in his series of lessons both a session on simile, "Comparisons: Spring is like. . . ," and another on metaphor. Edward Proffitt uses a variation on Koch's "I wish I were . . ." to teach the logic of metaphor. With it, students can learn that for a figure to work, each part must ring true, both in the literal and the figurative senses, as they do in the student example he includes:

> I wish I were curling rings of smoke,
> For then I'd waver and stretch into ribbons of blue ice.
> I wish I were crystal glass,
> For then I'd shatter into opaque clumps (134–35).

TEACHING RHYTHM AND SOUND WITH A LITERARY FOCUS

Poetry owes its archetypal, bedrock appeal to rhythm. No human culture is without music and dance, and all human beings respond emotionally to some kind of patterned repetition, whether it is a primitive drumbeat or a sophisticated symphony. Speculation that this appeal stems from the nine-month security of the fetus in close proximity to the beating of its mother's heart was given some measure of confirmation by studies of infants in hospital nurseries. The study determined that infants gained weight better and cried less when a recording of a beating heart was played in the nursery. And evidently there is a transference of the heart effect, for significant gains also resulted from further experiments that substituted strongly rhythmical music for the beating heart.[7]

Repetition: The Sound of Poetry

Perhaps this explanation accounts for the emotional persuasiveness of rhythmic prose as well as the all-but-universal appeal of strongly accented poetry. Rhythm also satisfies intellectually. By giving order to impressions and ideas, it helps make information accessible to our finite minds. On a less-generalized level, if those are correct who claim that the human mind is always striving after perfection, always seeking wholes, then rhythm satisfies us intellectually by establishing and perfecting a pattern, a whole.

Just as comparison is the key to an understanding of imagery, repetition is the key to an understanding of rhythm; and this concept can offer a systematic basis for our teaching of it. Poetry is always based on a patterned repetition of sound, whatever patterning system it employs.

TEACHING ABOUT DIFFERING REPETITIVE POETIC PATTERNS. Our students probably understand that all formal poetry is divided into regularly patterned lines; they also need to realize that the principle for the patterning may differ.

Koch Method.　If they have written poetry by the Koch method, they understand how rhythm can be created through a patterned repetition of opening phrases. They may be interested in exploring other ways of structuring repetition.

Japanese.　The principle underlying the pattern in Japanese poetry, for instance, is syllabic—based upon a specific odd number of syllables in each line. Like characteristic Japanese painting and flower arrangements, Japanese poetry appears to occidental eyes as gracefully asymmetrical. Their haiku, for example, consists of seventeen syllables arranged in three lines (5-7-5 syllables) and their tanka has thirty-one syllables arranged in five lines (5-7-5-7-7).

French.　We might point out, further, that Franch poetry is also syllabic, but it is arranged in stanzas with repetitive line patterns similar to our own, traditionally ending in rhymes of various kinds.

Anglo-Saxon.　Anglo-Saxon poetry, on the other hand, is patterned in quite a different way. Once student interest is piqued, they usually want to try to discover the pattern inductively. And they are quite able to do so if we supply them with copies of Caedman's "Hymn" or the following lines from *Beowulf* and let them ponder the poetry as they listen to a recorded reading.

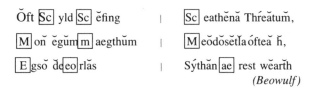

(Beowulf)

　　With great pleasure, our students can discover (through experiential learning) that, although the Anglo-Saxon line may have almost any number of syllables, it always has four strongly accented beats and the line is always broken in the middle by a pause, called a *caesura*. They will see immediately that Anglo-Saxon verse uses no rhyme and, when pressed for an alternative unifying concept, can be led to find the alliteration of (usually) three of the four accented beats (even if they are still unacquainted with the term alliteration). Students who know something about the development of the English language should not be surprised to discover that English metric poetry shares in the characteristics of both French and Anglo-Saxon verse by counting both accents and syllables.[8]

TEACHING TRADITIONAL ENGLISH METER.　Because English meter is at the root of traditional English-language poetry, we may want our students to become familiar with it in more detail.

Motivating. Occasionally students wonder why we bother to study formal rhythm and meter when most of the poems they write on their own are in free-verse. When I'm asked that question, I usually respond that the best free-verse poets are like the best abstract artists: they abstract from a solid technical understanding of the mechanics of their art. In order to paint a good impressionist, expressionist, or abstract version of a bowl of fruit, a student artist first acquires the skill to make a realistic drawing of the fruit. Similarly, our students' free-verse poetry will be better after they acquire technical knowledge and skill. And after our poetry study is over, I've seldom had a student-poet who didn't agree.

Introducing Metrics. A good way to begin is to present students with an inductive problem in English meter similar to the one they handled in Anglo-Saxon. We might read a stanza or two from Whittier's "Barefoot Boy" (or any very regular, strongly accented verse), and ask our students to clap to it or tap it out and determine what principle lies behind its rhythm:

> Bléssǐng | ón thěe | líttlě | mán, [˘]
> Bárefǒot | bóy wǐth | chéek of | tán [˘]

When they come up with four accented beats, all (but the last) followed by an unaccented syllable, we might tell them they are on their way to understanding all there is to know about meter, for they have discovered the combination of accent and syllable that makes up the English metric foot.

Teaching Terminology: Metric Feet. The smallest measure of poetry, the metric foot, consists of one accented beat and one or two unaccented beats, as is shown in Table 11–1.

Teaching Terminology: Lines. As our students will be able to discover for themselves, a metric foot consists of one accented syllable and at least one unaccented syllable. We count accented beats to determine how many feet are in a line. The odd thing is that we count them in Greek! If we are lucky enough to have students of Greek heritage, they will usually be delighted to count in Greek for the class, who are in turn delighted to see how closely the modern Greek numbers approach the names for the lines:

Table 11–1 English Meter

Foot	Accent	Sample Word
iam (iambic foot)	˘ ´	ǎbóut
trochee (trochaic foot)	´ ˘	líttlě
anapest (anapestic foot)	˘ ˘ ´	intěrcéde
dactyl (dactylic foot)	´ ˘ ˘	týrǎnnў

1 foot to a line = monometer
2 feet to a line = dimeter
3 feet to a line = trimeter
4 feet to a line = tetrameter
5 feet to a line = pentameter
6 feet to a line = hexameter
7 feet to a line = heptameter
8 feet to a line = octometer . . .

The lines are, in fact, labeled according to the number of times a particular metric foot is repeated in it—thus, for example, iambic hexameter, trochaic tetrameter, and so on. Though such technical discussion is undeniably tedious on the printed page, it need not be so in the classroom. There we can present the information through interactive clapping, chanting, and desk tapping.

Teaching Terminology: Stanzas. The metric line is repeated and arranged into a stanza of a particular number of lines, which is in turn repeats to form a poem, the totality of the whole repetitive pattern. Sometimes the pattern involves a mixture of kinds of feet in the lines; more often, it includes an arrangement of lines of different length (the ballad stanza of tetrameter-trimeter-tetrameter-trimeter, for instance), and occasionally the stanzas vary in length; but whatever arrangement is selected, repetition patterns it into a regular configuration that can be easily recognized and which the ear awaits with anticipatory pleasure.

EXPERIENCING METER. All this work on meter then needs to be reinforced by substantial practice until the metric lines sing in our students' consciousness. Our students can search for sample lines in their poetry books to illustrate all four kinds of feet. They can try to "dum-de-dum" samples of regular verse we provide for them to discover what kind of feet and how many feet to the line (iambic hexameter?). And they can attempt to write couplets in some of the more common or easier verse lines. Students almost always enjoy "learning how to dum-de-dum"; but because the work can be difficult for some of them, I would suggest lots of personal help and support, including, perhaps, turning some class periods into bustling workshops on meter, where those who have caught on quickly can help those who find the idea of meter harder to grasp.

TEACHING VARIATIONS ON THE ENGLISH METRIC LINE. When all the lovely cadences of English metrics are singing in our students' heads, it is time to teach variation, the methods poets use to change mere verse into poetry.

To demonstrate the necessity for such variation, we might return to "Barefoot Boy" or a poem with a comparable monotony of versification.

Singsong ten lines or so of "Barefoot Boy" aloud for our class and they will plead for mercy. "Why? What's wrong with this poem?" we might ask. "Dull, monotonous, boring," they will respond. "How come? What makes it that way?" And they'll notice that every line is a whole phrase or sentence, usually concluded by some mark of punctuation to make the voice drop, and further that there are hardly any marks of punctuation except at the ends of lines. If some students protest, "But you're reading it singsong," we might respond by asking them to try to read it themselves to see if the evenness of the accent does not promote that sort of reading. They might decide that the problem is that every line ends in a rhyme; but we could point to a poem like Robert Browning's "My Last Duchess," which—though also written in couplets—does not suffer from this problem. Their curiosity stirred, our students will want to know how the difference is achieved.

Purpose of the Regular Beat.   In order to understand why variation is important and how it is achieved, our students must realize that the purpose of the underlying meter is to provide a unifying beat out of which the individual rhythms of a poem can be created. The metric pattern, once established, acts as does the percussion music of a band or orchestra, creating a rhythmic unity from which the melody can depart and return. Joseph Malof puts it best when he writes:

> Most poems have, to some degree, a primitive, hypnotic pulse. But they also usually fight against the pulse, creating rhythmic tension or counterpoint. . . . [Thus] the poem itself is, rhythmically, the distortion of a perfect abstract pattern.[9]

Point and Counterpoint.   When the "hypnotic pulse" is permitted to remain too unencumbered, singsong effects are inevitable. Variation of "rhythmic tension" is created when the normal prose pronunciation of a poem runs counter to the established beat. Since the beat or meter consists of sound and no-sound, the poet can vary the rhythm by increasing or decreasing the expected (or regular) sound or pause.

Substituting Spondees and Pyrrhics.   Naturally, some such variation exists in the normal course of things. Our students are well aware that except when reading poetic lines for purposes of scansion, all accented syllables and all unaccented syllables are not pronounced with the same emphasis. But poets can deliberately accentuate the distinction for artistic effect, as Donne does, for instance, by substituting a spondee (a foot with two accented beats) for one of the iambs in these lines from "Batter My Heart," in order to bombard the sensibility of his readers:

> That I may rise and stand, o'erthrow me, and bend
> Your force / to break, / *blow, burn,* / and make / me new.

Poets are also free to make other conventionalized substitutions of accented sound, such as the substitution of a pyrrhic foot (two unaccented beats) for any duple (two-beat) foot or of an opening trochee at the beginning of an iambic pentameter line.

Varying Caesuras and End Stops. The most important variations from the established meter are achieved, however, through the use of pauses contrary to metric expectations, either by adding pauses (caesuras) within the lines or by avoiding the expected end-stop at the close (enjambment).

To demonstrate, we might choose to analyze the way Shelley, for instance, manipulates the pauses in "Ozymandias." Though the form of "Ozymandias" is a sonnet, a genre which can be as lyrical and musical as Shakespeare's "Shall I Compare Thee to a Summer's Day?" Shelley's ironic purpose demands an almost conversational tone. To obtain this tone, he disguises the Petrarchan rhyme scheme and the iambic pentameter by frequent enjambment and a clever manipulation of the caesura to keep the syntactic sense of the lines at variance with the metrical pattern.

If we duplicate triple-spaced copies of the poem or work with it on the board, our students will be able to discover for themselves how Shelley manages this feat. By working carefully through the poem, they will note that very few lines have identical caesura patterns. They will see also how Shelley begins with a regular first line to establish the beat, and gradually increases the variation. The second line has only one caesura and that coincides with the end of the first foot, though that line, like the first, is not end-stopped. The first caesura in the third line, however—and it's a major one—divides the third foot and the second divides the fourth:

> I met/ a trav/ [el]ler from/ an an/ tique land
> Who said: / ITwo vast/ and trunk / less legs/ of stone
> Stand in/ the des/ert . . . I near/ them,I on/ the sand,/I

Variation as Sound Effect. To show that poets use these techniques for a variety of purposes, we might read Shakespeare's Sonnet 29, "When in Disgrace," or Browning's "Home Thoughts from Abroad." In these poems, enjambment and the absence of caesuras force the reader to a breathlessness that imitates the exaltation of the skylark's song:

> . . . and then my state,
> Like to the lark at break of
>   day arising
> From sullen earth, sings hymns
>   at heaven's gate.
> (Shakespeare)

> That's the wise thrush; he sings
>   each song twice over
> Lest you should think he never
>   could recapture
> The first fine careless rapture!
> (Browning)

When our students, reciting the lines together, find themselves out of breath, and as they note the way Shakespeare finally permits them to let out their breath, to exhale on "h" sounds, they will discover for themselves poetic possibilities they might personally explore.

Teaching Sound Devices

Rhythm and meter are founded in repetition, and, with one exception, all the sound devices are also repetition-based. Repetition functions for emphasis. It calls attention to the word or phrase that repeats or that contains the repeating element and emphasizes the thought embodied within it. It is important that our students understand that every linguistic element can be repeated for poetic effect—though whether we want to teach them names for each of the specialized kinds of repetition is a matter for personal decision.

ALLITERATION. If we decide to teach the nomenclature, we might begin by telling our students that the repetition of *initial* sounds—either vowel or consonant—is known as alliteration:

> till *n*odding *n*ight—mad *n*aked summer *n*ight. (Whitman)

> The *g*rim, un *g*ainly, *g*hastly, *g*aunt, and ominous bird of yore. (Poe)

> *P*oets make *p*ets of *p*retty docile words. (Wylie)

Alliteration also works to reinforce other poetic effects. The bludgeoning impact of the spondee in the line from "Batter My Heart" quoted earlier, for instance, is strengthened by the initial alliteration of the "break, blow, burn."

ASSONANCE. Assonance is the repetition of all—initial and internal—vowel sounds. For example,

> From the m*o*lten g*o*lden n*o*tes . . .
> What a l*i*quid d*i*tty floats (Poe)

> In the s*u*n that is *you*ng *o*nce only (Dylan Thomas)

We may need to caution our students that assonance (like the other sound devices) refers to sound—not necessarily to letters. Letters, especially the vowels, have a variety of sounds. For assonance, for instance, to exist, the actual sounds must repeat, though the letters may differ. For example, in the Thomas quotation above, the "o" of "once" and "young" is assonant with the "u" of "sun." The "o" of "only," of course, is not.

CONSONANCE. Consonance is the repetition of all consonant sounds, whether initial or internal or concluding. For example:

> Over the bent wo*r*ld b*r*oods with wa*r*m b*r*east (Gerard Manley Hopkins)

> Our throa*ts* were *t*igh*t* as *t*ourniquets. (Karl Shapiro)

RHYME. Rhyme is the repetition of a final accented syllable, followed by nothing or by identical unaccented syllable(s):

They rigged out a shutter with sail and oar,
And threatened to pack off Gustavus Gore
On a voyage of penance to Singapore. (Rands)

There was an old person of Anerley
Whose conduct was strange and unmannerly. (Lear)

REPETITION OF SUFFIXES AND PREFIXES.   All of these devices have
the effect of adding interest, emphasis, mood, or excitement to the words or
phrases with which they are associated. The repetition of morphemes has the
same impact. We find, for instance, the repetition of prefixes—

"*un*hallowed and *un*sung"

—and of suffixes—

Deep into that dark*ness* peering, long I stood there, wonder*ing*,
fear*ing*, / Doubt*ing*, dream*ing* (Poe)

Ogden Nash has made his reputation by playing on common English suffixes:

I know not whether I am drifting sea*ward* or shore*ward*
My neck is stiff from my head trying to turn simultaneously
backward and foreward.

ONOMATOPOEIA.   The most striking sound device is probably onomatopoeia through which sound imitates meaning. Because of its comparative nature, onomatopoeia, the only nonrepetitive sound device, is closely linked
with metaphor and might even be considered "sound imagery."

Though we usually think of it in terms of such words as "plash" and
"bowwow," and the special effects Poe achieves in "The Bells," meaningful
sound is very much present in such effects as the breathless ecstasy of the
skylarks in the Shakespeare and Browning excerpts I quoted earlier, as well
as in the famous sneeze in Pope's *Rape of the Lock*, which we might want to
let our students read aloud together:

Sudden with starting tears each eye o'erflows,
And the high dome re-echoes to his nose.

Just as onomatopoeia is partly achieved in Pope's couplet through the assonance on "o," so it is often brought about through alliteration or consonance
or combination of them all. For example:

• The buzz saw snarled and rattled in the yard
• Our throats were tight as tourniquets.

PULLING IT TOGETHER.   The Sound of Poetry Student Guidelines sum
up sound strategy in a way that points up for our students its underlying
unity, the unity that stems from the principle of repetition.

STUDENT GUIDELINES

The Sound of Poetry

A. Rhythm: movement with regular recurrence.
B. Meter: patterned rhythm (of English poetry).
    1. Foot
        a. iambic: soft loud [- /]
           "Shall I compare thee to a summer's day?" (Shakespeare)
        b. trochaic: loud soft [/ -]
           "Blessings on thee little man" (Whittier)
        c. anapestic: soft soft loud [- - /]
           "For the moon never beams without bringing me dreams" (Poe)
        d. dactyllic: loud soft soft [/ - -]
           "This is the forest primeval. The murmuring pines and the hemlock."
    2. Line
        a. dimeter, trimeter, tetrameter, (1b & c), pentameter (1a), hexameter (1d), heptameter, octometer
        b. free verse—irregular rhythm
        c. blank verse—unrhymed iambic pentameter
        d. alexandrine—iambic hexameter
    3. Stanza
        a. couplet, triplet, quatrain
        b. sonnet: fourteen iambic-pentameter lines
        c. heroic couplet: iambic pentameter couplet
C. Variation
    1. Caesura
    2. Non-end-stopped line (making phrasal pattern at variance with metric pattern)
    3. Varying degree of stress on syllables (spondee and pyrrhic)
    4. Substitution of feet (accrusis (+) and catalexis (−))
D. Sound devices
    1. Onomatopoeia: the word imitates the sound; sound imagery.
        "How they clang and clash and roar." (Poe)
    2. Rhyme: repetition of final sound
        Masculine—"Bat/cat"
        Feminine—"batty/catty"
        Triple—"battiness/cattiness"
    3. Alliteration; repetition of initial sounds
        "What a *t*ale of *t*error now their *t*urbulency *t*ells." (Poe)
    4. Assonance: repetition of vowel sounds
        "This b*o*dy dr*o*p n*o*t d*o*wn" (Coleridge)
    5. Consonance: repetition of consonant sounds
        "And wa*s* a ble*ss*ed gho*s*t." (Coleridge)

continued

continued
6. Repetition of words and phrases:
"I galloped, Dirck galloped, we galloped all three." (Browning)
Sometimes used to achieve the effect of a refrain (repetition of a final line or lines, as in the old ballads)
"It's lilac-time in London; its lilac-time in London." (Noyes)

Sound Exercises

If our students are fully to enjoy reading and writing poetry, their ears will need to become sensitized to sounds, especially to the sounds of words. To achieve such a goal, Charles Rathbone has thought of a series of what he calls "soundful games, listening contests, and exercises that call on the ear to be discriminating."

SOUNDFUL GAMES.   Among these exercises are making lists of onomatopoeic words, of interesting words of more than six syllables, of brand names "that seem especially alliterative," and of members of such categories as "herbs and spices," "capital cities," "girls' names," "rivers," "vegetables," and "birds," all arranged in series with pleasingly rhythmical cadences. The contents of any of these lists may provide good subject matter for couplets, quatrains, and limericks later on.

Onomatopoeic Sentences.   Rathbone also recommends asking students to write a single long sentence that tries to "catch the sound of the actual pace" of an event, such as "the gradual slowing down of a long game of tennis, a train or subway coming into or leaving its station, the halls during the moments just before or after the bell or a race which includes a final sprint."

Contrasting Sentence Sounds.   Another Rathbone idea is to make contrasting sentences echoing the character and mood of ideas such as the following: "a short, cold shower, and a lengthy, hot bath; rush-hour driving and open freeway driving, Muzak and rock 'n' roll" (852–53).

Noise Poems.   One of Koch's assignments that also makes a useful sound exercise is his "noise" poem in which the students include at least one onomatopoeic word in each line.

PARTNER RHYMES.   We might also encourage our students to develop their sense of rhythm by writing what Sister Junette Morgan calls "partnership poetry." [10] For these poems, students work together supplying each other with rhymes for their couplets or quatrains. In a similar sort of partnership, the teacher might write the first and third lines of a few amusing limericks on the board (taking care to make the rhyming words easy) and, after some collaborative practice, ask the students to try to finish one themselves.

Birthday or Holiday Poems and Rhymes. Or students as a class can compose birthday cards, valentines, or get-well poems, appropriate to the occasion, in ballad quatrains or in whatever metric format the students suggest.[11]

A Caveat

Imagery is the language of poetry and rhythm is poetry's sound and major distinguishing feature. Thus the technical information concerning imagery and rhythm (some of the most important we have just surveyed) provides useful knowledge for our students if they are to read poetry with pleasure or write it with confidence. Divorced from these purposes, however, these technical details are interesting only as curiosities and trivia.

AVOID THE "LOOKEE THERE'S AN ONOMATOPOEIA" SYNDROME. The academic exploration of imagery and rhythm, therefore, must not be conducted in isolation from the poems that are their matrix and that provide the only justification for their study. In other words, the technical aspects of poetry should always be taught in conjunction with an interpretive reading of poems. For example, since "Ozymandias" offers a fine illustration of the manipulation of the caesura, the poem furnishes a good vehicle for teaching the possibilities for its use. If such training is to be meaningful, however, it should be preceded by a thorough exploration of the poem to discover what Shelley was trying to do in it so that the manipulation of the caesura may then be profitably presented as one method Shelley uses to achieve his purpose.

Again, Donne's "Batter My Heart" should not be presented as an example of paradox. Rather, the use of paradox might be explained in order to get at the meaning of the poem and the reason for its extraordinary effectiveness.

TEACHING POETRY IN A COMBINED CURRICULUM

In a combined poetry-study curriculum, students learn to write poems by reading poems and they learn to read poems by writing poems. Reading usually initiates the cycle.

Teaching Close Reading of Poems

Close reading of poetry is much the same as close reading of prose, but perhaps a bit more difficult because of the density and compactness of a poem. For this reason it offers especially good practice for students. As I often tell my own, "If you can close-read a metaphysical poem comfortably, you can read anything—history books, physics texts, anything."

Close-reading pedagogy is discussed in detail in pages 379–81 in Chapter 10. The Reading a Poem Closely Student Guidelines should be helpful to our students, but, of course, they can also be read usefully from a teacher's point of view.

STUDENT GUIDELINES

Reading a Poem Closely

1. *Read the poem aloud.* Poetry is as aural as music and is not meant to be read by the eyes alone. Listen to the poem as you read it. How does the sound contribute to the poem's meaning? To the emotional atmosphere the poem creates? Be on the lookout for such sound delights as the breathlessness of Shakespeare's skylark and the nasal quality of Pope's sneeze.
2. *Straighten out the poem's syntax.* You cannot begin to comprehend a poem unless you can understand what each of the sentences mean. Take, for example, the first lines of Shakespeare's Sonnet 73:

> That time of year thou mayst in me behold
> When yellow leaves, or none, or few, do hang
> Upon those boughs. . . .

The first thing to do is to cut through poetic inversion (not to mention four hundred years of language change) to discover what Shakespeare means: You see in me that time of year when a few yellow leaves (or none at all) hang upon the bough. Although it may sound prosaic, the first questions you must ask yourself when you begin reading a poem are: What is the subject of the first clause? What is the verb?

3. *Be sure you know the meaning of every word in the poem* — both literal and implied. If you are not really sure, look it up. Since poetry is such condensed expression, every word counts.
4. *Read literally.* This advice is particularly important when you approach metaphors and other imagery. Ask yourself, What exactly is the comparison? Then try to visualize it (or to imagine its smell, taste, or touch). Let's return to Sonnet 73:

> That time of year thou mayst in me behold
> When yellow leaves, or none, or few, do hang
> Upon those boughs which shake against the cold,
> Bare ruin'd choirs, where late the sweet birds sang.

What does Shakespeare intend us to think of when we read these lines? He compares his time of life with the autumn of the year. But in developing his images to make the time of the year more vivid and more specific, he extends the comparison to include himself as well. How can you get at Shakespeare's imagery? You can picture black, almost leafless branches silhouetted against a grey November sky. Try to feel them "shake against the cold" — as an old

continued

man might, perhaps. Then let the image in your mind of the bare boughs in silhouette transform itself into a silhouette of an equally bare "ruin'd choir," that is to say, the choir portion of one of the church or abbey ruins that dot the English countryside. Finally, imaginatively enter into Shakespeare's comparison of the special loneliness shared by the once lively choir loft and the once lively branches. Now that their respective choristers, the choirboys and the birds that once filled them with life and singing, are gone, the choir and the branches—and, by analogy, the poet himself—are left empty and useless and bereft.

5. *Note any unusual play of rhythm or diction, and decide what the poet means by it.* What effect, for instance, does Shakespeare achieve by breaking up his second line so frequently with pauses? And why does he break the logical ordering of the words?

> When yellow leaves, or none, or few, do hang

Might he mean to slow the reader down and add a tone of sadness? And what about the word "cold" at the end of the third line? Is it meant to stand as the object of the phrase "against the cold" in the second line? Or is it the first adjective in the words describing "choirs" in the third line? Or is it meant to "look before and after" and function in both ways? And what does Shakespeare gain by the addition of the adjective "sweet" in "where late the sweet birds sang"?

6. *Decide how the form contributes to the meaning of the poem.* For example, how does the three-quatrain-plus-a-couplet form of the Elizabethan sonnet help Shakespeare to organize his imagery in Sonnet 73? Similarly, how does Coleridge use the conventions of the medieval ballad to enhance the gothic effects of his "Rime of the Ancient Mariner?"[12]

Assignments

It is almost a maxim that for class-assigned student poems, the more structured the assignment, the better the poems created. We should, of course, be encouraging and responsive to poems students write on their own. But in requiring poems from the entire class, structured assignments ordinarily work better.

In teaching poetry writing as creative expression, we do best to follow Koch and provide structure for our in-class assignments. And in working with a combined curriculum, the most successful assignments are to write genre poems with content and metric conventions, such as ballads, sonnets, haiku—even villanelles.

STRUCTURED ASSIGNMENTS. To begin with, most students find these poems easier to write. Paradoxically, limits seem to offer greater freedom. The form is already provided, so all the students have to decide upon is the thought. Assignments to "Write a lyric about spring" or those that amount to "Write a poem according to the dictates of your heart" may cause students to feel foolish or threatened. And most importantly, a structured assignment seems to be capable of giving more students greater satisfaction and success. For once the terms of the form are fulfilled, once the metric (or rhythmic or syllabic) conventions are met, the poem is almost always good enough to be satisfying to the student poets and to be appreciated by their peers.

COLLABORATIVE POEMS. Though our students will compose their poems out of the fabric of their own lives and imaginations (and, surprisingly, "Whatever can I write about?" is scarcely ever asked when a poetry assignment is given), a class collaboration poem or two is sometimes a good place to begin. A collaborative poem gives the students a nonthreatening way to explore the content possibilities within the conventions of a genre and to practice inventing lines within the rhythmic limitations of a form. Haiku and ballads work particularly well in a class setting.

WRITING GENRE POEMS: NONMETRIC. The haiku, tanka, cinquain, or other formulaic poems avoid the technicalities of rhyme and meter, and, though they lack the appeal of a pronounced rhythm, even very young or inexperienced poetry writers quickly learn to write successful poems in these forms.

The Cinquain. "The cinquain is a *friendly* kind of writing to do," reports Tom Liner in *Inside Out.*[13] He recommends these five-line poems for his "slow kids" as well for "accomplished poets." Here's how:

> Line 1. One word (usually the subject)
>
> Line 2. Two words (usually describing the subject)
>
> Line 3. Three words (usually describing the subject in action)
>
> Line 4. Four words (usually expressing a feeling about the subject)
>
> Line 5. One word (summing up poem or repeating line 1.)

The following example, "Frog Is a Cinquain" was written by Terrill Brawner, one of Liner's students.

> Frog
> Funky warts
> Making foggy sounds
> Lovely, Madly, Slimy, Green
> Frog

Haiku. Because the Japanese formulaic poem the haiku (and also the tanka) counts syllables rather than words, it is a little more difficult than the cinquain. It also demands a higher degree of sophistication to meet the imagery requirements.

For, within the strict confines of seventeen syllables (line 1: five syllables; line 2: seven; line 3: five), the author of a haiku must set up a natural phenomenon, and make an observation upon it—or harder yet, have the poem itself imply some observation about life. And yet students have remarkable success with this form of poetry. The haiku they write and read to their classmates often evoke audible Oohs and Ahs. Freshman Heather Hoy's haiku is typical:

> Winged angel of life
> A nectar of motherhood
> Gentle bumblebee.

WRITING GENRE POEMS: METRIC.   Before students attempt to write a poem in a particular genre, they need to read many, many poems in that genre. They need to hear them read aloud, to read them aloud themselves— maybe even tap them out—and to play with them until the appropriate dum-de-dums are ringing in their ears.

Where to begin? The couplet has its advantages as a starting point, but the ballad form also works very well indeed.

Couplets.   Iambic tetrameter couplets are within the capability of even the most rank beginner and because of this accessibility make good early metric exercises. We can have the students chant tetrameter couplets:

> Dum de dum de dum de dum—
> Dum de dum de dum de dum

until they're engulfed in the sound. Then we can make up a spur-of-the-moment jingle—say,

> Once there was a pot of tea;
> It bubbled hot and nice for me.

and call upon our students to try their hand with similar silly ditties. Soon everyone has thought up such a couplet.

The heroic couplet (iambic pentameter), on the other hand, can present challenges beyond the capacity of beginners.

Ballads.   It is rare, however, to meet a student—of any age or background—who doesn't respond positively to ballad rhythms. And that should not surprise us. After all, for centuries preliterate people composed their songs and poems in ballad meter because songs in that meter were easily composed, easily remembered, and yielded strong emotional appeal. That rhythm, plus the primal mythic emotions of the stories of passion and violence ballads tell, leave few of our students unmoved.

Students respond well to the old folk ballads. While they are enjoying them, they can pick up knowledge of ballad conventions that will be useful in their own ballad writing. They learn about incremental repetition as "Edward, Edward" unwinds slowly to reveal the real horror that is the mother. They learn about ballad dialogue while they enjoy the humor when student readers act out the characters in "Get Up and Bar the Door." And they learn about "leaping and lingering" over scenes in "Sir Patrick Spens" while savoring its political ironies.

Students also especially enjoy such literary ballads as those of Coleridge, Noyes, Service, and Bob Dylan, while they see how writers can deliberately use the ballad form to serve their own purposes.

Dudley Randall's "The Ballad of Birmingham" works particularly well as a starter for their own writing because it uses almost all the folk-ballad conventions to tell a contemporary tale that overwhelms the reader with its ironic pathos.

And when it comes time for our students to try their own, the ballad stanza (the iambic tetrameter-trimeter quatrain, rhyming *abcb*) comes most naturally of all meters to native speakers of English; it works as well in singsong as the tetrameter couplet suggested above. And, of course, the ballad also offers alternative forms, such as the question-and-answer format employed by the composers of "Lord Randall" and "Edward," with which our more individualistic students might experiment. Furthermore, the repetition inherent in all works stemming from the oral tradition is easily mastered with the ballad and, once learned, will serve our students well in future poetic endeavors. Storytelling, appropriate to the ballad, comes naturally to inexperienced writers.

From a purely pedagogical perspective, whether we choose to organize our combined literature study generically (narrative poetry, then lyric poetry) or chronologically (past to present), or even by ease of understanding (from those requiring less to those requiring more literary sophisticationi), ballads, in every case, make a good starting point.

Sonnets.   If the contingencies of time permit only one major poem-writing assignment, the ballad would be a good choice for younger or less able students. But for students of at least average creative ability in the eleventh or twelfth grades or in college, a sonnet would probably provide the more profitable single experience. The more exacting format of the sonnet can offer our students greater challenge and the variations greater freedom. What is more, the lyrical nature of the sonnet affords a greater opportunity for self-expression, for a chance to explore that which lies closest to the late adolescent's thought and feeling.

Again students need to read many, many sonnets from the Renaissance up to the present day—from Shakespeare to e. e. cummings. They need not only to get a feel for the cadences of the sonnet rhythms, but also to understand the variety of what can be accomplished within its constrictions.

To offer choice, we should teach both the Elizabethan and the Italian rhyme schemes and especially the structural variations they imply. Will our students be more comfortable with *abab* or will they prefer to use the perhaps more difficult *abba* rhyme scheme? Will they want to build their sonnet with an introductory octave followed by a sestet resolution? Or will they prefer to develop a separate—though related—idea in each quatrain and wait for the final couplet for resolution?

Villanelles. Though few of our students will actually try a villanelle, we should not, I think, close the door to experimentation in this form. Some students, especially the gifted, are fascinated by the complex, but highly logical, French-Italianate form. And some simply fall in love with Dylan Thomas's "Do Not Go Gentle," Theodore Roethke's "The Wakening," or James Joyce's "Are You Not Weary." Some of the best student poems I have seen were written in this style.

Teaching Rhetorical Analyses

A whole-language unit on poetry can provide students with several kinds of writing opportunities. Most important among them are writing journal entries to respond to each poem they read and composing poems of their own. In addition, we might ask our students to write poem explications or critical analyses. A detailed discussion on teaching the rhetorical analysis may be found in Chapter 10, pages 375–84.

CLOSE READING. Close, interpretive reading precedes writing critical analyses. The Reading a Poem Closely Student Guidelines may be found on pages 490–91. These guidelines should help our students note enough of how an author goes about phrasing his or her ideas that they will be able to figure out their own notion of what the ideas the author is presenting are. They can just pull out their antennae and begin to read.

PLANNING THE PAPER. When our students have satisfied themselves that they have a clear understanding of their poem, they can plan their critical analysis. Having determined upon an interpretation, they should plan to support it with the formal, metaphoric, and sound effects they have noted.

We need to caution them, however, to use these discoveries only in an interpretative way. They need to understand that by themselves these details have almost no significance. When they set up their working thesis, they should NOT write, for instance:

> Shakespeare's "That Time of Year" is a sonnet with 14 lines of iambic pentameter verse and an Elizabethan sonnet rhyme scheme which divides it into a 4/4/4/2 pattern.

Instead they might write:

> In "That Time of Year," Shakespeare works on a separate comparison to his aging self in each of the three quatrains of the sonnet and concludes with an ironic comment on the rest in the final couplet.

A Sample Syllabus

The Syllabus Example offers suggestions for organizing six to eight weeks of combined-curriculum poetry study at the high school senior or college freshman level.

TEACHING STRATEGIES

Syllabus: Reading and Writing Poetry

PROJECT 1. ENJOYING POETRY
Poetry Jamboree

PROJECT II. DISCERNING THE NATURE OF POETRY
A. The language of poetry: Imagery
   Burns, "Red, Red Rose"; Noyes, "The Highwayman"
B. The sound of poetry: Repetition
   Poe, "The Bells"; Benét, "Mountain Whippoorwill"
   Variation: Shelley, "Ozymandias"

PROJECT III. SAVORING NARRATIVE POETRY
A. The ballad
   1. Reading ballads. "Lord Randall"; "Sir Patrick Spens"; "Edward"; "Bar-
      bara Allen." Pound, "The Goodly Fere"; Keats, "La Belle Dame Sans
      Merci," Randall, "The Ballad of Birmingham"
   2. Writing a ballad
B. Dramatic narrative
   1. Reading dramatic narratives. Browning, "My Last Duchess," "Soliloquy
      in a Spanish Cloister"; Eliot, "Love Song of J. Alfred Prufrock"
   2. Writing about dramatic narratives
      Write a critical analysis of Browning's "The Laboratory," Tennyson's
      "Ullyses," Hardy's "The Man He Killed," or another comparable poem.

PROJECT IV. RELISHING LYRIC POETRY
A. Reading lyrics through the ages
   15th c. medieval lyrics: "I Sing of a Maiden"; "O, Western Wind"
   16th c. Renaissance songs: Shakespeare, "Fear No More," "When Icycles
           Hang," "When Daisies Pied"; Campion, "There Is a Garden"
   17th c. Metaphysical poems: Donne, "The Sun Rising" Herbert, "Virtue".
   18th c. Ironic lyrics: Swift, "Elegy"; Prior, "To a Child of Quality"
   19th c. Romantic lyric: Wordsworth, "A Slumber Did My Spirit Seal";
           Coleridge, "Kubla Khan"; Houseman, "Loveliest of Trees,"
           "When I Was One and Twenty"
   20th c. Songs: e. e. cummings, "if anything happens that cant be done";
           Leonard Cohen, "Suzanne"; Hughes, "The Negro Speaks of
           Rivers"
B. Understanding Form
   1. Reading
      a. The haiku
         Assorted haiku

continued

   b. The sonnet
      Shakespeare, "That Time of Year," "When in Disgrace," "An Ex-
      pense of Spirit," "My Mistress' Eyes"; Milton, "When I Consider
      How My Light Is Spent"; Keats, "Bright Star," "Looking into Chap-
      man's Homer"; Wordsworth, "On Westminster Bridge," "On the
      Beach at Calais"; Donne, "Batter My Heart"; Gwendolyn Brooks,
      "First Fight, Then Fiddle"; Owen, "Sonnet"
   c. The villanelle
      Thomas, "Do Not Go Gentle"; Joyce, "Are You Not Weary";
      Roethke, "The Waking"
2. Writing a poem
   Write a sonnet (or a villanelle)

PROJECT V. EXPLORING A THEME: HUMAN MORTALITY

A. The question (Why is life, that is so sweet, so short?) Childlock Tich-
   bourne, "On the Eve of His Execution"
B. Reading the answers suggested by the poets
   1. The Christian answer
      Nashe, "Litany in Time of Plague"; Herbert, "Virtue"; Tennyson,
      "Crossing the Bar"; Donne, "Death Be Not Proud"; Shakespeare, "Poor
      Soul, the Center of My Sinful Earth"
   2. Aesthetic answer.
      Shakespeare, "Shall I Compare Thee to a Summer's Day"; Keats, "Ode
      to a Grecian Urn"
   3. Carpe Diem.
      Shakespeare, "O Mistress Mine"; Herrick, "To the Virgins to Make
      Much of Time"; Marvell, "To His Coy Mistress"
   4. Whimsical acceptance.
      Emily Dickinson. "Because I Could Not Stop for Death," "I Heard a
      Fly Buzz"
   5. 20th c. agonized acceptance.
      Ferlinghetti, "The pennycandy-store beyond the el"; Dylan Thomas,
      "Fern Hill"
C. Writing about mortality poems (a critical analysis)
   Compare two mortality poems and discuss either the different ways poets
   face the problem or two different poetic approaches to the same basic
   answer.

PROJECT VI. WRITING A POEM
         Student Choice

PROJECT VII. PUBLISHING: A CLASS POEM-BOOK
         All the poems written in the course of the unit,
         whether assigned or student-initiated, are collected,
         illustrated, and duplicated for a book with copies for
         all.

Intermixing the Expressive with the Scholarly

Lest our students begin to find work, such as that suggested in the syllabus above, too weighty and too academic and begin to forget about the intimate, expressive nature of poetry writing, we ought to interrupt the scholarly part of our study with occasional sessions in which our students can experience poetry again in a personal, nonstudious way.

TEN POETIC MINUTES. A number of teachers have been truly creative in thinking of ways to take students out of their schoolday selves and put them in touch with their own creativity. Beth C. Dakelman, for instance, asks her students to write for ten minutes a day on such "absurd or mind-tickling questions" as "Describe a pineapple"; "If you had one wish, what would you choose?" "If you could not be yourself, what would you be and why?" "Describe algae"; and "What is inside the secret chest you have just found in your backyard?"[14]

Another good idea, developed by Sister Agnes Ann Pastva, to stimulate the writing of journal poems is to bring to class a print of a vibrantly colored abstract painting or a roughly textured collage for students to "immerse themselves in until it begins to take on meaning."[15]

CREATIVE, EXPRESSIVE POETRY DAYS. Other teachers, especially those with younger students, prefer to take off most of a whole period once every week or so as a change of pace. When the day is regularly worked into the schedule, our students begin to look forward to it with anticipation. Any of the Koch projects work well in this format; see pages 464–67.

Another way to tease the poetic imagination during these periods is to prompt wondering about what lies "beyond." We can raise the question with our students by sending them to the window and, as Dakelman suggests, asking them to use their "X-ray vision" and see what is "beyond" the buildings, or the hills, or the trees (or whatever it is they can see from that window) (1272).

MIXED MEDIA. We can also let our students' own artistic responses lead them beyond the everyday. We might have them respond to a reading of "Kubla Khan" or "The Tyger," for instance, by drawing with pastels on dark construction paper. With those soft blendable colors they will ordinarily produce some magical and exciting drawings, which will in turn lead them into experimenting with imaginary realms in poems of their own. To augment the mood, we could play appropriate background music—something oriental for the Coleridge poem, for instance, and perhaps an instrumental version of "The Lion Sleeps Tonight" for the Blake.

Some Pedagogical Considerations

The central question in teaching poetry writing is how much should we participate? More than any other writing, perhaps, poetry is personal expression. If students' ownership of their own work is ever an issue, surely it is here. And yet we, with all our experience, are there to guide and advise.

WHERE TO HELP. We can — and should — help with the dum de dums or any other constraints that are part of an assignment. If we are fairly strict in having students meet such requirements, then we must supply all the help they need.

But beyond that, we must remember that we are dealing with an individual's creative mind here, a mind different from our own. So, though we can certainly offer suggestions — if we do so very gently and tentatively — we should never forget that the poem really does belong to the student.

When Students Come In with Their Own Poems. The situation is somewhat different when students bring their own nonassigned poetry to us. Maybe all they want to hear is "That's terrific!" — to which we might add, having searched for something good to praise, "I especially like your metaphor in the second stanza."

But maybe they want us to take their poem more seriously. Maybe they want us to approach it artist to artist. How do we find out? After our initial praise, we might ask what they especially like about the poem? Or we might ask if there is anything that makes the student uneasy about it — if we sense there is. And we should take up these hints. If he feels that he likes the parallelism in lines 5 and 6, we might show him how he could extend it to lines 7 and 8. If she feels there might be something wrong with the rhythm of line 3, we can help her put it to rights and maybe help line 5 too.

Sometimes a free-verse poem appears shapeless because the line demarcations are not rhythmically drawn. The serious student-poet might well appreciate our suggestions that she try experimentally rebreaking the lines in stanza 2 to make that stanza more parallel with stanza 1, and then decide which way works best. But again, we must phrase our suggestion tentatively. It is, after all, our student's poem.

GRADING POEMS. My best advice here is: Don't. Upon what grounds can we base a grade? I am not willing to judge a student soul on my tenuous assumptions about what constitutes good poetry. If we must give a grade, it should be a reflection of whether the student's poem, as revised, has met the specified criteria. If it has, then it deserves full credit. That is, if, for instance, the assignment is a to write a sonnet and include a simile, and the poem's meter is a regular iambic pentameter, the rhyme scheme is traditional, the topic is structured appropriately, and the simile suitably used, the work has surely fulfilled the assignment and deserves the credit. If it shows any special promise at all—and it's a rare student poem that doesn't have at least one creative touch to make the student proud—then the poem merits extra credit.

Creative Writing Club

A creative writing club not only affords an outlet for the creativity of students who like to write but also lends prestige to the occupation of writing and gives those who enjoy doing it their own place in the high-school sun. The meetings of the club should be pleasurable, the discussion of the poems, stories, and essays lively and encouraging. Negative criticism should restrict itself to advice on how the story, poem, or essay might be improved. It is important that the chairperson be a responsible leader, so that meetings are held at their regularly appointed time, that they are announced as they should be, and that the writings are reproduced in time for the meetings.

PUBLISHING.   Whatever other projects the creative writing club undertakes—contests, outings, the sponsorship of guest lecturers or readers—it should plan to publish an anthology of its writings once or twice a year. This anthology—to which all the students of the school might be asked to contribute—should be illustrated (it might even be a joint project with the art department or the art club) and it should be as professionally produced as possible. This attractive anthology should be sold for a small sum, not so much to offset its cost (though that too is, of course, important) as to increase its value on the campus.

ADVISING.   What should we do as adviser to a writing club? Without intruding too much, we must work to create the atmosphere of acceptance, enthusiasm, and organization that makes for happy and exciting meetings and successful projects. I have never known a creative writing club with enthusiastic student leadership and a sympathetic faculty adviser that did not become one of the more successful extracurricular activities in the school.

IDEAS FOR DISCUSSION OR ESSAY

1. Many teachers model scholarly activity by working along with their students. In that spirit, try out the following exercises in imagery and sound and evaluate their effectiveness.
   A. Composing New Images from Dead Metaphors. The following images long ago lost their impact. Find a new simile, metaphor, allusion, or other image to illustrate each of the abstractions.
   Sample Problem: Red as a rose.
   Sample Solutions: She blushed a painful tomato juice red.
                       Red as the cover of "Quotations from Chairman Mao"

1. Pure as the driven snow.
2. Ugly as sin.
3. Green as grass.

B. Creating Personifications. Turn the following abstractions into personifications.

Sample problem: Laughter

Sample solution: Her laughter hung in the air as if waiting to be recognized.

1. The sea
2. Autumn
3. A computer

C. Creating Hyperbole. Create a suitable hyperbole from each of the following superlative situations.

Sample problem: A truly excellent fiddle player.

Sample solution: He fiddled all the bugs off a sweet potato vine

1. True love
2. A politician with really disgusting ideas.
3. Hungry enough to eat a horse (dead metaphor)

D. Creating Allusions. Create an allusive metaphor or simile to illustrate each of the following.

Sample Problem: Your favorite toddler

Sample Solution: Two-year-old Susie, like the dormouse at the Mad Hatter's Tea Party, had the habit of falling asleep at the table.

1. One of your professors
2. Your room
3. A sports triumph

E. Illustrate the following from famous poems.

1. Hyperbole
2. Personification
3. Allusion

F. Create a line (or a couplet) in each of the following meters:

1. Trochaic tetrameter
2. Iambic pentameter
3. Anapestic [your choice]
4. Dactyllic [your choice]

G. Illustrate the following from famous poems.

1. Trochaic tetrameter
2. Iambic pentameter
3. Anapestic [your choice]

2. Try your hand at a sonnet, a ballad, and a haiku.

3. Do a close reading or explication of two of the following poems (or others comparable) and explain how you would teach them to a class:
   • Shakespeare's "Fear No More the Heat of the Sun"

- Dylan Thomas's "Do Not Go Gentle into That Good Night"
- Browning's "Soliloquy in a Spanish Cloister"
- Leonard Cohen's "Suzanne"

NOTES

The chapter-opening epigraph is from Ben Jonson, "To the Memory of Shakespeare."

1. Profitt, "Freshman English Once More," *CE* 38 (1976): 132–43.

2. Kenneth Koch, *Wishes, Lies and Dreams: Teaching Children to Write Poetry* (New York: Chelsea House, 1970); *Rose, Where Did You Get That Red? Teaching Great Poetry to Children* (New York: Vintage Books, 1973); *I Never Told Anybody: Teaching Poetry to Nursing Homes* (New York: Random House, 1977).

3. T. S. Eliot, *Selected Essays* (New York: Harcourt, 1932), 124.

4. Charles Rathbone, "Prelude to the Making of a Poem: Finger Exercises," *CE* 54 (1965): 854.

5. Baird Shuman, "Teasing Writing out of High," *CE* 62 (1973): 9.

6. Don M. Wolfe, Creative Ways to Teach English: Grades 7–12, 2nd ed. (New York: Oddysey, 1966), 71–72.

7. Yvonne Brackbill, et al. "Arousal Level in Neonates and Older." In *Journal of Experimental Child Psychology*, 4 (1966): 178–88.

8. We might refer students who are particularly interested in this sort of study to the few transitional pieces in middle English where the two forms seem to be vying together: for instance, *Sir Gawain and the Green Knight*, written in Anglo-Saxon alliterative verse stanzas which close with four short rhyming lines (abab), or lyrics, such as "The Blacksmiths."

9. Joseph Malof, "The Artifice of Scansion," *CE* 54 (1965): 858–59 See also James M. Reid, John Ciardi, and Lawrence Perrine, *Poetry: A Closer Look* (New York: Harcourt, 1963): 41–43, for a first-rate discussion and demonstration of metrical variation.

10. Junette Morgan, "Writing Poetry in Junior High," *CE* 57 (1968): 1013.

11. Suggested by Milton Kaplan, "Verse Writing in English Class," *CE* 55 (1966): 883.

12. From my *Writing Effectively*, 2nd edition, (New York: Harper, 1990), 398–400.

13. Tom Liner, *Inside Out: Developmental Strategies for Teaching Writing*, 2nd ed. (Portsmouth: Boynton, 1988), 87.

14. Beth Dakelman, "Think Tank and Mind Transportation: Teaching Creative Writing," *CE* 62 (1973): 1272.

15. Agnes Ann Pastva, "Writing Lessons that Work," *CE* 62 (1973): 1280.

□ □ □ **Part IV**

THE TEACHER

The teacher affects eternity; he can never tell where his influence stops.
—Henry Brooks Adams

□ □ □

□ □ □   **13**

Responding to Students' Work

The art of the teacher — at its best — is
the reinforcement of good things.
— Paul B. Diederich

⊔ ⊔ ⊔

Nothing we do as teachers of writing is more significant than the way we respond to our student's writing. In our responses to their papers we are communicating directly with our students at the point of their greatest sensitivity and vulnerability. What we say (or do not say) can provide an incentive for the sort of effort that results in genuine learning, or it can convince students that, since there is no possibility of that sort of accomplishment for them, there is no reason for them to exert the needed effort. In the simple act of marking papers, for instance, we undertake a tremendous responsibility. We must therefore bear in mind that the sheet of paper upon which we are busily scratching corrections is truly not an inanimate object we are commissioned to bring to perfection, but is, in a very real sense, an extension of a living, vulnerable, potentially able — or disabled — human being. The response process in the teaching of writing can be broken down into two tasks: responding to student papers and assigning grades. Each task presents formidable problems.

RESPONDING TO STUDENT PAPERS

When we attempt to define useful strategies for responding to student papers, we might reconsider our purpose in teaching composition and then find the strategies through which that purpose can best be implemented.

Helping Students Improve Their Writing

Improved student writing is our essential goal. How can it best be accomplished? Every assignment, naturally, does not result in a leap forward. But successful teachers agree, and research confirms, that when composition learning happens, it comes about as:

- A student writes a paper, as well as he or she can;
- An interventional interaction takes place;
- The student revises, taking this interaction into account — though not necessarily accepting the intervener's point of view

During the thinking-through or during the revising, the student experientially comes to grips with his or her particular writing demons and conquers them for this paper, with an understanding that carries over to the next paper.

VARIETY OF INTERVENTIONAL RESPONSES.   Successful intervention can come in various guises. It can come as a written response from us or from student peer-groups. It can come as an oral response from us informally, in conference, or taped, or from the student's classmates, outside friends, or family. And since, ultimately, it is the interaction that counts, it can come from the students themselves as they gain experience and learn to become their own readers.

Since the traditional view of what an English teacher does — perhaps our own view — is closely tied to our written response to student papers, let's begin here.

Writing Our Responses to Student Papers

Before our advice to our students can be of any practical use to them and their learning to write, we shall have to motivate them to make the effort necessary for this learning. The only way to convince people to exert effort to learn to do anything is to convince them both that (1) the thing is worth doing and (2) they are potentially capable of doing it well. How can we do this with our students' writing?

MOTIVATING STUDENT WRITING.   We teachers know that writing well is worth the effort (and sometimes the pain), because we know how necessary it is for communication and how important an aid it can be to clear and logical thought. How can we share this knowledge with our students? The only way we can convince them is to regard each of their papers as communication between them and ourselves.

Respond to the Writer's Thought.   If we consider our students' papers as messages to us rather than just as samples to be judged, we can engage in conversation about their message through our comments. We might write, "Snorkeling sounds like an exciting vacation" or, more personally, "I have always wanted to try snorkeling," or better yet, "You've described snorkeling so vividly, you tempt me to want to try it." Even a strictly academic paper can be made a vehicle of personal communication in this way; for instance, we might say, "Since you enjoyed Browning's evil Duke so much, you would probably be wild about his wicked Bishop. See me, and I'll find you a copy of 'The Bishop Orders His Tomb.' "

Interest More Important than Agreement. We need not feel we always have to agree with our students in our comments, however. Research confirms that the importance of a comment lies in the interest it shows.[1] We might write, for example, "Though your argument about the waste of state funds for the maintenance of life-terms is strongly put, you still have not convinced me that this savings would justify capital punishment. You might want to read — — —'s argument on it." Whenever appropriate, we might also comment upon the quality of the thinking evidenced in the paper, as, for instance, "Your economic argument is clearly spelled out, well exemplified, and convincing; but your political argument does not quite follow through. Come in and we'll work on it together," or "Though the reasoning seems a little confused in your second and third paragraphs—and I had a good deal of trouble trying to follow it—by the end of the paper you seem to have overcome the difficulty, and your points come out straight and clear. (It shouldn't be too hard to fix up the early work.)"

By viewing their papers as ongoing conversations, students may begin to see errors as impediments to that communication and to find some reason for correcting them. To provide our students with a valid purpose for learning to write, we must somehow convey to them that we take them seriously as thinkers and their papers seriously as a means of communicating their thought.

BUILDING CONFIDENCE. If we convince our students that we are interested in their ideas and in them as thinkers and as writers, we have progressed a good way toward solving the other half of the student-motivation problem: building their self-confidence, convincing them that they truly will be able to succeed at writing.

What else can we do? We can praise what we can sincerely praise.

Accentuate the Positive. Research has shown that positive reinforcement promotes a better attitude toward writing and can actually result in better writing. Alberta Goodman conducted a study, for example, which demonstrates that

> within an environment of acceptance and positive feedback, learners grow both in their self-concept of their ability to communicate and in their actual ability.[2]

Recording our enthusiasm for whatever is praiseworthy in our students' papers not only reinforces the desirable characteristics, but also demonstrates our belief in their potential for good writing. A liberal scattering of such comments as "A well-phrased sentence," "Funny!" "I found this paragraph touching," "Vivid description," "A striking word," or "You make us almost smell the hay!" encourages our students to further such efforts. At least one teacher habitually underlines in red any expression that seems to him "unusually interesting or effective," and manages to intersperse throughout his black corrections at least a few vibrant red incentives to student confidence.[3] Because of the importance of such incentives, we should make a real effort to find something we can honestly approve, even in—or perhaps especially in—papers our students will have to rewrite completely.

Minimize the Negative. If our students are to learn how to write, however, criticism cannot be totally ignored; but we can deliver it in ways designed to minimize its destructive effect on our students' self-image.

One easy method to protect student sensibility is to mark papers with a black or a blue or even a green pen—anything but the high-contrast red that speaks with such strong condemnation to students who find a quantity of it on their papers. The tone of our comments can be similarly hurtful to the sensitive student. When we must criticize, it should be in a matter-of-fact manner, with the underlying assumption that here's a point our student may not have known about before, but with a little effort he can easily master. Under no provocation should we employ a sarcastic tone. Even humorous sarcasm has a shrill personal ring.

It is of primary importance that criticism be perceived not as evidence of the writer's innate incapacity, an interpretation the insecure writer typically makes, but rather as recommendations for improvement.

Criticize Only the Correctable. Our phrasing of corrective notations should reflect our assumption that students will want to revise or rewrite. We might say, for instance, "Try adding some nonvisual sensory impressions and see how this paragraph will come alive" or "This sentence could stand some work—it now seems awkward and wordy." Negative comments should also be specific and posit remediation: not "This paper contains a level of error so high, I doubt your ability to pass," but "We will have to work on subjects and verbs in conference."

But since an overwhelming quantity of even the most constructively phrased criticism can damage our students' sense of their own worth, we should probably limit our marginal notations—especially on the papers of our less able students—to checking those problems to which we can reasonably assume their earlier training has introduced them. And surely we should not point out surface difficulties that will be subsumed by later readjustments. For instance, there is no use in asking them to work on subject-verb agreement in a passage that is irrelevant to the focus and should be deleted.

REVISION OPPORTUNITY ESSENTIAL. Such an assessment presupposes our students' understanding of their opportunity for revision. In fact, without such an opportunity (and the intervention that makes the revision meaningful), a teacher's notation of writing problems—though it still has the power to damage confidence and discourage the desire to write, unfortunately—has almost no positive effect on student writing, as a large number of studies have shown.[4] Without this opportunity, most students give one fleeting glance at our carefully annotated corrections, note the grade, and toss their paper hastily away.

To be blunt, our comments—despite the time, care, and affection we lavish upon them—do *not* have carry-over effect. Our students, almost without exception, understand the comments in context only. Even those rare writers of a "finished" paper who actually read our comment that, for example, a paragraph lacks coherence, or even a more constructive notation detailing how the paragraph might be made more coherent, will then write a similarly incoherent paragraph on their next paper. Real understanding of coherence may occur—and can only occur—when the student successfully revises the paragraph commented on and experientially gets a sense of what coherence or incoherence is. And only this sort of real, experiential understanding can affect the next composition. Simply put,

> Without revision possibilities, all the time and effort we spend annotating our students' papers is wasted.

The Problem of Time

But when we offer the possibility of revision, our thoughtful response to our students' writing can be very helpful indeed. Unfortunately, it also takes a great deal of time, so much time that it is questionable whether even the most dedicated of us can—or perhaps even should—undertake the process with a set of papers every week of the term. A number of solutions to this problem of time have been suggested, widely varying in their degree of usefulness.

TIME-SAVING IDEAS THAT DON'T WORK. We can reject out of hand the ideas of those who have simply given up assigning compositions and now limit their students' creative experience to the making of collages, video dramas, and slide shows, or doing grammar exercises for writing practice. For writing, of course, can only be learned by writing.

Assigned Papers Should Be Read. Nor should we give serious consideration to the recommendation that we assign a great many papers, but read only a few. The effect on students once they realize such a practice is occurring is like that on a person who has been talking animatedly and suddenly discovers that everyone else has left the room. Under such circumstances, even when all the papers are carefully filed, students cannot help but feel cheated and resentful.

What is more, many studies have shown that no increase in ability results from mere frequency of writing.[5] Unless a student's work receives a response and the opportunity to profit from that response, he or she will continue to make the same errors. Greater quantity of writing usually means only a greater quantity of the writing problems that prevailed in the first set of papers.

INCREASE THE QUALITY, DECREASE THE QUANTITY OF STUDENT WRITING. We need not feel we must assign a *new* theme each week. Since a number of studies confirm that much student growth in writing comes through the revising process, (see especially Hillocks [1982] cited in note 4 and the studies cited in note 5) even the most conscientious of us should feel free to "count" revision as "writing."

Assign Fewer, Though Revisable, Papers. It is more advantageous to our students' development if we assign fewer major themes but insist upon a thorough working of every theme we assign.

Assign Shorter Papers. Our assignments need not be lengthy. The processes our students must learn are as demonstrable in short papers as in long ones and, in fact, are usually easier for them to grasp when the work is short enough for them to comprehend the entire unity in their minds at once. When we shift the emphasis away from the quantity of our students' work—and of our own—we will all have more time to devote to the things that really matter, and we should, rather quickly, begin to notice an improvement both in our own time schedules and in the quality of our students' work.

Stagger the Assignments. Managing assignment deadlines so that student papers come in smaller batches may not reduce the paper load, but it does make it seem a good deal lighter.

Assign Some Expressive Work Where Our Comments Need Be Minimal. Those of us who nevertheless feel that students need to write each day or do some new thinking/writing at least once a week have yet another option. We can cut down on the accountable, revisable papers as I have suggested, and still have our students write new material regularly by requiring daily journal entries, or brief responses to their readings, or other expressive classroom exercises of a variety of kinds (see pages 405–7.)

We do not need to give this personal, expressive writing the careful, time-consuming comment that promotes revision. Nor would it be appropriate to do so. (See page 407.) Here, all we must provide is a sympathetic audience. Our students need only to know that we are reading what they write and that we care about their ideas. We can collect this material from time to time to read in batches, and we need not respond to every entry.

Furthermore, since having an audience of readers for this written expression is the main requirement, we can sometimes turn a set over to the students and have them read and respond to one another's work.

INCREASE THE QUALITY, DECREASE THE QUANTITY OF TEACHER COMMENT. Not only do students learn to write better through fewer (revisable), shorter assignments, but—perhaps surprisingly—research also shows that students learn better from shorter, more focused, teacher comment. When Hillocks studied the value of the length of teacher comments, he discovered that

> focused comments coupled with . . . revision produced a significant quality gain. . . . Indeed . . . the short comments [averaging 9–14 words, consisting of at least one compliment and . . . suggestions for increasing specificity or focus] were twice as effective as the long comments [averaging 22–41 words, with one or more compliments and very specific suggestions for improvement]. (*Research on Written Composition* 167)

Narrowing the focus of our comment is, of course, at least as important as brevity. Nancy Sommers's study of instructor's commenting styles demonstrates just how confusing scattershot commentary is to students.[6] But Hillocks offers advice we might all take to heart:

> A teacher who spends ten hours a week making focused comments on matters of specificity and focus . . . might expect to achieve comparable if not better results with only five hours of work. (*Research on Written Composition* 167)

PRIORITIES. Since we must be selective and focused in our comments, we will have to develop a system of priorities for marking papers.[7] The following order suggests the priorities inherent in an assignment—and in the teaching philosophy of this text.

Attending to the Aims of the Assignment. We need first to look at the student paper in terms of our purpose in making the assignment. If we have done a good job of sharing our goals with our students, we should find at least a few items to praise. And we may well also want to mark some places where revision in the goal area would be helpful.

Some teachers give assignments with a dual purpose, simultaneously working on both content and style. For example, a class learning to support their points more specifically and vividly, and writing a paper with that goal in mind, might also be having some difficulty with run-on sentences. The teacher might well suggest, after exercises or other practice, that these students be especially careful to check for run-ons in their editing of this support-centered paper. In marking this paper, the teacher would be sure to comment on vivid and specific support, but would also note any run-on sentences, as well as sentences where a semicolon or a comma and conjunction were used to particularly satisfying effect.

Insisting on Clarity. If our marking priorities are to mirror our teaching priorities, we will want to make sure our students are really getting across what they are trying to say before we worry too much about how they go about saying it. We should, therefore, consider focus and structure in our comments before directing our students' attention to stylistic concerns.

Some student papers, of course, do not have an organizing idea or a central point at all; others do not develop from their original commitment; and yet others branch off from their original idea in contradictory or irrelevant ways. All of these are serious difficulties that our students will have to concentrate on improving before they consider anything else. Almost invariably such problems will require conference work before the students proceed to revising. Other structural problems to which we should give priority are the arrangement of the supporting sections and the ordering of the material within these sections.

Stylistic Priorities.   But to those students whose papers exhibit a good understanding of focus and support we may want to suggest their exploring of stylistic questions. For example, we might comment upon the effectiveness of particular syntactic structures for particular rhetorical purposes, discuss ways to increase the vividness of their diction, or point out the differences between fresh and overworked language. We might even take up with them issues of imagery or tone.

Any one of these major structural or stylistic issues could provide focus for our terminal comment, a major marginal note, or a conference.

Individualizing Our Response.   Our priorities for commenting on an individual paper are thus dependent also on our assessment of the particular skills and needs of the student writer.

Commenting upon papers, unlike classwork, puts us into a one-on-one relationship, and thus the demands of fairness in no way require us to be uniform in our appraisal. Fairness, in fact, requires us to tailor our remarks to fit the needs of the individual student. For example, when Sharon, who is an editor of the paper, attempts a syntactically complex paragraph that doesn't quite work out, we might want to point up the fact that the difficulty lies in the faulty parallelism of the third and fourth sentences. But when Peggy, who can scarcely remember to start each sentence with a capital letter, makes a similar error, we would be wise to overlook it. Lou LaBrant puts the issue forthrightly:

> Corrections, suggestions for revision, and criticisms of content should be given in proportion to the ability of the student to use them. They are means to improvement, not penalties for being dull or inexperienced or incompetent. . . . It is poor teaching to demand what the teacher knows cannot be done. (359)

MARKING SURFACE PROBLEMS.   To what extent should we distinguish surface error? The question is not easy to answer, even though we can say that, except for nonstandard-dialect students (see Chapter 8), errors in spelling, capitalization, punctuation, usage, and—to some extent—syntax and diction should be regarded as minor problems in mechanics that should not worry us or our students too much.

Overlook Errors in Mechanics.   On the one hand, an abundance of corrections tends both to distract our students from concentration on the major problem and to make them feel that "getting it right" is a well-nigh hopeless job. Furthermore, many of these kinds of errors tend to sort themselves out once the students are sure of the structure of their composition and confident of their meaning. Mary Elizabeth Fowler, Carol Laque and Phillis Sherwood, among others, have noted this phenomenon, and Lou LaBrant has confirmed it experimentally, at least as far as the sentence fragment is concerned.[8]

Mark Egregious Errors.   On the other hand, many errors in mechanics are rather like open questions in our students' minds. Is it "i" before "e" or "e" before "i"? Should this phrase be set off by commas? Do you capitalize "university"? Other errors, though the result of carelessness not ignorance, nevertheless seemed right enough to the student to escape emending during proofreading. If we do not indicate this kind of half-understood mistake as error, we are confirming our students in the notion of their correctness; and if the sentences of which they are a part remain unrevised, this notion will receive further reinforcement through recopying in later drafts.

On balance, then, it would seem wisest to indicate minimally (by encircling, perhaps, or by a simple checkmark in the margin) those errors we judge to be in some way already understood by our students. As for the mechanical errors and stylistic infelicities they commit through complete ignorance—and much awkwardness of syntax and inappropriateness of diction is of this variety—these we might choose to ignore until class time or conference time can be spared from matters of greater importance to teach the principles involved.

Handling Errors in the Final Draft.   What about errors that persist into the final draft? For a number of years now I've used a system that my students tell me has been useful to them. I encircle significant errors on the graded paper, but withhold recording the grade until the student has corrected each error (on the final paper itself—no need for recopying). Correcting them in this way is a learning experience for the student because I do not specify the error. Motivated both by curiosity and the desire for a recorded grade, students are good-natured about "fixing up" their papers. What they seem to learn from the procedure, besides the kinds of error they are most likely to make and ways to correct them, is that though surface editing and proofreading are not nearly as important as thinking and writing, surface errors do bother readers and thus they are tasks of some significance.

MARKING TECHNIQUES.   The techniques we have been discussing for commenting effectively in writing on our students' papers are summarized in the Commenting Upon Student Compositions Teaching Strategies.

TEACHING STRATEGIES

Commenting on Student Compositions

1. Make all decisions in terms of the individual needs of the particular student.
2. Respond to the content of the composition in a brief dialogue with the student.
3. Find something to praise about the writing.
4. Keep comments brief.
   a. Focus discussion on one major problem.
   b. Prioritize points of comment. First address problems relating to the purpose of the assignment, then those involving focus and structure, and finally to problems of style, including those of grammar and mechanics.
5. Make all negative criticism specific and constructive.
   a. *Never* make a general disparaging statement.
   b. *Never* use sarcasm.
   c. Focus on items within a student's power to correct or improve.
   d. Avoid using a red pen or pencil.
6. Let the Alcoholics Anonymous creed be our guide in marking papers:

   > God grant me the serenity to accept the things I cannot change,
   > the courage to change the things I can change,
   > and the wisdom to know the difference.

ALTERNATIVE INTERVENTION RESPONSES.   There are a number of ways we can make sure students receive a helpful response to their writing besides our own written comments. We might try oral commentary, for instance. We could hold a one-on-one conference, instead of or in conjunction with our written comments. We might confer with our students informally during a writing workshop day. Or we might tape our comments instead of writing them.

Others might provide helpful responses. We might, for example, have students work with professional personnel from a campus skills center or with a lay reader, where this help is available. Or we might train exceptional students to do some of these response activities.

And surely, we should try having students respond to one another's papers in peer groups.

Teacher–Student Conferences

The most effective intervention in the writing process is the one-on-one conference. But conferences are not easy to handle effectively; the teacher is subject to a complex set of tensions. As Thomas Newkirk puts it:

> The teacher must balance two opposing mandates: on the one hand, to respond to the student, to evaluate, to suggest possible revisions and writing strategies; and on the other, to encourage the student to take the initiative, to self-evaluate, to make decisions, to take control of the paper.[9]

And yet when conferences do work, the student has an opportunity, in Newkirk's words, to "revise by talking" (327) and thus to come to terms with the structure of the current essay and perhaps to begin vaguely grasping a general sense of compositional structure that will be useful for later writing. It is then that the teacher becomes, again in Newkirk's words, "an active instrument in the student's search for meaning" (329), and that's no small accomplishment. (See pages 159–76 for a discussion of strategies for conducting such conferences.)

TIME CONSTRAINTS. Unfortunately, like commenting on student papers, responding with conferences takes a good bit of time—actually about the same amount of time per paper as commenting in writing.

Probably the best method for consistently conserving teacher time is to postpone the marking of those papers that require conferences. We might skim through each paper far enough to decide whether the author would profit from a conference on it. If one would be helpful, we need only give the paper a cursory reading and a quick note suggesting a conference.

First Reading at the Conference. For those sets of papers where we might want to confer individually with every student (the first set or two, perhaps, or those written for a particularly difficult assignment), we might forego all preliminary marking and rely instead upon our immediate response at the conference. Although inexperienced teachers might find the thought of responding to compositions "cold turkey" a bit harrowing, they will soon get the knack and gain the self-confidence to carry it off with aplomb.

It might help these teachers (as well as those of us who, though experienced, have thus far felt too conscientious to try this technique) to understand that this method not only helps to get our teaching load into practicable proportions, but that it also offers several advantages for our students. Primarily, in watching our unrehearsed response to their work, our students gain a sense of audience. For them we become what Barbara Fassler Walvoord calls "a transparent reader,"[10] a real reader who reacts to their words before their very eyes. Further, when students observe our rather mundane thought processes as we attempt to come to grips with what they have tried to say and with how they might make their way of saying it clearer or more effective, we offer an irrefutable demonstration of the importance of clarity. And possibly more importantly, the responding process itself loses some of the frightening mystique that produces anxiety in so many of our students. As Walvoord writes, after she conquered her own trepidation and began to read papers for the first time with her students in conference,

I discovered that being "real" to students is highly effective. If I made an evaluation and then changed it, well that's what sometimes happens when a real human being sits down to read somebody else's paper. If I could not immediately put my finger on what was "off" . . . I just asked the student to wait a moment while we wrestled with it. (146)

Taping Our Commentary

Some teachers have experimented successfully with commenting on papers by tape recorder, and some have adopted it as their everyday method. Spoken comment permits us to cover more material in greater detail and to personalize the communication with the sound and manner of our individual voices. It thus gives the student a more detailed analysis and more of a sense of audience. In fact, it provides the next best thing to a conference—though it lacks the interaction.

PROBLEMS.   On the other hand, the mechanical problems of making such a system work cannot be overlooked. Machines tend to break down, the quality of transmission cannot always be controlled, the message is necessarily temporary and sometimes hard to locate, and unless students have tape players at home, they may have to listen to their cassettes when conditions are not appropriate for concentration or have to wait for their turn at the available players.

PRAGMATICS.   Paul Anderson has learned to handle such problems. In fact, in his yearly survey, a consistent three-quarters of his students much prefer taped to written commentary. He offers the following advice:

1. Have students keep their paper and cassette together in an envelope with their names on each item.
2. Read through and check points on the paper before recording.
3. Use a microphone with an on/off switch to permit planning between comments.
4. Begin with an interested personalized comment, using the student's name.
5. Do not try to respond to every sentence, but concentrate discussion on the two or three major points checked out before.
6. Conclude by summarizing and suggesting specific revisions.
7. Since the taped message is only temporary, encourage students to take notes from it.[11]

Though the advisability of using cassette tapes for commenting on papers depends to a large extent upon the personality of the teacher and the circumstances in which the course is given, their use offers many of the advantages of conferences for those times when such meetings are not feasible.

Using Outside Help

Another important way to conserve the writing teacher's time is to yield to others some of the responsibility for responding to student papers. Although in recent years most scholarly attention has focused upon peer groups as a source for this help, most colleges and many school systems have a Writing Center—sometimes called a Skills Center, Learning Assistance Center, Student Enrichment Center, or Learning Resource Center. However it is named, it can be a real boon in our busy professional lives.

WRITING CENTERS. At most such centers I have encountered, the personnel are skilled and eager to help our students and to help us too. I recommend working closely with them. Ordinarily, such centers are set up to handle problems of mechanics and nonstandard dialects especially well—the very difficulties that are the hardest to work on in the nonbasic-writing classroom. Many are equipped with appropriate computer software. All are staffed by people experienced in diagnosing the source of writing problems and knowledgeable in finding solutions for them.

We should send to the center our students whose problems with mechanics are so great that they find it difficult to turn out acceptable papers even after they have caught on to the basics of structure, support, and audience. And we should also send to the center that student or two each semester who, for whatever reason, we seem unable to reach. It's good to have alternative writing teachers available to help these youngsters.

Once we have sent students to such a center, we need to keep in touch with the student and the center's personnel, and to follow up their tutoring as it seems appropriate.

LAY READERS AND STUDENT ASSISTANTS. The lay-reader program used to be widespread and some school systems still offer their faculty this option. In some institutions, especially skilled students serve similar functions.

Lay-reader/student-assistant duties vary. In one kind of program, the teaching assistant marks all assigned papers for mechanics, and then the teacher reads them for content and organization and adds the final notes. In another kind of program, the teaching assistant is responsible for marking some sets of papers completely, thereby enabling the lead teacher to hold more one-on-one conferences and to give more thorough consideration to the remaining assignments. In yet a third arrangement, teaching assistants serve almost as writing specialists; they sit in on the assignment days, mark first drafts, hold conferences, and help with revisions.

Evaluation. According to at least one study, students in classes with lay-reader assistance and those without it gained equally in their writing skills.[12]

Thus students do not seem to suffer if their teacher chooses this sort of support; indeed, when the teaching assistant is especially skilled, students probably gain.

Nevertheless, many teachers share T. A. Koclanes's reservations about such assistance:

> The evaluation of compositions . . . is not a job that can be handed over to a "lay reader" in order to free the teacher for more demanding tasks. In the teaching of English there is no more demanding task. ("Can We Evaluate Composition," 257)

Peer-Response Groups

In planning our writing program we will probably want to consider some use of peer response. (See pages 187–94, where the strategy is discussed from the revision process point of view.) Not only do peer response groups relieve us of some of the paper-marking pressure, but they also add another dimension to our students' writing experience. They provide them with an eager audience of their fellows and give them first-rate practice in the essential editing skills. They also give them another opportunity to get responses from real readers and to make revisions before *we* see their paper.

PREPARATION.   Peer response, however, requires careful preparation. Before we break our class into groups and set them to such a task, we must be certain that we have established in the full-class setting that atmosphere of acceptance, of expectation of differing views, and of understanding of one another's vulnerability that will make successful group work possible. And even after the groups are formed, we must not hesitate to make changes if we discover incompatibilities, subtle bullying, or other such problems.

GUIDING THE RESPONSE TASK.   Full-class discussion of papers can serve as a model for small-group discussion, but the groups will also need more specific guidance in exactly what they are supposed to do, and the individuals within the groups will need more specific standards from which to counsel one another and from which to edit their papers. Rather than imposing a set of guidelines upon our students, it is usually better to arrive at mutually agreed-upon criteria together. An older or more advanced class might want to set up a list of as many as a half-dozen important aspects of composition to check, while a less experienced class might want to start with just two or three important items, such as:

- Can the central idea be clearly understood?
- Does the rest of the paper consistently support the central idea?
- Are the supporting examples plentiful and vivid enough?

After the students have developed their guidelines, we should give them the opportunity to test them out and to practice with them in the whole class before working with them in their groups. The list should probably not remain static throughout the term, but expand and change as our students grow.

PEER INTERVENTION. Teachers have developed a variety of peer-response strategies.[13] But in general, students meet in groups of two, three, or four and comment upon each other's first drafts either orally or in writing. In the oral method, the students read their papers aloud, and each is discussed by the group in terms of the editing criteria decided upon and in terms of the specifications for the particular assignment.

With the written method, after they have discussed the assignment, students exchange papers and each evaluator responds in writing to an attached set of criteria. Each succeeding review may respond not only to the paper, but also to the remarks of the earlier evaluators. When the papers are returned, students can either revise them according to the critics' specifications or, if disagreeing or needing clarification, can call the group together for further discussion. We may wish to return the revised papers back to the groups, who can select those to be read to the entire class, to be put on the board, or to be included in the class's end-of-the-term publication.

EVALUATION. Peer response can be helpful to our students in a number of ways. It, like cold-turkey conferencing, provides them with a real audience that can foster in them that sense of audience so important to their work. Also, the process of looking for mechanical errors in their classmates' writing makes our students more skilled in looking for errors in their own. And, as a special dividend, it also makes them far more careful about their own proof-reading because of their reluctance to be caught by their peers with a page full of careless errors. Furthermore, the skills students learn in discussing or thinking through other students' papers to discover ways of improving them seem to carry over and help them edit their own work better.

Difficulties. Notwithstanding these benefits, a student group's ability to help students improve their papers is limited. Though even in the beginning the students usually do a fine job at helping each other clarify confused passages, adopt a more appropriate tone, and correct errors in spelling, punctuation mistakes, and run-on sentences and fragments, they are less able to rectify, or sometimes even to discover, problems of usage, diction, pronoun reference, and especially structure. And because of the pressure of dominant peer personalities, students sometimes are led into erroneous "corrections."

The central intervention task of helping students make structural global revisions or reorganization appears to be beyond the capabilities of most peer-response groups. A peer-group *prewriting* approach being researched by Lois Rosen and her colleagues at Penn State at New Kensington shows promise of eliminating what structural problems peers can eliminate ahead of time, before they become engraved in a finished first draft.[14] Currently, how-

ever, effective structural intervention in a written draft by peer groups remains problematical, so we probably should not employ peer response as a
total substitute for our own.

Nevertheless, the many benefits peer response offers both to us and to
our students recommend it strongly as an additional way of responding to
our students' work.

TEACHING STRATEGIES

Cutting Down the Work Load

1. Assign fewer papers. Count revision as writing.
2. Assign shorter papers.
3. Comment briefly. Focus the comment.
4. Intermix expressive writing assignments (journals and the like.) that need
   only occasional response.
5. Stagger assignments.
6. Conduct conferences without first fully reading the papers.

GRADING

Responding to our students' papers is a necessity in teaching writing; and, as
long as revision is permitted, the various interventions—despite their hazards—can play an important part in helping students learn to write better.
For most of us, grading, because it is required, is an equal necessity. Yet it
can be argued that assigning a grade is never totally fair, can be very destructive, and serves no useful purpose at all.

The Problem of Assigning Grades

We have all witnessed the damage caused by grades. We have all known
students who, having consistently received poor grades, have quit trying in
sheer frustration or whose entire lives have been marked by a sense of themselves as failures. We have also known many students of every stripe who, in
their eagerness to achieve, value the grade far more than their learning.

GRADE SOUNDNESS QUESTIONED.   What is more, despite the significance attached to the grades a student receives, their reliability is very
much open to question. Careful research reveals a distressing lack of
agreement in the assignment of grades among those who teach writing and
between a substantial proportion of these teachers and recognized writing
experts. Paul Diederich, for instance, discovered that when sixty distin-

guished readers graded three hundred student papers using nine ratings, "The result was nearly chaos. Of the 300 papers, 101 received all nine grades, 111 received eight, 70 received seven, and no paper received less than five." Vernon H. Smith's work, because of the greater size of his sample, is even more disquieting; he found that fully 52 percent of public school teachers from grades one through twelve markedly differed with a panel of experts and the rest of the teachers in the ranking of five student themes clearly distinguished from one another in quality.[15]

TEACHER OBJECTIVITY QUESTIONED. Diedrich's harsh characterization of English teachers as "capricious in judgment [and] full of prejudices" is surely true of few of us. Yet it is to a degree confirmed by the grades and comments Gary Sloan discovered on a significant number of the two thousand college freshman themes bequeathed him by a long-term department chairman.[16] The comments Sloan quotes are amusing in the whimsicality of the judgment and in the downright ignorance of English style they expose, but they must have been a good deal less amusing to the students to whom they were addressed and whose academic careers were dependent upon them.

Halo Effect. Few of us can altogether escape the "halo effect," through which our evaluation of a paper is in part determined by our first impression of students or by our overall opinion of their intelligence. Sometimes we are influenced by the neatness of our students' grooming or of their handwriting, sometimes by their politeness or manners, or sometimes even by whether they are male or female.[17]

GRADES SEEM TO BE HERE TO STAY. Nevertheless, despite the problems of assigning grades, they are a part of the educational system in the great majority of teaching situations we are likely to find ourselves in and are likely to remain so for at least some time to come. Experiments with pass/fail or credit/no credit have rarely been successful. Students have been so conditioned to think in terms of grades that when this incentive or goal is removed, the effort they devote to their studies almost inevitably declines. Teachers who have worked with the pass/fail procedure report that the abler students, feeling themselves overburdened—as so many students do, devote their energy to the classes where it "counts." Only the marginal students, relieved of the constant reminders of their lack of ability, seem to thrive under such a system—but, of course, the marginal student is, after all, working for a grade in a pass/fail situation, no less than in a graded one.

A WORKING SOLUTION. The only practical solution, therefore, would seem to be for us to try to put to good use whatever motivating force grades can lend us and at the same time try to find ways to avoid, to as great an extent as is possible, the abuses of the grading practice and the damages to our students that seem to be inherent in the system.

Strategies for Fair Grading

Consistency and fairness in theme grading is achievable. The intense activity in composition research in the last two decades is, to a large degree, predicated upon assessment instruments for comparing and evaluating student papers that are both valid and reliable—that is, that both measure what they are supposed to measure and do so consistently.[18] We can achieve a similar reliability and validity in our own classrooms by adopting the researchers' strategies. How? As we begin grading each batch of papers, we must be able to specify clear answers to two questions: What are my criteria for judgment? What are my standards of quality?

CRITERIA FOR JUDGMENT.   We need first to ask ourselves: What exactly am I looking for in these papers? What particular achievements will distinguish the excellent papers? What specific deficiencies will mark the poor ones? And to what extent should I be influenced by these achievements or deficiencies—that is, what proportion of my overall judgment should they sway?

Scales

Researchers have developed a number of scales offering varying criteria for judgment in answer to questions like these, scales that have successfully guided teachers in grading student themes. The best known, perhaps, is the Diederich Scale,[19] which assesses writing in the manner shown in Table 12–1.

A number of such scales, together with lists and explanations of the relevant criteria, are available through the National Council of Teachers of English.

Table 12–1 The Diederich Scale

	Low		Middle		High
General Merit					
Ideas	2	4	6	8	10
Organization	2	4	6	8	10
Wording	1	2	3	4	5
Flavor	1	2	3	4	5
Mechanics					
Usage	1	2	3	4	5
Punctuation	1	2	3	4	5
Spelling	1	2	3	4	5
Handwriting	1	2	3	4	5
				Total _____	

Developing Our Own Scale. We might adapt a professional scale to fit our individual needs in general or tailor one to make it more valid for a specific assignment. Or we might choose to develop a similar instrument of our own. Either option is supported by the research of John C. Follman and James A. Anderson, who tested four such professional scales and found that, when used by trained evaluators, they not only showed high reliability individually, but also correlated well with one another in their results. Better yet, they found that the results of yet a fifth scale, the Everyman Scale, "in which the rater's own particular criteria are used," were among the most reliable and consistent of the methods judged.[20]

These results, which were, by the way, contrary to the researchers' expectations, seem to indicate that what matters in grading is not so much the particular set of criteria employed, but rather the seriousness with which a scale is developed and the consistency with which it is employed.

Involving Our Students. It is often a good idea to have our students help us in developing the set of criteria by which most of their papers will be judged. In any case, we should share our criteria with our students and let them know exactly what the grade we put on their papers is based upon before they write even their first paper. Student involvement is important whether we plan to evaluate the overall quality of their writing or some particular aspect of it (for example, voice, sentence structure, or ways of opening or closing).

APPLYING THE STANDARDS. To apply such standards, we can approach a set of themes, skim through them rapidly until we find what seems to fulfill the criteria for a top paper, call it "A" or "B" or however the sample it most nearly approximates is labeled, and then use this paper as a touchstone and assign grades to the others accordingly. (Sample papers used in this way are known as anchors.) If we work carefully, when we are finished, we should have a continuum in which papers of equal quality (according to our criteria) have received equal grades and no paper has received a better grade than another paper of higher quality.

Having worked in this way with specific criteria to rank student themes and establish standards, most teachers find that they no longer need to depend upon essay-by-essay comparison with a physical scale because they have internalized the standards into their own thinking.

Grading the Nonaverage Student

Using scales of quality in this way, whether the scales are physical or internalized, works well in determining grades for "average" students—that is, for the students who by dint of effort and intelligent revision are sometimes capable of producing a paper comparable to the top-ranked compositions and who on a lazy day, or when they do not yet understand might also approximate papers on the lower end of the scale. The papers of a large number of our students can be accommodated without too much unfairness within the ranks of a well-constructed scale, and thus it would be a mistake to underestimate the value of such attempts at the formulation of universal standards.

But using such a scale to grade students whose talents are such that they can easily reach the top standard for writing even on their worst days or those who are not able to reach even the middle standard after many, many days of hard trying deprives the grade of its motivating force. For grades assigned to these students in this way will necessarily have very little connection with anything the students can do very much about.

THE NONAVERAGE DILEMMA. These "nonaverage" students, especially if we have a whole class of them, create a real dilemma for the conscientious teacher. Grading them by some universal standard for quality designed for the "average" student deprives them of the motivation essential to improving their writing. But grading them by nonstandard criteria (of effort, of improvement, or of relative place in the class, for instance) will give them an unrealistic notion of the quality of their work.

Such grades have no meaning outside the classroom walls, and those who rely upon grades (for determining, for example, who should be encouraged to seek a career in law or in medicine) may overestimate the abilities of marginal scholars, thereby setting them up for future failure, and underestimate the achievement of many of the very able in classes for advanced students.

SUGGESTED PRAGMATIC SOLUTIONS. Although the dilemma has a single root, our approach to it must vary with its individual manifestations. Let us consider the specific problems associated with varying classroom situations.

The Class Composed Entirely of Students of High Ability

Problem: The papers of any given assignment in this group, when ranked, will tend to distribute themselves, like those of any group, into the form of a bell-shaped curve, even though, when judged on a universal scale, the least successful paper might rank no lower than B.

        How can we use grades to indicate fluctuations in a student's work or to reward exceptional achievement, but still not penalize for their membership in this class those who find themselves only average in this group of outstanding students?

A Solution: The answer would seem to be to enlarge the number of gradations between A and B. The use of such intermedial gradations as A+, A+/A, A, A/A−, A−, A−/B+, B+, B+/B, and so on, will distinguish between the quality of papers within an assignment, will satisfy the need to show fluctuations in an individual's work, and will still permit the final A or B on the report card to provide the outside world with a realistic assessment of these students' high achievement.

The Class Composed Entirely of Less Able Students

Problem: Maintaining motivation without building false expectations.

A Solution: For any learning to take place, students must be convinced that effort that results in achievement will be rewarded. But, even though for class harmony we need to key most papers in every set proportionately to whatever the top grades are, we can occasionally assign higher grades to papers whose writers have achieved well beyond their usual work.

          In this way we will be adopting norm-referenced standards rather than any kind of absolute grading standards, it is true. But please note that effort is not the chief criterion, for mere effort will not suffice. The students' effort must lead to genuine achievement, though the grade for that achievement might be somewhat higher than that indicated on an absolute scale.

The Less Able or the Gifted Student within an Average Class

Problem: All of our students' work should improve throughout a term, including that of the less able and of the gifted students, but the relative position of these students in a class may not change. How can we motivate students whose papers, when balanced against their classmates, will almost always be much worse or considerably better than the rest?

A Solution: We need to give these students special consideration within the overall class structure. If the less able students put forth real effort and we help them channel it constructively, their papers should begin to show merit; and we must give that merit recognition. Thus, notwithstanding their relative rank in the class, by midterm, a median grade should be within their grasp and occasionally they should be able to achieve something even higher.

          We should make a similar kind of individual consideration for our gifted students so that they do not automatically receive the top grade but, using intermedial gradations, can receive a wide enough variety of grades to reflect fluctuations in effort and varying levels of achievement.

Guarding Ourselves against Unfair Grading Practices

The most important thing we can do to guard ourselves against personal unfairness in grading practices—capriciousness or prejudice—is to recognize that, as detached as we would like to be, we are all capable of this sort of discrimination. We each have to admit to ourselves that it could happen to us. Gayle Whittier writes about her surprise and chagrin when she realized that it had indeed happened to her:

> My rereading of Sarah's paper raised an interesting question: why did I check, say, a sentence fragment, in some papers (those to which I gave lower grades) while permitting one in others (those to which I gave higher grades)? My discrimination seemed to suggest that I extended license to high intelligence which I would not accord to the average or struggling student. And yet I had never had a sense of grading "unfairly" in so blatant a way.[21]

Being human, we all have our own biases, our own likes and dislikes. Certain characteristics in people appeal to us; certain characteristics annoy us. And unless we consciously recognize these predilections and guard against them, some of them will inevitably work their insidious way into our judgment of our students' papers.

GRADING ANONYMOUSLY.   The best way to protect ourselves, of course, is to grade anonymous papers. We might ask our students to put their names on the back of an inner sheet of their paper or in some other spot where we will not immediately notice it. Bluebooks can be turned in with the covers bearing student names rolled over. Some teachers even assign identification numbers, recorded in the grade book, to be used instead of students' names.

LEANING OVER BACKWARD.   Often none of these methods is feasible, however, or we learn to recognize our students' handwriting or we come to know their style. When such is the case, we have to come face to face with our own bias. If we think, for instance, "Oh, good! here comes an A paper!" whenever we recognize Robin's writing, or if, whenever we see one of Chris's themes, we are reminded once again of Chris's insolent mannerisms, we can smile a little at our own vulnerability and then lean over backward to give Robin's paper the careful evaluation it deserves and to separate our admittedly negative feelings for Chris from the document we have to mark.

COMPARING.   Another way to make sure we are grading our students' papers fairly and consistently is occasionally to exchange a set of papers with another teacher. Or we might read a set of themes and record their grades without actually marking the papers, put them away for a week, and then after we have marked them, compare the grades to see how consistent we have been.

Grading to Motivate

Using techniques and strategies such as those outlined in this chapter, we can go a long way toward making our grading system responsive to our teaching goals, consistent, fair, and free from capriciousness and prejudice. Unfortunately, all the fairness in the world still cannot eliminate a student's pain at receiving a low grade. There are some procedures, however, that we might use to help mitigate the misery.

SELF-EVALUATION. One method many teachers find helpful is to let students share in the evaluating process. Some of these teachers provide students with a set of criteria and have them evaluate their own papers or have them respond to a series of questionnaires throughout the revising process which culminates in the (sometimes optional) assignment of a grade. Mary Beaven suggests that questionnaires might include such questions as:

1. How much time did you spend on this paper?
2. (After the first evaluation) What did you try to improve, or experiment with, on this paper? How successful were you? If you have questions about what you were trying to do, what are they?
3. What are the strengths of your paper? Place a squiggly line beside those passages you feel are very good.
4. What are the weaknesses, if any, of your paper? Place an X beside passages you would like your teacher to correct or revise. . . .
5. What one thing will you do to improve your next piece of writing? Or what kind of experimentation in writing would you like to try?
6. (Optional) What grade would you give yourself on this composition? Justify it. ("Individualized Goal Setting" 153.)

Conferenced Term Grades. Other instructors avoid assigning a grade to individual papers, but rather once each report period have students bring all their revised papers to an evaluating conference at which the term grade is mutually determined.

Student-Recommended Term Grades. Some teachers, as each report period approaches, ask their students to recommend their own grades; and some of these teachers also ask their students to back their recommendation with a written defense. In those cases where the teacher and student disagree (and those who employ this system note these cases are surprisingly few), the disagreement is ironed out in conference.[22]

Method Evaluated. Though this sort of evaluation would seem to offer an excellent solution to the problems grading causes, in practice it does not always work out comfortably. The difficulty is not that students tend to over-grade themselves. This tendency, as Stephen Judy points out, can virtually be eliminated by a careful preparation in which the differences between "bad-faith" and "good-faith" evaluations are discussed.[23] Actually, more students become self-conscious and develop a false modesty that makes them undergrade themselves rather than overgrade. The real problem is the anxiety (of which undergrading is simply one symptom) that many students experience when self-evaluation is extensively employed.[24]

DELAYED GRADING. The best way to avoid the motivational—and sometimes psychological—damage that failing grades can wreak upon a student who is trying to do well is simply to avoid giving them. Is it possible to uphold realistic standards and still not give failing grades to students willing to put forth the effort needed to learn to write? Certainly. The answer lies in delaying the assignment of grades until students have produced satisfactory work.

General Delayed Grading. How? We simply do not assign grades to any paper we feel would profit from a thoroughgoing revision. When we explain our system to our students, we can be perfectly candid and tell them that our one purpose in teaching the course is to help them learn to write better and that it is our belief that much of this learning takes place during the rewriting process. But since rewriting takes time and is sometimes difficult, we are offering the possibility of a better grade to motivate them to do the work they need to do to learn to write well. In the meantime, we can point out the several options that are open to them when they receive their papers:

1. If their papers already have a grade, they can
   a. make the indicated surface corrections at the appropriate spots on the paper (or on the back, if more lengthy rewording is required) and turn it in to have the grade recorded.
   b. bring their paper in for conference, then choose to revise (for a possibly improved grade) or not as they think best.

2. If the paper does not have a grade, it means that we believe it would be improved by revision. The lack of a grade signifies either that the paper would earn a low grade as it stands or that it is quite good but, with just a little revising, it could become something really special. Students with ungraded papers can:
   a. sign up for a conference or rely on some other intervention activity to prime rewriting or
   b. decide not to revise and instead make the superficial corrections on their paper and return it with a note asking to be assigned a grade (but with the clear understanding that the grade might be low).

What usually happens in practice is that although the decision remains the student's, almost everyone opts for revision. Happily, when the revised drafts are complete, there is rarely reason to assign failing or even very low grades.

Since almost all the papers in a class's first set or two of assignments are likely to fall within this "revision-suggested" category, some of us save time by not annotating these papers and signing the whole class up for conferences.

CONTRACT-MASTERY SYSTEM. Another good way to minimize the negative effects of grades while promoting learning is what John V. Knapp calls the Contract-Conference-Mastery system.[25] In this system, students are given writing assignments in which progressively more writing skill is required throughout the term. Each paper must be completed satisfactorily before the student moves on to the next. The class is organized as a workshop and students bring each draft as they complete it to the teacher for (formative) evaluation and, until satisfactory, for guidance toward revision. In Knapp's version of the system, the student must complete the first two assignments to earn a D, the first four for a C, two more for a B, and all eight for an A.

Though this system shares some of the features of the Contract Technique, in which students contract to complete certain projects to be awarded certain grades, it avoids the disadvantages associated with that method. The emphasis in Contract Mastery is not on the quantity of projects completed but rather on the mastery of skills. Credit is awarded only to work satisfactorily accomplished. Not grades, but learning itself dominates the Contract-Mastery machinery, since students do not start out contracting for a particular grade, but rather are rewarded by the grade as they master each skill, building learning upon learning.

This method is a good way to teach writing because it permits students to work at their own speed, with the rate determined by their ability and the amount of effort they choose to exert, while ensuring that all of them will master at least the fundamental essentials of writing.

PORTFOLIO GRADING. Portfolio grading is another good delayed-grading approach. It occurs in a number of forms. The basic idea, however, is that students collect a term's work in a portfolio, revising each paper as far as they choose, and then at the end of the term select those papers that are to be graded. The teacher, or the class, set the number of papers to be judged and often also prescribe the genres to be represented.

Evaluating Process. In some versions of portfolio grading, students turn in their prewriting and all their drafts with one or all of their chosen papers so that their skills in the process of writing may also be evaluated.

Encouraging Metacognition. There is also a metacognition component in some portfolio approaches: in some of these, students introduce their portfolio with a memo explaining why they have selected the particular entries; in others, students keep a running commentary on their composing decisions and turn it in with the relevant papers.

Advantages. Some teachers consider portfolio grading fairer than grading every paper because a student is not penalized for a bad day or the inability to respond well to some incompatible topic. The method also encourages student writers to be more conscious of their writing decisions.[26] Portfolio evaluation combines some of the advantages of general delayed grading and of a contract system. As in delayed grading, revision is not only permitted, but encouraged. And as in a contract system, students are given a good deal of control over their own assessment.

Problems.   Although portfolio assessment generated much scholarly enthusiasm in the early 1990s,[27] teachers who have tried the method are not universally positive in their appraisals. Those not happy with it believe that portfolio grading, by backing up the entire grading process to the end of the term, gives them an almost intolerable workload at that already especially busy time. They also feel that this backloading of deadlines encourages students to indulge their natural human tendencies to procrastinate, and therefore instead of stimulating students to spend more thought and time revising each paper, as the method intends, it actually motivates last-minute cramming. Furthermore, some teachers who teach from a carefully coordinated set of assignments are also concerned that when students eliminate papers from their portfolios, they will be eliminating revision and reconsideration of assignments they consider vital for their students' growth.

In short, the teacher critics of portfolio assessment appreciate the method's encouragement of revision, but believe that other forms of delayed grading serve the same purpose without the disadvantages.

FINAL CONSIDERATION.   Whichever mode of evaluation we choose to use will be effective only to the extent that we believe in it as a way to help our students improve their writing and feel comfortable in using it. Grading is an intimate part of our teaching style and thus must, to some degree, be determined by our individual personalities and philosophies, a topic we will discuss in the final chapter.

IDEAS FOR DISCUSSION OR ESSAY

1. Through discussion develop a set of grading criteria with which all the members of the class (or of a group) can comfortably work.
2. Using the guidelines developed in #1, evaluate the following "Pre–World War II Letters to the Editor" written by the members of an eleventh-grade American history course and, working quickly, impressionistically assign a grade to each.

> To the Editor of the *Post:*
> Dear Sir:
> It is my opinion that at all cost we should stay out of War. In a sense we have already entered by selling arms. The War is none of our bussiness, we have not been directly atact and until we do we should cut off all ties with Europe. Selling arms isn't helping us to stay out of War, it helps our economy but eventually we will have to enter the War if we keep selling arms.
> Yours truly,

> Dear Sir,
>   I am not a war-loving person. I do not like violence. With the hard times that have hit America, I, at first, agreed with our policy of isolation. However,

I feel that this simply will no longer work. We must get involved with Europe. Japanese and German agression has to be stopped.

Hitler and his Nazis have already conquered Poland, Finland, Belgium, and other countries with his terrifying blitzkrieg. The blitzkrieg was as effective on the French, a major force, as it was on smaller forces. Now that the Nazis have captured France, they are ready to move on to Great Britain. World-wide conquest is obviously their goal.

Well, as much as we have tried to forget it, America is still part of the world, and if something isn't done to stop this agression, we too will be conquered. The Atlantic Ocean will not seem like such a large gap if Hitler and Mussolini add the French and British fleets to their own. It is time to fight for democracy at the sides of our foreign friends. It is the American people's duty to keep the world safe for democracy.

Take action now, before it is too late.

Editor:

I would like to express my views. on our problems we are having with Europe. I feel we are getting our selves in trouble. I dont see why we are getting involved in Europes affairs because only to kill off our own soldiers in awar. More Americans should disagree with FDR because its going to be your own lives your risking. We should limit ourselves to only the defense of the Western Hemisphere and keep our noses out of others affairs.

To the Editor:

In sight of the agressiveness in Europe I feel very strongly that action must be taken in some form by the United States. It is evident that Germany will not stop by appeasement. To remain isolated would mean our possible invasion. With Great Britain and France we should be able to beat the Axis Powers but alone would be a defeat over us and democracy. If we offer no resistance Hitler will have an open path to America. If we allow the over-run of Britain then our security of the Atlantic Ocean will not be protective. The German's will not listen to peace they want war and we cannot sit by and watch them destroy democracy in the world.

To the Editor:

I believe that in this time of "war" in many countries, the United States should make a strong stand. I feel we should be concerned about the affairs of other countries and their people, but we must think carefully before we run to help them. World War I is a prime example of how we tried to help, and the result was disasterous. We must examine every aspect of entering a war instead of being "suckered" into it, as in World War I.

The United States, however, cannot totally withdraw from the rest of the world and ignore what is happening to thousands of innocent people. I believe the United States should have a strong force prepared to defend themselves and their country because we never know what to expect. We need to let the other countries of the world know that we can fight if necessary, and we are willing to do so if the situation arises.

3. Discuss your evaluations and as a class (or as a group) set standards of quality agreeable to all. It would probably be a good idea to rank the sample compositions into a scale.
4. Using the criteria you have developed and the standards you have worked out, thoroughly comment upon and give a grade to one of the two papers below. Mark the other one for conference and write some notes explaining how you would conduct a conference whose purpose would be to help the author revise that paper.

> Dear Editor:
> I know that in the past decade our country has been in a great depression. Much poverty has struck each city, and well-paid workers are scarce. Although the United States is in an economics crisis we must be prepared for war. I am not encouraging war, but the citizens of our country should be aware of the problems between our neighboring countries which could soon envolve us. Facism is growing, Hitler is propoganding, and Japan's navy is increasing tremendously.
>
> It is good that the United States stays neutral and does not become agressive. Also that we are able to aid France and Great Britain in their war needs. If we should enter, we must find a way to strengthen our country with men and money.

> To the Editor:
> In my opinion, many people are thinking about the events which have occurred in the past. Our nation should be ready for any kind of conflict, and we're not. For example, in World War I we were not really quite ready. There were many innocent people killed in World War I so we should take precautions now so nothing like that happens. If the United States had something go wrong, we would be forced into war. The "good neighbor policy" would be good so it would insure that their would be no intervening in internal or external affairs.
>
> If Americans isolated themselves, like some thing is best, this would not solve the problem. Americans would be to otheres, weak and incapable of standing up for themselves. The Neutrality acts that were passed worked for the United States and they are good for the U.S. But for instance, let's say our merchant vessels, which are now unarmed, were attacked; they couldn't do one thing about it. So U.S. better think about it now.

NOTES

The part-opening epigraph is from Henry Brook Adams, *The Education of Henry Adams*.

The chapter opening epigraph is from Paul B. Diederich's "In Praise of Praise," *NEA Journal* 52 (1963): 58.

1. See, for example, Ellis B. Page, "Teacher Comments and Student Performance," *JEP* 49 (1958): 173–81; and M. E. Kelly, "Effects of Two Types of Teacher Response to Essays upon Twelfth-Grade Students' Growth," *DAI* 34 (1973): 5801A (Michigan State U).

2. Alberta Goodman, "Utilization of Positive Feedback in a Classroom Environment of Acceptance to Provide Enhanced Learner Self-Concept and Improved Written Performance," *DAI* 36 (1975): 6550A (U of Michigan).

A number of other studies show that positive comments positively affect writers' attitudes and motivation for writing; among them: Thomas C. Gee, "Students' Responses to Teacher Comments," *RTE* 6 (1972): 212–21 [from *DAI* 31 (1971): 3412-A]; E. Seidman, "Marking Students' Compositions: Implications of Achievement Motivation Theory," *DA* 28 (1968): 2605-A; and Alfred E. Stevens, "The Effects of Positive and Negative Evaluation in the Written Composition of Low Performing High-School Students," *DAI* 34 (1973): 1778A (Boston); R. M. Hausner, "Interaction of Selected Student Personality Factors and Teachers' Comments in a Sequentially-Developed Composition Curriculum." *DAI* 36 (1976): 5768-A; W. F. Taylor and K. C. Hoedt, "The Effect of Praise upon the Quality and Quantity of Creative Writing," *JER* 60 (1966): 80–83; T. S. Schroeder, "The Effects of Positive and Corrective Written Teacher Feedback on Selected Writing Behaviors of Fourth-Grade Children," *DAI* 34 (1973a): 2935-A; and P. F. Alpren, "Can Children Be Helped to Increase the Originality of Their Story Writing," *RTE* 7 (1973): 372–86.

See also Diederich's "In Praise of Praise," 58–59 and *Measuring Growth in English* (Urbana: NCTE, 1974), results summarized on 20; and Mary F. Hayes and Donald A. Daiker, "Using Protocol Analysis in Evaluating Responses to Student Writing" *Freshman English News* 13 (1984): 1–4, 10.

But also see note 4, which lists research demonstrating that without the opportunity for revision, teacher comment—even when it contains praise—does not stimulate a significant improvement in student writing.

3. As related by Lou LaBrant, "Marking the Paper," in *Teaching English in Today's High Schools: Selected Readins*, eds. Dwight L. Burton and Jack S. Simmons, 2nd ed. (New York: Holt, 1970), 352. I might add that this strategy provides a particularly good use for our red pen. Many teachers find that red is too invasive when we use it for corrections.

Other especially helpful discussions of techniques for commenting include T. A. Koclanes, "Can We Evaluate Composition?" *EJ* 50 (1961): 252–57; Don M. Wolfe, *Creative Ways to Teach English* (New York: Odyssey, 1966), 14–23; Carlton F. Wells, "Ten Points for English Teachers," *EJ* 55 (1966): 1080–81; Richard L. Larson, "Training New Teachers in the Writing of Comments on Themes," *CCC* 17 (1966): 152–155; and Donald Daiker, "Learning to Praise," in *Writing and Response: Theory, Practice, and Research*, ed. Chris M. Anson (Urbana: NCTE, 1989), 103–13.

4. Among them, John Paul Diedenhefer, "An Experiment in Grading Papers," *CCC* 27 (1976): 406–7; and Lois V. Arnold, "Writers' Cramp and Eyestrain—Are They Paying Off?" *EJ* 53 (1964): 10–15; and the Mary Hayes and Donald Daiker article on "Using Protocol Analysis," cited in note 2.

In *Research on Written Composition: New Directions for Teaching* (Urbana: NCRE and ERIC, 1986), George Hillocks, Jr. considers the research on this problem in some detail. See pages 156–68, where Hillocks reviews the research on the quality and effectiveness of teacher comments, including the work of Gee (1972), Seidman (1968), Stevens (1973), Hausner (1976), Taylor and Hoedt (1966), Schroeder (1973), Alpren (1973)—all cited more fully in note 2.

Hillocks also considered tape-recorded teacher commentary: D. R. Coleman "A Comparison between the Relative Effectiveness of Marginal-Interlinear-Terminal Commentary and of Audiotaped Commentary in Responding to English Compositions," *DAI* 33 (1973): 3945-A and K. E. Judd, "The Effectiveness of Tape Recorded Evaluations of Compositions Written by Seventh-Grade and Eighth-Grade Students, *DAI* 34 (1973): 1770-A.

Other scholars have studied the varying effects dependent upon where on the paper teachers placed their commentary: R. Stiff, "The Effect upon Student Composition of Particular Correction Techniques," *RTE* 16 (1967): 54–75 and E. J. Bata, "A Study of the Relative Effectiveness of Marking Techniques on Junior College Freshman English Composition," *DAI* 34 (1973): 62-A.

Other studies test the effectiveness of frequency of writing and teacher comment: D. L. Burton and L. Arnold, *"Effects of Frequency of Writing and Intensity of Teacher Evaluation upon High School Students' Performance in Written Composition,* ERIC (1964): ED 003 281; R. S. Sutton and E. D. Allen, "The Effect of Practice and Evaluation on Improvement in Written Composition." ERIC (1964): ED 001 274; and R. R. Clopper, "A Study of Contract Correcting as a Means of Significantly Increasing Writing and English Skills," *DA* 27 (1967): 3769-A.

Having examined the results of research in the various teacher-comment strategies on nonrevisable student papers, Hillock concludes:

> The results of all these studies strongly suggest that teacher comment has little impact on student writing. (165)

But in Hillocks own study, "The Interaction of Instruction, Teacher Comment, and Revision in Teaching the Composing Process," *RTE* 16 [1982]: 261–78), he discovered that when students are given the opportunity to revise from teacher comments—especially focused comments, they make a significant gain—nearly twice that of students who could not revise. And R. Beach found that students gained after teacher comments, when students were permitted revision, more than they did from the comments of fellow students; see "The Effects of Between-Draft Teacher Evaluation Versus Student Self-Evaluation on High School Students' Revising of Rough Drafts," *RTE* 13 (1979): 111–19.

5. For example, Paul Dressell, John Schmid, Jr., and Gerald Kincaid, "The Effect of Writing Frequency upon Essay-Type Writing Proficiency at the College Level," *JER* 46 (1952): 285–93; Frank Heys, Jr., "The Theme-a-Week Assumption: A Report of an Experiment," *EJ* 51 (1962): 320–22; Lois Arnold, 10–15; and James R. Squire and Roger K. Applebee, *High School English Instruction Today: The National Study of High School English Programs* (New York: Appleton, 1968), 137.

See also the studies Hillocks reviewed and I have cited in note 4: Burton and Arnold (1964), Sutton and Allen (1964), and Clopper (1967).

6. Nancy Sommers, "Responding to Student Writing," *CCC* 33 (1982): 148–56.

7. For a concise, comprehensive systemization of this topic, see Carolyn R. Boiarsky's "Revision Phases" in her *Technical Writing: Contexts, Audiences, and Communities* (Boston: Allyn, 1993), 274–75.

8. Elizabeth Fowler, *Teaching Language, Composition and Literature* (New York: McGraw-Hill, 1965), 139; Carol Laque and Phyllis Sherwood, *A Laboratory Approach to Writing* (Urbana: NCTE, 1977), 101; and LaBrant, 356–57.

9. Thomas Newkirk, "The First Five-Minutes," in *Writing and Response*, 317–18.

10. Barbara Fassler Walvoord, *Helping Students Write Well: A Guide for Teachers in All Disciplines*, 2nd ed., (New York: MLA, 1982), 145, 146.

11. Paul Anderson, Professor of English, Miami University of Ohio, from a private conversation, April 1979. For other suggestions, see Paul Briand, "Turned On:

Multi Media and Advanced Composition," *CCC* 21 (1970): 167–69; Stephen Vogler, "Grading Themes: A New Approach, A New Diversion," *EJ* (1971): 70–74; Enno Klammer, "Cassettes in the Classroom," *CE* 35 (1973): 179–89; and Robert Powell, "Grading Compositions on 33⅓ rpm Records," in *Patterns and Models for Teaching English*, ed. Michael Shugre et al. (Urbana: NCTE, 1964), 39–40.

For a thorough-going critique of casette commenting, see Russell A. Hung, "Technological Gift-Horse: Some Reflections in the Teeth of Cassette Marking," *CE* 36 (1975): 581–85.

12. Patsy S. S. Saiki, *The Composition Study: Summaries of Comparison of the Lay Reader Treatment with Other Treatments in Increasing Student Growth in Writing*, 1968–1969 (Honolula: Hawaii State Department of Education, 1970). Other helpful analyses of lay reader programs include: Paul Diederich, "The Rutgers Plan for Cutting Class Size in Two," *EJ* 44 (1960): 229–36, 66; Howard G. Getz, *Paraprofessionals in the English Department* (Urbana: NCTE, 1972); and Virginia M. Burke, "A Candid Opinion on Lay Readers," *EJ* 50 (1961): 158–64.

13. Among the most helpful sources on peer response are Mary H. Beaven, "Individualized Goal Setting, Self-Evaluation, and Peer Evaluation," in *Evaluating Writing: Describing, Measuring, Judging*, eds. Charles R. Cooper and Lee Odell (Urbana: NCTE, 1977), 148–53; Howard Pierson, *Teaching Writing* (Englewood Cliffs: Prentice, 1972), 26–30; James Moffett, *Teaching the Universe of Discourse* (Boston: Houghton, 1968), especially 193–98; Theodore W. Hipple, "The Grader's Helpers—Colleagues, Peers, Scorecards," *EJ* 61 (1972): 691–93; Irvin Peckham, "Peer Evaluation," *EJ* 61 (1978): 61–63; Francine Hardaway, "What Students Can Do to Take the Burden Off You," *CE* 36 (1975): 577–80; and Peter Elbow, *Writing without Teachers* (London: Oxford UP, 1973).

Studies demonstrating the effectiveness of peer evaluation include: Bob W. Ford, "The Effects of Peer Editing/Grading on the Grammar-Usage and Theme Composition Ability of College Freshmen," *DAI* 33 (1973): 6087A (Oklahoma); K. Bantam and G. Tutley, "The Effect of Peer-Evaluated Student Compositions on Writing Improvement," *English Record* 26 (1975): 26, 64–69; Roy C. Maize, "Two Methods of Teaching English Composition to Retarded College Freshmen." *JEP* 45 (1954): 22–76; and J. T. Sutton and E. D. Allen, *The Effect of Practice and Evaluation on Improvement in Written Composition*, Cooperative Research Project, #1993 (DeLand, Fla.: Stetson U, 1964).

14. Lois Rosen, from a presentation at the NCTE Spring Meeting, held in Richmond, Virginia, March 1993. See also pages 105–7 of this text.

15. Paul Diederich, "Grading and Measuring," in *Teaching Basic English Courses*, ed. Richard M. Bossone (New York: Van Nostrand, 1971), 386; Vernon H. Smith, "Measuring Teaching Judgment in the Evaluation of Written Research," *RTE* 3 (1969): 181–96.

See also Paul F. Schumann, "What Criteria Do You Use in Grading Compositions?" *EJ* 57 (1968): 1165.

16. Diederich, quoted in Vernon Smith, 182; Gary Sloan, "The Wacky World of Theme Marking," *CCC* 28 (1977): 37–73.

17. Diederich cites a large-scale study by Benjamin Rosner in which papers invariably achieved higher grades when they were marked "Honors Class" then when they were marked "Regular." Diederich concludes: "We find what we expect to find. If we think a paper was written by an honors student, it looks better then if we think it was written by a regular student ("Grading and Measuring," 393).

18. Using techniques developed to ensure the validity and reliability of research in composition, groups of graders repeatedly have achieved over 90 percent correlation of their evaluations. See especially Richard Braddock, Richard Lloyd-Jones, and Lowell Schoer, *Research in Written Composition*, eds. Charles Cooper and Lee Odell (Urbana: NCTE, 1963), 11–15; Charles R. Cooper, "Holistic Evaluation of Writing," in *Evaluative Writing* 18–20; and John C. Follman and James A. Anderson, "An Investigation of the Reliability of Five Procedures for Grading English Themes," *RTE* 1 (1967): 190–200.

See also Brian Hunt, "Reliability, Validity, and Holistic Scoring: What We Know and What We Need to Know," *CCC* 41 (1990): 201–13. In an essay most useful for its extensive bibliography, Hunt offers a critique of holistic scoring on the grounds that though it may be reliable, few have studied how valid it is.

19. Paul Diederich, *Measuring Growth in English* (Urbana: NCTE, 1974), 54. For examples of other such scales, see Cooper, "Holistic Evaluation," 9; Royal J. Morsey, *Improving English Instruction* (Boston: Allyn, 1965), 227–28; and Laque and Sherwood, *A Laboratory Approach*, 89.

20. As quoted in Nathan S. Blount, "Research on Teaching Literature, Language, and Composition," in *Second Handbook of Research on Teaching*, ed. Robert M. W. Travers (Chicago: Rand McNally, 1972), 1087. The scales tested included: California Essay Scale, Cleveland Composition Rating Scale, Diederich Rating Scale, Follman English Mechanics Guide, and the Everyman Scale.

21. Gayle Whittier, "The World We Never Made: Teaching Writing in a Literature Course," *CCC* 23 (1972): 181.

22. Examples of other self-evaluating questionnaires to be used individually or at evaluating conferences are included in Laque and Sherwood, 87; Walter Loban, Margaret Ryan, and James R. Squire, *Teaching Language and Literature* (New York: Harcourt, 1961), 535–39; and Michael Grady, "A Technique for Theme Correction," in *Classroom Practices in Teaching English*, Fifth Report (Urbana: NCTE, 1967), 77–81. Hardaway, "What Students Can Do," 580, also offers a questionnaire for peer evaluation. See also pages 182–83 in our text.

23. Stephen Judy [or Tchudi], *Explorations in the Teaching of Secondary English: A Source Book for Experimental Teaching* (New York: Dodd, 1975), 239.

24. For further discussion of the problem, see Beaven, "Individualized," 147–48, and Grady, "A Technique," 80–81.

25. John V. Knapp, "Contract/Conference Evaluations of Freshman Compositions," *CE* 37 (1976): 647–53.

26. Student metacognition of this sort is much praised by many experts in composition pedagogy; Brian Johnston in *Assessing English: Helping Students Reflect on their Work* (Sydney, Australia: St. Clair, 1983) typifies this point of view and expresses it well. There is, however, a minority viewpoint that considers self-reflection a hindrance to the natural learning processes. As Russell A. Hunt writes, "The more conscious many kinds of knowledge become, the less effectively they can be utilized." See "A Horse Named Hans, a Boy Named Shawn: The Herr von Osten Theory of Response to Writing," in *Writing and Response*, 91.

27. A number of professional conferences were devoted to its study—for example, Miami University's Fifth Conference on Composition Pedagogy: Portfolio Assessment, Oxford, Ohio October 1992. And a disproportionately large number of sessions and workshops at meetings of the NCTE and CCCC also attest to the strong interest in this strategy.

Assigning Writing

> The good writing assignment places the emphasis on the student as a thinker and on the development of his or her thoughts from the inception of the idea to the communication to an audience.
> — Stephen N. Judy and Susan J. Judy

☐ ☐ ☐

A good writing assignment is designed to make the wheels go round in students' minds, to stretch their understanding, and in the process to teach them something about the subject and enhance their writing skill. A successful assignment actually accomplishes these ends. But how can we devise writing assignments that will succeed? This chapter aims to respond to that question.

What are the components of a successful assignment? The answer is more complex than one would immediately think, because an assignment itself is more complex. In constructing an assignment we need to consider: topic or content, rhetorical context, how assignments can engage our students, introductory or prewriting activities, ways of presenting an assignment or explaining it to our students, and possible outcomes. All of these considerations go into devising a successful assignment. And we will need to examine them all.

INSTRUCTOR-ASSIGNED WRITING

But we should perhaps consider first the more basic question of whether we ought to give our students specific writing assignments or whether we should allow them to choose their own topic and audience.

Criticism of Writing Assignments

Some scholars and teachers argue that, since writing is an expression of the writer's thought, any teacher-made assignment necessarily puts constraints upon the writer's freedom of thought. We can help stimulate that thought, they assert, through a variety of heuristics and discussion strategies, but more formal assignments impose a teacher's ideas and thus stifle student creativity and intellectual freedom. Peter Elbow, for example, urges "writing without teachers"; Donald Graves argues that teacher-suggested assignments make students dependent and impede their inventiveness; and Nancie Atwell cautions us to "remember the centrality of ownership in students' growth as writers," insisting that "the piece of writing belongs to the writer."[1] Student-created assignments seem to work very well indeed in the workshop classrooms of these master teachers.

Endorsement of Writing Assignments

On the other hand, such assignment freedom is not for all of us. Other master teachers, such as Thomas Newkirk, have theoretical misgivings. He is "uncomfortable with . . . the metaphor of ownership" and writes:

> To a degree, the student owns his or her paper, but the paper is *intended* for others . . . and so, to a degree, the paper is also owned by its readers. . . . The expectations of the teacher, the course, and the academy must interact with the intentions of the student.[2]

Other teachers have pragmatic reasons for preferring to originate at least some of their writing assignments. As technical-writing instructor Carolyn Boiarsky points out, "Most writing in real life is assigned, from a gift necessitating a thank-you letter to Aunt Mary to a completed project initiating a memo to the supervisor." Furthermore, teachers report that many of their students consider a free-choice assignment the hardest of all. In their experience, students tend to write better papers—and write more willingly—when they can work within a good assignment.[3] And research supports this position. George Hillocks's meta-analysis of a series of important experimental projects strongly indicates that "specific assignments are effective when accompanied by effective instruction."[4]

As for my own practice, I usually offer my students a selection of specific assignments, and only occasionally suggest that they create their own topics. Invariably, however, one of my assigned choices is along the lines of "or another similar topic of your own choosing," and I encourage my students to follow up paths of thinking that intrigue them, some of which lead to topics varying widely from those I suggested. Conversely, when the assignment is a free choice, I have no compunction about making suggestions or helping students think through to a writing idea when they draw a blank.

DESIGNING AN ASSIGNMENT

What makes a good writing assignment? Our answer for each assignment will depend upon our purpose in making it. Our purpose is necessarily twofold: academic and rhetorical, what we hope our students will get out of the writing and what the shape of that writing should be.

Academic Goals

Academically, a good writing assignment must challenge our students to think, to give their growing minds a workout. It should also help them add to their knowledge of the topic and increase their skills in writing.

PURPOSE: GROWTH OF ACADEMIC KNOWLEDGE AND SKILLS. An assignment is part of a course and occurs at some particular point in time during that course. In terms of the course, then, we should decide first what *understandings* we hope our students will achieve at this time. We need to delineate the precise body of knowledge we want our students to explore while working on this particular assignment. "Explore" is the operative word here. A good assignment will not elicit some preordained information. Rather, it will delineate a do-able corner of information in which our students can let their minds roam freely.

We also should decide what *skills* we want our students to gain by writing this particular paper. Our assignment should build on skills acquired in earlier work. In Erica Lindemann's words, "Effective writing assignments encourage students to define progressively more complex rhetorical problems" (193).

Offering Experiential Work to Develop Skills. Most of the assignments in Dona Hickey's *Developing a Written Voice* provide good illustrations of assignments designed to give practice in a particular skill—in her case, putting voice into writing—and to give the student an opportunity to explore a special area of understanding. In a typical assignment Hickey sets up a detailed scenario with a persona—and a voice—for the student to identify with, and then asks the student to respond in writing to a situation that person is facing. She uses this strategy in the assignment quoted in part below. In addition, the assignment supplies a vehicle for students to consider the contrast in values of those who live in multicultural communities with those who live in unicultural ones and perhaps also to examine their own values in this regard. The assignment begins:

> You attended a private prep school. Now you are a junior at a large urban university. In the past two years many of your beliefs have been challenged, particularly your sociopolitical beliefs. . . . You have wrestled within; some of your values are in conflict, perhaps in transition. . . .

Hickey goes on to set up a rhetorical situation demanding sincerity, tact, and sensitivity in equal measure:

> Your best friend from high school . . . a sensitive, intelligent person . . . attends a local, private college in your hometown . . . with a homogenous

student population . . . where he or she has not had your experiences. . . .
Write a letter expressing how your experiences have had a profound effect on
certain values/beliefs you once shared.[5]

PURPOSE: THE GROWTH OF THE STUDENT. A writing assignment
is also part of a student's personal experience and occurs at a particular moment in his or her life. We need to plan our assignments so that they will
accommodate our students at this moment in their life experience.

A good assignment should offer the opportunity to practice skills students
have already learned, but to use them on material that is in some way new
and demanding. The best assignments thus offer both comfort and challenge.

Accommodating a Variety of Growth Stages.   Because our students
are at a variety of stages of intellectual growth, ability, and interest, we must
take care to construct assignments assessable to each of them. How? One
good way is to offer a variety of choices for each assignment. Students then
are free to select the topic that interests them at a level appropriate to them.
Alternatively, we might provide a single assignment that can be carried out
in a number of acceptable ways.

For example, an especially able or experienced student or class might respond best to the broadly independent assignment,

> Write a paper in which you show how Milton "justif[ies] the ways of God to
> man" in *Paradise Lost.*

But though an assignment such as this might be ideal for the gifted, most of
our students would flounder without more explicit guidance. For these students we might add suggestions of how they could accomplish the task:

> . . . You may wish to begin by summarizing the main points of Milton's
> argument as he presents them in the dialogue between God and the Son in
> Book III, and then show how Milton demonstrates and supports this argu-
> ment dramatically in the selections we have read from the epic.

To offer more specificity and variety we might also add:

> . . . To do so, you might select one of the following of Milton's techniques
> or a comparable method of your own choosing:
>
> • Milton's characterization of Satan, the deteriorating fallen angel
> • His characterization of Adam or of Eve
> • Milton's presentation of the relationship between Adam and Eve
> • Milton's use of a specific metaphoric structure
> • Milton's handling of his material as demonstrated by your analysis of an
>   especially significant passage or set of passages.

To engage the student more personally, we might also want to add another
option:

. . . An optional conclusion to your paper: How does Milton's seventeenth-century line of thought hold up when viewed from the perspective of your own twentieth-century values? If you would like to, add a conclusion expressing your answer to this question.

Rhetorical Goals

An important part of drafting the assignment is dependent upon the sort of paper we envisage. How can we help our students achieve it? How much guidance should we offer in phrasing an assignment? How important is it for the assignment to suggest a rhetorical context by providing information on audience, mode, or purpose?

RHETORICAL CONTEXT IN ASSIGNMENT DESIGN. When we seek scholarly guidance to help determine how firmly we want to root an assignment in a specific rhetorical context, we again run into conflicting views. And although there is less scholarly disagreement here than we found regarding the value of teacher-made assignments, the research results are certainly at variance with the widely accepted opinion incorporated in many student textbooks.

Although many textbooks work from the assumption that a good assignment must always specify audience, mode, and purpose, there are, in researcher G. Brossell's words, "grounds for questioning the presumed superiority of full rhetorical specification in essay topics."[6] Researchers who have controlled assignments for audience or mode have found no significant difference in the quality of the writing produced when these components are suggested and when they are not.

Audience Specification Questioned. In fact, all of the several studies that Hillocks reviews demonstrate that assignments with no specified audience (other than the teacher-grader) produce papers at least as good as comparable papers based on assignments that set up an audience—and often even better.[7]

Students appear to reject the semifalseness of setups with simulated audiences. For example, when P. Woodworth and C. Keech compared essays describing a personal experience written in any form they chose, with those written for an imagined "someone who is about to experience the activity for the first time" (63), the unspecified set were better. Nevertheless, a projected *real* audience may well be an effective incentive. For instance, a third set of the Woodworth and Keech papers, written by students who were assured that the audience projected for the assignment would actually be sent the essays, received the highest ratings. (See also page 551 for a discussion of successful assignments that are designed to be "published" or shared with a real audience.)

Mode Specification Questioned.   Specifying mode in assignments is also highly questionable. It is, of course, necessary for our students to be conscious of the genre we ask them to write in, whether personal narrative, rhetorical analysis, short story, or whatever. But though the classic topics or places of invention—definition, comparison, cause and effect, and the others now rather unhistorically called "modes of rhetorical discourse"—offer a plausible schema for diversifying assignments, I cannot recommend asking students to write "a definition theme, "a comparison-and-contrast paragraph," "a classification theme," or "an example paragraph."

Despite the neatness of such mode assignments, they demand making distinctions we cannot plausibly demonstrate. Students ask, with some justice, how can a person write a definition except by means of classification, analysis, example, or comparing and contrasting? How can one compare and contrast without using examples? More important, when students try to find paragraphs (or essays) that exemplify a single method of development throughout—other than the carefully choosen sample ones given in their textbooks—they have sparse success. Very few unmixed paragraphs (never mind essays) exist in professional writing, as research has demonstrated.[8]

And who among us, outside the English classroom, ever thought to herself or himself when sitting down to write, "I think I'll write some description today." As Stephen and Susan Judy put it, "The modal approach falsifies the way writers write" (47).

Purpose Specification Often Essential.   No writer can write well without a conscious purpose. Just how much of this purpose we should infuse specifically in our assignment is a delicate question. How we phrase the assignment can point the way clearly when we feel our students need a road map or can leave plenty of room for experimentation when we feel that our students need some freedom.

ROAD-MAP ASSIGNMENTS.   The single most prevalent and formidable problem in the papers of inexperienced writers is lack of focus. Road-map assignments can help students solve this problem. If, for example, we hope our students will write an expository theme with a point that is clear to the reader and supported persuasively, then we should phrase our assignment in a way that elicits such a paper. For instance:

> Write a brief essay explaining what you think poet So-and-so is getting at in "Such-and-Such" a poem. Support your interpretation with direct references to the poem. You may wish to pay close attention to So-and-so's use of metaphor.

Help with Focus.   If clear focus is our aim, then we should phrase the assignment so as to lead students to potential organizing ideas or working theses. For example:

> Professor X explains her position on the subject we have been studying in the quotation above. To what extent do you agree with it? Support or take issue with X's view by citing ideas from other works we have read, from videos we have seen, or from your own experience.

Help with Structure. If we want our students to overcome difficulties with organization in a complex assignment, we might phrase the assignment so that it guides them tactfully step by step into a structure for their papers. For example:

> Give your interpretation of what R. Author is saying in *Thus and So*, and explain it clearly for your readers through a close-reading analysis of the above passage. Then show how Author works out this theme through the various twists in the plot.

> If you do not think that the above passage from *Thus and So* reflects its author's meaning, choose a comparable quotation as the basis for your paper.

Avoiding Comparison Quandaries. Comparison or contrast essay topics are especially useful because through them our students have the opportunity to explore at least two separate sets of ideas. We must take particular care in drafting and presenting such assignments, however, because students are often confused by them. We can teach our students rather easily to organize such papers by working through the complexities of the alternative structural strategies with them (see pages 95–96). The real problem, however, is how to encourage students to express an appropriate point—or, indeed, any point—in these comparison-based papers.

Many students adopt "A and B are different" as a working thesis for any such assignments: "High school and college certainly are different experiences," "Those who favor gun control and those who believe in the unlimited right to bear arms have differing opinions," "Although both Macbeth and Richard III are Shakespearian villains, they are different in many respects." Whatever. We need somehow to forestall such limited views by our phrasing or presenting of the assignment. Students need to understand that the fact of difference can go without saying: it is the *why?* or the *how?* that is interesting enough to warrant their own writing and their readers' efforts in reading a paper on the subject.

Students need to be pointed toward a possible conclusion that might come out of the comparison. For example:

> Write an essay explaining in what single major way the differences between high school and college life (or junior high and high school life) have affected you.

> Write a paper comparing *Macbeth* and *Richard III* and showing how Shakespeare used differing characterizations of the villain to motivate the action of the two plays.

Contrast the views of those who favor gun control with those who believe in the unlimited right to bear arms and demonstrate why, in your opinion, one side has the best of the argument.

ASSIGNMENT CAVEATS. We need to guard against creating nonfocused assignments. Yet sometimes because of our desire to offer enough stimulus for our students' thinking, or sometimes because we just haven't had the time to settle back and clarify our own thought, we throw together an assignment that is a potpourri of good ideas—a melange meant to inspire, but doomed to confuse our students. For example, the following is NOT a focused assignment:

> FAULTY Compare two of the plays we have read so as to show how the author's theme is derived from the conflict and is developed through the pattern of imagery and whatever other development you choose to include so that the distinction between comedy and tragedy becomes clear to the reader.

Focusing Our Drafting. How can we tell when we construct a nonfocused assignment? It's not always easy because sometimes such assignments read very well. What we can do, however, is to try out ourselves every new assignment we propose. If we can't take the time to try it out, we can at least think through how we might write it. If we have trouble uniting the strands of the assignment or figuring out a plan for writing from it, our students are bound to have even more difficulty, and we will need to modify the assignment.

We can provide the broad spectrum of ideas we want to include to help stimulate student thought by offering a series of assignment selections and the opportunity to interlock them if the student so chooses. Or we can offer the broad spectrum in the presentation discussion or brainstorming sessions that will introduce the assignment. But we really should not include such breadth within a single segment of an assignment. A well-focused paper is far more likely to come from a focused assignment.

A Caveat for Road-Map Assignments. On the other hand, we also have to guard against assignments that are too controlling. Pointed phrasing of our assignments can provide students with guidance, as we have seen, in writing procedure, in formulating a working thesis, and in structuring their support for that thesis. For the most part, our students need and appreciate this sort of help. Nevertheless, we should take care that procedure does not overwhelm content in our assignments and that the structural scaffolding and the precise road-mapping of our assignment frees rather than constricts our students' creative thought.

DESIGNING AN ASSIGNMENT: INVOLVING THE STUDENT. To determine successful strategies and characteristics of a successful writing assignment, I conducted a survey of those who are in the best position to judge such success: the instructors who assign them. I asked them to share with me their most successful assignments.[9] A number of these that seemed most useful are included in the following discussion or in the Assignment Sampler at the chapter's end.

Engaging Strategies

Though the survey assignments vary widely, the great majority of them (94%) involve strategies designed to engage the student in some personal way with the subject matter. Many include a method of confronting students with what is to be learned and forcing them to grapple with that material or skill and to experience its implications. The fact that 94% of these successful assignments required personal involvement is particularly impressive when we realize that fully 86.5% of the assignments called for expository writing, a kind of writing that is not inherently personal.

Let us examine some of these assignment strategies. Although we may feel that some of the assignments exemplified are not relevant to our individual courses, we can perhaps derive from these successful assignments some useful techniques for engaging our own students.

ASSIGNMENTS FOR CREATIVE OR EXPRESSIVE WRITING. Some genres by their very nature engage writers. Few writers can remain aloof when composing creatively. Writing a poem, a story, or a play or composing personal narratives, letters, and journal entries are personal activities—and therefore personally involving—almost by definition. Some teachers even give their creative assignments a further personal touch. For example,

> **Photograph Poetry.** Both students and instructor bring to class photographs that have meaning for them. After the instructor points out significant details of his or her photograph, students jot down notes about their own and go on to write a poem about the picture. [David Schaafsma][10]

PERSONAL TOPICS AND APPROACHES. We can always expect to engage our students with an overtly personal topic. More than a quarter (25.5%) of the expository assignments submitted on the survey are about the students' life or involve them personally. Among them:

> **Family Problems.** Students identify a family problem they have some knowledge of and discuss it in terms of its causes and its consequences. [Thomas Whissen]

> **Ideal Love.** Students write a paper comparing and contrasting their ideal for a love relationship with that projected by TV advertising and programming, or their parents' ideal. [Michael Neuman]

Such assignments as these should touch a spark in a good number of our students. A word of caution though. In suggesting this sort of assignment, we should—despite their overall effectiveness—always allow alternative choices because some students become uncomfortable with such topics.[11]

Topics Concerning Student Life or Interests. Almost equally engaging—but without the problems posed for some students by truly personal subjects—are assignments involving topics of personal interest to most students. For example:

> **Campus Problems.** The class selects a problem on campus. The students are divided into groups and asked to brainstorm possible solutions to the problem before they write. [C. Russell]

Personal Response. Personal-reaction assignments offer an effective way for our students to respond to the works they study. These assignments enable students to explore the subtle insights of a work by relating them personally to it. For instance:

> **Booth's "Must Knowledge."** After reading Wayne Booth's "Is There Any Knowledge a Man Must Have," students evaluate their own educational goals and analyze them in terms of Booth's beliefs. [Linda Young]

> **Music Reactions.** Students write about their reactions to a musical selection, giving detailed description of images and feelings that occur to them at various parts of the composition. [Jack B. Fuesly]

EXPERIENTIAL OR DISCOVERY-BASED ASSIGNMENTS.

Perhaps the most effective assignments of all are those that engage students by involving them in figuring out data for themselves—and sometimes even in gathering the data. This method of learning, often referred to in this text as experiential or discovery-based—but also known as inquiry—is demonstrated clearly in Walter L. Bateman's *Open to Question: The Art of Teaching and Learning by Inquiry*, a book that includes some useful assignments as well. Bateman also provides the results of research that supports this mode of learning. Similarly, Hillocks's meta-analysis of pertinent research led him to conclude that inquiry assignments are "on the average nearly four times more effective than free writing and over two-and-a-half times more powerful than the traditional study of model pieces of writing" (249).[12]

Finding and Using Data. Respondents to the survey contributed a number of assignments in which students interact with a wide variety of stimuli or data. About 15% of the total are of this sort. They include writing from interviews of the elderly (for psychobiography), of Great Depression survivors (for a study of *Grapes of Wrath*), of friends (for sociological analysis and for philosophical analysis), and experiential interaction with such diverse stimuli as census data, television commercials, local places or events, philosophical syllogisms, and plagiarized papers. The following assignments are typical of this type:

> **Census Data.** In a census assignment, students find data related to given variables and list them in a brief table. Students then write a statement comparing their own assigned tract with that of the county and of the metropolitan area. [Robert D. Swartz]

> **Quaker Customs and Values on Campus.** Students work together on a survey of the fourteen Quaker colleges in the United States, to draw up a questionnaire on how much Quaker business procedure, worship, and social ideals figure in each campus's life. [Hugh Barbour]

In Someone Else's Moccasins. An interesting variation of discovery assignments are those that require writers to "walk a mile in someone else's moccasins." These rely primarily on simulations and, like Dona Hickey's voice assignment I summarized earlier, require students to immerse themselves in the material to be understood and written about. For example:

> **International Crises.** In class discussion students describe a number of crises and simulate them. Individual students are then assigned countries involved in a particular crisis and asked to write their country's stakes and likely behavior under the most likely contingencies in the crisis. [Edward Dew]

Simulations of this sort can also be remarkably imaginative, as, for instance, the following:

> **Becoming a Butterfly.** After studying Chuang Tzu, who could not tell whether there was a difference between being himself and being a butterfly, students are to imagine they are butterflies, so much so that they become butterflies. Then they write about whether or not they were able to do it. If they were, they write about how Chuang Tzu would explain the total transformation. If they were not, they write about how Chuang Tzu would explain why they were not able to. [Richard Yee]

Literary Moccasins. Some assignments carry this personal approach into literature. They require the student to identify with a character or the author and write (or reason) from that point of view. For instance:

> **Melville's "Bartleby."** After reading Melville's "Bartleby the Scrivener," students write a paragraph on what they would have done with or for Bartleby if they had been the narrator. [Michael Neuman]

> **Thoreau's Contemporary Evaluation.** Students write an essay about how Thoreau would evaluate present-day America. [Perry Lentz]

Decision-Requiring Assignments. Another sort of discovery assignment that engages the minds of our students are those that provide a piece of art, literature, or music, or a television program or movie as a source of data and require students to come to terms with it. Students can be asked to

- Evaluate
- Form an opinion about
- Analyze
- Justify or condemn
- Agree or disagree with
- Defend or take issue with
- Criticize or vindicate
- Contest, dispute, oppose
- Approve, consent, concur
- Respond to
- Propose alternatives to
- Or otherwise make decisions concerning it.

These terms all can be effective in setting up this sort of discovery assignment. The following examples are representative of this type:

> **Presidential Debate.** Students listen to a presidential debate, decide the winner, and write a one-page paper defending their decision. [Michael Neuman]

> **Joyce's *Portrait*.** In *Portrait of the Artist as a Young Man* Stephen Dedalus rejects his family, his country, and his church to find his own beliefs and way of life abroad. Students write a paper justifying or condemning his action. [D. W. Baker]

> **Problem of Evil.** Writing about the Holocaust, H. S. Kushner says, "I have to believe that the tears and prayers of the victims aroused God's compassion, but having given Man freedom to choose, including the freedom to choose to hurt his neighbor, there was nothing God could do to prevent it." Do you agree with the statement? Why? If you do agree, what are the main objections that could be brought against Kushner's position, and how would you respond to them? If you do not agree, what alternative would you propose, and how would you reply to the most crucial criticisms that could be brought against it? [Frederick Sontag]

Heuristics and Prewriting

The content of the assignment is what ultimately engages the student, as the assignments we have just looked at demonstrate, but many a successful assignment has the additional engaging quality of an effective heuristic to stimulate the writer's thought. Heuristics are techniques to help writers invent (in the Aristotelian sense) the ideas they need to write effectively.

An assignment that carries its own stimulation to the student's creative faculties has a head start toward success, as research confirms. Heuristics and other prewriting activities have been shown to improve student writing significantly. When a prewriting-suggestions variable was included in the research mix of Kahn and Johannessen's study, for example, the positive results were unmistakable. An impressed Hillocks comments:

[The assignment] which may come closest to helping students do their best work is that which provides suggestions for prewriting. (173)

SUCCESSFUL HEURISTIC STRATEGIES. Almost all of the successful assignments submitted to my survey include a heuristic component, either openly or implicitly. Almost 10% of the assignments contributed specify brainstorming. The rest were divided between strategies that relied upon internal stimuli—ways of bringing to consciousness thoughts and experiences stored in the students' memories or of stimulating their imaginations—and external stimuli: data, statistics, interviews, works of art or literature that get the creative juices flowing.

Brainstorming. When we introduce writing assignments to our classes, many of us include some sort of brainstorming activity as a matter of course. I found that many of the assignments submitted as "successful" particularly designate this exercise. The "Campus Problems" assignment summarized earlier is a good example. Another assignment the begins in brainstorming is the following simulation:

> **Space Capsule.** Students are informed about the *Voyager* spacecraft and the tape prepared by Dr. Carl Sagan and others. Students are then told that another solar system has been discovered and Earth nations are going to send a space probe to this solar system. The probe must contain information that will explain Earth to whoever is out there. The probe can contain one thirty-minute tape and one thirty-minute film. Students must plan the tape and film and write a formal essay about them. Before the actual writing, students throw out ideas, which are listed on the board. Students then make an outline format of their papers and go on to write. For extra credit or follow-up they may actually produce a tape or a script for a film. [Lauri Anderson]

Internal Stimuli. Other heuristics rely upon internal or external stimuli. Those that rely upon internal stimuli turn students inward to confront their own imaginations or thought processes. The Chinese Butterfly exercise discussed earlier embodies an especially effective use of internal stimuli. Most such heuristics, however, are either mnemonics that call up memories from which the students may invent their compositions or assignments that direct students to delve into, examine, or confront their basic values or goals. Typical among them is the following, which combines both strategies:

> **Childhood Experiences.** Students pick one or more childhood experiences and explain how these experiences helped shape their attitudes toward people of another race, religion, or politics. [D. W. Baker]

External Stimuli. Many kinds of good assignments begin with external stimuli. Sometimes the stimulus is as ephemeral as a word game:

Short Stories. The class is divided into three groups. Each group is given three words, such as *rock concert, grandmother,* and *mustard.* In five minutes, the students must make up a coherent story including the three words. The stories are presented to the class. [Clifford Hardie]

But usually the stimuli are more concrete. Almost all of the inquiry-method assignments I discussed earlier, for example, begin with a concrete external impetus. Students are both engaged and stimulated creatively by conducting interesting interviews or interacting with various data or statistics or art, music, theatre, movies, or written literature—or photographs. The Photograph Poem assignment I discussed earlier offers one example. Another good instance is this comparative religion assignment:

Chinese Landscape. Students are given a picture of a Chinese landscape and asked to write an essay describing and evaluating as many characteristics of Chinese religion as the landscape suggests. They then theorize why black-and-white painting "drove out" color painting and became dominant in Chinese culture. [T. Canby Jones] [13]

THE SECRET OF SUCCESSFUL ASSIGNMENTS.   What has the survey told us about assignments? That to be successful assignments must reach students—where they live and where they think. That formulaic "fill in the blanks" type topics are unproductive. And that it is a good idea to implement the assignment with a heuristic, to nudge the writer's thinking processes and start the creative juices flowing.

Presenting an Assignment

Our presentation of an assignment often determines how well our students will succeed at the writing they are assigned.

INTRODUCING THE ASSIGNMENT TO THE CLASS.   Time spent in making sure our students thoroughly understand what they will be working on and in involving them in the project is well spent. At the very least we will want to reserve time for our own oral presentation of the assignment and a full-class discussion of it.

Through Class Discussion.   We will want to make sure each student sees his or her way with complete clarity. We need to listen carefully to the questions our students ask, and if our own concerns about the assignment do not arise, we might gently raise them.

Besides our own presentation and class discussion, we might want to encourage a brainstorming session, as a number of the survey assignments suggest. Or we might want the students to break into groups to figure out the assignment and to do the preliminaries, but making ourselves available in case further questions should arise.

Using Prewriting Activities and Heuristics.   Prewriting activities and
heuristics should rarely be included in the written assignment. To make these
activities—the sort suggested in the survey—work effectively, we need to take
whatever class time is necessary to be sure our students understand exactly
what they are to do, to let them begin, and, in the process, to promote enthusiasm for the project.

Planning to Publish or Share an Assignment

Another important way to engage our students with an assignment is to let
them know, right from the start, how the results will be published. Even if
an assignment appears rather cut and dried, students are challenged to more
lively efforts if they know the assignment will be presented to their classmates
or to some wider forum.

A number of the survey assignments specify how they would be shared.
See, for example, Hardie's Short Stories assignment above. Another instructor suggests a library research project on controversial topics that would culminate not only in a paper but also a debate. Publication can also be achieved
through a letter home:

> **Article Critique.** Students choose at least three articles from the class read-
> ings and, in a letter to a parent or a significant adult in their lives, comment
> on and critique the point of view expressed in their selections. A copy of the
> letter is actually sent. [Robert Keller]

SHARING CREATIVE WORK.   It is particularly important that creative
work be shared. Short stories and poems need to be read aloud and/or published in a class literary journal and submitted to the school literary magazine. Plays should be performed. Note, for example, the following assignment, which can be almost endlessly adapted to fit whatever our students
are studying:

> **Church History Drama.** Students compose a miniplay dramatizing an im-
> portant historical scene (Luther's Proclamation, the Council of Trent, the
> Bonheoffor Trial, for example) to be presented for the class during the appro-
> priate time. [Dennis Voskvil][14]

But whatever the assignment, knowing that others will read it or hear it is so
important to students that we should make an attempt to read aloud, publish
in print, or put on the board at least some of the results of every assignment;
at the very least, a few people—the members of a peer group, for instance—
should share the work with the writer.

The Teaching Strategies that summarizes Designing an Assignment
should be useful.

TEACHING STRATEGIES

Designing an Assignment

A good assignment:

1. should reflect our purposes. It should do so in a way our students can easily deduce. It is usually a good idea to share our purpose with the students when we introduce the assignment.
2. should be clear. After reading an assignment, students should know exactly what they are expected to do.
3. should be brief, the briefer the better. The assignment should provide enough substantive detail for clarity and enough process detail to guide those students who need guidance, but not so much in either case as to restrict our students' imagination or their thought.
4. should be focused. An elaborate, diffuse assignment causes nothing but confusion. And whatever process details we choose to provide should also be focused. Students find theoretical discussions in assignments confusing. A few, sparsely worded, ordered steps should be sufficient.
5. should imaginatively and intellectually engage the student with the subject matter.

AN ASSIGNMENT SAMPLER

Every chapter in this text includes recommended assignments and exercises appropriate to the topic discussed. This section contains other assignments sent in by the surveyed instructors as well as some more suggested by teachers in books, articles, or interviews. I hope you find them helpful.[15]

Assignments for Creative Writing

- **Blob or Ork.** A mixed-media storytelling assignment at the junior high level, designed to stimulate the imagination and to enhance student skill in using precise and specific detail.

  Part 1: Students choose at least three crayons and, working privately, draw an alien creature. Only rule: It can't look human. Part 2: Teacher collects and redistributes alien pictures to other students, who then write a brief story about the creature. The story should make the creature live for the reader, but should not include purely descriptive details from the picture (such as red polka dots). Part 3: Then the stories are redistributed and a third student draws a picture from the story. [Norma Lane]
- **Sound Descriptions.** Students must describe the sound of a trumpet, clarinet, orchestra, or some other musical instrument or group. [Jack B. Fuesly]

- **Characterization and Dialogue.** Creative preparation for writing short stories or personal narratives.

    Exercise 1: Students try to capture in writing the details of the bodily movements, facial expressions, and so on, of classmates pantomiming a character in situations such as waiting in the principal's or dentist's anteroom, sitting on a the bench waiting to go into an important game, or walking down a dark street fearful of being followed.

    Exercise 2: Two students are given or invent conflict situations from which they develop and act out a dialogue with their audience supplying feedback. Then the class writes out a dialogue, including details about the appearance of the characters and the setting. [George Hillocks, Jr.]
- **Transitions and Foreshadowing.** Students are given a middle scene in a story around which they construct the rest, paying particular attention to foreshadowing, transitions, and other connecting threads. [David Phelps]

Inquiry Learning Assignments

- **The United Nations.** Students participate in a simulation dealing with the United Nations. The Security Council sessions are simulated and the students take active part in the process of clarifying and advocating the various positions within the conflicts put before them, and eventually settle the conflict peacefully. Students write a reaction paper to the simulation. [Ali Alavi]
- **Casework on Issues.** Students "examine a set of cases describing incidents of various kinds: drug abuse, homicide, divorce, or other less traumatic problems. They . . . generalize about the set of cases and support those generalizations from the data available. Working in small groups, they . . . formulate recommendations for the prevention of such problems and develop several arguments in favor of their recommendations." From these preliminaries they write their papers. [George Hillocks, Jr.]
- **Target Audience.** Students choose a magazine from a list and examine two or three issues. They then write a paper identifying the magazine's target audience in terms of income, social class, political and social values, education, religion, age, sex, interests, anxieties, attitudes, recreational habits, and so on, supporting their conclusion with specific examples from the magazines. [Ernest Fontana]
- **War Movies.** From a list of war movies (1949–1965) students select three and write an essay concerning such things as how the movies look at the act of war and what their attitude toward violence and killing is. [Ron Thronson]
- **Almanac Assignment.** Students address a central question about a fact from *Harper's Index*—or another almanac. They discuss the issues and implications of that fact, based on the question and, having explored answers to that question, argue for or against a particular answer. Examples of useful facts:

    —Silicone breast implant operations performed in the U.S. in 1986: 115,000

    —Percentage increase in the number of U.S. millionaires since 1980: 145%

    —Percentage of Japanese with IQs above 130: 10%; Americans: 2%

    —Percentage of American women who acknowledge that they wear uncomfortable shoes because they look good: 45%

    —Percentage of American 5th graders who report being in love: 39%

—Percentage of Americans who own running shoes but don't run: 70%

—Percentage of executive men who are single or divorced: 4%; percentage of executive women who are: 52%

—Budget per episode of "Miami Vice": $1,500,00; annual budget of the (real) Miami vice squad: $1,161,741.

[Brenda Jo Brueggemann]

- **Dominant Impressions.** A class experiences a place together (after a field trip, perhaps) and then makes up a joint list of some forty to fifty sensory details gathered at the site. Each student must decide what was his or her dominant impression of the place and then choose the details and an arrangement that will convey that impression to the reader. [Donald Murray]

Assignments That Help Students to Explore Their Values

- **Charity.** Students write a paper explaining whether helping a person in need is a moral obligation or a charitable service "above and beyond the call of duty." [Michael Neuman]
- **Conscientious Objectors:** To Be or Not to Be. Students are asked to write a paper discussing whether or not they feel it takes more courage to join the armed forces or to be a conscientious objector in a time of war. [D. W. Baker]
- **Getting What You Want.** Students explain the meaning of the following quotation: "In this world there are only two tragedies. One is not getting what one wants; the other is getting it." In writing their papers, students describe a situation in their own lives or in the life of someone else they know that would illustrate the quotation and comment on the writer's insight into human nature. [John O. White]
- **Love's Meaning.** Students write on "What is the difference between 'love' and 'like'?" [Sheila Murphy]
- **Nice Guys.** Students write a paper applying Leo Durocher's famous maxim, "Nice guys finish last," to life, and determining the extent to which it is true. [Michael Neumann]
- **Personal Values.** Students defend a value they hold by contrasting it with its opposite. [Thomas Whissen]
- **Plagiarism.** Students are given two papers, one of which is possibly "borrowed" from the other. Students pretend to be the assistant dean, to whom the professor comes with these two papers. The assistant dean has to decide what to do about the problem and write a letter of recommendation to the dean. The papers are not a word-for-word copy, and the second paper was written by a student who came to the school after the writer of the first paper had graduated. [Charles A. McLaughlin]
- **Education.** Students explain the implications of G. B. Shaw's comment that the only time his education was interrupted was when he was in school and discuss the extent to which they agree or disagree with his premise, supporting their observations with examples from their own experience. [John O. White]
- **Utopian Values.** Students construct a utopia based upon their personal values. They must deal with at least the following issues: size, location, private property, technology, government, civil liberties, system existence and survival in a world of

states of different types, feasibility, and how their utopia is better than existing societies. [Gary R. Johnson; also Stanley Blum]

- **Values Compared.** Students explain the important characteristics, attitudes, and values they share with their classmates and which ones make them different from their classmates. [Michael Neuman]

Assignments on Reading

- **Student Questions.** Students develop a question concerning some passage or point not understood in the assigned readings; or they develop a question concerning a basic assumption of the author or some notion they wish to propose. They write a paper in an attempt to answer their question. [Frederick Sontag]
- **Novel, Play into Movie.** Having read a work and then viewed the movie upon which it is based, students answer the following questions in a well-organized paper: (1) what characters, events, and themes were more vividly presented in the dramatic version than in the book? and (2) what changes would they have made in the production to make the work more effective if they were the director? [James Cool]
- **Poetry Revision.** Students are given two versions of a single poem—for example, by Wordsworth or by Frost. After studying both versions, they write a coherent essay on the effect of the revisions the poet made. [Respondent prefers anonymity]
- **Shakespeare's *Henry IV*.** After reading *Henry IV, Part 1*, students write a theme on the issue of "honor" and/or the issue of pragmatism, expediency, the "end justifying the means" in the play. [Perry Lentz]
- **Booth's "Must Knowledge."** Having read Wayne Booth's "Is There Any Knowledge a Man Must Have," students have a choice of essay assignments: they can

  —pretend to be a student representative to a commission making recommendations for a new plan of education at their university and decide what path they would recommend as most effective for educating students.

  —develop the idea that Booth's program is outdated and ineffectual, or the argument that our society and education system is reducing students to something less than they are.

  —write about the limitations and strengths of the education system as they see it. [Linda Young]

- **"Edward."** After reading the ancient ballad "Edward," students write a paragraph on the extent to which the mother is responsible for what happens to the son. [Michael Neuman]
- **Hawthorne's "Goodman Brown."** After reading Hawthorne's "Young Goodman Brown," students write a paragraph on whether or not Brown made the correct moral choice in the forest and why he isn't rewarded for doing the will of God. [Michael Neuman]
- **Hemingway's "Hills."** After reading Hemingway's "Hills Like White Elephants," students write a paragraph advising the lovers and explaining the basis for their advice. [Michael Neuman]
- **O'Connor's "Guests."** After reading O'Connor's "Guests of the Nation," students write a paragraph explaining what they would have done with or for the prisoners if they had been the narrator, and on what principle they would have acted. [Michael Neuman]

- **Thoreau's Evaluation of the Writer's Life.** Students write an essay about how Thoreau would evaluate where they are living and what they are living for. [Perry Lentz]
- **Heroism in *The Red Badge of Courage*.** Students explain how Henry Fleming's experiences in combat demonstrate and define Crane's view of the nature of heroism. They then compare that view to their own. [D. W. Baker]

IDEAS FOR DISCUSSION OR ESSAY

1. Choose one of the assignments included in the chapter or in the Assignment Sampler at its conclusion and either write an essay responding to it or think through carefully how you might respond to it, writing at least a working thesis and a structural plan organizing your ideas to support it.
2. Critique three assignment suggestions from the Assignment Sampler. Specifically, how is each effective? In what specific ways ineffective?

   Rephrase the three assignment suggestions you have critiqued as assignments addressed to students, incorporating your improvements.
3. Design an assignment.

   a. Specify the classroom situation for which you will be composing your assignment: the grade, intellectual level or mix of the students, subject currently being studied, and the purpose of the assignment.
   b. Write an effective assignment to fit these specifications.
   c. Analyze your assignment to show why it is effective.

NOTES

The chapter-opening epigraph is from Stephen N. Judy and Susan J. Judy, *An Introduction to the Teaching of Writing* (New York: Wiley, 1981), 48.

1. Peter Elbow, *Writing Without Teachers* (New York: Oxford UP, 1973); Nancie Atwell, *In the Middle: Writing, Reading, and Learning with Adolescents* (Portsmouth: Boynton, 1987), 95; Donald Graves, *Writing: Teachers and Children at Work* (Exeter NH: Heineman, 1983), 120. See also Lil Brannon and C. H. Knoblauch, "On Students' Rights to Their Own Texts," *CCC* 33 (1982): 157–66. among others.

2. Thomas Newkirk, "The First Five Minutes: Setting the Agenda in a Writing Conference," *Writing and Response: Theory, Practice, and Research*, ed Chris M. Anson (Urbana: NCTE, 1989), 328.

3. This is the response of most teachers I have interviewed. And it is reflected in the chapters devoted to assignments in such texts as: Stephen N. Judy and Susan J. Judy, *An Introduction to The Teaching of Writing* (New York: Wiley, 1981), 47–69; Gerald H. Cox's "Designing Writing Assignments" in *Teaching Prose: A Guide for Writing Instructors*, eds. Fredric V. Bogel and Katherine K. Gottschalk (New York: Norton, 1984), 87–107; and Erika Lindemann, *A Rhetoric for Writing Teachers* 2nd ed. (New York: Oxford UP, 1987), 191–207; and Carolyn Boiarsky, for example, in a private conversation.

4. George Hillocks, Jr., *Research on Written Composition: New Directions for Teaching* (Urbana: NCRC & ERIC, 1986), 239; Hillocks also discusses Graves Research, which reached a contrary conclusion; see "Break the Welfare Cycle: Let Writers

Choose Their Topics," in *A Case Study Observing the Development of Primary Children's Composing, Spelling and Motor Behaviors during the Writing Process* (ERIC ED 218 653, 1981a): 388–94. Hillocks cautioned, however, that Graves' project was limited to children grades 1–4, while the other researchers worked with older students.

5. Dona Hickey, *Developing a Written Voice* (Mountain View, Cal.: Mayfield, 1993), 224.

6. G. Brossell, "Rhetorical Specification in Essay Examination Topics," *CE* 45 (1983): 172, found that papers written from assignments with the most complete statements about rhetorical contexts scored the lowest and were the shortest (165–73).

7. Hillocks, *Research*, 170–73, where he analyzes the following studies: P. Woodworth and C. Keech, *The Write Occasion: Collaborative Research Study No. 1* (ERIC Ed 198–534); J. S. Metviner, "Rhetorically Based and Rhetorically Deficient Writing: The Effect of Purpose and Audience on the Quality of Ninth-Grade Students' Compositions," *DAI* 41 (1981): 3977-A; and E. A. Kahn and L. R. Johanessen, "Does the Assignment Make a Difference" Four Variations of a Writing Task and Their Effects on Student Performance," (U of Chicago, unpub. ms.).

8. In one example, Carol Feiser Laque and Phyllis A. Sherwood conducted a survey of 100 paragraphs from *Saturday Review*, 100 from *English Journal*, and 100 from letters to the *Richmond Times Despatch* and discovered that 56% used no single textbook method; 23% used examples; other methods were but scantly represented in the remaining paragraphs; see their *A Laboratory Approach to Writing* (Urbana: NCTE, 1977), 40–42.

My own informal study confirms their results; almost 90% of the paragraphs I analyzed were of mixed development. See also Richard A. Meade and W. Geiger Ellis, "Paragraph Development in the Modern Age of Rhetoric," *EJ* 59 (70): 219–26.

9. Of the 200 information requests I sent out to department heads chosen at random from institutions of varying sizes and locations in the United States, 70 teachers—38 in English and 32 from other disciplines—responded with 171 successful assignments, 63% English (42% Composition; 21% Literature) and 37% from the other disciplines.

How valid is the judgment of my respondents? Fairly reliable, I should think. After all, they derive their judgment that an assignment has been successful from the reaction of the students who write the papers. And only those instructors who are interested in writing assignments or in composition pedagogy took the trouble to reply. Those who received my inquiry and had other interests either ignored it or, as a number of them wrote, passed on the survey to their colleagues who were especially involved in this area.

10. This and the other example assignments have been cut to their bare bones and, in most cases, do not do credit to the style and detail of the originals. See notes 13, 14, and 15 for a list of the courses and institutions of those who have shared their assignments with us.

11. See page 303 in this text; also see Mike Rose, "Remedial Writing Courses: A Critique and a Proposal" *CE* 45 (1983): 109–28.

12. Walter L. Bateman, *Open to Question: The Art of Teaching and Learning by Inquiry* (San Francisco: Jossey, 1990). See also Hillocks, *Research*, 180–86; 211–16.

13. The following lists the courses in which the exemplified student-engaging and heuristic-including assignments were given and the institutions of the respondents at the time of the survey in 1990:

Schaafsma, Creative Writing, Grand Valley State College, MI; Whissen, Composition, Wright State U., OH; Neuman, Writing on Issues and Values, Capital U. OH; Russell, Communications, Rio Hondo, CA; Young, Advanced Composition, California State U; Fuesly, Humanities, Imperial Valley College, CA; Swartz, Geography and Urban Planning, Wayne State U. MI; Barbour, Religion, Earlham College, IN; Dew, Politics, Fairfield U. CT; Yee, Richard, Philosophy, Holy Name College, Oakland, CA; Lentz, English, Kenyon College, OH; Baker, English, Wabash College, IN; Sontag, Philosophy of Religion, Paragon House Publishers, New York; Anderson, Language and Literature, Suomi College, MI; Hardie, Creative Writing, Wilmington College, OH; and Jones, Religion, Wilmington College, OH.

14. The following respondents are quoted in the "Publishing or Sharing" section: Keller, Sociology, Hanover, IN; and Voskvil, Church History, Hope College, MI.

15. The following lists by subject heading data on contributors not mentioned earlier. They include:

Creative Writing. Norma Lane, 9th grade, Woodward High School, Cincinnati, OH. Hillcocks, *Research*, 129. David S. Phelps, English, U of Southern California, CA.

Inquiry Learning. Ali Alavi, Political Science, Wilmington College, OH; Hillocks, *Research*, 130; Fontana, English, Xavier U, Cincinnati, OH; Thronson, Communications, Chapman College, CA; Brueggemann, "Signs and Numbers of the Times: *Harper's* 'Index' as an Essay Prompt," *CCC* 41 (1990): 220–222; and Murray, *Writing Exercises from "The Exercise Exchange,"* ed. Littleton Long (Urbana: NCTE, 1976), 115–19.

Personal Values. White, "Who Writes These Questions Anyway?" *CCC* 39 (1988): 231–235; McLaughlin, English, U of Connecticut, CT; Johnson, Social Sciences, Lake Superior State College, MI; and Stanley Blum, Colonel White High School, Dayton, OH.

Assignments on Reading. Cool, International Literature, Wilmington College, OH.

□ □ □   **15**

The Personal Teaching Approach

Gladly teche.
— Geoffrey Chaucer

□ □ □

Probably the most cogent formula for successful teaching is simply to be ourselves. That teachers have much in common with actors is true. Like performers, we have to entertain, we have to cajole our audience, and we have to project a role. What we must remember is that the character we are projecting is our own.

TO BE OURSELVES

The maxim "To be ourselves" has two important ramifications: first, that we project the image not of a gigantic godlike figure shrouded by thunder clouds, who proclaims the principles of good writing from some distant Mount Olympus, but rather that of a real human being, near enough to our students to share the turmoil and the triumphs associated with learning to write; and second, that in choosing the way we want to teach and in deciding which strategies would be best for us to adopt, in Mrs. Willie Loman's words, "attention must be paid" to that individual essence within us that makes us what we are.

Be Real, Be Human, Be Warm

We must not be afraid to show that we are human, nor to let our real personality emerge before our students. If we have a lively and humorous side, our students will respond to it with joy. If we also have a thoughtful, serious side, glimpses of it at the appropriate moments may lead our students into the exciting world of serious thought. And we must be especially sure not to hide from our students the active curious mind that probably led us into teaching to begin with, for our own curiosity can enflame theirs, and in curiosity all real learning begins. We should also feel free to let the way we talk and the way we are reveal to our students our enthusiasm for our subject and our fondness for them.

IT'S OKAY TO HAVE FEELINGS. It's good for our students to understand that we too are human; so we must not be afraid to show our own vulnerability, and that we have feelings too. In this respect, we can serve as significant role models. If we are real—and our students respect us—they have permission to be real too, to be in touch with their feelings and to express these feelings in their writing.

IT'S OKAY TO BE WRONG. Nor should we hesitate to acknowledge when we do not know the answer or when we have made a mistake. Part of our students' education is to realize that no human authority is infallible, for in this way they learn to question, challenge, and probe for themselves. Furthermore, when our students realize not only that we teachers can be wrong, but also that we will own up quickly to our error without worrying too much about it, they can gradually rid themselves of their terror of making a mistake and become able to leave their sanctuary of silence and venture an untested answer in class discussion or in their writing.

Then, too, we can teach our students a good deal from the way we handle a point about which we are unsure. When we freely say we don't know but that we will look it up (or ask a student volunteer to look it up) and when we (or the student volunteer) report back the answer, we are holding up the scholar's constructive approach to ignorance for them to emulate. When we discover that we are wrong, our willingness to correct the mistake also gives our students a behavior pattern worth following themselves. By saying we do not know something, we also profit in a quite practical way, for our admission of ignorance when it is the case strengthens our credibility with our students about the things we really know.

IT'S OKAY TO HAVE VALUES. As our students come to know us better, we should not be afraid to let our values be clearly known. As good teachers, we must, of course, be accepting of students whose values differ from our own and open to the discussion of such values. Still within our own class we can insist upon those values, such as kindness or honesty, that are truly important to us. If cheating, for instance, is something we really abhor, our students have a right to know. It has been my experience that when students are aware of their teacher's repugnance for cheating (to continue the example), and have developed an affection or respect for her or him, the instances of cheating decline. Similarly, when students understand their teacher's predilection for kind behavior, for instance, they tend to help the teacher create a classroom ambience in which compassion flourishes and sarcasm and rancor are spurned.

Our Relationship with Students

Perhaps we should include in this discussion a word or two of warning about the pitfalls inexperienced teachers sometimes can tumble into in their desire to win the respect of their students.

NOT TOO DISTANT.   On the one hand, when novice teachers try to protect themselves from their own quite natural feelings of insecurity by adopting a stance of cold formality and distant "perfection," they run the danger of losing their students' goodwill. Especially when this stance is accompanied by what the students see as an unduly repressive system of discipline or classroom structure, they may respond by disliking the teacher and the subject and resolving to do only that work which is necessary to get them through a disagreeable term.

NOT TOO CLOSE.   On the other hand, students are perhaps even more uncomfortable with teachers who try to adopt the manners and symbols of their students' age group and, in short, attempt to be their "pal." Besides the slight embarrassment students experience when even very young teachers make the inevitable slips that clearly demonstrate the cultural gap between their "generation" and that of the students themselves, our students have no need for us to be their pals because they already have pals in abundance. What they do need from us—and truly appreciate when they find it—is a warm, friendly teacher who really cares about them and about their learning. Despite some superficial resemblances between this kind of teacher and the "pal" teacher, the differences are immeasurably great and are instantly recognizable by our students.

STUDENT-CENTERED TEACHING

Corollary to a decision to be ourselves as teachers might be a resolve to recognize our students also as individual human beings, a resolve that has inevitable consequences upon our view of our work. For with it our purpose becomes not merely to teach writing, but rather to teach our students to write. The Student-Centered Teaching Strategies provide a list of techniques that may be helpful in implementing a student-centered writing classroom.

TEACHING STRATEGIES

Student-Centered Teaching

1. We should try to get to know our students as individuals and gain a solid perception of the way each of their minds works and of their characteristic turns of thought.

continued

continued

2. When we teach new material, we will probably want, as often as possible, to elicit it from our students rather than to present it in lecture form. Often we would want to let them inductively or experientially discover the conclusions for themselves.

3. In class discussion, we would want to encourage student interaction rather than the strictly Socratic method of teacher question/student answer/teacher response, in which—to change the metaphor—the ball always has to be returned to the server before it can go anywhere else.

   One way to accomplish this interaction is for us not to concentrate our gaze exclusively on the student who is answering, but also to watch the faces of the other students to encourage a latent response from them before—or instead of—making our own.

4. Similarly, we should try to avoid repeating or rephrasing our students' replies, for this practice reinforces a teacher/student/teacher response pattern. If we feel the reply could not be heard or understood, we might instead ask a student to repeat it for the others.

5. From time to time we might share the writing task with our students, doing the assignment right along with them. We might also empathize with their writing difficulties by sharing memories of our own writing struggles.

6. We should be sure that our students fully understand our grading system. But in discussing it with them, we must be careful not to leave the impression that a good grade is what we value most. There must not be any question in our students' minds that their learning to write well is what really matters to us and that we consider grades important only as a tool to that end.

7. We should make ourselves available to our students and let them know that they are welcome to come to us for conferences. Because some students find it truly difficult to approach their teacher to ask for the help they need, we should go out of our way to let them know that we would really like to see them and plan our schedule accordingly.

8. Implicit in our manner and in our speech should be not only our enthusiasm for the art of writing and our belief in its importance, but also our firm conviction that each of our students truly can learn to do it.

OUR INDIVIDUAL TEACHING STYLES

The injunction "To be ourselves" also has a more personal and individual meaning. Though all of us share a common humanity and warmth, we all express it in different ways. Since teaching is about as personal an activity as can be undertaken, this individuality must, of necessity, permeate our teaching style.

Discover What's Comfortable

We will therefore only teach our best in a manner with which we can feel comfortable. For instance, some of us like to teach in a classroom that is buzzing like a beehive with constructive (and often quite noisy) activity. Others of us are happiest in a room where there is a quiet serenity that promotes thoughtful understanding. Which is the better way to manage a classroom? The answer is, of course, that the classroom in which each of us feels most at home, most capable of teaching his or her best, is the right kind of classroom for us. Much good learning has taken place in classes having both of these kinds of ambience and also in classes with the many different kinds of atmospheres in between. But it is almost impossible for teachers to do outstanding work using techniques with which they are not compatible or strategies against which they inwardly rebel.

EXPERIMENT. Since we cannot really be sure of how most methods would work for us until we try them out, however, we might approach our teaching experimentally. We might become eclectic, ferreting out as many good ideas as we can and trying the ones that seem good to us and with which we think we can work comfortably.

In this book, I have assembled a collection of such ideas for us to adopt or reject or shape to our own teaching style, in the hope that we will be able to discover for ourselves the methods through which each of us personally can best succeed in teaching our students to write.

Works Cited

Allen, Paula Gunn. *The Sacred Hoop*. Boston: Beacon, 1992.

Allen, Virginia. "Teaching English as a Second Dialect." [Columbia] *Teachers College Record* 68 (1967): 355–70.

Allsburg, Chris Van. *The Mysteries of Harris Burdick*. Boston: Houghton, 1984.

Alpren, P. F. "Can Children Be Helped to Increase the Originality of Their Story Writing." *RTE* 7 (1973): 372–86.

Anson, Chris M., ed. *Writing and Response: Theory, Practice, and Research*. Urbana: NCTE, 1989.

Arbur, Rosemary. "The Student-Teacher Conference." *CCC* 28 (1977): 338–42.

Aristotle. *Rhetoric*. Trans. Lane Cooper. New York: Appleton, 1932.

Arnold, Lois V. "Writers' Cramp and Eyestrain—Are They Paying Off?" *EJ* 53 (1964): 10–15.

Arrington, Phillip. "Reflections on the Expository Principle." *CE* 54 (1992): 314–32.

Ash, I. O. "An Experimental Evaluation of the Stylistic Approach in Teaching Written Composition in the Junior High School." *Journal of Experimental Education* 4 (1935): 54–62.

Asker, W. "Does Knowledge of Formal Grammar Function?" *School and Society* 17 (1923): 109–11.

Atwell, Nancie. *In the Middle: Writing, Reading, and Learning with Adolescents*. Portsmouth, NH: Boynton, 1987.

Axelrod, Rise B., and Charles R. Cooper. *The St. Martin's Guide to Writing*. 2nd ed. New York: St. Martins, 1988.

Baker, Sheridan. *The Compleat Stylist*. New York: Crowell, 1966.

———. *The Practical Stylist*. 7th ed. New York: Harper, 1990.

Bantam, K., and G. Tutley. "The Effect of Peer-Evaluated Student Compositions on Writing Improvement." *English Record* 26 (1975): 64–69.

Bartholomae, David. "Inventing the University." *When a Writer Can't Write*, ed. Mike Rose. New York: Guilford, 1985: 134–65.

——— "Released into Language: Errors, Expectations, and the Legacy of Mina Shaughnessy." *The Territory of Language: Linguistics, Stylistics, and the Teaching of Composition* ed. Donald A. McQuade. Carbondale: U of Illinois P, 1986: 65–88.

Bartley, Diane E., and Robert L. Politzer. *Practice-Centered Teacher Training: Standard English for Speakers of Nonstandard Dialects, Language and the Teacher: A Series in Applied Linguistics.* Vol. 27. Philadelphia: Center for Curriculum Development, 1972.

Bateman, D. R., and F. J. Zidonis. *The Effect of a Study of Transformational Grammar on the Writing of Ninth and Tenth Graders: NCTE Research Report #6.* Urbana: NCTE, 1966.

Bateman, Walter R. *Open to Question: The Art of Teaching and Learning by Inquiry.* San Francisco: Jossey-Bass, 1990.

Bata, E. J. "A Study of the Relative Effectiveness of Marking Techniques on Junior College Freshman English Composition." *DAI* 34 (1973) 62-A.

Beach, R. "The Effects of Between-Draft Teacher Evaluation Versus Student Self-Evaluation on High School Students' Revising of Rough Drafts." *RTE* 13 (1979): 111–19.

Bean, Rita et al., eds. *Survival through Language: The Basics and Beyond.* Pittsburgh: Pittsburgh U, School of Education, 1977.

Beardsley, Monroe C. "Style and Good Style." *Reflections on High School English.* Ed. Gary Tate. Tulsa: U of Tulsa P, 1966.

Beaven, Mary H. "Individualized Goal Setting, Self-Evaluation, and Peer Evaluation." *Evaluating Writing: Describing, Measuring, Judging.* Eds. Charles R. Cooper and Lee Odell. Urbana: NCTE, 1977.

Bender, F. "A Study of Teacher and Peer Comments in the Revising Process of College Writers." *DAI,* 51 (1990): 02A.

Bernstein, Abraham. *Teaching English in High School.* New York: Random, 1966.

Bizzell, Patricia. "Beyond Anti-Foundationalism to Rhetorical Authority: Problems Defining 'Cultural Literacy.' " 52 *CE* (1990): 661–82.

Blatt, Elaine, and Jane Bergman. "Career Research—A Multi-Discipline Approach." *Community College Frontiers* 7 (1978): 15–19.

Bleich, David. *Readings and Feelings: An Introduction to Subjective Criticism.* New York: Oxford UP, 1975.

Blount, Nathan S. "Research on Teaching Literature, Language, and Composition." *Second Handbook of Research on Teaching.* Ed. Robert M. W. Travers. Chicago: Rand McNally, 1972.

Bogel, Fredric V. et al. *Teaching Prose: A Guide for Writing Instructors.* New York: Norton, 1984.

Boiarsky, Carolyn R. "Revision Phases." *Technical Writing: Contexts, Audiences, and Communities.* Boston: Allyn, 1993.

Bogel, Fredric V. et al., eds. *Teaching Prose: A Guide for Writing Instructors.* New York: Norton, 1984.

Booth, Wayne. "The Rhetorical Stance." *CCC* 14 (1963): 139–45.

Boraas, J. "Formal English Grammar and the Practical Mastery of English." Diss. U. of Minnesota, 1917.

Bork, Sally. "*EJ* Work-Shop: Composition Starters." *EJ* 62 (1973): 1284.

Bossone, Richard M. ed. *Teaching Basic English Courses.* New York: Van Nostrand, 1971.

Bousefield, W. A., B. H. Cohen, and J. G. Silva. "The Extension of Marbe's Law to the Recall of Stimulus Words." *American Journal of Psychology*, 69 (1956), 429–33.

Bowden, S. P. "The Effects of Formal, Traditional Grammar Study on the Writing Ability of Secondary School Students." *DAI* 40 (1979): 1389-A.

Brackbill, Yvonne et al. "Arousal Level in Neonates and Older Infants under Continuous Auditory Stimulation." *Journal of Experimental Child Psychology* 4 (1966): 178–88.

Braddock, Richard. "The Frequency and Placement of Topic Sentences in Expository Prose." *RTE* 3 (1974): 287–302.

Braddock, Richard, Richard Lloyd-Jones, and Lowell Schoer. *Research in Written Composition*. Urbana: NCTE, 1963.

Bradshaw, James R. "An Experimental Study Comparing a Traditional Teacher Lecture Method with an Individualized Method of Instruction Business Report Writing." *DAI* 35 (1974): 3382A. Brigham Young U.

Brannon, Lil and C. H. Knoblauch, "On Students' Rights to Their Own Texts." *CCC* 33 (1982): 157–66.

Bressler, Charles E. *Literary Criticism: An Introduction to Theory and Practice*. Englewood Cliffs, NJ: Prentice, 1994.

Briand, Paul. "Turned On: Multi Media and Advanced Composition." *CCC* 21 (1970): 167–69.

Bridges, Charles W., Toni A. Lopez, Ronald F. Lunsford, eds. *Training the New Teacher of College Composition*. Urbana: NCTE, 1986.

Bridwell, Lillian S. "Revising Strategies in Twelfth Grade Students' Transactional Writing." *RTE* 14 1980: 197–222.

Briggs, T. H. "Formal English Grammar as a Discipline." [Columbia] *Teachers College Record* 14 (1913): 1–93.

Brooke, Robert. "Lacan, Transference, and Writing Instruction." *CE* 49 (1987): 679–91.

Brooks, Cleanth, Robert Penn Warren, and John Thibout Purser. *An Approach to Literature*. 4th ed. New York: Appleton, 1964.

Brophy, Jere E. "Teacher Praise: A Functional Analysis." *RER* 5 (1981): 5–32.

Brophy, Jere E., and Thomas L. Good. *Teacher-Student Relationships: Causes and Consequences*. New York: Holt, 1974.

Brossell, C. "Rhetorical Specification in Essay Examination Topics." *CE* 45 (1983): 165–73.

Brown, Clarence A., and Robert Zoellner. *The Strategy of Composition: A Rhetoric with Readings*. New York: Ronald, 1968.

Bruggeman, Brenda Jo. "Signs and Numbers of the Times: *Harper's* 'Index' as an Essay Prompt." *CCC* 41 (1990): 220–222.

Budz, Judith, and Terry Grabar. "Tutorial versus Classroom in Freshman English." *CE* 37 (1976): 654–56.

Burke, Kenneth. *Counter-Statement*. 3rd ed. Berkeley: U of California P, 1968.

Burke, Virginia M. "A Candid Opinion on Lay Readers." *EJ* 50 (1961): 158–64.

Burton, Dwight L., and Lois V. Arnold. *Effects of Frequency of Writing and Intensity of Teacher Evaluation upon High School Students' Performance in Written Composition*. Tallahassee: Florida State UP 1963.

Burton, Dwight L., and Jack S. Simmons, eds. *Teaching English in Today's High Schools: Selected Readings*. 2nd ed. New York: Holt, 1970.

Burton, Katherine. "Citing Borrowed Material." *Writing Exercises from "The Exercise Exchange*." ed. Littleton Long. Urbana: NCTE, 1976, 121–23.

Butterfield, Clair J. "The Effect of a Knowledge of Certain Grammatical Elements on the Acquisition and Retention of Related Punctuation Skills." Diss. U. of Iowa, 1945.

Calkins, L. M. "Case Study of a Nine Year Old Writer." *A Case Study Observing the Development of Primary Children's Composing, Spelling, and Motor Behaviors during the Writing Process, Final Report.* Ed. Donald H. Graves. Durham: U New Hampshire P, 1981.

Capossela, Toni-Lee. "Students as Sociolinguists: Getting Real Research from Freshman Writers." 42 *CCC* (1991): 75–79.

Carnecelli, Thomas. "The Writing Conference: A One-to-One Conversation." *Eight Approaches to Teaching Composition.* Eds. Timothy Donovan and Ben McClelland. Urbana: NCTE, 1980, 101–32.

Catherwood, Catherine. "A Study of Relationships between a Knowledge of Rules and Ability to Correct Grammatical Errors and between Identification of Sentences and Knowledge of Subject and Predicate." MA Thesis, U of Minnesota.

Christensen, Francis. *Notes toward a New Rhetoric: Nine Essays for Teachers.* 2nd ed. New York: Harper, 1978.

Clark, J. D. "A Four-Year Study of Freshman English." *EJ* (College Edition) 24 (1935).

Clopper, R. R. "A Study of Contract Correcting as a Means of Significantly Increasing Writing and English Skills." *DA* 27 (1967): 3769-A.

Clueth, Robert and Lee Ahlborn. *Effective English Prose: Writing for Meaning/Reading for Style.* Syracuse: Singer, 1965.

Coleman, D. R. "A Comparison between the Relative Effectiveness of Marginal-Interlinear-Terminal Commentary and of Audiotaped Commentary in Responding to English Compositions." *DAI* 33 (1973): 3945-A.

Coles, William, and James Vopat, eds. *What Makes Writing Good.* Lexington, Mass.: Heath, 1985.

Collignon, Joseph. "Why Leroy Can't Write." *CE* 39 (1978): 852–59.

Combs, Warren E. "Further Effects and Implications of Sentence-Combining Practice on Writing Ability." *RTE* 10 (1976): 137–49.

——. "Some Further Effects and Implications of Sentence-Combining Exercises for the Secondary Language Arts Curriculum." Ph.D. Diss. U of Minnesota, 1975.

Confrey, A. "Comments Made by Instructors on Student Themes." *Catholic Educational Digest* 24 (1927): 335–40.

Connors, Robert J. "The Rise and Fall of the Modes of Discourse." *CCC* 32 (1981): 444–55.

Connors, Robert J. and Andrea Lumsford, "Frequency of Formal Errors in Current College Writing, or Ma and Pa Kettle Do Research." *CCC* 39 (1988): 398.

Coon, Anne C. "Using Ethical Questions to Develop Autonomy in Student Researchers." *CCC* 40 (1989): 85–89.

Cooper, Charles R. "Holistic Evaluation of Writing." *Evaluative Writing: Describing, Measuring, Judging.* Eds. Charles R. Cooper and Lee Odell. Urbana: NCTE, 1977.

——. "Research Roundup: Oral and Written Composition." *EJ* 64 (1975): 72–75.

——. "Responding to Student Writing." *The Writing Processes of Students.* Eds. W.

Petty and P. J. Price. Buffalo: SUNY at Buffalo, Dept of Curriculum and Instruction, 1975.

Cooper, Charles R. and Lee Odell, eds. *Evaluating Writing: Describing, Measuring, Judging.* Urbana: NCTE, 1977.

———. *Research on Composing: Points of Departure.* Urbana: NCTE, 1978.

Cooper, H. *"Intervening and Expectation Communication: A Follow-Up Study to the "Personal Control" Study.* Hamilton, NY: Colgate UP, 1976.

Corbett, Edward P. J. *Classical Rhetoric for the Modern Student.* 3rd ed. New York: Oxford UP, 1990.

———. "The Theory and Practice of Imitation and Classical Rhetoric." *CCC* (1971): 243–50.

Cox, Beverly E., Timothy Shanahan, and Margaret B. Tinzmann, "Children's Knowledge of Organization, Cohesion, and Voice in Written Exposition." *RTE* 25 (1991): 179–212.

Cox, Gerald H. "Designing Writing Assignments." *Teaching Prose: A Guide for Writing Instructor.* Eds. Fredric V. Bogel, et al. New York: Norton, 1984.

Crabb, Alfred L., Jr. "Describing a Face." *Writing Exercises from the Exercise Exchange.* Ed. Littleton Long. Urbana: NCTE, 1976.

Crawford, C. C., and Madie M. Royer. "Oral Drill versus Grammar Study." *Elementary School Journal* 36 (1935): 116–19.

Crews, Frederic. *The Random House Handbook.* New York: Random, 1974.

Crowley, Sharon. *A Teacher's Introduction to Deconstruction.* Urbana: NCTE, 1989.

Cutright, Prudence. "A Comparison of Methods of Securing Correct Language Usage." *Elementary School Journal* 34 (1934): 681–90.

D'Souza, Dinesh. "Pied Pipers of Relativism Reverse Course." *Wall Street Journal* 27 July 1993.

Daiker, Donald. "Learning to Praise." *Writing and Response: Theory, Practice, and Research.* Ed. Chris M. Anson. Urbana: NCTE, 1989.

Dakelman, Beth C. "Think Tank and Mind Transportation: Teaching Creative Writing." *CE* 62 (1973): 1272–73.

Daly, John A., and Michael Miller. "The Empirical Development of an Instrument to Measure Writing Apprehension." *RTE* 9 (1975): 242–49.

———. "Further Studies in Writing Apprehension: SAT Scores, Success Expectations, Willingness to Take Advanced Courses and Sex Differences." *RTE* 9 (1975): 250–56.

Davis, M. W. "A Comparative Analysis of Sentences Written by Eighth Grade Students Instructed in Transformational-Generative Grammar and Traditional Grammar." *DA* 28 (1967): 213-A.

DeBeaugrande, Robert. "Forward to the Basics: Getting Down to Grammar." *CCC* 35 (1984): 362–367.

Deese, James, and Kaufman R. A. "Serial Effects in recall of Unorganized and Sequentially Organized Verbal Material." *JEP* 54 (1957): 180–87.

Deese, James and Steward H. Hulse. *The Psychology of Learning.* 3rd ed. New York: McGraw-Hill, 1967.

Dickie, Ollie T. "Turning the First Stone of Research." *EJ* 48 (1959): 36–42.

Diedenhefer, John Paul. "An Experiment in Grading Papers." *CCC* 27 (1976): 406–07.

Diederich, Paul B. "Grading and Measuring." *Teaching Basic English Courses.* Ed. Richard M. Bossone. New York: Van Nostrand, Reinhold, 1971.

———. "In Praise of Praise." *NEA Journal* 52 (1963): 58.

——. *Measuring Growth in English.* Urbana: NCTE, 1974.

——. "The Rutgers Plan for Cutting Class Size in Two." *EJ* 44 (1960): 229–36.

Doherty, Matthew. "The Missing Link: Rewriting." *EJ*, 54 (1965): 848–850.

Daiker, Donald, Andrew Kerek, and Max Morenberg, eds. *Sentence Combining and the Teaching of Writing.* Akron: U of Akron P, 1979.

——. *The Writer's Options: Combining to Composing,* 5th ed. New York: Harper, 1994.

Donovan, Timothy, and Ben McClelland, eds. *Eight Approaches to Teaching Composition.* Urbana: NCTE, 1980.

Dressell, Paul, John Schmid, Jr., and Gerald Kincaid, "The Effect of Writing Frequency upon Essay-Type Writing Proficiency at the College Level." *JER* 46 (1952): 285–93.

Dunning, Donald J. "A Derivative Approach to Creative Writing." *EJ* 54 (1965): 845–47.

Effros, C. "An Experimental Study of the Effects of Guided Revision and Delayed Grades in Writing Proficiency of College Freshmen." Final Report. West Haven Conn.: New Haven U, 1973. ED 079-764.

Elbow, Peter. "Closing My Eyes as I Speak: An Argument for Ignoring Audience." *CE* 49 (1987): 50–69.

——. "Reflections on Academic Discourse: How it Relates to Freshmen and Colleagues." *CE* 53 (1991): 135–55.

——. *Writing Without Teachers.* New York: Oxford UP, 1975.

Elbow, Peter, and Pat Belanoff, *Starting and Responding.* New York: Random, 1989.

Eliot, T. S. *Selected Essays.* New York: Harcourt, 1932.

Elley, W. B., et al. "The Role of Grammar in the Secondary School English Curriculum." *RTE* 10 (1976): 5–17.

English, Hubert M. "Linguistic Theory as an Aid to Invention." *CCC* 15 (1964): 136–40.

Faigley, Lester. *Fragments of Rationality: Postmodernity and the Subject of Composition.* Pittsburgh: U of Pittsburgh P, 1992.

——. "Judging Writing, Judging Selves." *CCC* 40 (1989): 404–05.

——. "Response to Bruce Holland." *CCC* 42 (1991): 89–90.

Faigley, Lester, and Stephen Witte. "Analyzing Revision." *CCC* 32 (1981): 400–14.

Fenner, James L. "Can Average Students Write? *EJ* 56 (1967): 725–38.

Fischer, Kenneth David. "An Investigation to Determine if Selected Exercises in Sentence-Combining Can Improve Reading and Writing." Ed.D. diss. Indiana U, 1973.

Fisher, Lester, and Donald Murray, "Perhaps the Professor Should Cut Class." *CE* 35 (1973): 169–73.

Fitzgerald, J., and L. R. Markham, "Teaching Children about Revision in Writing." *Cognition and Instruction* 4 (1987): 3–24.

Flanders, Ned. "Personal-Social Anxiety as a Factor in Experimental Learning Situations" *JER* 55 (1951): 100–10.

Flower, Linda. "Cognition, Context, and Theory Building." *CCC* 40 (1989): 282–311.

——. "Negotiating Academic Discourse." *Reading-to-Write Report No. 10.* Technical Report No. 29. Berkeley: Center for the Study of Writing at U of California, Berkeley and Carnegie Mellon.

——. "Writer-Based Prose: A Cognitive Basis for Problems in Writing." *CE* 41 (1979): 19–37.

Flower, Linda, and John R. Hayes et al, "Detection, Diagnosis, and the Strategies of Revision." *CCC* 36 (1986): 16–55.

——. "Problem-Solving Strategies and the Writing Process." *CE* 39 (1977): 450.

Follman, John C. and James A. Anderson, "An Investigation of the Reliability of Five Procedures for Grading English Themes." *RTE* 1 (1967): 190–200.

Ford, Bob W. "The Effects of Peer Editing/Grading on the Grammar-Usage and Theme Composition Ability of College Freshmen." *DAI* 33 (1973): 6087A. Oklahoma U.

Fowler, Mary Elizabeth. *Teaching Language, Composition, and Literature.* New York: McGraw, 1965.

Franklin, Phyllis, ed. *Profession 88.* New York: MLA, 1988.

Freedman, Sarah et al, eds. *Response to Student Writing.* Urbana: NCTE, 1987.

Fritts, Mildred. "The Effects of Individual Teacher Conferences on the Writing Achievement and Self-Concept of Developmental Junior College Writing Students." *DAI* 37 (1977): 4185A. ED138 988.

Frogner, Ellen. "Grammar Approach versus Thought Approach in Teaching Sentence Structure." *EJ* 28 (1939): 518–26.

Fry, D. J. W. "The Effects of Transformational Grammar upon the Writing Performance of Students of Low Socio-Economic Backgrounds." *DAI* 32 (1972): 4835-A.

Fulwiler, Toby. *College Writing.* Glenview: Scott, 1988.

Gale, I. F. "An Experimental Study of Two Fifth-Grade Language-Arts Programs: An Analysis of the Writing of Children Taught Linguistic Grammars Compared to Those Taught Traditional Grammar." *DA* 28 (1968): 4156-A.

Gates, Allan. "A Study of the Effects of Work Undertaken in an Independent Learning Center by Marginal Students at Marshalltown Community College." *DAI* 37 (1977): 7002A.

Gates, Henry Louis. *Figures in Black: Words, Signs, and the "Racial" Self.* New York: Oxford UP, 1987.

——. *The Signifying Monkey: A Theory of Afro-American Literary Criticism.* New York: Oxford UP, 1988.

Gayle, Addison, Jr. *The Black Aesthetic.* New York: Doubleday, 1972.

Gee, Thomas C. "Students' Responses to Teacher Comments," *RTE* 6 (1972): 212–21.

Gerber, John C., ed. *The College Teaching of English.* New York: Appleton, 1965.

Getz, Howard G. *Paraprofessionals in the English Department.* Urbana: NCTE, 1972.

Gibson, Walker. "An Exercise in Prose Style." *Rhetoric: Theories for Application.* Ed. Robert W. Gorrell. New York: Oxford UP, 1970.

Gliserman, Martin. "An Act of Theft: Teaching Grammar." *CE* 39 (1978): 791–800.

Goddin, M. A. P. "A Comparison of the Effect on Student Achievement of a Generative Approach and a Traditional Approach to the Teaching of English Grammar at Grades Three and Seven." *DAI* 29 (1969): 3522-A.

Golden, Ruth I. *Improving Patterns of Language Usage.* Detroit: Wayne State UP, 1960.

Good, Thomas L., and Jere E. Brophy, *Educational Psychology: A Realistic Approach.* New York: Longman, 1990.

——. *Looking In Classrooms.* 4th ed. New York: Harper, 1987.

Good, Thomas L, H. Cooper, and S. Blakey, "Classroom Interaction as a Function of Teacher Expectations, Student Sex, and Time of Year." *JEP* 72 (1980): 378–385.

Goodman, Alberta D. J. "Utilization of Positive Feedback in a Classroom Environment of Acceptance to Promote Enhanced Learner Self-Concept and Improved Writer Performance." *DAI* 36 (1975): 6550A, U of Michigan.

Gordon Brossell, "Rhetorical Specification in Essay Examination Topics." *CE* 45 (1983): 165–73.

Gordon, Edward J., and Edward S. Noyes, eds. *Essays on the Teaching of English: Reports of the Yale Converences on the Teaching of English.* New York: Appleton, 1960.

Gorrell, Robert M. "Freshman Composition." *The College Teaching of English.* Ed. John C. Gerber. New York: Appleton, 1965.

— — —, ed. *Rhetoric: Theories for Application.* New York: Oxford UP, 1970.

Grady, Michael. "A Technique for Theme Correction." *Classroom Practices in Teaching English*, Fifth Report. Urbana: NCTE, 1967.

Grasso, Mary Ellen. "The Research Paper: Life Centered." *CE* 40 (1978): 83–86.

Graves, Donald. "Break the Welfare Cycle: Let Writers Choose Their Topics." *A Case Study Observing the Development of Primary Children's Composing, Spelling and Motor Behaviors during the Writing Process.* ERIC ED 218 653, 1981a: 388–94.

— — . *Writing: Teachers and Children at Work.* Portsmith, N.H.: Heinemann, 1983.

Graves, Richard L. "A Primer for Teaching Style." *CCC* 25 (1974): 282–85.

Greene, H. A. "Direct versus Formal Methods in Elementary English." *Elementary English* 24 (1947): 273–85.

Guth, Hans P. *Words and Ideas: A Handbook for College Writing.* Belmont, Ca.: Wadsworth, 1969.

Hairston, Maxine. *Successful Writing: A Rhetoric for Advanced Composition.* New York: Norton, 1981.

Hamalian, Leo. "The Visible Voice: An Approach to Writing." *EJ* 59 (1970): 227–30.

Hansen, B. "Rewriting Is a Waste of Time." *CE* 39 (1978): 956–960.

Hardaway, Francine. "What Students Can Do to Take the Burden Off You." *CE* 36 (1975): 577–80.

Harris, C. E. *Effective Strategies in Peer Evaluation of Writing.* ERIC No. ED 272 897.

Harris, Joseph. The Idea of Community in the Study of Writing. *CCC* 40 (1989): 11–23.

Harris, Muriel. "Composing Behaviors of One- and Multi-Draft Writers." *CE* 51 (1989): 174–91.

— — . *Teaching One-to-One: The Writing Conference.* Urbana: NCTE, 1986.

Harris, R. J. "An Experimental Inquiry into the Functions and Value of Formal Grammar in the Teaching of English, with Special Reference to the Teaching of Correct Written English to Children Aged Twelve to Fourteen." Diss. U of London, 1962.

Harter, M. T. "A Study of the Effects of Transformational Grammar on the Writing Skills of Seventh Graders." *DAI* 39 (1978): 2794-A.

Hartwell, Patrick. *Open to Language.* New York: Oxford UP, 1982.

Hausner, R. M. "Interaction of Selected Student Personality Factors and Teachers' Comments in a Sequentially-Developed Composition Curriculum." *DAI* 36 (1976): 5768-A.

Hayes, Mary F. and Donald Daiker. "Using Protocol Analysis in Evaluating Responses to Student Writing." *Freshman English News* 13. 2 (1984): 1–4.

Henley, Joan. "A Revisionist View of Revision." *Washington English Journal* 8 (1986): 5–7.

Herrington, Anne J. and Deborah Cadman. "Peer Review and Revising in an Anthropology Course: Lessons for Learning." *CCC* 42 (1991): 184–99.

Heys, Frank Jr. "The Theme-a-Week Assumption: A Report of an Experiment." *EJ* 51 (1962): 320–22.

Hiatt, Mary. "Teaching the Writing of the Short Story." *EJ* 54 (1965): 810–17.

Hickey, Dona. *Developing a Written Voice.* Mountain View, Ca.: Mayfield, 1993.

Hillocks, George Jr. "The Interaction of Instruction, Teacher Comment, and Revision in Teaching the Composing Process." *RTE* 16 (1982): 261–78.

——. *Observing and Writing.* ERIC Clearinghouse on Reading and Communication Skills and National Council of Teachers of English, Theory into Practice Series. Urbana: NCTE, 1975.

——. *Research on Written Composition: New Directions for Teaching.* Urbana: National Conference on Research in English and ERIC Clearinghouse on Reading and Communication Skills, 1987.

Hipple, Theodore W. "The Grader's Helpers—Colleagues, Peers, Scorecards." *EJ* 61 (1972): 691–93.

Hoetker, James, and Gordon Brossell. "The Effects of Systematic Variations in Essay Topics on the Writing Performance of College Freshmen." *CCC* 40 (1989): 414–21.

Horning, Alice S. "Advising Undecided Students through Research Writing." 42 *CCC* (1991): 75–79.

Hoyt, F. S. "The Place of Grammar in the Elementary Curriculum." *Columbia Teachers College Record* 7 (1906): 1–34.

Hull, Glynda. "The Editing Process in Writing: A Performance Study of More Skilled and Less Skilled College Writers." *RTE* 21 (1987): 8–29.

Hunt, Brian. "Reliability, Validity, and Holistic Scoring: What We Know and What We Need to Know." *CCC* 41 (1990): 201–213.

Hunt, Kellogg W. and Roy O'Donnell. *An Elementary School Curriculum to Develop Better Writing Skills.* United States Office of Education Project No. 8-9093. Tallahassee: Florida: Florida State U, 1970.

Hunt, Russell A. "A Horse Named Hans, a Boy Named Shawn: The Herr von Osten Theory of Response to Writing." *Writing and Response: Theory, Practice, and Research.* Ed. Chris M. Anson. Urbana: NCTE, 1989.

——. "Technological Gift-Horse: Some Reflections in the Teeth of Cassette Marking." *CE* 36 (1975): 581–85.

Irmscher, William. *Teaching Expository Writing.* New York: Holt, 1979.

Jay, Gregory. "The Subject of Pedagogy: Lessons in Psychoanalysis and Politics." *CE* 49 (1987): 785–800.

Jensen, George H. and John K. DiTiberio. "Personality and Individual Writing Processes." *CCC* 35 (1984): 285–300.

Jeter, J. and O. Davis. "Elementary School Teachers' Differential Classroom Interaction with Children as a Function of Differential Expectations of Pupil Achievements, American Education Research Association annual meeting, 1973.

Johnson, Sabina Thorne. "Remedial English: The Anglocentric Albatross?" *CE* 33 (1972): 671–76.

Johnson, Sandy. "Sight, Sound and the Research Paper." *EJ* 58 (1969): 1031–63.

Johnston, Brian. *Assessing English: Helping Students Reflect on their Work.* Sidney: St. Clair, 1983.

Joseph, Albert. *Put It in Writing.* Cleveland: Industrial Writing Institute, 1977.

Judd, K. E. "The Effectiveness of Tape Recorded Evaluations of Compositions Written by Seventh-Grade and Eighth-Grade Students." *DAI* 34 (1973): 1770-A

Kahn, E. A., and L. R. Johanessen. "Does the Assignment Make a Difference: Four Variations of a Writing Task and Their Effects on Student Performance." U of Chicago, unpub. ms.

Kaplan, Milton. "Verse Writing in English Class." *CE* 55 (1966): 880–84.

Karp, M. "An Individual Method and a Group Method of Teaching College Freshmen the Mechanics of English Composition. *Journal of Experimental Education* 11 (1942): 9–15.

Katstra, J. et al. "The Effects of Peer Evaluation, Attitude Toward Writing, and Writing Fluency of Ninth-Grade Students." *JER* 80 (1987) 168–172.

Kelly, M. E. "Effects of Two Types of Teacher Response to Essays upon Twelfth-Grade Students' Growth." *DAI* 34 (1973): 5801A. Michigan State U.

Kelly, Lou. "Toward Competence and Creativity in an Open Class." *CE* 34 (1973): 644–660.

Kennedy, L. D., and A. D. Larson. "The Influence of Structural and of Traditional Grammatical Instruction upon Language Perception and Writing Ability." *Illinois School Research* 5 (1969): 31–36.

Kerner, David. "Jigsaw Puzzle in Exposition." *Writing Exerises from the Exercise Exchange.* Ed. Littleton Long. Urbana: NCTE, 1976.

Kinneavy, James L. *A Theory of Discourse.* Englewood Cliffs, Prentice Hall, 1971.

Kirby, Dan, Tom Liner, and Ruth Vinz, *Inside Out: Developmental Strategies for Teaching Writing.* 2nd ed. Portsmouth, NH: Boynton, 1988.

Kirschner, Samuel A., and S. Howard Poteet. "Nonstandard English Usage in the Writing of Black, White, and Hispanic Remedial English Students in an Urban Community College." *RTE* 7 (1973): 351–55.

Kitzhaber, Albert. "Rhetoric in American Colleges, 1850–1900." Diss. U of Washington, 1953.

Klammer, Enno. "Cassettes in the Classroom." *CE* 35 (1973): 179–89.

Kleinfeld, J. "Effective Teachers of Indian and Eskimo Students." *School Review* 83 (1975): 301–344.

Knapp, John V. "Contract/Conference Evaluations of Freshman Composition." *CE* 37 (1976): 647–53.

Koch, Kenneth. *I Never Told Anybody: Teaching Poetry Writing in Nursing Homes.* New York: Random, 1977.

——. *Rose, Where Did You Get That Red? Teaching Great Poetry to Children.* New York: Vintage, 1973.

——. *Wishes, Lies and Dreams: Teaching Children to Write Poetry.* New York: Chelsea, 1970.

Koclanes, T. A. "Can We Evaluate Composition?" *EJ* 50 (1961): 252–55.

Krause, W. Keith. *Murder, Mischief, and Mayhem: A Process for Creative Research Papers.* Urbana: NCTE, 1978.

LaBrant, Lou. "Marking the Paper." *Teaching English in Today's High Schools: Selected Readings.* Eds. Dwight L. Burton and Jack S. Simmons, 2nd ed. New York: Holt, 1970.

Laque, Carol Feiser, and Phyllis Sherwood, *A Laboratory Approach to Writing.* Urbana: NCTE, 1977.

Larson, Richard L. "The Research Paper in the Writing Course: A Non-Form of Writing." *CE* 44 (1982): 811–16.

——. "Teaching Before We Judge: Planning Assignments in Composition." *Teaching High School Composition.* Eds. Gary Tate and Edward P. J. Corbett. New York: Oxford UP, 1970.

——. "Training New Teachers in the Writing of Comments on Themes." *CCC* 17 (1966): 152–155.

Larson, Sidney. "Native American Aesthetics." *MELUS* 17 (1991–92): 53–67.

Lattin, Vernon E. "A Program for Basic Writing." *CE* 40 (1978): 314–15.

Lawson, Bruce, Susan Sterr Ryan, and W. Ross Winterowd, eds. *Encountering Student Texts: Interpretive Issues in Reading Student Writing.* Urbana: NCTE, 1989.

Lin, San-su C. "A Developmental English Program for the Culturally Disadvantaged." *CCC* (1965): 272–76.

Lindeman, Erica. *A Rhetoric for Writing Teachers.* 2d ed. New York: Oxford UP, 1987.

Long, Littleton, ed. *Writing Exercises from the Exercise Exchange.* Urbana: NCTE, 1976.

Lockerbie, Bruce. "The Speaking Voice Approach Joins the Rhetoric Parade." *EJ* 56 (1967): 411–15.

Love, Glen A. and Michael Payne, "The Research Paper: Does It Belong in High School?" *EJ* 56 (1967): 739–40.

Lubbock, Percy. "The Craft of Fiction: Picture, Drama, and Point of View." *Approaches to the Novel.* Ed. Robert Scholes. San Francisco: Chandler, 1961.

Lutzker, Marilyn. *Research Projects for College Students: What to Write Across the Curriculum.* Greenwood: Greenwood, 1988.

Lynch, James J. "The Conference Method in Teaching English Composition in Junior-Senior High School. *Bulletin of the National Association of High-School Principals.* 46 (1962): 119–20.

Lynn, William J. "Contrastive Approaches: An Experiment in Pedagogical Technique." *CE* 38 (1976): 144–52.

Macrorie, Ken. *The Perceptive Writer, Reader, and Speaker.* New York: Harcourt, 1959.

——. *Telling Writing.* Rochelle Park, NJ: Hayden, 1980.

——. "To Be Read." *EJ* (1968): 686–692.

——. *Uptaught.* Rochelle Park, NJ: Hayden, 1970.

Mailloux, Stephen. *Interpretive Conventions: The Reader in the Study of American Fiction.* Ithaca: Cornell UP, 1982.

Maimon, Elaine. *Writing in the Arts and Sciences.* Cambridge, Mass: Winthrop, 1981.

Maize, Roy C. "Two Methods of Teaching English Composition to Retarded College Freshmen." *JEP* 45 (1954): 22–76.

Malof, Joseph. "The Artifice of Scansion." *CE* 54 (1965): 858–59.

Marshall, Colleen. "A System for Teaching College Freshmen to Write a Research Paper." *CE* 40 (1978): 87–89.

Martin Bernal, *Black Athena.* New Brunswick, NJ: Rutgers UP, 1987.

Maynard, Howard A. Jr. "Student Perceived Teacher Effectiveness in Business Communications." *DAI* 35 (1974): 4867A. Georgia State U.

McAllister, Lois. "Tell Me What You Had in Mind." *EJ* 59 (1970): 231–34.

McCandless, Boyd R. and Ellis D. Evans. *Children and Youth: Psychosocial Development.* Dryden, 1973.

McClellan, James. "A Clinic for Misspellers." *CE* 40 (1978): 324.

McCracken, Timothy and Allen Ashby, "The Widow's Walk: An Alternative for English 101 — Creative Communications." *CE* 36 (1975): 555–78.

McCrimmon, James M. "A Cumulative Sequence in Composition." *EJ* 55 (1966): 427–28.

——. "Writing as a Way of Knowing." *The Promise of English: NCTE 1970 Distinguished Lectures.* Urbana: NCTE, 1970.

McManus, M. V. H. "A Study of Peer-Response Groups in a Tenth-Grade Writing Class." *DAI* 47 (1986): 08A.

McQuade, Donald A., ed. *The Territory of Language: Linguistics, Stylistics, and the Teaching of Composition.* Carbondale: U of Illinois P, 1986: 65–88.

McQuire, Edna. "College Freshmen on Writing in High School." *EJ* 51 (1962): 256–58.

Meade, Richard A. and W. Geiger Ellis, "Paragraph Development in the Modern Age of Rhetoric." *EJ* 59 (1970): 219–26.

Mellon, John C. *Transformational Sentence-Combining: A Method for Enhancing the Development of Syntactic Fluency in English Composition: NCTE Research Report No. 10.* Urbana: NCTE, 1969.

Metviner, J. S. "Rhetorically Based and Rhetorically Deficient Writing: The Effect of Purpose and Audience on the Quality of Ninth-Grade Students' Compositions." *DAI* 41 (1981): 3977-A.

Miller, Barbara D. and James W. Ney. "The Effect of Systematic Oral Exercises on the Writing of Fourth-Grade Students." *RTE* 2 (1968): 44–61.

Milligan, J. P. "An Evaluation of Two Methods of Teaching Written Sentence structure." *Elementary English Review* 16 (1939): 91–92, 106.

Mills, Helen. "Language and Composition: Three Mastery Learning Courses in One Classroom." *Journal of Basic Writing* (1976): 56–68.

Milic, Louis T. "Theories of Style and Their Implication for the Teaching of Composition." *CCC* 26 (1965): 66–69, 126.

Moffett, James. "I, You and It." *CCC* 16 (1965): 243–56.

——. *Teaching the Universe of Discourse.* Boston: Houghton, 1968.

Moran, Charles, and Elizabeth F. Penfield, eds. *Conversations: Contemporary Critical Theory and the Teaching of Literature.* Urbana: NCTE, 1990.

Morenberg, Max. *Doing Grammar.* New York: Oxford UP, 1991.

Morenberg, Max, Donald Daiker, and Andrew Kerek. "Sentence Combining at the College Level: An Experimental Study." *RTE* 12 (1978): 245–50.

Morgan, G. D. "A Study of the Writing Maturity of Students in a Linguistically-Based Composition Program at the Intermediate Level." *DAI* 31 (1971): 3178-A.

Morgan, Junette. "Writing Poetry in Junior High." *CE* 57 (1968): 1013.

Morsey, Royal J. *Improving English Instruction.* Boston: Allyn, 1965.

Murdock, B. B. Jr. "The Serial Position Effects of Free Recall." *JEP* 64 (1962): 482–88.

Murphy, Ann. "The Responses of College Freshmen to Three Modes of Instruction." *American Journal of Education* 89 (1981): 373–95.

——. "Transference and Resistance in the Basic Writing Classroom: Problematics and Praxis." *CCC* 40 (1989): 175–187.

Murray, Donald M. "Dominant Impressions." *Writing Exercises from "The Exercise Exchange."* Ed. Littleton Long. Urbana: NCTE, 1976. 115–19.

——. "The Listening Eye." *CE* 41 (1979): 13–18.

——. "Teach Writing as a Process not a Product." *The Leaflet.* New England Association of Teachers of English (1972): 11–14.

——. *A Writer Teaches Writing.* 2nd ed. Boston: Houghton, 1985.

Neeld, Elizabeth Cowan. *Writing.* 2nd ed. Glenview: Scott, 1986.

Neilson, "Writing as a Second Language: Psycholinguistic Processes in Composing." Diss. U of California at San Diego, 1979.

Neman, Beth S. "A Handbook for the Teaching of the Research Paper." *EJ* 56 (1967): 262–68.

———. *Writing Effectively.* 2nd ed. New York: Harper, 1989.

Newkirk, Thomas. "The First Five Minutes: Setting the Agenda in a Writing Conference." *Writing and Response: Theory, Practice, and Research.* Ed. Chris M. Anson. (Urbana: NCTE, 1989).

———. *To Compose: Teaching Writing in the High School.* Portsmouth NH: Heinemann, 1986.

Ney, James W. "Applied Linguistics in the Seventh Grade." *EJ* 55 (1966): 895–97.

Nielson, Brooke. "Writing as a Second Language: Psycholinguistic Processes in Composing." Diss. U of California at San Diego, 1979.

Nikoloff, Sayra B. *The Relationship of Teacher Standards to the Written Expression of Fifth and Sixth Grade Children.* Urbana: NCTE, 1967.

Noguchi, Rei B. *Grammar and the Teaching of Writing: Limits and Possibilities.* Urbana: NCTE, 1991.

Nugent, H. E. "The Role of Audience Awareness in the Writing of College Freshmen." *DAI* 41 (1979): 3279-A.

O'Donnell, A. M. et al. *Written Communication* 4 (1987): 90–99.

O'Donnell, Roy C. "The Correlation of Awareness of Structural Relationship in English and Ability in Written Composition." *JER* 57 (1964): 464–67.

O'Hare, Frank. *Sentence Combining: Improving Student Writing Without Formal Grammar Instruction: NCTE Research Report No. 15.* Urbana: NCTE, 1973.

O'Malley, William J. "Literary Craftsmanship: The Integration of Literature and Composition." *EJ* 52 (1963): 247–51, 268.

O'Neil, Wayne. "The Politics of Bidialectalism." *CE* 33 (1972): 433–38.

Oberchain, Anne. "Effectiveness of the Precise Essay Question in Programming the Sequential Development of Written Composition Skills and the Simultaneous Development of Critical Reading Skills." Master's thesis, George Washington U., 1971.

Odell, Lee. *Encountering Student Texts: Interpretive Issues in Reading Student Writing.* Eds. Bruce Lawson, Susan Sterr Ryan, and W. Ross Winterowd. Urbana: NCTE, 1989.

Olson, V. L. B. "The Effects of Revision Instruction and Peer Response Groups on Revision Behaviors, Quality of Writing, and Attitude Toward Writing of Sixth-Grade Students. *DAI* 47 (1986): 12A.

Page, Ellis B. "Teacher Comments and Student Performance." *JEP* 49 (1958): 173–81.

Pastiva, Agnes Ann. "Writing Lessons that Work." *CE* 62 (1973): 1276–80.

Payne, Lucille. *The Lively Art of Writing.* Chicago: Follett, 1965.

Peckham, Irvin. "Peer Evaluation." *EJ* 61 (1978): 61–63.

Pedersen, Elray L. "Improving Syntactic and Conceptual Fluency in the Writing of Language Arts Students Through Extended Practice in Sentence-Combining." Diss. U of Minnesota, 1976.

Peller, Gary. "Reason and the Mob: The Politics of Representation." *Tikkun* (July/August 1987).

Perl, Sondra. "The Composing Processes of Unskilled College Writers." *RTE* 13 (1979): 317–36.

Perrine, Lawrence. "Getting a Short Story Under Way." *Writing Exercises from the Exercise Exchange.* Ed. Littleton Long. Urbana: NCTE, 1976.

Perron, David. "An Exploratory Approach to Extending the Syntactic Development of Fourth-Grade Students Through the Use of Sentence-Combining Methods." Diss. Indiana U, 1974.

Perry, William G. "Cognitive and Ethical Growth: The Making of Meaning." *The Modern American College.* Ed. Arthur W. Chickering. San Francisco: Jossey, 1981.

——. *Forms of Intellectual and Ethical Development in the College Years: A Scheme.* New York: Holt, 1970.

Pierson, Howard. *Teaching Writing.* Englewood Cliffs, N.J.: Prentice, 1972.

Popkin, R. I. "A Study of Topic Sentence Use in Academic Writing." *Written Communication* 4 (1987): 57–66.

Petty, W., and P. J. Price, eds. *The Writing Processes of Students.* Buffalo: SUNY at Buffalo, Dept. of Curriculum and Instruction, 1975.

Powell, Robert. "Grading Compositions on 33⅓ rpm Records." *Patterns and Models for Teaching English.* Eds. Michael Shugre et al. Urbana: NCTE, 1964.

Profitt, Edward. "Freshman English Once More." *CE* 38 (1976): 132–43.

Pumphrey, Jean. "Teaching English Composition as a Creative Art." *CE* 34 (1973): 666–73.

Putz, Joan M. "Persuasion + Protection = Potency: A TA Approach to English 101." *CE* 36 (1975): 571–77.

Rank, Hugh. "Audience-Directed Writing: Magazines and Personae." *EJ* 1970: 405–08.

Rapeer, L. "The Problem of Formal Grammar in Elementary Education." *JEP* 4 (1913): 125–37.

Raskin, Victor and Irwin Weiser. *Language and Writing: Applications of Linguistics to Rhetoric and Composition.* Norwood, NJ: Ablex, 1987.

Raspberry, William. "Good Writing and Jazz: Lost Arts." *Washington Post* Writers Group, June, 1994.

Rast, Carlisle L. "The Beginning Research Paper." *EJ* 50 (1961): 469–71.

Rathbone, Charles. "Prelude to the Making of a Poem: Finger Exercises." *CE* 54 (1965): 854.

Raub, Donna Kay. "The Audio-Lingual Drill Technique: An Approach to Teaching Composition." Master's thesis, George Peabody College for Teachers, 1966.

Ray, T. J. "Describing Geometric Forms for Feedback." *Writing Exercises from the Exercise Exchange.* Ed. Littleton Long. Urbana: NCTE, 1976.

Reed, Horace B. "Implications for Science Education of a Teacher Competence Research." *Science Education* 46 (1962): 473–86.

Reid, James M., John Ciardi, and Lawrence Perrine, *Poetry: A Closer Look.* New York: Harcourt, 1963.

Reid, Joy. "The Radical Outliner and the Radical Brainstormer: A Perspective on Composing Processes." *TESOL Quarterly* 18 (1985): 529–34.

Ritchie, Joy. "Beginning Writers: Diverse Voices and Individual Identity." *CCC* 40 (1989): 152–74.

Robinson, Aurelia D. "An Investigative Study of Two Methods of Teaching Grammar: Conventional Instruction and Programmed Instruction." *DA,* 33 (1973): 6779A. Oklahoma U.

Roen, Duane H. "The Effects of Audience Awareness on Drafting and Revising." *RTE* 22 (1988): 75–88.

Rogers, Carl. "Communication: Its Blocking, Its Facilitation." *On Becoming a Person.* Boston: Houghton, 1961.

Rose, Mike. "Remedial Writing Courses: A Critique and a Proposal. *CE* 45 (1983): 109–25.

Rosenbaum, Peter. "On the Role of Linguistics in the Teaching of English." *Harvard Educational Review* 35 (1965): 341–42.

Rosenblatt, Louise. *Literature as Exploration.* New York, London: Appleton, 1938.

——. "Towards a Transactional Theory of Reading." *Journal of Reading Behavior* 1 (1969): 31–47.

Rosenthal, Robert, and Leonore Jacobson. *Pygmalion in the Classroom.* New York: Holt, 1968.

Royster, Sallibelle. "A Backward Glance at High School Composition." *EJ* 56 (1967): 1187–88.

Ruszkiewicz, John J. "The Great Commandment." *Training the New Teacher of College Composition.* Eds. Charles W. Bridges, et al. Urbana: NCTE, 1986.

Ryle, Gilbert. *The Concept of Mind.* New York: Barnes, 1949.

Saalbach, Robert P. "Teaching Students to Organize." *EJ* 48 (1958): 505–07.

Saiki, Patsy S. S. *The Composition Study: Summaries of Comparison of the Lay Reader Treatment with other Treatments in Increasing Student Growth in Writing.* 1968–1969. Honolula: Hawaii State Department of Education, 1970.

Saldivar, Ramon. *Chicano Narrative: The Dialectics of Difference.* Madison: U of Wisconsin P, 1990.

Samuels, Marilyn Schauer. "A Mini-Course in the Research Paper." *CE* 38 (1976): 189–93.

Sapir, Edward. *Language.* New York: Harcourt, 1921.

Sarason, Seymour B. et al. *Anxiety in Elementary School Children.* New York: Wiley, 1960.

Schroeder, Fred E. H. "How Not to Assign 'What-Did-You-Do-Last-Summer': A Cumulative Course in Writing Personal Narratives." *EJ* 57 (1968): 79–84.

Schroeder, T. S. "The Effects of Positive and Corrective Written Teacher Feedback on Selected Writing Behaviors of Fourth-Grade Children." *DAI* 34 (1973a): 2935-A.

Schultz, John. "Story Workshop: Writing from Start to Finish." *Research on Composing: Points of Departure.* Eds. Charles R. Cooper and Lee Odell. Urbana: NCTE, 1978.

Schumann, Paul F. "What Criteria Do You Use in Grading Compositions?" *EJ* 57 (1968): 1163–65.

Schwartz, Mimi. "Wearing the Shoe on the Other Foot: Teacher as Student Writer." *CCC* 40 (1989): 203–215.

Segal, D. and Nora R. Barr. "Relation of Achievement in Formal Grammar to Achievement in Applied Grammar. *JER* 14 (1926): 401–02.

Seidman, E. "Marking Students' Compositions: Implications of Achievement Motivation Theory." *DA* 28 (1968): 2605-A.

Seifert, Kelvin L. *Educational Psychology.* 2nd ed. Boston: Houghton, 1991.

Selzer, Jack. "Exploring Options in Composing." *CCC* 35 (1984): 276–84.

Seymour, Dorothy Z. "Black Children, Black Speech." *Commonweal* (1971): 175–78.

Shaughnessy, Mina P. *Errors and Expectations: A Guide for the Teacher of Basic Writing.* New York: Oxford UP, 1977.

Shaver, J. P. and D. Nuhn. "The Effectiveness of Tutoring Underachievers in Reading and Writing." *JER* 65, 3 (1971): 107–12.

Sheridan, Daniel. "Changing Business as Usual: Reader Response in the Classroom." *CE* 53 (1991): 813.

Shugre, Michael et al., eds. *Patterns and Models for Teaching English.* Urbana: NCTE, 1964.

Shuman, Baird. "Teasing Writing out of High-School Students." *CE* 62 (1973): 1269–71.

Sieminski, Greg C. "Couching Our Cutting with Compassion." *CCC* 42 (1992): 211–17.

Sledd, James. "Doublespeak: Dialectology in the Service of Big Brother." *CE* 33 (1972): 439–56.

Sloan, Gary. "The Wacky World of Theme Marking." *CCC* 28 (1977): 37–73.

Smith, Doris I. "Effects of Class Size and Individualized Instruction in the Writing of High-School Juniors." *DAI* 1 (1974): 2844A. Florida State U.

Smith, Eugene H. "Composition Evaluation: A Problem of Voice." *EJ* 56 (1967): 1189–94.

Smith, Myrna and Barbara Bretcko. "Research on Individual Composition Conferences." Urbana: ERIC, 1974. ED 091 70.

Smith, Susan Belasco. "Review of Ken Macrorie's *The I-Search Paper.*" *CCC* 40 (1989): 360–61.

Smith, Vernon H. "Measuring Teaching Judgment in the Evaluation of Written Research." *RTE* 3 (1969): 181–96.

Smitherman, Geneva. "Black English, Diverging or Converging?: The View of the National Assessment of Educational Progress." *Language and Education* 6.1 (1992): 47–61.

Smolin, Pauline. *How to Write a Well-Organized Paragraph* (Self Published, c. 1977).

Sommers, Nancy. "Responding to Student Writing." *CCC* 33 (1982): 148–56.

——. "Revision Strategies of Student Writers and Experienced Writers." *CCC* 31 (1980): 378–88.

Southwell, Michael. "Free Writing in Composition Classes." *CE* 38 (1977): 676–78.

Spalding, R. *Achievement, Creativity, and Self-Concept Correlates of Teacher-Pupil Transactions in Elementary Schools.* Champaign: U of Illinois P, 1962.

Squire, James R., and Roger K. Applebee, *High School English Instruction Today: The National Study of High School English Programs.* New York: Appleton, 1968.

Sternglass, Marilyn S. "Close Similarities in Dialect Features of Black and White College Students in Remedial Composition Classes." *Teachers of English to Speakers of Other Languages Quarterly* 8 (1974): 271–83.

——. "Dialect Features in the Compositions of Black and White College Students: The Same or Different?" *CCC* 25 (1974): 259–63.

Stevens, Alfred E. "The Effects of Positive and Negative Evaluation in the Written Composition of Low Performing High-School Students." *DAI* 34 (1973): 1778A. Boston U.

Steward, J. "The Effect of Diagramming on Certain Skills in English Composition," Diss. State U. of Iowa, 1941.

Stiff, R. "The Effect upon Student Composition of Particular Correction Techniques." *RTE* 16 (1967): 54–75.

Stotsky, Sandra. "Writing as Moral and Civic Thinking." 54 *CE* (1992): 794–808.

Strong, William. *Sentence Combining: A Composing Book.* 2nd ed. New York: Random House, 1982.

———. *Sentence Combining and Paragraph Building.* New York: Random House, 1981.

Sullivan, J. L. "A Study of the Relative Merits of Traditional Grammar, Generative-Transformational Grammar, or No Grammar in an Approach to Writing in Communication One at Colorado State College." *DA* 29 (1969): 2686-A.

Sullivan, Maureen A. "Parallel Sentence-Combining Studies in Grades Nine and Eleven." *Sentence Combining and the Teaching of Writing.* Eds. Donald Daiker, Andrew Kerek, and Max Morenberg. Akron: U of Akron P, 1979.

Newkirk, Thomas. "The First Five-Minutes." *Writing and Response: Theory, Practice, and Research.* Ed. Chris M. Anson. Urbana: NCTE, 317–331.

Sutton, D. G., and D. S. Arnold, "The Effects of Two Methods of Compensatory Freshman English." *RTE* (1974): 241–49.

Sutton, J. T., and E. D. Allen, "The Effect of Practice and Evaluation on Improvement in Written Composition." Cooperative Research Project, #1993. De-Land, Fla.: Stetson U, 1964.

Swift, P. W. "The Effect of Peer Review with Self-Evaluation on Freshman Writing Performance, Retention, and Attitude at Bronard Community College. *DAI* 47 (1986): 10A.

Symonds, P. M. "Practice versus Grammar in the Learning of Correct Usage." *JEP* 22 (1931): 81–95.

Tate, Gary, ed. *Reflections on High School English.* Tulsa: U of Tulsa P, 1966.

———. *Teaching Composition: 10 Bibliographical Essays.* Fort Worth: Texas Christian UP, 1976.

Tate, Gary, and Edward P. J. Corbett, eds. *Teaching High School Composition.* New York: Oxford UP, 1970.

Taylor, W. F., and K. C. Hoedt, "The Effect of Praise upon the Quality and Quantity of Creative Writing." *JER* 60 (1966): 80–88.

Taylor, Thomas. "Let's Get Rid of Research Papers." *EJ* 54 (1965) 126–27.

[Tchudi] Judy, Stephen. *Explorations in the Teaching of Secondary English: A Source Book for Experimental Teaching.* New York: Dodd, 1975.

[Tchudi] Judy, Stephen N. and Susan J. Judy. *An Introduction to The Teaching of Writing.* New York: Wiley, 1981.

Tchudi, Stephen N. and Susan J. Tchudi. *The English/Language Arts Handbook: Classroom Strategies for Teachers.* Portsmouth, NH: Boynton, 1991.

Thompson, C. L., and M. Middleton. "Transformational Grammar and Inductive Teaching as Determinants of Structurally Complex Writing." *California J. of Educational Research* 24 (1973): 28–41.

Tobias, S. "Test Anxiety: Interference, Defective Skills, and Cognitive Capacity." *Educational Psychologist* 20 (1985): 135–42.

Tobin, Lad. "Reading Students, Reading Ourselves: Revising the Teacher's Role in the Writing Class." 53 (1991): 333–48.

Travers, Robert M. W. ed. *Second Handbook of Research on Teaching.* Chicago: Rand McNally, 1972.

Turbill, *No Better Way to Teach Writing.* Rosebery, New South Wales, Australia: Primary English Teaching Assn., 1982.

Vitale, M. R. et al., "Effect of Sentence-Combining Exercises Upon Several Restricted Written Composition Tasks." *JEP* 62, No. 6 (1971): 521–25.

Vogler, Stephen. "Grading Themes: A New Approach, A New Diversion." *EJ* (1971): 70–74.

Ware, B. "What Rewards Do Students Want?" *Phi Delta Kappan* 59 (1978): 355–56.

Wagner, Linda Welshimer. "Practice without Pain." *EJ* 37 (1968): 221–22.

Walker, Carolyn P. and Elias D. David. "Writing Conference Talk: Factors Associated with High- and Low-Rated Writing Conferences." *RTE* 21 (1987): 266–285.

Wallace, David L., and John R. Hayes, "Redefining Revision for Freshmen." *RTE* 25 (1991): 54–64.

Walter Loban, Margaret Ryan, and James R. Squire. *Teaching Language and Literature.* New York: Harcourt, 1961.

Walvoord, Barbara Fassler. *Helping Students Write Well: A Guide for Teachers in All Disciplines.* 2nd ed. New York: MLA, 1982.

——. "The Red Pen Revisited: Teaching Composition through Student Conferences." *CE* 38 (1976): 188.

Weaver, Constance. *Grammar for Teachers: Perspectives and Definitions.* Urbana: NCTE, 1979.

Weiner, Bernard. "Achievement Motivation, Attribution Theory, and the Educational Process." *RER* 42 (1972): 203–15.

Wells, Carlton F. "Ten Points for English Teachers." *EJ* 55 (1966): 1080–81.

Werner, P. C. and W. S. Guiler. "Individual versus Group Instruction in Grammatical Usage." *JEP* 24 (1933): 140–51.

White, John O. "Who Writes These Questions Anyway?" *CCC* 39 (1988): 231–235.

White, Robert H. "The Effect of Structural Linguistics in Improving English Composition Compared to that of Prescriptive Grammar or the Absence of Grammar Instruction." Diss. U. of Arizona, 1965.

Whitehead, C. E., Jr. "The Effect of Grammar-Diagraming on Student Writing Skills." *DA* 26 (1966): 3710.

Whittier, Gayle. "The World We Never Made: Teaching Writing in a Literature Course." *CCC* 23 (1972): 175–83.

Wiener, Harvey S. "Media Compositions: Preludes to Writing." *CE* 35 (1974): 566–74.

Wilcox, Thomas W. "Synonymy and Tone." *Exercises from the Exercise Exchange.* Ed. Littleton Long. Urbana: NCTE, 1976.

Williams, James D. *Preparing to Teach Writing.* Belmont: Wadsworth, 1989.

——. "Covert Language Behavior During Writing." *RTE* (1983) 17: 473–49.

——. "Covert Linguistic Behavior during Writing Tasks: Psychophysicological Differences between Above-Average and Below-Average Writers." *Written Communications* (1987) 4: 310–28.

Williams, Joseph M. "Non-Linguistic Linguistics and the Teaching of Style." *The Territory of Language: Linguistics, Stylistics, and the Teaching of Composition.* Carbondale: Southern Illinois UP, 1986.

——. "Style as Meaning." *Introduction to The Prose Style of Samuel Johnson.* New Haven: Yale UP, 1941.

Wine, J. P. "Theory of Test Anxiety." *Test Anxiety: Theory, Research, and Applications to Reduce the Negative Implications.* Ed. I. Sarason. Hillsdale, NJ: Erlbain, 1980.

Winterowd, Ross "Topics and Levels in the Composing Process." *CE* 34 (1973): 701–09.

Witte, Stephen P. "Pre-text and Composing." *CCC* 38 (1987): 397–425.

Witte, Stephen P. and Lester Faigley. "Coherence, Cohesion, and Writing Quality." *CCC* 33 (1981): 189–204.

Wolfe, Don M. *Creative Ways to Teach English: Grades 7–12*, 2nd ed. New York: Oddysey, 1966.

Woodworth, P. and C. Keech, *The Write Occasion. Collaborative Research Study No. 1.* ERIC Ed 198–534.

Worcestor, David. *The Art of Satire.* Cambridge: Harvard UP, 1940.

Yodr, Albert C. "Dear Ann: I have a Problem." *Writing Exercises from the Exercise Exchange.* Ed. Littleton Long. Urbana: NCTE, 1976.

Young, Richard. "Invention, A Topographical Survey." *Teaching Composition: 10 Bibliographical Essays.* Fort Worth: Texas Christian UP, 1976.

Young, Richard, and Alton Becker, "Toward a Modern Theory of Rhetoric: A Tagmemic Contribution." *Harvard Education Review* 35 (1965): 456.

Subject Index

The following abbreviation is used throughout this index: *n* refers to an endnote (*nn.*, endnotes).

Name Index

The following abbreviation is used throughout this index: *n* refers to an endnote (*nn.*, endnotes).